UNDERSTANDING CONTEMPORARY ETHIOPIA

T0373917

GÉRARD PRUNIER
ÉLOI FICQUET

(*editors*)

Understanding Contemporary Ethiopia

HURST & COMPANY, LONDON

First published in the United Kingdom in 2015 by
C. Hurst & Co. (Publishers) Ltd.,
41 Great Russell Street, London, WC1B 3PL
© Gérard Prunier, Éloi Ficquet and the Contributors, 2015
All rights reserved.
Printed in India

Distributed in the United States, Canada and Latin America by
Oxford University Press, 198 Madison Avenue, New York, NY 10016,
United States of America.

A Cataloguing-in-Publication data record for this book
is available from the British Library.

ISBN: 9781849042611 (paperback)

This book is printed using paper from registered sustainable
and managed sources.

www.hurstpublishers.com

This book is dedicated to my Ethiopian daughters, Tana and Mehret. G.P.

Both editors wish to honour the memory of their late friend and colleague Jacques Bureau (1956–1998), who was their predecessor as the first director of the French Centre for Ethiopian Studies in Addis Ababa. More than anybody else, he helped us love and understand Ethiopia. G.P. & E.F.

CONTENTS

ABOUT THE CONTRIBUTORS

Gérard Prunier, PhD, is a renowned historian of contemporary Africa and author of the acclaimed *The Rwanda Crisis: History of a Genocide and of Darfur: The Ambiguous Genocide*, both published by Hurst.

Éloi Ficquet, PhD, is an anthropologist and historian, working on religion, ethnicity and power in Ethiopia. He was the Director of the French Center for Ethiopian Studies in Addis Ababa (2009-2012) and the chairman of the 18th International Conference of Ethiopian Studies in 2012. He is now assistant professor at the EHESS, Paris. Besides many articles on Ethiopian history and culture, he co-authored a *French-Amharic Dictionary* with Berhanou Abebe (2003) and he co-edited with Wolbert Smidt *The Life and Times of Lij Iyasu of Ethiopia* (LIT, 2014).

Stéphane Ancel, PhD, is a historian, who specialises in the evolution of the Ethiopian Orthodox Tewahedo Church since the nineteenth century. He has been a research fellow at Hamburg University in the ERC-funded project Ethio-SPARE program and he is currently working for the ERC-funded project Open Jerusalem (University of Paris-Est Marne-La-Vallée).

Shiferaw Bekele is a professor in history at Addis Ababa University. His areas of research are the economic, cultural and political history of Ethiopia from the late eighteenth to the twentieth century. He has published many essays and articles in journals and edited collections. He has (co-)edited several books of which the following two can be cited: *Kassa and Kassa* (Addis Ababa, 1990); *An Economic History of Ethiopia*

(Codesria 2001). He was the Executive Secretary of the Academy of Ethiopian Languages and Cultures and is founding fellow of the Ethiopian Academy of Sciences.

Giulia Bonacci, PhD, is a historian of migrations and diasporas, researcher at IRD, the French Institute of Research for Development. After her major work on the history of the settlement of the Rastafari community in Ethiopia, she has continued to study the migrations of African Americans and Caribbeans to Ethiopia and the social history of Pan-Africanism. The translation of her book *Exodus! Heirs and Pioneers, Rastafari Return to Ethiopia* was published in April 2015 by University of the West Indies Press.

Christopher Clapham, PhD, is Emeritus Professor in politics and international relations, Cambridge University. Among different research interests, he has been a keen observer of political evolution in Ethiopia and in the Horn of Africa since the time of Haile Selassie. His main publications on this field are *Haile Selassie's Government* (1969, Praeger); *Transformation and Continuity in Revolutionary Ethiopia* (1988, Cambridge). He has been the editor of the *Journal of Modern African Studies* published by Cambridge University Press since 1988.

Dereje Feyissa Dori, PhD, is a social anthropologist. He has conducted research on ethnicity and conflict in the Gambella region (western Ethiopia); Islam in contemporary Ethiopia; the political economy of development in the Afar region (eastern Ethiopia). He is currently adjunct professor at Addis Ababa University and Africa research director of the International Law and Policy Institute (Addis Ababa). In Germany he was a research fellow of the Max Planck Institute for social anthropology and he is currently Alexander von Humboldt Research Fellow. He published *Playing Different Games: The Paradoxes of Anywaa and Nuer Identification Strategies in Gambella, Ethiopia* (Berghahn Books, 2011).

Perrine Duroyaume is an urban expert and development program officer at F3E (France). She has been a research associate of the French Center for Ethiopian Studies. She has worked on several projects in Addis Ababa and other Ethiopian cities.

Emanuele Fantini, PhD, is a political scientist and a research fellow at the Department of Cultures, Politics and Society of the University of Turin. He has worked in the fields of development studies, the political sociology of state formation in Africa and water resources management. His current research focuses on the impact of the Pentecostal movement on social, political and economic issues in Ethiopia. He co-edited, with Jörg Haustein, a special issue of *PentecoStudies* (12/2 2013) "The Ethiopian Pentecostal Movement. History, Identity and Current Socio-Political Dynamics".

Patrick Gilkes has worked for many years as a journalist and political analyst on the Horn of Africa. Since 2004 he has been strategic planning adviser to the Ethiopian Foreign Minister. He is the author of *The Dying Lion* (1975).

René Lefort has been writing about sub-saharan Africa since the 1970s and has reported on the region for *Le Monde, Le Monde diplomatique, Libération, Le Nouvel Observateur*. He is the author of *Ethiopia: An heretical revolution?* (1982, Zed books).

Medhane Tadesse, PhD, is an expert in peace and security issues. He has taught at various universities in Ethiopia and abroad and has written extensively on armed violence, globalised security and diplomacy, militarisation, governance and humanitarian crisis in Africa. He is the editor of *The Current Analyst*, an online journal that examines issues relating to African peace and security.

Sarah Vaughan, PhD, is a research consultant, and honorary fellow at the School of Social and Political Science at the University of Edinburgh. She has taught African politics and social theory in Ethiopia and in Scotland. Her research interests include the sociology of knowledge, ethnicity and political interest, decentralisation and local government, transitional justice and conflict. She is co-author of *The Culture of Power in Contemporary Ethiopian Political Life* (Sida, Stockholm, 2003).

ABBREVIATIONS

AACG	Addis Ababa City Government
AAPO	All Amhara Peoples Organization
AAU	Addis Ababa University
ADLI	Agricultural Development Led Industrialization
AETU	All-Ethiopia Trade Union
AEUP	All Ethiopia Unity Party
ALF	Afar Liberation Front
AMISOM	African Union Mission for Somalia
ANDM	Amhara National Democratic Movement
ARENA	Union of Tigreans for Democracy and Sovereignty
AU	African Union
BBA	Building Block Approach
BPLM	Benishangul People Liberation Movement
CELU	Confederation of Ethiopian Labor Unions
CETU	Confederation of Ethiopian Trades Unions
CFA	Cooperative Framework Agreement
CIP	Complaints Investigation Panels
COPWE	Committee for Organizing the Party of the Workers of Ethiopia
CPA	Comprehensive Peace Agreement (Sudan)
CSA	Central Statistical Authority
CUD	Coalition for Unity and Democracy
EDORM	Ethiopian Democratic Officers Revolutionary Movement
EDP	Ethiopian Democratic Party
EDU	Ethiopian Democratic Union
EEBC	Eritrea-Ethiopia Boundary Commission

ABBREVIATIONS

EFFORT	Endowment Fund for the Rehabilitation of Tigray
ELF	Eritrean Liberation Front
ENDF	Ethiopian National Defence Forces
EOTC	Ethiopian Orthodox Tewahedo Church
EPLF	Eritrean People's Liberation Front
EPPF	Ethiopian People's Patriotic Front
EPRDF	Ethiopian People's Revolutionary Democratic FrontECFE: Evangelical Churches Fellowship of Ethiopia
EPRP	Ethiopian People's Revolutionary Party
ERIS	Electoral Reform International Services (UK)
ESM	Ethiopian Student Movement
ETA	Ethiopian Teachers' Association
ETB	Ethiopian Birr (currency)
EVASU	Ethiopian Evangelical Student Association
EWF	Ethiopian World Federation
FDI	Foreign Direct Investments
FDRE	Federal Democratic Republic of Ethiopia
FRELIMO	Frente de Libertação de Moçambique (Mozambique Liberation Front)
GDP	Gross domestic product
GERD	Grand Ethiopian Renaissance Dam
GNP	Gross national product
GPLM	Gambella People's Liberation Movement
GTP	Growth and Transformation Plan
HRW	Human Rights Watch
IFPRI	International Food Policy Research Institute
IGAD	Intergovernmental Authority on Development
IMF	International Monetary Fund
MIDROC	Mohammed International Development Research and Organization Companies
MLLT	Marxist-Leninist League of Tigray
MPLA	Movimento Popular de Libertação de Angola (People's Movement for the Liberation of Angola)
NBI	Nile Basin Initiative
NCO	Non-commissioned officer
NEBE	National Electoral Board of Ethiopia
NEPAD	New Partnership for Africa's Development
NGO	Non-governmental organization
NIF	National Islamic Front (Sudan)
OAU	Organisation of African Unity

ABBREVIATIONS

OFDM	Oromo Federalist Democratic Movement
OLF	Oromo Liberation Front
ONC	Oromo National Congress
ONLF	Ogaden National Liberation Front
OPDO	Oromo Peoples' Democratic Organization
PAIGC	Partido Africano para a Independência da Guiné e Cabo Verde (African Party for the Independence of Guinea and Cape Verde)
PFDJ	People's Front for Democracy and Justice (Eritrea)
PMAC	Provisional Military Administrative Council
POMOA	Political Office for Mass Organization Affairs
POW	Prisoner of War
RED	Real Estate Developers
REST	Relief Society of Tigray
SALF	Somali Abo Liberation Front
SEPDC	Southern Ethiopia Peoples' Democratic Coalition
SIM	Serving In Mission
SLM	Sidama Liberation Movement
SNNPRS	Southern Nations Nationalities and Peoples Regional State
SPLA	Sudan People's Liberation Army
SPM	Somali Patriotic Movement
SSDF	Somali Salvation Democratic Front
TFG	Transitional Federal Government (Somalia)
TGE	Transitional Government of Ethiopia
TNO	Tigray Nationalist Organization
TNPU	Tigray Nation Progressive Union
TPLF	Tigrayan People's Liberation Front
TSZ	Temporary Security Zone
TUSU	Tigray University Students Union
UDJ	Unity for Democracy and Justice
UEDF	United Ethiopian Democratic Forces
UEDP	United Ethiopian Democratic Party
UIC	Union of Islamic Courts (Somalia)
UN	United Nations
UNDP	United Nations Development Programme
USC-SNA	United Somali Congress-Somali National Alliance
WPE	Workers Party of Ethiopia
WSLF	Western Somali Liberation Front

YEMEN

Red Sea

Bab'el-Mande

ERITREA

SUDAN

DJIBOU

Agame

Teru

Enderta

Temben

Rayya

Yejju

Dewwey

Awsa

Shire

Tigray

Lasta

Albara r.

Simen

Welqayt

Wegera

Tekkeze r.

Armeceho

Begemdir

Wello

Yifat

Dembeya

Borena

Menz

Ka

ra

l. Tana

Gojjam

Shewa

Blue Nile

Agew

Awi

Abbay r.

Mecha

Awash r.

Qwara

l. Zway

Metekkel

Gudru

Gurage

l. Abiya

Gibe r.

Hadiya

l. Sha

Gumuz

Leeqa

Limu

Kambata

Beni

Wallaggaa

Wolay

Shangul

Jimma

Mao

Qelem

Komo

Dawro

Illubabor

Kafa

Gan

Gofa

Baro r.

Ari

Gambella

Maji

Nuer

Anuak

Omo r.

Akobo r.

SOUTH
SUDAN

ETHIOPIA
A "Rift-oriented" map of relief, rivers, and territorial identities

A rotation of 45° is applied to the usual orientation to the north, so that the Rift valley, which "cuts" the country into two parts, corresponds to the fold of the book. This change of perspective allows another visualization and understanding of the situation of the territories in relation to each other.

© E. Ficquet, 2014.

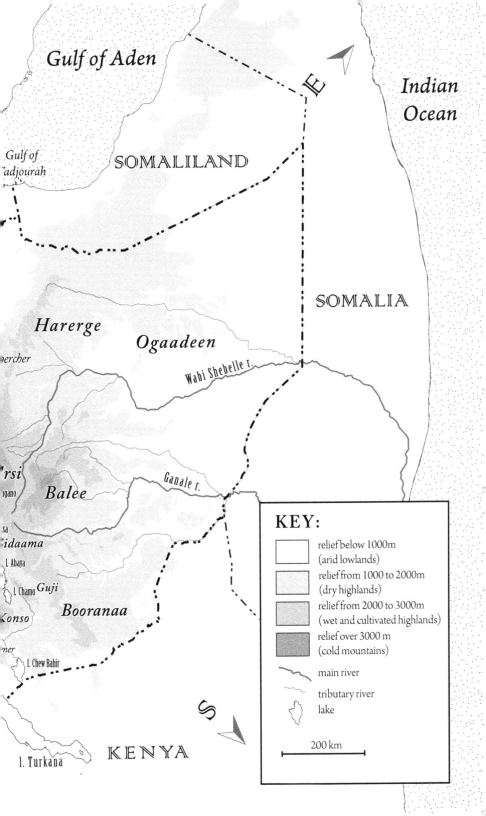

Gulf of Aden

Indian
Ocean

Gulf of
adjourah

SOMALILAND

Harerge

Ogaadeen

ercher

SOMALIA

Wabi Shebelle r.

rsi

ıgano

Balee

Ganale r.

sa

idaama

l. Abaya

l. Chamo *Guji*

Konso

Booranaa

ner

l. Chew Bahir

KEY:

relief below 1000m
(arid lowlands)

relief from 1000 to 2000m
(dry highlands)

relief from 2000 to 3000m
(wet and cultivated highlands)

relief over 3000 m
(cold mountains)

main river

tributary river

lake

l. Turkana

KENYA

200 km

ETHIOPIA - Administrative divisions since 1994
The Regional States of the Federal Democratic Republic of Ethiopia

Distribution of Population by Regions in 1994 and 2007

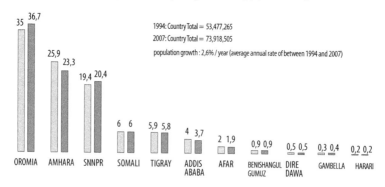

1994: Country Total = 53,477,265
2007: Country Total = 73,918,505

population growth : 2,6% / year (average annual rate of between 1994 and 2007)

OROMIA	AMHARA	SNNPR	SOMALI	TIGRAY	ADDIS ABABA	AFAR	BENISHANGUL GUMUZ	DIRE DAWA	GAMBELLA	HARARI
35 / 36,7	25,9 / 23,3	19,4 / 20,4	6 / 6	5,9 / 5,8	4 / 3,7	2 / 1,9	0,9 / 0,9	0,5 / 0,5	0,3 / 0,4	0,2 / 0,2

Source: Central Statistical Authority, Population and Housing Census, 2007.

ETHIOPIA - Administrative divisions before 1991

NB: The layout of these administrative divisions was established in 1942. Eritrea was included as a federal territory in 1952, then absorbed as a province in 1962. This territorial organisation was subject to a series of revisions and corrections on all levels, but its general aspect remained basically the same. In 1987 the Constitution of the People's Democratic Republic of Ethiopia created a new framework that was abandoned four years later, after the fall of the military regime in May 1991. Eritrea became officially independent in May 1993 and new federal administrative divisions based on ethno-linguistic boundaries were adopted with the 1994 Constitution of the Federal Democratic Republic of Ethiopia.

ETHIOPIA - Cities and Roads

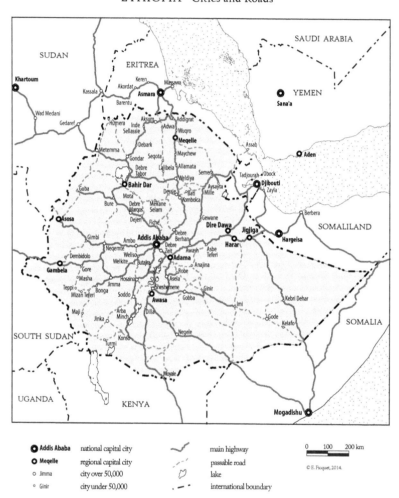

● **Addis Ababa**	national capital city	∿	main highway
○ **Meqelle**	regional capital city	⌁	passable road
○ Jimma	city over 50,000	◇	lake
○ Ginir	city under 50,000	·—·—	international boundary

0   100   200 km

© E. Ficquet, 2014.

Population of the major Ethiopian cities (over 100,000 inhabitants) :

Addis Ababa 2,738,248 | Dire Dawa 342,827 | Awasa 259,803 | Adama 222,035 | Bahir Dar 220,344 | Mekele 215,546 | Gondar 206,987 | Harar 183,344 | Dessie 151,094 | Jigjiga 125,876 | Jimma 120,600 | Shashemene 102,062 | Bishoftu 100,114.

Source: Central Statistical Authority, Population and Housing Census, 2007.

ETHIOPIA - Religions

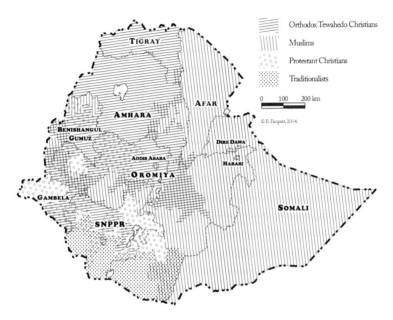

Source: Central Statistical Authority, Population and Housing Census, 2007.

Note on the making of the map: Religious groups are outlined when their followers represent more than 20% of the population at the level of *wereda* district. This allows for the representation of areas of religious coexistence.

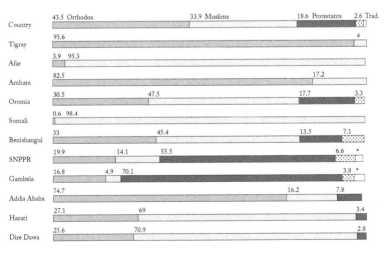

* Catholics: Country total: 0,8% - SNNPR: 2,4% - Gambela: 3,4%

ETHIOPIA - Orthodox Tewahedo Christians
and their major places of worship

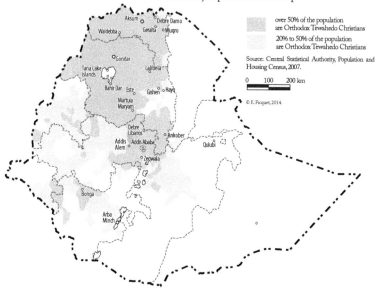

over 50% of the population
are Orthodox Tewahedo Christians

20% to 50% of the population
are Orthodox Tewahedo Christians

Source: Central Statistical Authority, Population and
Housing Census, 2007.

0   100   200 km

© E. Ficquet, 2014.

ETHIOPIA - Muslims
and their major places of worship

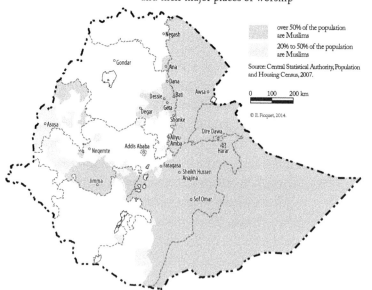

over 50% of the population
are Muslims

20% to 50% of the population
are Muslims

Source: Central Statistical Authority, Population
and Housing Census, 2007.

0   100   200 km

© E. Ficquet, 2014.

ETHIOPIA - Protestant Christians

over 50% of the population
are Protestant Christians

20% to 50% of the population
are Protestant Christians

Source: Central Statistical Authority, Population and
Housing Census, 2007.

0   100   200 km

© E. Ficquet, 2014.

INTRODUCTION

Gérard Prunier and Éloi Ficquet

Ethiopia is a land which, like Israel or Tibet, is often thought of first and foremost through myths before it is seen as a real country. Many people who would have some difficulty in precisely pinpointing Ethiopia on a map of the world have nevertheless heard about our hominid "grandmother" Lucy, the Ark of the Covenant, Solomon and the Queen of Sheba, the medieval quest for Prester John, as well as the more recent imperial figures of Menelik II and Haile Selassie I, the independence of the country during European imperialism in Africa, and the Lion of Judah, a symbol of sovereignty that has been used on covers of Rastafari reggae albums. The public at large also remember the images of recurrent famines that often end up negatively symbolizing Africa. The Power, the Glory and the Tragedies. Ethiopia is oversized in the public mind and it often tends to be oversized in the minds of its own inhabitants, who are the first to believe in the mythical quality of their motherland. It is one of the few countries in the world which has an *Encyclopaedia* devoted to it—not a universal encyclopaedia but a gigantic and erudite compendium of all things Ethiopian from the origins of time until 1974.[1]

That date is fully justified: 1974 was the year of destiny, the year when Ethiopia was suddenly thrown into the modern world. Seldom

1

has a date been so significant in the history of a people and of a nation. Today, as in France and Russia, there is a lingering consciousness of loss in the face of progress. No other country in Africa has known this experience. African countries were *decolonized* in the 1960s, which meant combining some continuity with a precolonial past with the irreversible changes due to colonialism. Their period of entry into modernity had been usurped by foreigners and the course of history had to be *restored*. But the Ethiopian case is just the opposite. Ethiopia had never been colonized and it lingered in a world where the Bible and the Prophets had more reality than Marx, Freud or Darwin. The Italian invasion of 1935 had been a warning shot but Orde Wingate and Emperor Haile Selassie had turned the clock back and repelled both fascism and the intrusion of the modern world. Thus for many lovers of Ethiopian culture, 1974 was the year of doom, of de-sacralization, of impiety. The country-as-myth which they had long cherished had come to a bad end. King Solomon had died a second death and Ethiopia had landed in the modern world with a painful thud. Then came the new narrative: communism, mass starvation, civil war, dictatorship, population displacements. After having long been the embodiment of a timeless biblically-rooted myth, Ethiopia had now been thrown into a pit of unmitigated evil that was in itself a new (counter)-myth. And then, in 1991, the same year that saw the final complete collapse of the Soviet "Evil Empire", communism was wiped off the face of Ethiopia and triumphant guerrilla fighters proclaimed the birth of a Brave New World. End of story.

In the last twenty years, under the leadership of its late Prime Minister Meles Zenawi, Ethiopia has been progressively—though reluctantly—*normalized*. Its bizarre shack-studded capital started to sprout skyscrapers, its Prime Minister rubbed shoulders with top world leaders in a way not seen since Haile Selassie, it started to lay out a giant infrastructural network built by illiterate peasants on the Chinese model, and it began to assert itself as a new regional power which was in the process of developing an original path towards economic growth. Its stated aim was to climb from the level of one of the poorest countries in the world to the level of a small emergent power. And, in many ways, this is where historiography lost track of Ethiopia.

Scope of the book

The last global study of Ethiopia was published in 1985,[2] and its main focus for reflection was: can we say that Marxism is now solidly embedded in Ethiopia? Since then dozens of books have been published on Ethiopia, covering famine, geopolitics, elections, religion, historical topics and polemical views for and against the present regime. But no attempt has been made to bring all these subjects between two covers and to produce a work that summarizes the main trends of contemporary Ethiopia. We felt that this was needed. A first attempt had been made (in French) a few years ago to do almost that—but not quite.[3] *L'Ethiopie contemporaine* tried to present the public with a more rounded study of traditional Ethiopian culture and history as well as recent events and processes that are deeply transforming the country. But when we started to translate it into English we were rapidly struck by a key problem: some elements of contemporary Ethiopia were either absent in that volume (for example urban development and evangelical churches) or had evolved so quickly since its publication that it now dealt with them incompletely. We then started not to translate but to rewrite and update the whole thing extensively. It took seven years and this is the result.[4] An imperfect, of course, but detailed wide-angle snapshot of the country which had not been attempted for nearly forty years.

Our goal in this work is therefore not to be exhaustive, but to be able to account in an accessible way for a wide readership, for the nature and evolution of Ethiopian political modernity since its foundation at the end of nineteenth century, and the ups and downs of the federal regime established in 1991, under the continuous leadership of Meles Zenawi, head of the Ethiopian People's Revolutionary Democratic Front (EPRDF), until his unexpected death in 2012. Ethiopia's "revolutionary and federal democracy" has become a political model which is quite unique, being an alloy of revolutionary theories, pragmatic neoliberalism and intrinsically Ethiopian customary practices.

In aiming to understand the logic of the present time and its historical background, this book focuses on the political, religious and economic issues that we believe provide the main basis for understanding contemporary issues. These analyses should provide a toolbox useful to all those who seek to discern the lines of evolution of this complex and in many ways hermetic country, or who seek to work, invest or travel there, or, in the case of the more and more "Ethio-descendants" who live abroad, who wish to trace their own roots there.

Some readers will undoubtedly regret that several aspects are not addressed, such as the cultural sector (in particular the music, visual arts and food for which Ethiopia has become internationally renowned), heritage management policies and touristic development, as well as more specific dimensions of state structure, such as the administration of justice or the significant strengthening of the army (which in a few years became a powerful military-industrial conglomerate). Other social issues are not covered here, such as public health, media and censorship, youth and its hopes, educational and academic policies. But we expect that the general framework provided here is a good opening that will help readers find in-depth knowledge from the abundant literature that exists on these issues.

With a view to providing informative and synthesizing contributions, annotations are sparse and chapters do not use a dense critical apparatus. However, each chapter includes a comprehensive bibliography, primarily designed to orient the English reader and point out the texts that are most readily available in most academic libraries and, increasingly, online. These bibliographies include some important works in the French, German and Italian languages which are essential for the scholarly study of Ethiopia. This field of study is indeed characterized by the great diversity of origin of the foreign observers (travellers, diplomats, experts, missionaries and so on) who have studied this country, written in collaboration with Ethiopian scholars, but about its myths and realities, its greatness and misery, and contributed, not without tensions and misunderstandings, to the modernization of its structures and to its international recognition.

Synopsis of the chapters

Ethnic diversity. In 2012 Ethiopia's population reached 91.2 million, the second highest in Africa after Nigeria. In Chapter 1, Éloi Ficquet and Dereje Feyissa highlight the geographical settings, the historical dynamics and the cultural characteristics of the diverse ethnic groups composing the Ethiopian population. The structural features of Ethiopia's geography, based on the dualism between well-watered highlands and dry lowlands, have left a strong imprint on human activities and social organizations. These determinations are outweighed, however, by the capacity of human groups to adapt to risks and to transform their environment through the combined effects of solidarity and greed, willingness and coercion. Over the last decade, the pace of development and social change has quickened in all kinds of sectors and has strongly impacted all Ethiopian societies, including those in the peripheries who used to be overseen by means of military control without much concern on the part of the government for their economic integration. The ongoing process of the infrastructural unification of Ethiopia, through roads and other investment, has entailed a levelling of the ways of life of the Ethiopian peoples, in spite of their continued cultural diversity. This material convergence is a major transformation of recent years that has not been sufficiently taken into account.

Religions. Besides linguistic and cultural differentiations, religions are another major dimension in Ethiopia's historical and current evolution. Like few other countries in the world, Ethiopia has been characterized by the long lasting establishment of three world religions: Christianity, Islam and Judaism (the latter to a lesser extent today since almost all Ethiopian Jews have been resettled in Israel after the first rescue operations in the 1980s). Throughout the long history of Ethiopian religions, clerics have been trained in the art of writing so as to preserve their knowledge and other kinds of instructions on documents, but they have also been experts in deciphering the mysteries of the invisible spheres. This intimate association between the more obvious, formal, written side of social life and the informal, esoteric, hidden dimensions is crucial to grasp in order to understand how politics has worked and continues to work in Ethiopia.

Orthodox Christianity. For centuries the Christian Orthodox Tewahedo Church of Ethiopia was considered the dominant framework through which Ethiopia could be understood. Today Orthodox Christians represent more or less one half of the Ethiopian population, concentrated in the northwest but also widely disseminated throughout the urban networks of the state structure. Without going far back into history, Stéphane Ancel and Éloi Ficquet start Chapter 2 at the end of the nineteenth century to show that the Church was instrumental in the unification of the kingdom and its dependencies around a common reinstated Christian identity. But quite quickly it became clear that without organizational changes in the clergy and the Church's complete submission to secular political authority, it could not continue playing this role. Therefore, the nationalization of the Ethiopian Church was its main challenge in the first half of the twentieth century. After the cutting of its historical umbilical cord to the Egyptian Coptic Church, the Ethiopian Church was forced to follow and adapt to political changes in Ethiopia. The Derg incarcerated and executed a Patriarch and nominated a new higher clergy who accepted revolutionary ideas. In turn, the EPRDF arrested the Derg's Patriarch, who fled into exile and was replaced by a new head who shared a common origin with the new secular leaders. These unceasing government interferences in clerical affairs led to the development of reformist movements that became a shelter for conservative oppositions.

Islam. In Chapter 3 Éloi Ficquet considers the case of Ethiopian Muslims, who make up approximately one third of the population (according to disputed statistics) and are spread over the eastern half of the country. Islam is also the common religion, albeit in significantly varying forms, of several of Ethiopia's neighbours. Since the early days of Islam, when companions of the Prophet took refuge at the court of the Ethiopian king, the participation of Muslims in the construction of Ethiopian nationhood has been an important issue. For a long time, in an imperial state originally built upon the supremacy of Christianity, Muslim subjects were discriminated against and marginalized. After the downfall of imperial rule the authorities moved towards more secular orientations. Muslims have been gradually recognized as having equal rights in a pluralistic society, but they are still the target of insinuations hinting that they could represent a security threat owing to their links with competing interests abroad. This misunderstanding was at the core of the recent protests by Ethiopian Muslims who claimed the right to be treated as genuine citizens in a pluralistic society. They argued that the state should focus on specific policies against extremist threats instead of relying on generalizations.

Protestant and Pentecostal movements. Besides the encounters and exchanges between the Christian Orthodox and Islamic communities, foreign Christian missionary movements also weighed on the course of Ethiopian history. In the seventeenth century Jesuit Catholic missions succeeded in converting the king to Roman Catholicism. This led to a civil war that resulted in the closure of the kingdom and internal theological controversies within the Orthodox Church. A ban on missionary penetration was progressively lifted in the nineteenth century. Missionaries' presence and activities were tolerated as long as they were content to proselytize among peripheral populations. Whereas Catholic missions kept a low profile by providing assistance to weak communities, Protestant churches were more assertive in their development goals and nurtured movements of political emancipation by fostering the use of local languages and the assertion of more autonomous identities. This caused the latter to be persecuted under the Derg. In Chapter 4, on the Evangelical movement and its current charismatic renewal, Emanuele Fantini explains the characteristics and common features of the different denominations encompassed under the label of "Pente". In the last two decades these churches have witnessed rapid expansion. Today Ethiopian Protestants represent almost 20 per cent of the population, even representing the majority in south-western regions. By their assertiveness, capacity for entrepreneurship, discourse against traditional beliefs and conduct, and use of the resources they get from their transnational networks, the various Protestant movements have become one of the major forces contributing to the birth to a "new Ethiopian man", in accordance with the developmental stance of the government. The potentially destabilizing consequences of such a radical transformation have often been overlooked.

Rastafari. In Chapter 5 Giulia Bonacci explores the Rastafari cult. There are only a few hundred followers of this Afro-Caribbean movement in Ethiopia, in the community of Shashemene. Their presence and image are, however, meaningful because their participation in wider Pan-African thought, their emphasis on the sacredness of Emperor Haile Selassie, and the great number of their sympathizers world-wide, attracted by reggae music and their way of life, have connected Ethiopia with a world-wide cultural network. The Rastafari have greatly contributed to the international promotion of Ethiopia as a holy land for the descendants of African slaves by reshuffling Biblical mythologies to fit them into the historical experience of black peoples' so as to restore their proud identities by fitting them into a globalized value system.

Political history of the modern state. The second section of the book traces Ethiopia's political history from the foundations of the modern state in the second half of the nineteenth century to the fall of the Derg military junta in the last decade of the twentieth century. During each period, despite internal disputes, the successive Ethiopian rulers all claimed they were driven by the same goals: sovereignty, modernity, unity. And they all were prone to the concentration of state power and economic assets in the hands of a small leading group. The heavy expansions of the bureaucracy and the army enabled state control and violence to be directed against subordinate and peripheral populations, whose chronic state of poverty was prolonged.

Tewodros, Yohannes, Menelik. In Chapter 6 Shiferaw Bekele provides a synthetic overview of the processes of nation- and state-building under the reigns of three kings of kings, Tewodros II (r. 1855–68), Yohannes IV (r. 1872–89) and Menelik II (r. 1889–1913). Each of them represented a distinct area of the Christian realm, respectively the west, the north and the south (the latter including the conquest of the east). Under the threat of foreign imperial ambitions and in the context of the scramble for Africa, these leaders boldly stirred up the Ethiopian spirit of independence and led their troops to historic victories. They were also visionary enough to recognize the warning signs that the world was changing in ways that would bring more than only military challenges. Facing the risk of being swallowed up by modernity and colonialism, they addressed the need for reforms by reshaping the traditional social and political structures into a centralized state. This implementation of modernizing and centralizing policies required new models and new technologies that were introduced with the financial and technical support of foreign powers, in particular through advisors and experts who were positioned at different levels of the state apparatus. The framework for understanding Ethiopia's development therefore has to include two dimensions: the existence of strong internal authority on the one hand, and the need for this authority to gain the support of external powers. Within this framework, all Ethiopian leaders had to skilfully negotiate with their international partners in order to carve open a space in which to develop according to their own vision and agenda— though they have also sometimes been able to take advantage of competition between different foreign powers.

Haile Selassie. For nearly sixty years, including five in exile, King of Kings Haile Selassie ruled over the evolution of Ethiopia from a feudal-like society based on power relations between provincial ruling families to a state with a centralized administration based, at least formally, on a conventional legal system and populated by well-educated individuals. This long reign is considered in Chapter 7 by Christopher Clapham who, as early as 1969, authored a perceptive study on the mechanisms of the Ethiopian government since the restoration of imperial rule after the victory over Italy in 1941.

Haile Selassie was probably the Ethiopian aristocrat of his time who had been the most exposed to Western education and values. His entourage consisted of intellectuals who were known as modernizers' or "Japanizers" since the Japanese Meiji era was their model for Ethiopia. He was genuinely convinced that significant reforms should be fostered—provided he remained the absolute ruler. After the short-lived Italian invasion—which had a durable modernizing impact on infrastructure—major breakthroughs were achieved, including the setting up of a provincial administration, the establishment of a new legal framework, the nationalization of the Church, and progress in higher education. On each issue His Imperial Highness was to occupy the centre of the chessboard. There was thus a widening contradiction between the actual attempts at modernization and the inherent conservatism of the regime. The system Haile Selassie established was based entirely on his person and it could not be transmitted to less talented heirs, who were trained in palace life but not in political competition. As Clapham puts it: "It was his own dominance that made the abolition of the monarchy inevitable". Constitutional monarchy was an illusion, just as the ideology of a multi-millennial monarchy had been. The very nature of his power meant that challengers would try to take over, by tricks or by force. The failed coup of 1960 was a warning shot. The backlash that followed accelerated the sclerosis of the regime, which from then on focused on factional rivalries and was deaf to appeals for social and economic evolution.

The Revolution and the Derg. In Chapter 8 on the 1974 Revolution Gérard Prunier shows that many factors converged to trigger mechanisms comparable to those that led to social revolutions in the agrarian empires of eastern Europe and the Balkans. The atmosphere of radical militancy inspired by the decolonization of other African countries amplified the frustration of the modernized urban elite, in particular the educated youth who found no job opportunities. The archaic structure of the economy, the inextricable cluster of land issues, the serious social inequalities, and the eruption of the "national question" were the most discussed factors. After mammoth street demonstrations in the spring of 1974, a military junta known as the *Derg* came to power and took the initiative from the leftist student movements. The main measure was to follow the slogan "land to the tiller" that had been initiated by Chairman Mao in China. Land collectivization was decided upon in 1975. In addition, the revolutionary regime recognized the diversity of cultures, religions and languages, but not to the extent of granting them political rights. The idea was that the revolution should mobilize the people as a whole without any distinction between the various peoples. Feudal Christian imperialism was replaced by a coercive military regime based on Marxist-Leninist ideology, and the task of ideological maintenance was transferred from the Church to the Army. In the bipolar context of the Cold War, the political fanaticism that characterized the leadership of Lt.-Col. Mengistu Haile Mariam was rationalized as an attempt to safeguard national unity against threats of foreign aggression or internal dislocation. With the support of the Soviet Union—and under pressure from it—the revolutionary military dictatorship tried to transform into a people's democracy. This process was completed in 1987, two years before the fall of the Berlin Wall and four years before the collapse of the Soviet Union and the destruction of Africa's largest army by a remarkably well-organized rebel guerrilla group.

Eritrea. In Chapter 9 Prunier discusses Eritrea, which formed a special case in Ethiopia's historical trajectory. Since antiquity, exposed to all kinds of trade and smuggling, Ethiopia's Red Sea façade had been open to overseas influences. After the opening of the Suez Canal in 1869 the Red Sea became an arena of competition among European powers and Eritrea became an Italian colony in 1890. The Italian colonial authorities devoted significant investment to turning it into a stepping-stone for fulfilling their ambition to expand their empire to cover the whole Horn of Africa. The historical experience of colonial discrimination, the interaction with Italian settlers, and the introduction of a modern economy entailed the emergence of a distinct Eritrean identity. After the Italian defeat in 1941, the process of decolonization under British supervision led to a short intermediary period of liberalization that favoured the formation of a civil society and further distanced

Eritreans from the Ethiopian empire. Haile Selassie claimed the "return" of Eritrea into his realm. But a ten-year-long federal union between Ethiopia and Eritrea (1952–62) failed to take into consideration the specificity of Eritrea. The country was then absorbed into a union with Ethiopia, but the Ethiopian framework of absolute imperial sovereignty did not correspond to the democratic aspirations of Eritreans. Resisting annexation by Ethiopia, this Eritrean liberal orientation transformed itself into a militant armed movement. For thirty years, the experience of guerrilla warfare and political indoctrination radically transformed the collective consciousness of Eritreans and their leadership. If tensions eased after the glorious days of independence in 1993, its competition with Ethiopia continued in the economic field and was exacerbated by disputes over monetary sovereignty. This led to a war over boundaries that broke out in 1998. Since the official end of the conflict in 2000 the two countries have not been reconciled, and the Eritrean regime has isolated itself with a form of totalitarian political and social delirium.

The Tigray People's Liberation Front (TPLF). In the wake of the Eritrean liberation movement, the national question was raised throughout Ethiopia by other peripheral components of the empire. After Eritrea was fully annexed into the Ethiopian Empire in 1962, not only coastal Muslim populations but also Christian highlanders dared to challenge the "mother nation". This struggle inspired other people, particularly among the younger generations, who found in the Eritrean struggle a model for contesting their subordinate situation in the Empire. In northern Ethiopia, Tigrayan militancy in favour of independence led to the creation of the TPLF in 1975. In Chapter 10 Medhane Tadesse traces the history of this movement from its foundation by a group of Marxist students, who managed to rally the local peasant population to the idea of armed struggle. Having a contiguous territory and ambiguous relations with the Eritrean People's Liberation Front (EPLF), the TPLF became a laboratory for political ideas. After several internal disputes and political trials this ideology of struggle forged the concepts and practices that are still the operating guidelines of the TPLF-led regime today. This movement acquired a national dimension by gathering around itself a coalition of other ethnic-based organizations that coalesced in 1989 into the EPRDF. Within the EPRDF, the TPLF executives have provided the ideological direction of the government, as well as much of its leadership.

11

Federalism and revolutionary democracy since 1991. The third and last section of the book deals with federal Ethiopia under the uncontested leadership of the EPRDF. In Chapter 11 Sarah Vaughan traces some of the dynamics and constraints of the three processes of decentralization, democratization and liberalization since 1991. From the onset of the government of transition, administrative units were reorganized according to mainly ethnic criteria and expectations were catastrophically high. When the constitution of the Federal Democratic Republic was ratified in 1994 the new Ethiopian leaders were suspected of pushing the country towards violent dissolution by using its ethnic fault lines as the basis for a new power structure. Yet, despite its internal contradictions, Ethiopian ethno-federalism still stands more than twenty years after its conception, and has not yet generated any major crisis. Tensions are high, violent outbursts erupt sporadically, but the most serious conflicts of recent years have been tied less to tensions between local groups than to national and regional issues. And when faced with these challenges Meles Zenawi's federal government has been both tough and, where necessary, flexible.

Elections. The admission of Ethiopia into the league of democratic nations implies the organization of elections whose results depend, in principle, on the people's judgement of the regime's behaviour. In Chapter 12 Patrick Gilkes reflects on the last two elections, held in 2005 and 2010. The May 2005 elections marked a significant change in Ethiopia's political history. If the pre-electoral campaign provided the country's first genuine electoral contest, the post-electoral crisis over the credibility of the results led the EPRDF to revise its model by turning to the well-off social elite, whom they recruited as model agents of change. Consequently, the 2010 elections left no space for dissent and the ruling coalition won 99 per cent of the seats. This obviously unrepresentative figure should not, however, be completely disregarded: a large portion of the public was ready to admit that the government had worked efficiently for the socio-economic transformation of the country.

Regional challenges. Ethiopia's ethnic question, its lack of access to the sea and its conflict with Egypt over access to the water of the Nile have remained critical issues for hundreds of years, influencing its development and defining its place on the regional geopolitical scene. In

Chapter 13 Medhane Tadesse describes the military and diplomatic actions of the EPRDF-led government in response to several challenges related to these issues: the Ethio-Eritrean war and its postponed resolution; the Somali conundrum and the threat of terrorism by self-styled Islamists; the conflicts in the Sudan and the South Sudan independence process; the development of the hydropower and irrigation potential of the Nile waters and the trial of strength with Egypt. Tadesse argues that diplomacy has been "more fruitful, if less dramatic, than the unilateral use of the military as a means of managing regional security". Ethiopia's involvement in African Union peacekeeping missions and cooperation with other international organizations were, for example, used in a rather successful strategy designed to block the emergence of a coalition of countries antagonistic to Ethiopia's regional policy imperatives.

Economic development. The proliferation of skyscrapers, the opening of clothes factories, the new cultivation of thousands of acres of arable land by foreign investors, and ambitious investments such as the Grand Ethiopian Renaissance Dam attest to Ethiopia's emergence as an "African Lion". In Chapter 14 on the dynamics of economic development, René Lefort acknowledges that the government has managed to get the country moving—and moving fast—in pursuit of ambitious growth objectives. However, statistical indicators have to be questioned, as do the paradoxes of a strongly state-led economy that aims not only to control strategic sectors and material resources, but also to orient people's lives towards development. The extreme concentration of economic assets in the hands of parastatal companies throttles the capacity of private investors to enter Ethiopia's market.

Urban renewal. One of the most striking features of Ethiopia's economic development is the expansion and transformation of its cities. Urban renewal is particularly visible in the capital city, Addis Ababa, which is dealt with as a case study in Chapter 15 by Perrine Duroyaume. What are the economic factors propping up the wooden scaffoldings that surround new skyscrapers, many of which remain empty? Where do the new freeways and railway lines lead? How does public planning work to organize the eradication of shantytowns, the mushrooming of condominium neighbourhoods and the expansion of residential areas far into the outskirts? The mechanisms of urban policy have attracted massive investment in real estate, leading to speculative excesses.

Meles Zenawi. The closing chapter by Prunier revisits the life and career of the late Ethiopian Prime Minister. Meles Zenawi was a paradox because his life straddled two different historical periods. His "first life" was that of a twentieth century revolutionary leader in the mould of Mao Zedong, Fidel Castro or Ho Chi Minh. But his "second life" progressively turned into that of a post-communist statesman on the Deng Xiaoping and Vladimir Putin model. Few leaders in Africa, if any, have reached his level of visibility and prestige, or motivated as much adulation or hostility. In a way, his biography is still not "closed", as the final judgement on his paradoxical personality has yet to be passed and will largely depend on the success or failure of the modernization process now underway in Ethiopia.

* * *

Ethiopia is engaged in such a frantic race towards modernity that both its successes and its failures are being constantly added to. Ideally this book (or at least some of its chapters) should be reissued or electronically updated every eighteen months, not only to keep pace with the transformations but also to try to assess how "timeless Ethiopia" is faring in the process. Ethiopian tourism promotion campaigns still try to evoke a majestic image of biblical solemnity wrapped in the nostalgic remnants of feudal grandeur. But from Axum to Konso, from Gondar to Harar, Ethiopia cannot be put under an inverted glass dome, and its inhabitants even less so. The nation is moving forward, at times in complex ways. This unique country is going through an entirely new period of growing pains and all its friends hope that this process will result in a democratic and prosperous future. That will require work.

Paris—Addis Ababa—Washington, 2009–2014.

1

ETHIOPIANS IN THE TWENTY-FIRST CENTURY

THE STRUCTURE AND TRANSFORMATION
OF THE POPULATION

Éloi Ficquet and Dereje Feyissa

According to its own calendar, Ethiopia entered the twenty-first century in September 2007 of the Gregorian calendar. This is an indication of how the country has avoided international norms for a long time, asserting its own difference. The symbolism of reaching the year 2000 was marked in the international community by the advancement of "Millennium Development Goals". Similarly, the celebration of the Ethiopian millennium, two years after the contested elections of 2005, provided an opportunity for the regime to herald a triumphant era of "Growth and Transformation". Ethiopia was to be reborn under firm state planning and control, and new-born Ethiopians were to be inculcated into the ideology of Revolutionary Democracy and imbued with the hopes of the African Renaissance. This latter concept, popularized by the South African President Thabo Mbeki in 1998, became the motto of the celebration of the fiftieth birthday of the African Union

15

at the brand new, Chinese-built headquarters of the pan-African organization in Addis Ababa in May 2013.

Ethiopia has become the second most populated country in Africa, behind Nigeria, having reached an estimated population of 91.2 million in 2012, based on the projection of the 2007 national census. This opening chapter will highlight the geographical settings, the historical dynamics and the cultural characteristics of the diverse ethnic groups that compose the Ethiopian population at this time of deep transformations. The structural features of Ethiopia, based on the physical dualism of well-watered highlands and dry lowlands, have left a strong imprint on human activities and the organization of society. These determinations are outweighed, however, by the capacity of human groups to adapt to risks and transform their environment through the combined effects of solidarity and greed, willingness and coercion. Over the last decade, the pace of development and social change has quickened in all kinds of sectors. There have been stunning growth of roads, towns and markets; expansion of commercial trade and tourism; increases of power and water supplies and spreading of communication technologies; investments in large scale irrigation schemes; building of schools and higher education institutions; and various other governmental and non-governmental projects. But in the last decade Ethiopia has also seen climate change and organizational inefficiency causing food insecurity; the spread of HIV/AIDS; the hopelessness of high youth unemployment and the loss of emigrants. Ethiopians at the beginning of the twenty-first century have new needs, desires, opportunities and obstacles, which have affected their sense of their local and national identities.

There is a mass of ethnographic and historical data to which one might refer in the academic domain of Ethiopian studies, but the editorial constraints of a single chapter will make for an overview rather than a detailed study. For each society or cluster of societies, the following sections will provide only bird's-eye views of landscapes, customary activities, traditional political organizations and contemporary challenges and cultural transformations.[1] By switching from one territory to another we will endeavour to capture Ethiopia's diversity of voices and perspectives on regional histories that depart from the mainstream national narrative. For a general review of the role of ethnicity in contemporary Ethiopian history and politics we refer to Sarah Vaughan's chapter in this volume.[2] The bibliography at the end of this chapter will provide references to the most accessible studies for English readers. Online open resources like Wikipedia and community websites also provide huge amounts of information, albeit often unchecked and uneven. Outsiders often take militant members of ethnic groups to be representative of their ethnicities, and the pseudo-scholarly mythologies that militants produce from reconstructed traditions are sometimes taken seriously. Readers who want access to more reliable and scholarly information are advised to refer to the five volumes of the *Encyclopaedia Aethiopica*, which offer detailed articles by Ethiopian and international specialists on the current state of knowledge on almost all of Ethiopia's languages and cultures.

The Habesha *or* Abyssinians: *the self-proclaimed core of Ethiopia's national identity*

The name Abyssinia sounds old fashioned when used to refer to the contemporary Ethiopian state, but it remains pertinent as a designation of its original nucleus. The English term "Abyssinian", like its close cognates in other European languages, derives from the term "Habesha" which in Ethiopia describes the cultural characteristics shared by the predominantly Christian highlanders who reside between Asmara (in central Eritrea) and Addis Ababa (in central Ethiopia). Most of these highlanders speak Tigrinya or Amharic, both of which belong to the Ethio-Semitic language family. However, the ethnic category Habesha is slightly vague: it encompasses groups with common linguistic roots and ancient historical ties, and therefore may also include the Gurage people, although to a "lesser degree" since their lifestyle differs slightly from that of a typical Habesha and they reside further south than other Habesha groups.[3] The peoples who refer to themselves as "Habesha" in the term's most extensive meaning make up about 36.7 per cent of Ethiopia's population (c. 19.9 million Amhara, 4.5 million Tigray, 1.9 million Gurage and 0.9 million Agew).[4] This section will focus on the northern Habesha societies, namely the Amhara and the Tigray, and some scattered or enclave minorities.

Although the ethnic labels of Amhara and Tigray are widely used to talk about Ethiopian matters in general terms, these meta-categories only partially correspond to the identities that Amharic and Tigrigna speakers take themselves to have, since these fluctuate between, on the one hand, quite strong local and regional territorial divisions[5] and, on the other hand, divisions on a national scale, not least that between the contemporary states of Ethiopia and Eritrea.

The mountains of north-west Ethiopia and central Eritrea constitute a particular environment whose temperate climate in a subtropical zone and fragmentation into plateaux have been favourable to the rise of a cereal-based agriculture, which is the main unifying trait of this cluster of societies.[6] Daily routines and domestic life are organized around the preparation of breads and pancakes (*enjera*) accompanied by spiced stews (*wet* or *tsebhi*), which are the staple foods and require the cultivation, storing and processing of cereals, of which the most highly regarded is a plant indigenous to Ethiopia, *tef*. Ploughs are used to prepare the soils. This technique is symbolic of the Habesha social order: in a hierarchical society, historically founded on the taxation of lower social groups, the ox plough represents the lowest link in the chain of authority to which everyone submits, and confers on their owners a minimal degree of dignity in the social pyramid.[7]

Before the 1975 land collectivization reforms, which are still in application today, land ownership in Habesha societies was regulated by a great variety of local systems that can be put into two main categories: untaxed lands, called *rist* that were shared between the members of an enlarged family group, and taxed lands, called *gult*, administrated by dignitaries or parishes.[8] This territorial organization favoured the church and the army as vectors of social mobility, and contributed to the mixing of populations. Having a written culture had been instrumental in the circulation and diffusion of ideas on a wide scale. The expansionist aims of the Christian kingdom were supported by a religious ideology in which Ethiopian Christians took over the role of the chosen people. This justified the subjugation, exploitation and enslavement of peripheral non-Christian societies, who themselves gradually assimilated elements of the Habesha ethos.[9] When this regional African power was challenged by the expansionism of colonial Christian powers, the Habesha clerical and political elite redefined the mould of Ethiopian culture by adapting it to the new foreign standards.[10] This process of unification, recodification and standardization of a modern national culture that was linked with urban centres was done at the expense of popular cultures and subaltern ethnicities.

AMHARA. The Amhara's central position in the highlands, their extension into the country's urban settlements, their role in the construction of the state apparatus, and the official status of the Amharic language all mean that they are sometimes seen as equivalent to (and conflate themselves with) the Ethiopian people per se. Their prime position is rooted in an age-old process which began in the fourteenth century with the emergence of the Christian Solomonic dynasty in Beta Amhara (corresponding to the southern part of today's Wollo region). The kings of Amhara gradually imposed their language and political mores on the territories under their sovereignty. Although learned clerical culture was expressed and transmitted through the written Geez language, the status of Amharic as the official language of the state was reinforced, expanded and modernized under the reigns of emperors Menelik II and Haile Selassie I. In recent political history, in particular since the 1960s, this primacy has been hotly contested by speakers of other languages, some of whose ideologues denounce assimilation into Amhara as a form of colonialism. The current ethno-federal regime has imposed certain formal territorial and institutional limitations on the Amhara people. However, this attempt to make the Amhara just one ethnic group amongst others is undermined by their considerable extension outside the limits assigned to them, as testified by the vitality of modern urban cultural production in the Amharic language both in Ethiopia and in international diaspora networks.[11]

TIGRAY. The Tigray people are also called Tigrayan or Tigrean in the academic literature. In Ethiopia, the various groups of Tigrinya speakers commonly identify themselves as Tegaru (the plural form of Tigray or Tigraway).[12] Whereas the term Tigrinya is used only to designate the language in Ethiopia, in Eritrea it not only designates the language but also the people. Meanwhile, Amharic speakers usually call them Tigre, but they should not be confused with the Tigre people, who are Muslims and live on the western lowlands of the Eritrean Red Sea coast. The variety and ambiguity of the forms of this ethnonym are indications of the rapid and still unsettled evolution of this identity in the ethno-political frameworks of Ethiopia and Eritrea, from a subaltern situation to a dominant political position in both countries since the 1990s. Tigray groups define the Habesha identity more narrowly, claiming that it is applicable only to them as an ethnonym, because their territory overlaps with that of the ancient Kingdom of Aksum and the Tigrinya language is directly linked with the ancient Geez language. But also noteworthy is the fact that Tigray oral traditions allow for the integration of Amhara and Tigray lineages, bearing witness to ancient and constant relations between these two peoples. When it comes to local political organizations and the management of land holdings, Tigray societies are characterized by the important role of village assemblies in decision making and the delivery of justice.

Current political trends have been influenced by the formation of the Italian colony of Eritrea in 1890, which disassociated the destinies of Ethiopian and Eritrean Tigray peoples. In Eritrea, Tigray highland Christians were the main members of the colonial indigenous elite, and were exposed to modern education as well as to racist and discriminatory behaviour from the colonizers. In Ethiopia, the contest for the royal crown after the reign of Yohannes IV placed the Tigray ruling families and commoners in a downtrodden position, causing in the following decades insurrectional movements collectively known as *Weyane*. The political grievances of the Tigrinya speaking community in the post-Yohannes IV period are inscribed in the expression "Zemene Shoa" (that is, the Shoan era), shorthand for the new and overbearing Shoa hegemony, which resulted in the economic deprivation and political decline of the Tigrayans. The peripheralization of the Tigray region, a former political centre, was a catalyst—effectively used by the Tigray People's Liberation Front (TPLF)—for the political and military mobilization of the Tigrayans, historically major actors in the making of the Ethiopian state. Currently, Tigrayan cultural identity is promoted within the Tigray Regional State, which uses Tigrinya as the language of the regional government and of primary and secondary school education.

The Tigrinya speaking groups of Eritrea and Ethiopia were brought together in the liberation wars provoked by the annexation of Eritrea by Ethiopia in 1962. A common culture of guerrilla resistance against the Ethiopian state was forged, with an emphasis on communal egalitarianism and self-reliance. But the Eritrean People's Liberation Front (EPLF) and the Ethiopian TPLF had contradictory strategies and ideologies, strengthening the development of separate Ethiopian and Eritrean Tigray identities. These quarrels are one of the sources of the border dispute between the two countries that has been ongoing since 1998.[13]

AGEW. The term Agew designates a very fragmented linguistic and cultural group, made up of scattered enclaves in Habesha territory. The principal groups are the Awngi to the west of Gojjam, the Khamir and the Khamta in north Lasta, the Kemant to the west of Gondar,[14] and the Bilin to the north, in the western Eritrean region of Keren. These groups can be considered to be the dispersed remnants of the ancient Cushitic societies that were established in the highlands. They have resisted the expansion of the Christian kingdom and its unification under the grip of Habesha political culture.[15] The Habesha have borrowed considerably from Agew material and popular culture, and Habesha languages, particularly Amharic, have been influenced by Agew languages. The Agew groups who were not assimilated were progressively pushed into the least productive lands and confined to the low social status of those who practice "impure" artisanal activities. The reason for this exclusion is that they are said to bear the "evileye" (*buda*), a malevolent supernatural power. Even if not ethnically Agew, isolated occupational minorities of craft workers (potters, blacksmiths, tanners, weavers) are still condemned to exist in the spatial and social margins. This kind of discrimination against craftsmen is not specific to Habesha societies but is found all over Ethiopia. The Agew have established an autonomous self-government in two zones of the Amhara Regional State: the Awi Zone and Wag Himra which are not territorially contiguous.

BETA ISRAEL. The Ethiopian Jews, often called Falasha from the pejorative name used by their neighbours, call themselves Beta Israel (House of Israel). Before they migrated to Israel they formed mainly Amharic-speaking dispersed communities. They specialized in handicrafts and were considered impure outcasts. The issue of the origin of this identity is complex. There are two competing scholarly views: one defends the hypothesis of an ancient settlement of Jewish migrants from Egypt or Yemen; the other argues that conversion to Judaism was a form of ideological resistance used by some Agew groups, who claimed alliance with the Chosen People of the Old Testament in reaction to the persecution they received from the dominant Christian Habesha society.[16] Their contemporary history is that of an absorption into the Jewish world, beginning with the setting up of European Jewish missions at the end of the nineteenth century and culminating, one century later, in their mass migration to Israel after their recognition by the Israeli law of right of return. The *aliyah* (immigration) was enabled by dramatic airlift operations. In 1984–5, Operation Moses rescued and transported 9,000 Ethiopian Jews from refugee camps in

Sudan. Operation Solomon transported another 15,000 in May 1991, just before the collapse of the Derg. A total of nearly 90,000 Ethiopian Jews migrated to Israel. The last episode concerned 2,000 so-called Falashmura, who were the leftover descendants of Ethiopian Jews who had converted to Christianity. In 2003 they were given Israeli visas on condition of conversion to Orthodox Judaism. A new page in the history of the Beta Israel has been opened since their relocation to Israel. They have struggled to integrate themselves into modern Israeli society by surmounting racist prejudice against black people and struggling for the preservation of their Ethiopian identity.

HABESHA MUSLIMS. Among the minorities who compose the Habesha social fabric, we also have to consider Muslims, who represent 4 per cent of the Tigray population and 17 per cent of the Amhara. Known as Jabarti, they are collected in village communities scattered in the Christian highlands.[17] Their isolation, endogamy, specialization in trade and weaving, religious practices and alimentary taboos confer upon them the characteristics of a casted group. The Argobba people (who number c. 150,000) also form a fragmented social complex, but show a greater territorial continuity, as they are made up of a succession of fortified villages on the still cultivable limit of the highlands, filling the gaps between Amhara, Oromo and Afar societies.[18] The Amharic speaking Muslims of Wollo represent 71 per cent of the population of this region, where conditions of tight interreligious mixing are common.

The HARARI *urban enclave.* The city of Harar, at the northern tip of the eastern Ethiopian plateau, has remote historical links with Habesha populations, for the Harari people (estimated to number 30,000 today) speak an Ethio-Semitic language that connects them to the Habesha cluster (in the widest sense of that term). Local popular traditions, partially confirmed by historical investigations,[19] assume that the first foundations of the place as a centre of Islamic teaching and missionary diffusion were laid down at the end of the thirteenth century by a holy man named Abadir, originally from Mecca, who is still venerated as the saint and protector of the city.[20] The regional hegemony of Harar reached its climax in the first half of the sixteenth century under *imam* Ahmad bin Ibrahim al-Ghazi, known by the derogatory name of Gragn ("the left-handed") for the war he led against the Christian kingdom. His eventual defeat led to the gradual decline of Harar's power.

After the Oromo of the Barentu moiety (see below) settled in the area in the second half of the sixteenth century, walls were built around the city by *Emir* Nur bin Mujahid and agreements were negotiated to maintain relations between the urban trading elite and their rural Oromo and Somali neighbours and suppliers of commodities. The Harari people were concentrated in the fenced city (called Jugol), where they developed an original model of urban civilization based on Sufi Islam. After the seizure of Harar and its surrounding region, named Hararge, in 1887 by the Shoan armies of Menilik (led by Ras Makonnen, the father of the future Haile Selassie) the city was transformed into a regional administrative centre, attracting a new population of Christians who dwelled outside the walls. Because of political repression under the imperial regime and then the confiscation of properties under the revolutionary regime, a large number of Harari migrated abroad, to the United States or the Arabian Peninsula. Under the current federal regime, the distinctiveness of the Harari language and culture has been recognized through the delineation of a regional state of its own. But management of this enclave has involved some tension because the Harari are a minority and constitute a cultural and political elite in a city that has become a multi-cultural melting-pot, where the Oromo, Somali and Amhara inhabitants play significant social roles.

The Oromo: *the demographic majority with a subaltern political role*

The Oromo people represent more than one third of the Ethiopian population (32.1 per cent in 1994; 34.5 per cent in 2007). The vast extent of their territory in Ethiopia—extending in the west to the borders of Sudan, in the east into the arid pastures they vie for with the Somali people, in the south along the Tana River into Kenya, and reaching as far north as the confines of the Tigray plateau—means that the different regional groups that make up the Oromo people are in contact with nearly all of the other ethnic groups of Ethiopia. 93.5 per cent of the 25 million Oromo in Ethiopia[21] live within the regional state of Oromiya.[22]

If the Oromo have a particularity it is the plasticity of their identity, which has adapted to the whole palette of social and cultural configurations that compose Ethiopia's diversity. From one region to another,

their way of life encompasses a large variety of agricultural and pastoral practices as well as modern urban activities. Another indication of
their diversity is their religious denominations. In 2007 47.5 per cent
of the population of Oromiya called themselves Muslims (mainly concentrated in the eastern zones and in the area of Jimma in the south-
west); 30.5 per cent were Orthodox Christians (concentrated mainly
in central areas); and 17.7 per cent were Protestants (concentrated
mainly in western zones).[23] 3 per cent still adhere to the traditional
Oromo religion. Under the label of *Waaqeffanna* (from the name of
the supreme sky-God, *Waaqa*), some intellectuals have attempted to
revive traditional beliefs and rituals like pilgrimages, with the aim of
reaffirming a transversal spirituality that links all Oromo.[24]

The diversification of the Oromo regional sub-groups has not taken
away several essential factors which tie this people to a shared identity:
a common language (Afaan Oromoo, also known as Oromiffa, which
belongs to the Cushitic family) of which the regional dialects are mutually intelligible; a sustainable rather than exploitative way of looking
at the relationship between nature and human beings; the high value
attached to cattle husbandry and the passion for horse-riding; a politico-ritual substratum based on the passing of responsibilities between
generations; and the conception of a shared past and present, which
gives the sense of a common destiny and forms a counter-narrative to
that laid down by the arbiters of Ethiopia's official history, which is
centred on the competition for power between Habesha groups and
casts the Oromo in the role of villains.

*A mainstream historical narrative written by rivals and outsid-
ers.* Often designated in historical sources by the name of "Galla",
which has strong pejorative undertones, Oromo were long described
in the historic literature of Ethiopian Christians as warriors, bandits
and heathens. This persisting representation was reproduced in
European travellers' accounts. The Oromo's bad reputation among the
Habesha was influenced by biblical depictions of the enemies of Israel,
and was caused by the conditions of their appearance on the Ethiopian
historical stage. Surging from the margins of medieval Ethiopia in the
middle of the sixteenth century after the devastating Muslim-Christian
wars, the Oromo clans threw themselves into a vast migration and
expansion into weakened territories that were more or less dependent
on the Muslim states in the east and the Christian kingdom in the west.

Because of their unconventional combat skills and fighting spirit they were feared as a scourge and a divine punishment. Progressively, between the seventeenth and eighteenth centuries, the different Oromo groups, who were pastoral nomads, took up sedentary forms of life on these new lands, assimilating the local societies into their clan structure assigning them subaltern status positions. By absorbing and adapting to parts of the local cultures that had preceded them, the Oromo clans reorganized themselves along territorial divisions and their economic, political and religious divergences increased.[25]

As they were assimilated into the social fabric of the lands in which they had settled, the Oromo ruling groups began to represent another kind of threat in the eyes of their Christian neighbours. By adopting the codes of the Amhara aristocracy (who in turn had adopted Oromo war codes, such as giving horse names to warriors) and through alliances, intermarriages and the might of their troops, some Oromo lineages became powerful parties in the political-military game. The picture of the treacherous alien replaced that of the unknown, ferocious invader in Habesha minds. This political competition intensified under the late eighteenth century Gondar kings, when Oromo ruling families reached the highest positions as a result of their alliances with the Christian aristocracy.[26] The following period, called the Era of the Princes, is generally described as a period of decline, but it can also be seen as having fostered a new, more pluralistic political order. This led in the nineteenth century to a movement of ideological resistance aimed at containing the rising Oromo political influence and restoring the lost Christian hegemony through reforms inspired by European modernity and nation-building policies. European powers were searching for footholds on the Red Sea route to Asia and they supplied their Ethiopian Christian partners with stocks of modern firearms. The kings of Shoa took advantage of the power they gained from this by extending their domination over Oromo lands and beyond to the south-west and south-east, claiming that they were recovering the lost provinces of the pre-sixteenth century Christian kingdom. Thus the contemporary state of Ethiopia was built on foundations that involved the military conquest of the Oromo and other neighbouring peoples, the violent crushing of their resistance, their political submission, the grabbing of their land and resources by settlers and the exploitation of their labour force.

Since the eighteenth century, some Oromo polities had been Christianized and incorporated into the Amhara Shoan power system, and some Oromo warlords were given high ranks in the military elite. Oromo troops, for example those led by the warlord *Ras* Gobana Dachi, played a major role in the conquest and subjection of other Oromo and non-Oromo territories. Other Oromo groups resisted forced incorporation into the Ethiopian Empire in various ways. In the face of the strength of the Shoan armed forces, spiritual and ideological resistance was the most viable means. And conversion to Islam (in the east) or to Protestantism (in the west) not only became a way of asserting and preserving the distinctiveness of Oromo identity, but was also a means of access to literacy. Ideological resistance was furthered by cultural movements that aimed at promoting Oromo identity (like the Mecha-Tulama association among western Oromo, or the Afran Qallo music band in the east).[27] The fully-fledged Oromo nationalist political movement was foreshadowed by local rebellions against the authoritarian rule and centralization policies of Haile Selassie's regime. The Oromo Liberation Front (OLF) was founded in the militant atmosphere at the beginning of the Ethiopian Revolution in 1974, and gradually militarized itself as the Ethiopian military regime became more radical. Its struggle was supported by Sudan and Somalia, who hosted Oromo refugee camps which doubled as OLF back-up bases. From exile, mostly in North America and Europe, intellectuals formulated an Oromo nationalist ideology modelled on those of other liberation movements. It is in the domain of history that this ideology found its most powerful voice, rehabilitating the Oromo from the roles of barbarian and villain assigned to them in official Ethiopian historiography.

In 1991 Oromo fighters took part in the final offensives against the communist military junta (the Derg) under the coordination of the rebel armies of the north. After the storming of Addis Ababa and the overthrow of the Derg, the OLF was at first integrated into the process of elaborating the Ethiopian federal constitution, but was quickly sidelined because of the radical nature of its claims for the independence of Oromiya (the Oromo nation). The political representation of the Oromo people within the new federal regime was shouldered by the Oromo People's Democratic Organization (OPDO), perceived to be one of the ethnic "satellite parties" of the ruling coalition, the Ethiopian People's Revolutionary Democratic Front (EPRDF). The federal constitution led to the delimitation of a very large Oromo territory, the Oromiya Regional State, whose boundaries correspond more or less to those in the maps produced by the nationalist ideologues. Inside this framework, the symbolic forms of autonomy granted to the Oromo are counterbalanced by a central political control that is all the more repressive as the demographic weight of the Oromo, their alternative political culture and their region's immense agro-industrial resources mean they continue to represent a potential threat to the interests of the nationally dominant Habesha groups.

Gadaa: *the generational political ideal of the Oromo.* From an internal Oromo perspective the account of history should also be guided by the idea of a cyclical turnover of generations. The active role played by generational groups in the management of communal affairs is encapsulated in the emic category of *Gadaa.* After intellectual reprocessing by foreign and Oromo scholars, it has become the most talked about and cherished value that is taken to express contemporary national Oromo sentiment. Indeed, *Gadaa* is seen as a specifically Oromo republican and egalitarian model, and is opposed to the hierarchical and authoritarian structure of the Christian Kingdom of Ethiopia. In practice, in most of the Oromo regional groups today leadership is not defined and organized through the application of generational *Gadaa* principles (except in some pastoral communities), but membership of *Gadaa* generational sets has retained a ritual meaning in many localities, in particular in the administration of customary justice.

In the still operating versions of the *Gadaa* system, particularly among Borana pastoralists, all males are gathered into sets defined neither by their age nor by their patrilineal lineage, but according to their membership of a generation. All sons of men belonging to one generation will form another single generation. As a generation gathers individuals of very different ages it is divided into five more sub-classes according to age. The sons of the members of class A will then form a class A'. In their turn, the sons of A'—the grandsons of A—will become members of A, according to the cyclical course of the system. Every eight years each class progresses into a different grade. Each grade is characterized by its own set of rights and responsibilities, from infant shepherds to young warriors, mature decision-makers and wise elders. In this way social roles are distributed in a life-long sequence, the exercise of leadership transiting from one generational class to another. What is more, the members of the generational class in charge of leadership and decisions of justice vote some of their fellows to become their representatives or chiefs. The gathering of generational class assemblies under the shade of venerable trees like the sycamore fig (*odaa*) is one of the most powerful symbols of the democratic ideal of the Oromo, oriented towards preservation of peace (*nagaa*) through the maintenance of a flow of arguments and blessings.[28]

In the sixteenth and seventeenth centuries, during the period of conquest and expansion of the Oromo clans, the role of leadership of *Gadaa* assemblies was paramount. The institution was weakened by the effects of distance between dispersed clans. Its egalitarian and trans-segmentary values were challenged by internal political evolution in the regions where Oromo settlers accumulated wealth and power over indigenous populations. The principles of elective leadership and generational changeover were gradually replaced by hereditary offices that led to the formation of monarchical institutions. In regions where *Gadaa* remained the main system of government, the Christian imperial conquest eventually put an end to the customary authority of *Gadaa* leaders, who were replaced by selected personalities among mighty lineages (in particular *Qaallu*, or priests of the traditional Oromo religion) to play the role of local customary authorities and tax-collectors.

It has also to be noted that *Gadaa* has never been the sole principle of the Oromo social order: its principles have coexisted with other forms of solidarity among kin groups associated with the hereditary transmission of ritual charges. Moreover, *Gadaa* is not specifically Oromo. Its form is shared by other societies in southern Ethiopia and bordering countries, for example the Dassanetch, Hor, Konso, Gedeo, Nyangatom, Toposa and Turkana.[29] In each of these societies there are variations in the size, duration, gradation and responsibilities of generation sets, but these are variations of a common political grammar that transcends ethnic divisions.

Short overview of the Oromo regional groups. Under the single ethnic designation of Oromo are found diverse regional entities. Historically, since the time of their great expansion and conquest, the Oromo clans were divided into two moieties, the Borana and the Barentu, who migrated and conquered new lands in different directions by splitting their *Gadaa* assemblies. The Borana oriented their migration towards central, western and southern regions. The Barentu expanded in eastern and northern directions. This early distinction continued to structure the representations of regional divisions from an Oromo perspective, but it was gradually overshadowed by the fixation of territorial entities that became official through administrative maps.

BORANA. In the semi-arid and bushy hills of a wide plateau straddling the Ethiopian-Kenyan border, the Borana-Oromo have a pastoral way of life mainly based on cattle herding and dependent on permanent deep wells. In the last few decades a series of severe droughts and conflicts have led many households to drop out of pastoral activities and seek aid and jobs in urban areas. The Borana-Oromo are understood by other Oromo to be the guardians of the most pure Oromo cultural values. This view is supported by the high density of sacred shrines and the presence of *Qaallu* of the Oromo religion and knowledgeable specialists of historical traditions. The Borana are also renowned for continuing to practice the rules of the *Gadaa* generational system through large ritual assemblies of decision and peace making.[30]

ARSI. The south-eastern highlands, from the shores of the lakes of the Rift Valley to the ridges of the Bale Mountains that arch over the plains of the Ogaden, form a vast territory occupied by the Arsi group. They practice a diversified agro-pastoral system based on cereal cultivation, exploiting climatic altitudinal contrasts. Historical tradition and scholarly debates have converged to identify the region south of Bale as the original cradle of the Oromo before their great expansion of the sixteenth century. In the course of this history, the Arsi group incorporated into its clan structure several pre-existing peoples who were under the authority of medieval Islamic states (in particular the sultanate of Hadiya and the lesser known sultanate of Bale).[31] In the last quarter of the nineteenth century, the conquest of Arsi territories by the imperial Christian armies took a dozen of years of harsh campaigns and violent repression (notably large-scale mutilation of prisoners) to overcome the fierce local resistance. *Gadaa* assemblies were thereafter forbidden and the Arsi practiced mass conversion to Islam as a form of ideological resistance against assimilation into the Christian empire. The fertile land was alienated by Christian Amhara settlers, who were locally perceived as colonizers. The persisting situation of land alienation, heavy taxation and religious harassment led to the outbreak of an armed revolt in the 1960s.[32] The recent spread of Salafi Islamic reform doctrine in this region has also been a response to the perceived marginalization and domination by a distant state structure.[33]

HARARGE. The north-eastern highlands of Hararge are centred on the religious, economic and political networks that have been controlled for centuries by the urban society of Harar and the Harari Ethio-Semitic speaking people. Despite being surrounded by Oromo settlers, and even becoming a minority within the walls of the city, the Harari retained their status as the literate upper class, made dominant over the rural Oromo commoners through their commercial relationships and the spread of Islam.[34] Since the end of the nineteenth century the Oromo farmers of this region have specialized in cash crops, the production of coffee being supplanted by the cultivation of *khat*, a mild recreational stimulant widely consumed in the Horn of Africa and Yemen, with Somalia in particular representing a very lucrative market.[35]

TULAMA *and* MECHA. The south-east of Shoa—that is, the region surrounding Addis Ababa—is inhabited by the Oromo of the Tulama and Mecha groups. These Oromo share many traits with the Habesha: in particular, cereal-based agriculture and the dominant influence of the Orthodox Tewahedo Church. From the beginning of the nineteenth century the Tulama and Mecha were gradually absorbed by the military structures of the Christian Kingdom of Shoa and played an important role in its expansion.[36] These farmers are now exposed to the inconveniences and the benefits of the huge transformations induced by agro-industrial development and the expansion of the periphery of Addis Ababa.

KARRAYU. In the lowlands at the foothills of the massifs of Shoa, the Karrayu raise their herds in the pastures of the Awash Valley, flocking to its banks in the dry season. The harnessing of the river to develop industrial irrigated agriculture and natural reserves has considerably diminished their pastoral area and increased their vulnerability to drought. This lack of resources creates conflicts with their Afar neighbours and pushes these nomads to seek employment in the plantations.[37]

WALLAGA. To the west of the Didessa River up to the frontiers of Sudan, the region of Wallagga was the seat of petty kingdoms founded in the first half of the nineteenth century.[38] The kingdom that eventually dominated was founded in the Naqamte area by a certain Moroda, who came from a minority faction of the Leqa clan. This monarchy flourished owing to the commercial benefits it received from its frontier position. Facing the conquering Christian armies of Gojjam and then Shoa, Moroda converted to Orthodox Christianity and took the Christian military title of *Dejazmach*. He played the card of integration into the Ethiopian Empire of Menelik by paying a tribute of gold. Paradoxically, choosing submission enabled the region to conserve a certain autonomy, making it today one of the most vibrant centres of contemporary Oromo particularism. At the beginning of the twentieth century Protestant missions were set up in the area, and they were to become the bedrock of the Mekana Yesus Church. The introduction of literacy in the Oromo language and the theological divergence with the central authorities were important factors that stimulated and canalized the training of several generations of intellectuals who were the initiators of the contemporary Oromo nationalist movement.[39]

GIBE. To the south-west of Ethiopia Oromo societies are organized around the city of Jimma, an ancient commercial hub on which converged all sorts of goods (ivory, civet, coffee) from the surrounding fertile region, which is suited to intensive agro-forestry and is crisscrossed by roads connecting markets to the commercial routes between Sudan and the Red Sea. The slave trade was their principal source of wealth in the eighteenth century. By imposing their rule and mingling with the neighbouring ancient indigenous societies (that were previously ruled by the Christianized Kingdom of Ennarya), the Oromo clans underwent important transformations in their own social organization. At the beginning of the nineteenth century the dispersal of the *Gadaa* assemblies gave rise to the formation of five Oromo monarchies (Guma, Gera, Gomma, Limmu and Jimma) on the medium altitude plateaux that are divided by the tributaries of the Gibe River, which flows into the Omo River. In order to reinforce their power by connecting themselves to regional and international trade networks, the sovereigns and ruling classes converted to Islam and invited to their side Muslim scholars from other Oromo Muslim areas such as Wollo and Harar.[40]

The pastoral peoples of eastern Ethiopia

The Afar and Somali peoples represent the two principal groups of lowland pastoralists in Ethiopia. Their languages belong to the eastern branch of the Cushitic family. Each forms a linguistic community with a homogeneous territory and culture despite internal divisions between territorial units and large clan groups. Except for a few minority groups, they predominantly believe in Islam, a religion whose cultural values are based on the similar lifestyle of ancient Arab camel herders. Ancient contacts between the African and Arabian sides of the Red Sea and Gulf of Aden, as well as the circulation of traders and Muslim clerics, have created multiple population admixtures.

The social organization of pastoral societies is caught between the two principles of locality and genealogy. Under the harsh conditions of very arid environments the struggle for survival requires knowledge and control of local scarce resources as well as the ability to travel long distance and to get assistance on the way. Every clan, lineage or lineage segment possesses its pastures and water points. They pasture their herds communally and unite to defend their settlements and animals. If not resolved by internal procedures within clans, conflicts over ownership and management of resources (land, cattle, water) are referred to mediating bodies such as councils of elders or ruling lineages in charge of large territorial units. Mobility is facilitated by the territorial dispersion of descent groups and by pacts of solidarity between families. These wide networks of mutual assistance are particularly required in hard times.

Ethiopian central government policies (where they exist), being dominated by the interests and perspectives of the highlander ruling class, have conflicted with efforts by pastoralists to protect their livelihoods and environment. Since the imperial seizure and subjugation of the peripheral lowlands a growing series of investments have been made in large-scale irrigation schemes, mineral extraction and road construction. These encroachments of modernity and development on pastoral lands have disrupted the fragile pastoral lifestyle.[41] The domination of cities over open spaces, progressively established through government control of administration and markets, has marginalized the mobile pastoral nomads who had hitherto been the masters of terrestrial communications. Nowadays social change and economic opportunities are predominantly found in the urban informal sector, where vulnerable nomadic groups can regroup in petty trade and manifold service jobs. These small time jobs constitute a safety net for supporting the subsistence of many uprooted families.

AFAR. About 70 per cent (1.3 million) of the Afar people live in Ethiopia. The figures are more approximate for the Afar living in the eastern lowlands of Eritrea (c. 300,000) and in the north and west of Djibouti (also c. 300,000, representing one third of Djibouti's population on three quarters of its territory). However, pastoralist people are constantly moving across boundaries and cannot be captured by statistics.

The Saho are linguistically and culturally related to the Afar, living to the north-east of them, mainly in Eritrea. They mainly practise transhumant cattle raising between the mountains and the coastal hinterland. Some of their subgroups who are in contact with Tigrinya-speaking societies are Orthodox Christians, notably the Irob (of whom there are c. 30,000 living in Ethiopia), who inhabit the contested area of Badme along the Ethiopia-Eritrea border.

The Afar territory forms a wide triangle, made of barren and empty lowlands, mainly inhabited on its fringes. The first edge of the triangle is drawn by the coast of the Red Sea, from the Bori peninsula to the bottom of the Gulf of Tadjourah. The second edge is limited by the foothills of the escarpment of the plateaux of Tigray, Wollo and Shoa. Being at a relatively cool altitude, these slopes offer more abundant pasture for transhumant seasonal migrations. Clashes often occur between pastoralists and mountain dwellers when they raid one another's herds in response to increased competition for land due to the government's expansion of cultivated areas on land traditionally used for seasonal grazing. Peaceful forms of exchange also exist in the form of a series of markets established in intermediary zones and connected by trade routes. Camel caravan trade used to be the link between the mountain and sea edges of Afar land. Among exchanged commodities, the extraction and trading of salt by the Afar was of vital importance for highlanders. Afar camel herders have suffered from competition provided by modern transport (first the Ethio-Djiboutian railway and later roads) but they have profited from trafficking smuggled goods and transporting illegal migrants seeking jobs in the Middle East.

The third edge of the Afar triangle is formed by a large strip of land on the eastern banks of the Awash River, including its terminal inland delta which ends in a series of lakes. The Awash and its non-permanent tributaries (Kessem, Borkenna, Mille and Golina) provide pastures and water holes to camel herds in the dry season on the route of the transhumant migrations to higher altitude areas. The vital relation of Afar pastoralists to their environment, based on the availability of water resources, has been seriously disrupted by the clearing of vast irrigated farming lands all over the Awash basin, which has hindered access to river banks, reduced water flows, and contaminated the rivers with pesticides and fertilizers.[42] Since the 1970s the vicinity of the Awash has become a contested border zone, with Somali Issa having settled in several spots of the riverine area. This Afar-Issa conflict is still one of the contentious issues in the sub-region, with a cross-border regional dimension involving the neighbouring states of Djibouti and Somalia.[43] The Afar deeply resent the loss of extensive lands in their traditional territories and are angry that the local balance of power has been upset because of the military support Djibouti provides the Issa (who are dominant in that state). On the other hand, Afar rebels in Djibouti have sought to mobilize the Ethiopian Afar in their defence.

Afar society is organized along both genealogical and territorial dimensions.[44] Each Afar belongs to one of the many patrilineal clans (*kedo*), which intermingle through links of kinship and pacts of alliance. Clans and sub-clans have their own oral traditions. They bear in their social fabric memories of a complex history of conflicts, natural disasters, population movements, integration of migrant minorities and incorporation of holy lineages of prestigious Arab ancestry. On the other hand, the regulation of land rights, water use and trade is the prerogative of authorities in charge of large territorial units (*bado*), usually referred to as sultanates. The largest and most powerful Afar sultanate is Awsa, established in the oasis of the terminal delta of the Awash River in the sixteenth century. The wealth derived from its agricultural resources and strategic position enabled this sultanate to extend its influence over all southern Afar lands. The northern inland Afar territories adjacent to Tigray used to be under the authority of the sultanates of Biru and Teru, and the sultanate of Goba'ad covered the south-west territories. The coastal area was divided between the sultanates of Beylul (north-east), Rahayta (central) and Tadjourah (or Tagorri, south-west). Beyond clan and territorial divisions the majority of Afar groups are divided into two moieties, the Reds (*Asayamara*) and the Whites (*Adoyamara*), which used to be rival political coalitions vying for the control of grazing lands along the Awash valley. Each traditional Afar polity, or sultanate, used to be headed by one of the two moieties; neither can pretend to have exclusivity over land resources and both are obligated to accommodate one another. This situation of coexistence has led to intermarriages and admixtures that have made the distinction between the two moieties very vague in some areas.

The Afar State is the only regional state within the Ethiopian federation where there are two political orders with very different bases of legitimacy: the historic Awsa Sultanate still co-exists with the new regional government, although their relationship is fraught with political tension. Ultimately, the political viability of the Awsa Sultanate is undermined by the competition with the regional government, based in Semera. Initially the EPRDF forged amicable political ties with the sultanate, which contributed to the regime change through the Afar Liberation Front (ALF). Upon his return from exile in 1991, the charismatic Sultan Alimirah convened a conference of clan elders to create what appears to be a "neo-traditional" regional government structure within the new Afar Regional State under the leadership of the ALF. Threatened by the emergence of a vibrant and autonomous centre of power and failing to co-opt the Awsa Sultanate, the EPRDF has sought to neutralize the power of the Afar traditional authorities by grooming new political elites dependent on the federal government. Since the mid-1990s, the EPRDF has in fact succeeded in gradually replacing members of Sultan Alimirah's families by capitalizing on corruption scandals involving members of the ALF's leadership. To mark the transfer of regional political power from the Sultanate to the new regional political leadership the regional capital was shifted from Aissaita, the seat of the Sultanate, to a newly built town at Semera. Unsurprisingly, this has generated political tension between the traditional authorities and the federal government-backed regional political leadership.

Politically marginalized since 1995, the Sultanate has, however, shown signs of revival with the coronation of a new sultan, Hanfare Alimirah, in November 2011. The high profile coronation ceremony, attended by dignitaries and traditional authorities from as far as Eritrea and Djibouti, has alerted the political elites within the regional state of Afar to the possibility that this represents the emergence not only of an alternative centre of political power but a very formidable one. On the other hand, the event was represented by the leadership of the Afar Regional State and the Ethiopian government media as a "cultural affair", reducing the new Sultan to the status of a mere "spiritual leader of the Afar". This is in sharp contrast to the Sultan's self-representation as the Afar's new political voice. The massive turnout during the coronation ceremony of Sultan Hanfare in 2011 was as much a vote of no confidence in the regional government as an endorsement of the historically legitimated alternative, the Awsa Sultanate.

SOMALI. The 4.5 million Somali Ethiopians are the third largest Ethiopian nationality, Tigray being the fourth with an almost equal number. They also represent around 30 per cent of the total Somali population (10 million in Somalia and Somaliland, 1 million in Kenya, 1 million in Yemen, 500,000 in Djibouti).[45] According to their clan division, three main groups can be differentiated. The north of the Somali Regional State, corresponding to the Shinile Zone bordering Djibouti, is mainly populated by the Issa clan, who as we have seen are dominant in Djibouti and compete with the Afar for the grazing areas of the Awash valley. The central part of the Somali Regional State, bordering Somaliland, is predominantly occupied by the Isaaq, who are the main clan confederation in Somaliland. Issaq pastoralists' access to the hinterland pastures of the highland area of the Haud in Ethiopian territory has been a major historical challenge for the delimitation of the border and for the management of conflicts. A key aim of the Ethiopian government in this region is the development of the road corridor between Jigjiga, the capital of the Somali Regional State, and the port of Berbera in Somaliland, which would offer an alternative to Djibouti for Ethiopian access to the sea.

Finally, to the southeast, the vast territory of Ogaden is named after the Ogaden clans who are part of the Darod clan confederation, which is dominant in southern Somalia. For the last four decades this territory has been characterized by chronic insecurity mainly due to fighting between the Ogaden National Liberation Front (ONLF) and the Ethiopian federal army, as well as sporadic intrusions by armed groups from Somalia. The Ogaden basin holds significant reserves of gas and crude oil that are being explored and may represent a major opportunity for the Ethiopian and regional economies if sustainable agreements can be found at regional and international levels to escape from the present situation of constant turmoil.[46]

There is also a sizeable Bantu community in the Ogaden basin (the Dobe and the Rheer Barre), which is distinguished by its status as a riverine agrarian minority alongside a dominant pastoralist majority. Paralleling the social cleavage between the Habesha and their Nilotic neighbours, the social boundaries between the Somali and the Bantu are drawn in the language of skin colour and phonotypical features, with the former "red" (light skinned) and the latter "black", as well as in reference to the stigma associated with the Bantu's experience of slavery. The Bantu are also looked down on for their hair texture, which the term *Rheer Barre* signifies ("people with kinky hair"). Animated by the new ethno-federal political structure, which is partly built on the project of ethno-cultural justice, the Somali Bantus, particularly the Dobe, have activated a separate political and social identity. Circumventing the Somali regional government, which promotes the "homogeneity" of the Somali Regional State, the Dobe directly appealed to the House of Federation, the Ethiopian parliament's second chamber, for recognition as one of the country's "Nations and Nationalities" (Ethiopian parlance for its ethnic groups).

The vast majority of Ethiopian Somalis have not been fully integrated into the Ethiopian national identity in their transition from "the enemy nation" during the imperial and Derg periods to the rank of an Ethiopian "nation" among other nations since the establishment of the federal political order in 1991. As Tobias Hagmann, one of the leading scholars on the Ethiopian Somalis, puts it, "the slow and incomplete incorporation of the Somali Region into the Ethiopian nation-state is an ongoing tale of the central government's repetitive yet futile attempts to establish a monopoly of violence by forceful and political means".[47] Only a small elite of young Amharic-speaking urban Somali have been assimilated into the national Ethiopian identity, and these have committed to the ruling party in exchange for high administrative positions. In recent years, however, an incipient reorientation of political identity is observable among the Somalis, who are embracing an Ethiopian national identity in return for a modicum of regional autonomy and new investment opportunities, which contrast with the disincentives of the Greater Somalia project, discredited by the state collapse and protracted civil war in Mogadishu.

The mosaic of peoples in the Southern Nations, Nationalities, and Peoples Regional State

Whereas the northern and eastern territories of Ethiopia are divided between very extended and populous ethno-cultural groups, who are differentiated by five major languages, the south-west quarter of the country presents a radically different configuration, with more than seventy languages officially spoken as well as a multitude of local dialectal variations. The great diversity of societies of the south-west is gathered under the institutional ceiling of the Southern Nations, Nationalities, and Peoples Regional State (SNNPR), in which the major groups have their own administrative zones.

To give some clarity to the structure of this mosaic, it is usual to classify these societies along linguistic categories by distinguishing Ethio-Semitic, Cushitic, Omotic and Nilotic speakers. Although these categories and their sub-groups have no other purpose than to bear witness to linguistic traits, anthropologists and historians tend to seek common cultural and historic traits in societies whose languages belong to the same family. The languages are taken to indicate the origins of the ancient societies from which these peoples descend. But ethnic unity goes beyond the simple frontiers of language. The complex history of each of these societies is reflected in the multiple layers of their social organizations. Ethnic groups are generally seen as definable, institutional entities, as if they had always existed. They are in fact the result of encounters between and amalgamations of populations from different places and of different statuses, and each resulting identity is like a communal roof under which individuals from different backgrounds have been gathered and sheltered.

An exception is made, however, for isolated groups of craft workers and hunter-gatherers, who play an essential role in local economies but are consigned to the social margins and assigned various statuses, from impure outcastes to experts in rituals. Through their marginal position they bind these societies together by forming a kind of trans-ethnic social category that contributes to exchanges of material and spiritual cultures.[48]

The peoples of the evergreen ensete *gardens.* The south-western highland regions of Ethiopia are known for their evergreen, neatly gardened landscapes, displaying the image of relative prosperity and cushioned from the famines that periodically touch the north of the country. This has to do not only with the high rain levels these lands benefit from, but also with the importance given by the societies that live there to the cultivation of the false banana tree, or *ensete*. Once grown, this perennial rhizome plant can tolerate irregular rainfall and can be harvested in almost any season. Its edible parts are the corm and the false-stem, which contain large amounts of starch. Its leaves and strong fibres are used for packing, ropes and building materials. The dough made of its pulp after fermentation has a rather low nutritional value, but it can be stored for several months and covers basic needs during periods of food shortage when other crops fail. Its high productivity allows it to be cultivated in small areas and it can be associated with the intensive production of vegetables, cereals and cash crops (coffee, *khat*, eucalyptus), as well as animal husbandry, the latter activity producing manure for soil fertilization. The productivity of home gardens varies according to altitude and soil fertility, which can vary dramatically over short distances. These characteristics ensure that these lands have high population densities and the appearance of food abundance. But this stereotype, which has prevailed for so long, is deceptive. In many neighbourhoods farming has become less productive because of population pressure, decreasing plot sizes and ill-advised agrarian development policies that have led to low productivity, unbearable levels of household debt, chronic poverty and food insecurity.

GURAGE. The common appellation Gurage corresponds to a name given by outsiders to the vague territory of a cluster of diversified populations (about fifteen territorial groups, comprising nearly 2 million people) who speak languages of the Ethio-Semitic family that relate them to the northern Habesha societies. Their ancient origins, as understood from mythological narratives, are linked with the historical expansions of the Christian kingdom since the early medieval era, through waves of migrations that involved military formations, trading communities, missionaries and other kinds of population movements prompted by warfare and natural disasters.[49]

In the course of their history the different Gurage groups have developed strong ties—through both peaceful exchange and conflict—with neighbouring Cushitic and Omotic speaking communities, with whom they share cultural habits and religious beliefs. Unlike the hierarchical social organization of the northern Habesha, Gurage political structures rest on acephalous ("headless") power relations between patrilineal descent groups or clans. Their disputes are resolved through meetings of either clan assemblies or councils of elders, who deliberate according to the rules of unwritten customary law.[50] The interreligious mixtures and the political divergences of Gurage societies show gradual levels of differentiation involving internal dynamics and external connections. The northern Kistane or Aymellel are predominantly Orthodox Christians. Their ancient links with northern Habesha polities facilitated their integration into the modern Christian empire. The central confederation of the "seven houses of Gurage" is an amalgamation of different clans who resisted absorption into the empire. The eastern Gurage (Welane and Silte, before their estrangement from the

Gurage cluster) are predominantly Muslim and attached to wider regional Islamic networks. Their resistance to Menelik's conquest took the form of an Islamic revivalist movement and a jihadist armed movement led by Hassen Enjamo.

After the forced or voluntary integration of the Gurage societies into the Ethiopian Empire, they migrated en masse to Addis Ababa, the newly founded capital city, a relatively short distance of 200 kilometres to the north-east of Gurage land. Gurage workers, particularly from the Kistane area, became the labour force for the early urban development of Addis Ababa, particularly in the construction and transport industries. Their entrepreneurship gradually spread to commercial activities. Gurage families still have a dominant position today in the emporiums of Piazza and Mercato. This continuous flow of migrant workers and businessmen for over a century has had a strong social and economic impact on rural neighbourhoods, particularly through the remittance of migrants' earnings, which is reinvested in rural development activities by self-help organizations.[51]

SILTE. For reasons of territorial and linguistic proximity the Silte (population 1 million) have long been classified as Eastern-Gurages. They are nearly all Muslims and conceive themselves as historically and culturally linked to Harar. They have claimed to be an independent ethnic identity, and this was granted in 2001 when a separate administrative zone was set up for them after a referendum in which they overwhelmingly voted for a separate identity.[52]

HADIYA *and* KAMBATA. The Hadiya (1.3 million) and Kambata (630,000) are Cushitic speaking peoples whose lifestyle is quite similar to that of the Gurage. The Hadiya are the remnants of a pre-sixteenth century Muslim medieval state that ruled mixed populations over a wide area covering a large part of today's Arsi and Sidama territories. The contemporary social structure of the Hadiya is characterized by egalitarian relations between neighbourhoods defined on the lines of patrilineal kinship.[53] Traces of early Islam were found in their syncretic cult (*fandano*), which disappeared after their conversion to Catholic and Protestant missionary churches. The neighbouring Kambata (including the Timbaro and Allaba groups) were linked in the pre-sixteenth-century medieval past to the northern Christian kingdom and were converted to Orthodox Christianity. They retained a stratified social structure based on the distinction between clans of noblemen and clans of commoners. Their ancient links with the Christian kingdom were reactivated after the conquest by Menelik's army, and the Orthodox Church attempted to regain its foothold by removing local syncretic cults. However, Catholic and Protestant churches established since the 1930s attracted the majority of the population.

SIDAMA. The Cushitic-speaking Sidama (3 million people) represent the most populous group in the SNNPR. Their mountainous territory on the eastern slopes of the Rift Valley offers similar conditions as the above-mentioned territories for intensive *ensete*-based agriculture. Sidama farmers are major producers of coffee, which has remained the main cash crop, in contrast to other groups which have abandoned coffee for *khat*. Their social and political organization is multi-layered. A trans-local authority is exercised by hereditary clan leaders who are in charge of maintaining peace and prosperity through rituals and divinatory powers. Local affairs are managed by councils of elders belonging to generational grades similar to those of the Oromo Gadaa system.[54]

Awassa, the capital city of the SNNPR, is also the seat of the Sidama Zone's administration. Since 2000 the question of its status has raised an intense controversy that has degenerated into an ethnic conflict. Awassa is located in Sidama territory on the shores of a lake bearing the same name.[55] Since it has become the regional capital under the federal regime it has seen a rapid growth from 70,000 dwellers in 1994 to 160,000 in 2007. This development has been enhanced by activities linked to the coffee market and by the construction of resorts, recreational sites and luxury villas on the lakeside. The federal authorities have proposed to give Awassa the status of chartered federal city, like Addis Ababa and Dire Dawa, since it has become cosmopolitan by attracting workers and investors from Welayta, Oromiya and neighbouring areas. This project was strongly rejected by the Sidama who held several protests that were severely repressed. Behind the confrontation between ethno-nationalist and federal perspectives, the main reasons for the disagreement are economic. Rural land belonging to Sidama lineages has been progressively transformed into high-value urban land, generating considerable profits. With a special administration, the management of the city and its flourishing business would be placed under the direct control of the government. It would also involve moving the Sidama zonal administration to another city and removing Sidama politicians and landowners from Awassa's affairs.

KONSO, GEDEO *and* BURJI. These groups (respectively numbering 250,000, 1 million and 70,000) are highland dwelling, Cushitic speaking societies that practice intensive agriculture. Their political system shares many common features with that of the Oromo, with a Gadaa-like generation-grading system being associated with the politico-ritual roles of clan chiefs.[56] The Konso are known in particular for their carvings on wood poles representing their heroic ancestors (*waka*). They do not cultivate *ensete*, but they practice irrigated agriculture on terraced fields. They cultivate the *moringa* tree, also known as the cabbage-tree; its boiled leaves constitute the staple food.[57]

OMETO (*Welayta, Gamo, Gofa and Dawro*). The meta-category of Ometo (subsuming a population of c. 3.7 million) includes various societies and their fragmented subgroups, who speak linguistic variants of the northern group within the family of Omotic languages.[58] In the 1990s the federal authorities attempted to unify all Ometo groups into a single administrative unit through the instrument of a common artificial language called We-ga-go-da (an abbreviation of the four main groups). This governmental initiative fell through on account of the reawakening of regional particularisms.

The WELAYTA (1.7 million people) were in the past the political core of this mountainous and fertile region overlooking the great lakes of the Rift Valley. It was the seat of a powerful kingdom that emerged in the thirteenth century, whose hierarchical and stratified power structure departed from the model of divine kingship combined with communal assemblies that was dominant in the other Ometo societies.[59] This populated and wealthy state developed trade relations with the northern Habesha Christian kingdom. In the eighteenth century power was taken over by a dynasty of kings who had migrated from Tigray. The kingdom was converted to Orthodox Christianity and undertook expansionist policies against its neighbours.

Despite its ancient links and religious affinities with the northern Christian kingdom, the king of Welayta, whose name was Tona, refused to acknowledge Menelik II's supremacy and pay him a heavy tribute. The consequence was the violent military conquest of Welayta by Shoan armies in 1894.[60] The monarchical institutions were destroyed and replaced by imperial appointees. The region, renowned for its agricultural wealth, became the main supplier of grain and meat for the imperial court in Addis Ababa. This marked the beginning of Welayta's economic decline, evident nowadays in the problems of land scarcity, soil depletion, food insecurity and chronic poverty. This decline is the consequence of imperial overexploitation, which continued through agricultural development programs based on the erroneous assumption that the legendary fertility of the land could not be exhausted.[61] The social structure of Welayta society has retained some remnants of the ancient kingdom in the form of stratified relations between patrilineal clans. Communal activities are dominated by Christian churches, in particular Pentecostal denominations that gave rise to self-made religious entrepreneurs who have saturated the spiritual market.

The GAMO, GOFA, and DAWRO societies (respectively 1.1 million, 0.4 million and 0.6 million people) that complete the Ometo grouping live to the south-west and west of Welayta. Their social structure is less stratified than the Welayta's. The Gamo are divided into about forty autonomous territorial and political entities (*dere*), each headed by a sacrificer-king (*kao*) who is the hereditary descendant of the founding hero of the locality. Beside this ritual charge, the maintenance of social order is the responsibility of democratic assemblies of elders and citizens.[62] The Gamo used to be predominantly Orthodox Christians, with inclusion of syncretic beliefs in local spirits. However, they have increasingly come under the influence of Protestant churches from Welayta.

KEFA. The Omotic speaking Kefa people (c. 1 million) and Shekacho people (c. 100,000) live further west in a mountainous area of dense forests, crossed by many rivers and with fertile, abundantly watered soils. These physical conditions have favoured rich and varied agro-pastoral activities and agro-forestry that stimulated commercial activities. The Kefa's main export products were ivory, coffee, civet musk, cardamom and slaves. The ancient Kingdom of Kefa was founded in the fourteenth century and became a mighty centralized state in the seventeenth century, after resisting the Oromo expansion.[63] This southern kingdom established an alliance with the northern Habesha kingdom. The ruling elite were converted to Orthodox Christianity, but lower classes continued their cults to local clan spirits (*eqqo*). Kefa was also linked to the Sudanese trans-Saharan trade routes, from which has come a significant number of Muslim merchant families. The aristocracy of Kefa was composed of clans possessing land rights linked to official functions. It was dominated by the Minjo clan from which the king was chosen. Most of the state functions were linked to a precise clan. This structure seems to have enabled the conservation of monarchical institutions in the long term. In 1897, the conquest of Kefa by the armies of Menelik put an end to the existence of this kingdom. The imperial government largely relied, however, on the ancient structures. The appointed governors of Kefa were assisted by local notables who formed a kind of indirect government and retained land rights on the formerly royal lands in the form of *rist* (inheritable land right). This society, quite isolated from the rest of the country, preserved a certain autonomy in the communal management of its land and forest resources.

Peoples of the south-western borders: ancestors' blessings vs. development prophecies

On the south-western borders of Ethiopia live several culturally and linguistically diverse peoples, who nevertheless share similar conditions of existence either because of their shared harsh environment or their common subaltern status, which has seen them ostracised—or, at best, ignored and neglected—since the conquest of their territories by the armies of Menelik at the end of the nineteenth century.[64]

In the current administrative division of the SNNPR the peoples of the south-western margins live in the South Omo Zone (575,000 inhabitants in 2007) and the Bench Maji Zone (650,000 inhabitants). The main groups living in the South Omo Zone are: MAALE (100,000); ARI (290,000); HAMER (50,000 including Banna, Bashada and Karo); TSAMAI (20,000); NYANGATOM (25,000); DASSANECH (50,000); MURSI (8,000); and BODI (7,000).[65] The main groups in the Bench Maji Zone are: BENCH (formerly known as Gimira, 300,000); ME'EN (140,000); DIZI (35,000); SURMA (or Suri, 30,000).[66]

Despite the diversity of languages and social habits that differentiate them, the traditional societies of south-west Ethiopia have similar social structures and ritual processes. Their particularities have been described by ethnographers since the second half of the twentieth century. Each local identity has been shaped and transformed by processes of inter-ethnic relations and conflicts over time.[67] Since each of these societies cannot be separately presented here, we will underline some common aspects of their politico-ritual language as well as mentioning in passing some of the ways in which they express their distinctness.

Besides pastoralism and agriculture, most of these societies rely on subsistence activities such as hunting and gathering, bee keeping, and fishing, depending on ecological variations between the hot and arid lowlands and the cooler, watered highlands. Although punished by the government, pillages, raids and vendettas have remained common and are effective ways of rapidly amassing cattle wealth. Nevertheless, agricultural activities remain the first means of subsistence, cattle being mostly reserved for rituals.

The continuity of a community from generation to generation is asserted through the collective memory of its ancestors,

who settled a given territory and imposed their domination at a precise time, fixed as time zero in mythological narratives. Power is transmitted either genealogically or generationally, to ensure the perpetuation and extension of the initial political architecture. The founding ancestors represent the origin of society and the source of life and fertility. Their descendants (through genealogical or generational lines) incarnate in a fashion these first beings and they have a role in the maintenance of land fertility, animal reproduction and communal prosperity. To benefit from the flow of "fertilizing blessings" emanating from ancestors, the junior members show their readiness to take over responsibilities by giving gifts to the seniors.

Since their incorporation into the political framework within Ethiopian national boundaries, the peoples of the south-western margins have been, like the other Ethiopian peripheral peoples, affected by the gradual introduction of globalizing factors. Protestant missionary ventures introduced literate education, new religious beliefs and individual aspirations. Ethiopian military garrisons brought the use of the national currency and the consumption of strong alcohol. Civil wars brought the AK-47, replacing spears as instruments of self-protection and symbols of virility.

The last decade saw a sudden speeding up of infrastructure investments that have changed the physiognomy of these barren lands. Until the end of the twentieth century, several days of difficult driving on bumpy, muddy, broken roads and tracks were necessary to reach the South Omo Zone. Since 2010 Addis Ababa can be reached from the South Sudan border in one day on new asphalt roads. The path for further development is open. The implementation of large-scale irrigated agricultural projects by the Ethiopian government (which champions the developmental state model and encourages foreign companies to invest in the lower Omo valley) has already cleared significant portions of cultivable lands, grazing areas and settlements of indigenous communities. In the South Omo Zone alone more than 250,000 hectares of land are apportioned to the state-owned sugar plantation, and the plan is to construct six of the ten envisaged sugar factories during the current phase of the Growth and Transformation Plan (2010–2015). These new investments deprive local communities of most of their prime grazing lands. They are also threatening the Pliocene/Pleistocene geological formations of the lower valley of the Omo River, which is on the World Heritage List for its hominid fossil sites. Moreover, the construction of massive hydroelectric dams on the upper course of the Omo River has affected the water flow, undermining the flood recession agriculture of populations living downstream. These developments also create new opportunities and jobs that attract migrant workers from the other parts of the country.

These rapid economic transformations are in line with a historical process of conquest, exploitation and acculturation that has moulded the Ethiopian national sphere and consciousness for centuries. It is too early, however, to predict the long-term social consequences of recent development projects—which do not appear to be conceived on sustainable grounds—on environments that are already particularly harsh. They may bring more material satisfaction and reduce poverty for some time. However, they may become an additional layer in the history of disasters that is already recorded in the strata of this land, the land from which mankind originated. For the time being, observers have noted the decline of ancient indigenous cultures, which are artificially maintained through the commercialization of ritual performances, traditional dress and body ornamentation as tourist attractions.[68]

Peoples of the western borders

Ethiopia and the two Sudans share a very long border (c. 700 km with Sudan, and c. 900 km with South Sudan). This long strip of peripheral lowlands was neglected because of its remoteness, its insecurity due to Sudan's civil wars, and colonial treaties that prohibited any kind of investment along the tributaries of the Nile in Ethiopian territory. These hindrances have gradually retreated: new roads are being built, the independence of South Sudan has gone some way to reducing instability, and the Ethiopian government has made bold announcements of its ambition to carry out development on a regional scale. It plans to take its share of the hydraulic resource of the Nile basin though large-scale investments in agriculture and the construction of the Grand

Ethiopian Renaissance Dam on the Blue Nile. The following descriptions of the social organization of the Ethiopian western frontier societies correspond more to historic rather than to current configurations, which are changing rapidly.[69]

The peoples of the Gambella Regional State. The Nuer, self-named the Naath (who number c. 150,000 in Ethiopia, and c. 1.7 million in South Sudan), and the Anuak (c. 90,000 in Ethiopia; c. 90,000 in South Sudan) are the two main ethnic groups of the Gambella Regional State (which had c. 310,000 inhabitants in 2007). They live in lowland territories situated on both sides of the Ethiopia-South Sudan border.

NUER. Since the second half of the nineteenth century the Nuer have expanded east in the direction of Gambella from their origins in the Upper Nile region of South Sudan, at the expense of first the Dinka and then the Anuak, both of whom have lost extensive territory to the Nuer. By the beginning of the twentieth century the Nuer had advanced as far east as Itang, which became the frontier between the Anuak and the Nuer—until recently when the demography tipped in favour of the latter. Nuer territorial expansion was accomplished as much through violence as through a dynamic system of assimilation of the vanquished and instrumental inter-marriage practices. The territory is often flooded during the rainy season, as the Akobo and Baro Rivers and their tributaries (which merge to form the Sobat River, which joins the White Nile in South Sudan) collect a lot of water and alluvial soil from the nearby highlands.

The Nuer are predominantly cattle-herders. They also cultivate maize, sorghum and tobacco on the flooded shores of lakes and rivers in the rainy season. The dry season villages are situated near rivers or waterholes; those of the rainy season are set at elevations spared by the floods. After the major ethnographic works published by Edward Evans-Pritchard (1940, 1956), the Nuer became the paradigm of the acephalous segmentary society. Disputes are regulated and contained by a principle of balanced opposition between lineages, understood as segments within larger tribes that do not depend on centralized leadership. But if we follow Douglas Johnson (1994), "heads" were in fact numerous in Nuer society, although they had no power or political authority, only a ritual and mediating role. This society was decapitated by the British colonial administration in order to hinder some Nuer spiritual leaders' resistance to external rule.[70]

Occupying the two border districts of Jikaw and Akobo, the Nuer in Gambella have for a long time been politically and culturally oriented to South Sudan, either through military mobilization by the Sudan People's Liberation Army (SPLA) or through taking alternative citizenship by joining South Sudanese refugee camps in order to gain access to basic social services such as education. The creation of the Gambella Regional State as one of the constitutive parts of the Federal Democratic Republic of Ethiopia has induced a reorientation of Nuer political identity: there is a new desire to "become Ethiopian". The 1994 national census revealed that the Nuer had transformed from an insecure minority in regional politics into the largest ethnic group, constituting 40 per cent of the regional population, by far outnumbering their main contenders, the Anuak, who constituted only 25 per cent; this demographic gap was even more pronounced in the 2007 census, according to which the Nuer now constitute 47 per cent and the Anuak 21 per cent. The new political structure and the radical changes in the demography of the region have put pressure on the Anuak, the other major contender in regional politics.

ANUAK. Unlike the Nuer and the wider Nilotic society, the Anuak possess few cattle and mainly depend on agriculture, fishing and gathering. Traditionally Anuak society was structured into two parallel forms of political organization. On the one hand, there were village heads called *kwari* (singular *kwaro*), who were entrusted with ensuring a balance between rival factions. On the other hand, there was a sacred monarch, drawn from one of two noble lineages known as *nyiye* (singular *nyiya*). The occupation of these positions and the possession of the emblems that are associated with them were objects of constant struggles which created a permanent cycle of overthrowing and accession to power, a form of political organization which Evans-Pritchard called ritual kingship.[71] These traditional social organizations have been deeply transformed by the effects of imperial conquest, the Derg's so-called cultural revolution, missionary works, civil wars, the displacement of refugees from Sudan, the resettlement of hunger stricken peasants from central Ethiopia, SPLA training camps, and models of education brought by NGOs.[72] New global economic processes such as the commencement of large scale commercial agriculture by foreign investors—most of which is in traditional Anuak territories—and the attendant sense of economic exclusion and relative deprivation are further provoking their ethnic sensibility.

48

The Anuak have responded to the externally induced socio-political and economic decline with various forms of resistance, which crystallized in the establishment of the Gambella People's Liberation Movement (GPLM) in the 1980s. Allied with the EPRDF and the OLF, which operated from bases in the Sudan, and claiming to represent Anuak ethnic interests, the GPLM took control over the newly created Gambella Regional State in the 1990s. Operating with the memory of historic territorial losses, the GPLM sought to contain Nuer territorial and cultural expansion, which has engendered talk of the Anuak people's extinction. Anuak political elites have also activated a political ownership claim over the rather multi-ethnic Gambella Regional State. To offset the Nuer's narrative of political entitlement based on their demographic strength, the Anuak have advanced historical justifications for their power claim, presenting the Nuer to the Ethiopian state as "outsiders" and "refugees". This has supplied them with the powerful political tool of framing local ethnic interests in national terms.

These conflicting political narratives and the changing state of alliances between the federal government/EPRDF and the Anuak and Nuer peoples have severely undermined the evolution of a cohesive regional political community, which could have better promoted regional interests in negotiations with the federal government. With a fragmented and weak political voice, Gambella has been thrust to the forefront of the so-called "land-grabbing" phenomena: local communities have lost extensive areas of prime land to transnational companies whose weak sense of corporate social responsibility is evident in their perpetual encroachment into areas way beyond those designated for investment. This state of affairs has created a very hostile relationship between the companies and local communities, a hostility which has already started erupting into deadly confrontations.

MAJANG. In the forest belt to the east of the Gambella Region live the Majang, who speak Koman (which is probably of the Nilo-Saharan language family).[73] With a population of c. 15,000, the Majang, also called the forest people, have been marginalized by their much larger and more powerful neighbours, including the Anuak and the highlanders who encroach into their forestlands. Resorting to continuous mobility as a strategy for coping with such encroachments, the Majang have recently acted along the lines of "if you can't beat them, join them". The spread of commercial farms—first government coffee plantations, then the farms of highlanders migrating away from their less resource-endowed northern highlands—has created a new land market which some members of the Majang society have sought to tap into by leasing or de facto selling their communally owned forestland. However, this has led to the pauperization of the Majang and the looming environmental disaster of the massive deforestation of the Majang forest, part of south-west Ethiopia's dwindling tropical rainforest. The potential problems that this might cause are added to by the fact that the major rivers of the Gambella region, which are tributaries of the White Nile, have their source in the multitude of streams in the forest.

Peoples of the Beni Shangul-Gumuz Regional State. The Berta (c. 200,000 people) and the Gumuz (c. 180,000 people) live on both sides of Ethiopia's border with Sudan. They are situated to the south of the Blue Nile, with the exception of certain Gumuz communities that still occupy the northern shores of this river.

BERTA. The Berta are also known by the territorial name of Bela Shangul, which refers to a sacred stone symbolizing their old political-religious organization.[74] The Sudanese Arabic name for them is Jabalawin, "the people of the mountain". After their incorporation into the Funj Sultanate of Sennar in the eighteenth century,[75] the Berta's land was conquered and administered by the Turco-Egyptians, and it was finally annexed to the Ethiopian Empire in 1898, under the supervision of *Ras* Makonnen.[76] The area was coveted by the Ethiopians for its gold, its slaves and the importation of goods smuggled through the Sudan. However, like Gambella, this area was neglected by the central authorities in the twentieth century, and was exposed to conflicts and humanitarian crises. The forced settlement of farmers from central Ethiopia modified the profile of the population and was a first step towards new agricultural policies. As with their counterparts the Anuak in the neighbouring Gambella region, the Berta's protests against their socio-political decline crystallized in the formation of a liberation movement in the 1980s, the Benishangul People Liberation Movement (BPLM). Also allied with the EPRDF and the OLF, and claiming to represent the Berta people's interests in regional politics, the BPLM took control over the newly created Benishangul-Gumuz Regional State. However, the BPLM's political power was short-lived as it became entangled with the Horn of Africa's geopolitics in the mid-1990s. The Berta, being Muslims and living on the Sudan-Ethiopia border, were susceptible to the political Islam agenda of the Sudanese National Islamic Front (NIF). The NIF in fact penetrated the BPLM in order to use it as a conduit for spreading political Islam to Muslim-inhabited areas of Ethiopia and beyond. The BPLM thus pressed for the adoption of Arabic as a regional language of government and sought increased self-determination, provoking the federal government to counter its political power and influence by favouring the Berta's neighbour, the Gumuz.

GUMUZ. Unlike the Berta, the Gumuz have long interacted with the northern highland Habesha society, for whom they historically consti-tuted "internal others", and who knew them by the pejorative term "Shanqila". They "inhabit an area that extends from Metemma south-wards through Gondar, Gojjam/Metekel, and across the [Blue Nile] up to the Didessa valley in Wollega, western Ethiopia. Linguistically, they belong to the Koman group of the Central-Sudanic branch in the Nilo-Saharan language family".[77]

Since the 1980s a government sponsored resettlement program has forced or encouraged thousands of northern highlanders to encroach on the land which the Gumuz use for shifting cultivation. The Gumuz area has attracted greater interest from central government and investors since construction of the Grand Ethiopian Renaissance Dam began at Guba, a Gumuz village near the Sudan border. This has been followed by the explosion of large scale agriculture which has appropriated a large tract of prime Gumuz land without compensation or measures to protect Gumuz economic and social interests. Like neighbouring Gambella, the Benishangul-Gumuz Regional State is conflict-ridden and lacks a cohesive political voice that could have better defended regional interests vis-à-vis the federal government and corporate investors.

Ethiopians on the move: internal and international migrations

Since ancient times the human geography of the Horn of Africa has been continuously reshaped by population movements along various routes and on various scales, from individual wanderings to mass migrations. In some cases migrations were voluntary (for example, in the case of pilgrims, students and traders), but more frequently peoples were compelled to move by such things as warfare, slave raiding and natural disasters.[78]

In the recent history of Ethiopia the expansion of the Christian empire in the second half of the nineteenth century led to significant shifts of populations from the north into the conquered territories of the south. Soldiers became settlers: they were given land rights on royal estates and were in charge of controlling the subjugated local populations. Garrisons were converted into urban centres, where the central administration established its representation. Merchants took hold of urban markets that were linked to nation-wide trading networks based on cash. Local populations were thereby trapped into administrative frameworks made to control and tax them. The aggravation of rural poverty, caused by excessive fiscal pressure, land scarcity and deteriorating ecological conditions, exacerbated the need to move, but there were few job opportunities for migrant workers. The construction of Addis Ababa and its expansion absorbed a considerable number of migrants. Apart from the capital city and some coffee, sugar cane and cotton plantations, the development of modern economic activities and the rate of urbanization were too slow to induce and sustain large labour migrations.

In the last quarter of the twentieth century, under both the Derg and the federal government, policies of resettlement were implemented to resolve the problem of land scarcity. Several hundred thousand people were encouraged or forced to move from overcrowded and ecologically fragile areas to less populated (though not empty) cultivable lands.[79] The Derg's command economy policies also introduced new models of urban settlement that were followed up in a more liberal fashion by the federal regime, leading to the acceleration of migration from rural to urban areas. Since the end of the 1990s all regions have been impacted by fast urban growth.

Before the last quarter of the twentieth century few Ethiopians travelled abroad voluntarily. The main reasons for international travel were trade, pilgrimage, study and diplomacy. But there is a long history of forced emigration of Ethiopians who, since antiquity, have been enslaved and sold abroad, in particular to the Middle East and India.[80] Until the end of the nineteenth century the profits generated by the enslavement of war prisoners and the civil populations of conquered areas were a strong incentive for the expansion of the Christian empire and had enriched its "trading partners" in neighbouring kingdoms.

The political economy of slave raiding was slowly curbed at the end of the nineteenth century because of international pressure.

As seen above, nation building and modernization agendas progressively introduced new dynamics of population movement. In this context international migration was marginal. In fact Ethiopia attracted small communities of immigrants, such as Armenians, Greeks and Yemenis, who were instrumental in the development of petty industries and trade. With the aim of developing the country and preserving its independence, the imperial authorities sent abroad a few hand-picked students who were charged with acquiring and bringing back modern intellectual and technical skills.[81] Most of them went to Europe or North America. After graduating many returned to their motherland where they were given high positions. The Ethiopian Revolution of 1974 and the fall of the imperial regime forced most such emigrants to stay abroad indefinitely and thereby become exiles. In 1977–8 the number of exiles increased as militants from opposition parties fled the Red Terror—the military regime's campaign of mass killings and torture. In the 1980s civil war and severe droughts led several hundred thousand vulnerable people to seek refuge in relief camps either elsewhere in Ethiopia or in Sudan. (Eritreans fleeing the Eritrean War of Independence since the 1960s had already experienced life in Sudanese refugee camps for the last two decades.) From Sudan, many Ethiopians and Eritreans sought asylum in Europe or North America, particularly after the Refugee Act of 1980 allowed Ethiopian and Eritrean immigrants into the United States. A particular consequence of the humanitarian crisis of the 1980s was the migration of almost the entire Beta Israel people to Israel.

After the fall of the Derg the borders were opened and more freedom of movement was granted to those Ethiopians who had sufficient resources to travel abroad. This gave a further impetus to migration. Some supporters and cadres of the Derg left the country for political reasons, but the majority of migrants sought jobs and new lives, being inspired by the success stories of fellow citizens who had previously resettled abroad. Since 2000 the number of Ethiopians leaving the country illegally has ballooned. Many try to reach Arab countries via Djibouti and Yemen, while thousands more head for Europe, Israel or South Africa, crossing deserts and seas by placing their lives in the hands of people-smugglers.

The successive waves of emigration have formed the layers of a worldwide Ethiopian diaspora that also includes a large number of descendants of Ethiopian-born migrants.[82] There is no accurate estimate of the size of this diaspora. The most important communities of Ethiopian migrants and their descendants are in North America, where they may reach as many as 500,000 people. Their concentration is particularly high in Washington DC and its vicinity, where they may number 250,000. There are also large numbers of Ethio-Americans in Los Angeles, New York, Toronto and many other North American cities. In Europe, the largest Ethiopian diaspora communities are mainly in Germany, Sweden, Britain and Italy. The migration of Ethiopian workers into Arab countries has significantly increased in the past ten years, particularly for female domestic workers. Their total number in the Middle East approaches 500,000 (around 200,000 in Saudi Arabia and 60,000 in Lebanon, and many are also in the Gulf Arab states and Turkey).[83] The worldwide diaspora perhaps numbers nearly 1.5 million.

Their financial resources, education, and experience of different kinds of jobs and ways of life, and the influential positions some of them occupy in international institutions and in the networks of the global economy, all mean that members of the diaspora have begun to play an increasingly important role in Ethiopia itself. Remittances (money transferred by migrants to their families at home) have become a vital source of currency for the Ethiopian economy and a powerful means of alleviating poverty.[84] The Ethiopian diaspora is also actively engaged in Ethiopian politics. Towards that end they maintain a very strong presence in cyber space, using social media to influence the political process at home. Many Ethiopian opposition parties have a diasporic constituency.[85] Besides money and politics, the diaspora also convey new cultural models and sets of values, which have modified the aspirations and worldviews of Ethiopia's youth. Furthermore, Ethiopians abroad are very proud of their roots and they actively promote the diverse Ethiopian cultures, in particular through food and music, in their countries of residence.

The Ethiopian government has taken measures to facilitate the return of Ethiopians settled abroad. One objective is to reverse the "brain drain" of the most educated and talented; the other is to attract investment from the most wealthy, so that they can contribute to the strategy for the economic growth and social transformation of the country. To this end, the government has issued a "yellow card" for the diaspora, which allows them to maintain de facto "dual citizenship". However, exposure to the political and economic standards of Western countries has accustomed Ethiopian emigrants to feel suspicious towards Ethiopia's bureaucracy, and to express freely their criticisms and frustrations in ways that may appear disconnected from the structure of the public sphere in Ethiopia today.

Conclusion

This chapter has endeavoured to introduce Ethiopia's diversity of regional settings by describing some of the various ethnic identities that compose the cultural fabric of the contemporary federal state. For each regional group and sub-group presented, our intention was to show that local specificities must be understood as results of historical interactions, forms of exchange and conflicts that have taken place over centuries. All Ethiopian ethnic groups have their own linguistic and cultural characteristics. They also share many features with their neighbours and with more distant societies as well. These intercultural contacts are deeply embedded in social structures and collective memories. In other words, the slogan of "unity in diversity" should be remembered while the many peoples, nations and nationalities of Ethiopia embark on the process of radically transforming their economic activities and lifestyles.

BIBLIOGRAPHY AND FURTHER READING

Abebe Kifleyesus, 2006, *Tradition and Transformation: the Argobba of Ethiopia*, Wiesbaden: Harrassowitz.
Abbink, Jon, 1990, "The Enigma of Beta Esra'el Ethnogenesis: an Anthrohistorical Study," *Cahiers d'Etudes Africaines*, 30, 120, pp. 397–449.
———— 1992, "Funeral as Ritual: an Analysis of Me'en Mortuary Rites (Southwest Ethiopia)," *Africa*, 47 (2), pp. 221–36.
———— 1993, "Ethnic Conflict in the 'Tribal Zone': the Dizi and Suri in Southern Ethiopia," *Journal of Modern African Studies*, 31 (4), pp. 675–82.
———— 1997, "Authority and Leadership in Surma Society (Ethiopia)," *Africa*, 52 (3), pp. 317–42.
———— 1997, "Competing Practices of Drinking and Power: Alcoholic 'Hegemonism' in Southern Ethiopia," *Northeast African Studies*, 4 (3), pp. 7–22.
———— 2000, "Tourism and its Discontents: Suri-tourist Encounters in Southern Ethiopia", *Social Anthropology*, 8 (1), pp. 1–17.
———— 2002, "Paradoxes of Power and Culture in an Old Periphery: Surma,

1974–1998," in D. Donham et al. (eds), *Remapping Ethiopia: Socialism & After*, Oxford: James Currey, pp. 155–72.

Abbute, Wolde-Selassie, 2009, "Identity, Encroachment and Ethnic Relations: the Gumuz and their Neighbours in North-Western Ethiopia", in G. Schlee and E.E. Vatson (eds), *Changing Identifications and Alliances in North-East Africa*, Vol. 1, New York: Berghahn.

Abeles, Marc, 2012, *Placing Politics*, Oxford: The Bardwell Press.

Abye, Tassé, 2004, *Parcours d'Ethiopiens en France et aux Etats-Unis. De nouvelles formes de migrations*, Paris: L'Harmattan.

Ali Birra, 2013, *Great Oromo Music. Ali Mohammad Birra*, ed. by F. Falceto and T. Osmond, Paris: Buda Records: *Ethiopiques* CD series n. 27.

Almagor, U., 1978, *Pastoral Partners, Affinity and Bond Partnership among the Dassanetch of South-West Ethiopia*, Manchester UniversityPress.

Anteby-Yemini, Lisa, 2004, *Les juifs éthiopiens en Israël. Les paradoxes du paradis*. Paris: CNRS Editions.

Ayalew Gebre, 2001, *Pastoralism under Pressure. Land Alienation and Pastoral Transformations Among the Karrayu of Eastern Ethiopia, 1941 to the present*, Maastricht: Shaker Publ.

Bahru Zewde, 2002, "Systems of Local Governance among the Gurage: The Yajoka Qicha and the Gordanna Sera," in Bahru Zewde and S. Pausewang (eds), *Ethiopia. The Challenge of Democracy from Below*, Uppsala, Addis Ababa: Nordiska Afrikainstitutet, FSS, pp. 17–29.

——— 2002, *Pioneers of Change in Ethiopia: The Reformist Intellectuals of the Early Twentieth Century*, Addis Ababa University Press, James Currey, Ohio University Press.

Bairu Tafla, 1987, *Asma Giyorgis and his Work: History of the Galla and the Kingdom of Shäwa*, Stuttgart: Franz Steiner.

Baker, Jonathan, 1992, "The Gurage of Ethiopia: Rural-Urban Interaction and Entrepreneurship," in J. Baker and P.O. Pedersen (eds), *The Rural-Urban Interface in Africa*, Uppsala: Nordiska Afrikainstitutet, pp. 125–47

Bartels, Lambert, 1983, *Oromo Religion: Myths and Rites of the Western Oromo of Ethiopia, an Attempt to Understand*, Berlin: D. Reimer.

Bassi, Marco, 2005, *Decisions in the Shade. Political and Juridical Processes among the Oromo-Borana*, Trenton, NJ: Red Sea Press.

Bauer, Dan F., 1977, *Household and Society in Ethiopia. An Economic and Social Analysis of Tigray Social Principles and Household Organization*, East Lansing, MI: African Studies Center, Michigan State Universtity.

Baxter, P.T.W., Hultin, J. and Triulzi, A. (eds), 1996, *Being and Becoming Oromo. Historical and Anthropological Enquiries*, Uppsala: Nordiska Afrikainstitutet.

Bender, M.-L. (ed.), 1976, *The Non-Semitic Languages of Ethiopia*, East Lansing: Michigan State University.

——— (ed.), 1981, *People and Cultures of the Ethio-Sudan Borderlands*, East Lansing: Michigan State University.

Braukämper, Ulrich, 2002, *Islamic History and Culture in Southern Ethiopia, Collected Essays*, Münster, Hamburg, London: Lit Verlag.
——— 2012, *A History of the Hadiyya in Southern Ethiopia*, Wiesbaden: Harrassowitz.
Brøgger, Jan, 1986, *Belief and Experience Among the Sidamo: a Case Study Towards an Anthropology of Knowledge*, Oslo: The Norwegian University Press.
Bulcha Demeksa, 2013, *My Life, My Vision for the Oromo and Other Peoples of Ethiopia*, Trenton, NJ: The Red Sea Press.
Bureau, Jacques, 2012, *The Gamo of Ethiopia. A Study of their Political System*, Oxford: Bardwell Press.
Carmichael, Tim, 2004, "Religion, Language, and Nationalism: Harari Muslims in Christian Ethiopia", in R.M. Feener (ed.), *Islam in World Cultures: Comparative Perspectives*, Santa Barbara, Denver, Oxford: ABC Clio, pp. 217–52.
Casanelli, Lee V., 1982, *The Shaping of Somali Society. Reconstructing the History of a Pastoral People, 1600–1900*, Philadelphia: University of Pennsylvania Press.
Chedeville, E., 1966, "Quelques faits sur l'organisation sociale des Afar," *Africa*, 36 (2), pp. 173–95.
Crummey, Donald, 2000, *Land and Society in the Christian Kingdom of Ethiopia: From the Thirteenth to the Twentieth Century*, Oxford: James Currey.
CSA (Central Statistical Authority), 1998, *The 1994 Population and Housing Census of Ethiopia. Results at Country Level, vol. 1 Statistical Report*, Addis Ababa.
——— 2010, *The 2007 Population and Housing Census of Ethiopia*. Addis Ababa.
Dereje Feyissa, 2011, *Playing Different Games: the Paradox of Anuak and Nuer Identification Strategies in the Gambella Region, Western Ethiopia*, Oxford: Berghahn publishers.
Dereje Feyissa and Hoehne, M.V. (eds), 2010, *Borders and Borderlands as Resources in the Horn of Africa*, Woodbridge, Suffolk: James Currey.
Dessalegn Rahmato, 2007, *Development Interventions in Wollaita, 1960s–2000s: A Critical Review*, Addis Ababa: Forum for Social Studies.
Donham, Donald L. and James, Wendy (eds), 1986, *The Southern Marches of Imperial Ethiopia*, Oxford: James Currey.
Ege, Svein, 1986, *Class, State, and Power in Africa: A Case Study of the Kingdom of Shawa (Ethiopia) about 1840*, Wiesbaden: Harrassowitz
Evans-Pritchard, E.E., 1940, *The Nuer: A Description of the Modes of Livelihood of a Nilotic People*, Oxford: Clarendon Press.
——— 1940, *The Political System of the Anuak*, London: Percy Lund, Humphries & Co.
——— 1956, *Nuer Religion*, Oxford: Clarendon Press.

Falceto, Francis, 2001, *Abyssinie Swing: A Pictorial History of Modern Ethiopian Music*, Addis Ababa: Shama Books.

Fernyhough, Timothy, 1989, "Slavery and Slave Trade in Southern Ethiopia in the 19th Century," in W.G. Clarence-Smith (ed.), *The Economics of the Indian Ocean Slave Trade in the Nineteenth Century*, London: Frank Cass & Co, pp. 103–130.

Fernandez, Bina, 2011, "Household Help? Ethiopian Women Domestic Workers' Labor Migration to the Gulf Countries," *Asian and Pacific Migration Journal*, 20 (3–4), pp. 433–57.

Ferran, Hugo, 2005. *Musique des Maale, Ethiopie méridionale*, Paris: Maison des Cultures du Monde.

Ficquet, Eloi, 2014, "Understanding *Lij* Iyasu through his Forefathers: The Mammedoch *Imam*-s of Wello," in E. Ficquet and W. Smidt (eds), *The Life and Times of Lij Iyasu of Ethiopia: New Insights*. Zürich, Münster, Berlin: LIT Verlag, pp. 5–29.

Freeman, Dena, 2002, *Initiating Change in Highland Ethiopia. Causes and Consequences of Cultural Transformation*, New York: Cambridge University Press.

Freeman, Dena and Pankhurst, Alula (eds), 2003, *Peripheral People. The Excluded Minorities of Ethiopia*, London: Hurst.

Fukui, K., 1979,"Cattle Colour Symbolism and Inter-Tribal Homicide among the Bodi," in K. Fukui et D. Turton (eds),*Warfare among East African Herders*, Osaka: National Museum of Ethnology.

Gamst, Frederick, 1969, *The Qemant: A Pagan-Hebraic Peasantry of Ethiopia*, New York: Holt, Rinehart and Winston.

Gebissa, Ezekiel, 2004, *Leaf of Allah: Khat and the Transformation of Agriculture in Harerge Ethiopia, 1875–1991*, Athens, Oxford, Addis Ababa: Ohio University Press, James Currey, Addis Ababa University Press.

——— (ed.), 2009, *Contested Terrain: Essays on Oromo Studies, Ethiopianist Discourses, and Politically Engaged Scholarship*, Lawrenceville, NJ: The Red Sea Press.

Getachew Kassa, 2001, *Among the Pastoral Afar in Ethiopia: Tradition, Continuity and Socio-Economic Change*, Utrecht: International Books.

Gibb, Camilla, 1999, "Baraka without Borders: Integrating Communities in the City of Saints," *Journal of Religion in Africa*, 19, pp. 88–108.

Gnamo, Abbas Haji, 2014, *Conquest and Resistance in the Ethiopian Empire, 1880–1974. The Case of the Arsi Oromo*, Leiden: Brill (African Social Studies Series 32).

Haberson, J., 1978, "Territorial and Development Politics in the Horn of Africa: The Afar of the Awash Valley," *African Affairs*, 77/309, pp. 479–98.

Hagmann, Tobias, 2005, "Beyond Clannishness and Colonialism: Understanding Political Disorder in Ethiopia's Somali Region, 1991-2004," *Journal of Modern African Studies*, 43 (4), pp. 509–36.

Hallpike, C.R, 2008, *The Konso of Ethiopia: A Study of Values of a Cushitic*

People, UK: AuthorHouse (revised edition of 1972 original edition, Oxford: Clarendon Press).

Hamer, John, 1987, *Humane Development: Participation and Change among the Sidama of Ethiopia*, Tuscaloosa: The University of Alabama Press.

Hassen, Mohammed, 1990, *The Oromo of Ethiopia, a History, 1570–1860*, Cambridge University Press.

Hutchinson, S.E., 1996, *Nuer Dilemmas, Coping with Money, War and the State*, Berkeley: University of California Press.

Johnson, Douglas, 1994, *Nuer Prophets: A History of Prophecy from the Upper Nile in the Nineteenth and Twentieth Centuries*, Oxford: Clarendon Press.

Kaplan, Steven, 1992, *The Beta Israel (Falasha) in Ethiopia: From Earliest Times to the Twentieth Century*, New York: New York University Press.

Knutsson, K.E., 1967, *Authority and Change: A Study of the Kallu Institution among the Macha Galla of Ethiopia*, Göteborg University.

Kurimoto, E., 1996, "People of the River: Subsistence Economy of the Anywaa (Anuak) of Western Ethiopia," in S. Sato and E. Kurimoto (eds), *Essays in Northeast African Studies*, Osaka, National Museum of Ethnology.

Kurimoto, E. and Simonse, S. (eds), 1998, *Conflict, Age and Power in North East Africa. Age Systems in Transition*, Oxford: James Currey.

Lange, Werner J., 1976, *Dialectics of Divine "Kingship" in the Kafa Highlands*, African Studies Center, University of California.

—— 1982, *History of the Southern Gonga (Southwestern Ethiopia)*, Wiesbaden: Steiner.

Leenco Lata, 2004, *The Horn of Africa as Common Homeland. The State and Self-Determination in the Era of Heightened Globalization*, Waterloo, Ontario: Wilfrid Laurier University Press.

Legesse, Asmarom, 1973, *Gada. Three Approaches to the Study of African Society*, New York: The Free Press.

—— 2000, *Oromo Democracy. An Indigenous African Political System*, Lawrenceville, NJ: The Red Sea Press.

Leslau, Wolf and Kane, Thomas L., 2001, *Amharic Cultural Reader*, Wiesbaden: Harrassowitz.

Levine, Donald L., 1965, *Wax and Gold.Tradition and Innovation in Ethiopian Culture*, University of Chicago Press.

—— 1974, *Greater Ethiopia: The Evolution of a Multiethnic Society*, University of Chicago Press.

Lewis, Herbert, 1965, *A Galla Monarchy: Jimma Abba Jifar, Ethiopia, 1830–1932*, Madison: University of Wisconsin Press.

Lewis, Ioan M., 1955, *Peoples of the Horn of Africa: Somali, Afar, and Saho*, London: International African Institute (Ethnographic Survey of Africa, 1).

—— 1961, *A Pastoral Democracy: A Study of Pastoralism and Politics among the Northern Somali of the Horn of Africa*, London: Oxford University Press.

Lyons, Terrence, "Transnational Politics in Ethiopia. Diaspora Mobilization and Contentious Politics," in T. Lyons and P. Mandaville (eds), 2012, *Politics from Afar: Transnational Diasporas and Networks*, London: Hurst, pp. 147–56

Maknun Gamaledin, 1993, "The Decline of Afar Pastoralism," in J. Markakis (ed.), *Conflict and the Decline of Pastoralism in the Horn of Africa*, Basingstoke: Macmillan in association with the Institute of Social Studies, pp. 45–62.

Markakis, John, 2011, *Ethiopia: The Last Two Frontiers*, Oxford: James Currey.

Messing, Simon, 1985, *Highland Plateau Amhara of Ethiopia*, edited by Lionel M. Bender, New Haven, CT: Human Relations Area Files, 3 vols. (originally: PhD, University of Pennsylvania, 1957).

Molvaer, Reidulf K., 1980, *Tradition and change in Ethiopia: Social and Cultural Life as Reflected in Amharic Fictional Literature ca. 1930–1974*, Leiden: Brill.

—— 1995, *Socialization and Social Control in Ethiopia*, Wiesbaden: Harrassowitz.

Morin, Didier, 2004, *Dictionnaire historique afar (1288–1982)*, Paris: Karthala.

—— 1995, *Des paroles douces comme la soie. Introduction aux contes dans l'aire couchitique (bedja, afar, saho, somali)*, Paris: Peeters.

Osmond, Thomas, 2004, "Waaqeffaanna: une association religieuse d'Ethiopie entre nationalisme ethnique et idéologie afrocentriste," *Politique Africaine*, 94, pp. 166–80.

—— 2014, "Competing Muslim Legacies along City/Countryside Dichotomies: Another Political History of Harar Town and its Oromo Rural Neighbours in Eastern Ethiopia," *Journal of Modern African Studies*, 52 (1), pp. 1–23.

Østebø, Terje, 2012, *Localizing Salafism: Religious Change among Oromo Muslims in Bale, Ethiopia*, Leiden: Brill.

Pankhurst, Alula and Piguet, François (eds), 2009, *Moving People in Ethiopia. Development, Displacement and the State*, Oxford: James Currey.

Perner, C., 1997, *Living on Earth in the Sky: the Anyuak. An Analytic Account of the History and the Culture of a Nilotic People*, Basel: Helbig & Lichtenhahn.

Planel, Sabine, 2008, *La chute d'un Eden éthiopien. Le Wolaita, une campagne en recomposition*, Montpellier: IRD.

Prunier, Gérard (ed.), 2007, *L'Ethiopie contemporaine*, Paris: Karthala.

Samatar, Said S., 1982, *Oral Poetry and Somali Nationalism. The Case of Sayyid Mahammad Abdille Hasan*, Cambridge University Press.

Schlee, Gunther, 1989, *Identities on the Move: Clanship and Pastoralism in Northern Kenya*, Manchester University Press.

Shack, William A., 1974, *The Central Ethiopians: Amhara, Tigrina and Related Peoples*, London: International African Institute (Ethnographic Survey of Africa, 4).

———— 1966, *The Gurage. A People of the Ensete Culture*, Oxford: Oxford University Press.

Shelemay, Kay Kaufman and Kaplan, Steven (eds), 2006, *Creating the Ethiopian Diaspora: Perspectives from Across the Disciplines*, Special Issue of: *Diaspora, Journal of Transnational Studies*, vol. 15 (2–3).

Smidt, Wolbert, 2010, "The Tigrinnya-speakers across the Borders: Discourses of Unity & Separation in Ethnohistorical Context," in M.V. Höhne and Dereje Feyissa (eds), *Borders and Borderlands as Resources in the Horn of Africa*, London: James Currey, pp. 61–84.

———— 2013, "The Term Habäsha: an Ancient Ethnonym of the 'Abyssinian' Highlanders and its Interpretations and Connotations," in Hatem Elliessie (ed.), *Multidisciplinary Views on the Horn of Africa*, Cologne: KöppeVerlag.

Solomon Addis Getahun, 2007, *The History of Ethiopian Immigrants and Refugees in America, 1900–2000. Patterns of Migration, Survival, and Adjusment*, New York: LFB Scholarly Publishing.

Stauder, J.,1971.,*The Majangir: Ecology and Society of a Southwest Ethiopian People*, Cambridge: Cambridge University Press.

Strecker, Ivo and Lydall, Jean, 1979, *The Hamar of Southern Ethiopia*, 3 vols, Hohenschäftslarn: Renner.

Taddesse Tamrat, 1988, "Processes of Ethnic Interaction and Integration in Ethiopian History. The Case of the Agaw," *Journal of African History*, 29, pp. 5–18.

Teferra-Worq Beshah and Harbeson, John W., 1978, "Afar Pastoralists in Transition and the Ethiopian Revolution," *Journal of African Studies*, 5 (3), pp. 249–67.

Tippet, A.R., 1970, *People of Southwest Ethiopia*, South Pasadena, CA: William Carey Library.

Tornay, Serge, 2001, *Les Fusils jaunes, Générations et politique en pays Nyangatom (Ethiopie)*, Nanterre: Société d'Ethnologie

Triulzi, A., 1981, *Salt, Gold and Legitimacy: Prelude to the History of a No-Man's Land, BeláShangul, Wälläggä, Ethiopia (ca. 1800–1898)*, Naples: Instituto Universitario Orientale.

Tronvoll, Kjetil, 1998, *Mai Weini: A Highland Village in Eritrea. A Study of the People, their Livelihood, and Land Tenure During Times of Turbulence*, Lawrenceville, NJ: The Red Sea Press.

Turton, David, 1988, "Looking for a Cool Place: the Mursi, 1890s-1990s," in D. Anderson and D. Johnson (eds), *The Ecology of Survival: Case Studies from Northeast African History*, London, Boulder: Lester Crook Academic Publishing/Westview Press, pp. 261–82.

Turton, David, 2004, "Lip-plates and the People Who Take Photographs: Uneasy Encounters Between Mursi and Tourists in Southern Ethiopia," *Anthropology Today*, 20, 2, pp. 3–8.

Vanderheym, J.-G., 2012, *An Expedition with Negus Menilek*, Oxford: The Bardwell Press.

Watson, Elizabeth, 2009, *Living Terraces in Ethiopia: Konso Landscape, Culture and Development*, Woodbridge: James Currey.

Worku Nida, 1996, "Gurage Urban Migration and the Dynamics of Cultural Life in the Village," in G. Hudson (ed.), *Essays on Gurage Language and Culture, Dedicated to Wolf Leslau*, Wiesbaden: Harrassowitz, pp. 133–51.

Yasin Mohammed Yasin, 2007, "The Regional Dynamics of the Afar and Issa-Somali Conflict in the Horn of Africa: An Afar View," in W.G.C. Smidt and Kinfe Abraham (eds), *Discussing Conflict in Ethiopia. Conflict Management and Resolution*, Berlin: LIT, pp. 23–8.

——— 2010, "Trans-Border Political Alliance in the Horn of Africa: The Case of the Affar-Issa Conflict," in Dereje Feyissa and M.V. Hoehne (eds), *Borders and Borderlands as Resources in the Horn of Africa*, Woodbridge, Suffolk: James Currey, pp. 85–96.

Young, J.,1999, "Along Ethiopia's Western Frontier: Gambella and Benishangul in Transition," *Journal of Modern African Studies*, 38 (2), pp. 321–46.

2

THE ETHIOPIAN ORTHODOX TEWAHEDO CHURCH (EOTC) AND THE CHALLENGES OF MODERNITY

Stéphane Ancel and Éloi Ficquet

Orthodox Christians today represent about half of the Ethiopian population. They are concentrated in the north-west but are also widely disseminated throughout the urban networks of the country. For centuries, the Christian Orthodox Tewahedo Church of Ethiopia was considered the dominant framework through which Ethiopia could be understood. A true pillar of Ethiopian history, from the fourth century AD the Church reinforced its territorial basis through a dense network of parishes, by providing the evolving Christian nation with powerful symbolic and ideological frames, and by helping it to spread out in the region. By forming links with other Christian powers, the Kingdom of Ethiopia and its Church defined themselves in a universal perspective on theological and eschatological grounds. At the end of the nineteenth century, the Church was instrumental in unifying the kingdom and its dependencies around a common Christian identity. Questions relating to the spiritual and temporal powers of the Church were central to its transformation as it was driven into modernity by the royal institution.

Terminological outline

The first problem that emerges in the study of the Ethiopian Church is that of its denomination. There exists today an official name, the "Ethiopian Orthodox Tewahedo Church", used in this article. Examination of terminology can serve as an introduction to the three constitutive aspects of the Church: the community, the dogma, and its place within Christianity.

Ethiopian Christians conceive of themselves as a *beta-kristian* ("house of Christians", or "church" in the Ge'ez language), by which they mean a community that gathers around a building at the centre of a sacred geography. Each church building owes its sacredness to the fact that it keeps a *tabot* (a wooden or stone replica of the Ark of the Covenant); the Ethiopian national myth locates the real Ark in Axum, the old capital of the kingdom, regarded as the site of the establishment of the first church. While throughout its long history the Ethiopian Church was content to refer to itself simply as a *betakristian*, the establishment of relations with other churches and the emergence of internal theological dissent pushed it to find a more precise description. Having followed the Coptic Church in its rejection of the conclusions of the Council of Chalcedon (451 AD), the Ethiopian Church was included among the Monophysite churches, which considered Christ to have a purely divine and non-human nature. Challenging the Council's classification, the Ethiopian Church began using the Ge'ez adjective *tewahedo* to define its position within the Christological debate. The meaning of this adjective is not, however, devoid of ambiguity, since it oscillates between the notion of the "union" of the natures of Christ and that of the "unity" of the Church.

The adjective "Orthodox" refers rather ambiguously to the position of the Ethiopian Church within Christianity. It is neither Catholic nor Protestant, and has no theological affiliation to the Slavic or Greek Orthodoxies. Because of its vaguely eastern geographic situation, the appearance of its rites and its being restrained to a national sphere, the Ethiopian Church was classified as "Orthodox" on the basis of a wide definition of the term. This in turn allowed for recent rapprochements, notably with the Ecumenical Patriarchate of Constantinople.

Lastly, the Ethiopian Church is Ethiopian. A deep-rooted ideological construction, whose history will not be developed here, underlies this label. Coined by Greek geographers, the toponym "Ethiopia" referred to a sacred territory after various references to it in the Old and New Testaments. It was later given new sacredness with the mission that Ethiopians assumed to preserve the Ark of the Covenant.

Religious authority under the Ethiopian monarchy

Before tracing the evolution of the Church within the history of the construction of the contemporary Ethiopian nation, it is crucial to describe the hierarchical higher ranks of the clergy.

Since its foundation, the leadership of the Ethiopian Church was divided between two figures: a foreigner, the Egyptian Metropolitan bishop or Abun, and a priestking, the King of Kings. Neither could claim to exert full religious authority since, in the eyes of the kingdom's ecclesiastics, the King was always suspected of being involved with political interests and the bishop represented a distant hierarchy subject to Egypt's Islamic authorities. Local responses to this ambiguous situation generated a decentralized organization founded on monastic networks.

The Coptic Patriarch. In theory, the highest authority of the Ethiopian Church was the Coptic Patriarch of Alexandria. Since the consecration of Saint Frumentius as the first Metropolitan bishop of Ethiopia by Saint Athanasius around the beginning of the fourth century AD, the bishop of Ethiopia—or Abun—had to be selected from among Egyptian monks and consecrated by the patriarch. Thus, upon the death of each Metropolitan bishop, the Ethiopian kings had to send ambassadors to Egypt with valuable gifts to ensure not only that the patriarch elevated a monk to the episcopal see and sent him to Ethiopia, but also, from the seventh century, that the transaction was endorsed by the Egyptian Muslim authorities.

It would be erroneous, however, to consider the patriarch the *de facto* head of the Ethiopian Church. He rarely engaged with the Ethiopian powers, and when he did it was usually to give his support to his representative if the latter encountered difficulties when taking office. Not until the middle of the nineteenth century did the patriarch travel in person to the distant diocese. His real powers were excommunication and potential refusal to designate an Abun. These powers were used rarely and only in the event of a profound disagreement with the Ethiopian monarchy. The Coptic Church could not afford to lose Ethiopia's support in the face of Egypt's Muslim authorities.

The Metropolitan bishop. The Metropolitan bishop was in charge of the direction and organization of the Ethiopian Church. Named abun in Ge'ez, or "our father", the bishop was the representative of the Patriarch of Alexandria in Ethiopia. He had few prerogatives, but they were vital to the functioning of the Church. His sacramental role was indispensable: he was the only individual allowed to consecrate kings, ordain the kingdom's priests, and consecrate *tabot*s. In the doctrinal sphere, as the guarantor of the Alexandrine faith, he had the power of excommunication.[1]

The bishopric, compulsorily occupied by an Egyptian, could remain vacant for a long time. This was a source of anxiety for the Church. But the urgency that it created also provoked a dynamic of perpetual renewal, preventing the sclerosis of the system. And through this intermittent but consistent link to Egypt, which was enhanced by pilgrimages to Jerusalem, Ethiopia benefited from contact with the Mediterranean world, which helped to maintain the vitality of its religious heritage. Each bishop, for example, brought in his luggage theological, canonical, and/or doctrinal works.

The King of Kings. Although the Ethiopian king, being crowned by the bishop, could not do without him, the former nevertheless had real authority over the latter and his Church, since he had a double role as a spiritual and temporal chief. The king had a say in terms of doctrine as a true representative of the Ethiopian faith. He convoked and presided over the councils, which no bishop could do. To the extent to which the king's decisions on religious faith did not contradict the principles of the Alexandrine faith, the bishop did not intervene. But in the event of a disagreement between the two on doctrinal matters, the bishop could only rely on the partisans of the Alexandrine faith among the Ethiopian ecclesiastics. The latter intervened less out of respect for the bishop than from eagerness to promote their own theological views against rival schools of thought.

The Ethiopian higher clergy. The structure of the Ethiopian higher clergy was not strictly centralized. The court clergy, which consisted of priests appointed by the King of Kings for functional tasks, did not constitute a "government" of the Church but served as a transmission belt between the royal power and the regional religious institutions, notably the monasteries, which exercised power locally. By giving them rights to land, the king gained the support of these institutions. The granting of titles to court representatives solidified the alliance by granting national visibility to selected religious institutions. This policy established a permanent link between some of the country's most important religious authorities and the court. In this way the king designated the chief of the Church of Axum, the *Nebura'ed*, who had a strong influence in the north of the country. The highly honorific title of *Aqqabe sa'at* was similarly granted to the abbot of the Hayq monastery, which was located at the heart of a vast monastic network in the centre of the country. Finally, the *Ichege*, the head of the Debre Libanos monastery, who was all-powerful in the south of the country, became a sought-after source of support for monarchs.

The nineteenth century and the new monarchical policy

Starting in the mid-nineteenth century, Ethiopian kings engaged in a policy of centralization, seeking to impose their administration over the local powers that had developed since the end of the eighteenth century. In the eyes of these reformist sovereigns, the Church could help unify the kingdom and its dependencies around a common Christian identity, and the clergy could act as agents of political reorganization through the network of monasteries and parishes that they administered. But it soon became clear that without an organizational change among the clergy and without its complete submission to royal power, the Church could not in fact assume such a role.

Alliances and conflicts between the bishop and the monarch. With the decline of the Solomonic dynasty linked to the slow extinction of the Gondar regime in the early nineteenth century, the young chiefs of regional armies who had aspirations to the royal throne were not able to ground their claims on dynastic legitimacy any longer. Instead, they needed the support of the bishop in order to be crowned. Once consecrated, they had to keep the upper hand over the Church's highest representative to be able to implement their coveted reforms of monarchical and ecclesiastical powers. The fiery Kassa Hailu, the future King of

Kings Tewodros II (1855–68), thus sided with Abuna Salama (1841–67) by pursuing a hostile policy against the heterodox movements that challenged the authority of his valuable ally.[2] Salama's successor, Abuna Atnatewos (1872–76), also knew how to take advantage of this game of alliances. Coming from Egypt after four years of conflict over the succession to the Ethiopian throne, he was instructed by the Coptic patriarch to crown *Dejazmach* Kassai of Tigray, turned King of Kings Yohannes IV (1872–89), who had given reassurances of his commitment against the implantation of Catholic missions in Ethiopia.[3]

Once ad hoc alliances collapsed, monarchs and bishops sometimes violently confronted each other. Since Tewodros II wanted to reform the kingdom by setting up an administration financed from a part of the lands owned by the Church, he suffered excommunication at the hands of Abuna Salama in 1864, which precipitated the decline of his reign.[4] When Khedive Isma'il of Egypt launched his troops to conquer Ethiopia in 1875, King Yohannes IV accused Abuna Atnatewos of maintaining relations with the Egyptian authorities and of being an unofficial agent of the invader, and as a result excluded him completely from the affairs of the kingdom.[5]

Four bishops for Yohannes IV. After the death of Abuna Atnatewos in 1876, King Yohannes IV asked the Coptic patriarch to designate several bishops. Following some bitter negotiations, Ethiopia received four bishops in 1883, all of Egyptian origin. The vacancy of the episcopal seat from 1876 to 1883 did not stop the King convening a council in 1878 to put an end to the Christological quarrels that had divided Ethiopian Christians for two centuries. In the absence of a Metropolitan bishop, Yohannes relied on a letter from the Coptic patriarch to assert the conformity of the kingdom's official doctrine to that of the successors of Saint Mark. The four new bishops arrived in 1883 and were settled in each of the kingdom's regions. Abuna Petros stayed in Tigray near the king, and was accorded the status of Metropolitan bishop. The other three were divided between the provinces where heterodox movements and Yohannes' main political rivals were established. Abuna Matewos went to Shoa next to Negus Menelik, Abuna Luqas to Gojjam next to Negus Takla Haymanot, and Abuna Marqos to Gondar, the centre of Ethiopian Christianity under the jurisdiction of King Yohannes.[6]

The presence of several bishops had the advantage of ensuring that the Metropolitan seat did not become vacant. Through this innovation in the religious domain, Yohannes ensured the stabilization of power relations with his rivals. Episcopal power thus began to acquire an embryonic local aspect, as its capacity to keep an eye on the local clergy was reinforced. Meanwhile, Abuna Petros ensured his role as Metropolitan by accompanying the King on his military campaigns, although he did not have genuine ecclesiastical authority over the other three bishops. The latter performed their roles in different ways. Abuna Marqos died shortly after his arrival in Gondar. Abuna Luqas hardly got involved with the politics of Gojjam. Only Abuna Matewos played a role in the politics of his province, Shoa, by setting himself up as the champion of the Alexandrine doctrine in a region where the heterodoxy of the "three births" was well rooted.

Menelik and Abuna Matewos. After the death of Yohannes IV in March 1889 on the battlefield against the Mahdist aggressions from Sudan, Menelik seized the succession—against the will of the deceased ruler—by having Abuna Matewos consecrate him as King of Kings Menelik II at Entoto Maryam, in the highland area of the future Addis Ababa. Abuna Petros, who stayed next to Yohannes IV until his death, lost his title of Metropolitan since he was no longer the "bishop of the King of Kings", but he remained bishop of Tigray and later his jurisdiction was extended to other provinces, as well as Eritrea. Abuna Matewos was elevated in his turn to the rank of Metropolitan, with the permission of the Coptic Patriarch Cyril V. Matewos maintained close ties with Menelik until the end of his reign. The Metropolitan increased his influence by reforming the church administration, in particular through the appointment of *Liqa Kahenat* priests in the provinces. These clergymen were traditionally responsible for monitoring small sub-parish churches. Abuna Matewos obtained from Menelik II permission for them, under his authority, to collect taxes in certain areas, thus providing him with a significant source of revenue and power.[7] The Emperor even made Abuna Matewos his ambassador by sending him to Jerusalem and St Petersburg in 1902.[8]

The role of Abuna Matewos was key during the crisis in the succession that followed Menelik's death in 1913. The Shoan dynasty opposed the heir to the throne, Lij Iyasu, son of Ras Mikael of Wollo and grandson of Menelik, taking a dim view of the ascension of a Muslim dynasty from Wollo, recently converted to Christianity. Letting himself be used as an instrument of the conspiracy, Abuna

Matewos excommunicated the young prince on 27 September 1916—the Ethiopian Holy Cross day—accusing him of having renounced the Christian faith and embraced Islam. Matewos' move can be understood by the fact that Shoa was the keystone of his episcopal power; he therefore could not overlook the support of the regional aristocracy. But it is also important to stress the danger that the ascension of the Wollo dynasty represented for him. When Lij Iyasu decided to promote his father *Ras* Mikael to the dignity of Negus of Wollo in 1914, Yohannes IV's former Metropolitan Abuna Petros was designated to perform the coronation. He stayed in Wollo until he was regarded as the bishop of the province and accompanied the new Negus during the offensive that he undertook in 1916 against the troops of Shoa. During this conflict between regional powers, the fate of the Ethiopian episcopate was also at stake, since the winner could elevate its bishop to the status of Metropolitan. After Mikael was defeated, Abuna Petros followed him into prison and died in captivity in 1921 in Addis Ababa.[9]

Zewditu (1917–30), daughter of Menelik II, was crowned Queen of Queens on 11 February 1917 by Abuna Matewos. Ras Tafari Makonnen, the future Haile Selassie, at the time the governor of Harar and the main instigator of the overthrow of Iyasu, became plenipotentiary regent and heir to the throne.

Changes in the status of the Abun between 1917 and 1959

Between 1916 and 1930 two factions fought over the role of the *Abun* and his place within the monarchical institution. On one side, a young generation of intellectuals and senior officials led by the regent Tafari pushed for reform of the state and the statutes of the Metropolitan. For them, the construction of a centralized state had to be achieved with the Church providing an ideological glue based on an Abyssinian Christian identity with the Abuna as its chief. In addition, they wanted the Church to communicate and promote the decisions of the state. This implied that the monarchy would control the appointment of the Abuna, who would in turn have the right to appoint the bishops in the provinces. On the other side, the conservative old guard, led by Abuna Matewos, was unwilling to concede any changes whatsoever in the status of the Metropolitan or the Church. They condemned the idea of undermining a centuries-old tradition that prevented political interference in purely ecclesiastical affairs.

The visit of Ras Tafari to Cairo in 1924. In the summer of 1924, Ras Tafari Makonnen travelled to Cairo for a protocol visit to King Fuad and the Coptic patriarch. Ras Tafari articulated his demands to Patriarch Cyril V (1874–1927) and the council of the Coptic community. He requested that, upon the death of the ageing Abuna Matewos, the practice of consecrating an Egyptian monk should be abandoned and that an Ethiopian monk should be selected instead. Moreover, while the Coptic patriarch would retain the right to designate the Metropolitan bishop, the latter should be allowed to select the bishops, who should be Ethiopian. These demands got a cold reception from the Coptic community. Ras Tafari returned to Ethiopia empty handed.[10] Through the weekly magazine *Berhanenna Salam* ("Light and Peace"), which was established in January 1925, progressive intellectuals launched a hostile campaign against Abuna Matewos and denounced the capitulation of the Ethiopian Church to the Copts.

The trial of strength between Ras *Tafari and the Coptic Patriarch Cyril V: 1926–1930.* In September 1926, Ras Tafari, despite failure in Egypt, managed to grant more powers to the Ichege. Things stepped up following the death of Abuna Matewos in December that year. In need of a new Abuna to crown him as King of Kings, Ras Tafari resumed negotiations with Cairo to obtain an Abuna who could consecrate Ethiopian bishops. Facing the opposition of Patriarch Cyril V of Egypt (1874–1927), Ras Tafari determined that from then on the Ichege would be in control of the financial and executive powers of the Church. In response to this provocation, Patriarch Cyril refused to name a new Abuna, and it was only after his death in 1927 and the crowning of Ras Tafari with the title of Negus that negotiations resumed; they were completed in 1929.[11]

Yohannes XIX (1928–42), the new Coptic patriarch, chose as Metropolitan an Egyptian monk who took the name of Abuna Qerellos VI (1929–50), but did not grant him the right to consecrate bishops. However, the Copts agreed on a compromise: three Ethiopian monks were allowed to be consecrated bishops in Cairo in June 1929. This was a great victory for Negus Tafari.[12] The prelates who were selected to integrate the Ethiopian episcopate were all chosen from among his allies. Some time later, during the trip of the patriarch to Addis Ababa in February 1930 for the crowning of Tafari Makonnen as King of Kings Haile Selassie I, the Ichege Gebre Menfes Qiddus was appointed to the episcopal role for the southern territories under the name of Abuna Sawiros, thus initiating the fusion of both roles.[13] Haile Selassie I now had a clergy designated by him and under his command, and capable of controlling territory and transmitting his decisions. The Ethiopian prelates consequently undermined the authority of Abuna Qerellos, whose only remaining power was the right to consecrate the monarch.

The Italian occupation and its consequences. The Italian occupation of Ethiopia from 1936 to 1941 caused a blow to Haile Selassie's reform policies. The new masters of the country attempted to dissociate the Church from the monarchy. The Italians killed several churchmen, including the bishop of Wollo Abuna Petros, who they accused of resisting their power. In an effort to weaken the links between Ethiopia and British-controlled Egypt, the Italian authorities also tried to separate the Ethiopian Church from the Coptic patriarchy. Having initially collaborated with the occupying power, Abuna Qerellos opposed the Italian project of separating the churches in 1937. Sent to Rome later that year, he took refuge in Alexandria on the pretext of being sick. In need of a Metropolitan, Marshal Graziani convened an assembly of Ethiopian clergymen to elect a new Metropolitan on 27 November 1937. Abuna Abraham, bishop of Gojjam, was elected. On 28 December 1937, the Coptic Holy Synod declared the election illegitimate and excommunicated the new Metropolitan.[14] Ignoring the patriarch's interdiction, Abuna Abraham and his successor Abuna Yohannes designated eleven bishops in order to constitute a full ecclesiastical hierarchy.[15]

In January 1941, Haile Selassie led an attack to reconquer his kingdom, supported by British troops. Based in Khartoum, the monarch-in-exile received a letter from Abuna Qerellos expressing his aspiration to join the campaign. Haile Selassie replied that Ichege Gebre Giyorgis was right next to him, had been designated in 1934, and now represented the true authority of the Church. Abuna Qerellos consequently stayed in Cairo throughout Ethiopia's reconquest, losing any credibility he had left in the eyes of his Church and his flock. However, while Haile Selassie wanted an acquiescent Church led by the Ichege, it was out of the question to simply inherit the structure left by the Italians, with a collaborationist Metropolitan who had been excommunicated by the Copts. He therefore asked Abuna Qerellos to return to Ethiopia and resume his duties.[16]

The Egyptian delegation that accompanied the Metropolitan in June 1942 to Addis Ababa returned to Cairo with a series of proposals from Haile Selassie regarding the links between the Ethiopian Church and the Copts of Egypt.[17] He requested the recognition of the Ethiopian bishops designated during the Italian occupation, the consecration of an Ethiopian Metropolitan who would have the right to designate bishops upon the death of the Abuna Qerellos, and the creation of a synod of Ethiopian bishops that would participate in the election of the Coptic patriarch. The Coptic Holy Synod rejected all these proposals in February 1945 but accepted an agreement in principle regarding Ethiopian participation in the election of the patriarch.[18] The situation seemed completely deadlocked. The reaction in Ethiopia was strong, and another press campaign against the Copts was launched. The Metropolitan was described as an ignorant individual who was serving the interests of Islam, and his incapacity to designate bishops was perceived as a deliberate ploy on the part of the Copts to weaken the Ethiopian Church. Never had Abuna Qerellos been so isolated.[19]

Autonomy. In 1946 a new patriarch, Yusab II, was elected in Cairo. On 15 July 1948 he consecrated five Ethiopians, including the very influential Ichege Gebre Giyorgis, who was close to Haile Selassie and became Abuna Baselyos.[20] It was also agreed that upon the death of Qerellos, an Ethiopian Abun entitled to designate bishops would replace him. Abuna Qerellos died in Cairo in October 1950 after five years away from his diocese. On 14 January 1951 Abuna Baselyos became the first Ethiopian archbishop of Ethiopia invested by the Coptic patriarch. Haile Selassie's gamble had succeeded: a Metropolitan who had the right to constitute a true hierarchy capable of supporting an efficient provincial administration now led the Ethiopian Church. The Abun was subjected to monarchical authority since he owed his new position to the efforts of the sovereign. Yet the status of the archbishop still left the Ethiopian Church under the heel of the Coptic patriarchate. Two events precipitated the definitive separation of the two Churches: an institutional crisis within the Coptic Church, and the Egyptian Revolution led by Gamal Abdel Nasser.

Autocephaly. Under the rule of Colonel Nasser, the position of the Coptic community within the Egyptian political chessboard was more contested than ever. In addition, the Coptic patriarchate suffered a

73

very serious institutional crisis between 1954 and 1956.[21] Patriarch Yusab II died in November 1956, and the process of electing a new patriarch turned into a complex diplomatic and military contest. The fact that the Ethiopians obtained the same number of votes as the Egyptians in the Holy Synod for the election of the patriarch deeply troubled the Coptic community. The possibility of an Ethiopian becoming Coptic patriarch and the fear that the See of Saint Mark could be transferred to Addis Ababa distressed the Copts who were already being ill-treated by their own government. For their part, the Ethiopians were suspicious of an election that in their view was under Nasser's control.[22] In the end, Ethiopia obtained the right to have its own patriarch who could designate bishops outside Ethiopia if he wished. But the Coptic patriarch continued to consecrate his Ethiopian counterpart. The Ethiopian patriarch's appointment remained subject to the approval of the Coptic patriarch and of the King of Kings. In June 1959, Haile Selassie went to Cairo and met Nasser. During his stay, Patriarch Cyril VI of Egypt appointed Abuna Baselyos head of a new autocephalous Church of Ethiopia.

By becoming autocephalous the Ethiopian Orthodox Tewahedo Church entered a new phase in its history, in particular in its relation to the state. Freed from its dependence on the Coptic Church, it immediately came under the tutelage of the monarchy.

An ecclesiastic administration dominated by the monarch: 1942–1974

The monarch took control over the Church through two parallel strategies. The first was to obtain from Egypt the right to have an Ethiopian patriarch and Ethiopian bishops. The second was to put all the country's parishes and monasteries under a centralized authority.[23] In 1926 a central administrative entity within the Church was created to deal with fiscal matters. A decree of 30 November 1942 introduced a tax on the lands owned by the Church, placing under the jurisdiction of a central ecclesiastical council the income of every parish throughout the territory. Not only did this decree limit the financial autonomy of the churches and monasteries, it also subordinated the appointment of priests to the control of this council. Tax collectors faced local opposition, strengthened by the fact that their appointment depended less on the ecclesiastical council than on the government itself.[24]

Not satisfied with having subjected the new Ethiopian patriarchate to his personal authority, Haile Selassie acquired a court clergy that was able to compete with the episcopal authority. A few months after the consecration of the first Ethiopian patriarch, it was decided that the *Liqa Seltanat* Habte Maryam Werqeneh would hold the positions of manager of the Holy Trinity Cathedral in Addis Ababa (founded in 1943) and the government's director of religious affairs. Benefiting from the influence of the theological college that was affiliated to the Holy Trinity Cathedral in 1948, and utilizing a budget amounting to approximately 20 per cent of the revenue that the state extracted from the Church, Habte Maryam Werqeneh undertook the development of religious associations in Addis Ababa and the launch of newspapers and radio programmes.[25] Although concentrated in the capital, his initiatives were in direct competition with the patriarchate, which was largely inert.

Abuna Tewoflos, bishop of Harar since 1951, was elected in April 1971 as the successor to Abuna Baselyos. His main priority was to complete the centralization of the Church management. In 1972 he sought to install in each of the country's parishes a council composed evenly of priests and laymen elected by local clergy and parishioners.[26] Responsible for the management and fiscal matters of the parishes, these councils constituted the first echelon of a pyramidal administration linking all the churches to the patriarchate.[27] The councils were the most blatant expression of centralization of Church finances, and put an end to the fiscal autonomy of the parishes. In addition, the patriarchate retook the initiative in the development of the Church in response to the troublesome Liqa Seltanat. Had Haile Selassie not intervened in person, Abuna Tewoflos would have designated Habte Maryam bishop of the southern provinces, a position that would have effectively kept him away from Church affairs.[28]

The Ethiopian Church in the world and ecumenical relations

Since 1959, the Ethiopian patriarch has had the power to appoint bishops and archbishops abroad. Missions were established in the Caribbean, Africa, and the Middle East. Churches were also founded in countries with substantial Ethiopian diasporas, for example in the United States and Europe. The development of foreign missions was undertaken simultaneously with the development of missions within Ethiopia in those regions where followers of the Ethiopian Church were a minority. These regions, south and west of the northern Ethiopian high plateaux, were opened by Haile Selassie to Catholic and Protestant missions in 1944. While this decision formalized the position of the different Christian churches in the territories, tensions remained. Relations with Catholics continued to be imbued with resentment. Relations with Protestant churches, domestic or not, were even more troubled, for Protestant missions were generally established in remote areas where they could gain more autonomy and local power.

Since becoming a member of the World Council of Churches in 1955, the Ethiopian Church has been involved in ecumenical relations, in particular with Orthodox Churches. In 1961, the Ethiopian Church was invited to the first pan-Orthodox conference in Rhodes, organized by the Patriarchate of Constantinople. A series of meetings between the Ethiopian Church (pre-Chalcedonian) and the Orthodox Churches (Chalcedonian) followed, with the objective of establishing a genuine dialogue between the two traditions under the supervision of the Ecumenical Patriarchate of Constantinople.

The Church and the 1974 Revolution

By the time the revolution erupted, the Church had a consubstantial link with the monarchical regime. In May 1974, the patriarchate requested that the Church should be represented within the new government. But in August the provisional government, by then under the control of the army, announced the separation of Church and State. The patriarchate reacted vigorously, demanding that the rules for the election of the patriarch should be included in the planned new constitution and that Christianity should be declared the official religion of the state. In spite of the vigour of these statements, the Church was disunited: disagreements between the higher and lower clergy became manifest on 12 March 1974 during a gathering in Addis Ababa of about a hundred priests who were challenging the policy of hierarchical centralization implemented by the patriarchate. At the highest level of the ecclesiastical hierarchy dissent intensified, aggravating longstanding differences, most importantly between the patriarch and the clergy of the Holy Trinity Cathedral, and between the patriarch and Archbishop Yohannes of Tigray who had refused to vote for him during the 1971 election. Although the position of Liqa Seltanat had been abolished on 15 August 1974, and Habte Maryam had been arrested, the position of Abuna Tewoflos had not become easier. Makonnen

Zawde, the chief administrator of the Church, clashed with him.[29] Having failed to obtain any answer to his public statements in May and August and being contested by his own administration, Abuna Tewoflos kept a low profile. In September, on the day of the Ethiopian New Year and the day before the King of Kings was arrested, he recognized the revolution.

If the promulgation of the secularity of the state in August put an end to the preponderance of the Ethiopian Church in the country, the agrarian reform announced on 4 March 1975 resulted in an unprecedented blow to the Church's revenue. The decree abolished the Church's land ownership and liberated peasants from their obligations to the institution. The Church therefore lost all of its land revenue, which constituted the largest share of its economic power. The clergy's reaction was intense, but they failed to prevent implementation of the reforms. Moreover, the establishment of peasant associations in charge of supervising the reforms challenged the predominant position of the clergy in the countryside. The decree of 26 July 1975 on urban landed property completed the reduction in the Church's land resources.

The takeover of the Church by the revolutionary power: 1976–1991. Yet the goal of the new government was not to destroy an institution that could still be useful for the consolidation of its power, as it had been useful to Haile Selassie. The takeover of the Church by the revolutionary military junta, the Derg, was done under the leadership of Lieutenant-Colonel Atnafu Abate, its Vice-President. Gathering members of the clergy and laymen in a committee around him, he launched a purge with the explicit goal of fighting corruption among Church leaders. Between late 1975 and early 1976, individuals considered undesirable by the regime were imprisoned or sidelined. The purge reached even to the highest levels. Abuna Tewoflos was accused of corruption, of committing acts of injustice under the previous regime, and of having contacts with counter-revolutionary elements. He was deposed on 18 February 1976 and later incarcerated. He was executed in August 1979 along with other top imperial officials.

Abba Melaku Wolde Mikael, until then relatively unknown among the public, was elected patriarch of Ethiopia under the name of Abuna Takla Haymanot on 18 July 1976 by a college of ecclesiastics and laymen. Having been an ascetic monk based in the Wolayta region, and lacking a modern education, the new patriarch had the exact opposite character to that of Tewoflos. He was therefore well suited to the post from the perspective of the revolutionary regime. The Coptic Church in Egypt, led by Patriarch Shenouda III, protested vigorously against his appointment, and refused to recognize him. The Copts complained it was illegal to appoint a new patriarch while his predecessor still lived and had not abdicated. Furthermore the enthronement of an Ethiopian patriarch still could not be made without consecration by the Coptic patriarch, as stipulated by the 1959 agreement.[30] Some reluctance also existed amongst the members of the Ethiopian Holy Synod, who considered in this "apolitical" monk a puppet of the new power. The majority of the recalcitrant bishops, branded as reactionaries, were asked to retire. In January 1979 Abuna Tekle Haymanot consecrated thirteen new bishops. The leadership of the Ethiopian Church radically changed: out of fourteen bishops only three kept their position. Furthermore, *Qes* Solomon, who was "an enthusiastic supporter of the revolutionary regime",[31] was named as director general of the Church.

The reshuffling at the top of the Church's hierarchy went along with reform of the parish administration. Issued in 1972, the first proclamation on the parish councils did not fit in with the new political and social context. The new administration therefore amended the reforms of Abuna Tewoflos. It was vital for the Church, deprived of land revenue, to rationalize and thereby maximize the collection of donations from the faithful. Parish councils were therefore reintroduced in 1976, and from 1978 the clergy could be paid with locally collected allowances.[32] Because it introduced the participation of laymen in the management of parishes, this system was often described as a form of "democratization" of the Church, a principle well in line with those of the new regime.

The spirit of the revolution entered the Church and its members adopted the discourse of the new state by promoting popular democracy and development. Despite its atheism, the Derg did not attempt to eradicate the Orthodox Church or Islam, but leaned on religious institutions in order to spread its ideology and control rural localities. Therefore, the patriarchate launched a series of seminars throughout all dioceses to instruct the clergy and the faithful on the compatibility between the principles of socialism and the Bible. In return for its cooperative attitude, the Church survived. There was even an upsurge in church attendance as people found in ritual activities a shelter from political turmoil.

After the death of Abuna Takla Haymanot in May 1988, the patriarchal election was held on 28 August 1988. The Synod ratified the choice of the government by electing Abuna Merkorios, the bishop of Gondar, who was also a member of the Parliament. Like his predecessor, the new patriarch remained extremely close to the regime, being a hard line supporter of Ethiopian national unity and the war against Eritrean liberation.

The change of regime in 1991 and the election of Abuna Paulos

After the rebel forces of the Ethiopian People's Revolutionary Democratic Front (EPRDF) overthrew Mengistu in May 1991, Abuna Merkorios tried to hang on to his seat. However, the new regime, like every previous regime, could not work against a hostile and dissident Church. The transitional government needed the full support of the Church. The patriarch was thus forced by the government to abdicate. For more than one year he was under house arrest. On 3 July 1992 the Ethiopian Holy Synod elected a new patriarch, Abuna Paulos.

Since the end of the nineteenth century, the designation of a new patriarch after a regime change had become a tradition in the history of the relations between the state and the Church.[33] By electing Abuna Paulos, the bishops of the Holy Synod perpetuated this link of interdependence and expressed their will to turn the page from the years of the Derg.

Abuna Paulos, whose first identity was Abba Gebre Medhin, was originally a monk from the historic monastery of Abba Garima near Adwa in Tigray. He was one of the most educated high-ranking clerics of his generation. He studied at the Theological College of the Holy Trinity in Addis Ababa, then in the United States at St Vladimir Orthodox Theological Seminary, being thus exposed to the issue of relationships with other Oriental and Eastern Orthodox Churches. When the Revolution broke out, he interrupted his studies and returned to Ethiopia, being summoned by his patron Abuna Tewoflos, who gave him responsibility for ecumenical affairs. He was among the five bishops who were ordained by Abuna Tewoflos in 1975, without government approval. Because of this reshuffling of the episcopal hierarchy—which was considered an act of defiance—Abuna Paulos and the other bishops were imprisoned in 1976. He was released in 1983 and sought refuge in the United States until the fall of the military dictatorship. There he resumed his doctoral studies in theology at Princeton University. In 1986, while still in exile, he was elevated to the rank of archbishop despite being a leading figure of the opposition to the Derg.

One year after the fall of the military junta, Abuna Paulos was elected to the position of patriarch. This was meaningful in several ways. His Tigrean origin was an unambiguous indication that authority had shifted to a new ruling elite, and his election was also presented as the reinstatement of the righteous succession to Abuna Tewoflos, who had been uncanonically eliminated and replaced. His intellectual profile and international experience were also well suited to the task of rebuilding ecumenical relations with other Churches. As a victim of the Derg's abuses, he also built relations with conservative groups who were nostalgic for the imperial regime, for example by attending the funerals in 1993 of sixty high dignitaries assassinated by the Derg, and by presiding over the burial of Haile Selassie in 2000.

Several challenges faced the new patriarch. The reorganization of the Church and its administration had to take place in the context of a new political framework and new spiritual aspirations and practices from the faithful, to which the Church had to adapt. Despite the unquestionable international skills of the patriarch and the modern style he instilled into the Church, his authority was contested and weakened by divisions at various levels.

The separation of the Eritrean Church

The first significant act of Abuna Paulos as patriarch, undertaken reluctantly, was the separation of the Ethiopian and the Eritrean Churches. Shortly after the Eritrea independence referendum in April 1993 the Eritrean clergy asked the Coptic Patriarch Shenouda III to grant Eritreans autonomy from the Ethiopian Church. Abuna Paulos and Abuna Filipos, the Archbishop of Eritrea, ratified the separation, and the Coptic Holy Synod approved the autocephaly of the Eritrean Church on 28 September 1993.

This was an extremely thorny issue. Opponents of the regime denounced what they saw as the dismembering of Ethiopia's spiritual heritage. The patriarch was not in favour of the split, but he managed to ensure a peaceful resolution of the affair. The shrinkage of the Ethiopian Orthodox Tewahedo Church within the new post-Derg political context was the logical consequence of its earlier separation from the authority of the Coptic Church. Since 1959 the Church had completely fallen under the control of the state and so its evolution was unavoidably linked to political changes. After the Eritrean separation was accepted in principle, its formal implementation took some years, in particular because of the need to train the bishops who would compose the Synod and elect a patriarch. In April 1998 the autocephaly of the Eritrean Orthodox Tewahedo Church was completed with a ceremony in Cairo, without the presence of the Ethiopian patriarch. The Coptic Patriarch Shenuda III anointed Abuna Filipos as the first patriarch of Eritrea.

Thereafter, during the conflict on the borders between Ethiopia and Eritrea, the patriarchs of the two churches made joint efforts to show their solidarity and promote peace. Patriarch Abuna Filipos died in 2002, aged 101. He was succeeded by Patriarch Abuna Ya'eqob, who died in December 2003. Abuna Antonios took over the patriarchate, but he resisted the interference of the Eritrean government in religious affairs and refused to take measures against reformist groups within the Church. In January 2005 the Eritrean Synod, siding with the government, deprived Abuna Antonios of executive power. In January 2006 he was removed from office, his pontifical insignia were confiscated and he has been detained under unknown conditions.[34] The fourth patriarch of the Eritrean Church, Abuna Dioskoros, was appointed in April 2007. Neither the Coptic nor the Ethiopian patriarchates recognized this election as legitimate, and most Eritrean Orthodox Christians in the diaspora consider Abuna Antonios to be the only legitimate patriarch. This controversy over the Eritrean Church leadership is one of the consequences of a policy of strict Eritrean government monitoring of all religious groups that participate in activities outside state-sanctioned institutions.

The dissidence of the EOTC Synod in exile

Besides the separation of the Eritrean Church, a further consequence of the change in the Ethiopian government was that those exiles who rejected the new state created a dissident Ethiopian diaspora Church.

After he was deposed and replaced, the former patriarch Abuna Merkorios was kept in custody. His partisans helped him to escape the country in October 1993. He first took refuge in Kenya, from where he declared himself to still be the legitimate head of the Ethiopian Church, and established a dissident Church. His first supporter was Abuna Yeshaq, who was the Archbishop of the Western hemisphere (that is, the diaspora in North America and Europe) and who had supported the Derg in the name of the preservation of national unity. He had already made his feelings clear in September 1992, when he refused to recognize the abdication of the former patriarch and the election of Abuna Paulos. He gathered around him a group of high-ranking clergymen exiled in the United States and Canada—for example Abuna Melke Tsadeq, Abuna Zena Marqos and Abuna Elyas, to mention only the most well-known. Their opposition to Abuna Paulos was strengthened by the separation of the Eritrean Church, which made the transition all the more unbearable to them.

When the deposed Patriarch Merkorios left Kenya and settled in the US in 1997, the dissenting bishops formed around him the "Legal Holy Synod in Exile", which rapidly took control over a number of Ethiopian parishes abroad, mainly in North America but also in Europe and Australia.[35] It attracted many supporters of the political opposition to the EPRDF, who are found in large number in the Ethiopian diaspora. On 21 January 2007, the exiled bishops felt strong enough to take a further—critical—step forward in their challenge to the authority of Abuna Paulos. Merkorios consecrated thirteen new bishops to guide the faithful of his Church and to consolidate its structure by establishing dioceses in charge of the nearly sixty churches scattered throughout North America and the rest of the world. "By so doing, [the dissident Church] solidified its official split from the mother Church in Ethiopia."[36] However, a number of diaspora communities, particularly in America, felt that this division was the result of political issues interfering in religious affairs, and consequently declared their neutrality and independence from any affiliation to a higher ecclesiastical hierarchy, modelling their congregational management on that of Protestant churches.

These three options—obedience to the domestic Ethiopian Church, dissidence or neutrality—show the different ways of being an Ethiopian Orthodox Christian abroad. Maintaining reciprocal links between diaspora and domestic communities has thus become a driving factor in the evolution of the EOTC. Ethiopian parishes export young ordained priests and ritual paraphernalia to the diaspora, and receive in return financial support and senior priests with international expe-

rience, who want to revitalize themselves at home and climb the ecclesiastical ladder.

In response to these divisions, Abuna Paulos committed himself to
ecumenical relations, his area of specialization, trying to end the isolation the Ethiopian Church had suffered from since its separation from
the Coptic community. In 1993, soon after his election as patriarch, he
visited the Ecumenical Patriarchate in Istanbul. His Greek counterpart
visited Addis Ababa in 1994. Theological rapprochement between
Chalcedonians and non-Chalcedonians seems to be far from being
achieved, however, and the time when "Orthodox Ethiopians" will
become simply "Orthodox" still seems distant.

The rise of Evangelical churches and the counter-attack
of Orthodox reformist movements

Another challenge that has gradually weakened the position of the
EOTC has been the erosion of the community of the faithful, which
represented 50.6 per cent of Ethiopia's population in the national census of 1994. This reduced to 43.5 per cent in 2007. This decrease is
mainly explained by the headway made by Evangelical and Pentecostal
Protestant churches (which have increased from 10.2 per cent of the
population in 1994 to 18.5 per cent in 2007); the Muslim population
has remained broadly stable (32.4 per cent in 1994; 34.0 per cent in
2007). A vibrant and fast growing force in the south of the country
and urban centers, Evangelical churches have been competing with the
Ethiopian Church by recruiting from Orthodox families, disseminating a combative message through modern media, and introducing new
models of piety.

In order to curb this trend, and revive the devotion of the faithful and
enhance their participation in the development of the Church, the
Ethiopian patriarchate undertook a new strategy of communication and
indoctrination. A unique message had to be spread throughout the
Ethiopian clergy. The Sunday Schools department, established in 1973,
was reactivated to lead new efforts in the education of the Orthodox
youth and to increase their participation in the Church.[37] The patriarchate tried to further democratize religious knowledge by using a lay association run by students, called Mahibere Kidusan ("Association in the
Name of the Saints"). Founded in the 1980s, the original purpose of
this association was to provide religious teaching in higher education

institutions. It progressively became a tool of communication, in charge of spreading the scripted message from the patriarchate to the provinces. Newspapers, magazines and theological works published by the association have been distributed in book stalls throughout Ethiopia.

But in delegating the dissemination of its doctrine to an association, the patriarchate placed itself in a position that created tensions. Using modern communication technologies (radio, the press and, to a lesser extent, the Internet) and broadcasting an uncompromising message, Mahibere Kidusan has taken on the mantle of being the new radical movement at the heart of the Church. Its discourse is aimed at restoring the original identity and values of Christian Orthodox Ethiopians by extending to the laity practices that used to govern only priests, such as strict observance of fasting, sexual abstinence, and celebrating marriage by taking communion. More generally, it idealizes a past in which Christian values were dominant. The association has also published lampoons of Islam, which openly subverts the official stance of the patriarchate and the government, who advocate interreligious tolerance.

In general, Mahibere Kidusan's teachings express conservative Ethiopian thought. By focusing on moral issues and sidestepping political controversies, the association has been able to translate into religious language arguments that could not be voiced by the political opposition, which has been weakened and silenced since the contested elections of 2005. It has won support particularly from well-off, educated, young members of the urban middle class. These supporters gradually felt strong enough to criticize Patriarch Abuna Paulos, whom they considered to be too careless about the deterioration of the Church and too subservient to the government. This dissent was influential enough to create divisions within the Holy Synod. The disruption was such that in 2009 the association was threatened with excommunication and dismantlement.

In addition to this intellectual and educational movement, Ethiopian Orthodox Christianity has been also transformed at the grassroots level by the emergence of charismatic figures and the revival of traditional practices such as exorcism, healing rituals and prophecies. A significant role is played by hermit monks, called *Bahtawi*s, who live strict ascetic lives. They disregard the authority of the Church hierarchy because they place themselves directly under God's rule, believing they can access divine revelation through their mystical powers. For instance, *Bahtawi* Gebremedhin of Entoto, on the heights of Addis

Ababa, attracts crowds of people whom he treats with prayers and holy water (*tsebel*), which is believed to cure all kinds of diseases, including AIDS.[38] In 1997 another hermit monk, *Bahtawi* Fekade Selassie, who was known for his prophecies and harsh criticisms of the government and Church leadership, was shot dead on the premises of St Istifanos Church in central Addis Ababa, presumably by one of the guards of the patriarch. This was a shock for many of the faithful, who blamed increasing authoritarianism. In the same church the *Memehir* (Master) Girma Wondimu performs what people believe to be "miracles" by practicing exorcism. His weekly sessions are attended by a large local audience, and many more watch videos of him on the Internet. These healers address the spiritual and psychological needs of believers who are strained by the daily hardships of existence and the struggle to adapt to modernity. They draw on ancient traditional beliefs and practices that were found in the margins of mainstream orthodoxy.[39] These traditions have been reactivated, made more visible and adapted to modern life in reaction to missionary incursions by Pentecostal cults based on charismatic healing.

In its long history the EOTC has been periodically agitated by doctrinal disputes and charismatic movements. The conservative youth leaders and intellectuals and the neo-traditional healers who have all appeared in the last two decades have been serious challengers to the authority of the patriarch, but they have not destabilized the whole institution of the patriarchate. On the one hand, Patriarch Abuna Paulos was a modernizer and he was mainly criticized for having introduced several innovations. By accompanying the general transformation of Ethiopian society, the patriarchate reduced its exposure to internal dissent. On the other hand, the patriarchate kept a strong institutional control over the majority of parishes. Since their establishment in 1972 and their amendment under the Derg, the existence of parish councils has put an end to the autonomy of the parishes. Each church throughout the country has become a constitutive block of the Church's administrative structure. After the theological college in Addis Ababa reopened in 1994, church administrators of a new kind appeared throughout the country, whose role is to enforce regulations handed down by the national centralized structure of the patriarchate. If the decision to open up local church administration to laymen was initially aimed at preparing the way for radical changes, ultimately the system has mostly helped perpetuate the position of local notables within parish communities.

Constantly assailed to make donations, the faithful are burdened with making heavy contributions for the support of the clergy and the maintenance of churches. Through their financial involvement and their participation in religious associations, parishioners can achieve the prestigious position of notable, devout, or active member of a community. Such involvement can assuage the anxiety that results from seeing one's local identity being diluted by a perpetually evolving national identity. In addition to this participation in community life, there has been a boom of religious associations. These associations offer their members the possibility of restoring bonds broken by rural exodus, in particular through mutual aid to help people cope with the economic costs of funeral ceremonies.

Further evidence of the commitment of Orthodox parishioners to the vitality of the Church is provided by the evolution of architecture. In addition to their contributions to the maintenance of ancient churches, their financial efforts have also helped construct magnificent cathedrals—characterized by a cross-shaped plan, high walls, large stained-glass windows and prominent domes—that can be seen and heard from far away. The Trinity Cathedral in Addis Ababa, built in 1942, used to be unique, as the church of the king. The construction in 1997 of the cathedral of Bole Medhani Alem in Addis Ababa, the second largest in Africa, using community funds, introduced a new model that quickly spread into many provincial towns. Local communities are proud of these buildings, which are a powerful sign of the revival of Ethiopian Christianity. Cathedrals have also enabled a change in the involvement of the faithful in the liturgy, as they are no longer systematically packed outside the church, as in traditional round-shaped churches, but can stay inside in front of priests and take a more active share in the celebration. This evolution in the style of worship is testified to by the popularity of religious hymns on recorded cassettes and mobile phone speakers. All of this is a way of responding to the threat to the Orthodox Church from the attractiveness of Protestant churches, which enjoy playing music and singing during services.

From Abuna Paulos to Abuna Mathias: continuity and beyond

During the twenty years in which Abuna Paulos was patriarch (1992–2012), the Ethiopian Church underwent transformations that influenced the spiritual and social life of the faithful. An observer of the

Ethiopian Church summarized the major issues that it has been confronted with as follows: "Orthodox Christians have been challenged to re-evaluate their institutions on multiple fronts, to balance the notions of tradition and territoriality on which their religion is based with multiple competing conceptions of the Ethiopian future, and with the mass perspective shift that global economy, secular government, and narratives of modernity bring about."[40]

The patriarchy of Abuna Paulos was closely associated with the transformations undergone by the whole of Ethiopian society under the leadership of Meles Zenawi. The new political setting posed several challenges to the Church: the separation of the Eritrean Church, the schism of the diaspora community, and the competition with other Christian denominations in a newly open religious "market". Furthermore, after the new regime was established, the Ethiopian Church had to comply with Meles Zenawi's developmental goals, which aimed at transforming the Ethiopian psyche from one that valued fatalistic acceptance and endurance of difficulties (to be rewarded in the afterlife) to one at home in a market economy (in which rewards, in the forms of money and consumer goods, are given in this life). This shift in moral values led to the exacerbation of internal doctrinal controversies and criticisms of the patriarch to a level never experienced before, but Abuna Paulos's international experience, knowledge of ecumenical issues, and his sense of modernity balanced by his link to the old imperial regime have contributed to the stable transformation of the Church. His main achievements have been the modernization of Church administration, the improved training of the clergy, the increased participation of the laity in the Church, the implementation of developmental activities, and the strengthening of international and ecumenical relations.

Strikingly, the Patriarch and the Prime Minister unexpectedly died within a week of one another, at the end of August 2012. The shock was immense for the whole Ethiopian nation. Suddenly both political and spiritual powers were absent. After weeks of national mourning and the celebration of the Ethiopian New Year, the government affirmed its continuity through the confirmation of Haile Mariam Dessalegn, the former Deputy Prime Minister, as the new Prime Minister. For the first time in Ethiopian history a Protestant became the head of state. In a secular state, his denomination should be considered as a neutral fact, made inevitable by the religious diversity of the members of the government. Meanwhile, the interim period before the election of a new patriarch was managed by the designation of Abuna Nathanael as caretaker patriarch by the Holy Synod.

During this period negotiations were undertaken to bring about reconciliation between the national and the exiled synods. The President of the Republic, Girma Wolde Giorgis, even wrote a letter to the patriarch in exile to convince him to return home. This initiative was dismissed as an unconstitutional interference. The attempts at reuniting the Church ultimately failed, however, because of the refusal of the dissidents to recognize any other patriarch than Merkorios.

The patriarchal election was held at the end of February 2013. 800 voters were drawn from archbishops, representatives of ancient monasteries and the fifty-three dioceses as well as from the faithful, the Sunday schools and the clergy. None of the well-known rivals of the late patriarch were among the candidates. This was not seen as the proper occasion to show internal dissent. Abuna Mathias was elected on 28 February 2013 and enthroned on 3 March.

The new Patriarch is a figure of continuity. Like his predecessor he was born in the region of Tigray (in 1940). In 1978 he was appointed archbishop in Jerusalem, from where he denounced the Derg regime. He fled in exile to Washington D.C. where he was a spokesman for the opposition to the Derg. He was reintegrated into the Holy Synod in 1992 after the appointment of Abuna Paulos. He actually stayed in Washington, where he was based as the archbishop of North America until 2009. Being the representative of the official EOTC, he made efforts to reach reconciliation with the dissenting parishes in the diaspora. Between 2009 and 2012 he was back in Jerusalem as archbishop. His background and international profile, very similar to that of Abuna Paulos, indicate that the EOTC will continue to be a cooperative actor in the Ethiopian government's national development strategy.

BIBLIOGRAPHY AND FURTHER READING

Abbink, Jon, 2003, *A Bibliography on Christianity in Ethiopia*, Leiden: Africa Studies Centre (working paper n° 52) (http://www.ascleiden.nl/pdf/working-paper52.pdf).

Alexander, George, 2012, "The Detained Patriarch, Persecuted Christians and a Dying Church", *Orthodoxy Cognate Page*, 18 January 2012, http://theorthodoxchurch.info/blog/news/2012/01/the-detained-patriarch-persecuted-christians-and-a-dying-church/ (last access April 2013).

Ancel, Stéphane, 2011a, "Territories, Ecclesiastical Jurisdictions and Centralization Process: the Improvement of the Ethiopian Patriarchate Authority (1972–1983)", *Annales d'Ethiopie*, 26, pp. 167–78.

—— 2011b, "Centralization and Political Changes: the Ethiopian Orthodox Church and the Ecclesiastical and Political Challenges in Contemporary Times", *Rassegna di Studi Etiopici*, 3 (Nuova Serie), pp. 1–26.

Ayele Teklehaymanot, 1988, "The Egyptian Metropolitan of the Ethiopian Church", *Orientalia Christiana Periodica*, 54 (1), pp. 175–222.

Bairu Tafla, 1977, *A Chronicle of Emperor Yohannes IV (1872–1889)*, Wiesbaden: Franz Steiner Verlag.

—— 1986, "Titles, Ranks and Offices of the Ethiopian Orthodox Tawahdo Church: a Preliminary Survey", *Internationale Kirchliche Zeitschrift*, 76, pp. 293–304.

Binns, J., 2013, "Out of Ethiopia—a Different Way of Doing Theology", *International Journal for the Study of the Christian Church*, 13 (1), pp. 33–47.

Boutros Ghali, M., 1991, "Ethiopian Church Autocephaly", *Coptic Encyclopedia*, 3, pp. 980–84.

Boylston, Tom, 2012 a, "The Shade of the Divine: Approaching the Sacred in an Ethiopian Orthodox Christian Community", PhD Thesis: London School of Economics.

—— 2012 b, "Orthodox Modern", *FocusOnTheHorn*, 2 July 2012. http://focusonthehorn.wordpress.com/2012/07/20/orthodox-modern-religion-politics-in-todays-ethiopia-part-1/ (last access April 2013).

Caulk, Richard, 1972, "Religion and State in Nineteenth Century Ethiopia", *Journal of Ethiopian Studies*, 10 (1), pp. 23–41.

Chaillot, Christine, 2002, *The Ethiopian Orthodox Tewahedo Church Tradition: A Brief Introduction to its Life and Spirituality*, Paris: Inter-Orthodox Dialogue.

Chernetsov, Sevir, 2003, "Ethiopian Orthodox (Täwahedo) Church. History from the Second Half of the 19th Cent. to 1959", *Encyclopaedia Aethiopica*, vol. 1, pp. 421–24

Crummey, Donald, 1972, *Priests and Politicians: Protestant and Catholic Missions in Orthodox Ethiopia, 1830–1868*, London: Oxford University Press.

—— 1978, "Orthodoxy and Imperial Reconstruction in Ethiopia, 1854–1878", *Journal of Theological Studies*, 29 (2), pp. 427–42.

Doulos, M., 1986, "Christians in Marxist Ethiopia", *Religion in Communist Lands*, 14 (2), pp. 134–47.

Engedayehu, Walle, 2013, "The Ethiopian Orthodox Tewahedo Church in the Diaspora: Expansion in the Midst of Division", *African Social Science Review*, 6 (1), article n° 8. http://digitalcommons.kennesaw.edu/assr/vol6/iss1/8 (last access April 2013).

Ephraim Isaac, 1971, "Social Structure of the Ethiopian Church", *Ethiopia Observer*, 14 (4), pp. 240–88.

—— 2013, *The Ethiopian Orthodox Täwahïdo Church*, Trenton, NJ: The Red Sea Press.

Erlich, Haggai, 2000, "Identity and Church: Ethiopian-Egyptian Dialogue, 1924–1959," *International Journal of Middle East Studies*, 32 (1), pp. 23–46.

Getatchew Haile, 2003, "Ethiopian Orthodox (Täwahedo) Church. History from Ancient Times Till the Second Half of the 19th Cent.", *Encyclopaedia Aethiopica*, vol. 1, pp. 414–21.

Goricke, F. and F. Heyer, 1976, "The Orthodox Church of Ethiopia as a Social Institution", *International Yearbook for Sociology of Knowledge and Religion*, 10.

Haile Mariam Larebo, 1986, "The Orthodox Church and the State in the Ethiopian Revolution, 1974–1984", *Religion in Communist Lands*, 14 (2), pp. 148–59.

—— 1987, "The Ethiopian Orthodox Church and Politics in the Twentieth Century: Part 1", *Northeast African Studies*, 9 (3), pp. 1–18.

—— 1988, "The Ethiopian Orthodox Church and Politics in the Twentieth Century: Part 2", *Northeast African Studies*, 10 (1), pp. 1–24.

Heidt, A.M., 1973, "L'Église éthiopienne orthodoxe d'aujourd'hui: interview avec l'abuna Théophilos, patriarche d'Éthiopie, et l'abuna Samuel", *Irenikon*, 46 (4), pp. 491–6.

Hermann, Judith, 2010, "Le rituel de l'eau bénite: une réponse sociale et symbolique à la pandémie du sida", *Annales d'Ethiopie*, 25, pp. 189–205.

Imbakom Kalewold, 1970, *Traditional Ethiopian Church Education*, New York: Columbia University: Teachers College Press.

Kaplan, Steven, 2007, "Matewos", *Encyclopaedia Aethiopica*, 3, pp. 867–8.

Marcus, Cressida, 2002, "Imperial Nostalgia: Christian Restoration & Civic Decay in Gondar", in W. James et al. (eds), *Remapping Ethiopia: Socialism & After*, Oxford; Athens, OH; Addis Ababa: James Currey; Ohio University Press; Addis Ababa University Press, pp. 239–56.

—— 2008, "Sacred Time, Civic Calendar: Religious Plurality and the Centrality of Religion in Ethiopian Society", *International Journal of Ethiopian Studies*, 3 (2), pp. 143–75.

Marcus, Harold, 1987, *Haile Sellassie I: the Formative Years, 1892–1936*. Berkeley/Los Angeles/London: University of California Press.

Mersha Alehegne, 2010a, "Qerellos VI (*Abunä*)", *Encyclopaedia Aethiopica*, 4, pp. 291–92.

—— 2010b, "Täklä Haymanot (*Abunä*)", *Encyclopaedia Aethiopica*, 4, pp. 839–40.

—— 2010c, "Tewoflos (*Abunä*)", *Encyclopaedia Aethiopica*, 4, pp. 938–9.

Murad, K. 1950–1957, "La dernière phase des relations historiques entre l'Église copte d'Égypte et celle d'Éthiopie (jusqu'en 1952)", *Bulletin de la Société d'Archéologie Copte*, 14, pp. 1–22.

Nosnitsin, D., Fritsch, E., and Dimetros Weldu, 2003, "Churches and Church Administration", *Encyclopaedia Aethiopica*, vol. 1, pp. 740–4.

Sergew Hable Sellasie (ed.), 1970, *The Church of Ethiopia. A Panorama of History and Spiritual Life*, Addis Ababa: Ethiopian Orthodox Church.

Shenk, C., 1972, "The Italian Attempt to Reconcile the Ethiopian Church: the Use of Religious Celebrations and Assistance to Churches and Monasteries", *Journal of Ethiopian Studies*, 10 (1), pp. 125–35.

Shiferaw Bekele, 2010, "Petros (*Abunä*)", *Encyclopaedia Aethiopica*, 4, pp. 139–40.

Stoffregen-Pedersen, Kirsten, 1990, *Les Éthiopiens*, Turnhout, Belgium: Éditions Brepols.

Taddesse Tamrat, 1972, *Church and State in Ethiopia (1270–1527)*, Oxford: Clarendon Press, 1972.

Young, Allan, 1977, "Magic as a 'Quasi-Profession': The Organization of Magical Healing among Amhara", *Ethnology*, 14, pp. 245–65.

3

THE ETHIOPIAN MUSLIMS

HISTORICAL PROCESSES
AND ONGOING CONTROVERSIES

Éloi Ficquet

This chapter will review the long lasting issue of the participation of Muslims in the construction of Ethiopian nationhood and the related challenge of how to maintain coexistence and mutual tolerance between religious groups.[1] From perhaps the tenth century, independent Muslim polities neighboured the Christian kingdom of the north-western Ethiopian highlands. Although mutual recognition grew out of trade relations, competition and distrust sometimes led to conflicts between these powers and the Christian kingdom. In the second half of the nineteenth century an imperial state was built up on Christian allegiance. Muslim subjects were forcefully incorporated into the new territorial framework of the Ethiopian state, in which they were discriminated against and marginalized. After the 1974 revolution and the downfall of imperial rule, the authorities moved towards more secular orientations. Muslims have been gradually recognized as having equal rights

93

in a pluralistic society. However, they still have to struggle—internally within their communities and externally by confronting government interference—against the suspicion that they could be vectors of external threats emanating from the wider Islamic world.

Number, distribution and visibility of Muslims in Ethiopia

Today Muslims represent a large portion of the Ethiopian population. Around one Ethiopian in three adheres to Islam. This has been the official estimate since the first statistical surveys in the 1960s and has been confirmed by every national census since 1984.[2] The last census, undertaken in 2007, showed that 33.9 per cent of Ethiopians (25 million out of 74 million) were Muslims, up from 32.8 per cent in the 1994 census. There has been some discussion about whether or not this stable proportion of one third is accurate. Some observers have asserted that this is an underestimation, fabricated and constantly repeated by the Ethiopian authorities and foreign scholars. Some web columnists even claim that Muslims could make up the majority of the Ethiopian population, but such statements are made without providing factual data convincing enough to support them.

On a map of Ethiopia's religions three main blocks appear. The eastern regions (Afar, Somali, eastern Oromiya) are predominantly Muslim and the north-western regions (Tigray and Amhara) are Orthodox Christian. Protestant Christians are concentrated in the south-west—in the Southern Nations, Nationalities, and Peoples' Region (SNNPR) and Gambella. This snapshot picture is highly contrasted and should not hide the fact that a high number of Ethiopians experience much more complex situations of interreligious coexistence, particularly in towns and some densely populated rural areas. A focus on Muslims in each region shows different kinds of situations. Almost the entire populations of the Afar and Somali regions follow Islam (95 per cent and 98 per cent respectively). Muslims are a small minority in Tigray (4 per cent). They are found in a larger proportion in Amhara (17 per cent), their number being high in its eastern districts of Wollo and Shoa, bordering the Afar and Oromiya regions. The situation is similar in the SNNPR, where Muslims (14 per cent) are concentrated in the north-eastern areas bordering Oromiya, particularly the Gurage and Silte zones. In the Benishangul Gumuz Region, which borders Sudan, Muslims make up 45 per cent of the population. The region with the largest number of Ethiopian Muslims is Oromiya. They represent 48 per cent of Oromiya's population, and Oromo Muslims represent 51 per cent of all Ethiopian Muslims. They are concentrated in the regions of Jimma, Illubabor, Arsi, Bale, and in the surroundings of Harar.

In recent years the size of the Muslim population has remained quite stable in relative terms, but their visibility has significantly increased in the public sphere and this may have given the impression of a sudden rise in their number. For example, regulations on the construction of mosques have been eased,[3] Muslim clothes (including the *hijab* for women and *qamis* for men) have become quite common in the streets, and Islamic spiritual songs in Arabic and Ethiopian languages are often heard coming from loudspeakers in Muslim-owned music shops.

Such public expressions of Islamic identity represent a significant break from the past. The next sections will review the evolution of the situation of Ethiopian Muslims, from their status as a minority group to their struggle for recognition and civil rights.

Muslims in north-east Africa, before their incorporation into the state of Ethiopia

For centuries Islam has been taught, practised and debated within the territorial framework that is identified today as the state of Ethiopia. The proximity of Arab countries facilitated the early diffusion of Islam into Ethiopia and helped maintain a continuous flow of new ideas from the international Islamic community. However, this geographical situation does not fully explain the attractiveness of Islam in the Ethiopian setting. Among the many factors, let us emphasise two. First, the principles of Islam consider as equals all humans who fear and accept the supreme authority of Allah, beyond cultural divisions and without the mediation of a clerical hierarchy above the rest of the society.[4] Second, through the medium of Arabic, Islam provides access to a written language of international communication. Through its egalitarian and intercultural values Islam contributed to the lifting of barriers between north-east African societies and linked many of them into trans-regional networks that helped the circulation of goods, ideas and people. Despite its universal outlook, it did not remove the roots of local conflicts, but it generally shifted priority to the maintenance of peaceful interaction between Muslim groups, regardless of their cultural differences.[5]

In the context of the global history of Islam, Ethiopia is characterized by the longstanding coexistence of Muslim communities side by
side with a powerful Christian state. Unlike other ancient Christian
communities in Africa (for example, in Egypt, the Maghreb and
Nubia), who were reduced to the status of political minorities by Arab
conquerors and progressively converted to Islam, the ancient Ethiopian
Christian Kingdom of Aksum established early relations with emerging Islamic powers and contained them on the fringes of its realm.

The establishment of this *modus vivendi* is recalled by the famous
story of the first *hijra* (migration). When the first followers of the
Prophet Muhammad fled persecution in Mecca, they took refuge in
Aksum under the protection of the king or *negus* (*najashi* in Arabic
traditions). As a token of gratitude, the Prophet is said to have
instructed his followers not to invade Ethiopia as long as Ethiopians
did not attack Muslims.[6] This episode in early Islamic history reflects
a certain level of mutual respect and understanding between Christians
and Muslims in Ethiopia, which has been maintained over centuries.

As the two religions share a wide set of common references, concepts
and values, differences between rival societies were translated in
Ethiopia into a kind of agreed ideological dualism. Exchanges were
facilitated by a clear division of socio-economic roles. Of course, such
a model of coexistence could not work without competition. Peaceful
interactions were frequently overshadowed by low intensity conflicts
in contact areas. However, clashes were generally not primarily triggered by religious differences.

In the Middle Ages, between the tenth and sixteenth centuries,
Christian and Muslim polities continued their expansion southwards,
driven by similar dynamics and means. Holy men—Christian monks
and Muslim sheikhs—travelled into the "wilderness" to convert hea-
then societies on the periphery of their respective polities. Their mastery of religious texts was the source of their charisma and the aura of
conviction through which they spread their beliefs and converted local
populations. They then helped smooth the process of integration of
these groups into the political and economic spheres of the Christian
and Muslim polities. In short, tax-collecting royal armies followed
Christian monks; caravans followed Muslim sheikhs.[7] Permanent
Muslim settlements were gradually strung out along trade routes, connecting trading posts and their hinterland with the international networks that travelled through the Red Sea. Areas of medium altitude

were their favoured environments. One advantage of such environments was that they collected waters flowing from escarpments. Another was that they were high enough for their inhabitants to gain an overhead view of traders and conflicts coming from the lowlands.[8]

In the sixteenth century, hegemonic ambitions on both sides led to an escalation of warfare that culminated in the Islamic invasion and occupation of the Christian kingdom between 1529 and 1543. This *jihad* was led by Imam Ahmad bin Ibrahim, known as Gragn "the Left-handed", who fought to establish a strong and unified Muslim East African state. A Portuguese expeditionary force sent to support the critically endangered Christian kingdom killed him. His army collapsed and disbanded after his death and his successors failed in their attempts to regain lost territories. On both sides this devastating conflict was followed by a long period of decline, disintegration and reorganization of regional powers.

This period of confrontation and reshaping of local powers gave opportunities for literate and charismatic men—*ulama* and *awliya*[9]—to circulate between polities and gain "employment" as advisers, healers and peacemakers. Some of them came from Arab countries and some even claimed to descend from Sharifian lineages linking them to the family of the Prophet Muhammad. Their knowledge, charisma and origins conferred on them great prestige, which was in turn bestowed upon their hosts and protectors. Conversion to Islam spread from elites to local populations in a process that incorporated local beliefs by translating them into the transnational words and codifications of Islam. This wave of Islamization had a strong impact on Oromo polities (in the areas of Hararge, Wollo and Gibe) that were connected to trade routes through the interregional and international networks of Islam. This missionary impetus corresponded to a wider scale reform movement in the Muslim world, carried out by old (Qadiriyya, Shadhiliyya) and new (Tijaniyya, Ahmadiyya) Sufi mystical orders.

Muslims and the making of Ethiopia in the nineteenth and twentieth centuries

In reaction to the expansion of Islam there was a re-awakening of Ethiopian Christian nationalism in the second half of the nineteenth century. The formation of the modern state of Ethiopia is the result of policies of expansion and modernization centred on the Christian

Kingdom of Ethiopia (for details of this process see Chapter 6 in this volume). This process was carried out through the conquest of peripheral territories and peoples, many of whom were Muslims or had been previously exposed to Islamic influence. From this period onwards, a large number of Muslims have become nominally Ethiopians. They have found it challenging to actually become true citizens, for they have been faced by authorities who, more or less officially, consider them as deviant from the genuine Ethiopian identity and as potential enemies linked to external rivals.

The strategy of building a Christian hegemony over neighbouring Muslim territories was based on the memory of the religious wars of the sixteenth century, and was nourished by a belief that the reconquest of lost provinces would revive the golden age of the medieval empire and open a new prosperous era for a Greater Ethiopia. This Christian expansionism, partly driven by irredentism—that is, the desire to annex land on the grounds of prior historical possession—was further encouraged by the international context, in which Muslim countries (of which Egypt was particularly at the forefront of the Ethiopian consciousness) were occupied by European powers. The Ethiopian leaders of the second half of the nineteenth century—Emperors Tewodros II, Yohannes IV and Menelik II—aimed to elevate Ethiopia to the rank of the major powers in a world dominated by European Christian colonial empires. Furthermore, the Europeans gave some direct and indirect assistance to Ethiopian Christians—selling them firearms and giving them technological advice—which made the difference on the battlefields.

Violent means of annexation, including attempts to force mass conversion, and oppressive occupation regimes generated resistance from Muslim communities. The annexation policy also sharpened the hostility of Islamic anti-colonial movements in neighbouring countries, such as Mahdist Sudan[10] and Somaliland, where Muhammad Abdille Hassan, the so-called "Mad Mullah", led a rebellion against colonial forces. Some peripheral groups who still practiced indigenous religions also converted to Islam in order to protect themselves against Christian domination and predation.[11] Being aware of the risk of setting up Muslims against his nation-building policy, Emperor Menelik II adopted a more conciliatory approach.

After victory in the Battle of Adwa against the Italians in 1896, Ethiopia's independence was secured against the threat of colonial invasion, and international treaties guaranteed its boundaries. To consolidate the nation within its expanded framework the crown needed the participation of all Ethiopians, including the recently absorbed Muslim communities and polities. Muslim areas were of particular importance since they had become "buffer zones" between the core of the kingdom and the bordering countries under colonial rule, and they connected Ethiopia to the world through international commercial networks. Menelik understood that Muslims were the economic lungs of the country. Therefore, his government tolerated their distinctness as long as they practised their faith discreetly[12] and accepted Christian domination even in Muslim-majority regions.

In 1909 Menelik designated his only grandson, *Lij* Iyasu, as his heir to the throne of the Empire. Iyasu was sixteen years old when the Emperor died in 1913. Though educated as a Christian prince, he was the son of a Muslim lord of Wollo, who had converted to Christianity following a pattern of political conversions that had been quite common in this territory since the end of the eighteenth century.

During his short reign Lij Iyasu tried to accommodate religious diversity by regularly visiting Muslim chiefs and making alliances with them. He paid respect to them through symbolic acts such as wearing Muslim dress, and he did not hide his Muslim ancestry, being proud of incarnating the alliance between the two sacred dynasties of King Solomon and the Prophet Muhammad. His political behaviour indicates that he probably had in mind a kind of syncretic fusion of the two religions, or at least an equality of status, that would abrogate religious discrimination and strengthen the future of Ethiopia. His many marriages with Christian and Muslim women from ruling families of all Ethiopian regions can be understood in this conciliatory perspective. He was also concerned with geopolitical issues. In the context of the First World War he sympathized with Turkey and Germany against France, Britain and Italy. Indeed, these three colonial powers had agreed to share Menelik's empire after his death and senior officers who tutored him warned Iyasu against this threat. The way he governed has remained unclear and misunderstood by most historians, who have generally reduced his reign to his impetuous and immature nature. His benevolent attitude towards Islam was provocative to conservative challengers. Playing on his ambiguous behaviour, they employed the communication technologies of the time (press propaganda, doctored photographs) to convince the public that Iyasu could not be crowned because he had, they said, converted to Islam. He was excommunicated and deposed in September 1916, captured in 1921 and kept in custody until his murder in 1935.[13]

After this contested interregnum, the Shoan Christian aristocracy firmly reasserted their domination. Menelik's daughter Zewditu was crowned Empress and power was exercised by *Ras* Tafari Makonnen, who had the title of Crown Prince and the role of regent plenipotentiary until his coronation as King of Kings Haile Selassie in 1930. This man was the very opposite of Iyasu in every facet of life and politics. As he was the son of Ras Makonnen, the conqueror and governor of Harar, his background and perspectives were fundamentally bound to the policy of Christian domination over Muslim territories. For this purpose he favoured the settlement of Christian soldiers on Muslim lands. Ethiopian Muslims "seem to have accepted their subordinate position as part of the natural order of things".[14] Their resignation was the result of the harsh military control imposed on them to prevent any expression of discontent.

The Italian fascist occupation authorities between 1935 and 1941 exploited the resentment of Ethiopian Muslims against Christian oppression. Following the colonial principle of "divide and rule", they took measures favourable to the emancipation of Muslims such as building new mosques (no less than fifty), allocating grants for pilgrims to Mecca, and supporting Islamic education and publications in Arabic. This policy had the purpose of undermining Ethiopian anti-colonial resistance, which the Italians considered essentially Christian-driven.[15] Indeed, since Muslims were barred from the Ethiopian imperial army and were forbidden to own firearms, they were neither able nor inclined to fight alongside the patriots.

This short episode of Italian rule had a considerable impact on Ethiopian Muslims' self-awareness. First, the extended rights they were temporarily granted provided a memory that spurred on their later struggles for recognition. Secondly, pilgrimages, education trips and imported books exposed the most learned to the currents of ideas circulating in the Muslim world, amongst which was the fundamentalist Salafi movement from Saudi Arabia which became an influence on Ethiopian Islam from then on.[16]

The Italian East African Empire was defeated in 1941 with the help of British troops. Haile Selassie's monarchy was restored. Some retaliatory measures were taken against Muslim leaders on account of their collaboration with the enemy, but the Emperor also followed a policy of appeasement and co-option of Muslim notables. However, the centralization of power undertaken by the Emperor to reestablish his authority worsened the marginalization of local Muslim leaderships. In eastern Ethiopia the post-World War II situation led to particular developments. The planned independence and unification of British Somaliland and ex-Italian Somalia stirred up the Somali nationalist movement in Ethiopia. The idea took hold of building a "Greater Somalia", including Ethiopia's Somali territories, identified as land populated by "Western Somalis", which were then under British provisional administration. Somali ambitions also included the incorporation of eastern Oromos with whom they shared common cultural features and a similar past. The Somali Youth Club, the first Somali political organization (established in 1943), opened an office in Harar where local grievances were gathered in a petition forwarded to Arab countries. This movement, which marked the deterioration of the international image of Ethiopia as a tolerant country, was severely crushed by the imperial authorities in 1948.[17] Later in the 1960s, Somalia's independence and unification encouraged the outbreak of a rebellion in Bale, rallied by eastern Oromo Muslims. In the same period, Muslim lowlanders were the first to protest against Ethiopia's annexation of Eritrea in 1962. They formed the first armed liberation front before Christians took over the leadership of the insurrection.

It would be simplistic, however, to imply that ethno-nationalist movements and those who demanded religious freedom had the same goals. The political movements were concerned with economic problems and the defence of autonomous ethnicities. They were guided by worldwide left-wing ideologies such as Pan-Arabism or Third-Worldism that gave priority to modern development understood in a secular perspective, religions being criticized for supporting backward social orders. On the other hand, activists for religious rights among Ethiopian Muslims were not leaning towards radical action. Their aspiration tended to be national integration; they wished to be recognized as no less Ethiopian than any other citizen and to enjoy equal rights.

By virtue of Ethiopia's longstanding resistance to colonialism, Emperor Haile Selassie liked to pose as a hero of African independence. While he hosted Africa's independent countries at the headquarters of the Organization of African Unity in Addis Ababa, he could not appear as a persecutor of his own population. He therefore tried to silence expressions of discontent rising from Muslim communities by coming up with half-hearted measures such as allowing local Muslim *shari'a* courts to settle legal disputes pertaining to private affairs.[18]

Such compromises hardly satisfied the demands for religious freedom. The dissatisfaction of Ethiopian Muslims converged with the growing frustrations of other social groups. At the beginning of 1974 a popular uprising erupted against the social and economic dead-ends of the imperial administration. In April, after a series of strikes held by students, low rank clergymen, taxi drivers, prostitutes and public officers, tens of thousands of Muslim residents of Addis Ababa took the street to add their voices to the general protest. This huge demonstration was a historical landmark. It marked "the culmination of a sense of indignation and an organized expression of their pent-up anger and discontent which had been simmering for many years".[19] A petition of thirteen requests was submitted to the government asking for equal rights and freedom of worship. The demand that the official designation of "Muslims living in Ethiopia" (which implied that Muslims were aliens) should be changed to "Ethiopian Muslims" significantly emphasized national consciousness.

The popular movement was followed by a military coup triggered by the most radical faction within the army. The Emperor was deposed in September 1974. The Derg promised to prioritize Ethiopia and to treat all Ethiopians equally irrespective of their religious differences. It granted religious freedom to Ethiopian Muslims and declared official the observation of Muslim holidays. The Muslim Council was formally established in 1976. It was, however, nothing more than a *de jure* body without proper function.[20] And such policies were abandoned after the Derg shifted to a scientific socialist ideology, which considered all religions backward and reactionary. Thereafter, all religious denominations were persecuted indiscriminately. In eastern Ethiopia Muslims in particular were hit hard as they were suspected of having sided with the Somalis during the Ogaden War of 1977.[21] Every religious authority was considerably weakened by the Derg's authoritarianism. However, religious sentiment in the populace was reinvigorated and transformed, with resort to clandestine ceremonies.

At another level, the implementation of a command economy had heavy consequences for Muslim businessmen. They were denounced as exploiters and plotters against the economy and accused of sabotaging the revolution by increasing prices. A number of them were arrested and executed. Their financial position was undermined by the nation-alization of trading companies and the confiscation of rented housing.

Muslims under the Ethiopian People's Revolutionary Democratic Front: from satisfaction to protest

The military socialist dictatorship of the Derg, led by Mengistu Haile Mariam, eventually collapsed in May 1991. It was defeated by a coali-tion of ethno-nationalist guerrillas under the leadership of the Tigray People's Liberation Front (TPLF), which became a national party ori-ented towards revolutionary democracy, the Ethiopian People's Revolutionary Democratic Front (EPRDF). Religion had not been a priority for the rebel groups. Their struggle against the Derg was guided by radical Marxist principles that were atheistic. However, they had to respect the denominations and beliefs of the population to win and retain public support.

Under the leadership of Meles Zenawi, the main goal of the transi-tional government was to build ethnic federalism, designed to accom-modate the country's diversity with the purpose of greater national integration. The religious factor was not taken into account in the lay-ing out of the ethnic regions, which were based mainly on the criterion of linguistic homogeneity. An efficient way to neutralize religious issues was to give freedom to the faithful, while monitoring them softly, to let them accept and respect the secular constitutional frame-work and the newly established political order.

The Federal Constitution of Ethiopia, adopted at the end of 1994, promulgated religious freedom and equality of rights. Article 11 pro-claimed the separation of state and religion through three clear-cut points: "1. State and religion are separate; 2. There shall be no state religion; 3. The state shall not interfere in religious matters and religion shall not interfere in state affairs". Article 25 affirmed the equality of all citizens without any denominational discrimination and Article 27 guaranteed freedom of worship, including the right for believers to "establish institutions of religious education and administration in order to propagate and organize their religion".

This constitutional commitment to secularism was followed by mea-sures allowing Muslims to practice their faith more openly. The three main festivals (Id al-Fitr, Id al-Adha [or Arafa] and Mawlid) of the Muslim calendar became public holidays; procedures for the construction of mosques and schools were eased; and restrictions on pilgrimage to Mecca were lifted, as was the ban on importing or printing religious printed materials.[22] Furthermore, the representation of Muslims in regional government and assemblies enhanced their participation in national affairs. However, the first fly in the ointment appeared in early 1995 when the Supreme Council for Islamic Affairs, the Majlis, was reactivated and reorganized. Elections of regional and national representatives stirred up an internal power struggle; the leadership, which was loyal to the national government, was pitted against independent and supposedly more representative personalities. In early 1995 this quarrel led to an outbreak of violence in the compound of the Anwar Mosque of Addis Ababa that was severely repressed by the police.

All in all, Ethiopian Muslims welcomed the EPRDF's liberal religious policy, which allowed them to take significant steps towards being recognized as fully-fledged citizens. Nevertheless, religion being a competitive arena, the new openness generated internal debates and external tensions. To review recent trends and protests in Ethiopian Islam, four issues need to be considered:

(a) Ethiopian Islam has gone through a general revival and Ethiopian Muslims have strengthened their relations with the Arab world;

(b) An increasing number of Muslims have opted for radical tendencies motivated by desire for more rigorous moral standards rather than by political goals;

(c) Both (a) and (b) have contributed to the hardening of inter-religious tensions;

(d) Suspicions that Ethiopian Muslims are accommodating extremist Islamist cells has led the state to monitor Muslim organizations, restrict freedom of expression and impose a preferred form of religion. In response, since the beginning of 2012, many Ethiopian Muslims have started to express their disagreement. Irritation has grown into anger, leading to weekly mass protests against what many consider unconstitutional state interference in religious affairs.

The Islamic revival and Ethiopian Muslims' tighter links
with the Middle East

By allowing more religious freedom, the EPRDF created a favourable environment for a movement of revival within Ethiopian Islam. Indeed, Ethiopia's other religious groups have also experienced renewed popular interest in religion, its values and its spiritual resources. Several factors have increased both the demand for and supply of religion. A growing number of denominational schools have disseminated religious ideas using diverse models of education.[23] The revival in Islam has also been enhanced by the availability of Islamic literature in the form of magazines, newspapers, music, imported Arabic materials, and translations from Arabic, as well as writings by Ethiopian and foreign Muslim writers.[24] Moreover, in a political sphere dominated by one party silencing divergent voices, religion has appeared as a protected and attractive sphere for debating societal issues. Hence, religion has "surfaced as a force for social mobilization".[25]

Furthermore, the opening of the country's borders and the development of telecommunication networks exposed Ethiopians to foreign influences and stimulated their connectedness with the Ethiopian diaspora. For Ethiopian Muslims, contacts with the outside world were and remain particularly oriented towards the regional neighbours along the Nile, the Red Sea and the Gulf states. Contacts have been established through pilgrimage to Mecca, Islamic higher education programmes and legal and illegal labour migration.

In particular, the employment of Ethiopian domestic workers in the Arab world has significantly increased in the past ten years.[26] Lines of young Ethiopian women (most of them from Muslim areas) queuing every evening at check-in desks at Bole International Airport for Middle East destinations are the visible side of this emigration.[27] A great deal of trafficking is also done behind the façade of legal brokerage. Reports of mistreatment and abuse regularly appear in the news, disclosing the hard conditions of exploitation and harassment Ethiopian maids abroad are confronted with.[28] Despite these hazards, the relatively high level of income earned by migrant workers, as well as the emphasis that is put on success stories locally, have made emigration an attractive route to social advancement among young generations.

The financial returns from these human flows are high. On the one hand, remittances (money sent home by emigrants) have become a vital resource for many Ethiopian families and communities. On the other hand, Ethiopian students and religious personalities are connected to networks that attract and funnel diverse sources of funding for supporting philanthropic projects or mosque building. These links have especially strengthened Saudi and Emirati influences on the Ethiopian Muslim way of life and religious practice. This influence was also amplified by the economic success story of the Ethio-Saudi billionaire investor Sheikh Mohammed Al Amoudi, owner of the largest private Ethiopian conglomerate. Outside the economic sphere, cultural and spiritual norms are channelled and constantly updated through Ethiopia's large satellite television audience. And, recently, websites developed by members of the Ethiopian diaspora in the US and Europe have offered information and perspectives on Ethiopian Muslim concerns from the point of view of Muslims who have experienced life in secular Western countries.[29]

Radicalization: the increasing attractiveness of Salafism

Under the general term of Salafism, radical Islamic movements reinterpret the roots of Islam to advocate strict and literal observance of religious rules.[30] In the name of the absolute oneness of Allah (the doctrine of *tawhid*), Salafists challenge some of the established practices of Islam, particularly Sufi practices, and condemn some teachings and spiritual exercises as heresy (*bid'ah*) and idolatry (*shirk*). Hence, dominant traits of Ethiopian Islam, which have become embedded in local cultures, such as the celebration of the Prophet Muhammad's birthday, the worship of saints, visits to shrines and therapies for removing evil spirits, are castigated by Salafis as misleading and backward in comparison with the Arab model of Islamic purity. Such Arab teachings are reinforced by Salafism's capacity to give access to a wide range of resources and business opportunities.

Salafism was first introduced into eastern Ethiopia by pilgrims and students returning from Saudi Arabia in the 1940s. The reformist ideas they had been exposed to matched local aspirations for change in the eastern Oromo regions of Arsi, Bale and Hararge. Yet the audience for Salafi ideas remained limited to small circles and their dissemination was checked by the strong mystical Sufi tradition in Ethiopian Islam. Such doctrinal confrontation has been carried into internal debates in the Ethiopian Muslim community. Salafis are viewed by their opponents "as rigid literalists, as narrow-minded and as ignorant of the diversity of Islamic scholarship. They are criticized for separating themselves from the current societal debate, labelled as backward and accused of playing a destructive role in the development of the Muslim community in Ethiopia."[31]

Yet an increasing number of Ethiopian Muslims have drifted towards the values and models of behaviour of radical Islamic movements, among which Salafism has been the most influential.[32] This movement has spread from its foothold in the eastern Oromo areas of Arsi and Bale. It has gained some influence in other areas of the Oromiya Regional State (for example, Harar and Jimma), and in Addis Ababa and the Muslim areas of the Amhara Regional State (eastern Shoa and Wollo) and the SNNPR (Silte). But compared to the deeply rooted Sufi institutions, shrines and pilgrimages, the actual penetration of Salafism greatly varies from place to place. Organizations funded by Saudi Arabia have played an instrumental role in the dissemination of Salafi doctrines. Among these, the Ethiopian Muslim Youth Association (linked to the World Association of Muslim Youth) and the Aweliyya School and Mission (see note 23) have played particularly noticeable roles. However, although foreign funding has provided incentives for the proliferation of Salafi institutions, the construction of mosques and schools could not be achieved without the financial contribution of local communities,[33] and neither could their premises be maintained without regular attendance.

In a context dominated by dramatic economic and social transformations, many of Ethiopia's young Muslims have perceived Salafism to offer an appropriate response. State-driven development programmes combined with liberalizing policies have led to the emergence of new categories of business people and a shift away from traditional values and economic positions. In other words, Salafism, among other religious movements, can be understood as a moral and religious response to a changing environment and an attempt at redefining and enhancing Muslim self-consciousness.

Given the absolute control of the ruling party over politics, Salafism's influence has remained confined to moral, lifestyle and ritual spheres. It has not overflown into the political game in the same way that it has in neighbouring countries, where movements of political Islamism struggle for the strict application of *shari'a* law and drag extremist groups in their wake. Nevertheless, Salafism in Ethiopia, as elsewhere, is not a cohesive movement, and some minority extremist groups, particularly the Takfir wal Hijra, have erupted onto the Ethiopian political landscape by refusing to recognize the constitution (which they consider to be idolatry), pay tax or carry national ID cards.

Interreligious tensions

Similar dynamics of religious transformation and radicalization have also been at work in the practices and discourses of the Christian Orthodox and Protestant churches. This has in turn stirred up inter-religious debates and competition. Indeed, a common pattern in reformist speeches is to highlight the threat of being overcome by challengers from other denominations, who are generally portrayed as "fanatical" and "aggressive". Ironically, the same epithets are often applied to the reformers themselves by their coreligionists, who see them as internal challengers.

Besides reciprocal invectives, carried out through the publication of controversial pamphlets, the most frequent expressions of tension between religions take place through appropriations of public space. A sign of this sharpened competition has been the increasing use of loudspeakers to broadcast sermons and spiritual songs. The most controversial issue is the construction of places of worship, mosques in particular. In Addis Ababa, as well as in most of the major towns of the country, the authorization given to Muslim communities after 1991 to build large, highly visible and architecturally ambitious mosques helped transform urban landscapes. In many cases, this was strongly challenged by Orthodox Christian residents of the neighbourhoods where new mosques were built, mainly through legal battles over the ownership of the land, which generated bureaucratic delays in building. Enmity was also expressed by the throwing of stones at mosques (under the cover of darkness).[34] Attempts to build the first ever mosque in the Christian sacred city of Aksum were foiled by the angry protests of members of the Orthodox Church. Some disputes led to violence and bloodshed. In the last ten years some sporadic interreligious clashes have also been reported in the south-west of Ethiopia, particularly in Oromiya, where Christian communities (generally Protestant-Evangelical, rarely Orthodox) have been harassed and attacked and their churches burnt by groups of the majority Muslim population, who themselves have been infuriated by acts of provocation, such as incendiary speeches and the profanation of the Qur'an.

However, these occasional outbursts of interreligious violence have never escalated into larger conflicts. The harshest disputes have been severely repressed by the authorities and generally contained at a local level.[35] The other factor helping to preserve the status quo is the general opinion that the longstanding tradition of tolerance between Christians and Muslims should be retained as a cementing national value.[36] An optimistic picture of peaceful and harmonious relations has been emphasized in official discourse and praised by foreign observers.

In practice, everyday forms of coexistence oscillate between overt denominational differences and cultural commonalities. Clothing and food habits are the most usual criteria of differentiation. The most rigorously respected norm is the prohibition on eating the meat of animals not slaughtered in the traditionally accepted religious ways. Different religious communities often comment in a derogatory way on one another's norms, though such talk is also sometimes softened by jokes and people sometimes play with and contest religious boundaries. Similarly, memories of past conflicts can be softened by stories of individual friendships. And religious differentiation is counterbalanced by occasional transgressions of boundaries between groups, for instance in pilgrimages undertaken by Orthodox Christians and Muslims alike, springing from their shared beliefs in the spiritual and charismatic powers of holy figures. Cases of interreligious marriages, involving the conversion of one of the two spouses, are rare but not unheard of. Conversion is similarly unusual but is not impossible for individuals who want to reshape their faith to suit their aspirations.

In the social sphere at large there are a number of common cultural practices that are not tagged by religious norms. This kind of secular "interstitial space" plays an important role in the circulation of individuals beyond denominational identities for the purposes of social and professional mobility. The currents of religious radicalization have worked against these "grey areas" by erasing the remnants of religiously-neutral culture and struggling against modern secular norms by prescribing alternative models of behaviour determined by religious norms and denominational identities.

Confrontations on regional and national levels

From the perspective of the Ethiopian government, Islamic fundamentalism has been a sensitive issue since the violent clashes at the Anwar Mosque in February 1995. These internal disputes alerted the authorities to the development of radical trends linked to external influences. The suspicion was heightened by regional and global events. In June 1995 foreign Islamic militants backed by the Sudanese regime attempted to assassinate the Egyptian President Hosni Mubarak during his visit to Addis Ababa. This event provided confirmation that Ethiopia was not immune to the challenges posed by political Islam in neighbouring countries.[37] The regional proliferation of jihadist insurgent groups, particularly al-Itihaad al-Islamiyya in Somalia, was observed with scrutiny and fear by the Ethiopian authorities. The 9/11 terror attacks in New York put these regional struggles and geopolitical issues into a larger perspective. Ethiopia's military intervention in Somalia against the Union of Islamic Courts, launched in December 2006, was motivated by hegemonic ambitions and desire for international recognition of Ethiopia's stabilizing role in regional security. But instead of being welcomed and praised as liberators, the Ethiopian troops fuelled further tensions that were aggravated by al-Shabaab's radical insurgency.

In this context, characterized by an upsurge in both internal interreligious confrontations and external extremist threats, the risk of violent actions by radicalized groups could not be neglected. The government has acted against this threat by gathering local intelligence and using targeted interventions. Muslim organizations have been monitored carefully to prevent contagion of radical thoughts. The government has declared more and more openly and frequently its wariness about Islam, which it perceives as a vehicle for evil foreign influences. As long as only small groups were targeted in this way, the majority of Ethiopian Muslims could accept such bold statements from the government. However, the situation began to deteriorate in mid-2011, after the government shifted to a strategy aimed at training Muslim leaders in constitutional values on religious matters. This was done through the promotion of an anti-Salafi movement, called al-Ahbash, considered by its promoters to be moderate and politically acceptable, though its detractors lambast it as sectarian and contentious. In any case, this project backfired, sparking an Arab Spring-like protest—the very thing the government was trying to prevent.

The al-Ahbash controversy and the wave of protest since mid-2011

The confrontation started in mid-July 2011, when a series of regional workshops were organized by the Ethiopian Supreme Council of Islamic Affairs with the support of the Ministry of Federal Affairs. The purpose of these workshops was to instruct community representatives, scholars and heads of mosques on the rights and duties of the Constitution regarding religious matters, as well as to warn them against the threats of religious extremism, and to train them in how to refute fundamentalist arguments. Some participants in the workshops were indignant about what they considered an intolerable attempt to re-educate Muslims. Another matter of discontent, which became very controversial thereafter, was the fact that some of the instructors came from Lebanon and distributed to the attendees teaching materials and books in Arabic published by the Lebanon-based organization known as al-Ahbash.

The Association of Islamic Charitable Projects (in Arabic: Jam'iyyat al-Mashari' al-Khayriyya al-Islamiyya), founded in the 1930s, became in the 1980s the official front of the al-Ahbash religious movement, which became a prominent Sunni faction in Lebanese politics in the 1990s. "Al-Ahbash" is Arabic for "the Ethiopians", and the movement is linked to Ethiopia by its founder and ideologist, the prominent scholar and Sufi sheikh, Abdullah Muhammad Yusuf al-Harari al-Habashi (1920–2008). The two final attributes (*nisba*) of his name indicate he was from the city of Harar in Ethiopia, hence the name of his followers.

The sheikh left Ethiopia in 1947 after having been involved in the disputes that arose in Harar over the challenges posed by pan-Somali nationalism and Islamic radicalism (see above). Allegedly, he worked against secession from Ethiopia and thwarted the development of Salafi-oriented schools.[38] What exactly happened during this agitated period is still very controversial. Apparently the confrontation was so heated that Sheikh Abdullah was branded as *shaykh al-fitna*, "the sheikh of strife". Being, like his adversaries, banned from Ethiopia, he travelled to Saudi Arabia, Jerusalem and Syria, where he completed his spiritual education. He settled in Lebanon, where he developed his works and attracted students. In his numerous writings, Sheikh Abdullah al-Habashi has argued for the plurality of potential interpretations of Islam, and has favoured interreligious tolerance, the rejection of violence and submission to secular ruling authorities, as well as acceptance of modern clothes and behaviour for women. Al-Habashi's theological essays are particularly critical of all the tenets of Salafism, which he attacks as misleading innovations and deviations, wrongly professing knowledge of the roots of the religion. He criticizes Salafis for their misuse of *takfir* (tagging other Muslims as infidels), for their political project of Islamic absolutism aiming at the restoration of the caliphate, and for their justification of violence in pursuit of this purpose.[39]

The doctrine of al-Habashi is a mixture of different lines of thought (the Shafi'i school of Islamic jurisprudence, Sufism, elements of Shi'ism and discourses on Christian-Muslim coexistence) that are found in Ethiopian Islam, but his interpretations are so personal and even singular that his ideas cannot be considered as a typical expression of Ethiopian Islam. The other characteristic feature of this movement is its ability to make use of communication technologies, which has contributed to the rapid expansion of its regional and international networks, first through radio programmes, then through early use of the internet in the form of multilingual online chat groups. Several branches of the movement were established in Europe and North-America, where it reached a wide audience[40] attracted by its apparently moderate message.

The meaning of "al-Ahbash" also alludes to the historical tradition of the first *hijra* (see above), the migration to Ethiopia of the first followers of the Prophet Muhammad, who found asylum in the non-Muslim state and accepted its rules—a story that is meaningful to Muslims who find themselves in the minority in countries worldwide. In Ethiopia itself, the sheikh was known and respected as a high profile scholar, but the presence and influence of his organization were negligible until its recent irruption into public debate.

Behind its apparent political correctness—served by an up-to-date communication strategy—there lies a highly contentious facet of the al-Ahbash movement. In its verbal war against its Salafi opponents, al-Ahbash uses methods castigated by its own doctrine: defamation, declarations of exclusion from Islam, intimidation and political collusion. Their detractors have condemned them as a propaganda vehicle used by Syria's secular, Alawite-dominated regime to combat Islamic fundamentalism. Al-Ahbash's followers are remembered in the Lebanese public consciousness for having demonstrated in early 2001 in support of Syria by brandishing clubs, knives and axes. And conflicts fought with rhetoric and symbols have sometimes become violent in Lebanon's contested politico-religious arena. The cycle of violence culminated in 1995 with the assassination of al-Ahbash's leader, Nizar Halabi. In 2010 some al-Ahbash-affiliated armed groups fought in the streets of Beirut against Hezbollah partisans. The relations between the two parties, both of whom are pro-Syrian, had deteriorated after the assassination of the former Lebanese Prime Minister Rafiq Hariri in 2005, of which al-Ahbash was suspected.

By allowing al-Ahbash clerics to disseminate their teachings in Ethiopia through a programme of seminars instigated to combat the development of religious extremist outlooks, the Ethiopian authorities inadvertently imported some of the explosive issues of the Middle East. The initial intention was to curb the spreading of Salafi doctrines by reinvigorating Ethiopian Sufi Islam through the promotion of al-Ahbash's new ideas, which were understood to be moderate and easily acceptable to Ethiopian Muslims since they emanated from an influential Muslim scholar of Ethiopian origin. For the older generation, however, al-Ahbash's ideas revived dormant polemics from the 1950s, hitting their consciousness like a boomerang. For the majority of the younger generation, on the other hand, these ideas were completely new, and it was easy to accept the criticism that they came from a foreign, sectarian, quarrelsome tradition.

After the first series of workshops, during which the controversy began, the Majlis, backed by the government, stuck to its plans by assigning "certified" preachers to mosques and Islamic schools throughout the country. Large numbers of Muslims in the capital city and in different regions expressed their shock and concern. The official aim of controlling Muslim opinion was perceived as an attempt to interfere in religious affairs and a violation of the principle of the separation of state and religion. The authorities took the first expressions of disagreement by Muslims—which ranged from anger to mockery, whether voiced in private circles, within mosques or through the Muslim press—as confirmation of the spreading of radical Islamist positions. Actually, the feelings of confusion and discontent raised by the controversy were present among the Muslim population as a whole, and not just its radical and militant elements, but the developments provided a context that Salafi militants could exploit, by defending, quite paradoxically, the liberal principles of secularism, in order to reach a wider audience.

Instead of seeking a way out of this tangled situation, the government remained unyielding in its resolve to fight radicalism and refused to change its strategy, arguing that its role was to inform the public about their constitutional rights and duties. It therefore took stronger measures to curb the organizations that were heading up the protests. The Aweliyya School in particular was in the midst of the turmoil. As seen above, this general teaching institution was founded in the 1960s, with the support of Saudi funds. The school has become the *alma mater* of many members of the Ethiopian Muslim business elite and it played an informal role as a rallying point for Muslims before the formal establishment of the Majlis. Since the establishment of the secular Federal Democratic Republic of Ethiopia, the state's policy on Muslim affairs has consistently relied on recognizing the Majlis as the only official, elected and representative body of the Muslim community on regional and national scales. This institution was empowered with the capacity to license and monitor all kinds of organizations related to the practice and teaching of Islam (mosques, schools, charities). Therefore its role has been contested by the Muslim community, which sees it as an executive arm of the state, going beyond its accepted role of representing and advocating the community's concerns, and trying to control religious institutions without any written law establishing its authority to do so.[41]

Thus, behind the theological dispute on al-Ahbash there was a fundamental conflict over the legitimacy and representativeness of religious institutions in a still partially settled legal framework. For the "Aweliyya network", formed by that school's faculty, students and alumni, the al-Ahbash controversy offered an opportunity to reaffirm their influence and legitimacy as respected spokespersons of the Muslim community, challenging the moral and political authority of the Majlis. In return, the Majlis used its authority to thwart this well-established, well-known competitor. The Majlis's first step, in September 2011, was to withdraw the licence of the International Islamic Relief Organization, the Saudi NGO that was funding the Aweliyya School, on the legal grounds that its action was not confined to humanitarian relief. This was followed, in December 2011, by the dismissal of the Aweliyya School's Arabic teachers and administrators and their replacement by appointees faithful to the Majlis administration.

This was the straw that broke the camel's back. To Aweliyya's affiliates and sympathizers this decision was an unacceptable abuse of power. The first consequence was that the negotiations that were being undertaken behind the scenes to try to find a way out of the crisis were stopped. The second consequence was a pro-Aweliyya demonstration in the school's compound on 4 January 2012, gathering at least 2,500 protestors—the first mass protest since the violent repression of the 2005 post-election unrest. This was the first of a series of demonstrations that went on for more than a year, giving rise to a kind of social movement unprecedented in the political history of Ethiopia. Almost every Friday after the congregational *juma'a* prayer the showdown continued, with Aweliyya School and Anwar Mosque at the epicentre. The wave of protest spread throughout the great mosques in a number of towns in Muslim regions. In many cases the crowd overflowed onto the streets, though in a peaceful manner. The protests focused on issues of religious freedom, the organizers being careful not to deviate into other political matters.

The norms of the institutional framework of Ethiopian revolutionary democracy prescribe that any concern or demand from civil society, if not self-censored, should be channeled and processed through the language and procedures of the ruling party and its delegated authorities, such as the Majlis. The government did not react immediately to the outbreak of protest, as if its intention was to show that it was lenient in the sphere of denominational issues and respectful of religious freedom. In official statements, the demonstrations were minimized to a problem created by an insignificant number of troublemakers and the government seemed to favour letting local mediation find a compromise.

The situation deteriorated, however, to the point where an intervention was deemed necessary. When the intensification of the weekly protests presented the signs of a revolt, the Muslim problem suddenly became a major matter of concern. The time had come for the government to take urgent action and show its determination to enter into a trial of strength with a significant, though hard to measure, portion of the Muslim population. On 17 April 2012, three months after the first demonstrations, Prime Minister Meles Zenawi gave a speech in the parliament in which he blamed the protesters for promoting the extremist Salafist ideology, implying they were the agents of a conspiracy connected with al-Qaeda jihadist cells that had recently been uncovered in Arsi and Bale. After exposing the nature of the threat, he strongly reasserted that the government would not hesitate to crack down on any group engaged in the disruption of peace and stability in the country, regardless of their ethnic or religious nature. The government followed through on this hard line in the subsequent months, despite the blatant gap between the apparent reality of the protests and the seriousness of the charge.

The hardening of the government's position exacerbated the crisis. Protesters were infuriated to be demonized as terrorists. The security forces were sent to break up the demonstrations, and used tear gas and brutal beatings. In most cases, the police's interventions were not met by violent reactions from the protesters like stone-throwing or looting, which would likely have led to even more severe repression, justified on the grounds of public safety. Indeed, the strength of this social movement has been the self-control of the crowds, who have stuck to the strategy of non-violence by remaining impassive in the face of arrests, injuries and even killings. Facing charges of religious extremism and terrorism, the protesters presented a contrary face to the public and the international media, being conscious that the success of their movement and the diffusion of their demands depended mainly on their image.

With this purpose in mind, the protesters adopted new communication strategies, more or less following the models of recent and ongoing unrest in Arab countries. Calls for demonstration and slogans spread through SMS messages; news, opinions and grievances circulated on internet social media (Facebook, Twitter); in-depth analyses of the situation were published on blogs along with comment sections; and videos of the demonstrations posted on platforms like YouTube and spread by Ethiopian media (Esat, Bilaltube) were widely watched in the Ethiopian diaspora. There was also a shift in rhetoric from religious utterances to secular arguments whose scope was that of a civil rights struggle. The first demonstrations were characterized by the loud incantation in unison of "*Allahu akbar*", following a mode of expression that characterized some of the recent movements of protest in Arab countries like Yemen. But the rallies gradually adopted secular mottoes like *dimsachen yisema* ("let our voice be heard"), which became the brand of the movement. Their communication strategy also encompassed visual elements, including secular symbols: yellow cards were waved in warning, white ribbons were worn as signs of peace, and mouths were plastered to symbolize the lack of freedom.

The religious dimension was not eliminated, however. For example, *mawlid* ceremonies were organized under the designation of the "Programme of Unity and Solidarity" (*ye andinetinna ye sedeqa programme*). This ritual celebration of the birth of the Prophet Muhammad and his holy deeds is performed by the recitation of spiritual poems. It is a popular practice in Sufi Islam, but is firmly rejected by Salafis. Celebrating this ritual was intended to show that the struggle was not in the hands of religious extremists, guided by anti-Sufism, but by protesters with a conciliatory view of Ethiopian Islam in all its diversity. However, opponents of the movement criticized the way religious gatherings were hijacked to disguise political meetings. Another meaningful development on the politico-religious level was the message of solidarity sent in May 2012 to Ethiopian Muslim protesters by the Ethiopian Orthodox Church Synod in exile (in Washington, DC), which is influential among those in the Ethiopian diaspora who oppose the EPRDF. This statement reflected the fact that part of the Christian population—at least those exposed to ideas from the diaspora—did not consider the Muslim movement to be an Islamist threat but saw it rather as an expression of civil society's demand that the state withdraw its control over religious activities.

The government, in an attempt to find a way out of the crisis, eventually accepted one of the protesters' demands, namely the election of new members of the Majlis. However, the organization of the election became the matter of further disputes over whether it should be held in the offices of *kebele* (neighbourhood) administrations under state supervision, or in mosques. Another contentious issue was that the protest movement institutionalized itself through a self-appointed committee of representatives, the "Muslim Solution Finding Committee", composed of seventeen prominent scholars linked to the Aweliyya network. This initiative was perceived by the authorities as a trick to bypass the Majlis. In July 2012 the protests intensified before the celebration of Ramadan (coinciding with the annual African Union meeting in Addis Ababa). And the context became even more strained by leaks concerning the deterioration of the health of the Prime Minister. The executive was paralyzed but it could not show any sign of weakening and its reaction became harsher. A wave of arrests was carried out against the leaders of the protest, their supporters and journalists. These raids by the police provoked violent clashes the week before the beginning of the Ramadan.

The Muslim fast went off quietly, however. Its closure, marked by the celebration of the Id al Fitr, was the occasion of some rallies aimed at reawakening the protest, but a few days later the death of Prime Minister Meles Zenawi was announced. The subsequent period of national mourning was a moment of respect and national unity that could not be spoiled. During this caesura there was some anxiety about the formation of a new government, with the protestors hoping that there would be an amnesty for detainees. However, there was no power vacuum after the death of Prime Minister Meles and no major change in government strategy. The former Deputy Prime Minister Haile Mariam Dessalegn was sworn in as the new Prime Minister on 21 September 2012. He expressed his commitment to continue the policy and legacy of his mentor and predecessor. The elections for the Majlis were held in the beginning of October 2012 despite the protesters' complaint that it could not be a fair process as long as their representatives were detained. The outcome of the poll, described as "free and democratic" in the self-serving statements of the authorities, confirmed the stranglehold on the Majlis by affiliates of the party.

The protest went on, each side standing firm. On the one hand, the government remained inflexible in front of the demonstrations. In the official discourse, the crowds of protesters were once again played down as representing only a minority of activists. On the other hand, the stubbornness of the protesters did not decrease, motivated as they were by their collective determination to defend their religious rights and have their imprisoned leaders released. In October 2012 a new wave of demonstrations led to violent clashes in Wollo. In November the federal court charged the members of the self-appointed arbitration committee and other leaders of the protest with plotting acts of terrorism and attempting to establish an Islamic state. In January 2013 the protest was launched again on the anniversary of the movement. The authorities responded with a documentary film aired on national television aimed at denouncing the threat of "jihadist movements" (*jihadawi harekat*) on Ethiopia by drawing parallels between the Ethiopian Muslim protest movement and Islamist insurrections in other African countries (al-Shabaab in Somalia, Boko Haram in Nigeria), notwithstanding the fact that the Ethiopian movement has been largely non-violent, non-underground and open-faced. The conspiracy theory presented by this film corresponded to the indictment against the detained figures of the movement, before any trials had taken place. The protesters and their supporters condemned the methods used by the authorities for lambasting Muslim dissenters, through judicial decisions and media coverage based on groundless fabrications. They continued to express their indignation loudly in the mosques' yards, in the streets and on online social networks. Another major development, in July 2013, was the killing of a pro-government Muslim preacher in Dessie, Sheikh Nuru. The government blamed extremists for this action and organized demonstrations to condemn the protesters' drift towards terrorism.

Conclusion

The outcome of the trial of journalists and leaders of the protest may determine whether the movement will persist or fade away. The fact that this trial has been postponed indicates a will to give a chance to mediation. Already in the recent past some opposition figures charged with serious offences have been released or allowed to go into exile. From the government's point of view, defendants who are convicted and given harsh sentences could become martyr-type figures in whose name a more radical movement might arise. From the protesters' point of view, as long as they are protesting in the name of general and secular principles they can keep the advantage of the positive image they have gained in national and international public opinion. However, the actors and observers of the movement should be careful not to let a politically correct agenda become a façade used to hide more radical aims.

This, at least, is the situation as of July 2013. It is still too early to assess the long-term effects of this social and religious movement, which is unprecedented in Ethiopia. But what can be said is that through their political mobilization a significant number of Ethiopian Muslims have opened a new chapter in the process of their integration into the Ethiopian nation. There has been a considerable evolution indeed since the first half of the twentieth century, when Muslims were assigned the status of "tolerated aliens" under the theocratic state. The recognition of their fully-fledged citizenship was partially initiated by the revolutionary military regime and was then completed by the federal regime, which adopted a secular system of government. However, the regulation of relations between the state and religious communities still needs some fine-tuning. While all religious communities need to recognize the necessary limitations of their activities under the rule of law, the balance between actions undertaken in public life and private values can only be maintained if the government guarantees freedom of thought and expression.

BIBLIOGRAPHY AND FURTHER READING

Abbink, Jon, 1998, "An Historical-Anthropological Approach to Islam in Ethiopia: Issues of Identity and Politics", *Journal of African Cultural Studies*, 11 (2), pp. 109–124.

———— 2011, "Religion in Public Spaces: Emerging Muslim–Christian Polemics in Ethiopia", *African Affairs*, 110/439, pp. 253–74.

———— 2014, "Religious Freedom and the Political Order: the Ethiopian 'Secular State' and the Containment of Muslim Identity Politics", *Journal of Eastern African Studies*, 8 (3), 346–65.

Awol Allo and Abadir M. Ibrahim, 2012, "Redefining protest in Ethiopia: what happens to the 'terror' narrative when Muslims call for a secular state?", *OpenDemocracy*, 23 October 2012 (http://www.opendemocracy.net/awol-allo-abadir-m-ibrahim/redefining-protest-in-ethiopia-what-happens-to-terror-narrative-when-musl) (latest access on June 2013).

Beydoun, K.A., 2012, "The Trafficking of Ethiopian Domestic Workers into Lebanon: Navigating Through a Novel Passage of the International Maid Trade", *Berkeley Journal of International Law*, 24 (3), pp. 1009–1045.

Braukämper, Ulrich, 2002, *Islamic History and Culture in Southern Ethiopia: Collected Essays*, Berlin: LIT Vlg.

Carmichael, Tim, 1997, "Contemporary Ethiopian Discourse on Islamic History: the Politics of Historical Representation", *Islam et Sociétés au Sud du Sahara*, 11, pp. 169–86.

———— 1998, "Political Culture in Ethiopia's Provincial Administration: Haile Selassie, Blata Ayele Gebre and the (Hareri) Kulub Movement of 1948", in M. Page et al. (eds), *Personality and Political Culture in Modern Africa*, Boston: Boston University African Studies Center Press, pp. 195–212.

De Waal, Alex (ed.), 2004, *Islamism and its Enemies in the Horn of Africa*, Bloomington: Indiana University Press.

Dereje Feyisa, 2011. "The Transnational Politics of Ethiopian Muslim Diaspora", *Ethnic and Racial Studies*, 35 (11), pp. 1893–1913.

———— 2013, "Muslim Struggle for Recognition in Contemporary Ethiopia", in P. Desplat and T. Østebø (eds), *Muslim Ethiopia*, pp. 25–46.

———— 2013b, "Religious Conflict Analysis in Ethiopia", Research Report Submitted to Norwegian Church Aid.

Desplat, Patrick and Terje Østebø, (eds), 2013, *Muslim Ethiopia. The Christian Legacy, Identity Politics and Islamic Reformism*, New York: Palgrave Macmillan.

Erlich, Haggai, 1994, *Ethiopia and the Middle East*, Boulder, CO: Lynn Rienner.

———— 2007, *Saudi Arabia and Ethiopia: Islam, Christianity, and Politics Entwined*, Boulder, CO: Lynne Rienner.

Fauvelle-Aymar, François-Xavier and Bertrand Hirsch, 2010, "Muslim Historical Spaces in Ethiopia and the Horn of Africa: A Reassessment", *Northeast African Studies*, 11 (1), pp. 25–53.

Ficquet, Eloi, 2006, "Flesh Soaked in Faith: Meat as a Marker of the Boundary between Christians and Muslims in Ethiopia", in B. Soares (ed.), *Muslim-Christian Encounters in Africa*, Leiden: Brill, pp. 39–56

Ficquet, Eloi and Smidt, Wolbert (eds), 2014, *Life and Times of* Lïj *Iyasu of Ethiopia: New Insights*, Berlin: LIT Vlg.

Fernandez, Bina, 2011, "Household Help? Ethiopian Women Domestic Workers' Labor Migration to the Gulf Countries", *Asian and Pacific Migration Journal*, 20 (3–4), pp. 433–57.

Nizar Hamzeh, A. and R. Hrair Dekmejian, 1996, "A Sufi Response to Political Islamism: Al-Ahbash of Lebanon", *International Journal of Middle East Studies* 28 (2), pp. 217–29.

Gori, Alessandro, 1995, "Soggiorno di studi in Eritrea ed Etiopia. Brevi annotazioni bibliografiche", *Rassegna di Studi Etiopici*, 39, pp. 81–129.

——— 2005, "Contemporary and Historical Muslim Scholars as Portrayed by the Ethiopian Islamic Press in the 1990s", *Aethiopica*, 8, pp. 72–94.

Haustein, Jörg and Terje Østebø, 2011, "EPRDF's Revolutionary Democracy and Religious Plurality: Islam and Christianity in Post-Derg Ethiopia", *Journal of Eastern African Studies*, 5(4), pp. 755–22.

Hussein Ahmed, 1994, "Islam and Islamic Discourse in Ethiopia (1973–1993)", in Harold G. Marcus (ed), *New Trends in Ethiopian Studies*, Lawrenceville, NJ: Red Sea Press, vol. 1, pp. 775–801.

——— 2001, *Islam in Nineteenth-Century Wallo, Ethiopia: Revival, Reform and Reaction*, Leiden: Brill.

——— 2006, "Coexistence and/or Confrontation? Towards a Reappraisal of Christian Muslim Encounter in Contemporary Ethiopia", *Journal of Religion in Africa*, 36 (1), pp. 4–22.

——— 2007, "History of Islam in Ethiopia", *Encyclopaedia Aethiopica*, vol. 3, pp. 202–8.

——— 2009, "The Coming of Age of Islamic Studies in Ethiopia: The Present State of Research and Publication", in S. Ege et al. (eds), *Proceedings of the 16th International Conference of Ethiopian Studies*, Trondheim, pp. 449–55.

Ishihara, Minako, 1996, "Textual Analysis of a Poetic Verse in a Muslim Oromo Society in Jimma Area, Southwestern Ethiopia", *Senri Ethnological Studies*, 43, pp. 207–232.

Kabha, Mustafa and Haggai Erlich, 2006, "Al-Ahbash and Wahhabiya: Interpretations of Islam", *International Journal of Middle East Studies* 38 (4), pp. 519–38.

Kemal Abdulwehab, 2011, "Review of Abdulfätah Abdällah, 2008–2010, *The History of Addis Abäba Mosques*, vol. 1 & 2, Addis Abäba", *Annales d'Ethiopie*, 26, pp. 311–18.

Miran, Jonathan, 2005, "A Historical Overview of Islam in Eritrea", *Die Welt des Islams*, 45 (2), pp. 177–215.

Østebø, Terje, 2008, "The Question of Becoming: Islamic Reform Movements in Contemporary Ethiopia", *Journal of Religion in Africa*, 38, pp. 416–46.

——— 2010, *Islamism in the Horn of Africa. Assessing Ideology, Actors, and Objectives*, Oslo. International Law and Policy Institute (ILPI). Report no. 2/2010.

——— 2012, *Localising Salafism. Religious Change among Oromo Muslims in Bale, Ethiopia*, Leiden: Brill.

Peebles, Graham, 2012, "Migrant Nightmares: Ethiopian Domestic Workers in the Gulf," *Dissident Voice*, July 3 2012, http://dissidentvoice.org/2012/07/migrant-nightmares-ethiopian-domestic-workers-in-the-gulf/ (latest access on June 2013)

Seri-Hersch, Iris, 2009, "Confronting a Christian Neighbor: Sudanese Representations of Ethiopia in the early Mahdist Period, 1885–89", *International Journal of Middle East Studies*, 41, pp. 247–67.

Trimingham, John S., 1952, *Islam in Ethiopia*, London: Oxford University Press.

Vangsi, J., 1985, "Note sur l'appartenance religieuse en Ethiopie", *Archives des Sciences Sociales des Religions*, 59 (1), pp. 113–129.

4

GO PENTE! THE CHARISMATIC RENEWAL OF THE EVANGELICAL MOVEMENT IN ETHIOPIA[1]

Emanuele Fantini

The significant growth of the Evangelical movement in Ethiopia in the last twenty years has been officially certified by the 2007 Population and Housing Census, counting almost 14 million Protestants, 18.6 per cent of the population, compared with 43.5 per cent Orthodox Christians, 33.9 per cent of Muslims and minor percentages of Catholics and traditional faiths.[2] As a consequence Ethiopia is the African country with the highest numbers of Evangelicals in absolute terms, more than in countries more often associated with their presence, such as Nigeria, Uganda, Kenya, and the Democratic Republic of Congo.[3] In the early 1960s, Protestants were estimated to represent less than 1 per cent of the population,[4] rising to 5.5 per cent in the 1984 census and 10.2 per cent by the 1994 one. This shows that the Ethiopian Protestants have the highest growth rate of all the religious denominations in the country and represent "one of the fastest growing evangelical churches in the World".[5]

Evangelical Christianity is not a new phenomenon for the Ethiopian society. Its presence in the country dates back to the nineteenth century with the arrival of the first missionaries. However, the rapid expansion it has witnessed in the last two decades represents one of the major forces contributing to reshaping of Ethiopian society and the equilibrium between Christianity and Islam in the whole Horn of Africa. In spite of its relevance and its sensitiveness, the Evangelical movement in Ethiopia has received little attention in academic studies or from national or international observers. The occultation of church records and member profiles during the persecution by the Derg communist regime contributed to relegation of Pentecostalism among under-documented social phenomena. Accounts by foreign missionaries and church members remain the only available sources to retrace the history of the Evangelical movement in Ethiopia. Most of them are limited to the local context of a single mission or church, while only a few rise to the level of national relevance.[6] The reestablishment of religious freedom in 1991 under the current regime contributed not only to the considerable expansion of the Evangelical movement, but also to retracing of sources, collection of testimony and consolidation of archives. This material has supported more recent and ambitious attempts to draw a comprehensive history of the origin and evolution of the movement as a whole,[7] providing an account of the various narratives as well as of the meaning and political implications of their differences and contradictions,[8] and exploring the *place of* Evangelicals in the broader context of religious pluralization and competition in Ethiopia and the Horn of Africa.[9]

Comprehensive studies and analysis of the Evangelical movement in Ethiopia are further challenged by its plasticity and internal pluralism. The present contribution will therefore begin by addressing the issue of definition and denominations, in order to highlight different groups of churches officially recorded under the above statistics. It will subsequently identify common features that the movement shares with global Pentecostalism as well as those peculiar to the Ethiopian context in light of the specificity of the historical trajectory of the country. Finally, it will point to the most pressing issues posed to contemporary Ethiopian society by the rise of the Evangelical movement and its charismatic renewal.

The "Pente label": historical roots, different groups and common trends

Protestants, Evangelical, Pentecostal, Born Again (*dagem lidet* in Amharic) Christians: in current popular speech in Ethiopia all these terms are used interchangeably and frequently subsumed in the vernacular expression *Pente*. Internal divisions within the movement, the blurring of theological differences between main denominations, and the mushrooming of new churches and ministries increase the difficulty of finding a common definition and uniform categorization. The controversy surrounding its definition or even its nature as a homogeneous object of analysis might constitute a first feature that the Ethiopian case shares with the global movements described as Neo/Post/New-Pentecostalism or Charismatic Christianity.[10]

Therefore, in order to grasp the multifaceted character of the current *Pente* wave in Ethiopia it is first of all necessary to clarify the different typologies of groups encompassed under the official label—or Babel definition—of "Protestants" used in Ethiopian statistics, ranging from the traditional Evangelical denominations implanted by missionaries to small independent churches established around the charisma of a single pastor.

Traditional Evangelical denominations. The great majority of believers belong to a few big churches descended from the activities of early European and North American missionaries, like the Lutheran Mekane Yesus Church and the Baptist Kale Heywet Church (both with over 4 million members) or the smaller Mennonite Meseret Kristos (around 230,000 members).[11] The presence of foreign Protestant missionaries in the country is recorded since the nineteenth century, with the arrival of the Church Missionary Society (Anglican) and Swedish and German missionaries with a Lutheran background under Emperor Tewodros, and the first establishment in 1904 of an Evangelical community in Wollega. Their activity developed discreetly in the presence of the oldest and strongest autonomous Christian church in Sub-Saharan Africa, the Ethiopian *Tewahedo* Orthodox Church. It was only during the reign of Haile Selassie that missionaries gained a significant presence. Between 1918 and 1931 several missionary societies, like the Sudan Interior Mission, established missions in Ethiopia, particularly in the south-western region, which were the beginnings of modern missionary activities, combining evangelization with the provision of basic social services. Following the parenthesis of the Italian occupation, during which there was official persecution of the Evangelical Churches leading to the expulsion of foreign missionaries, their presence was again legally recognized through the "Regulations Governing the Activities of

Missions" issued by Haile Selassie in 1944. The Emperor considered the missionaries as allies in his efforts at modernization of the country, particularly because of their educational efforts. However, in order not to compromise his privileged relationship with the Orthodox Church, he divided the country between "Open Areas", where missionaries' evangelization and development work was allowed, and "Closed Areas", where only the Orthodox Church was allowed to operate. Practical demarcation of these areas was entrusted to the Ministry of Education. The "Open Areas" were mostly the various peripheries of the Empire: the southern and western regions as well as the eastern lowlands, predominantly Muslim. The "Closed Areas" roughly covered the northern and central highlands. As for the capital Addis Ababa, it was considered a free territory for all denominations.

The expulsion of foreign missionaries by the Italians had accelerated the transfer of responsibility to an Ethiopian leadership, which later favoured the growth of national evangelical churches. Thus, the establishment in 1959 of the Ethiopian Evangelical Church of Mekane Yesus shows the desire of Ethiopians to create their own national church and emancipate it from the influence of foreign missionaries, incorporating within Lutheran theology some traits borrowed from the local culture and Orthodox religious practices such as child baptism. This was followed by the creation of the Meserete Kristos Church in 1962 and the Kale Heywet Church in 1963. Within the Ethiopian context, all these denominations have been traditionally labelled as Evangelical, and to this day they remain the biggest and most influent of all Evangelical denominations. They have inherited from their missionary past a strong geographical implantation in the "Open Areas" of traditional Evangelical presence, such as Wollega in Western Oromia, Gambella and the southern areas of the country nowadays incorporated in the Southern Nations, Nationalities and People Region (SNNPR),[12] as well as a significant commitment to humanitarian activities through their "developmental wings" working in partnership with international faith-based NGOs.

Classical Pentecostal churches. A second group of churches regrouped under the label "Protestant" are those stemming from the Pentecostal movement that penetrated Ethiopian Christian communities from the mid-1960s onwards. With a higher level of autonomy from any external influence when compared with the traditional Evangelical groups,

Pentecostalism in Ethiopia rapidly moved towards the creation of national independent churches. The first Pentecostal missionaries in Ethiopia were Anna-Liisa and Sanfrid Mattson who established the Free Finnish Foreign Mission in 1951 and started to operate in Addis Ababa in 1956. They were later followed by the Swedish Pentecostals amongst whom the most influential was the Philadelphia Church Mission founded by Karl and Ruth Ramstrand in 1960 in Awasa.

In parallel to these initiatives, the Pentecostal movement witnessed autonomous "multiple beginnings"[13] promoted by national groups directly or indirectly connected to missionary work. The revivals sprang within the student circles in Addis Ababa and other towns like Nazareth, Harar and Awasa. Two moments can be considered pivotal in bringing together these different experiences and shaping their sense of belonging to a common movement. The first was the Awasa Conference organized by the Swedish Pentecostal Mission in 1956, gathering for the first time a great number of young believers and sympathizers from all around the country and exposing them to the teachings of Pentecostal doctrines. The second was the prayer meetings promoted by Addis Ababa University students which culminated in the four-day Conference of 1966. From there emerged an Ethiopian leadership affirming the need to consolidate the movement around a common vision and unitary framework, emancipating it from missionary control. The most relevant step following these gatherings was the decision in 1967 to form a new church, the Ethiopian Full Gospel Believers Church (*Mulu Wengel* in Amharic), which became the first independent Pentecostal church in Ethiopia and still today represents the largest of the traditional Pentecostal denominations. It was followed by two others, the Ghennet Church and the Heywet Birhan Church, which had been started through the work of Finnish and Swedish missionaries and were to become autonomous in 1977 and 1978.

In their initial stages, these churches were an urban phenomenon, mainly attracting young and educated believers. The leadership consisted not of people raised within traditional Evangelical churches but rather of university students coming from an Orthodox background[14] and later exposed to the Finnish Pentecostal or the Philadelphia mission. Their dynamism was pivotal in influencing the evolution of the broader *Pente* movement beyond the borders of their respective churches. Later, the commitment shown by Pentecostals in underground religious activities during the period of Derg persecution contributed to spread their beliefs, styles and practices to other mainline Evangelical denominations. Even today prominent figures and groups that emerged during the Pentecostal renewal of the 1960s play a leading role in the consolidation of the whole *Pente* movement and its expansion through the establishment of new churches.[15]

New independent churches and ministries. A third wave of the *Pente* movement could be traced to the climate of religious freedom created by the 1995 Federal Constitution, which led to the formation of several neo-Pentecostal or neo-Charismatic independent churches. These groups can be associated with the broad phenomenon of new African "spirit" movements, encompassing the huge variety of "divergent African churches that emphasize the working of the Spirit in the church, particularly with ecstatic phenomena like prophecy and speaking in tongues, healing and exorcism".[16] Just as elsewhere in the world, the picture of these groups in Ethiopia is rapidly and constantly changing because of the tumultuous proliferation of new cults, making the changes hard to catch. The most prominent churches, in the spotlight for their public visibility and activism, seem to be the Beza International Church, the You-Go City Church, the Exodus Apostolic Reformation Church and the Unic 7000 Church.

These groups have originated mainly out of the autonomous initiative of the organized clergy, usually with a background of militancy within traditional Evangelical or Pentecostal churches but also influenced by living and training abroad, in countries like Kenya, South Africa or the USA, where believers had gone either to escape Derg persecutions or to pursue theological studies. In a break with traditional denominations, they usually do not belong to the main network representing Evangelical and Pentecostal groups, the Evangelical Churches Fellowship of Ethiopia (ECFE). As an alternative coordinating space, several of these leaders recently created the Ethiopian Pastors Conference.

In spite of limited membership and dimensions—often confined to a single see in Addis Ababa or other cities—these churches are exceptionally vocal and active. At ease with modern media like satellite TV and the internet and backed up by professional fellowships or parachurch activities, they are particularly effective in attracting young and educated people as well as the middle class of main urban centres. This dynamism and public visibility should be accurately weighted in order not to overestimate their influence and penetration, especially outside

Addis Ababa and other main urban areas. These churches seem to rely strongly on the international sphere. They rely on their leaders' and members' contacts abroad, in particular within the Ethiopian diaspora. They are eager to establish branches in the US and Europe—increasingly considered as new lands for re-evangelization—and to affiliate with international networks in order to address foreign communities living in Ethiopia, mostly other African nationalities but also the recently immigrated Indian or Chinese communities.

Becoming Pente. Nowadays, in popular speech, all these different churches and groups are known as *Pente*. The genesis of the term is not completely clear. Most sources agree that it appeared for the first time in the aftermath of the incidents that took place in Debre Zeit in 1967, following an attack by local residents on a gathering of hundreds of youths belonging to the Pentecostal movement.[17] Under the Derg it was used to label traditional Pentecostals with a mocking tone, and it contributed to the political persecution of all the Protestant churches.[18] Later, *Pente* became the popular term to designate the broader spectrum of groups included in the official statistics under the label of Protestants. Having lost most of its disparaging connotation, the term seems nowadays to be accepted and even adopted by the majority of the *Pente* themselves, although most of them would prefer the term "Born Again Christians", which has fewer overtones.

So we will use the term *Pente* as a broad definition encompassing all the above different denominations, when not referring to a specific church typology—Evangelical, Pentecostal, neo-Pentecostal or neo-Charismatic—so as to analyze this pluralistic movement as a unitary social phenomenon. Undoubtedly, from an institutional perspective the *Pente* movement remains fragmented. Despite appeals to unity by several church leaders and intellectuals and the fact that most of the believers belong to a few big churches, *Pente* expansion proceeds mainly through the division and multiplication of groups. In 2007, 628 different *Pente* denominations, churches, ministries and faith-based organizations were listed in the register of the Ministry of Justice.[19] These groups vary considerably in size, relevance and record of historical presence in the country. Most of them remain minor entities, but their vast majority—around 85 per cent—does not belong to any of the two bodies (EFCE and Ethiopian Pastors Conference) trying to coordinate and officially represent the *Pente* constellation.

This fragmentation can mostly be interpreted as the result of personal initiatives and agendas of religious entrepreneurs rather than disputes on theological issues. In fact, the choice of the term *Pente* aims specifically at reflecting the Charismatic Renewal that, in Ethiopia like elsewhere in the continent, "has fundamentally altered the character of African Christianity".[20] In the last twenty years, traditional Pentecostal theological positions and spiritual and liturgical practices, as well as Charismatic emphasis on the Gifts of the Spirit, have spread to mainline Evangelical denominations and nowadays characterize the whole *Pente* movement.[21] The blurring of doctrinal differences and the emerging of common worship styles are further facilitated by circulation and pulpit sharing among pastors of different cults, as well as by the religious nomadism of believers, often shifting among, and attending services in, various churches.

So we must investigate the *Pente* movement as a coherent phenomenon, characterized by a common repertoire of theologies, imaginaries, and notions as well as by techniques of organization and proselytism, shaped by the encounter with Ethiopia's specific historical trajectory.

The global Gifts of the Spirit: innovation and modernity

The Charismatic Renewal blowing within the *Pente* movement in the last years has contributed to the spread of the religious repertoire commonly associated with global Pentecostalism: reference to Baptism in the Holy Spirit with its significance of radical transformation of the individual and society manifested through the gifts of the Spirit, such as speaking in tongues, prophecy, healings, and exorcism; the interpretation of prayer was personal and intimate, and seen as an immediate communication with God; the performative power of the faith aimed at satisfying desires and vanquishing fears through divine protection and empowerment. All these typical Pentecostal notions have extended to the older more traditional Evangelical Churches like Mekane Yesus and Kale Hiwot.

This is accompanied by rejection of social and religious practices consolidated within the Ethiopian Orthodox Church, like burial ceremonies and other rituals, commonly associated by *Pentes* with "local tradition" and "culture" and therefore regarded as deviating from the original meaning and truth of the Scriptures. On the contrary, the modern and innovative character of worship styles and practises are considered by *Pente* followers as a key factor behind the success and expansion of their movement. Therefore, in reaction to the archaism of the use of Ge'ez by the Orthodox Church, *Pente*s use local languages in preaching and ceremonies, in order to render religious messages more intelligible to the people. Paradoxically, they also switch to English as a sign of distinction and adhesion to the ethos of global modernity. In parallel to this, building on the translation into local languages and dissemination of the Bible inaugurated by early missionaries, *Pente*s encourage constant reading and studying of the Scriptures, both individual and in group, as well as their literal interpretation.

The innovative character and appeal of *Pente* religious messages have been further enhanced through the introduction of electric musical instruments and new styles of singing and gospel choir, as well as of more dynamic and emotional registers in preaching and worship. A strong tradition of resort to modern media, from Radio Voice of the Gospel since the 1960s to satellite TV channels and the internet in current times, has been pivotal in contributing to the diffusion and circulation of *Pente* messages. Historically radio waves were crucial in overcoming the barriers between "Open Areas" and "Closed Areas" set by Haile Selassie. Nowadays the internet and satellite TVs are decisive in reinforcing participation in transnational Pentecostal networks and transmitting ideas and messages that can circumvent the strict regulations of the national media system.

In terms of organizational structure, most of the *Pente* churches, particularly those belonging to the new neo-Charismatic wave, are autonomous and not accountable to any institutional hierarchy. Their flexibility is further increased by the integration of traditional liturgical activities through the action of a vast array of ministries, parachurch bodies and the like. *Pente*s cultivate an articulated relationship with the world of development NGOs. Mainline Evangelical churches have created their own development wings. Mekane Yesus runs a Development and Social Service Commission and Meserete Kristos Church its Relief and Development Association. Those work in close cooperation with North European and American faith-based organizations, such as Norwegian Church Aid or World Vision, in providing basic social services and carrying out humanitarian work.[22] Other churches, like Mulu Wengel, mainly rely on believers' funds to support their developmental wings. More recently, the preaching of several pastors and groups has absorbed the approach of the global fight against poverty that is promoted by international institutions[23] and adopted in the official government discourse, discussing notions such as good governance, accountability and the fight against corruption. This common focus feeds a growing practice of conferences, workshops and training sessions animated by religious leaders, who address church members as well as civil servants and government institutions.

This combination of theological notions, worship styles and organizational structures is intensely oriented towards proselytization, targeting not only other Christian communities but also Muslim constituencies.[24] Historically the youth and student milieu has been the elective territory for evangelization by Evangelical and Pentecostal churches, through pioneer experiences like the SIM Youth Centre and the Mekane Yesus Hostel targeting the students of the Addis Ababa University campus. This tradition has been revived by the Ethiopian Evangelical Student Association (EVASU), currently operating on all the country's university campuses, facilitating inter-denominational cooperation and contact among believers.

This focus has allowed the *Pente* movement to establish a strong presence in urban areas and to gain the adhesion of its educated milieu. Thanks in particular to the dynamism of the first young Pentecostals,[25] the movement has managed to rise from the peripheries where missionaries and traditional evangelical churches had been originally confined, reaching and flourishing at the geographical, political and economic centre of the country. Thus, even though the latest census portrays the Protestant churches as based mainly in rural areas,[26] *Pente*s are today primarily perceived as an urban phenomenon.

This significant growth of the Ethiopian *Pente* movement can be partially explained by a feature that it shares with other forms of global Pentecostalism: its effectiveness in elaborating religious and cultural responses to the process of social transformation associated with modernity and globalization. With the growing impact of globalization and modernization on the African continent, the flexibility of Pentecostalism seems to provide for a "contextualised Christianity", through a "style of worship and liturgy (…) that offers tangible help in this world as well as in the next".[27] Salvation becomes "holistic".[28]

Tensions surrounding a certain idea of modernity embraced by the educated elite and ruling class[29] and its contradictory and paradoxical results for the whole society[30] have traditionally been a main driver of Ethiopian historical developments. In this context, Pentecostalism has provided adequate spiritual notions and moral codes to fulfil the quests and aspirations of the university students who have been confronted by the process of modernization initiated by Haile Selassie.[31]

The current expansion of the *Pente* movement seems to confirm the "selective affinity" between Pentecostalism and globalization described by Harvey Cox in reference to Max Weber's theory of the Protestant ethic and the spirit of capitalism.[32] Similarly to what was observed by Ruth Marshall concerning the Pentecostal revolution in Nigeria, the Ethiopian *Pente* churches have been successful in finding an effective response to the context of radical insecurity—material, political, ideological, and ontological—linked to the insertion of the country within the process of neo-liberal globalization.[33] The answer seems to be articulated through resorting to a new syntax, elaborated by mobilizing and originally combining the political imaginary of the public space (related to the "modern" themes of good governance, leadership, and so on) and the "force of the invisible" (the power of the spirits, healing, miracles and the fight between the realm of God and the realm of Evil).[34]

The specificities of the Ethiopian case: autochthony, persecutions, and coexistence with a federal and developmental state

In associating *Pente*s with concepts like modernity and globalization, caution should be observed to avoid rigid determinism and univocal explanations of complex and ultimately intimate phenomena. In fact, some of the most intriguing analyses of the relationship between political innovation and religious identity—in Africa[35] like elsewhere in the World[36]—have demonstrated how these are part of a multifaceted single phenomenon rather than separated forces. They show an ambivalent relationship of exchange and "antagonistic interdependence"[37] around the issue of modernity, which has to be investigated in the light of its insertion within the historical trajectory of each country.

An autochthonous movement. When it is compared with the rest of Sub-Saharan Africa, the first specific feature of an Ethiopian history in the religious sphere is the absence of the colonial factor and the existence of a long established autochthonous Christian church. The Ethiopian Orthodox Church has been co-existent with the project of state building through the assimilation of all the different peripheries to the Abyssinian core of the Empire.[38] Its privileged relationship with the Ethiopian government and the popular consideration of Orthodox

Christianity as a key component structuring the national identity of Ethiopians—although highly controversial, because failing to accommodate the historical presence of Islam in the country—initially forced *Pentes* to operate through light structures and a low profile.[39] Later it contributed to the popular perception of them as being alien to the national culture and driven by foreign influence and interests, with all the negative connotations that such a perception implies.

As a reaction, the *Pentes* are eager to stress the autochthonous character of their movement and are proud to portray their churches as truly autonomous, stressing the Ethiopian nationality of their historical leaders. The assertion is usually summarized by the motto "the Gospel for Ethiopia by Ethiopians", implying also the idea that "native ministers engage in evangelistic activities more effectively than foreigners."[40]

This narrative might contrast with the traditional portrayal of Pentecostalism as a global movement, charged with a transnational drive and "able to escape from the aura of transcendence attributed to the sovereign state".[41] However, the indigenous nature of the *Pente* movement is not derived from the incorporation or the prevalence within its cult of elements pertaining to local cultures or traditions. Rather it is affirmed by emphasizing the independence of Ethiopian *Pente* churches from alien forces, the diminishing role of pastors of other African nationalities and the financial support received from abroad. Thus *Pentes* tend to describe their movement not as a religion imported from abroad, but rather as a response inspired by the Spirit to demands arising from within the Ethiopian society. These narratives might be accentuated to counter the common feeling of mistrust towards foreign influence, perceived as a threat to national cohesion and uniqueness, as well as a precaution to avoid drawing excessive attention and suspicions from a government that has a problematic relationship with the Ethiopian diaspora in the USA.

The insistence on the autochthonous character of the *Pente* movement does not imply that it developed in isolation from the rest of the world. On the contrary, it underlines the ability to evolve at the interface between transnational flows and local aspirations, appropriating global ideas and interpreting them to reform existing religious repertoires. This attitude was for instance evident during the emergence of the indigenous Pentecostal leadership within the student movement during the 1960s in dialectical relationship with foreign missionaries and the Orthodox Church. Nowadays, a similar assertive attitude towards the international sphere could be found in the programmes of re-evangelization of the West that animate Ethiopian *Pente* followers and their churches abroad, although official ambitions have until now been only partially translated into practice.

The persecution experience and its consequences. The perception of the *Pente* as an alien movement, with a destabilizing potential for national identity and social cohesion, has been among the causes of a long record of persecution. Historical marginalization of early missionaries under imperial rule was later followed by their expulsion during the Italian occupation. Despite the official relaxation by Haile Selassie through the "Regulations Governing the Activities of Missions", ostracism persisted after the war and was fuelled by the rise of Pentecostals in the 1960s. Perceived as heretical and sectarian, they were the victims of official condemnation by the Orthodox hierarchy and of popular distrust on the part of Orthodox believers, occasionally leading also to physical attacks. This was matched with institutional harassment by the government, which rejected the official registration of the Mulu Wengel Church in 1967 in spite of the existing legislation. The episode was followed by years of considerable oppression, including mass detentions, physical abuse and public defamations. In some cases, the first Pentecostals were even marginalized by mainstream Evangelical churches and missionaries, worried by the "emotional stirring" that were claimed to emanate through the gifts of Holy Spirit.[42]

The persecution increased under the Derg regime, despite initial sympathy for the 1974 Revolution in some *Pente* circles. *Pente*s were attracted by the message of liberation from imperial oppression in the peripheries where they had their traditional constituencies and appreciated the occasion to put an end to the longstanding dominant position of Orthodox Christianity as state religion. However, complying with Communist orthodoxy in forbidding all public religious manifestation and activism, the Derg shut down churches and congregations and imprisoned *Pente* leaders. Among the most serious events was the execution of Gudina Tumsa, Secretary General of the Mekane Yesus Church, in 1979.[43] *Pente* churches, like other religious groups, were forced into underground activities and home church practices.

The extent and degree of persecution varied from church to church, according to the different stances taken on the Revolution, the strategy of cooptation or repression adopted by the Derg and the relations established by religious groups with liberation movements, such as the links between the Mekane Yesus Church and the Oromo Liberation Front guerrillas.[44] But nowadays *Pente*s from different churches and backgrounds seem to share a common narrative on the experience of persecution. The tradition of oppression is echoed in the comments on clashes and incidents that sporadically erupt in the country with other religious denominations, as well as of the social ostracism by relatives and friends that the *Pente* disciples still complain of as a consequence of their conversion.

Moreover, recurrent arguments in this narrative underline the paradoxical effects of persecution in reinforcing the strength of the *Pente* spiritual message and its diffusion throughout the country. In fact, marginalization contributed to the forging among early Pentecostals an identity of "holy, separated and messianic communities"[45] and later to produce a "narrative of moral superiority on account of the suffered persecution"[46] by different governments and other religious groups. This identity was completed through adhesion to strict moral codes, in particular regarding sexual behaviour and abstinence from smoking, alcohol and traditional dances. Often explicitly associating persecution with the experience of the apostles and the first Christian communities, *Pente* followers consider it as a necessary sacrifice for the spread of their message. As a consequence, these experiences reinforce their worship and evangelizing, and improve their ability to survive in hostile contexts. Their small and autonomous congregations are animated by a strong sense of solidarity and ecumenical collaboration developed during the Derg regime. That experience has been interpreted as crucial in opening the way for the diffusion of Pentecostal practices and styles throughout mainstream Evangelical churches, given their particularly active role in the underground churches. More broadly, it contributed to laying of solid foundations for the expansion of the whole movement in the last twenty years.

Ambivalent relations with ethnic federalism. In terms of identity and allegiance, the *Pente* movement entertains an ambivalent relationship with the federal structure of the contemporary Ethiopian state. In fact, this arrangement is characterized by a contradictory approach to religion. On the one hand, the official discourse aims at separating ethnic and religious boundaries, in an attempt at depoliticize the second. Among the criteria used to identify "belonging to nations, nationalities or people" the federal Constitution quotes the sharing of "intelligible language, common culture, similar customs, common psychological make up and predominantly contiguous territory",[47] without mentioning the religious factor. On the other hand, as Østebø writes, throughout Ethiopian history religion and ethnicity "have mutually informed each other, contributing to the creation and reinforcement of both ethnic and intra-religious boundaries".[48]

The consequences of this contradiction are operating within the *Pente* movement, whose plasticity nurtures a plurality of identities and allows multiple and negotiated belongings. In some cases, the *Pente* message promotes a discourse of individualization and the creation of networks going beyond ethnic boundaries. Being Born-Again entails a break with the past and its burden in terms of traditions and divisions, it promotes belonging to a new community superior to ethnic identity, the "kingdom of priest and holy nation" announced in the Scriptures.[49]

Moreover, *Pente*s are often associated with a message of personal salvation, social atomization and individual separation radically different from the ideological construction behind ethnic federalism, which respects community group rights before those of the individual. The *Pente* message fits well with the aspiration to embrace modernity that is expressed by the educated young generations. It also accommodates the feelings of the urban and cosmopolitan Ethiopians of mixed origins who fail to pigeonhole themselves within the official ethnic structure. Furthermore, in its more radical declension, it provides an opportunity to subvert traditional or institutional forms of power and knowledge, offering an "alternative civic identity" in the context of a closed political space.[50]

In other cases, the use of local languages in preaching and reading the Scriptures, or the condemnation of traditions and superstitions associated with the Orthodox Church, contributes to reinforcing the identity of specific ethnic groups. In traditional areas of early missionaries and later Evangelical and Pentecostal presence, like those of the current SNNPR or the Wollega zone in Oromia region, *Pente* is the religion of the majority.[51] In these areas, while the conversion to Orthodox Christianity was traditionally associated with military incorporation and political assimilation of the local elites, missionaries' schools represented the only opportunity to be educated in a non-Amharic and non-Abyssinian context for people belonging to subaltern groups. Hence, *Pente* affiliation could represent an opportunity to bolster one's opposition to the Amhara and later Tigrean political establishment associated with the Orthodox Church. But it could also contribute to fuelling and amplifying intra-ethnic conflicts, like those that repeatedly erupted in Jimma (western Oromia) between 2006 and 2011 or the inter-ethnic tensions around the issues of autochthony and allogeny of different religious groups.

These examples show how the plasticity of the *Pente* movement and its horizontal organization in autonomous and relatively independent churches allow for an effective tinkering with identities. This enables many Ethiopians to respond to the challenge of structuring themselves as political and moral subjects within the contradictory structure of ethnic federalism, that is, to reconcile (post)modern aspirations channelled by globalization with "traditional" allegiances. Paradoxes and ongoing tensions between these contradictory paths are exemplified by the controversy surrounding the creation of ethnic branches of national churches, like the Oromo groups reorganizing themselves within the Mekane Yesus Church or the student associations demanding worship and services in local languages instead of Amharic or English.

Coexistence with a secular and developmental state. The contradictory relationship with the ethnic federalist architecture of the state contributes to the ambivalence of *Pente* engagement in public and civic affairs. Under confrontational regimes, like those of Haile Selassie and the Derg, their political stand was relatively clear. *Pente*s rejected and opposed government interference in religious affairs. Thus their fight for religious freedom represented an alternative to compliance with the regime and later offered a "model of civil disobedience with their effective underground structures".[52]

However, this stance did not translate into the elaboration of an ideological and systematic political alternative to the Derg regime. In fact, as long as the government did not conflict and interfere with their faith, several leaders of the *Pente* movement continued to serve as civil servants in prominent positions under the Derg. They were particularly appreciated for their professional skills and educated profiles, but refrained from joining the one party state and disclosing their religious faith.[53] Several of them pursued their careers under the present regime.

Attitudes towards civic engagement and the political system are less sharp within the current context of religious freedom. On the one hand, the new climate allows an increased presence of *Pente*s in the public space. It facilitates a shift from the millenarian refusal of compromise with the World, with which Pentecostalism is often associated, to a new season of public engagement, with churches encouraging active involvement of believers in politics and economic development. This shift is often pursued in the name of a holistic approach to salvation that aims at reconciling the spiritual and material dimensions. Thus, the consolidation of local political leaderships from different ethnic backgrounds within the federal framework has led to the promotion of political leaders at the regional (particularly in southern and western areas) and national level, whose *Pente* faith is widely known.[54] The institutional recognition of the freedom of religious association allowed the formation of professional fellowships promoting Christian politicians, as well as lobbying activities by groups like the Christian Lawyers Association or workshops, training and prayer sessions for *Pente* political leaders.

On the other hand, the secular attitude of the current government has inspired a cautious control of the church potential in terms of political mobilization. Religious affairs are officially relegated to the private sphere and assigned to the scrupulous monitoring of the Ministry of Federal Affairs. That ministry's mandate consists in the institutional cooptation of religious leaders to promote social cohesion in the country, especially on sensitive occasions like elections, and to settle interdenominational conflicts. This policy has until now prevented contentious political stands by various churches, direct involvement of pastors in the political arena or the founding of parties with religious inspiration. As a result ethnic allegiance remains the main vector for political mobilization. Besides, the rigid ideology of the ruling party coalition, the Ethiopian People's Revolutionary Democratic Front (EPRDF), shelters it from pressures that could arise from religious groups. Hence *Pente* believers divide themselves equally between government and opposition coalitions. And they tend not to publicize any direct political engagement, in order not to compromise their churches with a single political faction, as that would offer additional grounds for internal divisions within the movement.

The originality of the Ethiopian historical trajectory also helps shape the relationship of the *Pente* movement with the economic sphere. Pentecostalism, in Africa like elsewhere in the world, has been traditionally associated with a neoliberal economic approach. Some analysts see a direct cause and effect connection between the two phenomena, considering Pentecostalism as organic to neo-liberalism through the forging of individualistic and flexible personalities that are intrinsically adapted to neoliberal policies. Other studies on the contrary interpret Pentecostalism as a response to the economic and social transformations due to the retrenchment of the state preached by the neoliberal agenda. From this perspective, Pentecostalism is described as a movement providing spiritual and material support to alleviate poverty and deprivation caused by structural adjustment programmes, or facilitating the translation and interpretation in vernacular terms of the disorienting effects of globalization. Once again, the multifaceted nature of the *Pente* movement invites a more nuanced understanding of its relationship with the economic sphere, avoiding univocal causality and deterministic explanations but focalizing rather on the plurality of economic strategies and practices that it can pursue. In Ethiopia, the elaboration of economic notions and their turning into practical economic choices by *Pente*s should not be analyzed in the context of a neoliberal retreat of the state alone. On the contrary, it should be seen within the framework of the transformation of state action and its involvement in the economy—through monopolistic control of strategic sectors like telecommunications and strong influence over resources distribution—in official compliance with the paradigm of the developmental state. In this respect the *Pente* movement, through professional fellowships and networks, parachurch activities and ministries, development initiatives, members' donations, and separate community organizations, offers alternative channels to the governmental ones for the delivery of social and economic services, resource accumulation, access to international funds, and the pursuance of careers, mundane aspirations, and social mobility.

Despite a vocal discourse on the need to promote Christian values and interests in the national economy, in order to counter the Islamic domination of commerce and to tackle the corruption of the system imputed to the action of Evil forces, the development of a flourishing *Pente* economic community has not materialized yet. *Pente* business fellowships and economic activities remain at an infant stage. Until now, their limited dimensions do not represent a significant challenge to the economic and financial establishment, controlled by the EPRDF affiliated enterprises and Sheikh Mohamed al-Amoudi's business group.

Hence, rather than being a competing force, *Pente* economic actors and ventures seem to offer a sheltered space to negotiate roles and positions with the economic establishment and to prosper in the niches of the free market allowed by the current government. First of all, their quest for individual and social transformation seems to entail a "selective affinity" with the transformation of the Ethiopian economy towards a more market oriented direction. It is also in coherence with the official discourse of the Growth and Transformation Plan, through which the government aims at reaching the status of a middle-income economy by 2015. Then the vast majority of *Pente*s openly reject the Prosperity Gospel as a theological degeneration and practice alien to the Ethiopian socioeconomic culture. *Pente* churches try to offer, with different tones and nuances, a moral justification of economic success, of exclusive lifestyles and conspicuous consumption, striking a balance with traditional discretion and suspicion of economic prosperity and wealth.

Finally, in a country with a relatively short experience of free market economics, *Pente* economic networks and fellowships, through a rigid doctrine and practice of the self, allow the acquisition and enforcement of a discipline conducive to entrepreneurship. The inculcation of this discipline is matched with practical training in marketing and other business techniques, as well as the opportunity to test them through the participation in economic and financial ventures.

Open questions: Pente *expansion, secularism and religious pluralism in Ethiopia*

The set of spiritual notions, codes of action and material practices developed at the interface between global flows and local peculiarities contributes to structuring of the *Pente* phenomenon as a coherent field for the formation of moral and political subjects. Thus *Pente* trajectories come to exemplify the contemporary struggle by Ethiopians to define their identity against the unresolved questions of ethnic federalism, to renovate traditional practices of equilibrium between adhesion and dissidence vis-à-vis a feared political authority, and to cope with the contradictions of the country's insertion into the a neoliberal economy.

In the future, a major test for the ambitions of the *Pente* movement will be firstly of its capacity to confirm the steady and exceptional expansion rate of the last twenty years and to cope with the reactions that this causes in the rest of Ethiopian society. In the past, the growth and consolidation of the movement have been mainly related to local dynamics, such as the end of official persecution and the solidity of local religious entrepreneurs, rather than with exogenous factors such as the action of transnational missionaries from Asia or America as in other African countries. Growing investment in transnational networks, particularly by new independent churches, as well as in the education sector through the development of theological colleges, suggests the need to assess the influence of North American Pentecostalism in terms of theological thought, codes of action, circulation of teachers and the flow of resources channelled through the Ethiopian diaspora.

Furthermore, the internal divisions and the proliferation of churches, together with the individualistic approach to religion and the spiritual nomadism of the faithful, might challenge their capacity to transmit their faith to their offspring. This applies particularly in the urban context where multiple religious allegiances coexist within the same family. Future expansion will probably rely on the attitude towards proselytism. While the official discourse on evangelization openly targets Muslim areas, the record seems to indicate that conversion still occurs mainly among Orthodox believers.[55] This trend has already helped to spark more confrontational and fundamentalist reactions in the Orthodox camp, such as the strict return to tradition preached by the influent *Mahbere Qiddusan* movement. The evolution of ecumenical relationships among different Christian denominations towards more tensions is a matter of growing concern.

These trends should be investigated within the broader issue of the effects of *Pente* expansion on religious pluralization and competition within the Ethiopian political space. Until now, research into the relation between Christianity and Islam in the region has focused mainly on the Ethiopian Orthodox Church for the Christian side.[56]

Pente churches are perceived as alien to the tradition of mutual toleration and as backed by international interests attempting to jeopardize the national cohesion and stability of the country. This interpretation tends to over-emphasize the peaceful coexistence between Islam and Christianity in Ethiopia and to overlook its conflicting aspects.[57] The *Pente*s are inspired by an assertive attitude towards proselytism and have introduced a more aggressive and Manichean vocabulary in the discourse, brandishing references to spiritual warfare and liberation from evil forces. Furthermore, the adhesion to transnational networks might be a channel for intrusion within the national public debate of global contentious issues such the rise of Islamic fundamentalism or resistance to American imperialism.

The exploitation of these issues has to be seen in the light of their overlapping with local simmering tensions stemming from socio-economic competition or ethnic boundaries. In addition, *Pente* impact on interfaith coexistence should be assessed in relation to the dynamics occurring inside other religious groups, such as the internal controversies shaking the Orthodox Church or the reformist aims of some Muslim fringes. The combined effects of these dynamics seem to feed antagonistic discourses and confrontational occupation of public spaces, resulting in religious clashes with an increasing and unprecedented frequency.[58] The controversial contribution to this escalation made by the growing complex of religious media, enjoying a relatively high degree of freedom compared with their secular colleagues, is preoccupying. Furthermore, given its geopolitical implications, the effects of the *Pente* expansion on the renovated and contentious religious presence in the Ethiopian public sphere need to be evaluated within the broader context of the complex interplay of politics, war and identity in the Horn of Africa.[59]

The increasing vocal presence of religion in the Ethiopian public space has not resulted so far in the direct involvement of spiritual leaders in politics or the emergence of religious political parties. The current government has proved effective at controlling the mobilization potential of religion and maintaining ethnic allegiance as the main vector for political participation. Nevertheless recent developments have showed that religion is "actively and assertively constructed by communal leaders and religious entrepreneurs as the normative, dominant identity of citizens" and that "antagonistic religious discourses tend to fill the space vacated by politics with the decline of democratic debate and freedom".[60]

The internal pluralism and flexibility of the *Pente* movement, coupled with its lack of accountability to institutional hierarchies, might allow it to avoid external control and influence. This however raises questions about the ability of the movement to fully make its influence felt as a coherent force in political lobbying, in cultural debates and in continued social presence.

Even if the *Pente*s do not represent a force trying to destabilize the current political system, several of the developments within the movement do challenge the official approach of secularism and separation between state and religion affirmed in the Constitution (art. 11).

First of all, a shift in the internal division of work among different religious institutions might lead to more direct action by churches in crucial issues like community development, human rights advocacy and conflict resolution. Involvement in these fields has been in fact forbidden by the 2008 Regulation on Civil Society Organization to all "international" NGOs receiving more than 10 per cent of their budget from abroad, which included the main developmental wings of *Pente* churches. The direct assumption of responsibility for these activities by churches is already happening and its consequences for institutional relation with the government will need to be cautiously monitored in the next years.

In addition, the radical character of the *Pente* experience casts an ambiguous shadow over the literal interpretation of Ethiopia as an "Ancient and Holy Nation" as mentioned in the Bible. In their combat for the Realm of God against the Realm of Evil, *Pente*s have publicly embarked on a crusade against corruption and promotion of their own view of "good governance". The consequences of this discourse of transformation and moralization of the public space cannot be entirely understood in terms of political rationality. In fact, this discourse entails a spiritual dimension and produces a "prescriptive regime"[61] that sets its own norms and codes of action towards the formation of moral and political subjects. Therefore, in describing the extraordinary rise of the *Pente* movement in the last few years and its impact on contemporary Ethiopian society, we should bear in mind what is properly *Pente*, that is, the complexity of an approach to spiritual salvation and practices of faith that are not reducible to the political, social and economic logics of this world.

BIBLIOGRAPHY AND FURTHER READING

Abbink, Jon, 2011, "Religion in Public Spaces: Emerging Muslim-Christian Polemics in Ethiopia", *African Affairs*, 110/439, pp. 253–74
Anderson, Allan, 2004, *An Introduction to Pentecostalism. Global Charismatic Christianity*, Cambridge University Press.
Bahru Zewde, 2002, *Pioneers of Change in Ethiopia: The Reformist Intellectuals of the Early Twentieth Century*, Athens: Ohio University Press.
Bax, Mart, 1987, "Religious Regimes and State Formation: Towards a Research Perspective", *Anthropological Quarterly*, 60 (1), pp. 1–11.
Bayart, Jean-François (ed.), 1993, *Religion et modernité politique en Afrique Noire*, Paris, Kharthala.
Corten, André, 2006, "Un religieux immanent et transnational", *Archives de Sciences Sociales des Religions*, 133, pp. 135–151.

Corten, André and Mary, André (eds), 2000, *Imaginaires politiques et pentecôtismes. Afrique/Amérique latine*, Paris: Khartala.

Cox, H., 2006, "Spirits of Globalisation: Pentecostalism and Experiential Spiritualities in a Global Era", in Stralsett, S. J. (ed), *Spirits of Globalisation, The Growth of Pentecostalism and Experiential Spiritualities in a Global Age*, London: SCM Press, pp. 11–22.

Crummey, Donald, 1972, *Priests and Politicians: Protestant and Catholic Missions in Orthodox Ethiopia, 1830–1868*, Oxford: Clarendon Press.

Donham, Donald, 1999, *Marxist Modern. An Ethnographic History of the Ethiopian Revolution*, Berkeley: University of California Press.

ECFE—Evangelical Churches Fellowship of Ethiopia in partnership with Dawn Ministries, 2005, *National Mission Research. The Harvest Force and the Harvest Field of Ethiopian Evangelical Churches*, Addis Ababa.

EEA—Ethiopian Economic Association, Ethiopian Economic Policy Research Institute, 2008, *The Role of Faith Based Organization (FBOs) in Development in Ethiopia: Past Contributions and Future Prospects*, Addis Ababa.

Eide, Øyvind M., 2000, *Revolution and Religion in Ethiopia. The growth and persecution of the Mekane Yesus Church 1974–85*, Oxford: James Currey.

Gascon, Alain, 2005, "Éthiopie: la croix contre la croix. Fédéralisme et prosélytisme des Églises penté", *Hérodote*, 119 (4), pp. 95–109.

Getachew Haile, Lande, A. and Rubenson, S. (eds), 1998, *The Missionary Factor in Ethiopia*, Frankfurt: Peter Lang.

Halldin, V., 1977, *Swedes in Haile Selassie's Ethiopia (1924–1952): A Study in Early Development and Co-Operation*, Uppsala, Stockholm: Almquist & Wiksell International Distributors.

Haustein, Jörg, 2008, "Brief History of Pentecostalism in Ethiopia, on the website of the European Research Network on Global Pentecostalism", http://www.glopent.net/Members/jhaustein/ethiopia/brief-history-of-pentecostalism-in-ethiopia (latest access on September 2014)

———— 2009a, "Navigating Political Revolutions. Ethiopia's Churches During and After the Mengistu Regime", in Koschorke, Klaus (ed.), *Falling Walls. The Year 1989/90 as a Turning Point in the History of World Christianity*, Wiesbaden: Harrassowitz, pp. 117–36.

———— 2009b, "*Pentecostal and Charismatic Churches in Ethiopia 2009*", http://www.glopent.net/Members/jhaustein/ethiopia/pentecostal-charismatic-churches-in-ethiopia (latest access August 2011).

———— 2011a. *Writing Religious History: The Historiography of Ethiopian Pentecostalism*, Wiesbaden: Harrassowitz.

———— 2011 b, "Charismatic Renewal, Denominational Tradition and the Transformation of Ethiopian Society", in Evangelisches Missionswerk Deutschland (ed.), *Encounter Beyond Routine. Cultural Roots, Cultural Transition, Understanding of Faith and Cooperation in Development*, International Consultation, Academy of Mission, Hamburg, 17th-23rd January 2011, Hamburg: EMW.

Haustein, J. and Fantini, E., 2013, "Guest Editorial: The Ethiopian Pentecostal

145

Movement—History, Identity and Current Socio-Political Dynamics",
PentecoStudies, 12 (2), pp. 150–61.

Hibou, Béatrice, 1998, *Economie politique du discours de la Banque mondiale en Afrique: du catéchisme économique au fait (et méfait) missionnaire*, Paris: Les Etudes du CERI, 39.

Hussein Ahmed, 2006, "Coexistence and/or Confrontation?: Towards a Reappraisal of Christian-Muslim Encounter in Contemporary Ethiopia", *Journal of Religion in Africa*, 36 (1), pp. 4–22

Johnstone, Patrick and Mandryk, Jason, 2010, *Operation World*, Colorado Springs: Biblica Publishing.

Marshall, R., 2009, *Political Spiritualities. The Pentecostal Revolution in Nigeria*, University of Chicago Press.

Østebø, Terje, 2008, "The Question of Becoming: Islamic Reform Movements in Contemporary Ethiopia", *Journal of Religion in Africa*, 38 (4), pp. 416–46.

Samson Estephanos, 2007, *Evangelical Churches Directorate*, Addis Ababa.

Tadesse Tamrat, 1972, *Church and State in Ethiopia, 1270–1527*, Oxford University Press.

Tadesse Tamrat, 1998, "Evangelizing the Evangelised: the Root Problem between Mission and the Ethiopian Orthodox Church", in Getachew Haile et al. (eds), *The Missionary Factor in Ethiopia*, Frankfurt: Peter Lang.

Tibebe Eshete, 2009, *The Evangelical Movement in Ethiopia. Resistance and Resilience*, Waco, Texas: Baylor University Press.

Tronvoll, Kjetil, 2009, *War & the Politics of Identity in Ethiopia. The Making of Enemies & Allies in the Horn of Africa*, Oxford: James Currey.

Wolf, E.R., 1991, *Religious Regimes and State Formation. Perspectives from European Ethnology*, Albany: SUNY Press.

5

FROM PAN-AFRICANISM TO RASTAFARI

AFRICAN AMERICAN AND CARIBBEAN 'RETURNS' TO ETHIOPIA

Giulia Bonacci

On 7 November 1964 Noel Dyer, a Jamaican Rastafari[1] who had migrated to England, took the train from London to Dover. After arriving in Paris, he worked for three months in order to be able to continue on his way to Spain and Morocco. From there, he set off towards the east. He crossed Algeria, Tunisia, Libya and Egypt on foot, went beyond the Aswan dam and over the desert to reach Sudan, where he got arrested by the authorities, because he did not have a visa. He spent three months in prison until the Ethiopian Ambassador in Khartoum heard about the Rastafari who wanted to go to Addis Ababa on foot and authorized him to enter Ethiopia. It took Noel Dyer more than a year to complete his journey from England to Ethiopia. It was an exceptional journey, which shows at least two things in addition to his personal determination.

The first is the violence of the racial discrimination and economic marginalization that he had experienced first in Jamaica and later in

England, and which had led him to leave. This violence is one of the common denominators for most Africans and people of African descent in the Americas and Europe. The root cause of their traditions of resistance is the backdrop against which they draw their identity and their political objectives. The second is the power of the imagination and the ideologies that led Noel Dyer to tie his identity, freedom, redemption, and future to that of Ethiopia. At the heart of this imagination, the racial identification with Ethiopia on the basis of skin colour is central, whatever Ethiopians may think of it. For Noel Dyer and others, Ethiopia is that mythical, biblical land where milk and honey flow. It is also a political reality, Ethiopia having been, with Liberia, the sole sovereign and independent state in sub-Saharan Africa until the end of the 1950s.

Noel Dyer is the only one to have come on foot. However, since the end of the nineteenth century many people of African ancestry, from the Americas and the Caribbean, have come to settle in Ethiopia and tied their lives to those of the Ethiopians. They formed a constant presence, even if their contribution to the development of the country remains little known. They are the reflection of a peculiar representation of Ethiopia, both sacred and sovereign. And by coming to live in Ethiopia, they have embodied the paradoxes of those engaged in fulfilling the Pan-African ideology, which postulates the unity of destiny and cause of Africans at home and abroad.[2]

The Ethiopian prophecy

It was with the Bible that the term "Ethiopia" first crossed the Atlantic Ocean. The Bible did not travel with the human cargo, but on the decks of European ships, including slave ships, and in the hands of churchmen including those who approved slavery. In the King James Bible of 1611, all the terms designating black people were translated by the word "Ethiopia" following the Greek usage. For the enslaved or freed communities in the Americas, the Bible, in spite of its association with the slave-owners, had two great assets. First, the numerous references to Ethiopia and Ethiopians offered a model with which the descendants of Africans could identify and thanks to which they could call themselves Ethiopians. Second, the history of the Exodus and the metaphor of the Hebrews, a divinely elected people reduced to slavery, offered them an archetype of deliverance and liberation. Verse 31 in

Psalm 68 is the reference to Ethiopia that is the most known. The verse goes, "Ethiopia shall soon stretch forth her hands unto God".[3] Interpreted by black congregations, it represented their aspirations: the promise of an imminent liberation and their active role in the prophetic destiny attributed to Ethiopia. This biblical interpretation was further reinforced with the victory of Ethiopian troops over the Italians at Adwa in 1896. Beyond its religious significance, Ethiopia then came to be seen in addition as a mighty sovereign state, successfully fighting against white imperialism. The Emperors of Ethiopia came to represent both a religious and a political power that was significant for a then colonized Africa and for all the oppressed black people in the world.[4]

This embodiment of black religious power and nationhood started to attract black people to Ethiopia at the end of the nineteenth century. The Haitian Benito Sylvain made four trips to Ethiopia and represented Emperor Menelik II at the first Pan African Conference convened in London in 1900 by the Trinidadian barrister Henry Sylvester Williams. Joseph Vitalien from Guadeloupe became the personal physician of Emperor Menelik and the first tutor of the young Tafari Makonnen, the future Emperor Haile Selassie. When these Caribbean and African American people started to come to Ethiopia they were faced by a strong racist reaction from the European legations in Addis Ababa which did not want to see the development of a close relationship between them and the Ethiopians. At first they were only a few, but more were to come, encouraged by the teachings of Marcus Garvey.

A Jamaican born in 1887 and a printer by trade, Marcus Garvey created the Universal Negro Improvement Association (UNIA) in Kingston in 1914. A few years later, the UNIA was moved to New York and Marcus Garvey developed a black nationalist programme that brought him a following of millions[5] in the Americas, Europe, and Africa. Charismatic and controversial, Marcus Garvey called for the return of black people to Africa and used Ethiopia as a metaphor to designate both the continent and the black people in exile. Moreover, Garvey urged black people to see God in their own image, that is, "to see God through the spectacles of Ethiopia".[6]

In 1930, moved by the promise of liberation contained in the Ethiopian prophecy, Arnold Josiah Ford, originally from Barbados, settled in Ethiopia along with some of his disciples. Leader of a congregation of Black Jews[7] of whom there were many in the Harlem of that era, he was a musician and a composer, and author of "The Universal

Ethiopian Anthem", the hymn of Marcus Garvey's organization. Ford was well received by the Ethiopian authorities and he was given land, but he lacked the capital that could enable him to bring about a rapid development. And then another event became a major obstacle to black settlement in Ethiopia: the Fascist invasion of Ethiopia in 1935.

The Pan-African cause of the twentieth century

As the war approached, Ethiopia became a cause to defend. On this occasion, the first grand pan-African international mobilization took shape. In a few weeks the attention of Blacks in the entire world was focused on Ethiopia, the pan-African press circulated news on the war, and thousands of "Ethiopian" volunteers, American citizens and colonial subjects, were ready to take up arms to defend Ethiopia. The war had become a metaphor for the anti-colonial struggle, and Ethiopia was supported by songs written for the occasion, by massive demonstrations, by fund-raising, and by the boycott of Italian businesses in New York, sometimes followed by riots and other militant actions. This mobilization around the defence of the sovereignty and integrity of Ethiopia was one of the great moments of Pan-Africanism in the twentieth century.[8]

After the liberation of Ethiopia in 1941, a generation of Pan-Africanists committed itself to participate in the reconstruction of the country. They were teachers, professionals, technicians, journalists, photographers, and administrators. John Robinson, an American aviator who had already fought against the Italians as a military pilot in 1936, returned to Ethiopia in 1944. In a few years, he trained more than eighty air force cadets who later became the first Ethiopian civilian and military pilots. David A. Talbot, a Guyanese journalist, succeeded a black American, William Steen, as editor of the *Ethiopian Herald*. He also broadcast on the radio, and was in charge of English publications in the Ministry of Information. Mignon Ford, from Barbados, opened the Princess Zenebe Worq School in 1941, and Dr Tomas Fortune Fletcher, an American, became the director of the Medhane Alem School. The examples are numerous, and they illustrate the importance Ethiopia had in the lives of these professionals who identified themselves with the country and felt directly concerned by its reconstruction. Some stayed only until the end of their contracts but others, like Mignon Ford or David Talbot, remained in Ethiopia until the end of their lives.

The Ethiopian government was shaping for itself a clear pan-African policy by recruiting and inviting black people to come to Ethiopia. Furthermore, as a token of appreciation for the support showed by the black people of the world during the war, Emperor Haile Selassie granted to the members of the Ethiopian World Federation (EWF) five gashas, equivalent to 200 hectares, of fertile land in the outskirts of Shashemene, a southern market town.[9] The Ethiopian World Federation had been established in New York in 1937 by order of the Emperor with the objective of centralizing the moral and financial support offered in the Americas for the Ethiopian war effort. Headed by an Ethiopian, Melaku E. Beyen, it published a newspaper, *The Voice of Ethiopia*, organized fundraising and informed the public with news of the war. National and international branches were quickly established. The first settlers on the Shashemene land grant were Helen and James Piper. Born in the tiny Caribbean island of Montserrat, they had lived in the USA and were Garveyites, Black Jews and members of the Ethiopian World Federation. They came as part of the pan-African generation involved in the reconstruction of Ethiopia, and after a couple years spent working in Addis Ababa, went on to settle on the Shashemene land.

However, by the end of the 1950s, pan-Africanism began a major transformation as it was appropriated by the new African elites. The Pan African Congress in Manchester in 1945 saw the strategies of the anti-colonial struggle being put to the fore by young leaders like Kwame Nkrumah and Jomo Kenyatta. In the eyes of black Americans fighting for their civil rights, the significance of Emperor Haile Selassie, considered "the father of Africa", started to be outshone by the "sons", the heads of states of the new independent countries. The changes brought about by the process of decolonization inspired black Americans in their struggle more than the Ethiopian model, which began to be considered as an autocratic and ageing regime, struggling for its survival against a coup d'état (1960), peasant revolts and the Eritrean problem.

But the image of Ethiopia as a sacred sovereign state began to be glorified by a new and different population not previously noticed, the poor blacks coming out of the ghettoes of Kingston, Jamaica. This was no longer the African or pan-African elite, the intellectuals of the grand congresses, the trade union leaders or activists engaged in the anti-colonial armed struggle; it was the Rastafari.

The Rastafari and Ethiopia

The Rastafari were heirs to the ideologies of Ethiopianism and Pan Africanism and heirs to Marcus Garvey's black nationalism. Their contribution lies in their social practice, their cultural contributions and their resilient engagement with Ethiopia. The early Rastafari of the 1930s were accustomed to cultural resistance, and like many other Jamaicans they had travelled to Central America and the United States. As a result, they had familiarized themselves with the international lexicon of pan-African and racial unity.[10] The Rastafari relayed the conviction that Ethiopia had a prophetic destiny in which they could take part, and, rejecting their status as colonial subjects, they identified with Ethiopians and declared allegiance to this Black Empire rather than to the British Empire.

Emperor Haile Selassie occupied a central place in the cosmology and practices of the Rastafari. The black communities had noticed his first political actions while he was still *Ras* Tafari.[11] A delegation sent to the United States in 1919, the gradual abolition of slavery in Ethiopia, the admission of the country into the League of Nations in 1923 were all measures that had given Ras Tafari considerable prestige. On several occasions, he had invited black people to come and settle in Ethiopia. His coronation on 2 November 1930 made him Emperor Haile Selassie I, King of Kings and Lord of Lords, Conquering Lion of the Tribe of Judah, Elect of God, and Light of the World—all titles with a Biblical significance, used by Ethiopia's sovereigns since the nineteenth century to legitimize their political power. In Jamaica, only one step was needed for sensitized congregations to interpret these dynastic and messianic titles as proof that the man who had been crowned on that day had a divine nature and would play a role in the realization of the prophecy that announced their liberation. This interpretation made the Rastafari movement both religious and political, and it was at first harshly repressed in Jamaica.

The beliefs and practices of the Rastafari formed a critique of the colonial society in which they found themselves. Their hairdo, the *dreadlocks* (literally meaning "terrifying knots"), symbolized their religious consecration, in reference to their Nazarene vow (see Numbers, 6 in the Bible), as well as their rejection of European aesthetic norms imposed by colonial society. They created ritual organizations and social structures through which they transmitted their history orally to the younger generations. The contribution of Rastafari to the collective Jamaican consciousness is now recognized. By opposing the image of Africans associated with the infamous chains of slavery, and by reversing the colour line to claim the black body as the site of divinity, in the image of Haile Selassie I, they participated in the exorcism of racism on which Jamaica was grounded.[12]

In Jamaica, as in most slave societies of the Americas, claiming the right for people of African ancestry to return to Africa caused major social movements and involved people representing a wide spectrum of society.[13] For the Rastafari, repatriation to Africa or Ethiopia was a pillar of their faith. Both an imperious necessity understood in terms of human rights and a gateway for their redemption, repatriation to Africa had to be achieved by whatever means necessary. Various attempts at leaving Jamaica for Africa had already failed, but an announcement in 1955 by the Ethiopian World Federation that a land grant was available in Ethiopia had raised high hopes among the Rastafari. In 1961 the Jamaican government sponsored a Back to Africa mission to study the settlement possibilities in five African countries. However, despite encouraging conclusions, the results of this Back to Africa mission were somewhat forgotten in the enthusiasm of Jamaica's independence in 1962.

It was the state visit of Haile Selassie to Jamaica in 1966 that eventually encouraged Rastafari to pack up and leave. On his Caribbean tour, the Ethiopian Emperor visited Haiti, Barbados, Jamaica, and Trinidad and Tobago. In Jamaica, ten thousand people were waiting for him at Kingston airport, overwhelming the protocol and national security forces. Far from putting an end to the Rastafari movement—as the British had hoped—the visit of Haile Selassie brought Rastafari into the limelight. They were invited to official receptions, and in a speech in the National Arena Haile Selassie declared that "Jamaicans and Ethiopians are blood brothers".[14]

The first group of Rastafari left for Ethiopia in 1968. It was composed of three adults and four children, and they were followed the following year by another group made of members of local 43 and 31 of the Ethiopian World Federation. Leaving behind them fearful families, the Rastafari started to fulfil their claim to repatriation.

The Shashemene settlement

The Jamaican Rastafari arriving in Shashemene by the end of the 1960s found a few people already living on the land grant: Helen and

James Piper, the first settlers, a handful of Black Americans, Baptists, Muslims and one Rastafari, as well as Noel Dyer who had arrived a few years before. Rastafari from Kingston continued pouring in, some members of the Ethiopian World Federation, and members of the Twelve Tribes of Israel, an organization founded in 1968 as a splinter group of the Ethiopian World Federation. It had developed its own doctrine and was very keen on the issue of repatriation. The relationship between those who were already there and the newcomers was not easy, as more people meant further distribution of the five gashas of land and a power struggle for their administration. Those early Jamaican settlers eventually petitioned the Ethiopian government and saw the land grant divided among twelve households in July 1970. It was an amazing achievement for poor black people coming out of the Kingston ghettos to find themselves masters of fertile land acreages in Ethiopia. While no further lots were arranged for other Rastafari arriving in the early 1970s, the Shashemene settlers built their houses and ploughed the land with the local peasants, reproducing the unequal labour relationships then prevalent in Ethiopia.

Although well received by the Imperial regime, they had to face the 1974 Ethiopian revolution and the large-scale land nationalization of 1975. Associated with the Emperor on account of their faith, they lost everything, their houses, their crops, and their right to land. The pan-African motivation of the Shashemene settlement could not withstand the massive social and political change that was overtaking Ethiopia. Some Shashemene settlers left because they felt threatened, a few stayed and a few continued to arrive during the years of the Derg, the military regime. They shared with the Ethiopians the hardships of curfew and food rationing, and struggled to survive in war-torn revolutionary Ethiopia.

Apparently Colonel Mengistu Haile Mariam, leader of the new regime, admired the continued presence of these foreigners who wanted to be Ethiopians and had not abandoned the country while thousands of native Ethiopians had fled abroad. But living in Shashemene was not easy. The image the settlers had of Ethiopia turned out to be in sharp contrast to the reality of the country. The peasants around Shashemene, the town's businessmen, and the civil servants had great difficulties understanding why these people came from all over the world to share their fate. The Ethiopians sometimes supported, assisted, and nourished them; at other times they stole from them, chased them away and even killed them. Following many petitions from the Rastafari, eighteen lots of land were granted in 1986 by local authorities so as to accommodate growing families piling up in small clapboard houses. That was the last time land was formally granted by the Ethiopian government to the Rastafari in Shashemene.

With the change of regime in 1991, Rastafari resumed coming to Ethiopia. An international coalition of Rastafari organized in 1992 a month-long celebration of the Centenary of Haile Selassie (born in 1892), thus putting Ethiopia back at the centre of the Rastafari movement. During the 1990s, and particularly around the millenniums in 2000 and 2007,[15] hundreds of Rastafari came to settle in Ethiopia to contribute to the country's development. The former location of the land grant had been absorbed into the town of Shashemene, exacerbating the fragility of the community which lacked papers and land holding titles. The neighbourhood is now known as "*Jamaica sefer*", even though about fifteen nationalities are living there. This reflects the internationalization of the Rastafari movement. In the 1970s, while the Ethiopian Empire collapsed under the impact of social change, the Rastafari movement had spread beyond the boundaries of Jamaica. Because of reggae music, the Rastafari artists had broadcast their identity to the world, and in turn Rastafari from all over the world had arrived in Shashemene, sometimes from as far as Sweden, New Zealand, Chile, Japan and South Africa. Rastafari communities had meanwhile developed in Addis Ababa, Bahar Dar, Awassa and Debre Zeit.

Despite their small numbers in relation to Ethiopia's population,[16] the Rastafari represent a particular figure in the Pan African relationship. They play a special role in the contemporary global representation of Ethiopia, as they learn Amharic in the Western capitals, agitate for the return of Ethiopian treasures looted by the British at Maqdala, and produce hagiographic discourses on Ethiopia, glossing over the subjects of war, famine, and poverty familiar to the international media. In Ethiopia they are a unique type of foreigner as most of them have left everything to live with Ethiopians in Ethiopia. They claim to be "Ethiopians" even though they cannot help sticking to their own identities. Although their culture is sometimes embarrassing to the Ethiopians,[17] they nevertheless build schools and clinics, and develop businesses and services. They attract tourists, they invest, and they bring up their children in the country. Nevertheless, their contributions remain unrecognized, and their integration is not easy. Bob Marley is now celebrated in the country and adopted as a cultural reference by Ethiopia's youth.[18] Yet, there is no government policy to facilitate the settlement and integration of Rastafari. Nor is there any legal or financial assistance from pan-African institutions.

Interestingly, the last ten years have witnessed a convergence between the Rastafari presence and the discreet but growing nostalgia for Emperor Haile Selassie's regime. Despite some legal restrictions[19] the symbols of the *ancien régime* are nowadays visible in Addis Ababa, marketable to the tourists, and a number of Ethiopian associations openly express their proximity to Ethiopia's royalty. As an example of this convergence, one of these Ethiopian associations, the Emperor Haile Selassie I Memorial Foundation, organized on 22–24 July 2011 the first pilgrimage to Ejersa Goro, the birthplace of the former Emperor, in collaboration with the Rastafari community. Although the two parties express their involvement in this pilgrimage in different ways, it was the first time since 1974 that Ethiopians and Rastafari were working together on a tribute to Emperor Haile Selassie.

Conclusion

Ethiopia has assumed a central place, as much imagined as real, in the development of Ethiopianism and pan-Africanism. Although Ethiopia was not affected by the trans-Atlantic slave trade for which trading posts were established along the whole western coast of Africa, it has been chosen by generations of African American and Caribbean militants as a symbol of freedom, redemption, and sovereignty. At the beginning of the twenty-first century, pan-Africanism is trying to acquire new dimensions. The African Union has succeeded the Organization of African Unity (OAU, founded 1963), and a sixth region, that of the diaspora, has been established, even though discussions on the definition of this African diaspora and on the modalities of its claim to the eventual acquisition of an "African citizenship" are still going on. On the occasion of a conference held in Kingston in 2005, which included the African Union, South Africa and the Caribbean states, the contribution of Rastafari as the guardians of the vision of the founders of pan-Africanism was recognized and celebrated.[20] The resilience of the Rastafari in holding on to their identity, and their complete support for the last Ethiopian Emperor, Haile Selassie I, even more than thirty years after the downfall of the Empire, offers to the Ethiopians another representation of themselves and their legacy, located at the heart of the pan-African ethos.

BIBLIOGRAPHY AND FURTHER READING

Bonacci, Giulia, 2010, *Exodus! L'histoire du retour des Rastafariens en Ethiopie*, Paris: L'Harmattan.

———— 2013a, "The Ethiopian World Federation: a Pan-African Organization among the Rastafari in Jamaica", *Caribbean Quarterly*, 59 (2), pp. 73–95.

———— 2013b, "L'irrésistible ascension du *ras* Täfäri dans les imaginaires noirs", *Annales d'Ethiopie*, 28, pp. 157–76.

———— 2013c, "La fabrique du retour en Afrique. Politiques et pratiques de l'appartenance en Jamaïque (1920–1968)", *Revue Européenne des Migrations Internationales*, 29 (3), pp. 33–54.

Brotz, Howard, 1964, *The Black Jews of Harlem. Negro Nationalism and the Dilemmas of Negro Leadership*, London: Macmillan.

Chevannes, Barry, 1994, *Rastafari: Roots and Ideology (Utopianism & Communitarianism)*, Syracuse University Press.

———— 1997, *Rastafari and Other African-Caribbean Worldviews*, Rutgers University Press.

———— 1998, "Rastafari and the Exorcism of the Ideology of Racism and Classism in Jamaica" in N.S. Murrell, Spencer, W.D. and McFarlane, A.A. (eds), *Chanting down Babylon, The Rastafari Reader*, Kingston: Ian Randle Publishers, pp. 55–71.

Drake, S.C., 1970, *The Redemption of Africa and Black Religion*, Chicago/Atlanta: Third World Press, Institute of the Black World.

Garvey, Marcus, 1986, *The Philosophy & Opinions of Marcus Garvey. Or, Africa for the Africans*, Dover: The Majority Press.

Geiss, I., 1968, *The Pan-African Movement. A History of Pan-Africanism in America, Europe and Africa*, New York: Africana Publishing Co.

Harris, Joseph, 1994, *African-American Reactions to War in Ethiopia, 1936–1941*, Baton Rouge: Louisiana State University Press.

Hill, Robert, 2001, *Dread History. Leonard P. Howell and Millenarian Visions in the Early Rastafarian Religion*, Chicago/Kingston: Research Associates School Times, Miguel Lorne Publishers.

MacLeod, Erin, 2014, *Visions of Zion. Ethiopians and Rastafari in the Search for the Promised Land*, New York: New York University Press.

Scott, William R., 1993, *The Sons of Sheba's Race: African-Americans and the Italo-Ethiopian War, 1935–1941*, Bloomington: Indiana University Press.

Ullendorf, Edward, 1968, *Ethiopia and the Bible*, London: Oxford University Press.

6

MONARCHICAL RESTORATION
AND TERRITORIAL EXPANSION

THE ETHIOPIAN STATE IN THE SECOND HALF
OF THE NINETEENTH CENTURY

Shiferaw Bekele

The second half of the nineteenth century made modern Ethiopia in many ways. The era witnessed a continuous reconstruction of the state, which then shaped the nature of developments in the next century. The reinvigorated state then expanded the territorial extent of the kingdom, adding many more ethnic groups than before and giving rise to new challenges in the twentieth century. This enabled the much-expanded country to withstand the threat of the expansionist powers, mostly Britain and Italy, and to keep its independence in a continent that was being colonized from one end to the other. Yet, it lost a part of a historic province (Hamasen, Akele Guzay and Serae, the highlands of Eritrea) to Italian colonialism. The troubled relationship with that former colony of Italy formed one of the dominant themes in the political history of the second half of the twentieth century and threatens to remain important even in this century.[1]

The restoration of the powers and glories of the monarchy lay at the heart of the process of rebuilding the state. This process commenced in 1853. The need for reform stemmed from the political situation of the period called *Zemene Mesafint*, meaning literally "the Era of Lords" (1769–1855). The lords were the *Were Sheh* rulers (sometimes known as the Yejju dynasty) who exercised actual power over the kingdom for seven decades (1786–1853). In this period, the polity was at its weakest. The kings of the Solomonic dynasty were mere *rois fainéants* in the hands of the Were Sheh rulers who governed the country in their name. But they never acquired legitimacy in the eyes of the regional nobility who constantly challenged them. The result was a continuous civil war that sputtered on and off, in one province or another, throughout the period.[2]

In all the turmoil between the 1770s and the 1850s, the legitimacy of the Solomonic kings was never questioned. And all the direct members of the dynasty, even those who were distantly related, prided themselves on their blood connection. The society at large treated them with special consideration, even if each region and each province had its own dynastic ruling house. All these families (with the exception of the Muslim chiefs of Wollo) based their claim to rule their respective domains on an invented or real descent from the Solomonic dynasty. Their standing vis-à-vis each other was affected as much by their degree of closeness to the Solomonic dynasty as by their military prowess or the resources they commanded.[3]

There was therefore a contradictory process in Ethiopia in the Era of Lords. On the one hand, the credibility, power and authority of the Solomonic monarchy had never reached such a low point, while on the other, the legitimacy of the dynasty never waned. For this reason, the Were Sheh rulers never dared to abolish it and take its place or replace it by another dynasty. Nor did they keep the throne empty for any length of time. This fixation on the Solomonic dynasty was not the obsession of the Were Sheh rulers alone. Lord after lord who aspired to control the throne and to rule in the name of the king invariably chose a direct member of this family (a son, grandson or brother of a former king) as puppet *Negus*. They aspired to assume the position of regency because the regency would allow them to exercise all the actual powers of the monarchy.[4]

The Were Sheh rulers never acquired the full authority of the kingship, with perhaps the exception of *Ras* Gugsa (fl.1799–1825) who seems to have effectively ruled over the whole polity. He was obeyed by the nobility in general and imposed his will on the people. Traditions collected from different regions agree that he established peace and effectively governed the kingdom for his whole reign. But his successors (Yimam 1825–28; Marye 1828–31; Dori 1831 and Ali II 1831–53) were made of a different stuff. They never managed to exercise full authority around the country. They were constantly challenged by one or another regional lord. In many cases, they did not win decisive victories. Even members of their own extended family were thorns in their side throughout their stay in power. As a result the kingdom declined into being a rather weak polity. The end result was an atmosphere of uncertainty, constant troop movements, frequent battles followed by looting and mayhem among the people. Thus, the sunset years of the *Zemene Mesafint* were disturbed years.

This weakness reflected directly on the Ethiopian Orthodox Church. It too suffered from this debilitation of the kingdom. The monarchy had always constituted the central administration of the Church up to its complete collapse in the 1780s. The king, rather than the bishop, ran the Church. He regularly appointed the major national ecclesiastical dignitaries—abbots of the major royal monasteries, the *Ichege*, the *Aqabe Sa'at*, and other leading figures. He sat down in judgement on church related disputes and, finally, he looked into doctrinal matters. He called and presided over "religious councils" (synods) to decide on sectarian controversies. They were actually in most cases like royal courts during which sentences were meted out on the recalcitrant sects. The bishop was directly answerable to the king. Below the king, regional governors ran the church and appointed the heads of the monasteries and other regional ecclesiastical dignitaries within their domains. Members of the aristocracy and the nobility—not only men but also women—built, patronized and ran individual churches, or were appointed by the king or by the regional lord to administer specific monasteries. They ran these institutions (for example appointing the clergy) and endowed them with land and other property. Very often they would use their positions, influence and connections to persuade the king to endow "their" churches with extensive lands from which they themselves would become the major beneficiaries.

Thus, the Ethiopian Church was run not by an ecclesiastical administrative structure in the true sense of the word but rather by a state hierarchy, which considered managing the Church one of its functions. The power, authority and glory of the crown rubbed off on the prelates and enhanced their authority, prestige and standing in society. The removal of the monarchy from the centre of power in the last quarter of the eighteenth century deprived the Church of its national administrative institution. The *Zemene Mesafint* was therefore a bad period for the Church. It lacked national leadership. Its problems were further compounded by the doctrinal controversies that steadily sapped its strength and debilitated it. The Were Sheh rulers who were supposed to exercise all the powers and authority of the kingship because of their position as the regents were expected to carry out all the kingly functions of running the Church. Nevertheless, they did not take their duties seriously and the result was that the Church was left in limbo. They neglected the Metropolitan (*Abun*) or they banished him outright. They were surrounded by Muslim lords, clerics and soldiers rather than by their Christian counterparts, as they found the Muslims more amenable to their wishes. So the Church found itself in the rather unenviable situation of an orphan.

To complicate matters, the danger of Egyptian invasion loomed large on the western horizon (Egypt had ruled the Sudan since 1821). Christian Ethiopians saw in this a danger linked to the steady expansion of Islam inside their country. It was in this context of an Islamic upsurge and the absence of peace and stability that Tewodros emerged and inaugurated a new era in Ethiopian history.

For this reason, the *Zemene Mesafint* came to be seen by the populace as a period of disorder, chaos and lawlessness, as a period when there was no central authority, as an era of incessant civil wars between the regional lords for supremacy or, as often as not, for sheer raiding and looting. Were Sheh rulers are remembered as the inept lords of Begemdir fighting irresponsibly with the equally irresponsible rulers of Gojjam or Semien or Tegray or Lasta or Wallo. Historians like to draw parallels between this era and the Biblical Era of the Judges in the history of Israel "when there was no king in Israel: every man did that which was right in his own eyes." (Judges 21:25). "For Ethiopia", in the words of Paul Henze in his general history of Ethiopia, "the second half of this formulation could better be phrased: every leader did what he thought advantageous to him and his region."[5]

The rise of Tewodros II and the restoration of the monarchy (1855–1868)

Tewodros brought the *Zemene Mesafint* to an end in 1853 when he decisively defeated *Ras* Ali II (1831–53), the last Wara Sheh ruler, at the battle of Ayshal in Gojjam on 29 June 1853. It was not an easy road. He had to fight every inch of the way to supreme power. He was a formidable warrior. His brilliant victories over far larger armies and his exceptional exploits on the battlefield seem to have captured the imagination of the Ethiopians of his generation and subsequent generations were to see him as a larger than life hero.

For all his fame among Ethiopians (Tewodros is a household name literally), our knowledge of the man leaves much to be desired. We only know the outline of his life. He was born around 1820—nobody is sure about the exact date of his birth—in the town of Gondar. His given name was Kassa (Tewodros was his regnal name). His father must have been a member of the nobility who died early in his son's life, while our knowledge of his mother is rather fuzzy. She seems to have belonged to a family of the high clergy which had fallen on bad days, so that she was forced to become a peddler of *kosso* (herbal medicine) on the open market of Gondar. Hence, in his years of prominence, he was constantly insulted as the son of the *kosso* vendor.

This family background gave him a reasonable starting point for his future career because his paternal half-brother, Dejazmatch Kenfu, was an important lord of the period, who governed a major province (fl.1826–39). After finishing church education, his brother took him into his court as a page, this being a way of training young members of the nobility in manners, administration, justice and the politics of the day. Kenfu was a marcher lord as he governed the frontier districts with Egyptian Sudan. Kenfu fought one major battle with the Egyptians (1838) and emerged as the victor. This must have left a lasting imprint on the mind of the teenager Kassa, who must have drawn a few conclusions of long lasting significance—the need for a modern army equipped with up-to-date firearms and the need to modernize state and society.

Kenfu died in 1839 and this left Kassa an "orphan" because he had to look for another master. The years following the death of his half-brother are the most obscure in the young man's life. Eventually in the early 1840s we find him a rebel in the western lowlands. He must have proved himself a tough rebel because the governor of the province was forced to concede his demands to bring him back to peaceful life.

Kassa kept going into rebellion several times and emerging more powerful out of each round. After the second rebellion he was given the hand of none other than the daughter of Ali II, and his third rebellion was so strong that the rulers agreed to raise him to the high rank of *dejazmach* and to make him the governor of the former provinces of his half-brother, in the hope of making him a loyal lord. This was in 1848. His last rebellion was the most decisive because it enabled him to defeat several powerful lords one after another, the last being Ali II himself. This was in June 1853. He did not show any sign of ruling in the old way as a king-maker in his turn. Instead he claimed full-fledged monarchical rank with the highly symbolic regnal name of Tewodros ("the one brought forth by God") on 11 February 1855. In so doing, he announced far-reaching changes in the political history of the ancient polity.[6]

His coronation meant the abolition of the old Solomonic dynasty, which had ruled the country in a direct line since 1270. The dynasty had led the country through thick and thin. It certainly did not save the country from incessant rebellions and civil wars, but it had acquired a religious and a political legitimacy. Even during the height of the fratricidal wars of the late eighteenth and early nineteenth centuries, nobody wanted to replace it. All the coalitions of lords were faithful to it and sought to rule in its name by putting a member of the dynasty on the throne. So if anything demonstrated the blind loyalty of the Ethiopians to the dynasty, it was precisely the *Zemene Mesafint*, the period in which the monarchy was at its weakest. Now Tewodros did away with it at one stroke. It is true that he claimed that he had Solomonic blood, even if it was through a rather distant relationship. Nobody took him seriously. The son of a *kosso* vendor on the open market of Gondar (whatever the truth of that insult) would never qualify for the *royal bed* of the country (the Ethiopians did not have the tradition of sitting their kings on thrones, it was on beds that the kings sat and thus the Amharic for bed, *alga*, became the synonym for throne). Indeed, the young king faced the serious problem of legitimacy from day one. While he planned to march to the two important provinces not yet brought under his rule, Wollo and Shoa, in the weeks following his coronation, his enemies were conspiring to organize a widespread rebellion against him. Unlike him, they hailed from the more illustrious and established regional dynasties.

The lack of legitimacy was one side of the coin. The other side was the bold vision, which the sheer act of the coronation inaugurated—of a strong, centralizing monarchy. In bringing about the restoration of the kingship, Tewodros was addressing the problem that had bedevilled the Ethiopian state since the last quarter of the eighteenth century—a weak monarchy.

His plan to march first to Wollo and then to Shoa seems to have been motivated by a number of factors. Wollo and the adjoining province of Yejju were the native area of the Were Sheh dynasty whose rule Tewodros had brought to an end. Ali II and his mother Menen had quite naturally fled to Wollo after their final defeat in June 1853 and they were busy organizing resistance and a possible comeback. Tewodros was also driven by the hope of converting the local Muslim population to Christianity. The Ethiopian polity had been a Christian state since the conversion of Ezana to Christianity in the fourth century, but since the last quarter of the eighteenth century, Islam had made strong inroads among the Wollo Oromo.[7] The menace of Egyptian expansion heightened the danger of Islam in the eyes of the rulers. Tewodros, who was a near mystic, hoped to address both the political and the religious problem.

His march to Shoa was intended to reunify that old province with the kingdom. Shoa had developed its own state institutions over the last century and a half, until it had evolved into a full-fledged kingdom. Recapturing Shoa was the dream of more than one king of Gondar. After a few weeks of festivities and preparations, the new king set out from Debre Tabor in April 1855. He quickly subdued the chiefs of Wollo while Ali and his main followers disappeared into remote gorges and mountain fastnesses. He appointed a member of the local ruling house to govern the province from Meqdela, a mountain stronghold that Tewodros's suicide later in 1868 would raise to the status of an icon in the minds of educated Ethiopians of the second half of the twentieth century.

It must have been with a tremendous sense of euphoria that the young monarch proceeded to Shoa. The kingdom put up a clumsy resistance that was quashed without much difficulty; its king died of natural causes and the nobility surrendered the young son of the king, Menelik.

But this first success was somewhat deceptive and he spent the following months fighting off a string of provincial rebellions—in Gojjam, in Semien, in Wollo—that were to prove more and more intractable as time went on, driving his punitive measures to become increasingly harsh and brutal.

But Tewodros was also the first Ethiopian king in over two centuries to think of forging a close relationship with European powers. He believed that he could do so on the basis that both the European states and his own state were Christian and that, for this reason, either Britain or another leading European power would help him in his confrontation with Muslim Egypt. He believed that one or the other of these states would extend to him "technical assistance", in today's parlance—namely, skilled men who could teach his people the military crafts he needed. But he does not seem to have grasped the facts about the international leading powers of his time. Britain and France had great colonial empires and were vying with each other for even greater empires and influence. In this rivalry, they cared little for religious solidarity. They were rather driven by the hard-headed pursuit of their national interests and had a dim view of the powers and capacities of African kings and polities. For them an African monarch was no more than a tribal chief with pompous titles. Racism was the order of the day in Europe at the time.

Unaware of this situation, Tewodros wrote a letter to Queen Victoria in 1862 in which he explained to her how and why he came to power and the danger his country faced from Egypt. His request was simple—technical assistance and help from his Christian brothers in his confrontations with the Muslim foes. He laid great hopes on his initiative. The British however were not impressed and did not even bother to send back a courtesy reply. When their letter never came, Tewodros was deeply offended. He did not have different options to express his feelings to the British. So he had recourse to a rather undiplomatic measure—he put the Europeans at his court in custody until the British responded to him. It was a move that finally gave a jolt to the bureaucrats in London. They sent a courteous but empty letter. This made things worse and Tewodros decided to add their consul and envoy to the hostages. When finally it dawned on the British that the matter was very serious, they decided to send an army to secure the release of the hostages and punish the king. They spent considerable sums of money and fitted out a big expeditionary corps which landed at Zula, a little to the south of the harbour town of Massawa, at the end of 1867.

In the meantime, Tewodros's situation in the country had not improved. He had never succeeded in fully quelling any of the rebellions and establishing peace and order. In fact, the rebellions had slowly expanded over the whole kingdom. By 1865, it was clear that his days were numbered. The vision of a centralizing monarchy and a strong state foundered on the hard rock of regional resistance. By the end of 1867, when the British were preparing to land their expeditionary force, the Emperor controlled only a few districts around his capital. Three powerful lords had already emerged as potential successors and they were busy positioning themselves to take over the "bed" of Tewodros. They were Gobaze of Lasta, Kassa Mercha of Tegray and Menelik of Shoa.

In fact, as early as 1865, Menelik had declared himself "King of Kings of Ethiopia", the traditional title of the Ethiopian emperors. He controlled no more than his native province and so the title served more as a proclamation of his aspirations rather than an expression of the reality. As for Gobaze, he was busy establishing his suzerainty over the lords of central Ethiopia. Kassa's opportunity to strengthen himself came through the British. When they landed at Massawa, they asked him to collaborate with them by opening the road through which they would pass and supplying them with provisions. In return, they promised firearms. Kassa jumped at the offer.

As a result, the British did not face any resistance on their way to Meqdela, the mountain stronghold that Tewodros had converted into his last fortress. Abandoned by his people and surrounded by his enemies, he waited for the last duel with the British. When they reached Meqdela, he went into his last battle on 13 April 1868, the Good Friday of that year. His troops were mown down by superior firepower, killing the army commander Gebre, one of his best generals. On the third day, when the British stormed the fortress Tewodros committed suicide rather than surrendering. This romantic suicide fired the imagination of subsequent generations of Ethiopians and fuelled their national pride. They saw in it an act of undaunted courage and defiance against a much superior enemy. The British released the hostages and then marched out of the country without trying any form of occupation or control. On their way out, they kept their promise and gave some of their (outdated) firearms to Kassa. This changed the balance of forces between the three regional potentates who were vying for national power.[8]

It is traditional among historians to discuss the complex legacy of Tewodros. He left Ethiopia more divided than when he found it; and yet he started the process of national revival, which his successors kept building on. He had envisioned his national revival to be guided by a strong monarchy but he had opened the way for regional potentates to aspire for the kingly "bed" by abolishing the Solomonic dynasty. To make up for his lack of legitimacy, he had come up with a neo-Solomonic identity which his successors later built on by putting forward their own claims of belonging to the hallowed dynasty, weaving symbols and rituals around it. Tewodros had attempted to address some of the fundamental issues of the day, and one of these was the question of strengthening the Ethiopian Orthodox Church, then an important arm of the state as we have seen. He also took measures to contain Islam, at least in Wollo. These twin policies were not successful in his days but his successors were to implement them with a greater degree of success. His move to reunify Shoa was a seminal measure because it put on the national agenda a policy of territorial expansion as an integral element of the rebuilding of a powerful state. Yet in the years following his death, Ethiopia was once more territorially divided and ruled by three "kings" for the next ten years.

Ethiopia divided: a decade of competition for the kingly bed (1868–78)

The competition for the kingly bed passed through two stages. The first was between the three lords (Gobaze, Kassa and Menelik), which we have already mentioned; it lasted three years (1868–71). In that first phase the three lords—Gobaze, Kassa and Menelik—all aspired to the position of king of kings. Gobaze was the first to assert his claim. Shortly after the death of Tewodros, he got himself crowned and took the name of Tekle Giyorgis. But his army was quickly routed and the hapless king was captured, blinded and relegated to a mountain top where he died.

The second phase (1872–78) was between Menelik, who had assumed the title of King of Kings as early as 1865, and Kassa, who had become Emperor Yohannes IV in 1872. For six years (1872–78), the kingdom was divided into two more or less equal halves ruled by these two monarchs. Yohannes devoted the years 1873 to 1875 to the task of establishing his authority over all the provinces of the kingdom—that is, over the central and southern regions. Menelik too prepared himself for the final showdown. The powerful lords of Begemder, the central provinces and Gojjam "entered" into Yohannes's court one after another. Just before Yohannes confronted Menelik, the Egyptians moved into the territory he controlled by way of Massawa and marched to the Mereb River. He suspended all activities in central Ethiopia and veered to the north to face the Egyptians. Fortunately for him, he scored a quick victory over their "superior" army at the battle of Gundet in October 1875. Egypt was humiliated and its imperial ambitions over Ethiopia were frustrated. But it decided to try again, sending a much bigger and better equipped army. The two sides met in Akkele Guzay (today part of Eritrea) and Yohannes defeated the invaders again in March 1876. It took him some time to stabilize the situation in the northern frontier provinces, so it was only in late 1877 that he could turn his attention to his last rival.

Menelik did not sit idle either. He made strenuous efforts to prepare himself for the final showdown with Yohannes. Nevertheless, Yohannes's army had been armed with firearms left behind by the British, which gave him the edge over the other lords and had ensured his victory over Tekle Giyorgis. He was now even more strengthened by arms collected from the battlefield where he had defeated the Egyptians. And his army was now fully battle tried. Yohannes marched into Shoa in the spring of 1878 and when Menelik realized that the enemy enjoyed a clear superiority over his own forces, he decided to "enter"—to recognize the suzerainty of the Emperor and to abandon his title of king of kings, settling down to that of simple king, ready to pay tribute. On the other hand, Yohannes did not feel strong enough to demand that Menelik abandon his kingship. Therefore, the two compromised in March 1878 and after many years of turmoil, Ethiopia came again to have a single monarch who was recognized by all the lords of the country as their suzerain. The new sovereign was a strong ruler with a formidable army under his command who became the law of the country.[9]

This year (1878) marked in fact the culmination of the long process started by Tewodros in spite of the serious weaknesses from which the kingship had suffered. One of these was the fact that the monarchy was no more than a regional court glorified as a national institution. The fact that Yohannes maintained his court for much of his reign in Tegray (in Adwa in the earlier years and in Mekelle in his later years) went far to underscore the regional character of his kingship. For this reason it did not really enjoy a higher legitimacy than the claim of any other lord belonging to a regional ruling house.

Now that his status as the supreme sovereign of the country was confirmed by his last and most powerful rival, Yohannes turned his attention to the other major political and religious problems of the country—the divisions within the Ethiopian Orthodox Church and the growing expansion of Islam. As the king of the country, it was his duty to give guidance and leadership to the Church. The Church had been rocked by sectarian divisions since the first half of the seventeenth century. The situation had sunk to the lowest depths during the *Zemene Mesafint*, when the Church was paralyzed. Tewodros had been the first to address the issue even before he put the crown on his head, when he had summoned the Metropolitan and the leading ecclesiastical officials in and around Gondar to his court in the summer of 1854. During this gathering he ruled that the sectarian tendencies were outlawed and Orthodoxy reaffirmed through the preponderance of the authority of the Metropolitan. Like much else that he initiated, this was a false start. He quarrelled with the bishop and other leading Church dignitaries only two years later and the Church renewal had ground to a halt. But Yohannes took it up again. He summoned all the leading ecclesiastical dignitaries, and the leading spokesmen of the three sects, and held a council at Boru Meda in Wello in the presence of all the major lords of the country including Menelik. He ruled that the sects should abjure their doctrines and take the Orthodox line again or else face excommunication and persecution. The presence of the regional lords gave weight to the ruling. It was implemented around the country. The Church was finally reunited. After a century of neglect, the monarchy gave it a strong leadership and direction. Henceforth, Ethiopian Orthodox Christianity revived and expanded.[10]

He also addressed the question of Islam, and here he adopted a hard line of suppression. He declared to the people of Wollo that they had to convert to Christianity or face persecution. This decree was not as successful as that reorganizing the Church, as it met with the hard resistance of the Wollo Muslims. Yohannes responded with even harsher repression.[11]

Whatever the specific nature of the policies he adopted, it is clear that during 1878 the strong state the Ethiopians had been dreaming of since the last quarter of the eighteenth century had emerged. It was this state that was later to organize the territorial expansion of the country, eventually making it twice as large as it had been up to then. It was also this state that managed to withstand the powerful imperialist onslaughts of the subsequent two decades and ensured the survival of Ethiopia, the only independent traditional state in a colonized African continent.

Foreign aggression and internal expansion (1878–96)

The most remarkable feature of Ethiopia after 1878 was its dynamic expansion in the western, southern and south-eastern directions. It was Menelik who organized this empire building. He was not the first to start it. Nevertheless, expansion reached a high point under his command. He launched it as one of his major agendas soon after his declaration of rebellion against Tewodros in 1865. Between that year and 1878, he set out on a series of campaigns that eventually pushed the limits of his territory all the way to the Gibe River in the west.

He also moved his capital from northern Shoa further to the west, to Entoto, in the hills overlooking the present city of Addis Ababa. Entoto remained a major centre of his activities until 1886 when he decided to create a "modern" city and founded Addis Ababa. Menelik's armies marched out of Entoto in two principal directions—western and southern. The expansion to the west was commanded by the redoubtable general Ras Gobena Dachi, who had entered the service of Menelik from the beginning of his reign. Most of the western territories inhabited by the Oromo were conquered by this general between the years 1879 and 1886.

The expansion to the south split into two directions. One of them was into the Rift Valley, into areas inhabited by the Silte, the Kambata and the Hadiya, after which the army pushed further south into Wolayta. The other direction was to the Arsi and Bale plateau. The plateau was conquered between 1882 and 1890—a rather protracted undertaking because of the stiff resistance put up by the local population. The last major conquest was the Harar plateau, which was incorporated at the beginning of 1887. In the same year commenced the slow process of establishing Ethiopian rule over the Somali-peopled lowlands.

Ten years after the submission to Yohannes, Menelik had dramatically increased the size of the country he controlled. His success can be explained by several factors. First he was able to integrate the Shoan Oromo and the Gurage into his administration and into his forces very early in his career. This enabled him to recruit a much larger army than he could otherwise have done. Moreover, his success attracted able-bodied men from the northern provinces and the former soldiers of the armies of Tewodros and Tekle Giyorgis who had been cast adrift upon the death of their masters. This swelled the ranks of his armies and in all the engagements after 1878 he was able to put into the field more troops than any of his foes.

Even though Yohannes was the King of Kings and Menelik his vassal, the latter's court became a greater centre of attraction not only to many men of central Ethiopia but also to people from overseas. Foreigners of many hues and colours—merchants and adventurers, diplomats and missionaries, men of shady character and noble figures—flocked to the court in Entoto. Among them were arms dealers whose usefulness Menelik appreciated. Italy and France competed to sell arms to the Shoan king, allowing Menelik to equip ever larger armies and ensuring a technological advantage over any potential adversary after 1882.

The leadership factor occupies an important place here. Menelik's diplomatic genius was recognized by friends and foes alike, by Ethiopians and foreigners in his own lifetime. He was a man with a tremendous organizational capacity and a military strategist of no mean proportions. In addition he showed himself to be a first class tactician in the battles in which he participated as a commander. In addition to his own personal leadership qualities, he surrounded himself, for the most part, with men of high calibre, both Ethiopian and foreign.[12]

A combination of these factors goes a long way towards explaining the remarkable success of Ethiopia in carving out an empire at a time when the Europeans were scrambling all around it to build their own empires on the continent. Yet, empire building was never a smooth ride, particularly for those who were being conquered. The Ethiopian empire was built by iron and fire.[13] Tears, suffering and blood was the fate of many conquered communities. A considerable proportion of their arable land was confiscated and given to the Ethiopian soldiers and their commanders. Some of the peasants were turned into the serfs and tenants of the conquerors. The obligations were onerous. All this had of course an ethnic dimension—a good proportion of the conquerors were Amhara and even the Oromo and Gurage soldiers spoke Amharic and professed Orthodox Christianity. Regardless of their real origins these traits made them "Amhara" in the eyes of the local population.[14]

The tribulations of the conquest and the hardships the empire brought remained engraved in the historical memory of the conquered people. The expansion brought into the Ethiopian polity over 90 per cent of the Oromo people (a small segment fell under British rule in what later became Kenya) and they came to constitute the largest ethnic group in the country. With the onset of modernization and the spread of Western ideas of equality in the twentieth century, some of the Oromo elite did not see any reason why they should be subjected to the rule of other ethnic groups. They nursed the memory of the circumstances in which their people were incorporated into the country. In like manner, as the country entered the twentieth century, the Somalis found it difficult to identify themselves with the old Ethiopian state. Identity is not something that comes easy. It takes time to forge a nation out of an empire—out of a cauldron of peoples, cultures and religions. All this was left for the future.

At the time, there were new challenges as a young European imperialist power came barging in with a hungry appetite for land even before the Ethiopian empire formation was consummated. That country was Italy.

The story of Italy's aggression against Ethiopia was a rather complicated and long affair. Italy first established its control in 1869 over a small port on the Red Sea, Assab. It was in 1885, over a decade and a half later, that the Italians took over Massawa courtesy of the British. As soon as they landed in the historic port, they set out into the interior. This brought them face to face with Yohannes. But at that time he was locked in a dangerous combat with the Islamist rulers of the Sudan, the Mahdists.

The Mahdists had risen against their Turco-Egyptian rulers, expelled them from the Sudan and established the Mahdiyya state in 1885. They managed to encircle some of the retreating Egyptian troops in frontier towns between Eritrea and the Sudan (Kassala was the most important garrison) and along the Ethio-Sudan boundary line. The British who had by now become the masters of Egypt decided to persuade Yohannes to help the Turco-Egyptian forces to break out of their besieged garrisons so as to leave for their country.[15] After some negotiation, the Ethiopian sovereign agreed to help his former enemies. In return, the British would restore the districts occupied by the Egyptians over ten years earlier. But this agreement was never fully implemented by the British. It was the Italians rather than the Ethiopians who eventually took over the old occupied territories which now constitute the lowland provinces of Eritrea.

The Ethiopian king found himself in serious trouble after making this agreement. The Mahdists would never forgive him for extending assistance to their mortal enemies who also happened to be his enemies. On the other hand the British, who had refused to restore Massawa to Ethiopia but had agreed to keep it themselves, decided to hand it over to the Italians who were driven by a keen desire to carve out a colonial empire in the north-eastern corner of Africa. The clashes with Mahdist forces came first because Yohannes had to send his armies to relieve the Egyptian garrisons. From the latter part of 1884 onwards, the two sides got engaged in a ferocious war that was to last five years. It was in the midst of this complicated situation that the Italians landed at Massawa and started to inch their way into the interior. Ethiopia protested but to no avail.

In January 1887, the Ethiopians scored their first dramatic victory over a small but well equipped Italian unit at a place called Dogali, not far from Massawa.[16] This did not deter the colonizers. The next year Yohannes led a big army and reached the lowlands not far from Massawa. His foes dug in. It was not easy for Ethiopians to dislodge a fortified enemy, owing to their lack of modern artillery. In the meantime, the Mahdist forces had scored a devastating victory over an Ethiopian army in the west, had marched all the way to the historic city of Gondar where they burned down churches and killed men, women and children or took them into slavery. The Ethiopian situation was very dire.

To complicate matters, Yohannes received rumours that his two very powerful vassals—Negus (king) Teklehaimanot of Gojjam and Negus Menelik of Shoa—were conspiring against him. So he decided to turn his attention to the south to deal with his recalcitrant lords. He made a forced march to Gojjam where he devastated that province in order to punish its lord.

This forced march into Gojjam also became an unintended way of disseminating rinderpest into central Ethiopia. It had been brought into the Massawa area, perhaps by the cattle the Italian army had bought on the Arabian or the Indian market in late 1887 or early 1888. The disease quickly spread in Gojjam, moved very fast to other parts of the country and devastated the cattle. This led to a great famine that came to be called by the people of Ethiopia *Kifu Qen* (the Terrible Period).

Then Yohannes marched to the Ethio-Sudanese borderlands to deal with the Mahdist threat. On 9 March 1889, the two sides got locked in a major battle during which Yohannes was mortally wounded, leading the Ethiopian army to disband. Much more than the Mahdist victory, what turned out to be of far-reaching consequences for the future history of the country was the death of Yohannes.

Following the death of this Emperor, Menelik simply proceeded to assume the imperial office. He did not have to work much for this because by this time he was clearly the most powerful lord in the empire, both in terms of natural and human resources and because of the strength of his armies. The lords of central Ethiopia who had been loyal to Yohannes found it politically wise to submit to the Shoan king without much ado. But while the court of Yohannes had been no more than a regional court, the old Solomonic monarchy had been a truly national institution, supreme over provincial interests and identities. When Tewodros had abolished the Solomonic dynasty and taken its place, his rule became identified with his native province of Quara. It was the same with Yohannes whose Tigrean association was underlined even more by the fact that the king maintained his court for much of his reign in his native region rather than in Gondar or Debre Tabor. So, as a result, succession for Menelik did not pose any particular challenge of legitimacy.

But the Tigrean nobility did not see it that way. They were bitterly disappointed that the crown had been taken out of their region. And although they could not marshal resources to get it back, they nursed a form of resentment which got passed down to their descendants, all the way down to the twentieth century.

But at the time Menelik wanted the Italians to recognize him as the King of Kings of Ethiopia—an important consideration in order to deny his Tigrean and other rivals the opportunity of getting firearms and other help. On their part, the Italians were anxious to obtain the new ruler's recognition of the strip of land they had occupied in the hinterland of Massawa. They were also hopeful that Menelik would accept the status of an Italian protectorate. In the treaty that the two sides signed in the same year in the locality of Wichale, the wishes of the signatories were fulfilled with the exception of the protectorate issue, which was worded in an ambiguous manner. Nevertheless, when the Italians claimed that Ethiopia had become their protectorate, Menelik protested and expressed repeatedly his determination to maintain independence.[17] So Italy had no choice but to go to war to impose its rule on a country that was not yet colonized by the major colonial powers. The war of invasion started in 1895.

Ethiopia was in a much stronger position to face the Italians in 1895 than it had been before. It was under a strong state and its natural and human resources had grown greatly. On 1 March 1896 the climax of the war took place at Adwa. The Ethiopians won the day with a resounding victory and that victory ensured their survival in the new colonial era.[18]

Indeed, survive they did, but with a historic part of their polity amputated by Italy. These were the highland districts and a considerable proportion of the lowlands of what became the colony of Eritrea. The Ethiopians always regretted this fact in the future decades, much in the same way the French bitterly resented the cession of Alsace and Lorraine to Germany in 1871. When they got the opportunity after the Second World War, the Ethiopians carried out a protracted diplomatic struggle to win it back. They succeeded. In the meantime, however, things had changed in Eritrea. The people were not exactly the same as their grandfathers who had been separated from their Ethiopian brethren at the end of the nineteenth century. Colonial rule had changed their mentality and profoundly modified their sense of identity. And this led to a protracted and bitter war to separate from Ethiopia— another major theme of Ethiopian history in the second half of the twentieth century.[19]

The victory of Adwa gave immense prestige to Menelik both at home and abroad. The neighbouring colonial powers (Britain and France) and the former aspirant colonizer, Italy, hastened to sign treaties of friendship and boundary agreements. Thus, Ethiopia acquired the shape it has today in the years following that victory. On 26 October 1896 Italy agreed to recognize the full sovereignty and independence of Ethiopia and also agreed on provisional boundary delimitation between Eritrea and Ethiopia. With Italy thus renouncing its protectorate claims over the African polity, the British and the French decided to follow suit, and they recognized the sovereignty and independence of Ethiopia in 1897. In addition, they signed boundary delimitation agreements (the British between their colony of British Somaliland and Ethiopia and the French between their colony of French Somaliland—today's Djibouti—and Ethiopia). Later, two negotiations were conducted with the British to delimit the boundary between the Sudan and Ethiopia on the one hand (1902) and between Kenya and Ethiopia (1908) on the other.

Menelik signed four delimitation agreements with Italy, three of them regarding Eritrea and Ethiopia (1900, 1902, 1908) and the fourth (1908) regarding Somalia and Ethiopia. These four agreements with the Italians turned out to be constant sources of friction between the two sides after they were signed since the Italians, unlike the British and the French, were dragging their feet. They continued to harbour expansionist designs towards Ethiopia and because there was no clear demarcation, the boundaries between Ethiopia and the two former Italian colonies became explosive issues in the first half of the twentieth century, which eventually led to the brief Italian conquest of 1935–41. And in a way we can say that both Eritrea and Somalia are problems that still haunt today's Ethiopia.[20]

In any case, at the end of the nineteenth century, Ethiopia succeeded in overcoming colonial pressures; it obtained international recognition as a sovereign state, no mean achievement at the height of colonialism; it got its boundaries delimited. And yet the underlying challenge remained: modernization. There was growing realization among the rulers that, if their country had to keep its independence, it had to modernize.

The last years of the Menelik era to 1916

Menelik responded to that challenge, albeit in haphazard fashion, partly because he was not prepared by background and by education to confront the problem and partly because the parameters of modernization escaped him. He therefore agreed to the building of a railway line to the coast (construction started in Djibouti in 1897, the line reaching Dire Dawa in 1902 and Addis Ababa in 1917), had telegraph and telephone lines erected, started the process of modern education (the first public school was opened in 1907), and acquired a number of technical tools (cars, machines) for which there was only scant need at the time. A seminal measure he introduced was the establishment of ministries and a council of ministers in 1907. This move was no more than cosmetic at the time, but once introduced the institutions took a life of their own. Therefore 1907 is taken as the year which saw the beginning of the modernization of the millennia-old Ethiopian state.[21]

The regional foundation of the kingship since the coronation of Tewodros in 1855 continued to characterize the monarchy. The court in Addis Ababa was still regarded as a Shoan court. And this perception and the concomitant reality came out fully in the protracted succession strife that followed the incapacitation of Menelik from 1907 onwards. Menelik was getting old and he was also suffering from a serious illness. The question of who would succeed him became urgent. He addressed it by naming his grandson Iyasu (he did not have a son) as his successor in 1909, a choice that was far from popular with various circles at the court. The powerful consort of the ailing king,

Taytu, wanted to keep the reins of power in her firm hands and Iyasu was not her grandson. She started to jockey for position but, after a period of crises, she was removed from power in 1910. Then there was another attempt by Ras Abate (1911), which again generated a political crisis. The forces loyal to the heir apparent overcame the challenge. After 1912, Iyasu started to operate as the ruler of Ethiopia even though the old king was still alive, if only barely. Menelik was suffering from a form of complete paralysis that had left him speechless and unconscious. He finally died in 1913.

Born in 1897, Iyasu was only fifteen when he took the reins of power into his hands in 1912. A couple of years later, the First World War broke out, which complicated matters for the young ruler. He had neither the experience nor the personal discipline that would have allowed him to carry out his duties as a monarch. He surrounded himself with sycophants and alienated a large number of the powerful lords by his irresponsible decisions and his unruly youthful behaviour. The move that eventually undid him was his diplomatic approach to Mohamed Abdille Hassan, dubbed the "Mad Mullah" by the colonial authorities in British Somaliland. Iyasu also befriended several important Muslim families and even visited mosques. This was not behaviour expected from a Christian monarch and it turned the Christian nobility against him. In addition, his Islamic sympathies alienated the colonial powers, since the Ottoman Empire was trying its best to use its position as the seat of the Caliphate to turn Islamic communities against France, Britain and Italy at the height of the Great War.[22]

Iyasu was overthrown by a coalition of lords in a coup d'état in September 1916. The obscure daughter of Menelik, Zewditu, was propped up on the throne while the young Ras Tafari Makonnen (the future Haile Selassie) was designated as the heir apparent. For the next fourteen years, the two ruled the country in uneasy tandem. And it was only with the accession of Tafari to power in 1930 that Ethiopia can be said to have truly entered the twentieth century.

In spite of its long history, Ethiopia entered the twentieth century with a state ruled by a monarchy that was basically a Shoan monarchy. Its people, its chiefs and the newly incorporated provinces had not yet adopted an Ethiopian national identity. The traditional national ethos, symbolism and historical experience that constituted the foundation of the identity of the people of the historic core of Ethiopia could not easily be used for the newly incorporated people of the empire because they had strong religious and ethnic traits, distinct from those of the Shoans. These underlying factors gave the empire a considerable fragility. Realizing these dangers, Haile Selassie was to make serious efforts at creating a modern and secular Ethiopian nationalism. He exerted tremendous efforts to make his court a truly national institution. But he did not fully succeed because many of the civil wars and conflicts which the country went through after the World War II sprang precisely from the ethno-regional forces that refused to accept the Ethiopian national identity.[23]

Whatever were the shortcomings of colonialism, Africa—with the exception of Ethiopia—was initiated into modernization by the white rulers. Unlike their brethren elsewhere on the continent, Ethiopians were guided into the modern world by their own rulers who themselves did not have a deep knowledge of the new global forces. The ruling class in the second decade of the twentieth century did not count a single person with university education. Tafari inherited literally a handful of Ethiopians with experience of travel to Europe where they got some education. These were neither competent nor sufficient in numbers for the enormous task of national transformation.

The economy was still largely at the stage of barter exchange. Crude media of exchange (bars of salt, bullets, rifles, etc.) were also used. An imported silver coin (the regionally circulating Maria Theresa thaler coin) was used only for luxury items and for the purchase of strategic commodities (firearms and land for example). With an economy not yet monetized and no valuable minerals, Ethiopia would be hard put to find the wherewithal for the financing of modernization. The external environment was not very suitable, either. European powers considered Ethiopia an anomaly because it was not colonized. And they believed that the best avenue for its development was colonization. The international organizations—the UN, World Bank, IMF, etc.—that were to lend money or provide assistance in other ways to the developing countries were still far off in the future.

When all is considered, it can be said that Ethiopia entered the modern era with enormous structural disadvantages which its national pride was at great pains to hide under the mantle of its past glories.

BIBLIOGRAPHY AND FURTHER READING

Abdussamad H. Ahmad and Pankhurst, Richard (eds), 1998, *Adwa Victory Centenary Conference*, Addis Ababa: Institute of Ethiopian Studies.

Abir, Mordechai, 1968, *Ethiopia, The Era of the Princes. The Challenge of Islam and the Re-unification of the Christian Empire, 1760–1855*, London: Praeger.

Arnold, Percy, 1992, *Prelude to Magdala*: *Emperor Theodore of Ethiopia and British Diplomacy*, ed. by R. Pankhurst, London: Bellew.

Bahru Zewde, 1991, *A History of Modern Ethiopia, 1855–1974*, Athens: Ohio University Press.

———— 2002, *Pioneers of Change in Ethiopia. The Reformist Intellectuals of the Early 20th Century*, Oxford, Athens, Addis Ababa, James Currey: Ohio University Press, Addis Ababa University Press.

Bairu Tafla (ed.), 1977, *A Chronicle of Emperor Yohannes IV (1872–89)*, Wiesbaden: Franz Steiner.

Bairu Tafla, 2000, *Ethiopian Records of the Menilek Era. Selected Amharic Documents from the Nachlaß of Alfred Ilg 1884–1900*, Wiesbaden: Harrassowitz.

Biasio, Elisabeth, 2004, *Prunk und Pracht am Hofe Menileks: Alfred Ilgs Äthiopien um 1900. Majesty and Magnificence at the Court of Menilek: Alfred Ilg's Ethiopia around 1900*, Zürich: Verlag Neue Zürcher Zeitung.

Brownlie, Ian, 1979, *African Boundaries: a Legal and Diplomatic Encyclopaedia*, London: Hurst.

Bulatovich, A., 2000, *Ethiopia through Russian Eyes. A Country in Transition (1896–1898)*, Lawrenceville, N.J.: The Red Sea Press.

Caulk, Richard A., 1971 a, "The Occupation of Harar: January 1887", *Journal of Ethiopian Studies*, 9 (2), pp. 1–20.

———— 1971 b, "Yohannes IV, the Mahdists, and the Colonial Partition of North-East Africa", *TransAfrican Journal of History*, 1 (2), pp. 22–42.

———— 1972, "Religion and State in Nineteenth Century Ethiopia", *Journal of Ethiopian Studies*, 10 (1), pp. 23–42.

———— 2002, *"Between the Jaws of Hyenas": A Diplomatic History of Ethiopia (1876–1896)*, Wiesbaden: Harrassowitz.

Crummey, Donald, 1969, "Tewodros as a Reformer and Modernizer", *Journal of African History*, 10 (3), pp. 457–69.

———— 1975, "Society and Ethnicity in the Politics of Christian Ethiopia During the Zemene Mesafint", *International Journal of African Historical Studies*, 8 (2), pp. 266–78.

———— 1986, "Banditry and Resistance: Noble and Peasant in 19th Century Ethiopia", in D. Crummey (ed.), *Banditry Rebellion and Social Protest in Africa*, London, J. Currey/Portsmouth, NH: Heinemann, ch. 6.

———— 1988, "Imperial Legitimacy and the Creation of Neo-Solomonic Ideology in the 19th Century Ethiopian History, 1830–1868", *Cahier d'Etudes Africaines*, 28/109, pp. 13–43.

Donham, Donald L. and James, Wendy (eds), 1986, *The Southern Marches of Imperial Ethiopia: Essays in History and Social Anthropology*, Oxford: James Currey.

Erlich, Haggai, 1986, *Ethiopia and the Challenge of Independence*, Boulder, CO: Lynne Rienner Publishers.

—— 1994, *Ethiopia and the Middle East*, Boulder, CO: Lynne Rienner.

—— 1996, *Ras Alula and the Scramble for Africa: A Political Biography. Ethiopia & Eritrea, 1875–1897*, Lawrenceville, NJ: The Red Sea Press.

Ficquet, Eloi and Smidt, Wolbert (eds), 2014, *The Life and Times of* Lïj *Iyasu of Ethiopia*, Berlin, Münster, Zürich: LIT Verlag.

Fontaine, Hugues, 2012, *African Train. Un Train en Afrique. Djibouti-Ethiopie*, Addis Ababa: CFEE, Shama Books.

Gebru Tareke, 1991, *Ethiopia: Power and Protest. Peasant Revolts in the Twentieth Century*, Cambridge University Press.

Henze, Paul, 2000, *Layers of Time: A History of Ethiopia*, London: Hurst.

Hussein Ahmed, 2001, *Islam in Nineteenth-Century Wallo, Ethiopia: Revival, Reform and Reaction*, Leiden: Brill.

Jonas, Raymond, 2011, *The Battle of Adwa: African Victory in the Age of Empire*, Cambridge, MA: The Belknap Press of Harvard University Press.

Mac Dye, W., 1969 [1870], *Moslem Egypt and Christian Abyssinia*, New York: Negro University Press. [Reprint of an 1870 work by a former US Civil War officer who had joined the Egyptian army and taken part in the attempted conquest of Ethiopia]

Marcus, Harold, 1975, *The Life and Times of Menelik II, Emperor of Ethiopia (1844–1913)*, Oxford: Clarendon Press.

Marsden, Philip, 2007, *The Barefoot Emperor: An Ethiopian Tragedy*, London: HarperPress.

Molvaer, Reidulf K., 1994, *Prowess, Piety and Politics. The Chronicle of Abeto Iyasu and Empress Zewditu of Ethiopia (1909–1930) Recorded by Gebre-Igziabiher Elyas*, Cologne: Rüdiger Köppe.

Pankhurst, Richard, 1968, *Economic History of Ethiopia, 1800–1935*, Addis Ababa, Haile Selassie I University Press, Evanston: Northwestern University Press.

Paulos Milkias and Getachew Metaferia (eds), 2005, *The Battle of Adwa: Reflections on Ethiopia's Historic Victory against European Colonialism*, New York: Algora.

Prouty, Chris, 1986, *Empress Taytu and Menelik II: Ethiopia, 1883–1910*, Trenton, NJ: Red Sea Press.

Rubenson, Sven, 1964, *Wichale XVII: the Attempt to Establish a Protectorate over Ethiopia*, Addis Ababa: Institute of Ethiopian Studies.

—— 1966, *King of Kings Tewodros of Ethiopia*, Addis Ababa, Nairobi: Oxford University Press.

—— 1976, *The Survival of Ethiopian Independence*, London: Heinemann.

Seri-Hersch, Iris, 2010, "'Transborder' Exchanges of People, Things, and Representations: Revisiting the Conflict Between Mahdist Sudan and Christian Ethiopia, 1885–1889", *International Journal of African Historical Studies*, 43 (1), pp. 1–26.

Shiferaw Bekele, 1990, "The State in the Zamana Masafent (1786–1853): An

Essay in Reinterpretation", in Tadesse Beyene, Richard Pankhurst, Shiferaw Bekele (eds), *Kasa and Kasa: Papers on the Lives, Times and Images of Tewodros II and Yohannes IV (1855–1889)*, Addis Ababa: IES/AAU, pp. 25–68.

Tadesse Beyene, Pankhurst, Richard and Shiferaw Bekele (eds), 1990, *Kasa and Kasa: Papers on the Lives, Times and Images of Tewodros II and Yohannes IV (1855–1889)*, Addis Ababa: IES/AAU.

Tadesse Beyene, Tadesse Tamrat and Pankhurst, Richard (eds), 1988, *The Centenary of Dogali: Proceedings of the International Symposium, Addis Ababa-Asmara, January 24–25 1987*, Addis Ababa: Institute of Ethiopian Studies.

Triulzi, Alessandro, 1981, *Salt, Gold and Legitimacy: Prelude to the History of a No-man's Land: Bela Shangul, Wallaga, Ethiopia (ca. 1800–1898)*, Naples: Istituto Universitario Orientale.

Zewde Gebre Sellassie, 1975, *Yohannes IV of Ethiopia. A Political Biography*, Oxford: Clarendon Press.

7

THE ERA OF HAILE SELASSIE

Christopher Clapham

Origins and rise to power, 1892–1930

The mid-twentieth century in Ethiopia, from 1916 through to the revolution in 1974, was dominated by a single man, Emperor Haile Selassie. Despite efforts by successor regimes to expunge him from the public record, he had a critical impact on the formation of modern Ethiopia, and for many years was virtually coterminous with the country in the eyes of the outside world. His legacy, mixed and contested though it is, remains central.

Despite the regal aura that he assumed after his accession to the throne in 1930, he was not in the direct line of succession, and gained power—like virtually all Ethiopian rulers of the last hundred and fifty years—by force. He was the younger son of Emperor Menelik's cousin and close confidant *Ras* Makonnen, who until his death in 1906 was governor of the strategically and economically vital south-eastern province of Harar. His genealogical claim to the throne, such as it was, derived from Makonnen's descent through his mother from King Sahle-Selassie of Shoa. The future Haile Selassie, who was known until 1930 by his given name of Tafari, was born near Harar in 1892, and received a mixture of traditional church education and tutoring by Catholic Capuchin friars. Although his father's death when he was only thirteen deprived him of both political and emotional support, he was clearly destined for high office, and was himself appointed governor of Harar at the age of seventeen. Already at that time he proved politically adept, a slight, withdrawn, calculating individual, capable of holding his own in the tangled and factionalized politics of the period that followed Menelik's mental disability and eventual death in 1913.

The brief reign of Menelik's grandson, Iyasu, has inevitably been obscured by that of his cousin and near contemporary. Since his overthrow opened the way to Haile Selassie's eventual rise to the throne, demonizing him served to promote the legitimacy of his successor, and he was generally dismissed during Haile Selassie's reign as a serial womanizer and secret convert to Islam. Conversely, Haile Selassie's detractors presented Iyasu as a far-sighted prince who sought to reconcile the longstanding divisions between Ethiopia's Christians and Muslims, in order to create a united Ethiopian nation. Even if Iyasu had such a strategy, however, his tactics in pursuing it were disastrous. He showed little interest in day-to-day administration, spending much of his time travelling especially around the Muslim eastern regions of the country, and ignoring the class of courtiers and aristocrats, overwhelmingly Shoan and entirely Christian, who had acquired interests and influence in an increasingly important central government. Though Tafari was careful to protest his allegiance to Iyasu, his own power base in Harar was deeply associated with Christian rule over a strategically vital Muslim area, and was directly threatened by Iyasu's entente with Islam. The decisive break came in mid-1916, when Iyasu removed Tafari from Harar and reassigned him to Kaffa—a wealthy province in the south-west, but by no means Harar's equal in political terms. At the same time, Iyasu's association with Islam and hence with Turkey aroused deep suspicions from the British and French, especially in the context of the First World War, in which Turkey was allied with Germany. It also presented threats to Allied, and especially British, imperial interests.

Tafari's role in the coup d'état that overthrew Iyasu in September 1916 has never been fully elucidated. Characteristically, he remained behind the scenes while others made the running, but he emerged from the coup, which elevated Menelik's daughter Zawditu to the throne, with the title of *ras* and the status of heir to the throne. There is some question as to whether he was also accorded the status of regent, but in practice he became head of the central government administration, within a complex political order in which he had little control over provincial government outside his own fiefdom of Harar, and in which his role even in central government was restricted by other powerful actors, and major decisions had to be referred to the Empress. The story of the following decade is one in which Tafari—presenting himself as the leader of the "modernizing" forces in Ethiopia, in contrast to the "traditionalists" led by the Minister of War, *Fitawrari* Habte-Giyorgis—gradually and skilfully accumulated power, until by 1930 he emerged as the unchallenged ruler.

One key element in this strategy was his control over Ethiopia's foreign relations, and his use of external linkages mediated through the leading foreign embassies in Addis Ababa, in order to compensate for his relative weakness in domestic politics. His modernizing measures always retained a cautious streak, and he was deeply aware of the need to carry a consensus among leading political figures; but he was the undoubted favourite of the British and French, the two colonial powers which with Italy (which always maintained a more ambivalent attitude) at that time controlled all of Ethiopia's neighbouring territories. One important initiative was securing Ethiopia's admission to the League of Nations in 1923, a move which ultimately failed to secure the country's independence against Italian aggression, but nonetheless marked its formal acceptance as an equal member of the community of nations. It also had significant domestic political implications, in that the main obstacle to Ethiopia's accession was the issue of slavery, the eradication of which helped to extend the control of the central government, in which Tafari had the major role, over provinces governed by his rivals.

In 1924, Tafari embarked on the first extensive foreign visit by any Ethiopian ruler, with a tour of Europe that included France, Italy and the United Kingdom. He protected his position at home by taking with him a large retinue, including two of the most powerful provincial rulers, Ras Haylu and Ras Seyoum. Diplomatically the trip was a failure, since he was unable to persuade the then colonial powers to allow Ethiopia unrestricted access to the sea through any of their possessions; he was however able to use Ethiopia's membership of the League to force the retraction of an Anglo-Italian accord that had sought, without reference to Ethiopia, to define their respective spheres of influence in the country. The most important result of the visit was to bring himself and his country to the attention of the European public, and also to other Africans and people of African descent. The RasTafarian movement in Jamaica reflected his name and title at that time.

Domestically, Tafari was preoccupied with the two key elements in the construction of an effective central administration, money and skilled personnel. By far the most important source of government revenue was customs duties, which could be readily levied at the port of entry, and did not entail the politically difficult task of extracting resources first from the peasantry, and then from their immediate overlords. Tafari established a centralized customs administration, undermining the ability of provincial governors to raise money from both foreign and domestic trade; he was greatly helped by the fact that the railway from Djibouti, which after reaching Addis Ababa in 1916 rapidly became Ethiopia's main trade artery, ran through the Harar region which he controlled. The railway also enabled him to move loyal troops rapidly to Addis Ababa at times of political crisis. In addition Tafari had promoted an educated class of Ethiopian administrators, recognizing that in this way he could build up a cadre of officials loyal to himself, and thus undermine the power of other vested interests. Most of these officials, who only reached high office after 1941, came from relatively humble backgrounds, and were correspondingly dependent on their patron for advancement. Among those who figured strongly in the post-war government were Wolde-Giyorgis Walda-Yohannes, who started his career as a dresser in the Menelik Hospital, and the three brothers Makonnen, Aklilu and Akala-Warq Habta-Wald. He founded a school named after himself, the Tafari Makonnen School, in 1925, and took a close personal interest in the young Ethiopians who were sent abroad for further education, most of them initially to France.

Although Tafari effectively controlled the central government by the mid-1920s, the provinces were another matter, since most of them were ruled by well-established noblemen and notables who were all but independent of central management. Jimma, and Benishangul on the Sudanese border, were still governed by their pre-conquest Muslim dynasties, under Sultan Abajifar and Sheik Khojali respectively. From Yirgalem, Menelik's fierce old Gurage general *Dejazmatch* Balcha responded to repeated summonses to come to Addis Ababa, "If Tafari wants me, let him come down here into Sidamo and get me". Some governors, especially in border regions such as Tigray, were even in a position to maintain independent contacts with foreign powers: before 1935, the usual means by which Tigrayan notables travelled to Addis Ababa was through Asmara and Massawa, by ship to Djibouti, and thence by rail to the capital. But time was on Tafari's side, and one by one the autonomous rulers either died or miscalculated. When in 1928 Balcha arrived in Addis Ababa with a personal army of five thousand men, his troops were induced to desert him and he was arrested—eventually to die fighting the Italians in 1936. When the last of the great magnates, Empress Zawditu's husband Ras Gugsa Wolle of Gondar, came out in open rebellion in early 1930, Tafari sent against him a central government army including a single aeroplane, piloted by a Frenchman, which so terrified Gugsa's troops that they deserted, leaving him to be killed. The following day, Zawditu herself died, leaving the way open for Tafari to assume the imperial throne.

Haile Selassie's early reign: invasion, exile and restoration, 1930–1941

Marking a formal break with his earlier life, Tafari took the throne name Haile Selassie, or Power of the Trinity, which was also his own baptismal name. He immediately assumed a consciously aloof and imperial demeanour, well suited in any event to his own character, and a dignity which deserted him only under the most intense stress. Despite the circuitous means by which he had attained the position of supreme leadership, he constantly asserted—and gave every impression of believing—that his authority derived directly from God. While retaining an extremely shrewd and calculating political mind, he was always deeply aware of the importance of the trappings of power.

The earliest public acts of the reign were designed to impress the new ruler and his country on the consciousness of the outside world, and in the process to establish his authority in the minds of his subjects. The coronation—never in earlier reigns a particularly noteworthy event—was invested with a previously unknown level of pomp and ceremonial, not least for the benefit of the foreign dignitaries, including one of the younger sons of the British King George V, who came to Addis Ababa for the occasion. Coronation day on 2 November subsequently became (along with liberation day on 5 May and the Emperor's birthday on 23 July) one of the three main public holidays of the regime. The first anniversary, in November 1931, provided the occasion for the public promulgation of Ethiopia's first written constitution, a document largely drafted by a leading Ethiopian intellectual of the time, Tekle-Hawariyat Tekle-Maryam, and based on the 1889 Meiji Constitution of Japan. It was presented as a gift by the Emperor to his people, and the contemporary official iconography showed a beam of light issuing from the Trinity (enthroned in the heavens), illuminating Haile Selassie (symbolically located at the mid-point between heaven and earth), and diffused, in the form of the constitution, to the masses waiting with outstretched arms below. The document both proclaimed Ethiopia's modernity for external consumption and unequivocally insisted on the emperor as the sole ultimate source of power domestically, arousing some disquiet from members of noble lineages, who viewed him as no more than the first among equals. Although a two-chamber parliament was established, this had no direct elections and no more than titular powers.

As Emperor, Haile Selassie could undertake far more systematic modernizing measures than had been possible when he was merely regent. The remaining provincial lords who still retained some autonomous status were rapidly brought into line. The grasping Ras Hailu made himself so unpopular with his own subjects in Gojjam that he could be brought down; he was confined to Addis Ababa, while Gojjam was handed over to Haile Selassie's cousin and trusted supporter Ras Imru. Ras Kassa, another cousin and member of the imperial family whose genealogical claim to the throne was stronger than Haile Selassie's, was appointed to Gondar. In Tigray—always a special case because of its distinct language, its close relations with Italian Eritrea, and the hankering of its rulers for the imperial throne once occupied by Yohannes IV—the daughter of Ras Seyoum was married to Haile Selassie's eldest son, while his local rival *Dejazmatch* Haile Selassie Gugsa married the Emperor's daughter. The wealthy province of Jimma, still nominally ruled by Sultan Abba Jifar, was brought under effective central control.

A flurry of other modernizing measures sought to convert Ethiopia into an effective unitary state. A national currency was instituted, with the conversion of the Egyptian-owned Bank of Abyssinia into the new and government-owned Bank of Ethiopia, freeing Ethiopia from the dependence on a fluctuating international silver market imposed by the use of the superb Maria Theresa thaler. A road-building programme, later overshadowed by that of the Italians, sought to bring the provinces into closer touch with (and hence dependence on) the capital, and in turn with the international market. For the first time, a significant foreign trading community, largely consisting of Greeks, Armenians and Lebanese, was established in Addis Ababa. Increasing numbers of schools were opened. Foreign advisers, drawn from many different countries in order to lessen the risks of dependence on a single outside power, were brought in to provide technical expertise in the reform of the state apparatus. They came from countries including France, Switzerland, the United States, the United Kingdom and Greece; the most sensitive task, that of training a modern army, was entrusted to Swedes and Belgians, whose countries did not harbour ambitions in the region. None were recruited from Italy. The advisers' task was a difficult one, not least because Ethiopians retained a considerable (and justifiable) suspicion of foreign motives, and in an era of colonialism few Europeans were accustomed to working under African control. All in all, nonetheless, the opening years of Haile Selassie's reign can plausibly be regarded as a period of rapid and fairly effective state-building.

This effort was completely overshadowed, however, by the threat to Ethiopia's independence presented by Fascist Italy. It may be doubted whether Italy had ever completely abandoned the imperial ambitions cut short by the defeat at Adwa in 1896, or had fully accepted Ethiopia's status as a sovereign independent state. At the time of Haile Selassie's visit to Italy as regent in 1924, when Mussolini had only recently attained power, Italian proposals for Ethiopian access to the sea through Assab so clearly reflected a colonial agenda that they were unacceptable to the Ethiopians. Italian diplomatic reports during the 1920s presented the picture of a backward and barbarous state, in terms that would justify intervention as a civilizing mission. A network of Italian consulates in northern Ethiopia collected military intelligence and sought to establish close relationships with prominent local noblemen.

The state-building measures that characterized the first years of the new Emperor's reign thus also served a strategic purpose, to pre-empt any claim by Italy to annex Ethiopia on "humanitarian" grounds. In other respects, however, Haile Selassie's diplomacy was unusually inept, in that he failed to develop sufficiently strong relationships with either France or the United Kingdom to induce them to offer significant resistance to Italy's increasingly evident ambitions. France would have been the most suitable ally, since it had strong commercial links with

Ethiopia through Djibouti and the Franco-Ethiopian railway but had no other territorial stake in the region, in sharp contrast to the British with whom Ethiopia shared long frontiers in the Sudan, Kenya and British Somaliland. British hegemony in Egypt also reinforced a long-standing concern for the Nile waters, and hence for control of the areas of north-western Ethiopia that drained into the Nile. Given that European diplomacy was at this time intensely concerned with the rising threat from Nazi Germany, and that both Britain and France were prepared to buy Italian support or at least neutrality by offering Mussolini slices of their own territories in Kenya and Chad respectively, it may be questioned whether any efforts on Haile Selassie's part would have been successful; but in any event, Ethiopian foreign policy placed far too much emphasis on the paper guarantees against aggression provided by the League of Nations, which were to prove worthless.

A significant Italian military build-up in Eritrea developed from 1932, three years before the eventual invasion, with a lower level of activity in Italian Somalia, which was very much a secondary front. The first major diplomatic incident nonetheless took place in this area in 1934, when a combined British and Ethiopian mission surveying the frontier between Ethiopia and British Somaliland found Italian troops occupying the watering place at Walwal in the Ogaden, well inside Ethiopian territory. The subsequent clash was shrilly presented by Mussolini as an example of Ethiopian aggression, even though the wrong was entirely on the Italian side. To this and other provocations, Haile Selassie responded with determined resort to diplomatic mechanisms, while taking great care to do nothing that could plausibly be presented as provocation on Ethiopia's part. The troops on Ethiopia's borders with Italian territories, for example, were held well back from the frontier, so as to prevent any incident that could be exploited for propaganda purposes. This did nothing to deter the eventual invasion that was launched early in October 1935, at the start of the traditional campaigning season after the end of the rains, but it did at least ensure that this would be recognized as an unequivocal case of international aggression.

It said much for Haile Selassie's nation-building efforts that only a single Ethiopian notable, his Tigrayan son-in-law Haile Selassie Gugsa, defected to the Italians; an almost united country thus confronted the invaders. The discrepancy in modern weaponry was however decisive. In sharp contrast to the Adwa campaign forty years earlier, when the Ethiopians were able to fight on terms that at least approached the technological level of their enemies, the advent especially of air power had made a massive difference. The Ethiopian armies were destroyed as much by bombing, and later by the extensive use of the supposedly banned mustard gas, as by ground-based operations. Haile Selassie himself had no military credentials, and although he moved his headquarters to Dessie, nearer the northern front than Addis Ababa, he left the conduct of operations in the hands of the Minister of War, Ras Mulugeta, and the principal provincial governors. Their troops overwhelmingly consisted of traditional peasant levies, with no more than a small contingent from the newly trained army. Eventually, with the northern front crumbling, Haile Selassie felt obliged to conduct an attack himself, at Mai Chew in southern Tigray in April 1936, as much for honour's sake, and to fulfil the expected obligations of an emperor, as for any hope of success. It predictably failed, and organized Ethiopian resistance on the northern front collapsed. Haile Selassie, shocked and depressed, made his way back by circuitous routes to his capital.

The decision as to what to do next, as the Italian armies closed in, lay between going into exile and continuing the struggle from abroad, or else retreating westwards with the remaining Ethiopian forces into areas not yet occupied by the enemy. Some argued that continued resistance, or a martyr's death in the manner of Tewodros, was the only honourable course. Haile Selassie opted for exile, and although this earned him some criticism for deserting his country in its hour of need, in the event it proved to be the wisest option. Taking advantage of the fact that the Italians had inexplicably failed to pursue their campaign in eastern Ethiopia, from southern Eritrea or Somalia, energetically enough to cut the railway line, he left Addis Ababa for Djibouti, where he embarked on a British warship, leaving Ras Imru to retreat westwards to Gore in order to maintain a formal presence within the country. On 5 May 1936, the Italians entered Addis Ababa, and established an east African empire stretching from the Red Sea to the Indian Ocean.

After a stop in Jerusalem, Haile Selassie travelled to the United Kingdom, which he left to address the League of Nations Assembly in Geneva on 30 June. The speech to the League, drafted by Lorenzo Taezaz, was the most memorable in that organization's undistinguished history, and dramatically contrasted the promise of collective security with the horrors inflicted on Ethiopia. Delivered with unquenchable dignity, it established Haile Selassie on the world stage, and presaged the forthcoming Second World War, while the poignant question with which it ended, "What answer shall I take back to my people?", anticipated his eventual return. It did nothing, however, to induce the League to take any effective action, or to restore the Emperor's own immediate fortunes. For the following four years, he lived in exile in the small English city of Bath, remaining in touch as best he could with resistance leaders within Ethiopia. Only after Italy's entry into the Second World War in June 1940 did he once more gain an international role, when he was flown by the British to Khartoum to help foster resistance to the Italians in Ethiopia.

The years of occupation counterpoise two linked narratives, those of Italian empire-building on the one hand and Ethiopian resistance on the other. Italian rule was from the start imposed with the brutality to be expected of a Fascist state. Ethiopian leaders, including the Emperor's son-in-law Ras Desta, and the three elder sons of his cousin and confidant Ras Kassa, were lured to surrender by promises of clemency, and then summarily executed. An attempt on the life of the Italian Viceroy, Marshal Graziani, by two Eritreans in February 1937 was followed by a bloodbath in Addis Ababa, and the murder of many of Ethiopia's graduates and of the monks at the ancient monastery of Debre Libanos. Predictably, this brutality was counterproductive, and the Italians could never muster the manpower and organization that would have been required to hold down by force a large country with spectacular topography and very limited communications. Several leading Ethiopians, including Ras Seyoum in Tigray and the discredited Ras Hailu in Gojjam, were induced to accept titular office under the Italian regime, but were never invested with significant powers. In 1938, Graziani was replaced by the Duke of Aosta, a member of the Italian royal family and by all accounts a humane and decent man, who attempted to institute a policy of reconciliation. Though this represented a marked improvement, it came too late to bring about any widespread Ethiopian acceptance of Italian rule.

Any hope that its East African empire might prove economically beneficial to Italy was soon dissipated. Not only were the military and administrative costs of maintaining the empire high, but Italy had neither the time nor the capacity to develop any significant sources of revenue. The main legacy of empire was the road network, radiating out from Addis Ababa, which represented a major feat of engineering and for many years provided the backbone of the national transport system. The urban infrastructure was likewise extended, especially in Addis Ababa and in towns such as Gondar and Jimma that served as regional headquarters for the Italian administration. But the attempt to settle Italian peasant farmers in Ethiopia proved an abject failure, and as Ethiopian resistance became increasingly organized and effective, so Italian administration largely retreated to the towns and the lines of communication between them.

This resistance derived from the very earliest days of the occupation. The rapid collapse of the imperial armies left Ethiopian governors still in control of many parts of the country, while Ras Imru continued to lead the titular government in western Ethiopia until his capture in December 1936. Several officials in the imperial regime, including Abebe Aregay and Takele Welde-Hawariyat, took to the countryside and remained under arms throughout the five-year occupation, even launching a daring though futile attack on Addis Ababa. The areas of greatest resistance were the core highland regions of Shoa, Gojjam and Begemdir, with the "patriots", or *arbeññyoch* as they were called, being especially active in Gojjam; but resistance took place throughout the country, including Oromo and other areas conquered only in the late nineteenth century, where the Italians sought—with some success—to present themselves as liberators from Amhara imperialism. The traditional woolly coiffure of the patriot fighters later became the model for the "Afro" style in the United States and elsewhere.

Resistance bands under the command of particular patriot leaders, even though they often co-ordinated their activities, did not add up to any single organized campaign. Different leaders were fiercely jealous of their own independence, and sometimes at odds with one another. Some of them regarded Haile Selassie as having betrayed his country by fleeing to Europe, and some of the more intellectual ones even dabbled in republicanism. Haile Selassie himself was too far away to exercise any co-ordinating role. An *impasse* therefore remained, until Mussolini's entry into the Second World War on the side of Germany in June 1940. This instantly transformed the situation, since on the one hand the substantial Italian military force in north-east Africa gravely threatened the British position in the Middle East, while on the other hand this force was isolated from its homeland, and itself vulnerable to extinction. Strategic considerations therefore dictated a rapid assault on Italian East Africa, which despite the early Italian conquest of

British Somaliland could be launched from Sudan and Kenya. Haile Selassie, still resident in Britain, provided an obvious focus for the reconquest of Ethiopia and was flown out to Sudan, where he was only grudgingly received by British officials still steeped in colonial attitudes. On the broader diplomatic scene, however, and with an eye especially on the United States, it was essential to present the defeat of the Italians in Ethiopia as a liberation from Fascist rule, not merely as an extension of the British Empire, and for this the Emperor was indispensable.

The defeat of the Italians in north-east Africa proved rapid and decisive. Largely the work of British imperial forces, in which the Indian and South African armies played an important part, the major offensives were from Sudan into Eritrea, and from Kenya into Somalia. The decisive battle of the campaign, with heavy casualties on both sides, took place around Keren in Eritrea. In the south, the attacking forces advanced rapidly along the Somali coast to Mogadishu, then north to Harar and Dire Dawa, and along the line of rail to capture Addis Ababa on 6 April 1941. Haile Selassie entered Gojjam directly from Sudan in January, as part of a small force under the command of the legendary Orde Wingate, which included two battalions raised from Ethiopian exiles. This route was chosen because of the strength of the Ethiopian resistance in the province, and Haile Selassie—despite misgivings on the part of some of the patriot leaders—was once more almost universally accepted as Emperor. He entered Addis Ababa on 5 May 1941, and resumed his imperial role. The final pocket of Italian resistance, at Gondar, succumbed in November 1941.

The restored monarchy, 1941–60

The position in which Haile Selassie found himself in May 1941 was an awkward one. Although he regarded himself as the emperor of an independent state, and was so regarded by his people, he had been restored to power by an army under British command, many of whose commanders treated Ethiopia (along with Eritrea and Somalia) as occupied enemy territory, and some of whom sought to incorporate the country into the British colonial empire. With the Second World War still in its early stages, Allied military control of the region was strategically important, especially with respect to the campaign in North Africa. Although British colonial ambitions were rapidly abandoned, and Ethiopia recognized as an independent state under the emperor's authority, he still needed British military and financial assistance in order to re-establish his government. A formal agreement was signed in January 1942, which while recognizing Ethiopia's independence still retained a special status for the British, as against other foreigners, notably in the military field and in the provision of foreign advisers to the Ethiopian government. This struck at Haile Selassie's preference for playing different outside powers against one another and avoiding dependence especially on any state with colonial ambitions in the region. He invited an American, John Spencer, who had briefly served as a legal adviser before the Italian invasion, back to Addis Ababa, knowing well that the British—dependent as they now were on the United States, in the context of war—were in no position to object. British military assistance continued to be needed, notably in 1943 when the *weyane* rebellion in Tigray (whose name was subsequently given to the Tigray People's Liberation Front, which claimed to be the second *weyane*) was crushed with the aid of British aircraft. A second agreement with the British in December 1944, by which time any military threat to the region had disappeared, removed the status accorded them in the 1942 agreement, though much of the Somali-inhabited part of Ethiopia, known as the "reserved areas", remained under British administration for a further ten years.

Given the problematic nature of the relationship with Britain, which until the early 1950s controlled all of Ethiopia's neighbours save only French Somaliland, Haile Selassie shrewdly turned to the United States as an alternative source of support. The USA was at this time rapidly expanding its global alliances, to exercise its new superpower status, and—at a time when almost all of tropical Africa was still under colonial rule—an ally in north-east Africa had much to offer, especially in the context of burgeoning American concern with the Middle East. The foundations were laid at a meeting between Haile Selassie and the US President Franklin Roosevelt in Egypt in 1943, when FDR was returning from the Tehran summit. Particularly important was a US mission to train a modern Ethiopian army, on a scale significantly greater than anything attempted before 1935. An Ethiopian detachment performed well as part of the UN force in the Korean War, while enabling the Emperor to demonstrate his commitment to the principles of collective security that had so cruelly failed to protect Ethiopia against Italian aggression in 1935. A further critical benefit was US support for Ethiopian claims on Eritrea, in return for which the United States gained a military communications facility just outside Asmara, which until the advent of satellite technology formed a key link in its global command and intelligence network. American development aid was also forthcoming, especially for education.

The period from the end of the World War II through to 1960 represented the high point of Haile Selassie's regime. Political power was tightly concentrated in the palace, under the close supervision until 1955 of Wolde-Giyorgis Wolde-Yohannes, who held the ancient title of *tsehafe tezaz*, translated as Minister of the Pen. Given his closeness to the Emperor, formidable personality, and grasp of administrative detail, Wolde-Giyorgis became effectively prime minister, even though that post was formally held by a dignified but ineffectual nobleman, *Bitweded* Makonnen Endalkachaw. He was the leading member of a class of courtier-politicians through whom Ethiopia was governed under Haile Selassie. Others included the Habte-Wold brothers, with Makonnen as longtime Minister of Commerce, and Aklilu as Foreign Minister and subsequently Prime Minister. Most of them came from modest backgrounds, while some were recruited through the court and the complex network of relationships that linked the Ethiopian aristocracy and the imperial family. Most came from Shoa, though the influential Minister of Finance, Yilma Deresa, was an Oromo from Wellega, and a few were Tigrayans; the core Amhara provinces of Begemder, Gojjam and Wollo were almost entirely unrepresented. All were Christian, a small number being Lutherans and Catholics, while the great majority were Ethiopian Orthodox. None, however, represented broader political constituencies, whether regional, ethnic, religious or ideological; the entire system of government was intensely focused on the palace, and its inevitable internal rivalries were fought out, not over issues of policy or representation, but over factional squabbles for the Emperor's support. Although Haile Selassie was extremely adept at manipulating factions within this narrow political elite, the consequence was that the politics of the palace became increasingly divorced from developments in the country as a whole, with eventually disastrous effects.

Overtly, the government was committed to the universal principles of "modernization" and "development", with special rhetorical emphasis given to education, which was always closely associated with the Emperor himself. The University College of Addis Ababa, later extended to become Haile Selassie I University, was established in 1951, with colleges for agriculture, building, and public health. The educational system as a whole, however, rested on a very narrow base, with a high concentration in Addis Ababa and little presence at all beyond the major provincial towns. Economic development was similarly concentrated, especially in Addis Ababa and satellite towns along the line of rail to the south. Although a "five-year plan" was promulgated as early as 1957, this amounted to little more than rhetorical aspiration, and developments in the key area of agriculture were heavily affected by the interests of major landowners, who in turn were closely linked to the regime. The showpiece agricultural development scheme, in the Awash valley south and east of Addis Ababa, consisted essentially in large plantations for sugar (run by the Dutch HVA company) and cotton (run by the British company Mitchell Cotts). These encroached heavily on the dry-season grazing areas of Afar and Kereyu Oromo pastoralists, while also bringing significant financial rewards to the Afar Sultan Ali-Mirah of Awsa. From the 1960s, an ambitious Swedish aid programme sought to turn the Arsi highlands into the breadbasket of Ethiopia, with considerable success in terms of enhanced food production, albeit at the price of intensified class divisions between landowners and the indigenous peasantry. It was symptomatic that such initiatives could be launched in areas that had been incorporated into Ethiopia during the late nineteenth century, whereas the regime did not dare to touch historically Ethiopian highland regions, in which land was controlled not by landlords but by the Amhara or Tigrayan peasantry. The most agriculturally productive of the Amhara regions, Gojjam, was also the most politically disaffected, and even an attempt to measure land there in 1968 aroused a spontaneous peasant revolt, and had to be rapidly abandoned.

Nowhere were the political limitations of the regime more disastrously exposed than in Eritrea, which remained under British administration for a decade after its capture from the Italians in 1941. Ethiopia had plausible claims on the territory, which would provide it with independent access to the sea, both because parts of it had formed part of Ethiopia for a very long period prior to 1890 and because it had served as the base for attacks on Ethiopia in both 1896 and 1935. The Tigrinya-speaking Orthodox Christian community of highland Eritrea retained close links with northern Ethiopia, and formed the core of a significant "unionist" movement (favouring union with

Ethiopia) which was supported by the government in Addis Ababa but equally had a local base. Attempts by the great powers to agree on Eritrea's future foundered as a result of growing Cold War rivalries, leaving the issue to be settled by the UN General Assembly, when US support was critical in passing a resolution federating the territory with Ethiopia—a solution that effectively made it part of Ethiopia, while establishing a locally elected government with a high level of autonomy. This arrangement took effect from September 1952, giving Ethiopia its own port for the first time since the loss of Massawa to the Turks in 1555.

As a result of Italian rule, and also during the short period of British administration, Eritreans had however developed a separate identity from other Ethiopians. The British period, and the political process aroused by protracted discussion of the territory's future, had led to the formation of an independent press and of political parties, both completely absent to the south. Economic development was significantly greater than in Ethiopia. The government in Addis Ababa was quite incapable of developing any working relationship with an elected and autonomous Eritrean administration, and systematically sought to reduce it to the same level of dependence as other provinces within the Empire. This goal was achieved in 1962, when (under heavy pressure) the Eritrean assembly was induced to dissolve itself, and the territory was placed under direct imperial rule. Success at one level, however, translated into catastrophe at another. Eritrean alienation from the central government was already growing rapidly, and the suppression of the federation helped to push it into growing support for armed opposition.

Attempts to provide an institutional framework for enhanced political participation were no more than cosmetic. On the twenty-fifth anniversary of his succession, in 1955, Haile Selassie promulgated a revised constitution, under which for the first time the Chamber of Deputies would be elected by popular suffrage; the Senate continued to be appointed by the emperor. The new Constitution was in some degree prompted by the federation with Eritrea, which had created an embarrassing contrast between the popularly elected Eritrean administration and government of the rest of the country by an emperor who claimed to rule as the "elect of God". The executive branch of government, however, continued to come entirely under the emperor's control; there were no political parties, and the elected chamber could provide no effective representation of local issues or identities, or even exercise its formal constitutional powers with regard to legislation and the budget. So far from bridging the gap between the regime and the people whom it governed, the new Constitution merely drew attention to its unbridgeability.

By the late 1950s, the regime's difficulties were becoming increasingly apparent. *Tsehafe tezaz* Wolde-Giyorgis, who like many other strongmen had started to presume on his position to an extent that offended his master, was dismissed in 1955, removing a stabilizing presence at the centre, and greatly intensifying the level of factional conflict. Rival security chiefs, competing for the Emperor's ear, increased the sense of insecurity. Young educated officials were alienated by the regime's immobilism and—for the first time in Ethiopia's history—looked enviously to other parts of Africa that appeared to be making rapid progress towards democratic self-government. They sensed that Ethiopia, once the pride of the continent, was being "left behind". These tensions erupted in December 1960, in a coup d'état that attempted to seize control of Addis Ababa while Haile Selassie was away on a state visit to Latin America, depose him, and replace him with Crown Prince Asfa Wesen at the head of a reforming government.

Central to the plot was a family relationship between Mengistu Neway, commander of the imperial bodyguard, and his younger brother Germame, epitome of the younger generation of radical modernizers. It very nearly came off. Most leading members of the regime were enticed to the palace and immobilized, and only luck enabled two other generals to escape and organize resistance based on other elements in the armed forces. On this occasion, Haile Selassie's tactics of playing off rival factions, in the armed forces as elsewhere, served him well. After a short but violent fight, the rebels were defeated, and the Emperor returned to resume control. In a final act of violence, prefiguring the events of 1974, the rebels turned machine guns on the notables imprisoned in the palace, killing many of them. It is very doubtful whether, as was sometimes later claimed, the coup d'état would, if successful, have led to a democratically modernizing Ethiopia. Germame Neway and his colleagues had no democratic credentials, and viewed most of their fellow citizens as backward and obscurantist. One of their first actions was to adjourn parliament indefinitely. Their goal, like that of their successors fourteen years later, was national transformation with themselves in command. They did however shatter the illusion of permanence and stability that had hitherto surrounded the regime.

The empire in decline, 1960–74

The period between the 1960 coup d'état and the 1974 revolution was suffused with the sense of an era nearing its end. Haile Selassie was already 68 years old in 1960, and—in a social structure and political system highly dependent on individual leadership—there was no sign of any likely successor. Though social change, and a measure of economic development, continued, and the country (outside Eritrea) was broadly peaceful, there was no evident solution to the political *impasse* into which the regime had fallen. A number of token changes were announced: in 1966 the Prime Minister, Aklilu Habte-Wold, was formally accorded the power to appoint his own ministers, but this made very little difference to the appointments, and did nothing to endow him with any independent political status; a Ministry of Land Reform was established in the same year, but was in no position to make any changes that might challenge established interests. Despite his collaboration with the 1960 plotters, explained as having been "under duress", the Emperor's eldest son Crown Prince AsfaWesen remained heir to the throne, but he was in bad health, and had never in any event shown any sign of the dynamism needed to rule and reform a fractious country.

One significant pointer to the future lay in the growth of an active and radical student movement. In December 1960, the students at the University College of Addis Ababa had immediately and spontaneously demonstrated in favour of the new regime. They were subsequently pardoned by a forgiving Emperor, and for a while the student body remained quiescent; but from the mid-1960s, aided by the expansion in student numbers that followed the conversion of the Emperor's former palace into a new university campus, radical and sometimes violent student protest became a regular occurrence. Marxism-Leninism became the preferred, indeed almost universal, ideology of student radicals, and the language in which the political issues of the day were discussed—the national question, the land question—came to echo that of pre-Soviet Russia. Indeed, the parallels between these two pre-revolutionary societies increasingly seemed evident. Ethiopian students abroad, both in Europe and in North America, formed their own organizations, which could debate the issues facing their homeland in terms unrestricted by the surveillance that accompanied such discussions inside Ethiopia itself. The different movements, though united in their Marxism, conceived these issues in significantly different ways, which in turn affected the vicious factional conflicts in early revolutionary Ethiopia.

Though students seemed to be—and indeed were—a small, privileged and urban group in late imperial Ethiopia, they formed linkages with other potentially dissident elements in Ethiopian society that extended their beyond the politics of the campus. One important constituency was junior army officers, who in the later years of the imperial regime were often conscripted directly from secondary schools into the military, and resented their inability to pursue civilian careers while they retained contacts with their former classmates in the university; army officers were prominent among those who attended evening and part-time courses in the university, and several of these later emerged in prominent positions in the revolutionary regime. The attempted coup had in any event raised the political profile of the army, and on several occasions during the 1960s the regime was forced to grant pay increases to soldiers which it could ill afford. Searching for an issue that would resonate beyond their own elite interests, student politicians came up with the slogan, "land to the tiller", directly taken from the Russian model. Most students came from urban backgrounds, and had little if any contact with the countryside, which they tended to regard as a backward zone inhabited by traditionalist peasants; but the call for land reform was to have an impact after 1974 that few of them can have foreseen.

Most dangerously of all, students raised the "national question", the question of the identity, organization and place in the political order of the different ethnic groups of which the country was composed. One early form which this took was the creation of local self-help organizations, in which city-dwellers from a particular group or area would raise funds to pay for development projects in their places of origin. Usually headed by a prominent official from the area concerned, and operating within the conventions of the imperial system (by, for example, soliciting donations to the project from the Emperor), they nonetheless helped to create hitherto absent connections on ethnic lines. Some, notably the Gurage organization (which could draw on a wealthy business community with a very high level of social solidarity), were very effective. However, the creation in late 1966 of a pan-

Oromo organization, Macha Tulama, under the leadership of an Oromo general instantly aroused government concern, and the organization was forcibly suppressed.

The situation in Eritrea never got entirely out of control during the imperial era, as was to happen later, but nonetheless grew steadily more difficult, escalating from mere banditry in the western lowlands in the early 1960s to provide a serious insurgent threat by the early 1970s. In 1967, Haile Selassie spent a month in Eritrea, distributing largesse and an aura of imperial benevolence throughout the province—a characteristic and entirely ineffectual response to what was basically a problem of political representation, which in turn the regime was incapable of managing. Eritrean students in Addis Ababa increasingly differentiated themselves from their fellow students, and sometimes defected to join the Eritrean Liberation Front, which, however, at this time remained divided and ill-organized. The creation of the EPLF, and its transformation into a formidable insurgent army, was a post-revolutionary development. The neighbouring region of Tigray was at this time governed by the dynamic Ras Mengesha Seyoum, great-grandson of the Emperor Yohannes IV, who was married to Haile Selassie's granddaughter, and remained entirely loyal.

Elsewhere, there was a serious revolt in the southern province of Bale between 1963 and 1970, fuelled largely by misgovernment and land alienation, and supported from across the frontier by the newly independent Somali Republic. This was eventually managed through a combination of military containment and some political concessions—the leader of the revolt, Wako Gutu, was given a minor imperial title and left in peace—but without any fundamental rectification of the conditions that had caused it. Most of Ethiopia remained peaceful, and most student radicals believed—in keeping with Stalin's writings on the national question in the Soviet Union, in which they were well versed—that ethnic conflict was basically no more than a manifestation of class exploitation, and could be rectified by land reform.

While the imperial regime during the 1960s was coming under increasing threat, its diplomacy was outstandingly successful. While Haile Selassie and the empire he ruled seemed anachronistic to many of his own subjects, in much of Africa he was a figure of legend; a much published photograph showed the future Kenyan leader Jomo Kenyatta, as a student in London in 1935, demonstrating against the Fascist invasion of Ethiopia. He—or possibly his advisers, notably the

Foreign Minister Ketema Yifru and the Prime Minister Aklilu Habte-Wold—recognized that this prestige could be tapped to raise the Emperor, and hence the country, to a role of continental leadership. This was achieved by the Addis Ababa summit of African heads of state in May 1963, which established the Organization of African Unity, with Haile Selassie as its first chairman, and Addis Ababa as its permanent headquarters, and thus the diplomatic capital of Africa. The advantages were more than personal: in particular, Ethiopia secured almost universal support for the principle that the "territorial integrity" of African states would be respected by their fellows, a principle reinforced at the Cairo summit in 1964 by an explicit declaration that African states would respect the frontiers inherited on their accession to national independence. While this principle reassured the leaders of newly independent states, with their artificial colonially-created frontiers, it also provided Ethiopia with powerful continental support against the Eritrean secessionists, and against the claims by the Somali Republic (which had united the former Italian Somalia and British Somaliland) to the vast Somali-inhabited area of south-eastern Ethiopia. Much of Haile Selassie's time in his later years was occupied by a constant round of state visits and diplomatic meetings, but it is doubtful whether this had any significant impact on the regime's inability to avert the coming cataclysm: its defects were structural, not simply personal, and there was nothing by this time that an ageing Emperor could do to correct them.

Ethiopia's triumphs on the continental scene compensated for, but did not remove, difficulties in its relations with its own neighbours. The Somali Republic, coming to independence in a flush of national enthusiasm, claimed not only south-eastern Ethiopia but north-eastern Kenya and French Somaliland (the Côte Française des Somalis, or the Territoire Français des Afars et des Issas, as it was called at this time) as part of its national territory. While any direct military threat was to remain insignificant until the mid-1970s, covert Somali support for dissident movements within Ethiopia (like the Wako Gutu rebellion in Bale noted above) added to the regime's problems. Somalia's resort to Soviet military assistance in pursuit of its territorial ambitions intensified the incorporation of the Horn of Africa into the Cold War structure of alliances, just at a time when with Ethiopia's continued relationship with the United States was being questioned in Washington, both as a result of US involvement in Vietnam and because American policy planners sought to avoid too close an association with a clearly failing regime. It became progressively more difficult for Ethiopia to obtain the US military aid that it sought in order to ward off the Somali threat, and pursue the intensifying war in Eritrea.

Relations with the Arab world were also awkward, as indeed they have always been for Christian Ethiopia. The Eritrean insurgency of the ELF received considerable support from Iraq and Syria, which in turn was brought into Eritrea through Sudan. Covert Sudanese backing for the Eritrean rebellion was in turn countered by covert Ethiopian support for the rebels in southern Sudan. The presence of African Arab states in the OAU on the one hand limited their overt support for the ELF, but on the other led to Arab leverage on African states in the conflict with Israel; when, late in 1973, the OAU recommended its members to break diplomatic relations with Israel, over continued Israeli occupation of Egyptian territory, Ethiopia reluctantly complied in order to retain its standing in the organization.

The 1973 Arab-Israeli war, and the associated oil embargo and rise in global oil prices, were among the factors that finally precipitated the collapse of the imperial government in Ethiopia. Simultaneously, a serious famine in northern Ethiopia and especially in Welo—news of which was suppressed by the government in order to avoid adverse publicity, while no measures were taken the relieve starvation—undermined the sedulously promoted image of the Emperor as the caring father of his people. A strike by taxi drivers, protests by teachers over educational policy, disaffection in the lower ranks of the army, and the perennial volatility of student politics, all helped to precipitate demonstrations in Addis Ababa late in February 1974 that rapidly escalated out of control. Haile Selassie responded by dismissing the Aklilu government, appointing first Endalkachew Makonnen (son of a previous Prime Minister) and then the reformist nobleman Mikael Imru as Prime Minister, and setting in motion a process of further constitutional reform. The sudden opening up of the press, and an accompanying wave of free discussion, debate and demonstration, encouraged the belief that Ethiopia might peacefully be transforming itself into a free and democratic country. This belief was always deluded: the brief moment of freedom in mid-1974 represented no more than a sudden release of pressure, unaccompanied by the changes in social attitudes, creation of institutional mechanisms, or resolution of major underlying policy issues that would have been needed to convert it into a new and stable form of governance. Behind the scenes a committee of the armed forces, soon to be known as the Derg, was being organized as an alternative source of power. The progressive dismantling of the old regime—known as the "salami revolution" because it proceeded slice by slice—was the prelude not to the creation of a democratic Ethiopia, but to the transfer of power to a very different kind of dictatorship. Haile Selassie's deposition and arrest on 12 September 1974 effectively signalled the end of imperial Ethiopia, though the Crown Prince, who was sick in London and never returned, was for a while formally declared as his successor. One of the greatest of all Ethiopian rulers was quietly murdered the following year.

Conclusion

The era of Haile Selassie continues to evoke contradictory attitudes. For some, it was a period of peace and national unity, a golden age by contrast with the upheavals and violence that followed, when Ethiopia was governed skilfully and with a light hand, and its inherent conflicts and contradictions were kept at least relatively under control. For others, it was a period of repressive feudalism, built on injustice and inequality, when government was dedicated to the service and glorification of a single man, and opportunities to secure peaceful reform were spurned. Symptomatically, after Haile Selassie's body was recovered from the old palace after the fall of the Mengistu regime, the government of Meles Zenawi—very much a product of the pre-1974 generation of disaffected students—refused to allow him a state funeral; the legacy of hatred went too deep.

Yet there is very little question about the place of Haile Selassie in modern Ethiopia: the judgement of history can already be grasped. His reign represented the final stage in the construction of a centralized imperial state. The project of Tewodros II, Yohannes IV and Menelik II was finally achieved, and was moreover achieved with great skill, and with the minimum of force required to subdue an always fractious country. Despite the failure to avert the Fascist invasion and occupation, Haile Selassie was deeply aware of developments in the outside world, and adapted to these in a way that primarily served his own position, but in the process also generally advanced the interests of the Ethiopian state. That he appeared to be an anachronism by the end of his own reign, when he was 82 years old, was by no means so remarkable as the fact that he remained in control of developments for so long, and retained an ability to adapt to changes inconceivable in his youth in late nineteenth and early twentieth century Ethiopia.

The problem was that this project of centralized imperial state formation was itself deeply flawed, and its eventual achievement merely revealed the weakness of its foundations. For one thing, by concentrating power so exclusively in his own hands, Haile Selassie prevented the development of alternative political institutions—not that this would have been an easy task, in a society so geared to personal leadership as Ethiopia—and obstructed any process that might have permitted the conversion of the emperorship into a constitutional monarchy, capable of surviving changes in political leadership. It was his own dominance that made the abolition of the monarchy inevitable. More basically still, the project of imperial centralization destroyed any mechanisms through which political power could be linked to changing social forces in a highly diverse country; there was no form of representation, other than that provided by the inadequate and highly personalized operation of the imperial court. Politicians could acquire no power base of their own, because that would necessarily challenge and dilute their dependence on the emperor—a deficiency that was most clearly illustrated by the failure to manage the federal structure in Eritrea, but which equally applied to the rest of the empire.

But this empire itself was flawed. First of all, it was built on a legacy of conquest that brought with it both an extremely unequal landholding system and a structure of governance that necessarily privileged a central and largely Shoan elite; while the regime in fact constantly evaded calls for reform, it is unlikely that it could have carried out such reforms without fatally damaging its own existence. Even if the structures of social and economic inequality were destroyed, moreover, and the system of imperial government entirely swept away, Ethiopia would still face deep-seated problems in incorporating its diverse peoples into any common and participatory political system. These problems were left to Haile Selassie's successors. The judgement on his own reign was that he did what he could, very skilfully, within the highly constricting circumstances in which he operated, and which he was in no position to transcend.

BIBLIOGRAPHY AND FURTHER READING

Badoglio, Pietro, 1937, *The War in Abyssinia*. With a Foreword by Mussolini, London: Methuen.

Bahru Zewde, 1984, "Economic Origins of the Absolutist State in Ethiopia (1916–1935)", *Journal of Ethiopian Studies*, 17, pp. 1–19.

—— 2002, *Pioneers of Change in Ethiopia. The Reformist Intellectuals of the Early 20th Century*, Oxford/Athens/Addis Ababa: James Currey/Ohio University Press/Addis Ababa University Press.

Clapham, Christopher, 1969, *Haile Selassie's Government*, New York: Praeger, 1969.

Darley, Major H., 1969, *Slaves and Ivory in Abyssinia*, New York: Negro University Press.

Del Boca, Angelo, 2012, *The Negus: The Life and Death of the Last King of Kings*, Addis Ababa: Arada Books.

Gebru Tareke, 1991, *Ethiopia: Power and Protest: Peasant Revolts in the Twentieth Century*, Cambridge University Press.

Greenfield, Richard, 1965, *Ethiopia: A New Political History*, New York: Praeger. [Under a very general title, this is in fact an excellent contemporary analysis of Haile Selassie's regime by one of his personal advisers; it features the only detailed history of the failed 1960 coup]

Halldin, V., 1977, *Swedes in Haile Selassie's Ethiopia (1924–1952): A Study in Early Development and Co-Operation*, Uppsala/Stockholm: Almquist & Wiksell International Distributors.

Hess, Robert L., 1970, *Ethiopia: The Modernization of Autocracy*, Ithaca, NY and London: Cornell University Press.

Kapuscinski, Ryszard, 1978, *The Emperor: Downfall of an Autocrat*, New York: Vintage Books.

[Reprinted by Penguin Books, 2008. Although factually inaccurate, this is a literary mood piece which powerfully evokes the declining years of the Haile Selassie regime]

Marcus, H.G., 1983, *Ethiopia, Great Britain, and the United States (1941–1974): The Politics of Empire*, Berkeley: University of California Press.

—— 1987, *Haile Selassie I: The Formative Years (1892–1936)*, Berkeley: University of California Press.

Mockler, Anthony, 1984, *Haile Selassie's War*, New York: Random House.

Perham, Margery, 1969, *The Government of Ethiopia*, Evanston, IL: Northwestern University Press.

Sbacchi, Alberto, 1985, *Ethiopia Under Mussolini: Fascism and the Colonial Experience*, London: Zed Press.

Spencer, John H., 1984, *Ethiopia at Bay: A Personal Account of the Haile Selassie Years*, Algonac, MI: The American Library.

Steer, G.L., 1936, *Caesar in Abyssinia*, London: Hodder and Stoughton.

8

THE ETHIOPIAN REVOLUTION
AND THE DERG REGIME

Gérard Prunier

The word "revolution" has been overused and misused during the course of the twentieth century, to the point where it ended up losing its initial meaning: "a radical upheaval of the political and social order using violent means". This is one of the reasons why the unique and surprising political upheaval that took place in Ethiopia in the last quarter of the century has often not been properly taken into perspective. The event was unique in Africa[1] where, even if some of the anticolonial struggles had been wrapped in "socialist" trappings, they were aimed primarily at removing colonialism. The case of the former Portuguese colonies is particularly noticeable from that point of view. In spite of the Marxist-Leninist rhetoric of the Frelimo, the MPLA and the PAIGC—and the Soviet Bloc support they enjoyed—it was easy to analyze the social transformation that took place as a simple appropriation of the colonial state by a native African bourgeoisie, at times with strong internal neo-colonial traits. The social order that was being fought was essentially that of a foreign domination. But its elimination was not accompanied by any serious attempt at a radical social transformation.

This was completely distinct from what took place in Ethiopia where the revolution, even though it ended in a bloody military dictatorship, nevertheless aimed, from its very beginnings, at a radical transformation of the post-feudal order embodied by Emperor Haile Selassie. A further cause for the present lack of interest—or even of understanding—concerning what the revolution was all about is the discrediting of the very idea of socialism since the collapse of the Soviet Bloc. "Communism" is not seen in the early twenty-first century as a utopia but simply as a form of totalitarianism. Its motivating social reformist outlook, perverted and bent out of shape as it might have been by the practice of Stalinism, is today completely discounted or seen as a form of mental aberration that only affected naïve souls. And since the Ethiopian brand of "socialism" was probably the most brutal apart from the Cambodian version, its deeper initial social nature has been completely occulted by its later descent into violence.

The problem is not to "rehabilitate" the Ethiopian revolution (too many of its policies cannot withstand any form of ethical questioning). It is rather to reassess a phenomenon that is now doubly misunderstood because of our contemporary ideological transformation, and because of the difficulty to comprehend the mind-frame of the actors at the time.

The causes of the revolution

Why did Ethiopia experience a genuine social revolution while this phenomenon remained unknown elsewhere on the African continent? Basically because the history of the social structures of Ethiopia is in fact closer to those of Eastern Europe than to those of the African continent. This parallel that brings Ethiopia close to Russia actually became so evident during the years of the revolution that it struck the Russians themselves who at times were completely fascinated by traits that strongly reminded them of historical situations that ran similar to aspects of their own history and culture. This ran from the Byzantine cultural underpinnings of both cultures to the Russian participation in Menelik's conquests. And of course to the later course of a revolution which fascinated the Russians.[2] But if we had to summarize in a single sentence the main cause of the revolution we could say, imprecise as this would be, that *it came from the incapacity of a post feudal socio-political system to modernize itself when faced with the challenges of the transformations of the second half of the twentieth century.* That system was strongly defined and coherent, solid as long as it held but also rigid and coercive when it became dysfunctional. It was a traditional authoritarian monarchical institution which, in its unabashed absolutism, seemed to belong more to pre-modern Europe than to "Africa". Hence the focus on the person of the Emperor who, even though he was not the *cause* of the revolution, nevertheless represented, by his social conservatism and his personal anachronism, a living symbol of the systemic dead end where the country had become locked towards the end of his reign.[3]

Paradoxically one of the first causes of the revolution was the Emperor's success in re-centralizing the empire after the Italian defeat. Since the end of the *zemene mesafint* (era of the princes) in 1855 the re-centralization of power had been at the heart of all the political—and military—efforts of Tewodros, Yohannes and Menelik. All three of the modernizing *Neguses* had slowly built up a kind of "imperial Jacobinism", bringing more power to the centre and slowly whittling away what was left of it on the periphery.

The Second World War and the British intervention presented Haile Selassie with a unique occasion to de-feudalize Ethiopia; which did not mean at all to democratize it but more simply to centralize it. The success of this process brought with it a new burden. Centralization was accompanied by a heavy expansion of the imperial bureaucracy and of the army.[4] The costs of these new structures were high and, somewhat in the way of France before the 1789 revolution, implied a reassessment of the whole tax base. While the feudal nobility had seen its wings increasingly clipped both militarily and administratively, its economic weight remained enormous and it had no intention to accept added taxation whose burden, once more, had to fall on the peasant masses.

The economy remained archaic and industry, which was a new post-war phenomenon, employed barely 60,000 people on the eve of the revolution and represented only 15 per cent of GNP. Almost 70 per cent of investment was in the hands of foreign capitalists and the Ethiopian capitalists were mostly aristocrats who played the role of local partners but had no real autonomy. The regime had tried to develop a modern agriculture and the various economic plans[5] had massively favoured the mechanized sector at the expense of traditional agriculture. But modern mechanized agriculture operating on large acreages represented only a tiny proportion of the food production and tended to focus on export crops or raw materials for the nascent agro-industries. These tended to serve the limited needs of the urban population which could afford to purchase its products. This agricultural "modernization" relied on both the land and the capital coming from the nobility and had led to what René Lefort called "a form of mechanized feudalism".[6] The economy remained split between a large traditional agricultural sector living essentially at the level of subsistence[7] and a small "modern" sector linked to urban consumption and export.

Demographic growth kept pushing new waves of population towards the cities, at a level that was lower than in the formerly colonized parts of Africa but was still far from negligible. In the twenty years preceding the revolution Addis Ababa had grown from 300,000 to 700,000 and several provincial towns (Bahir Dar, Shashamene, Dire Dawa) had more than doubled in size. But the growth of the monetary sector of the economy had not kept pace and urban unemployment was running at 40–50 per cent. At the same time as the economic substratum was tensing up under the effects of a surface "modernization" which did not improve the lives of the peasants or those of the unemployed urban masses, the Emperor, still in the name of that same "modernization", kept introducing new administrative reforms which increased the tensions without bringing visible benefits.

Education had developed considerably but without the young graduates seeing their chances of employment increase in proportion to their years in school. The state was obsessed with mere statistical progress in education. Enrolment numbers would grow 10 per cent per year in primary education and 15 to 20 per cent in the secondary system. But since the budget did not keep pace, per capita spending per student actually decreased, the whole thing resulting in the mass production of larger and larger numbers of poorly educated school-leavers who could not find jobs. Further up, in spite of a very severe policy of selection at university entrance exams, the result was to inflate the numbers of students who ended up in a social cul-de-sac. In the radical political climate of the 1960s, this gave birth to a large militant student movement which was to have an even greater impact on Ethiopian society than their comrades had in Berlin, Paris or Berkeley.[8] This was because this semi-educated and radicalized youth was facing not the development of the capitalist mass-consumption society but rather something more akin to the 1905 Russian aristocracy. The old feudal elite was at times trying to really modernize itself through its association with foreign investors; but most of the time it was content to occupy the key bureaucratic positions of the administration upper ranks where it would keep playing a "new" bureaucratic version of the old feudal quarrels of yesteryear. To offset their power, the Emperor, who was still obsessed with keeping all the threads of power ultimately in his own hands, played the card of the educated young men who were beginning to filter up from the small middle class and the lower ranks of the aristocracy.

These "new men", in the Roman sense, were fighting each other and clashing with the old aristocracy, all for the greater benefit of the Emperor who, through these palace intrigues, managed to keep the whole system under his personal control. But the end result was to combine a heavy Byzantine-type bureaucracy with the inefficiency of permanently feuding administrative factions. Institutions such as "the Parliament" or "the Constitution" were hollow structures which had created expectations they could not satisfy. The press, professional associations and trade unions were kept under tight control by a nit-picking security system which tended to paralyze social interaction and to breed frustrations. The system remained broadly efficient at handling the status quo but extraordinarily incompetent at facing change and modernization.

This left the army as a key separate element of the social order. The Ethiopian army was certainly the best on the African continent, apart from South Africa. Well trained and well equipped through American help, the military institution intimately embodied the contradictions of the global Ethiopian society. The superior officers were graduates from the Military Academy in Harar and would complete their training by attending advanced courses abroad, particularly in the US. Middle-ranking officers, coming from less well-to-do families, were trained at the Holeta Military Academy, less prestigious than the Harar one. As for the NCOs and the rank-and-file soldiers who came from the urban proletariat or the peasantry, they were trained directly within their units. Army salaries were not very generous and were supplemented by private family resources in the case of the officers. But this army was an operational army which had not stopped fighting over the last twenty years, either on the country's borders (the 1963–64 war with

Somalia) or in the repression of various insurrections, the most complex of those being of course the Eritrean revolt.[9] Militarily, dissidence in Eritrea had slowly began to move from the level of a revolt to that of a full-scale war and the army felt ill-treated and ill-considered, given its constant efforts and sacrifices. Organized and conceived as an element in the centralizing policy of the state, the army could not but be viscerally aware of the difficult nationality problem which the high-handed attitude of the Shoan Amhara nobility seemed to consider as a non-issue. As a result the armed forces were in a complex situation: riven by unacknowledged class-conflicts, fiercely nationalistic and attached to the centralizing policy of the state, they were also humiliated by their perfunctory treatment at the hands of the Emperor and of the high nobility which took them for granted. These forces were heavy with anger, suffering and frustration. And they had guns.

A spontaneous popular uprising starts the revolution (1974)

Against this background of progressive social slippage and muted conflicts specific events started to trigger developments resulting in unexpected consequences. The first of these was the 1972–3 food shortage which slowly grew to famine level. The results of the famine did not by themselves trigger the revolt. It was limited to Wollo and Tigray and worse famines had occurred before.[10] But the dearth of food products drove prices up over the whole national territory, not just in the famine areas. Besides the media development and the increased political consciousness there were more critical attitudes to a hitherto highly respected sovereign. The 1973 famine was severe even if definitely less damaging than the 1888–92 one. But it was the first one in Ethiopia's history to be strongly mediatized both inside the country and abroad.

The image of Emperor Haile Selassie as "Father of the Nation" was brutally dented by the reality of the old man's callous senility. The contrast between the prestigious international image of the Emperor, the luxury in which he and his courtiers were living and the indifference towards the tragedy his people was going through combined to create a disastrous effect.[11] For the first time the slogans of the student movement, which had so far seemed almost sacrilegious to the ordinary population, began to bite into the public consciousness. A second factor which played a significant role in the situation was the 1973 oil shock which led to a massive rise in petrol prices. In Addis Ababa the price of petrol at the pump jumped by 95 per cent on 1 February 1974, and the drivers of the collective taxis which made up most of the public transport system were not allowed to raise their prices to offset the cost.[12]

And, at the same moment, the Ministry of Education announced a reform aimed at limiting the number of the students allowed to enrol, which threatened both their immediate situation and their future since teaching was one of the main outlets for the overflow of young graduates. The taxi drivers and the teachers both decided to go on strike on the same day, 18 February. In an already tense situation, thousands of demonstrators poured into the streets, goaded on by the revolutionary students. The small urban working class of Addis Ababa joined in after a call to strike was aired by the Confederation of Ethiopian Labour Unions (CELU). The CELU was a very moderate and reformist organization, without the slightest Marxist leanings. But the Emperor had never allowed it to unionize the civil service and it felt that this was a great opportunity to enter a domain so far inaccessible. In a few days the CELU's membership went up by 40 per cent and reached 120,000 members. By then everybody had taken to the streets, from the lower ranks of the clergy to the prostitutes, in what quickly became a mixture of socio-economic demands and a mass psychodrama in which the general public was shouting down a stale and moth-eaten regime that had no more capacity to offer a future. The Emperor seemed to be in a state of shock. He did not seem to understand what was going on and he gave up on one thing after another. He arbitrarily brought gas prices down, gave up on the reform of the educational system, accepted the unionization of the public service and replaced his unpopular Prime Minister Aklilu Habte Wold with Endelkatchew Makonen. But it was very late in the day and the shadow of the praetorians was beginning to loom on the revolutionary scene.

A first military mutiny had taken place way down in Sidamo in mid-January and had received no attention.[13] But on 25 February the 2nd Division which was fighting in Eritrea mutinied as a corps. A feverish agitation spread among the units and several started to ask for a salary increase. But the demands soon went beyond simple material ones. Between March and June 1974, several *derg*s (committees) were created in various regiments. They had different ideological and political colorations, ranging from simply reformist organizations to violently revolutionary ones.

The "First *Derg*" under Colonel Alem Zewde was a middle of the road one, aiming at a structural reform of the army but without challenging the authority of the Emperor. Even this was too much for the conservative groups at the court who countered by creating another structure under Brigadier Abebe Abiye, who had been in charge of repression in the army after the coup of 1960. Brigadier Abebe Abiye's group was supposed to devise a programme of repression within the army to bring it back in line and reassert the authority of the Emperor, as had been done fourteen years before.

But the times had changed and soon a "Second *Derg*" appeared, regrouping in a clandestine organization middle ranking officers and even NCOs who shared a radical left-wing revolutionary orientation. Those three groups started to struggle among themselves for control of the newly Provisional Military Administrative Council (PMAC) which had been set up to bypass the Army General Staff. The PMAC relied on the armed might of the 4th Division in the capital and on 26 April it arrested over two hundred civilians, high-ranking members of the civil service and aristocrats. By then, the target of the PMAC revolutionaries was now not even the imperial power—which had been so weakened—but their moderate rivals who were trying to set up a constitutional monarchy or a conservative republic.

By July, in the hope of staving off the rapidly increasing slide to the left, the Emperor accepted the resignation of his Prime Minister and his replacement by the "Red Prince", Ras Mikail Imru, an aristocrat known for his broadly reformist views. Ras Imru was the last chance for the reformist cause. To control the rise of the radical military, he fired Brigadier Abebe Abiye and replaced him as Defence Minister by a popular military hero, General Aman Andom.[14] General Andom was not a Derg member. But his trip to Eritrea, where he was welcomed by enthusiastic crowds, was a success. This did not please the radical officers who combined simplified left-wing views with a rabid form of nationalism. They suspected General Aman Andom of favouring some form of autonomy for Eritrea and they countered it by launching a violently nationalist programme dubbed *Ityopia Tiqdem*, "Ethiopia First".

Meanwhile the Derg, which felt it had to destroy the imperial mystique before deposing Haile Selassie, had launched a massive psychological campaign aiming at destroying the aura that still surrounded the old monarch. He was accused of being a thief,[15] of being indifferent to the recent famine[16] and of having fled abroad in a cowardly way at the time of the Italian invasion. Endelkachew Makonen and several members of the former government and nobility were arrested while businesses belonging to the imperial family were nationalized. The old Emperor appeared stunned. Several times he refused either to flee abroad or to arrest the PMAC leaders, not seeming to comprehend the process that was unfolding.[17] On 12 September he was arrested and taken into custody. His death was announced on 27 August 1975, supposedly from natural causes.[18]

General Aman Andom was made Prime Minister in replacement of Ras Imru. The 1955 Constitution was abolished, the parliament was dissolved and on 19 October 1974 special courts martial were created to try people who were to be charged for conduct relating to the famine. All strikes became illegal and a curfew was instated.[19] Hundreds of former government dignitaries were arrested. The PMAC then announced that all the students were to be mobilized in the so-called *zemetcha* (campaign) and "collaborate in educating the masses". This was in fact the beginning of what Professor Edmond Keller has aptly called "a socialist revolution by the back door".[20]

Why had the army come to embody a revolutionary movement which had started as a genuine popular movement? A good summary was given by Claudio Moffa when he wrote:

> In spite of the clear political character of their demands, neither the students nor the working class nor other sections of the urban population (not to speak of the peasants) had managed to give birth to a coherent organization that could operate nationally.... In this situation, the power vacuum that had happened could not be filled by any other social group except the Army, the only organized force existing in the country. And it was with this Army that all "parties" would henceforth have to deal with.[21]

The students, who had begun to realize that the army had no intention to share power with them, began to agitate for the creation of a new civilian government. The CELU had come to the same conclusion and started to support the students' demands, trying to launch a general strike. The strike was nipped in the bud by the army which arrested all the trade union leaders. The air force, whose personnel was more highly educated than the land army, began to get restless and the PMAC started to arrest "counter-revolutionary officers".

By then General Aman Andom had paradoxically become the last obstacle to a military dictatorship. He was deposed as Prime Minister and died resisting arrest on 23 November while, on the same day, the Derg shot sixty of the former top politicians and members of the aristocracy in an Ekaterinburg-type massacre.

On 20 December the PMAC announced its Ten Points Programme, defining the aims of the Ethiopian Revolution as the army saw it. In the name of *hibretesebawinet* ("socialism"), a new word it had just invented, Ethiopia would remain united (this was for the Eritreans), the state would take total control of the economy and a great national socialist party would be created. The next day the new regime announced that all the students enrolled for the *zemetcha* campaign would be sent to the countryside, to give literacy classes to the peasantry, safely far from the cities. The army did not want any "socialist" rivals in the urban areas where its power was being established. The popular revolution had ended and the new secret military junta had taken over.[22] The civilian component of the revolution now realized it would have to fight for its life.

"White Terror" against "Red Terror": the struggle for the control of power (1975–8)

How can we define the group of people who had taken power through this lopsided struggle? It was of course a military group. But it was not the "military elite", as is often the case in military coups in Africa or the Middle East.[23] The Derg was a conspiratorial group of junior officers and NCOs that carried its own "class struggle" within the military establishment itself. It was mysterious and by the end of 1974 only the name of its President, Teferi Bante, had been made public. Nobody was really sure of its real structure and the first Vice-President, Mengistu Haile Mariam, later to emerge as the real leader, was at first half hidden in the shadows.

The internal convulsions of the "Committee" remained secret, all the more so as they became bloodier and bloodier. The first victim had been the first organizer of the Derg, Major Tefera Tekle Ab, who "disappeared" in 1974. By mid-1975 three key leaders—General Getachew Nadew and Majors Sisay Habte and Kiros Alemayu—were killed. The Derg President, Brigadier-General Teferi Bante, was shot during a gunfight inside the old Imperial Palace in February 1977 where eight members of the "Committee" were killed. It was then that Lt Colonel Mengistu Haile Mariam began to come out of his grey comfort zone and to show himself as the hidden hand behind these purges. The final figure of this deadly ballet was reached in September 1977 when Vice-President Colonel Atnafu Abate was himself executed, in the company of forty-six other officers. Mengistu Haile Mariam had finally emerged as the undisputed master of the bloody junta.

But these internal spasms were not occurring in a political void. The Derg had all the while to contend with the organized elements of the civilian movement that had preceded it and was trying to survive under the military dictatorship. There were many groups[24] but two especially played a major role, Mei'son[25] and the Ethiopian Peoples Revolutionary Party (EPRP). Mei'son was close to "orthodox" Communist Parties and had a strong French tinge.[26] It also had a largely Oromo membership, something that would later open it to accusations of "nationalist deviationism". The EPRP was the direct descendant of the Ethiopian Student Association in the US. It was also more "leftist", in 1960s parlance, and its membership tended to be more Amhara. This resulted in a number of tactical choices. Mei'son displayed a measure of concern for "revolutionary legality" while the EPRP tended more towards a conspiratorial approach. Mei'son was closer to the centralizing policies of the military while the EPRP tended to be open to the Eritrean struggle. Mei'son, in true Soviet tactical style, believed that Ethiopia was not yet ready for a full socialist revolution, while the EPRP was "maximalist" and demanded the immediate establishment of a full Communist society. Given this logic Mei'son felt it could collaborate with the army "to create the objective circumstances of the transition towards a genuine socialist society" while the maximalist EPRP was soon to plunge into an armed face-off with the Derg. These were genuine differences in revolutionary strategy that the Derg, which cynically used the socialist phraseology for its short-term tactical power gains, could not have cared less about.

All industries and trade were nationalized and the "bourgeois" CELU was disbanded and replaced by a "revolutionary" trade union confederation, the All-Ethiopia Trade Union (AETU), totally controlled by the army. On 4 February 1975 all land was nationalized and distributed to the peasants.[27] Faced by such an array of "socialist" measures, even if they were taken largely in a short-term tactical perspective, it was difficult for the civilian groups to dissent.[28] This is where the parting of the ways between Mei'son and the EPRP became unavoidable. Mei'son, faithful to its "gradualist" approach, accepted to work with the Derg while the EPRP branded the army as "fascist" and embarked in a policy of open confrontation with the rising dictatorship. Mei'son and the small groups cultivated by the Derg agreed to enter into a new structure, the Political Office for Mass Organization Affairs (POMOA), imagined by the army as an organization to "mobilize the masses". The EPRP refused to collaborate and plunged into the armed struggle. The small party was well grounded in the cities, particularly in Addis Ababa, where the educated youth was largely behind it.

On 16 September 1976 the EPRP, now branded as "anarchist", was declared to be "an enemy of the revolution". This was the beginning of an urban civil war where the Derg unleashed its own "Red Terror" against the alleged "White Terror" of the youth organization.[29] From late 1976 to the end of 1978, Ethiopia was to live through two particularly atrocious years. In true revolutionary fashion the EPRP was sure that the Derg, which did not have deep popular roots, could not survive an armed confrontation. It started killing army officers at random and the regime answered these killings blow for blow. The violence started as a precise targeted exchange, but with an escalation in the killings it became broader and less precise. The families of the militants often became victims of their sons' engagement. The EPRP started to recruit children as killers and the Derg went as far as replying by the indiscriminate massacre of entire classrooms of school children, "for the example". The horror reached a kind of apex during the few days of 20 April to 1 May 1977 when more than one thousand students and secondary school pupils were massacred to stop the EPRP from sabotaging the May 1st "popular demonstration" the regime had planned. Those terrifying years were to have a durable effect on Ethiopian collective psychology and to deeply alter the population's perception of politics.

The bloodletting had reached such frantic levels that the country seemed to be on the brink of some kind of a total collapse. This tempted the Somali dictator Mohamed Siad Barre into intervening and trying to wrench the Somali-populated region of the Ogaden from Ethiopian control.[30] For several years Siad Barre had been remote controlling a Somali guerrilla movement in Ethiopia, the Western Somali Liberation Front (WSLF). But in July 1977 he stopped pretending that the WSLF was "Ethiopian" and sent his regular army in support of a general guerrilla offensive in the Ogaden. For a time, the situation of the Derg looked desperate, not because of the WSLF alone, but because the enemies of the "Socialist" military had been multiplying over the last few months. The urban areas, as noted, were torn apart by the "Red Terror" struggle with the Ultra-Left. In the countryside many regions had seen guerrilla groups arise against what they still perceived, in traditional Ethiopian fashion, as the "Imperial Centre": the EDU and TPLF in Tigray, the OLF in Oromo areas, the SALF in Bale and the ALF among the Afar. None of these movements had the capacity to overthrow the regime alone. But their multiplication was draining the resources of the army which had to fight simultaneously on five or six fronts. To make things worse for the Derg, the Eritreans, who felt their enemy weakening, had launched a major offensive which had brought them control of nearly 80 per cent of the former Italian colony. During the summer of 1977, when the Somali offensive added its external weight to these multiple internal revolts, it looked as if the military regime was nearing the brink of total collapse. The final blow seemed to come when Mei'son, which had made the choice of "critically supporting" the Derg, decided that enough was enough and joined the opposition. Colonel Mengistu declared a state of national emergency and called for mass mobilization. Tens of thousands were conscripted. But this by itself would not have been enough if the international diplomatic landscape had not been suddenly altered.

For some months the Derg had been negotiating with the Russians. The Soviet Union had started to invest in the Horn of Africa in the 1960s, through help to the Somali Republic. Because of its irredentist ideological basis—uniting all the Somali people under one flag— Mogadishu had refused to sign the OAU Charter whose Article 4b enshrined a clearly-set preservation of colonial borders. The Somali Republic had started on its unification programme by fusing the former colonies of British Somaliland and Somalia Italiana. But it still wanted Djibouti, the Kenyan Northern Frontier District and the Ethiopian Ogaden. Up to the early 1970s, all these entities were part of US-protected territories, which, in the Cold War logic, opened a broad opportunity for Moscow's diplomacy. But the 1974 Ethiopian revolution had put all this into question and the Russians had started secret negotiations with the military regime. The situation was paradoxical since the Somali invasion had been prepared with the help of Red Army military advisers and the Somali Army was 100 per cent equipped with Russian weapons. But as the Derg was on the verge of collapse, for Moscow the time had come for a quick decision. The Derg's demise would have opened the way either for a classical military dictatorship which would probably have turned towards the US[31] or else for a ultra-left civilian takeover, with militants who would have been hostile to the USSR. In both cases Moscow would have lost out.

So it decided to switch alliances and in December 1977 engineered for the benefit of the Derg the type of massive military air bridge which it was to use again two years later for the benefit of Babrak Karmal in Afghanistan. Besides their own military advisers and very large quantities of military equipment, the Russians ferried South Yemeni troops[32] and several thousand Cubans. These combined forces went on the offensive at the end of January 1978 and within three months, owing to their superior equipment and firepower, had retaken all the ground lost to the Somali in the Ogaden. The US Secretary of State, Cyrus Vance, had obtained from Brezhnev a promise that the Soviet-led offensive would stop at Somalia's border and that the communist armies would not occupy the country, as they certainly could have done if they had wanted. By March 1978 the war was over and the Somali state, which had been entirely built on the ideology of national unity, entered into a deep crisis which would eventually lead to its total disappearance in 1991.

As soon as he was free from the Somali threat, Mengistu launched a major offensive in Eritrea which pushed the EPLF back and regained most of the ground the guerrillas had occupied during the last eighteen months. But this did not really change the situation in the north because the Derg was incapable of thinking up a coherent strategy beyond its policy of absolute centralism. On 20 November 1978 Mengistu went to Moscow to sign a "Treaty of Friendship and Cooperation" which put Ethiopia solidly in the Soviet orbit. For the time being, the triumph of the "socialist" military regime was complete. But the problem then was what to do with its victory.

The attempt at institutionalizing a communist regime (1979–1987)

The Soviets wanted to see Ethiopia turn itself into a standard "People's Republic" on the pattern of the eastern European countries. The Derg did not disagree but it was traversed by deep contradictions between its component parts and had to find a way of doing what Moscow wanted. Since 1976 the regime had created a Committee for Organizing the Party of the Workers of Ethiopia (COPWE) which was supposed to prepare the birth of the great single Marxist-Leninist party. But the contradictions had been going on for a long time and had resulted in very little because COPWE needed both to take into account the Ethiopian constraints *and* satisfy at the same time the ideologues in Moscow who were getting all the more concerned as considerations of orthodoxy showed that the reality of "communist" power was slowly dissolving itself into a sea of bureaucratic confusion, political contradictions and economic shortages. So it took eight long years for COPWE to phase itself out and become the Workers Party of Ethiopia (WPE).

The new party was enthroned on 12 September 1984 during a gigantic popular show choreographed by the North Koreans. The date picked had been chosen so as to coincide with the tenth anniversary of the revolution and it cost between $120m and $150m, at a time when the country had once more plunged headlong into one of its murderous famines. The massive expenses undertaken at a time when the country was again suffering—the bill for spirits and other alcoholic drinks alone amounted to more than $2m—were seen both in Ethiopia itself and abroad as an insult to the dying peasantry. But the Derg did not care. In many ways, just as Haile Selassie's coronation had been in 1930, it was first and foremost a solemn declaration of power—*mengist*. The new regime was trying to set itself up as a new dynasty. And its policies soon headed for a completely independent, bizarre and contrary form of "Ethiopian socialism" that not even its Soviet godparents approved of. The main traits had to do with population transfers and villageization.

Since famine had been a major factor in the explosion of the revolution in 1974, its return ten years later under a "socialist" regime that prided itself in its pro-peasant policies was a black spot for its self-image. Worse, the regime could only alleviate the famine with Western aid, particularly American.[33] For Mengistu this was an unacceptable situation. Ethiopia should not be dependent on foreign countries, particularly capitalist ones.

If we look at Ethiopia's human geography, we immediately notice that the "historical north" is much more populated than the lowlands of the south and west. For the head of the Ethiopian state, the solution was deceptively simple: let us transport the starving people from the exhausted lands of Wollo and Tigray and resettle them around Gambella or in Gamo Gofa. But this "solution" was not feasible for a number of reasons: the transporting of people was carried out in extremely brutal ways, killing more than 50,000 settlers; there was nothing prepared at the destination sites to help the re-accommodation of the incoming people; the northern peasants were suddenly transported from a malaria-free ecosystem to a different one in the lowlands where malaria killed them in large numbers; and the local populations at the new sites had no sympathy for these "humanitarian invaders" who were seen as coming to take over their lands.[34]

The amount of money budgeted by the government to pay for the transporting of the people being resettled was completely insufficient and mortality was bound to be massive. The population transfer programme finally ground to a halt in January 1986 after 591,000 had been deported. Was this a "Khmer Rouge"-like annihilation campaign as some human right militants pretended at the time?[35] Not really. The transported villages did not look like concentration camps even if people were dying there. There was no barbed wires or watch towers.[36] So what lay behind this self-destructive form of "aid"? Largely it was two converging forces. One was the traditional authoritarianism of Abyssinian culture, where *mengist* (the state power) is all powerful and quasi mystical. The second was the military nature of the operation. The men who ran it were dim-witted and talking to them was appalling. It was a simplified military logistics approach to a complex problem combining agriculture, climate, ecology, demographic growth and an archaic peasant culture. The whole process could not even be questioned because it had the dual seal of approval of the Abyssinian state and of its present "socialist progress" incarnation.

Then what about villageization, the other pillar of the Derg's policy of social engineering? The idea of villagization was another false good idea. Ethiopian rural dwellings are dispersed. So regrouping them would theoretically allow the government to provide more easily and at a lower cost all the public services (running water, school, dispensaries) that the rural habitat lacked. The problem, as the Tanzanians had already experienced when they had tried the same thing some ten years earlier, was that it was much easier to move people by force than to provide them with the proper services later.[37] Contrary to the population transfers which implied moving people 1,000 or 1,500 km at a time, villagization would take place within a restricted perimeter of some 40 to 60 kilometres. But the numbers involved were much higher. Mengistu wanted to "villageize" at least seven million people. Here the movement was generally on foot, dismantling the houses or even carrying them whole on people's shoulders. Once set in motion both processes had acquired a "socialist" label, as if Karl Marx's main social aim had been to re-engineer the lives of African peasants. The policies had become a basic tenet of *hibretesebawinet* and any rational argumentation that ran counter to these would be attacked as an ideological heresy.[38] Still, bad as the process was, the "concentration camps" image was not correct. But these "open" villages were nevertheless traps for the peasants who had been obliged to join them, for the same reasons as in Tanzania: they were too far from the outer ring of fields, which led to the abandonment of some of the cultivated areas; some markets had become too distant; crop theft became frequent; too many small livestock around the villages themselves led to overgrazing on too small an area, leading in turn to massive killing of animals and later to a dearth of animal production, both milk and meat and a lot of time was wasted in walking to the fields and back. Meanwhile the promised "collective equipment" never materialized or when it did, it was of cheap "communist" quality and did not work. The only benefits were for the government which obtained two things: better fiscal returns and a higher degree of security control making it harder for the guerrillas to obtain support from the harassed peasantry.

In terms of agricultural policy, many of the errors committed in the USSR in the 1930s were replicated in Ethiopia, particularly in terms of collectivization. Between 1980 and 1985, the collective farms, which represented only 5 per cent of cultivated areas, received 43 per cent of the investment in the agricultural sector and their returns represented less money than what had been invested in their development.[39] There again, ideology had replaced common sense.

Actually this obdurate approach can call into question the very nature of the regime. Were Mengistu and his close associates really "Communists"? Their civilian allies and/or opponents of the EPRP and Mei'son had been. But the military? In his remarkable study on the revolution,[40] Gebru Tareke shows time and time again how the very men in charge of carrying out these policies did not really understand what they were doing and seem to believe in fallacies. Then why do it? The answer might be at two levels. On the one hand these simple souls were nationalists. They believed that "Marxism" (about which they knew next to nothing) would provide them with a quasi-magic blueprint for "development". They trusted their Eastern European advisers just as later generations would trust the World Bank and the IMF. Thus the "revolutionary institutions"—the Constitution, the 835-member *Shengo* (legislature) frozen in its liturgical formalism, the local *kebele*s (neighbourhoods) in towns, the Peasant Associations in the countryside, the collective farms, the single party, the single "Trade Union", the controlled press which nobody read—were not *really* seen as practical measures but rather as some kind of scriptural formulas which would almost magically arrive at some wonderful results. The deep imprint of extremely ritualized religion was obvious in the deeply obedient approach to ideology displayed by the regime during those years. What mattered was neither actual understanding nor pragmatic efficiency but *faith* and a belief in miracles.

The fall of the regime (1988–1991)

For a while, after the famine, it looked like the regime had reached a kind of cruising speed and might survive. But the structural problems it faced were enormous:

• It was under attack from a whole number of guerrilla groups, one of which, the TPLF, wanted to go all the way to Addis Ababa. The Eritreans could have been sidetracked by offering them independence, even though it would have meant a major policy reversal for the Derg, and those operating in the peripheries did not have the military capacity to go all the way and take over the centre of power, but the TPLF could neither be resisted indefinitely nor be fobbed off.
• The Derg needed enormous amounts of weaponry which the Soviets had provided so far. But from 1985 Gorbachev launched a new course in Soviet policies, both at home and abroad. In 1989 the Russians evacuated Afghanistan and they started to explain to Mengistu that their help would have to end soon.
• The United States, which had long considered the main anti-Derg fronts with a great deal of suspicion—they were after all avowedly Marxist themselves—began to feel that military aid could replace the humanitarian aid which had been provided during the famine. Using the services of two of their allies in the region, Saddam Hussein in Iraq and Jaafar al-Nimeiry in the Sudan, they started to transfer limited but not negligible quantities of military equipment to the EPLF, under the unspoken understanding that some of it would be later transferred to the TPLF.[41]
• Inside Ethiopia, the erratic Derg policies towards the peasantry had alienated it permanently. Given the traditional attitude of deference towards authority, many peasants still obeyed superficially but dissented in practice, cheating on their taxes, not carrying out the

instructions of the regime and trying to hide their young men from military conscription. Those youths who were forced to go anyway did not want to fight. As soon as they arrived in Eritrea they would desert in droves, to the point where the EPLF, which could not feed them, would shove them over the border into the Sudan, from where they would try to go back to their areas of origin on foot.

The 1988 defeat at Af Abet, which Gebru Tareke aptly called "Ethiopia's Dien Bien Phu",[42] was a tipping point. After Af Abet, the TPLF turned into a conventional army that could get re-supplied while its opponents could not. In May 1989 the Army tried to overthrow Mengistu in a desperate and poorly organized coup. Mengistu, who was in Pankow (East Germany) countered the coup masterfully[43] and several of the rebel superior officers, including the commander of the air force, committed suicide. Some of the TPLF's prisoners started to join their captors in special units that were created to marshal them and turn them against their erstwhile comrades. The regime, abandoned by the collapsing Soviet Empire, was on its last legs. When Mengistu came back from East Germany he half-heartedly started his own economic and social mini-*perestroika*. But contrary to the Russian model, it was not accompanied by any political liberalization. In early 1991 the TPLF, now reinforced by whole units of POWs who had decided to join the insurgency, went on the offensive and approached Addis Ababa. In Eritrea the EPLF gained control of the whole province. On 21 May 1991, while his army was making a desperate last stand at Dekemhare, Mengistu fled ignominiously, to take refuge in Zimbabwe. He had exalted the memory of Emperor Tewodros and his last supporters had expected him to die in battle or by his own hand. But his inglorious flight at least preserved the capital from a bloody fate.[44]

Conclusion

What have been the effects of the largest movement of revolutionary social transformation to take place on the African continent since the end of decolonization? At the material level, not much. Mengistu's "socialist utopia" did not leave anything behind. But there were many intangible changes that make today's Ethiopia a very different country from the one that plunged into the revolution in 1974. The biggest and still unresolved problem is that of landholding. The land nationalization decree of February 1975 has been changed but in multiple ambiguous ways that stopped short of two things: going back to the pre-revolutionary situation or privatizing land outright. The land problem in today's Ethiopia has become extraordinarily complex and is unlikely to remain as it is. Where will it go is still hard to decide. But one thing is sure: its transformation will be at the heart of the country's evolution in the coming years. From the agrarian point of view—and Ethiopia still is and will remain for many years a mostly agricultural country—the revolution is not yet over.

Another momentous change brought about by the revolution is a drastic change in the status of the Muslim population. Muslims in today's Ethiopia have become *de jure* and *de facto* full citizens. The acquisition of full civic rights has been an essential transformation in a country where they had been second class citizens since the sixteenth century. This transformation has had a soothing effect on Ethiopian religious relations where the growth of radical fundamentalism seen in the rest of the Islamic world is perhaps less threatening. It does not mean that the phenomenon does not exist, but it is muted and culturally blended. Today most Ethiopian Muslims are still Ethiopian first and Muslim second. This might not last, but it has so far limited the development of radical Islam in spite of the violence occurring in neighbouring countries such as Somalia and Sudan. This stabilization of Ethiopian Islam is one of the few undiluted achievements of the revolution.

Another benefit of the revolution is the fact that the people count. Full-fledged democracy still remains a future target in Ethiopia. But the heavy social weight of the aristocracy is gone and the opinion of ordinary people has become a key element of the political game. Although the Derg was probably more anti-democratic than the monarchy it had abolished, its discourse was democratic. The *notion* that the ordinary people mattered was a new concept. That Haile Selassie had certainly, in his own way, wanted the good of his people is undeniable. But the idea that the people themselves could discuss and contribute to their own welfare was obviously completely foreign to his political and philosophical world view. The Derg, which did not practice it, rhetorically enthroned the *principle* of democracy. It is obvious that this principle has taken root and will not leave the scene. How it will embody itself in the future is hard to say. But its very existence is a product of the revolution.

The role of violence has also shifted. Up to 1974 violence was an accepted part of society. It was supposed to be ritualized, channelled and controlled, or else it erupted into *shiftannet* (armed dissidence). Such a course obviously still exists, but it has lost a great part of its legitimacy and cultural acceptance. The Derg's orgy of violence has had a kind of immunizing effect on the social body. Violence is not anymore a simple acceptable fact as it had been for centuries.

And finally the revolution has opened Ethiopia to the world. Before 1974 the outside world was a bizarre and forbidding universe that had to be mediated through the emperor himself, through a select group of aristocrats and through a few intellectuals. The revolution has opened the door to the outside winds. There is still a tendency in Ethiopian culture to try to filter and control these influences because, for many centuries and with some reason, Abyssinia has seen the world as a threat. But there is a kind of unspoken agreement on the fact that the outside world is here and will stay here. It does not mean that "globalization" is automatically welcome and fondly adopted. But Ethiopia has begun to see itself as a part of the world and not only as its centre.

BIBLIOGRAPHY AND FURTHER READING

Africa Watch, 1991, *Evil Days: Thirty Years of War and Famine in Ethiopia*, London: Africa Watch.

Andargachew Tiruneh, 1993, *The Ethiopian Revolution, 1974–1987: From an Aristocratic to a Totalitarian Autocracy*, Cambridge: Cambridge University Press.

Aregawi Berhe, 2009, *A Political History of the Tigray's People Liberation Front (1975–1991)*, Los Angeles: Tsehai Publishers.

Bahru Zewde, 2014, *The Quest for Socialist Utopia: the Ethiopian Student Movement (1960–1974)*, London: James Currey.

Balsvik, Randi R., 1985, *Haile Selassie's Students: The Intellectual and Social Background to Revolution, 1952–1977*, East Lansing, MI: African Studies Centre, Michigan State University.

Clapham, Christopher, 1988, *Transformation and Continuity in Revolutionary Ethiopia*, Cambridge University Press.

Clay, J.W. and Holcomb, B.K., 1986, *Politics and the Ethiopian Famine (1984–1985)*, Trenton, NJ: Red Sea Press.

Dawit Wolde Gyorgis, 1989, *Red Tears*, Lawrenceville, NJ: Red Sea Press.

Del Boca, Angelo, 1995, *Il Negus. Vita e morte dell'ultimo Re dei Re*, Rome: Laterza.

Dessalegn Rahmato, 1991, *Famine and Survival Strategies: A Case Study of Northeast Ethiopia*, Uppsala: Nordiska Afrikainstitutet,

Donham, Donald, 1999, *Marxist Modern: an Ethnographic History of the Ethiopian Revolution*, Berkeley, CA: University of California Press.

Eide, Ø. M., 2000, *Revolution and Religion in Ethiopia (1974–1985)*, Oxford: James Currey.

Ergas, Z., 1980, "Why did the Ujamaa Village Policy Fail? Towards a Global Analysis", *Journal of Modern African Studies*, 28 (3), pp. 387–410.

Eshetu Chole, 2004, *Underdevelopment in Ethiopia*, Addis-Ababa: OSSREA.

Fontrier, Marc, 1999, *La chute de la junte militaire éthiopienne (1987–1991): Chroniques de la République populaire et démocratique d'Éthiopie*, Paris: L'Harmattan, ARESAE.

Gebru Tareke, 1991, *Ethiopia: Power and Protest: Peasant Revolts in the Twentieth Century*, Cambridge University Press.

—— 2009, *The Ethiopian Revolution*, New Haven, CT: Yale University Press.

Gill, G. J. (ed.), 1974, *Readings on the Ethiopian Economy*, Addis Ababa: Haile Selassie University, Institute of Development Studies.

Gilkes, Patrick, 1975, *The Dying Lion. Feudalism and Modernization in Ethiopia*, New York: St. Martin's Press.

Glucksman, André and Wolton, Thierry, 1986, *Silence on tue*, Paris: Grasset. [To be mentioned only for documentary purposes; this is a Cold War propaganda work of dubious factual value]

Gyenge, Zoltan, 1976, *Ethiopia on the Road of Non-Capitalist Development*, Budapest. [the symmetric opposite of the book mentioned above]

Hiwot Tefera, 2012, *Tower in the Sky*, Addis Ababa University Press.

Jean, François, 1986, *Ethiopie: du bon usage de la famine*, Paris: MSF.

Kapuscinski, Ryszard, 1978, *The Emperor: Downfall of an Autocrat*, New York: Vintage.

Keller, Edmond, 1988, *Revolutionary Ethiopia: From Empire to People's Republic*, Bloomington, IN: Indiana University Press.

Kiflu Tadesse, 1993, *The Generation*, 1st vol., Trenton, NJ: The Red Sea Press.

—— 1998, *The Generation*, 2nd vol., Washington, DC: University Press of America.

Lefort, René, 1983, *Ethiopia: An Heretical Revolution?* London: Zed Press.

Makonnen Araya, 2011, *Negotiating a Lion's Share of Freedom: Adventures of an Idealist Caught Up in the Ethiopian Civil War*, Raleigh, NC: Lulu.com.

Markakis, John, 1974, *Ethiopia, Anatomy of a Traditional Polity*, Oxford University Press.

—— 1987, *National and Class Conflict in the Horn of Africa*, Cambridge University Press.

Markakis, John and Nega Ayele, 1978, *Class and Revolution in Ethiopia*, Nottingham: Spokesman.

Messay Kebede, 2011, *Ideology and Elite Conflicts. Autopsy of the Ethiopian Revolution*, Lanham: Lexington Books.

Mohamed Yimam, 2013, *Wore Negari: a Memoir of an Ethiopian Youth in the Turbulent '70s*, Bloomington, IN: X-Libris.

Moffa, Claudio, 1980, *La rivoluzione etiopica. Testi e documenti*, Urbino: Argali.

Pankhurst, Alula, 1992, *Resettlement A Famine in Ethiopia: the Villagers' Experience*, Manchester University Press.

Pankhurst, Richard, 1986, *The History of Famine and Epidemics in Ethiopia Prior to the Twentieth Century*, Addis Ababa: Relief and Rehabilitation Commission.

Prunier, Gérard, 1994, "Population Resettlement in Ethiopia: the Financial Aspect", in *Etudes éthiopiennes, Actes du 10e Congrès international des études éthiopiennes, Paris 20–26 août 1988*, Paris: Société Française d'Études Éthiopiennes, pp. 683–89.

RRC, Relief and Rehabilitation Commission, 1985, *The Challenges of Drought: Ethiopia's Decade of Struggle in Relief and Rehabilitation*, Addis Ababa: The Relief and Rehabilitation Commission.

Thomson, Blair, 1975, *Ethiopia, the Country that Cut Off its Head: A Diary of the Revolution*, London: Robson Books.

Young, John, 1997, *Peasant Revolution in Ethiopia: The Tigray People's Liberation Front (1975–1991)*, Cambridge University Press.

9

THE ERITREAN QUESTION[1]

Gérard Prunier

On 23 May 1993, following thirty years of war and two years of *de facto* autonomy, the Ethiopian province of Eritrea officially became an independent state. For the international community this outcome, which put an end to over half a century of legal ambiguities and embarrassing diplomatic contradictions, brought a general feeling of relief. There had been no departing from respect for article 4b of the Organization of African Unity Charter, given the fact that Eritrea had been a colony of Italy while Ethiopia had retained its independence.[2] Nevertheless, in spite of a marked war-weariness on the part of the populations and of the smooth official declarations, five years later war broke out again between the former heartland and its former province.

What had happened? There is no single clear-cut answer to what is probably one of the most vexing geopolitical problems on the African continent. Eritrea and its "problem" are, like the Israelo-Palestinian conflict or the "Irish question", one of these atrociously complicated historical conundrums where cultural divergences and past offences combine to produce an unmanageable whole. Most of the time, passion—on both sides—overcomes any attempt at an objective examination of the problem. Obviously the next few pages will not allow us to bring a satisfactory answer to such contradictions. But we hope nevertheless to provide the reader with a number of elements that will enable him to consider the problem with a minimum of objectivity.

How the contradictions of the past extended into the present

Today, what is it that we call "Eritrea"? It is a territory of 124,000 km^2 stretching between the 18th and the 13th degree of latitude north and the 36th and 43rd of longitude west. This space is divided into three broad natural regions. First, the central heartland or *kebessa* represents about 45 per cent of the total. Located at a fairly high altitude (between 2,000 and 3,000 metres) the *kebessa* region covers the three central provinces of Akele Guzzay, Saray and Hamasien and extends a bit to the north into the mountains of Senhit and Sahel. The geography and climate make it a direct extension of the Ethiopian *dega* and *weyna dega* territories.[3] Then we have the hot lowlands of the west[4] that go down by stages towards Sudan which they strongly resemble, making a wide half-circle from the Sahel in the north to the Gash-Setit region in the south. And finally we have Dankalia, representing about 10 per cent of the country's surface, stretched out as a kind of long probing finger along the Red Sea coast from the Sudan to the border with Djibouti in the south. Flat and arid, this is one of the hottest places on earth.

The population numbers something in the vicinity of six million,[5] divided into nine distinct ethno-linguistic groups. Two of those—the Tigrigna speakers (50 per cent) and the Tigre (30 per cent)—represent by themselves over three quarters of the total. Religiously the divide is about 50 per cent Christians[6] and 50 per cent Muslims, the Christians populating mostly the *kebessa*, with the Muslims living in the lowlands.

The first question that must be answered about Eritrea is whether it constitutes a long-standing entity historically different from Ethiopia and now finally managing to regain a long-denied independence (this is the view of the Eritrean nationalists) or is simply an Ethiopian province torn from its Fatherland by illegitimate secessionists (this is the antagonistic view of the Ethiopian nationalists). At the risk of being unpopular, we have to say that both views are crudely simplified and ultimately incorrect. On this let us quote a few words from the American historian Tom Killion in the introduction to his *Historical Dictionary of Eritrea*: "The projection in time of the term "Eritrea" and the name "Eritreans" as used in this book about the pre-colonial past should be seen as a convention for writing and does not imply in any way the existence of such an identity before 1890."[7]

This disclaimer is all the stronger as Tom Killion was known to be a leading supporter of the Eritrean nationalist approach. But his intellectual honesty obliged him to recognize that basic fact, although it is still far from being universally accepted by his intellectual camp.[8] On the other side many contemporary Ethiopian nationalists still deny the right of contemporary Eritrea to have a distinct national existence and refuse to admit its population's visceral commitment to an independence that thirty years of constant struggle should have established beyond the shadow of a doubt.

How then can we account for the existence of two such deeply contradictory views of the Eritrean reality? First of all, both are based on feelings rather than on any dispassionate attempts at analyzing the elements at our disposal. And then we have the problem of history and the transformations that it brought to a fluid and changing environment which both sets of nationalisms want to view as a static a-temporal entity.

If we go back to the first semi-centralized political structure in the region, the Aksumite Empire, we can see that it was neither "Ethiopian" nor "Eritrean" even if it embodied elements of both. The Aksumite empire covered roughly the present Ethiopian province of Tigray and the Eritrean highlands (*kebessa*). But neither the rest of Ethiopia nor the Eritrean lowlands were under its control,[9] even though the extensive nature of its commercial network brought the Empire to control the other shores of the Red Sea, in today's Yemen. The decline of Aksum during the fifth and sixth centuries was caused by a series of foreign conquests (the Sassanid Persians in Arabia, the nomadic Beja tribes of the Sudan to the west, the Arabs in Egypt) which slowly contributed to isolation of an empire that lived essentially from its control of regional commerce. From the seventh century onwards, the Eritrean highlands became semi-autonomous, accepting the intermittent dominion of the Abyssinian emperors as long as it did not become too pressing, while in the lowlands the Hadareb and Beni Amer nomads lived within the cultural sphere of today's "Sudan"—

which of course did not exist then as a political entity since "the Sudan" did not acquire its present form before the Turco-Egyptian conquest of 1821.[10] It was only during the reign of Emperor Amda Syon (1314–44) that Abyssinia managed to extend its control over the Tigrigna-speaking highlands of today's "Eritrea". This control was ever more fluid as it descended along the slopes of the *kebessa* towards the coastal lowlands,[11] and the small Sultanate of the Dahlak Islands (later occupied by the Turks) actually ruled over both the coastline and the port of Massawa. As for the western Eritrean lowlands, they were part of the "Sudanese" Sultanate of Sennar.[12]

The period of feudal anarchy known in Ethiopian history as *zemene mesafint* (1769–1855) further eroded the already largely theoretical control of the Abyssinian monarchy over the *kebessa* and allowed for the development of regional Tigrigna-speaking micro-dynasties sitting astride present-day Eritrea and the Ethiopian province of Tigray. Emperor Yohannes IV, himself a Tigrean, managed to reimpose a certain amount of Abyssinian control over the "Eritrean" highlands. But he was soon faced by a new brand of enemies, the Turco-Egyptians. Nominally a vassal of the Ottoman Empire, Egypt was at the time a semi-modernized state that had managed to hire a large number of European and American expatriate technicians and military officers. It was bent on conquest, half on the pattern of the traditional Ottoman plunder and half because colonies had become, over the last half century, a kind of "badge of cultural superiority", separating the "civilized people" from the "savages"; the modernizing regime in Cairo definitely wanted to be seen as belonging to the first category. As a result the years 1865–85 were particularly critical for Abyssinian independence since the Egyptians first occupied the whole Red Sea coastline, then crept from there up to the eastern highlands and slowly infiltrated the western lowlands from their Sudanese rear base occupied since 1821. By 1870 they launched an attempt at conquering the whole of Abyssinia.

In those pre-Berlin Conference days, the Western powers looked with approval on this expansion of a state which, although Muslim, was seen as "civilized", deferring to Europe and flattering it in its desire to emulate it. As a result Eritrea could easily have become an Egyptian colony if the Sudanese heart of Cairo's empire had not suddenly exploded under the blows of the Mahdist uprising in 1881. During the next four years Mohamed Ahmed "al-Mahdi" conquered the Northern Sudan by kicking out the Turco-Egyptian occupiers, in spite of the support given to them by London. This was the unexpected event that was suddenly going to quicken the pace of the European colonization of Africa.[13] Britain, deeply worried both about the danger of Mahdist "contamination" in East Africa (the rhetoric sounds like a forerunner of the twenty-first century discourse about al-Qaida) and about the spread of French influence from its base in the Red Sea colony of Obock,[14] found an original defence, the use of the nascent Italian imperialism. Recently unified, Italy was the weakest of the "Great Powers" and dreamed of acquiring colonies, both to export its excess demographic growth and to be admitted into the ranks of the "serious" European nations which were then just beginning to start their notorious "Scramble for Africa". London then decided to support Italian colonial ambitions in the Horn of Africa,[15] on the understanding that Rome would block the French expansion on the Red Sea coast and contain the Mahdist expansion coming from the Sudan. London recognized the Italian occupation of Massawa and Italy took advantage of the death of Emperor Yohannes IV[16] to launch an attempt at occupying the Ethiopian highlands with the support of the British.[17] On 1 January 1890 King Umberto proclaimed the existence of *la colonia primogenita*, "the first-born colony", the first projection abroad of Italian power since the disappearance of the Venetian empire in the seventeenth century. From that moment on, it was Italy that started to define the outline of what was to later become an "Eritrean" identity.

From external control to the growth of an autonomous identity

The beginnings of the Italian colonial occupation were thought of in Rome as a period of transition which, at least in the mind of the Prime Minister Francesco Crispi, would only be a transitional stage before an outright conquest of the whole of Abyssinia. Crispi had a very simplified vision of colonization, directly driven by the demographic problems of Italy at the end of the nineteenth century and the underdevelopment of its agriculture. For the Prime Minister who could declare in a speech given in Palermo in 1889, "Ethiopia is opening to us. Large areas which are ripe for colonization will soon become available as receptacles of Italian fecundity," Ethiopia was simply a future colony of settlement, ready to absorb the overflow of the poor rural population of the *Mezzogiorno*. In May 1889 Crispi had signed with Menelik the Treaty of Wichale which was supposed to define the Italian zone of occupation in the north of Abyssinia. Not only did Rome not respect the borders defined by the Treaty, it had two different versions of the Treaty drawn up, the Italian version differing widely from the Amharic one and placing Ethiopia implicitly under an Italian Protectorate! Meanwhile, both to satisfy British demands and to broaden the space available for colonization, the Italian forces were pushing the colony's limits in all directions, towards the south-east up to the limits of the French colony in Obock, westwards until the Mahdist resistance stopped their expansion into the Sudanese lowlands and southwards as long as the rest of Abyssinia did not come to the aid of the assaulted Tigray province.

Thus one can see that the territorial shape and the present borders of Eritrea are not the direct outcome of an internal evolution but the simple product of Italian military operations. Crispi sent to Eritrea a land administrator, Leopoldo Franchetti, whom he put in charge of "opening" the land to Italian colonial occupation. Franchetti's brutal and clumsy policy of land expropriation resulted in the 1894 revolt led by Bahta Hagos. The revolt was crushed fairly easily and the Italians drew from it two false conclusions: the military ease of the repression led them to underestimate the capacity of the Ethiopians to fight back;[18] and they felt that, rather than trying to seize too much land in Eritrea proper, it would be better and more "balanced" in terms of future land alienation to conquer the whole of Ethiopia. This led to the 1896 war during which Italy tried to take over the whole of Abyssinia, only to be defeated and beaten back at the battle of Adwa (March 1896). The event had a massive impact, as, even more than Gordon's defeat at Khartoum eleven years earlier, it was a clear example of a European military force defeated by "savages". This led to a real change in Italian colonial policy vis-à-vis Eritrea, with the arrival of a "modern" Governor, Ferdinando Martini. During the ten years of his term of office (1897–1907) Martini completely transformed the colony. He reconciled his administration with Menelik, gave up his predecessors' policy of land seizure[19] and resolutely set about laying the foundations for a small modern industrial base.

The next twenty-five years saw a steady development in that same direction, creating a kind of "golden age" of Italian colonialism in Eritrea. Such a view has to be expressed with care. Recent political analysis has tended to consider "colonialism" as an unmitigated evil; the reality is much more complicated. The real unmitigated evil was often essentially cultural and psychological. Oppression, even if it is benign and economically beneficial, has in the long run a destructive cultural effect. Hence the large differences between some of the worst colonial situations (South Africa, the Belgian Congo) and considerably milder ones (Uganda, Senegal, Sudan). But Eritrea, once purged of its colonial fanatics after 1896, was definitely on the mild side, a definitely better place than (to stay within the Italian framework of reference) either Libya or Somalia. The Eritreans eventually drifted into a "co-colonial" position like a number of other people in Africa (the Baganda in Uganda, the Tutsis in Rwanda and Burundi). Eritreans became agricultural workers,[20] mechanics, clerks, soldiers in the colonial army, slowly moving into a form of modernity that was largely unknown at the time in Ethiopia. Their social and ethnic distinctions, while remaining very strong, tended to be lessened, mollified, made more amenable to trans-group social intercourse. In other words a proto-identity, a global "us" as well as a global "them", began to develop. And to develop not only in reaction to colonization, but also through colonization as well. This did not mean that the Eritreans loved the Italians or considered them with total awe and respect. But neither did they hate them globally, as was at times the case in both Libya and some parts of Somalia.[21] And—perhaps more important— they had been changed by them in many subtle ways that were not obvious to their southern relatives.

In many ways Fascism's second wave brought about a strange new effort at reshaping identities. In 1932, when Mussolini began to seriously consider preparing the conquest of Ethiopia, he massively developed the European presence in the colony. There were only 4,188 Italians in Eritrea in 1931, but by May 1936 their numbers had swelled to 350,000! The army was a main component of that population, having gone from 7,500 men in 1928 to 60,000 on the eve of the invasion. The conquest of Ethiopia (1935–36) was followed immediately afterwards by a wave of industrial and commercial investments which were supposed to benefit the whole of Africa Orientale Italiana (AOI) but which were in fact largely concentrated in the old colonial heartland of Eritrea.[22] The settler population brought by Mussolini dispersed a bit but tended nevertheless to remain in Eritrea. By the time AOI was incorporated, 15 per cent of the Eritrean population was Italian and there were more Italians (53,000) than natives (45,000) in the capital Asmara. This was a unique situation on the continent where even in heavily "white" colonies such as the Rhodesias and Kenya such ratios were never reached. Only in Algeria did the European proportion grow to comparable numbers. This phenomenon contributed to a further transformation of Eritrean culture if we look at it in comparison with neighbouring Ethiopia.

But AOI was suddenly erased from the map in late 1941, when the British army and its allies totally demolished the Italian forces. There was no common policy towards the ex-Italian colonies, given that in late 1943 Italy switched from being a fighting member of the Axis to a complex situation of "co-belligerence" within the Allied camp. Thus Libya was considered as a kind of *res nullius* which the Americans and British dealt with in a purely military fashion; Somalia was occupied by the British who for several years toyed with the idea of a pan-Somali construction, and Eritrea was also occupied by the British but in a completely different spirit. Knowing that it would probably not stay durably in Eritrea (and never really seriously trying to do so) Britain launched a kind of social and political experiment in the country which, even if it was motivated by an open and liberal intent towards the native population, was to have potentially dire consequences. This period of British administration (1941–52) was short and is today largely forgotten. But it played an essential role in the transformation of Eritrean identity, driving it even further away from its Ethiopian references.

The reason was that Britain introduced in the territory a series of measures that were quite exceptional for an African colony in the 1940s. It started by the recruitment in the British administration of a number of Eritreans who had served under the Italians, offering them a fair level of promotion. Education was transformed and brought in many more children than during the Italian period. English began to be taught and was eagerly embraced by the educated segment of the population. The teaching of Tigrigna and Arabic spread as well[23] and newspapers in these languages started publication. Trade union organization began and grew rapidly among urban workers and civil servants. By 1947 the administration authorized the creation of political parties. Eight or ten immediately appeared and started to agitate for the support of segments of the population as there was now talk of the rapid election of a territorial assembly.

In fact this rapid pace of political development was somewhat artificial because London had no clear idea of what it wanted to do or could do. There were several schools of thought. The straight annexation option, which aimed at taking over the whole of AOI, did not appear very feasible as both Washington and the UN consensus were hostile to it. Another "solution" was to work for a separation of Tigray from Ethiopia and joining it with the *kebessa* part of Eritrea to create an independent (but British influenced) "Greater Tigray" while the western lowlands would be attached to the Sudan.

But since Emperor Haile Selassie was radically opposed to any separation of Tigray from Ethiopia, a third plan was hatched in 1949, called the "Bevin-Sforza" plan from the names of its British and Italian sponsors, aiming at dealing with the whole of AOI.[24] Eritrea would be divided, its western lowlands would go to Sudan while the *kebessa* and Dankalia would be united, in one way or another, with Ethiopia. The UN General Assembly adopted the Bevin-Sforza plan by 37 votes against 11, but the plan was nevertheless abandoned because of anti-Italian riots in Libya. This unexpected factor brought the whole fate of Eritrea back to square one, causing Eritrean public opinion, whose awareness was growing by leaps and bounds given the political progress of the territory, to really start to fret.

The collapse of the Bevin-Sforza plan accelerated the creation of the first overtly pro-independence movement, the Independence Bloc.[25] This in turn worried the Emperor who stepped up his support for the pro-Ethiopian Unionist Party. The Ethiopian secret service started by trying to vilify the campaigners for independence as tools of the Italians (because of the limited pro-Italian membership in the Independence Bloc) and, when this proved not to be enough, launched a campaign of targeted murders against the Bloc leaders.[26]

The climate became such that it led to serious rioting in February 1950 in Asmara. The UN Commission of Inquiry floundered in total confusion, its five members eventually coming up with three separate reports contradicting each other, one advising reunion with Ethiopia, another arguing in favour of a federation and the third recommending a ten-year UN Trusteeship followed by independence. The result was to bring everything back to the drawing board, and in December 1950 the UN General Assembly voted Resolution 390 A (V), in favour of a Federation between Ethiopia and Eritrea. But there were to be another twenty months between that decision and its implementation, and the British Military Administration had time to organize a legislative election before the full proclamation of Federation.

These elections (the last free ones Eritrea was ever to know, up to this day!) are quite interesting since they give a kind of instant snapshot of the political landscape at the time. Out of the assembly's 68 members, 32 belonged to the Unionist Party (UP) which advocated total union with Ethiopia, 18 had been elected under the banner of the Eritrean Democratic Front (EDF),[27] 15 were members of the Muslim League (ML) which was still considering possible partition with Sudan but leaning more towards full-fledged independence, and three were traditional tribal leaders. We can thus see that the members were divided almost evenly between supporters of union with Ethiopia and supporters of independence. But the members did not just happen to hold these views. *All* of the UP parliamentarians were Christian Tigrigna speakers while *all* of the EDF or ML elected representatives were Muslim lowlanders.[28]

This created a dangerous ethno-political identity split, meaning that a lot would depend on how the Federation experience would be lived. Eritrean identity, imprecise as it might be, was by then a completely unavoidable fact. But it was imprecise in its forms of expression and, although it is not politically correct to say so today, some of the later supporters of independence started their political careers as UP unionist members. Most Eritreans could have adapted to some form of federation if the Emperor had understood that his new subjects had to be dealt with in quite a specific way, so as to accommodate their particularities: that is, what their complex older history and their more recent colonial past had made them into. But the problem was that it was exactly that understanding of the specificity of Eritrean feelings that the Emperor and his closest advisers[29] did not have.

The Federation was eventually officially proclaimed on 15 September 1952, and it was to lead to disaster. Barely a year later, a British civil servant who was in charge of overseeing its application was already complaining in a letter to the Foreign Office that Tedla Bairu[30]

> has reduced the ministers to the rank of mere employees who are forbidden to take any decision, never calls a cabinet meeting, has closed down the only independent newspaper that was still published, blocks the transmission of any financial audit to the Parliament, stops the opposition MPs who have been elected in partial elections to sit in Parliament and keeps postponing any discussion of the problem of customs[31] (…) It seems that his way of conducting business is such that total union with Ethiopia is bound to happen within a short time.[32]

The Emperor was not even trying to hide his game, declaring in a public speech in September 1954, for the second anniversary of the proclamation of the Federation, "The day when the population of the Mareb Melash[33] (…) would opt for a complete union with Ethiopia rather than a simple federal link, would be for me a day of great happiness".

But in the meantime a deliberate form of sabotage blocking the functioning of the Eritrean government was hardly the best way to endear himself to the Eritrean public, and he was beginning to cause irritation and lose support among even the pro-Ethiopia Christian highlanders. As we already briefly hinted earlier, the problem of such a policy, which was driven by instinct and prejudice rather than by analysis, was Haile Selassie's temporal disconnect. The Emperor saw himself as the Saviour of Ethiopia, the legitimate and necessary master of an unruly and dangerous body politic. Whether fissiparous tendencies came from rebellious feudal lords or democratically-minded young politicians made very little difference for him. Power, *mengist*, that old Abyssinian obsession, had to be absolute and had to be in imperial hands.[34] For him any form of power "check and balance", even a democratic one, could only be seen as equivalent to the feudal obstructions the Ethiopian throne had been fighting to contain and eliminate for the past hundred years. An Eritrea moving along the path of democratization and social transformation could only be seen by the Emperor as a kind of foreign body which should be brought back down to the general level of the rest of the Empire. How could he accept the idea of democratic legitimacy in Eritrea when he was doing everything he could to fight against it in Ethiopia proper?[35]

In spite of its limitations and backwardness, the Eritrean body politic was definitely more advanced that the Ethiopian one along the road towards both social modernity and some form of democratic political expression. Federation with Ethiopia had been a form of cultural revenge against colonialism, but it had failed to deliver the hoped for path to social transformation that it had been expected to bring. From now on, it was through the organization of a revolutionary movement aiming at independence that this newly discovered modernity would try to assert itself.

The years of struggle

Federation survived till 1962 in a climate marked by the steadily grow-ing manipulations by the Addis Ababa authorities. The elections between 1956 and 1960 were tainted by the constant intimidation of non-Unionist candidates and eventually led to a parliament mostly controlled by Ethiopia. But even then, when the legislative assembly was controlled from Addis Ababa, that assembly repeatedly refused to willingly abrogate the Act of Federation, which was eventually declared to be abolished on 14 November 1962 by the Emperor's representative.

The writing had been on the wall for some time and small groups of anti-unionists had created the first "revolutionary" movement, the Eritrean Liberation Movement (ELM), from exile in Sudan as early as 1958. This first nationalist organization combined in a strange way a rather moderate programme (return to an effective federation) with conspiratorial and semi-terrorist tactics; its militant network was dis-mantled after the 1963 demonstrations against the abolition of the Federation, and this gave rise to another movement, the Eritrean Liberation Front (ELF), better organized but almost entirely made up of western Muslim Lowlanders.[36] Born in Cairo in 1960, the ELF is the grandmother of all further Eritrean political movements, still fondly referred to as "*al-Jebha*" (the Front) or even "*Ummi*" (our mother) even by those who have been long divorced from it. It was to be the matrix from which all the armed Eritrean political movements came, many of them to later disappear in the turmoil of fratricidal conflicts.[37]

The first military operations of the Eritrean guerrilla campaign started on a very limited scale. On 1 September 1961 Hamid Idris Awate, a former *askari* of the Italian Army and an ELM sympathizer, was the first man to lead an armed attack on the Ethiopian forces. His little group could not really be called a guerrilla force, with all the later connotations of a clearly defined political armed struggle; it was more of a band of *shifta* (political bandits) like those who used to harass the British troops in the post-war years. At the beginning the military oper-ations remained very limited and all took place in the western lowlands whence most of the fighters came.[38]

After 1966, a number of young Christians slowly began to join the rebellion. But tribal and religious allegiances had remained very strong and many of the young Christian recruits were killed by the very people they had come to join.[39] These murders caused tensions inside the ELF where young educated men created the *Islah* (reform) movement in 1968. Many of these young men started to debate among themselves, criticizing the policies of the external leadership. But the external council was relying for support on the extreme religious and ethnic feelings of the zone 1 and 2 commanders who were asked to crush the reformist challenge. The internal massacres restarted, leading many young reformists, who were mostly Muslims but had Christian comrades with them, to split from the ELF mainstream, creating the ELF/PLF (Popular Liberation Forces).

It was the ELF/PLF that was later to give birth to the EPLF, the organization that eventually succeeded in winning the war. But at the time they were far from it. The haemorrhage of fighters drove the ELF into an attempt at reforming itself during its First Congress in 1971. The struggle was out in the open between the supporters of a non-sectarian nationalist line and those who could not shed the "Arab" and "Muslim" line. The contradictions became such that in February 1972 the ELF militarily attacked its younger challenger. This fratricidal war lasted for two and a half years, until September 1974, when pressure from the base forced the two leadership groups to talk. The situation was evolving quite fast with the explosion of the revolution in Ethiopia proper and the constant arrival of new Christian recruits who were pushing for reconciliation and unity.

Faced with this mounting emergency the ELF/PLF leadership decided on a clean organizational break and created a new front, the EPLF. The new organization was immediately faced with a major political and military choice. Owing to the revolution the Ethiopian army was disintegrating and losing any form of discipline and restraint, committing massive massacres and other human rights violations. The EPLF offered its wayward "mother" an alliance and both organizations went on the offensive in conventional war style. Within months they had occupied almost the whole of the territory and besieged Asmara. Among the two, the EPLF had won the more spectacular successes and this had allowed the younger organization to draw a steady stream of new recruits, both Christian and Muslim, highlanders and lowlanders.

But the scene of the conflict had widely broadened with the attack by Somalia on Ethiopia. Since 1969, Siad Barre's Somalia had been the regional ally of the Soviet Union, pampered by Moscow as a counterweight to Haile Selassie's pro-American Ethiopia. But now, with the onset of a full-fledged revolution openly claiming to be Marxist-Leninist (even if its various components were fighting each other over what was meant by that label), Moscow had to choose.[40] This war between an old protégé and an aspiring new one was unfortunate for the Russians. But broad considerations ranging from cultural affinity to strategic importance and from military weight to tactical opportunity led Moscow to switch sides right in the middle of the battle for the Ogaden. Soviet military aid immediately started pouring into Ethiopia and Communist allies (Cubans, South Yemenis) quickly followed. The Somali army fell back in disarray and the Communist reinforcements were quickly turned around so that they could be brought to bear in Eritrea as well.

Between July and December 1978, the Derg launched a series of violent and coordinated attacks that forced the Eritrean fronts to withdraw and abandon their newly occupied areas.[41] The EPLF managed an orderly retreat towards the Sahel but the ELF retreated in confusion towards Sudan and over 10,000 of its fighters disbanded themselves. That Front practically ceased to exist on the ground inside Eritrea. But its leadership went on monopolizing the aid distributed by Arab countries and kept speaking abroad in the name of "the Eritrean resistance". With his back to the wall, Ahmed Nasser, the ELF president, agreed to talk with Derg representatives in conversations sponsored by the Russians. But what he was offered was akin to surrender and he dared not sign. The negotiations broke down and the ELF was so weakened that it gave the order to its last remaining troops to abandon the frontline and withdraw to Sudan.[42] The EPLF condemned this as "treasonable" and attacked its former ally.

By late 1980 the ELF had been completely defeated and its last fighters had withdrawn to Sudan or had abandoned their former organization and joined the EPLF. The ELF then sank into internecine fighting, the leaders blaming each other for the defeat and finally murdering each other in Sudan. When its old leader Osman Saleh Sabeh died of natural causes in 1987, his death marked the final demise of the old Front. A new Islamist current began to appear in the ruins of the Front and in 1988 the first Islamic fundamentalist Eritrean organization, Jihad Eritrea, began to operate. But its limited recruitment never amounted to more than a shadow of what the old ELF had once been.

For the EPLF, the years of defensive entrenchment in the Sahel turned into the heroic years of the guerrilla campaign, still celebrated today in the national Eritrean mythology as a kind of golden age. The Front cleverly developed its technical and medical capacities, it started making and servicing a lot of the equipment it was using, produced clothes, taught children and generally tended to develop a kind of Utopian and Spartan counter-society that both embodied its socialist ideals and gave it a tremendous practical capacity.[43] Its ideology, a mixture of populism and revolutionary Marxism, demanded complete obedience from its cadres and it was enforced with a near fanatical ideological zeal and a cold-blooded brutality in case of disobedience. In 1987 the Front organized its Second Congress, resulting both in a tightening of discipline and in a spectacular personal success for Issayas Afeworqi who was elected to the position of Secretary General. Major historical figures of the nationalist movement such as Wolde Ab Wolde Maryam and Ibrahim Totil joined the rejuvenated organization.

As the Americans felt that the Gorbachev-led USSR was vacillating in its resolve to support the Derg, they used a leading ally in the region, Saddam Hussein, to step up their military aid to the EPLF.[44] This allowed the EPLF to launch a major offensive in March 1988 during which the Front managed to occupy the key garrison town of Af Abet, which the demoralized Ethiopian Army did not defend very energetically. In Af Abet the Front captured a large quantity of heavy military hardware (artillery, tanks, vast quantities of fuel and ammunition) which enabled it to turn itself into a conventional army almost overnight. American and Iraqi help increased and the Front decided to renew its military cooperation with the Tigrean Peoples Liberation Front (TPLF) with which it had been in conflict since 1985.[45] Since the TPLF was better placed geographically to finish off the Derg, the EPLF supplied it with a large part of the equipment captured at Af Abet. After its victory at the battle of Shire in February 1989, the TPLF took control of the whole of Tigray Province, but its southward progress was difficult as the Tigrean Front met considerable ethnic resistance in the Amhara-populated regions. In February 1990 the EPLF captured Massawa after a major battle during which it lost 3,000 men and the Derg army twice that number. Losing Massawa meant that the Ethiopian forces could not be resupplied by sea at a time when the TPLF successes had cut off the land routes. By then it was obvious that the Derg had lost the war. But its army clung fiercely to the ground in a typically Ethiopian display of desperate courage. Thousands fell on both sides in the terrain between Asmara and the coast before the insurgent forces finally captured the Eritrean capital in May 1991. Practically at the same moment the TPLF, which had finally managed to reach Shoa Province at the beginning of the year, entered Addis Ababa practically without fighting, thus sparing the capital the major destruction a final defence would have caused.[46] This twin victory put an end to both thirty years of civil war and seventeen years of a "revolutionary" regime which had sunk into a brutal military dictatorship without any real perspective beyond its own survival.

The Eritrean question within the context of independence

The accession to power in Addis Ababa of a new regime politically allied to the EPLF allowed the Eritrean Front to organize the independence of its territory in close agreement with the new Ethiopian government. In May 1993, in an internationally-supervised referendum, 99 per cent voted for independence.[47] Ethio-Eritrean relations were at first as good as they could possibly be after such a long conflict. But while the twin victory had been an excellent short-term opportunity, there was not enough time afterwards to face numerous problems that remained between the old Abyssinian core and its secessionist offspring. The difficulties were supposedly economic but they had deeper and more intricate causes as well.

As we saw in the first section of this chapter dealing with the colonial period, Eritrea had been designed by its Italian godfather as an industrial nucleus which should have been the core of a wider, agricultural development area. Neither the British Military Administration period, nor the Federation, nor the unilateral union had altered that basic framework. As a result the small Eritrean economy found itself painfully dependent on an Ethiopian hinterland which had always been seen as a "natural outlet" for northern industrial production. But after 1993 the limited but real economic development of Ethiopia in general and of Tigray in particular started to interfere with that "preordained" pattern. If we summarize the arguments of the two sides, which quickly veered into polemics, the Eritreans complained that the new Ethiopian manufacturing capacities were undermining their exports[48] while the Ethiopians accused their erstwhile ally of exploiting their underdevelopment. In addition Asmara insisted on the creation of a separate currency (both had kept the birr as common currency after 1991) in the mistaken belief, grounded in the Eritrean feeling of superiority, that this new currency would be stronger than the birr.[49] Addis Ababa eventually accepted this but the new Eritrean currency, the nakfa, predictably started to slip and within months of its creation was worth twenty times less than the birr. Asmara saw this withering of its treasured new symbolic currency as an Ethiopian plot.

But behind these accusations there was a whole past which had not always been one of brotherly cooperation, even during those days when both Fronts had fought against the Derg. At the time when Marxism was their common ideology they had had strong divergences concerning their choice socialist countries of reference; the TPLF had been pro-Chinese and later pro-Albanian while the EPLF had struck a more independent path towards a kind of "national communism". The EPLF also had a long tradition, due to its important Muslim component, of cooperating with "Arab socialist" regimes. These diverging views had had severe military consequences, with the two Fronts breaking up their alliance and even fighting each other sporadically between 1985 and 1988. Then, after the split, their views on the nationality question had been completely opposite, Eritrea opting for a heavily centralized approach while the Ethiopian regime had chosen a more federal path. It was these differences that between 1993 and 1997 gave the frequent discussions about the economic difficulties a rough and tense background. These contradictions were real and simple goodwill would not have been enough to dispel them. But they did not amount to such a heavy load that they would irremediably lead to a resumption of the conflict.

In many ways, it was a basic political and cultural disconnect which eventually caused a return to war. And this disconnect reached a long way back. The Eritreans had been the "soldiers of Empire" in the Italian colonial context[50] and they had also been its skilled workers. They were secretly proud of that heritage, which the Ethiopians, Tigreans included, considered offensive. The Tigreans "had supplied much of Eritrea's casual labour to the point where "Agame" [Tigreans] acquired a pejorative connotation among highland Eritreans. Agame and other Tigreans also made up the *makalay aylet* class of landless rural labourers and tenant farmers."[51] These old forms of prejudice and discrimination resurfaced during the war and coloured the relationship between the Eritrean EPLF and the Tigrean TPLF. It gave rise to what we could call a "big brother/little brother" relationship. When the TPLF started fighting the Derg, the Eritrean guerrillas had already been in the field for fourteen years. Their experience and their numbers bore no relationship to those of the small band of *woyane* fighters who had taken to the bush in 1975. Issayas Afeworqi considered himself to be the inheritor of a whole Eritrean tradition of Eritrean superiority which he carried over into his relationship with the TPLF. The tanks used by the Tigreans to take Addis Ababa had been captured by the EPLF at Af Abet three years before and given to the TPLF as a sovereign gift.

In many ways Issayas was constitutionally incapable of working with the TPLF on an equal basis and still looked down on his "*makalay aylet*" cousins as a subordinate kind. It was hard for him to realize that once the TPLF was in control of Ethiopia, its priorities would become national rather than parochial. But could this "neo-imperialist" view be counterbalanced by other trends within the EPLF? Unfortunately not. The new government was a victim of the "guerrillas in power" syndrome, wellknown in a whole bevy of other African countries (Angola, Mozambique, Guinea Bissau, Uganda, Rwanda, Burundi, Southern Sudan, South Africa). In all these cases the leading organizations (and their founding fathers) developed a political monopoly which tended to veer into strong authoritarianism. This was the Eritrean path after 1993. By the time of independence, Issayas Afeworqi had become the absolute master of Eritrea.

This entrenchment of authoritarianism was the one cause that federated all those mentioned above, eventually leading to a renewal of the conflict with Ethiopia. The exaggerated centralism of the Eritrean regime precluded any check and balances which might have stopped the clumsy slippage into a useless conflict based on archaic prejudices and unreasonable political analysis. The conflict that started in May 1998 was both outdated and pointless since none of the two adversaries had any "war aims" beyond claims to small border territories that were strategically and economically without value. The real causes of the war were the ones we have outlined, but their deeply buried cultural and historical nature was too tenuous to be structured into war planning. The outside world did not understand the causes of the conflict and resorted to the quip of calling it "two bald men fighting over a comb".[52] The expression was picturesque, even though it simply reflected a bewilderment that precluded any possibility of mediation.[53] The result was two years of atrocious slaughter (between 50,000 and 80,000 combined casualties) and an overall military expenditure of over \$4.5bn which neither side could afford.[54] After two years of a bloody stalemate during which the two armies confronted each other in World War I style with long meandering lines of trenches, the Ethiopian forces rediscovered the virtue of movement and outflanked their enemy in the west (May 2000). The war was over militarily within a few weeks but dragged on diplomatically until December when a cease-fire was finally signed. The diplomatic game was as obscure and confused as the war itself had been and resulted in a state of no-peace, no-war which is still lingering at the time of writing. But this opaque conflict was to have major consequences on the internal fate of Eritrea itself.

The global political structure of the PFDJ[55] was shaken by the whole chain of events and the iron dominance of Issayas Afeworqi was suddenly thrown into question. Critics initiated a move towards the creation of a constitution and the process soon came under the stewardship of Eritrea's leading intellectual figure, Bereket Habte Selassie. The post-war Eritrean political establishment suddenly came alive, launching a whole movement of internal reform. On 5 May 2001 an "Open Letter to All the Members of the PFDJ" was signed by fifteen leading members of the party, ending with those words: "How can the present crisis be resolved? When the President is ready to be governed by the constitution and the law and when the legislative and executive branches perform their legal functions properly.". This was of course anathema to Issayas Afeworqi who regrouped his supporters and started to arrest his opponents. June to August 2001 was a period of great tension and great hopes. But Issayas cleverly used the September 11th 2001 al-Qaida attack on the Twin Towers to make his move. Realizing that the world's attention was completely polarized by what had happened in New York and that his hands were suddenly free, he struck on 18 September, still known today by the Eritrean opposition as "Black Tuesday". He arrested all the signatories of the 5 May letter that were in the country, a bevy of democratically-minded PFDJ cadres, hundreds of civilian dissenters, true or imaginary, and all the independent journalists, closing down all their newspapers in one fell swoop.[56] What had been up to then an authoritarian regime became overnight one of the tightest dictatorships on the planet.

Paradoxically, even though the President's personal stature was shaken, his enormous personal prestige kept many of the rank-and-file Eritreans loyal to his person. But the few PFDJ leaders who sided with him (Yemane Gebre Ab, al-Amin Mohamed Said, Abdallah Jaber) lost their personal credibility, particularly since they were not among the heroes of the independence struggle. The constitutional project was buried and the system tightened to an incredible degree. No independent organization was allowed and in May 2002 thirty-six independent churches—mostly Pentecostal Christians and the Jehovah's Witnesses—were banned and many of their members arrested.[57] 2,000 are estimated to still be in detention today. Military service expanded to an enormous degree, with all young people of both sexes being drafted between the ages of 18 and 40 and a military reserve created for all the men between 40 and 50. Since the conscripts could be used in discretionary fashion for civilian work, including productive work on the private property of party cadres and officers, and since their pay was barely symbolic, this measure turned the whole population of Eritrea into potential slave workers.[58] Young people began fleeing in the hundreds and, as the years went on, in the thousands. Many were shot dead while fleeing. Sanctions against those captured were drastic, leading to the creation of forced labour camps. The repression increased the human haemorrhage, the small nation of Eritrea becoming the second source of international refugees on the African continent and the fourth in the world, with an estimated 500,000 refugees having fled abroad since the end of the war in 2000 and adding themselves to the 250,000 who had left during the war of independence but had never returned home. The new refugees flee not only to the Sudan but even to the territory of their former enemy, Ethiopia. They even cross into Somalia, in spite of the permanent war, in order to reach the harbour of Bosaso from where they sail to Yemen. Many try to chance it across the Sahara all the way to Libya from where they reach Italy. Both routes have been extremely hazardous and the poorly documented loss of lives has been massive. Large numbers have fled towards Israel by way of Egypt but they have been preyed upon by the Sinai Beduin, many of whom are suspected to work in cahoots with members of the Eritrean Military Secret Service in order to facilitate ransom payments. This has resulted in a major human rights disaster.

Given the limited capacity of the Eritrean economy to provide for the life of the new nation, its survival is tightly linked to the support of the large Eritrean diaspora in Europe, America and the Middle East. This diaspora used to contribute 2 per cent of its income to the EPLF during the war and kept doing so after independence, as long as it saw its efforts being channelled into the development policies of the new state. But the futility of the 1998–2000 war, the political repression that followed it and the rapid choking of all forms of civil liberties and human rights cooled the enthusiasm of the Eritreans living abroad. Today the Issayas dictatorship has taken to coercing its citizens into paying this "contribution" by a variety of measures (persecution of relatives living in Eritrea, travel restrictions for home visits, financial seizure of property) which some diaspora members have started to challenge in international law courts.

The flavour of this tragedy is contained in the title of one of the most recent studies on Eritrea: it is called "Soldiers, Martyrs, Traitors and Exiles".[59] This dismal but apt title sums up the present state of Eritrea. How long it will remain relevant is hard to tell. But the odds are against a durable institutionalization of the dictatorship on the North Korean model. The exit of Issayas Afeworqi from the political scene, be it peaceful or violent, will very probably result in a radical change of tack—even though the basic tenet of independence is unlikely to be challenged, even by the strongest anti-Issayas activists. The present tragedy keeps contributing, like the now distant Italian colonial past, to the further shaping of a distinct identity. Both the PFDJ loyalists and the dissident groups which are trying to structure themselves into a coherent form of opposition now operate according to parameters that are most distinctly non-Ethiopian.

Culturally the Eritreans remain a part of the complex *habesha* (Abyssinian) galaxy. But their historical and political identities are moving ever deeper into a world of their own, albeit a tragic one. The chasm started by colonialism, deepened by the failure of the (re)union and dug even deeper by the war of independence, has now resulted in an irreversible transformation. Eritrea's pain used to be attributed to the colonizers and later blamed on the Ethiopians. Eritreans, like many other people in history, now have to face—and remedy—their own failures. Blaming it on President Issayas Afeworqi is an easy way out, similar to making Stalin responsible for the failure of the Soviet Union. Eritreans will have to explore the deeper causes which allowed a heroic, self-sacrificing and deeply honest movement of national liberation to degenerate into a tyrannical dictatorship now relying on a form of party cronyism verging on gangsterism. This form of soul-searching which has occurred in countries as varied as Germany, South Africa and post-Vichy France has also failed in many other places where prejudices proved stronger than lucidity. Between the possible paths of catharsis, civil strife or stagnation, the future remains uncertain for that detached part of the old Ethiopia. And the future relations between the two sister countries, now stuck in a toxic no peace, no war situation, will depend to a large extent on the outcome of the process.

BIBLIOGRAPHY AND FURTHER READING

Abbink, J., 1998, "Briefing: The Eritrean-Ethiopian Border Dispute", *African Affairs*, 97/389, pp. 551–65.

Alemseged Abbay, 1998, *Re-imagining Identity: the Divergent Paths of the Eritrean and Tigrayan Nationalist Stuggles*, Lawrenceville, NJ: Red Sea Press.

Aregawi Berhe, 2009, *A Political History of the Tigray's People Liberation Front (1975–1991)*, Los Angeles: Tsehay.

Andebrhan Giorgis, 2014, *Eritrea at a Crossroads: A Narrative of Triumph, Betrayal and Hope*, Houston: Strategic Books.

Bereket Habte Selassie, 2009, *The Crown and the Pen*, Trenton, NJ: Red Sea Press.

—— 2011, *Wounded Nation*, Trenton, NJ: Red Sea Press.

Bernal, V., 2004, "Eritrea Goes Global: Reflections on Nationalism in a Transnational Era", *Cultural Anthropology*, 19 (1), pp. 3–25.

Bozzini, David, 2011, "Low-Tech State Surveillance: The Production of Uncertainty among Conscripts in Eritrea", Surveillance and Society, 9 (1/2), pp. 93–113.

Clapham, Christopher, 1969, *Haile Selassie's Government*, New York: Praeger.

Caulk, Richard A., 1986, "'Black Snake. White Snake': Bahta Hagos and His Revolt Against Italian Overrule in Eritrea, 1894", in D. Crummey (ed.), *Banditry, Rebellion, and Social Protest in Africa*, Oxford: James Currey/Portsmouth, NH: Heinemann, pp. 293–310.

Connell, D., 1993, *Against all Odds: A Chronicle of the Eritrean Revolution*, Trenton, NJ: Red Sea Press.

—— 2005, *Conversations with Eritrean Political Prisoners*, Trenton, NJ: Red Sea Press, 2005.

Dell'Oro, Erminia, 1988, *Asmara addio*, Pordenone: Edizione dello Zibaldone.

Dorman, S.R., 2005, "Past the Kalashnikov: Youth, Politics and the State in Eritrea", in J. Abbink and van Kessel, I. (eds), *Vanguard or Vandals. Youth, Politics and Conflict in Africa*, Leiden: Brill, pp. 189–204.

Erlich, Haggai, 1996, *Ras Alula and the Scramble for Africa. A Political Biography in Ethiopia and Eritrea (1875–1897)*, Lawrenceville, NJ: Red Sea Press.

Gaim Kibreab, 2008, *Critical Reflections on the Eritrean War of Independence:*

Social Capital, Associational Life, Religion, Ethnicity and Sowing Seeds of Dictatorship, Trenton, NJ: Red Sea Press.

———— 2009, "Forced Labour in Eritrea", *Journal of Modern African Studies* 47 (1), pp. 41–72.

———— 2009, *Eritrea: A Dream Deferred*, Oxford: James Currey.

Iyob, Ruth, 1997, "The Eritrean Experiment: a Cautious Pragmatism?", *Journal of Modern African Studies*, 35 (4), pp. 647–73.

———— 2000, "The Ethiopian-Eritrean Conflict: Diasporic vs. Hegemonic States in the Horn of Africa, 1991–2000", *Journal of Modern African Studies*, 38 (4), pp. 659–82.

Jacquin-Berdal, D. and Plaut, M. (eds), 2005, *Unfinished Business. Ethiopia and Eritrea at War*, Lawrenceville, NJ: Red Sea Press.

Killion, T., 1998, *Historical Dictionary of Eritrea*, Lanham: The Scarecrow Press.

Kuhlman, T., 1990, *Burden or Boon? A Study of Eritrean Refugees in the Sudan*, Amsterdam: VU University Press.

Munzinger, W., 1967, *Ostafrikanische Studien*, New York: Johnson Reprint Corporation.

[Reprint of the Swiss 1864 edition. Excellent ethnographic studies on several Eritrean peoples. Written by a Swiss adventurer and explorer who became governor of Massawa before being killed while taking part in the Egyptian attempt to conquer Ethiopia.]

O'Fahey, R.S. and Spaulding, J.S., 1974, *Kingdoms of the Sudan*, London: Methuen.

O'Kane, D. and Redeker Hepner, Y. (eds), 2009, *Biopolitics, Militarism, and Development: Eritrea in the Twenty-First Century*, New York: Berghahn Books.

Okbazghi, Yohannes, 1991, *Eritrea: A Pawn in World Politics*, Gainesville: University of Florida Press.

Pateman, R., 1990, *Eritrea: Even the Stones are Burning*, Trenton, NJ: Red Sea Press.

Perham, M., 1969, *The Government of Ethiopia*, Evanston, IL: Northwestern University Press.

Pollera, A., 1935, *Le popolazioni indigene dell' Eritrea*, Bologna: Licino Cappelli.

[In spite of being a product of Fascist ethnography, a valuable contribution to the study of the Eritrean populations.]

Pool, D., 1993, "Eritrean Independence: The Legacy of the Derg and the Politics of Reconstruction", *African Affairs*, 92, pp. 389–402.

———— 2001, *From Guerrillas to Government: The Eritrean People's Liberation Front*, Oxford: James Currey.

Poscia, S., 1989, *Eritrea, colonia tradita*, Rome: Edizioni Associate. [Far from its apparently polemical title, probably the best study of the complex inner rivalries and fighting within the Eritrean guerrilla movements.]

Ramm, A., 1944, "Great Britain and the Planting of Italian Power in the Red Sea (1868–1895)", *English Historical Review*, 59, 234, pp. 211–36.

Redeker-Hepner, T., 2009, *Soldiers, Martyrs, Traitors and Exiles. Political Conflict in Eritrea and in the Diaspora*, Philadelphia: University of Pennsylvania Press.

Reid, R. (ed.), 2009, *Eritrea's External Relations*, London: Chatham House.

Taddia, Irma, 1986, *L'Eritrea colonia (1890–1952)*, Milan: Franco Angeli. [A reference work on the Italian colonial period. To be read together with the work of Tekeste Negash for an overall view.]

Tekeste Negash, 1986, *No Medicine for the Bite of a White Snake: Notes on Nationalism and Resistance in Eritrea, 1890–1940*, University of Uppsala.

—— 1987, *Italian Colonialism in Eritrea (1882–1941): Policies, Praxis and Impact*, Stockholm: Almqvist & Wiksell.

—— 1997, *Ethiopia and Eritrea: The Federal Experience*, Uppsala: Nordiska Afrikainstitutet.

Tekeste Negash and Tronvoll, K., 2000, *Brothers at War: Making Sense of the Eritrean-Ethiopian War*, Oxford: James Currey.

Trevaskis, G.K.N., 1960, *Eritrea, a Colony in Transition (1941–1952)*, Oxford University Press. [The period of British administration in Eritrea.]

Tronvoll, Kjetil, 1998, "The Process of Nation-Building in Post-War Eritrea: Created from below or Directed from above?", *Journal of Modern African Studies*, 36 (3): 461–82.

—— 1998, *Mai Weini: A Highland Village in Eritrea. A Study of the People, their Livelihood, and Land Tenure during Times of Turbulence*, Lawrenceville, NJ: Red Sea Press.

Wrong, Michaela, 2005, *I Didn't Do It For You: How the World Betrayed a Small African Nation*, London: Fourth Estate/Harper Collins. [A vivid and interesting work which is unfortunately smitten by the romantic aura of the Eritrean liberation struggle and blind to the present Eritrean situation.]

Young, J., 1997, *Peasant Revolution in Ethiopia*, Cambridge University Press.

Zewde Retta, 2000, *Yä-Ertra Gudday*, Addis Ababa. [in Amharic]

10

THE TIGRAY PEOPLE'S LIBERATION FRONT (TPLF)

Medhane Tadesse

After a sixteen-year armed struggle in the countryside against the Derg and several armed groups in northern Ethiopia, the Tigray People's Liberation Movement (TPLF) came to power in 1991. Since then the TPLF-led Ethiopian People's Revolutionary Democratic Front (EPRDF) has ruled Ethiopia alone, although an ultimately unsuccessful attempt at power sharing was made during the initial transition period.

The successful transition had much to do with the character and history of the TPLF, which was instrumental in forming the EPRDF and has provided the ideological direction of the government, as well as much of its leadership. Upon assuming power the TPLF embarked on the difficult task of restructuring the Ethiopian state. Attempts by generations of rulers of Ethiopia to centralize the state were reversed in 1991 when the Front spearheaded an innovative and bold experiment of transferring authority to regional administrations based on ethnicity.

The TPLF was founded in 1975 by a group of Tigrayan university students most of whom were active participants in the Ethiopian student movement. In the mid-1980s the TPLF established a Marxist-Leninist vanguard organization and in 1989 the Front formed the EPRDF, which gave it greater Ethiopia-wide legitimacy and carried the party to victory in 1991. By defeating several armed groups, and finally the Derg, the TPLF fought its way to the helm of power in Ethiopia. Achieving an outright military victory meant that the TPLF faced little opposition either within or outside the EPRDF. It also meant that it could gain the approval of its proposed constitution and pursue its programs of political and economic reform largely unhindered. Its major challenges were the war with Eritrea and achieving democratic government at home; it was these challenges that critically defined its own future and the direction of the country.

After it had amended but not seriously altered its program in the face of dramatically changed international circumstances (an insurrection by the Oromo Liberation Front (OLF) in 1992–93, Islamist incursions from Sudan and Somalia, the defeat of the Eritrean army in the war of 1998–2000, a measure of economic progress, and small democratic advances) it was a shock when the TPLF's Central Committee divided in acrimony in March 2001. In the following years many of the most senior members of the Front were dismissed, marginalized, or jailed as the movement went through convulsions that spread to the other sections of the EPRDF and to the army. Meles Zenawi, Prime Minister, chairman of both the TPLF and the EPRDF, together with his close followers quickly assumed the upper hand in the contest and then initiated what was held to be a wide-ranging program of internal reform. Compounding this, the shock of an ambiguously contested election in 2005 left the Front with no other choice but regrouping under one strongman advocating a developmental state agenda.

The early rise of the TPLF

The genesis of a substantial number of the post-1974 opposition groups goes back to the Ethiopian Student Movement (ESM) of the late 1960s and early 1970s. In their attempt to integrate the "universal truths" of Marxism-Leninism into an Ethiopian context, Ethiopian students touched upon the question of nationalities.[1] This proved to be controversial and threatened the unity of the movement. As a result less serious as well as more serious advocates of the question of nationalities emerged from the Ethiopian Student Movement in the late

1960s and early 1970s. This, among others, was the main factor behind the progressive polarization of the Student Movement and later the violent conflict among anti-Derg opposition groups in Tigray, particularly the war between the TPLF and the Ethiopian People's Revolutionary Party (EPRP), which resulted in the defeat of the latter and its expulsion from Tigray. It is the irony of "political fortunes" in Ethiopia that seemingly large, popular and renowned pan-Ethiopian organizations such as the EPRP disintegrated and were consequently weakened, while those whose political programme was not much appreciated were able to survive and become powerful over time. Indeed, few expected that the TPLF would eventually emerge as a dominant force in Ethiopian politics.

In 1972, Tigrayan students established the Tigray University Students Union (TUSU) to promote Tigrayan culture and historical pride, to identify the problems of Tigray and to deal with issues such as the formation of a Tigray Nationalist Organization (TNO) and later the Tigray Nation Progressive Union (TNPU). In 1974, however, the radical nationalist faction gained the upper hand. The Union discussed the national question in general and the problems of Tigray in particular, the means of struggle (peaceful or armed), and the strategy and objectives of the struggle. Finally, it resolved in favour of waging an extended nationalist armed struggle.[2] It is widely believed that student support for the self-determination of nationalities alarmed the Haile Selassie regime. As a result the regime launched harsh measures against the students. Thereafter the radical students were forced to look for other methods of struggle. Most of them left the country to prepare themselves for armed struggle. With the demise of the Haile Selassie regime in September 1974, the TNPU was already recruiting members to leave for rural Tigray in order to start an armed struggle against the Derg. Tigrayan students were already pointedly determined to create their own political organization and decided on a Tigrayan nationalist movement rather than a multinational one.[3]

Operating from isolated areas in the largely marginalized northern territory of Tigray, the student-led TPLF was avowedly Marxist and committed to Maoist notions of protracted people's war based on the peasants. It made its zone of operation in the localities of Tigray, which are known to have been influenced by the protracted war in Eritrea.[4] As Tigray was home to several armed groups, the TPLF had to rely on a military survival instinct. Unlike the other groups the TPLF gave great emphasis to rural armed struggle and worked hard to strengthen its guerrilla army. In spite of its leftist dogmatism it was not naïve as far as the primacy and indispensability of the military struggle was concerned. It might have increasingly shown flexibility in many other areas such as land tenure, trade and commerce that directly impacted the peasants upon whom the movement depended, but it remained committed to the pre-eminence of military survival and its position on nationalities. Stealth focus on both helped the Front in several ways. It proved effective in mobilizing Tigrayan peasants gradually, providing an organizational structure for uniting other oppressed nations in struggle; the EPRDF was formed in 1989, and also created a basis for establishing a post-Derg political order.

Ideological foundations

The TPLF repeatedly declared that the ever-increasing national prejudices and hatred had made conditions extremely difficult for class alliances and for a joint struggle of the oppressed and oppressor nationalities towards a common goal. What the TPLF was actually putting into words was that although all Ethiopian nationalities were suffering from class oppression, the national contradiction was so intense that it became impossible to wage a joint class struggle. Although exaggerated somewhat, this belief, coupled with what the TPLF termed the chauvinist and opportunist stance of multinational organizations, particularly the EPRP, is considered to have been the main cause, not only of the nationalist way of struggle, but also of the TPLF's call for the creation of an independent republic of Tigray. The February 1976 "Manifesto" declares that the first task of the nationalist struggle will be the establishment of an Independent Democratic Republic of Tigray.[5] At that juncture, the TPLF could have been taken as immature and narrowly nationalistic in scope.

Unsurprisingly, the startling political position of the TPLF coupled with other tactical military considerations resulted in bloody battles between the group and pan-Ethiopian armed groups such as the Ethiopian Democratic Union (EDU) and the EPRP. Moreover, the "Manifesto" created serious controversy within the TPLF. Nonetheless, after serious introspection and internal evaluation, certain postulates were amended over a nine-month period. Specifically, the fundamentalist approach pertaining to the establishment of an independent republic of Tigray was moderated and described by the same leadership as a dangerous tendency towards narrow nationalism. Consequently, it was declared that the primary objective of the national struggle should be the establishment of a democratic Ethiopia based on voluntary and democratic principles.[6] In spite of this revisionism, the TPLF always kept a plan in reserve and never rejected the principle of the right to self-determination, which had belonged to the foundation of the Ethiopian Student Movement in particular and the Ethiopian Left in general. This principle, undoubtedly, remained the key element of the political programme of the Front.

The conviction that Ethiopia's primary contradiction arose from state domination by the Amhara over the country's oppressed nations, including Tigray, was non-negotiable. This argument further concluded that only national (that is, ethnically based) movements could successfully confront the Derg and provide the means for replacing the centralised state with the desired nation-based federation. Later on, the TPLF realized that it was important to give its programme the semblance of a broader ideological framework. Refuting the view that the nationalist tendency is always bourgeois in orientation, the TPLF argued that under a set of revolutionary conditions attention to the national question could serve the oppressed. TPLF leaders rejected the dominant notions of proletarian revolution and pan-Ethiopian struggle in favour of a focus on the peasantry, an emphasis on the national question, and an espousal of Tigrayan nationalism. Quoting Lenin's statement that the national question is not usurped by the bourgeoisie, the TPLF argued that it could, indeed, be directed in a revolutionary and democratic way.[7] It is worth remarking how these two concepts were to be married later on in the slogan "revolutionary democracy". Revolutionary democracy or *Abiotawi Demokrasi*, therefore, seems to have taken on its final contours with the emergence of a Marxist faction within the TPLF. Ideologues and communist elements of the Front formed a pre-party organization known as the Organization of Vanguard Elements in 1983, which became the Marxist-Leninist League of Tigray (MLLT) in 1985.[8] Without neglecting the nationalist theme, the declared objectives of the MLLT were also designed to suit a pan-Ethiopian situation.

The TPLF brashly reasoned that the national struggle could neutralize not only national oppression, but also any kind of oppression (including that of the bourgeoisie). It appears, therefore, that the TPLF had also borrowed from Stalin's theory the idea that oppressed ethnic groups have the right to struggle against all forms of oppression. This indicates that, in the eyes of the TPLF, the national question was the preferred path to total emancipation of the oppressed masses.[9] In its 1983 *Peoples' Democratic Program* the Front justifies why the national question is central to the question of democracy, arguing that a demo-cracy could not materialize in Ethiopia without solving the national question democratically. The Front contended that failure to solve the national question in a revolutionary democratic manner was, indeed, undemocratic, declaring that nobody could claim to be a true democrat and to have established a democratic system without allowing Nations, Nationalities and Peoples (ethnic groups) to exercise all their demo-cratic *and* human rights, including the principle of self-determination.

Applying this thesis to the Ethiopian scene, the TPLF became certain that the national struggle in its revolutionary and democratic form not only could achieve national freedom and independence, but was also the only way forward for the total emancipation of all oppressed nationalities. In this context, the national question had ceased to be part of the old *bourgeois* democratic revolution. Hence, in a very rudi-mentary way, the TPLF developed and refined a program of national self-determination, popular administration, revolutionary democracy, and a commitment to the social and economic advancement of the country based on the peasantry. This had practical benefits for mobi-lization and transformation in support of the armed struggle. It helped the front to link the economic survival of the peasantry to the political and military fortunes of the TPLF. The pillar of this success was the system of elected village assemblies, known as *Baito*s. These gave Tigrayan peasants an unprecedented democratic control over local affairs. Clearly, the *Baitos* system has been widely admired for its suc-cess in promoting land redistribution, environmental protection and social reforms. This gradual evolution in doctrine and the resultant policy formulation of the MLLT clearly reveal one thing. From narrow nationalist tendencies, the national struggle in Tigray became articu-lated in such a way as to create a direct link between nationalism (the national question) and democracy.

This introductory scene, which spans a period of two decades from the heyday of the Student Movement to the establishment of the MLLT (from circa 1969 to 1985), is pivotal to an understanding of the ideo-logical orientation and political dogma of the TPLF/EPRDF and the constitutional dispensation which came into being during the transitional period and unleashed the restructuring of the Ethiopian state. It must be stressed that unlike most African governing groups, the TPLF has been a profoundly ideological movement of a Stalinist variant which came to power through a lengthy armed struggle on the basis of peasant support and a commitment to a revolutionary transformation of society. This specific political character of the TPLF heavily affected its relations with other political/armed groups.

Thriving in a complex insurgency: the TPLF and Ethiopian armed groups

The notion of protracted war and ideological/political correctness meant that the TPLF entered only into short term "tactical alliances" with groups that shared its opposition to the Derg even if they did not have compatible political programmes. But the TPLFs long term view of the conflict remained firm and ensured that its objectives were not subject to alteration because of these alliances, a position that defines the political position of the TPLF to this day. The TPLF might have had several plans for Ethiopia but political compromise with any group or entity was not one of them.

The early years of the struggle were very challenging as the plethora of armed groups in northern Ethiopia literally sandwiched the TPLF on all fronts. The TPLF's area of operation between 1975 and 1978 was mainly eastern Shire, eastern Axum and eastern Adigrat, all adjacent to Eritrean territory. While both Eritrean fronts remained ambivalent to its formation, most Ethiopian opposition groups were hostile to the creation of the TPLF. During the early years of the struggle the TPLF fought with almost all armed groups in northern Ethiopia one after another. This defined its political and security orientation.

The bloody and hazardous battles with both Eritrean and Ethiopian opposition movements also defined its character. They may well have instilled a sense of fearlessness and military excellence. Using effective mobilization techniques, a detailed appraisal mechanism, systematic propaganda, and persistent political work that combined cultural symbols, the TPLF was able to overcome the difficulties faced by the environment in which it was operating. Besides, in the early days of the revolution no group took the TPLF seriously and it was seen by many (EPRP, EPLF, ELF, EDU) as an organization hastily formed to confuse and weaken the revolutionary struggle. Indeed, the fact that during the initial years the group was underestimated and ignored by all the actors in the country, including the government, was a blessing in disguise.

The TPLF was helped by the fact that the Derg was late to come to western Tigray and it was helped further when the Derg continued to ignore the seriousness of the challenge posed by the TPLF. The military focus of the Derg was on the EDU and the EPRP while the TPLF used the respite to prepare itself militarily. It is a political irony that the eventually most powerful group in the country was relegated to a side show on the Derg's radar for many years. Partly because of its military preoccupation in Eritrea and the Ogaden and partly because it underestimated the potential threat from the TPLF, the government did not launch significant military campaigns in the region until 1978, although there were cases when the government made efforts to eliminate TPLF "suspected" members and supporters during the Red Terror. Furthermore, the relative lack of attention from the government provided the TPLF with an opportunity to expand its operations in Tigray.

Two years into the beginning of the armed struggle the TPLF was in a position to militarily engage with its opponents, one after another, at a time of its own choice. But when it started the fighting was nonetheless tough and revelatory. TPLF combatants had to fight to the death just to survive as a group. The bloody battles with the EDU in 1977 were fatal and fateful. Indeed, it was the brutal and bloody war with EDU that defined the military fortunes and character of the TPLF. It was a time of adversity in which the TPLF barely thrived. The doggedness and tenacity with which the TPLF won the war had a huge impact on the military position of the TPLF beyond Tigray.

The successive battles with the Ethiopian Democratic Union (EDU) in western Tigray were not only important in holding a chunk of territory; they but greatly added to the military clout of the Front and put the group in a much stronger position vis-à-vis other groups, particularly the EPRP. It was during this time that a spirit of valour and fearlessness was instilled among TPLF fighters, creating a view of their own bravery as greater than that of other groups. The military significance of the war with EDU thus cannot be overstated. It marked the beginning of the TPLF as the dominant military force in Tigray.[10] In less than two years the "provincial" TPLF had become a disruptive military force in a complex national emergency involving the whole country.

The violent struggle with the EPRP in the years between 1975 and 1978 also played a role in the development of the TPLF. Both organizations engaged in a serious struggle, each working hard to gain supremacy over the other in the urban as well as rural areas of Tigray. The conflict was multi-dimensional. It involved propaganda, the organization of the people, the setting up of "popular" committees and judiciary bodies as well as covert and overt armed conflicts in the towns and rural areas of Tigray. The TPLF gave a great deal of emphasis to the military aspect of the struggle, on the basis of which the EPRP accused it of being a "Focoist" and right wing petty bourgeoisie organization with strong fascist inclinations. On the other hand the TPLF criticized the EPRP as an artificial military group which didn't have a fighting spirit. The TPLF's view was that, militarily speaking, the EPRP didn't have what it takes. The TPLF, certainly, did not lead a complacent or secondary military life.

Moreover the EPRP tried to exploit the rift between the TPLF and the Tigray Liberation Front (TLF) and presented it as a clash between the regional groups of Adwa and Agame respectively. Given the support the EPRP had from both Eritrean fronts (ELF and EPLF) the TPLF was bent on dislodging the group from Tigray. Both organizations also accused each other of collaborating with the Derg authorities during the Red Terror in order to eliminate the members of the other group in the towns of Tigray. The conflict was so bloody and confused that the Derg had difficulty in identifying its targets in most towns of Tigray. It is reported that, aside from Addis Ababa, the Red Terror took its biggest toll in Tigray. Beginning in mid-1977 tension built up between the two organizations and they were no longer on speaking terms. The struggle for supremacy over Tigray would enter its final stages with the bloody conflict in rural areas. Lack of information and poor preparation as well as wrong timing contributed to the military defeat of the EPRP at the hands of the TPLF. The TPLF was able to integrate itself with the people of Tigray. It defined its political position in a way that articulated the grievances of the people. Leaders and fighters of the front operated alongside the people living the life of the poor peasant. Over time the refined political and military position of the TPLF, through a series of corrective measures, produced disciplined, well-politicized and gallant fighters, laying the ground for decisive victories over its opponents.

The fact that the EPRP had entered into a conflict with the TPLF just when it emerged from its victory against the EDU is a major variable. Like all military actors in the country the EPRP seriously misjudged when and how to enter a conflict with the TPLF—with catastrophic results. Winning the war against the major pan-Ethiopian nationalist force in Tigray paved the way for the TPLF dominance of Ethiopian politics in the years to come. TPLF leaders have apparently come to view the EPRP as a kind of Frankenstein monster that needed to be stamped out. This episode cleared the major obstacle at the national level and ultimately defined the political fortunes of the TPLF. Hence the TPLF actually won the war as early as in 1978, way before its final "official" victory of May 1991.

Managing other powerful adversaries: the TPLF and the Eritrean Fronts

Another major complication faced by the TPLF during the early years of the struggle was its relationship with the Eritrean People's Liberation Front (EPLF) and the Eritrean Liberation Front (ELF). Though it provided token military assistance and training the EPLF was apprehensive about the TPLF and didn't regard it as a viable organization in the fight against the Derg. The conflict with the EPRP in Tigray also had a bearing on the TPLF's relations with both Eritrean fronts; both the EPLF and later the ELF are reported to have tried to force the TPLF into accepting to become subservient to the "giant" EPRP, showing their patronizing attitude to the TPLF. Indeed, one of the preconditions for accepting trainees from Tigray by the EPLF was that the TPLF should support the EPRP. Both Eritrean fronts, particularly the EPLF, tried to marginalize the TPLF because of the military balance of power (as the EPLF perceived it). This was mainly true before the TPLF defeated the EPRP in Tigray. No doubt, the EPLF preferred to deal with the EPRP because at that stage it was perceived to be a promising organization, leading many observers to believe that sooner or later it would topple the Derg. Eritrean armed groups have had a long record of underestimating the TPLF and this appears to be the reason why the EPLF pursued a policy of fully marginalizing the TPLF after it signed a co-operation agreement with the EPRP. In a joint statement released by the EPLF and the EPRP in August 1976, the two groups agreed to support each other militarily, politically and materially.[11] Besides, the EPLF was suspicious of the TPLF's relations with its arch-enemy the ELF.

During those years the ELF had a military presence in Western Tigray, so there were some attempts to establish military contacts between the TPLF and the ELF, and that might have discouraged the EPLF from approaching the TPLF. Indeed the support provided by the ELF to the TPLF was relatively more substantial than the EPLF's cooperation. Gradually, clear differences in ideology and means of war further complicated the relations between the two. Not surprisingly, the EPLF began to entertain the idea of engaging with the TPLF and soften its position when the balance of military power in Tigray changed in favour of the TPLF.[12] A consistent trend throughout the armed struggle was the fact that the TPLF had to show its military might to be accepted as a partner and a credible force by Eritrean forces in general and the EPLF in particular.

In 1978, the EPLF tried to ingratiate itself with the TPLF through conciliatory tones and by appreciating the value of cooperation. Owing to the closeness of political and organizational features—the EPLF at least officially adopted a radical socialist line which seems to have attracted the TPLF—and exhaustion from the war with EDU and the EPRP, the TPLF was badly in need of some assistance and cooperation from the EPLF. The two fronts signed a cooperation pact in 1978, the same year the TPLF chased the EPRP from Tigray.[13] Eventually, tension developed between the TPLF and the ELF. From the very beginning the two groups had a troubled relationship. Being a veteran liberation movement the ELF had a demeaning view of the TPLF. Their area of operations being one and the same, both fronts had a series of unresolved border and administrative issues. The ELF was active and had influence over large rural areas of north-western Tigray between Badme and Adi-Hageray, areas contested during the recent war between Eritrea and Ethiopia. Evidently the TPLF was not ready to play the role of a puppet, as the ELF would have liked it to do. Moreover, politically speaking they were antagonistic and contradictory to each other. Although in 1975–76 the TPLF learned a lot from the brief joint military operations with the ELF against the Derg, it developed a great deal of aversion towards the ELF's arrogant behaviour as well as its politically backward tendencies.[14] There were huge differences on multiple fronts, from the issue of nationalities to the Eritrean question and popular participation in the struggle. Clearly, the TPLF approached the ELF in the early days because of difficult circumstances and not out of veneration or strategic partnership. The brief period of partnership was used, for what it was worth, as a military lesson during the formative years of the TPLF—the rest is ideology and politics.

While the military preponderance of the TPLF attracted the attention of the EPLF it increased the apprehension of the ELF. After clearing the EDU from western Tigray it was a matter of time before the TPLF become a major threat to the very survival and longterm interests of the ELF. Clearly, the ELF was averse to the TPLF's way of doing things, such as organizing the peasantry and carrying out land reform. For the TPLF, the very idea of land reform was a major element of its political programme and ideological orientation. The attempt to address peasant problems and organizing them for the struggle was, indeed, the major source of strength for the TPLF. This and the right to self-determination had been the hallmark of the front that differentiated it from all political and armed groups in the country, which ultimately gave it a huge military and political advantage. A contributing factor in the mutual mistrust was the fact that the ELF had close relations with the Tigray Liberation Front (TLF), which had been eliminated by the TPLF. The TPLF also developed grudges against the ELF due to its support of the EDU and the EPRP against which it was fighting for supremacy over Tigray. The fact that Eritrean fronts were helping anti-TPLF armed groups and were unable to check the rise of the TPLF can be explained in several ways—weak planning, poor judgment, ill-conceived views, a less sound political base and dismal popular mobilization. The astuteness with which the TPLF effectively used its weak position and managed to conceal it, as well as its selection of timing to make alliances and enter into armed confrontations, is a telling commentary on the complex turn of events and twist of coincidence that helped it to wear away all military challenges and grow into a major player in Ethiopian politics.

Thus, the ELF had long incurred the TPLF's disfavour and by 1979 both groups were clearly at loggerheads. The dynamics of the initial conflict between the ELF and the TPLF were, from all angles, separate from inter-Eritrean rivalry. However, the timing was perfect for the TPLF as it was around that time that the EPLF, after years of protracted warfare, found it opportune to strike against the common enemy, the ELF. Hugely attracted by TPLF's military prowess and its war footing against the ELF, the EPLF seemed to have decided to conduct a final onslaught against the ELF in western Eritrea. In mid-1979, the ELF became restless and prepared for war behind the TPLF lines in western Tigray. The first battles between the ELF and the TPLF were fought in late November 1979 when the ELF invaded the very base of the TPLF at the Belesa River in central Tigray. Highly weakened by internal squabbles, the ELF was unable to resist the TPLF counterattack. Successive battles led to the military decline of the ELF and its eventual defeat by the EPLF in 1981.[15] The TPLF was instrumental in the defeat and disintegration of the veteran Eritrean armed movement, unequivocally putting its footprint in the war of Eritrean independence and the future of Eritrea. It was in the early years that the TPLF dealt with veteran Eritrean and Ethiopian political/armed movements, which cleared the way for the post-1991 dispensation in both countries. By the end of 1979, the EPLF and the TPLF were the only major armed groups in Eritrea and Ethiopia respectively. The TPLF's fast rise from obscurity to military dominance was unexpected by many. Less than four years after its establishment, the TPLF, under the most unfavourable circumstances, had been able to decisively deal with the TLF, EDU, EPRP and the ELF. By the early 1980s, the TPLF had become the most powerful opposition group in northern Ethiopia surpassed, militarily speaking, only by the EPLF. Very soon however the imbalance militarily would be changed in the TPLF's favour.

Compared to the TPLF, which engaged with peasant conditions that in turn increased its obsession with fundamental ideological convictions, the EPLF was just a military organization. Nurtured as a tiny military force in the Sahel mountains isolated from its own population the EPLF had the fascination of a military institution which defined its character in the years to come. Any aspect of cooperation between the two would remain tactical and mostly characterized by short termism. As early as 1981 the TPLF made it clear that its alliance with the EPLF was only tactical and not strategic. The notion of ideological correctness, mounting military strength and the requirements of warfare meant that the TPLF entered short-term "tactical" alliances with groups that shared its opposition to the Derg even if they did not have compatible political programmes. But the TPLF's long-term view of the conflict and its negative perceptions of other armed groups remained firm and ensured that its objectives were not subject to alteration because of these short term alliances. The TPLF had always been deeply ideological and the sheer necessity of survival in a hostile environment seemed to have forced its leaders to frequently refer to the broader Marxist literature. The frequent joke at the time was that with no foreign alliances apart from a difficult relationship with the EPLF, the TPLF leadership had to look to Marx, Stalin, and Mao for inspiration and so eventually finished by seeking solace in Albania's Enver Hoxha.

As the TPLF advanced in the 1980s it increasingly challenged the EPLF in a number of areas, the most persistent disagreement being over their different interpretations of national self-determination and the role and character of the Soviet Union. With a large and menacing military offensive of the Derg in sight the political differences were temporarily dampened, which gave way to a brief tactical military cooperation. In 1982 the TPLF resolved in favour of defending the Sahel mountains during the Red Star Campaign, the largest offensive of the Derg against the EPLF. It was during this time that the TPLF attracted the attention of the military leadership in Addis Ababa. It is remarkable that the Derg was almost unaware of the alarming rise of the TPLF. It was not until the late 1980s that it fully understood the military threat posed by the group. Apart from the occasional skirmishes, between November 1976 and early 1983 the government launched six major offensive campaigns against the TPLF; none of these campaigns achieved their goals. The TPLF mostly avoided conventional resistance whenever the military balance of power was in favour of the government. The front during this time largely depended on guerrilla warfare to destroy government forces stationed in the different parts of Tigray. In a series of victories it won over government forces the front was able to increase its stockpile of weapons.

As much as it played a leading role in the disintegration of the ELF, the TPLF decided to save the Eritrean Revolution, and by implication the EPLF, from destruction by blunting successive offensives of the Derg army. As long as the TPLF continued to engage in tactical military alliances the multi-faceted political differences were kept under wraps, but the rapid expansion of the TPLF in the mid-1980s brought these differences to the fore.

A leap forward: ideological reinforcement and organizational advancement

Given the developing enmity from the EPLF, it was imperative for the TPLF to secure independent supply lines for the fast growing armed struggle against the Derg. And it had to do it fast. In September 1984 the TPLF constructed its own supply line through Welqait in western Tigray to the Sudan, which ended up leading to a break between the two organizations in 1985. 1985 was also a year of significant advance for the TPLF in many aspects. It held a Party Congress and a crucial reassessment was made on the history of its ten years of struggle. The front was digging in for the long haul. After a series of discussions from the top down to the smallest unit, the front purged some its leaders such as Aregawi Berhe and Giday Zeratsion for political and disciplinary reasons. This served as a precursor to the formation of the Marxist-Leninist League of Tigray (MLLT) and the rise of Meles Zenawi as the leader and chief ideologue of the Front.[16] The 1985 TPLF congress also considered the need for a permanent base area. In 1985–86 the rebels destroyed the bridge on the river Tekezze, blocking the Welqait-Tembien-Adi Da'ero roads, and established a permanent base area at Kazza and Dajana. The group utilized this brief moment of respite and soul searching to develop the ideology of the TPLF, shift the orientation from Tigray to Ethiopia, and carry out the necessary research to better pursue the objectives of the movement, particularly in the military sphere. Armed with new conceptual ammunition, both military and political, the TPLF braced itself for the second phase of its struggle clearly aimed at its major enemy, the Derg. By about the mid-1980s the TPLF had been able to acquire a sufficient quantity of light weapons but it had almost no heavy weapons. But its string of military successes had now put it in a position to begin to acquire them.[17]

The TPLF made further advances and was able to control more territory. In late 1988 and early 1989 the Front conducted a series of successful military operations which made it difficult for the Derg to fully concentrate on the war in Eritrea. With the Derg's demise in sight the TPLF and EPLF were busy and highly agitated; their alliance was resumed in 1988, but the differences remained and would resurface at the time of the war that broke out a decade later between Eritrea and Ethiopia. In March 1988 the EPLF won a decisive victory over the highly concentrated and well-equipped government forces at Af'abet.[18] This was accompanied by a decisive military victory on the Shire Front by the TPLF, another turning point in the war against the Derg. The battle of Shire proved the excellent military capabilities of the TPLF. Sudden and unexpected, the battle of Shire inflicted a decisive blow to the government.[19] Events following the battle not only changed the military balance of power dramatically in favour of the TPLF, subsequently the main component part of the EPRDF, but also drastically shortened the path to final victory over the military government of Ethiopia. After the battle of Shire the EPRDF and EPLF went on coordinating their offensive operations against the government army. In the post-Shire war between the TPLF and government forces, despite considerable casualties on both sides, all battles were fought a smaller scale, making the battle of Shire a landmark in the history of the protracted war in Ethiopia. The TPLF, for many years confined to the hills and the borderlands with Sudan, would penetrate as far south as northern Shewa, and capture the capital in less than two years.

The TPLF, right from the start, had displayed organizational and military effectiveness. This is largely attributed to a persistent focus on military discipline and political orientation. The main and decisive factor in the TPLF's victory over its opponents was its political and military superiority. Throughout the protracted war the TPLF effectively politicized the people and was particularly capable of successfully integrating itself with the rural population. The front was not only able to get popular support in Tigray but also in neighbouring regions. The TPLF's multi-faceted propaganda activities indeed resulted in its being politically superior to the government in both Tigray and adjacent regions. Equally important in conducting war and developing a bond with the peasants, according to TPLF leaders, was the development of a system of evaluation (plans and programmes of accountability) of leaders, known as *gim gema*.[20] First taken up by intellectuals, who had always dominated the movement, it then spread to the guerrilla army and was soon deemed to be crucial for the development of military skills as well as making commanders answerable to their fighters. From the army, evaluation systems spread to the liberated territories and were introduced to the local councils, mass associations and militias where they gained popularity as the best means of ensuring the accountability of leaders and administrators, a function they continue to retain.

Hence, during the late 1980s, the TPLF's military successes against the Derg allowed it to expand beyond its traditional northern base of operations. They also prompted the TPLF to develop political and organizational roots in the areas through which they were advancing. This led to a search for ethnic organizations at the regional level which could be depended upon as allies, both in the struggle against the Derg and in the subsequent restructuring of Ethiopia along ethno-regional lines. The TPLF thus had to woo and win over several ethnic armed groups.

Where national movements existed and were judged to be ideologically compatible, the TPLF sought to forge alliances. Where suitable movements did not exist, it encouraged their creation. The Front, then, established the EPRDF as a federation of various sub-organizations (TPLF, EPDM, OPDO and EDORM) in 1989 to serve as an umbrella for the expanding constellation of allied regional parties. This enabled the TPLF to form alliances with (and in practice to dominate) parties representing other nationalities. In its first National Congress (17–23 January 1991), the TPLF-dominated EPRDF adopted a political and economic programme premised on the TPLF's long-standing interpretation of the national question. Suffice it to say, then, that the influence of the TPLF was so pervasive that its political orientation, logically, became the political programme of the new umbrella Front.

EPRDF victories in strategic towns in northern and central Ethiopia between April 1990 and April 1991 shattered the morale of the Ethiopian Defence Force and the Derg in early May 1991. The peace negotiations between the TPLF and the Derg, which were held in Rome in 1989 and 1990 and later in May 1991 in London, were only perfunctory as the military dominance of the rebellion had become overwhelming. In the end the TPLF-led EPRDF forces seized the capital on the morning of 28 May 1991 and a Provisional Administration was instituted on 1 June 1991.

The TPLF and the transition

After the TPLF-led EPRDF had entered Addis Ababa it organized a conference to map out the country's future but, significantly, the organizations invited were national but regionally-grounded either as liberation fronts or groups recently organized, frequently at the behest of the TPLF. As an ideologically-driven party, and true to its character and history, the EPRDF was suspicious and careful not to admit those organizations it considered detrimental to the creation of an ethno-regionally structured state.[21] A whole bevy of ethnic parties were created specifically to participate in the Conference. The Addis Ababa conference revolved around the rights of the country's nationalities which were approved, including a right to secession. The TPLF's outright military victory, and its domination of the transitional conference that was a product of that victory, ensured that its will prevailed. Upon completion of the conference the Transitional Government of Ethiopia

273

(TGE) was established and the TPLF Chairman Meles Zenawi assumed the presidency. An EPRDF-dominated Council of People's Representatives was set up and it adopted the resolutions of the Addis Ababa conference as an interim constitution. But before much progress could be made on these plans, regional elections were organized for June 1992 causing the Oromo Liberation Front (OLF) to revolt as it could not see an independent role for itself in this new dispensation.

The complete victory of the TPLF over all its opponents over the preceding years and the Derg in 1991, the Front's administrative competence, a measure of pragmatism, the invaluable experience of developing a close understanding of the country's peasants, and a belated appreciation of the changed international context had produced—at least until the war with Eritrea and the 2005 elections—a generally smooth transition. Outright military victory also meant that the TPLF could gain the approval of its constitution and predetermined political processes and pursue largely unhindered its programme of political and economic reform. While the Transitional Charter left the formal structures of the emerging Federal States to be defined by the Council of Representatives, and ultimately by the constitution-drafting process, the new political framework was already evolving as regional parties began to fight for control over local administrations and imposed their mark on the political and social landscape. The transitional period (1991–4) was not all-inclusive and was, therefore, characterized by tension as ethno-regional forces tried to challenge the EPRDF Army in their own localities. The most immediate challenge to the TPLF-led EPRDF derived from the friction between the Front and the OLF. The OLF had played an important but secondary role in the Addis Ababa conference, and being a party to the London conference was given the next largest group of seats in the Council of People's Representatives after the EPRDF, and promised that its forces would be integrated with those of the national army. However, at the end of 1991 and in early 1992, regional power struggles escalated into intense conflicts, predominantly in the Oromiya and Ethio-Somali National Regional States where the armed wings of the respective regional political movements clashed both with each other and with the forces of the EPRDF.

The OLF in particular had grown increasingly disenchanted with the TPLF's domination of the transitional government, as it seriously doubted the Front's commitment to the right of nationalities to secede from the Ethiopian federation and, after alleging intimidation and

274

other irregularities in the elections, withdrew from the government and launched a failed insurrection. It was in this inauspicious climate that preparations were made for the elections of Regional and District Councils in June 1992.[22] The political differences between the OLF and the EPRDF were minimal; they revolved mainly around the sharing of power in an ethnically structured political system. And yet the eventual clampdown on the OLF, in which around 20,000 combatants were captured against minimal army losses, foreclosed the possibility of power sharing in the post-1991 Ethiopia. In December 1994 the TPLF-led government approved a constitution which led to the creation of a federal state of ten regions. This paved the way for national elections in May 1995 which in the absence of major opposition parties, produced a massive victory for the TPLF and its allies, and on 24 August the country was formally proclaimed the Federal Democratic Republic of Ethiopia (FDRE). Upon assuming power the TPLF embarked on the demanding task of restructuring the Ethiopian state. Attempts by generations of rulers of Ethiopia to centralize the state were reversed in 1991, with the coming to power of the TPLF-led Ethiopian People's Revolutionary Democratic Front (EPRDF), which facilitated the independence of Eritrea and has pursued an innovative and bold experiment of transferring authority to ethnically based regional administrations. The EPRDF's great experiment, designed by the TPLF to give legitimacy to ethnic nationalism, which has brought decades of war to Ethiopia, together with the formation of a system of ethnic-based regional administration, inevitably ensured its dominance.

It could safely be argued that the overall democratic process from 1995 to 2000 had been tailored to maximize the influence of the TPLF. As a result political change could only have come from within the EPRDF and not from the opposition. While the EPRDF had not closed the door to power sharing, it held that forces like the OLF must accept the 1994 Constitution, by implication the *status quo*. The overall political supremacy of the EPRDF at the end of the 1990s was the product of its having secured the political, military and organizational balance of power in its favour. Having achieved an outright military victory against the Derg in May 1991, the Front thereafter faced no coordinated national armed opposition. As a result, the post-1991 security situation in Ethiopia depended, by and large, on the capacity of the EPRDF to employ the instruments of violence at its disposal. Ultimately, the "politics of co-optation" and growing inter-National

Regional State dialogue and cooperation brought about the consolidation of EPRDF rule, the gradual withering of a viable national opposition and a struggling civil society. As discussed earlier, the TPLF maintains only a nominal commitment to liberal democracy, which it had rhetorically adopted in order to appease outside donors; its own preference was for a very different form of "revolutionary democracy", in which a revolutionary democratic party with a "correct line" would be the one to authentically represents the interests of the broad masses of the population, while rival parties—which could not by definition represent those interests—were judged to be illegitimate.

This TPLF-led transition clearly showed that by initiating a guided programme of democratization, the Front had achieved its goals of peace—it established a workable constitution, carried out programmes of economic and political reform and above all cemented its hegemonic status, which enabled it to freely implement its revolutionary political ideology. To recapitulate, the EPRDF's democratic nationalism had to tolerate a careful and limited programme of democratization without undermining the intended route and the end result. Meanwhile most of the success of the transitional period can be attributed to the EPRDF's economic policies and the capacity of the Front to carry them out. Upon assuming power in May 1991 the EPRDF was confronted with an economy that was on the brink of collapse, a state devoid of funds, and a discontented civil service dominating the bureaucracy. The incoming government quickly introduced some reforms by officially encouraging markets, opening up trade and privatizing state farms and other largely bankrupt state holdings, liquidating of the hated state agricultural marketing corporation. TPLF leaders who had revered Enver Hoxha of Albania only months before triumphantly entering Addis Ababa had to show a great deal of pragmatism and adapt to the changing international context. Ethiopia's economy started to grow and witnessed some structural changes immediately after the end of the transition period. Indeed, international financial institutions applauded the economic changes and continued to support the TPLF's economic transformation policies, owing largely to the clever way in which TPLF leaders managed their relations with the West and multilateral financial institutions.[23]

In the second half of the 1990s the TPLF-led EPRDF extensively reformed the state and the economy, demonstrating its administrative competence by managing successive droughts and domestic security.

Ethiopia's government has operated a state-dominated market economy since rebels overthrew a socialist military regime in 1991. While
private investment has been encouraged in areas including agriculture
and manufacturing, government enterprises continue to control or
monopolize financial services, transport, energy and telecommunications. Good security, governance and encouraging levels of economic
development were unfortunately disrupted by the outbreak of the
Eritrean-Ethiopian war in May 1998.

The war with Eritrea and internal crisis

The EPLF and TPLF carried forward their differences and the resultant
mutual suspicion even while they worked to maintain a shaky military
alliance to overthrow the Derg. Historical animosity and mutual suspicions, different, if not opposing, political trajectories, and prevalent
economic and border issues might be considered as major factors in the
conflict. None of these differences were publicly on display during the
Eritrean independence referendum. However, that such differences
should produce war has more to do with the perceived military invincibility of the EPLF (on which its internal and external legitimacy, as
well as its economic and the foreign policy, was based) than with border disputes that were never a problem for the two organizations or
the people who lived in the areas in question. Evidently, the calculus of
both regimes was to resolve outstanding issues, which in turn became
the main drivers of the sudden outbreak of the conflict and the way it
played out. The EPLF, unaware of the regional distribution of power
and the fact that TPLF leaders had become masters of a historic state,
overwhelmingly and fatally counted much on their own perceived military invincibility.

The notion of Eritrean military invincibility has been at the core of
the EPLF's internal and external legitimacy. The fact that the TPLF
had long changed the military balance in its favour and would not tolerate anything that might undermine its dominant position in Ethiopia
was consistently ignored by the leadership in Asmara. The history and
character of the TPLF were duly overlooked, its organizational and
military qualities forgotten. Like the Derg, the EPLF was oblivious to
the clout and dynamism of the TPLF. And the fact that the war shattered that sense of invincibility, and the political and foreign policy
issues associated with it, would not be forgotten or forgiven; hence, a

long drawn out feud between the two. True to its instinct, intelligent sequencing and accurate reading of its internal and external environment the TPLF decided to accommodate the EPLF in every way possible. The new government entered various economic and security pacts with Eritrea that many felt served Asmara's interests more than those of Ethiopia. That the EPLF thought such pacts would be accorded long-term implementation was a critical misjudgement. Unaware of the changing environment and the nature of the state the TPLF had captured, the EPLF neglected dispute resolution mechanisms because of its perceptions of its military invincibility.[24] Having spent more years in the bush and given its historical superiority in armaments, the EPLF was irritated to find itself at the helm of a country much smaller and less influential than Ethiopia.

Meanwhile, the TPLF encouraged the EPLF leadership and the Eritreans to vote for outright independence, eventually eliminating the possibility of the EPLF tampering with the new dispensation and power consolidation process in Ethiopia. The hint that the EPLF and the Derg were major potential troublemakers in the event of a power sharing agreement was never overlooked. The EPLF was allowed to feel superior and continue its rapacious policies, with only rare notes of protest from the government in Addis Ababa. The TPLF leadership bears part of the responsibility for the rising temptation of the EPLF to follow dangerous options. The sagacity with which the TPLF managed the relationship with the EPLF during the post-1991 period says more about the nature of the Front. However, given the narrative it has regarding its relations with Eritrean fronts and the pattern of behaviour of the EPLF, it is difficult to understand how TPLF leaders could have been so ill prepared for the military attack from Eritrea.[25]

Though caught unprepared for the Eritrean invasion of its territory on 12 May 1998 the Ethiopian government bounced back swiftly, illustrating the TPLF's organizational leadership and the capacity and depth of the Ethiopian state. The TPLF leadership quickly mobilized the country and conducted successful offensives that ultimately resulted in the defeat of the Eritrean army and control of a chunk of Eritrean territory. The Algiers Agreement in 2000, largely dictated by Ethiopia, marked the culmination of the war and subsequent stalemate between Ethiopia and Eritrea. While the TPLF leadership demonstrated considerable skills at mobilization and war making, its handling of the diplomatic front both during and after the war exposed its inexperience. This weakness was compounded by a focus on internal power struggles due to the untimely outbreak of the TPLF crisis. The Ethiopian government could be said to have pre-emptively announced its acceptance of the ruling by the Ethio-Eritrean Boundary Commission (EEBC), which awarded the disputed areas controlled by Ethiopia to Eritrea.[26]

The end of the war brought an increasing need to assess the TPLF's ten-year performance and prepare the ground for conventions of the Front and the EPRDF. The course and outcome of the war with Eritrea had far-reaching consequences for the TPLF. The war saw an unexpected change of power relations within the TPLF.[27] The ultimate victory over Eritrea can be attributed to the hard-line positions of the group that challenged Meles' leadership during the war. While Meles repeatedly urged caution to his colleagues, it was in fact the so-called "hard-liners" in the TPLF who clearly had the support of the majority of Ethiopians in their resolute determination to achieve an unambiguous victory over Isayas and his army. But in the wake of the victory Meles astutely marginalized and then dismissed the very people who were most responsible for the victory over Eritrea. It appears that the majority of the TPLF favoured a swift and decisive military victory not only to demolish Eritrean pretensions, but also to make clear that Ethiopia would not become an agent of the West, and to assert the country's dominance in the Horn of Africa. The group around Meles in turn were more pragmatic about the war because they felt that the conflict seriously undermined economic development upon which the future of Ethiopia depended. Crudely, however, some in the first group began to view Meles as an agent of the West, while his group tended to view the militants as traditionalists and die-hard Marxists.

The first major dispute broke out over how to conduct the war and these in turn overlapped with personal differences, which led to the development of factions. Critical in this early period were disagreements over recommendations made by the OAU on the Technical Arrangements to end the war. After a raucous and extensive debate the Central Committee divided 17 to 13 to reject the generally conciliatory proposals and, significantly, Meles voted with the minority. This marked the beginning of concrete divisions within the leadership. It also made clear the acrimony developing between Meles and other members of the Central Committee, and many now believe that bitterness over the issue was a direct precursor to the subsequent crisis. It could be argued that had the war not broken out at this time an evaluation of the Front would have taken place, and in a much more positive atmosphere that might have saved the party the grief it was to endure. The results of that struggle can be seen in the departure of many senior members of the Front, the demoralization of many others, the increasing shift in power to Meles, and the greater significance given to the Amhara component of the EPRDF at the expense of the TPLF. Differences among the EPRDF leadership, and in particular its TPLF core, had risen periodically, but the Eritrean war proved the catalyst in dividing the leadership.

While his opponents held that an assessment of the war with Eritrea could serve as a point of departure, the group associated with Meles contended that the objective should be to carry out a ten-year evaluation of the EPRDF's rule. During the summer of 2000 Meles presented a paper to the Central Committee denouncing Bonapartism, which argued that the TPLF's leadership was suffering serious decay and becoming distant from its constituency. The TPLF Central Committee had indeed debated Bonapartism, after which at the end of February the Meles-sponsored report gained the support of the TPLF Central Committee by a small majority of 15 in favour to 13 opposed, after considerable lobbying by the Meles group. His rivals then walked out and Meles seized the moment to consolidate his power. Meles called a conference of the TPLF cadres in Mekelle in which he appealed to Tigrayan nationalism and raised slogans that suggested that if he lost his battle with the dissidents then Tigray would also be lost and, furthermore, that the survival of the party was at stake. Again the dissidents walked out of the meeting and Meles again carried the vote. Meles effectively promoted an idiosyncratic narrative of an endangered TPLF. With the dissidents effectively frozen, Meles and his allies began what they called *Tehadso*, or "renewal".[28] Dubbed a ten-year assessment of the EPRDF the "renewal" became a full-scale attempt to cleanse the organization and root out the allies of the dissidents and those labelled as politically degenerate or decadent.

* * *

The crisis of 2001 is a watershed in the history of the TPLF and changed the nature of the Front. The result was a shift in power from Tigray to the central government in Addis Ababa, from the instruments of the party to the state, and from a grouping of the TPLF Central Committee to Meles.[29] There has since been a marked decline of collective leadership and an increasing dependence upon one leader: Meles. In addition, the TPLF had lost leaders of great integrity and experience in the party and army. Since then members have become increasingly passive, opportunistic and no longer certain of their commitment. There are now doubts about their willingness to endure the kind of sacrifices that they had willingly suffered in the past to advance the interests of the party. In the aftermath of the crisis the party and state largely united under a single leadership, furthering Meles' move to assuming disproportionate power in the Ethiopian state. After weakening the TPLF in the course of marginalizing his opponents, Meles had increasingly become dependent upon his control of state organs, of key elements of the TPLF, of his ANDM allies, and of a small entourage. Thus in the last years of the Meles Zenawi administration, the Front had to increasingly confront a crisis of legitimacy and an ideological decline, resulting in the emergence of a minority regime, relying on the prominence of a ruling security establishment. Today the quest for a broader political power base and an overhauled ideology continues.

BIBLIOGRAPHY AND FURTHER READING

Abebe Zegeye and Pausewang, Siegfried (eds), 1994, *Ethiopia in Change: Peasantry, Nationalism and Democracy*, London: British Academic Press.

Aregawi Berhe, 2009, *A Political History of the Tigray People's Liberation Front (1975–1991), Revolt, Ideology, and Mobilisation in Ethiopia*, Los Angeles: Tsehai Publishers

Bahru Zewde, 2014, *The Quest for Socialist Utopia: The Ethiopian Student Movement (1960–1974)*, Woodbridge, Suffolk: James Currey.

Balsvik, Randi R., 1985, *Haile Selassie's Students: The Intellectual and Social Background to Revolution, 1952–1977*, East Lansing, MI: African Studies Centre, Michigan State University.

Hammond, Jenny, 1999, *Fire from the Ashes: A Chronicle of the Revolution in Tigray, Ethiopia, 1975–1991*, Lawrenceville, NJ: The Red Sea Press.

Kahsay Berhe, 2005, *Ethiopia: Democratization and Unity. The Role of the Tigray's People Liberation Front*, Münster: Monsenstein und Vannerdat.

Medhane Tadesse, 1992, "EPRP versus TPLF, 1975–78: The Struggle for Supremacy over Tigray," MA thesis, History Department, Addis Ababa University.

——— 1999, *The Eritrean-Ethiopian War: Retrospect and Prospects*, Addis Ababa: Mega Enterprise.

Praeg, Bertus, 2006, *Ethiopia and Political Renaissance in Africa*, New York: Nova Science.

Tesfatsion Medhanie, 1997, *Eritrea & Neighbours in the 'New World Order':
Geopolitics, Democracy and 'Islamic Fundamentalism'*, Berlin: LIT Vlg.

Young, John, 1996, "The Tigray and Eritrean Peoples Liberation Fronts: A
History of Tensions and Pragmatism", *Journal of Modern African Studies*,
34 (1), pp. 105–120.

――― 1997, *Peasant Revolution in Ethiopia: the Tigray People's Liberation
Front*, Cambridge: Cambridge University Press.

Young, John and Medhane Tadesse, 2003, "TPLF: Reform or Decline?",
Review of African Political Economy, 30, 97, pp. 389–403.

11

FEDERALISM, REVOLUTIONARY DEMOCRACY AND THE DEVELOPMENTAL STATE, 1991–2012

Sarah Vaughan

A revolutionary reform agenda?

In 1991 the incoming Transitional Government of Ethiopia (TGE) led by the Ethiopian People's Revolutionary Democratic Front (EPRDF) inherited a centralized, authoritarian state and the ruins of a command economy from its military Marxist predecessor. The EPRDF, now a coalition of four ethnically-defined organizations, came to power by force of arms, emerging from the civil wars that had engulfed much of northern Ethiopia and Eritrea, as well as the wider Horn area, for several decades. Devastating conflict had centred upon control of the state, for it was the state that had exercised a virtual monopoly over access to resources and decision-making.[1] Conflict had precipitated enormous movements of refugee and displaced populations in and around Ethiopia, and driven hundreds of thousands into service under army conscription, or to take up arms against it.[2]

The new government publicly committed itself to three trajectories of fundamental reform, set out in a "charter" or compact for government adopted in July 1991, which, given the *de facto* separation of Eritrea,[3] would steer the remainder of the country through a transition. These were: decentralization of the state, with the introduction of a system of "ethnic" or "multinational" federalism; democratization of its politics, under a multi-party electoral system; and liberalization of the economy, in a neo-liberal international climate. Federal decentralization, democratization, and socio-economic advancement were all seen as mechanisms for the resolution of conflict and removal of its deeply rooted causes. The EPRDF itself identified the extreme centralization of power under a "rentier state", and its "ethnocratic" concentration in the hands of an elite from a single ethnic group—at the expense of the country's other impoverished, oppressed, and exploited populations—as the central root of Ethiopia's modern political history of war, famine, and underdevelopment. The federal solution the organization proposed was widely welcomed, despite anxieties about its ethnic formulation. "Self-determination" was expected to mean an expansion of popular access to decision-making and control over resources, which would encompass the great majority of Ethiopia's agricultural and pastoral producers, democratize relations between them, and release their potential for socio-economic development and competitive politics.

More than two decades later, much has changed. Ethiopia's economy is booming and sections of it have opened up significantly. Federalism and *woreda*-level decentralization have had a profound impact on the architecture of the state and the services it provides, particularly to the poor; and the country has taken exemplary strides to reach Millennium Development Goals. Four rounds of federal, regional and local elections have shaped the trajectory of the country's politics in key ways—many of them highly problematic. Nevertheless the continuities are also strong. The state continues to dominate, even monopolize, strategic sectors of an economy in which many in the private sector feel marginalized. The radical devolution offered by the federal constitution still seems a long way off, and development continues to be planned from on high. Most important of all, the EPRDF has continued to administer the overwhelming majority of the population in the four large central regions throughout the period, with its allies or affiliates governing in the peripheries almost as consistently, regardless of a succession of challenges from opponents.

This is not what liberal democratic observers in 1991 expected or hoped for, and over the last decade an alternative non-liberal narrative

284

has emerged to conceptualize these processes. Under the paradigm of the Ethiopian "developmental state" processes of economic liberalization, decentralization and even democratization are seen as centrally managed, and desirably so. For members of the ruling party, the EPRDF's "vanguard leadership" of this state-driven process is essential to achieving socio-economic growth that is broadly inclusive, sustainable, and not open to capture by wealthy elites or "rent-seekers". For its critics, this arrangement preserves intact the fundamental problem of twenty years previously: the extreme concentration of state power in the hand of a leadership the legitimacy of whose rule they question. This chapter traces some of the dynamics—and constraints— of the three processes of decentralization, democratization and liberalization[4] since 1991, exploring these contradictions.

Federalism and decentralization: devolution of power or deconcentration of responsibility

The federal architecture. The introduction of federalism involved redrawing administrative and political boundaries, so as to carve up the empire state into a series of federated units drawn around the major ethnic or language groups constitutionally referred to in Ethiopia as "nations, nationalities and peoples".[5] Ethiopia has more than seventy recognized language groups, of vastly different population sizes, and there is particular heterogeneity in the south-west of the country. The 1991 Charter ascribed broad rights of "self-determination" to all of these groups: to preserve, promote, use, and develop their own culture, history, and language; to administer their own affairs in their own territories, and participate equitably in central government; and to secede from the arrangement if they felt their rights had been denied or abrogated.

These principles underpinned both a transitional period of government and the establishment of the Federal Democratic Republic (FDRE) in 1995. The FDRE constitution formalized the division of the country into nine federated National Regional States (*kilil*s), "delimited on the basis of settlement patterns, identity, language and the consent of the people concerned" (Articles 46 and 47). The groups in question are those "who have or share a large measure of a common culture, or similar customs, mutual intelligibility of language, belief in a common or related identities, and who predominantly inhabit an identifiable contiguous territory" (Article 39). The nine States (Afar, Amhara, Benishangul-Gumuz, Gambella, Harar, Oromiya, Somali, SNNPRS/the Southern Nations, Nationalities and Peoples' Regional State, and Tigray) are asymmetrical on every social indicator, with vast differences in population size, demographic distribution and profile, developmental indices and resources. The SNNPRS (five separate kilils in the initial 1992 configuration) constitutes a kind of "federation within a federation", made up of a series of ethnic administrative units (zones and "special" *woredas*) encompassing 56 recognized groups. Gambella, Benishangul Gumuz and Harar also retain administrative mechanisms to accommodate ethnic diversity at the sub-regional level.[6] Two large municipalities (the federal capital Addis Ababa, and Dire Dawa in eastern Ethiopia) remain separately administered under the Federal Government.

As a result of these arrangements, both constitutional provision and legal, political, economic, and administrative order in contemporary Ethiopia are based essentially upon ethnicity, upon the collective identities of Ethiopia's nations, nationalities, and peoples. The system, often referred to as "ethnic federalism", is a highly unusual one, which has been met with controversy both internationally and domestically. In 1991, for instance, the reforms contrasted squarely with integrationist nation-building currents then reaching a peak in other parts of Africa—most notably in Eritrea and South Africa, both of whose governments publicly expressed concern about the Ethiopian experiment. Given the contemporary disintegration of the former Yugoslavia, and the collapse and fragmentation of neighbouring Somalia, many considered a process of "ethnicizing" politics in Ethiopia to be inexplicable, irresponsible and dangerous. Ethiopia's new leaders justified their radical initiatives as attempts to resolve the problems of the past, and increasingly conceptualize Ethiopia's nationalities in terms of their shared histories of oppression, downplaying the more apparently "primordial" or intractable aspects of their collective profiles.[7]

The politicization of ethnicity. It is a widespread criticism that, in ushering in ethnic federalism, the EPRDF has been responsible for introducing ethnicity into politics in Ethiopia. In fact the politicization of ethnicity predates both the organization and its coming to power. The nineteenth century expansion of the relatively homogeneous Abyssinian polity to form the modern Ethiopian Empire state brought a swathe of

FEDERALISM, DEMOCRACY AND DEVELOPMENT

heterogeneous groups under an Amhara, or Amharicized, imperial ruling class, which exercised a near monopoly of economic privilege and
social status, controlling land, exploiting production, and excluding
the majority of the population from government. The administrative
elite, to which many from other groups assimilated, practised a crude
form of cultural suppression and integration, establishing the Amharic
language and culture, and Orthodox Christianity, as passports to
power. The imperial state was founded on what has been called an
"explosive [...] correlation of ethnic, cultural and class differences"
that made it inherently unstable.[8] In order to stabilize it, the imperial
administration of Haile Selassie I was centralized, bureaucratized, and
militarized. The military was used to quell ethnic and regional uprisings in Bale, Eritrea, Gojjam, the Ogaden, Sidamo, and Tigray provinces, until it finally overthrew the Emperor in 1974.

At this time, ethnicity became irreversibly politicized, with the further expansion under the Derg of an imperial school system which had
educated, and rendered conscious, the elites of many of Ethiopia's ethnic groups. Unlike its imperial predecessor, the military government
promoted the *cultural* emancipation of ethnic groups, established an
Institute for the Study of Ethiopian Nationalities, and introduced a literacy campaign in the major local languages. It refused, however, to
grant political rights to Ethiopia's nationalities, and centralization was
entrenched with increasing brutality. This fanned the rise of organized
opposition in the form of the Eritrean nationalist EPLF and the ethno-
nationalist EPRDF and Oromo Liberation Front (OLF).

The EPRDF's ideas about ethno-nationalism had been honed in
Tigray, where from 1975 its elder partner the Tigray People's
Liberation Front (TPLF) fostered Tigrayan nationalist sentiment and
resistance, out of a popular sense of grievance at what they saw as the
region's socio-economic and cultural neglect through the twentieth
century. Prior to the Italian colonization of Eritrea, and the southward
shift of power with the expansion of the Ethiopian empire state, the
northern Tigrigna-speaking areas had been at the centre of the
Abyssinian polity. The memory of this lost political status, and the re-
imagining of historical precedents of resistance, such as the so-called
weyane rebellion in Tigray in the wake of the defeat of Mussolini,
fuelled support for the TPLF.[9] The Tigrayan nationalists used language
and historico-cultural symbols (the ancient stelae at Axum) to mark
their local commitments; but they also delivered relief and rehabilita-

287

tion assistance throughout the 1980s, and promised a rehabilitated and reinvigorated Tigray, under autonomous government within a democratized Ethiopia.

By the time the EPRDF, EPLF and OLF finally defeated the regime in 1991, a series of smaller ethno-nationalist movements, operating amongst the Afar, Somali, Sidama, Anywaa and other populations, was also ranged against the Derg. Ethnicity, then, was not introduced into Ethiopian politics in 1991, but had been thoroughly politicized for several decades. Whilst ethnic or multinational federalism has undoubtedly rendered these identities newly and differently relevant to political life, this has had complex and diverse results, about which there is much debate.

The transitional period 1991–1995: empowering ethnicity. The Transitional Government (TGE) appointed a Boundary Commission to propose an "ethnic map" of the new political units; a proclamation establishing them followed in January 1992. The visible involvement of non-EPRDF organizations in the controversial project was a particularly important coup. Whatever the subsequent complaints of the opposition, there were relatively few from the TGE who were not implicated in the mapping. The spectrum of participants helped force compromise and speed decisions, reining in the more ambitious claims of powerful players, whilst deflecting and defusing conflict within the group. The balance also lent a degree of transparency and legitimacy to the outcome, which the TGE could claim was "thrashed out around the table". Plural and enthusiastic involvement veiled both the extent to which the process was managed and the logical absurdity of "granting self-determination" to groups in parts of the country that had neither demanded nor fought for it.

In practice it was current language use that became the single effective criterion applied by the commission in drafting the map. This was considered a more visible and conclusive indicator of ethnic boundaries than, for instance, historical precedent. The TGE Commission was dismissive of claims based on history, fearing their open-ended potential for dispute, and preferring to deal in currently verifiable demographics.[10] Even this was not straightforward. The commission drew on the work of the Derg's Institute for the Study of Ethiopian Nationalities, which in the 1980s had established that only around 30 out of 580 *woreda*s were monolingual, and rejected language as a basis for administrative division. In 1991 there was little argument within the TGE about adopting the policy, only about its implementation. Difficult issues were postponed (like the issue of Dire Dawa), side-stepped, or siphoned off for separate negotiation by interested parties (as in the case of Harar). The core of the work was finished within a few months.

There was clear political rationale for haste. All ethno-national parties in the TGE sought stability, the reduction of controversy, and the rapid and peaceful demarcation of units of local government, which each could then seek to colonize. By contrast, the subsequent periods of dispute, debate, violent conflict and adjustment associated with these boundaries have continued to be protracted and painful. If ethnic groups sought selected historical precedents for markers and materials with which to categorize and label their identities and stake out their territories, the hasty administrative revisions of 1991 contributed additional resources to complicate this process.

A Constitution Commission was appointed to draft a range of constitutional proposals and questions for popular discussion, and subsequent debate and ratification by a Constituent Assembly elected in 1994. Two issues proved controversial during the constitutional debates: the inclusion of a right of secession and the retention of land in state ownership—both challenged then and since by the political opposition. When the FDRE constitution was finally adopted, it was premised on strong residual sovereignty for the regional governments, tempered both by formal requirements to follow a framework of federally sanctioned policy directions (Chapter 10) and by the practical importance of the flow of subsidies from the federal centre.

The first federal government, 1995: reining in ethnicity? During the first federal government, there was an observable and orchestrated move by the centre to claw back control over what some have described as an "ethnic free-for-all" in the establishment of the federation. During the early 1990s, groups of all sizes, claims, and degrees of credibility had been encouraged to organize and mobilize for self-determination (Vaughan, 1994). Now, however, the federal government started to push for the "efficient" reconsolidation of some zones, regions, and political parties, particularly in the SNNPRS. In 1997, the EPRDF's parties were amalgamated, and a number of separate "non-viable" zones—Kaffa and Sheka, Bench and Maji in the south-west for example—were unceremoniously stuck back together: much to the disgust of those in towns that lost jobs, construction, and budget control to ethnic neighbours and competitors.

Separatist claims were either rejected or deferred through the 1990s, including notably recalcitrant campaigns by the Silte and the Welaiyta. The ruling party seems to have been taken aback at the enthusiasm with which its own cadres were involved in spearheading local drives for autonomy, responding to new and appealing local incentive structures. Opponents who had always feared that ethnic federalism would lead to the balkanization of the Ethiopian empire state felt that the government was, in this period, attempting something akin to repacking Pandora's box, in Eshetu Chole's resonant image (1994). A clear integrating impetus characterized federal policy, which refused to countenance "fragmentation". The centre's hand was strengthened as a resurgence of pan-Ethiopian nationalism greeted the outbreak of war with Eritrea in May 1998.[11]

Also of concern as the war erupted was the poor quality of governance, with the corresponding instability, in the pastoralist periphery of the state. Four regional states were struggling with federal self-government: the Muslim pastoral Afar and Somali areas to the east, and the mixed areas of Benishangul-Gumuz and Gambella on the western border with Sudan. These areas had been governed for a century by envoys and civil servants from the centre. Corruption, embezzlement and instability thrived as undereducated and inexperienced officials applied the enticing resources attendant on abrupt political promotion to communal or clan rivalries. Central interference to curtail the activities of more independent minded politicians at any sign of incipient secessionism (as in the Somali kilil and Berta zone) often complicated matters further. In 1997, teams of federal advisers were despatched by the federal Prime Minister's office, to provide the so-called "emergent states" with professional and technical "'support". When it emerged that the supportive role encompassed investigation of funds given to the kilils in federal budget subsidies, and control of political matters, tensions rose. The progress of the war with Eritrea saw the grip of the federal government and National Defence Forces (ENDF) tighten on these regions as governance issues gave way to concern for the security of state borders.

Second wave decentralization from 2002: building the woreda. A second federal government was elected in May 2000 amidst high drama on the battlefields along the northern border with Eritrea. A major shake-up within the leadership of the ruling party in 2001 (further discussed below) ushered in a "second wave" of decentralization under federalism, shifting its focus from the (usually ethnically defined) *kilil* or zone to the (usually demographically defined) *woreda* or district. The devolution of budgeting, expenditure and accounting to *woreda*s had been a stated objective of government decentralization for much of the previous decade, but was introduced abruptly in 2002. Since then, *woreda* "block grants" have been provided according to regionally designed subsidy formulae, involving a range of per capita and unit cost related calculations. These have gradually evolved over the last decade to favour unit costs of service provision, a formula pioneered in the SNNPRS. In combination with the expansion of nationally devised development "packages", a uniform national approach to *woreda*-focused service delivery has furthered the perception of this second phase of the consolidation of the federal state as one of "centralised decentralisation". Close analysis of local political activity presents a mixed and contradictory picture.[12]

The scope for *woreda*-level decentralization was initially greeted with much scepticism, primarily regarding *woreda*s' capacity for the administration of funds. Reform was pushed through remarkably quickly in the four large regions, with strong investment of political capital and international aid.[13] Capacity building became the watchword from 2002, when a new federal super-ministry was established to spearhead it, and the number of civil servants assigned at *woreda* level grew from around 150,000 in 2002 to more than 400,000 at the end of the decade. These systems of local government were established more quickly in the densely populated highland agricultural areas administered by the EPRDF than in the lowland periphery, where *woreda* structures still barely existed. In 2002 the two-speed evolution of the federation was formally acknowledged with the establishment of the Ministry of Federal Affairs, given explicit responsibilities in relation to the four weaker states on the periphery.

Early beneficiaries of change during the period of reform and "renewal" in the early 2000s were the Welaiyta, Silte, and Sheka ethnic groups which were finally granted their own administrative units, in a move that served to encourage a fresh spate of claims. In March 2002, also in the southwest, a militant Sheko-Majengir movement sought to wrest its own territory by force, and the ensuing violence claimed many lives. An investigation implicated local administrators and police in reprisal killings, and a number were brought to court. Two months later, several protestors were killed when police used live ammunition to disperse a demonstration against changes to the relations between the southern capital city of Awassa and the surrounding Sidama zone. Sidama separatism has rumbled on, coming to a head in 2005, when a long-standing impetus for a distinct Sidama *kilil* was fuelled not least by incautious promises made by local EPRDF cadres in the context of stiff electoral competition. The ethno-nationalist demand subsided with the appointment of a Sidama to the SNNPRS presidency, and a personal appeal from the Prime Minister not to destabilize the federation: presumably deferred rather than resolved, in view of the strongly held feelings in play.[14]

A recalcitrant periphery: conflict and federal intervention. The control of territory remains a particularly intractable area of conflict where communities are mobile. Thus long-standing disputes between Afar and Somali pastoralists over rights to grazing, water, and control of the land over which they migrate with their herds have caused border disputes between their two *kilil*s. Conflict sporadically affected traffic on the road to the port of Djibouti, bringing down the wrath of the federal government. In October 2004 the federal government supported referenda designed to resolve similar disputes between Somali and Oromo communities and their respective regional governments. Local gerrymandering (in this case often shifting voters rather than boundaries) meant that the process was only marginally successful in resolving conflict, and problems have continued in several parts of that border.

From December 2003, the federal government also turned its attention to conflict between Anywaa, Nuer, and highland communities in the western border region of Gambella, invoking emergency powers of intervention. In 1991, following the close association between the pastoralist Nuer and the Sudan People's Liberation Front, which had been supported by the Derg, the Anywaa benefited from the change of government, winning political control of the regional state in which they claimed to be the largest indigenous group. The 1994 census indicated otherwise and heavy-handed Nuer attempts to bring about a more equitable balance of power raised alarm amongst the Anywaa. The situation was complicated by the presence of large numbers of refugees from conflict in the Sudan, often Nuer and other populations encamped on land traditionally regarded by the Anywaa as their own. An additional factor was the high educational, economic, and employment status of many highlanders relative to the indigenous communities they lived amongst, and escalating tension saw a series of attacks. One such triggered reprisal killings in Gambella town, manifold conflict, and the involvement of the federal army, which drove thousands of Anywaa across the border into Sudan, and exposed the extent of inter-communal tension that had been allowed to brew under the surface of the federal dispensation.

Sporadic conflict has continued in Gambella. As with other conflicts in border areas, the government has since the early 2000s blamed its escalation on Eritrean support (finance, logistics and training) for armed opponents. Much more serious has been the conflict in the Ogaden. Much of the Ogaden National Liberation Front (ONLF) withdrew from the TGE and returned to armed struggle in 1993, when a vote on regional secession was thwarted. Between 2004 and 2006 it grew to a fighting force of several thousand, with regional and cross-border support from areas of Somalia controlled by the Islamic Courts Union. It carried out a lethal attack on a Chinese oil exploration camp at Abole in April 2007 to draw the attention of a government distracted by post-electoral domestic politics and Islamist threats from Somalia. The military crackdown in the region between 2007 and 2009 drew international criticism. Latterly the ENDF has been replaced in the region with a local ethnic-Somali "special" police force, regarding which concerns have grown again about human rights violations. Although its counter-insurgency clearly weakened the ONLF, the government has not capitalized on a series of 2010 peace deals with Ogaden nationalist and Islamic factions to strike a comprehensive agreement to end the conflict. Poor security in parts of the Somali Region does not threaten the regime, but it wrecks lives and livelihoods, undermining whatever promise federalism might have held there.

The federal arrangement in Ethiopia has provided a new framework within which to accommodate ethnic diversity. It has not eliminated conflict, but has for the most part succeeded in reducing and diluting it and diverting it away from the state centre. In something of a social revolution it has broadened the access to state jobs, budgets and education which the majority of the country's social and language groups enjoy, whilst also fostering incentives for local politicians to make instrumental and often divisive appeals to ethnic emotion as well as national interest: something the regime decries as "narrow nationalism". Many communities have now strongly invested in the federal arrangement, and it is hard to see it either reversed or fundamentally revised without resistance. The day-to-day operational strength of the federal arrangement remains obscured by the fact that the EPRDF and its allies have administered all levels of government, so that many aspects of constitutional and inter-governmental relations remain opaque or untested in practice. This single party dominance leaves open two significant issues. First, whilst ethnic and social access has broadened under federalism, political access has not been similarly plural; rather it is increasingly comprehensively mediated through ruling party membership. Secondly, the federal project has not secured a full national consensus, and remains divisive and contested, a problem magnified by loud diaspora objections.

Revolutionary democracy and multi-partyism

The reform of the Ethiopian political system under a series of ostensibly liberal institutions was designed to create an elected, representative, and plural legislature, an independent judiciary, and an accountable executive. The Derg's authoritarian one-party state of the immediate past was a "ghost at the feast" as the parties met to consider the future, and the need for political and economic transformation was clear to all. The early 1990s climate of political conditionality for aid and the demise of the Soviet donor bloc meant that some form of "liberal democracy" seemed to emerge as the only viable option. A series of charter, constitutional, and legislative provisions for multi-party competitive politics, based on regular elections to a multi-level parliamentary system, was quickly put in place.

The national consensus that the EPRDF sought to form behind the federal project ran into opposition from both ends of the domestic political spectrum. Pan-Ethiopian nationalists, many resistant to the secession of Eritrea, opposed in principle what they expected would be the dismemberment or fragmentation of the country under ethnic federalism. EPRDF policy-making gave emphasis to rural peasant communities, and such concerns were raised particularly amongst urban, multi-ethnic and educated groups, who felt their interests marginalized. A number of opposition political organizations represent this constituency, led by the Ethiopian Democratic Party (EDP) which came to prominence in 2000, by the Coalition for Democracy Unity (CUD, later the UDJ) which emerged in 2004 to significant success in the 2005 poll, and most recently by Medrek, which united a number of these parties in the run up to the 2010 poll. Whilst the EPRDF belatedly turned its attention to recruiting support and members from amongst educated and intellectual groups after 2001, opposition to it remains strongest in urban areas.

Meanwhile, an increasing number of the ethno-nationalist leaders of Ethiopia's various communities, who had enthusiastically endorsed the introduction of federalism in 1991, complained that in practice the concessions granted proved shallow, with power remaining tightly controlled at the centre. They included the Southern Ethiopian People's Democratic Coalition (SEPDC), active particularly in Hadiya and Kambatta but increasingly across the SNNPRS, and the relatively small Oromo National Congress (ONC), both of which joined Medrek in an unprecedented show of unity with the pan-Ethiopianists. Both groups of critics have their diaspora-based counterparts which operate outside the legal electoral framework of the country, many committed to armed opposition. They include the pan-Ethiopian People's Patriotic Front (EPPF) and Ginbot 7,[15] and the ethno-nationalist Oromo, Sidama, and Ogaden National Liberation Fronts (OLF, SLM, and ONLF), many of which date back to the 1970s when they were active against the Derg. Strong diaspora support for both wings of opposition was boosted in the wake of the 2005 elections.

In 1991, legislating to provide for the core principles of reform provided the first tasks of the new parliament. Seats allocated in the TGE's new legislature, the Council of Representatives, reflected the political balance of power at the time, along with an attempt at a relatively comprehensive ethnic representation. EPRDF parties retained a substantial majority, alongside representatives of other ethnically based liberation movements that had opposed the previous regime, a raft of newly-established parties representing the smaller ethnic groups, and a number of new and older pan-Ethiopianist groups (although several long-standing Ethiopian nationalist groups were excluded). The parliament elected the EPRDF chairman, Meles Zenawi, as Head of Government, and ratified a selection of ministers reflecting the hierarchy of influence across the spectrum of political organizations represented. A National Election Board was set up in 1991, legislation was drafted for the conduct of federal, *kilil* and *woreda* elections, and the first polls were held in June 1992.

Magnanimity or managed exclusion? The Transitional Period, 1991–1995. At the beginning of the transitional period, observers were pleased both with the liberal democratic nature of the political reforms undertaken by the TGE and with the surprisingly inclusive manner in which they were being implemented by the coalition government. Those middle-class and "intellectual" members of ethnic groups, particularly from the south, whom the EPRDF had encouraged to form their own parties and join the TGE in senior positions spoke of the "magnanimity of the EPRDF" which, despite its decisive military victory, seemed to have committed itself to sharing power. Many took the coalition at face value, and assumed that they were being offered a permanent place at the table, representing rural constituents amongst whom they had done little to mobilize political support or establish party political organizational infrastructure. They thought of the EPRDF as a northern party (operating in Amhara and Tigray, and some parts of Oromiya only), and saw themselves as taking over a complementary role in the south, and on the peripheries.

It was only in the run-up to the first *kilil* and *woreda* elections in mid-1992 that it became clear that the EPRDF did not intend to leave the rest of the country to its opposition colleagues in the TGE. Despite objections from the OLF, it had been agreed that the EPRDF forces would operate as a national army for the duration of the TGE. The EPRDF had made careful preparation for the organization's swift move into the south, with a caucus of several hundred cadres from southern ethnic groups separately organized, mobilized, and trained well before the fall of the Derg. They were positioned to move quickly into their home areas as the government forces collapsed, to talk to elders and opinion-formers in their own groups. During the summer months of 1991 they fanned out across the south of the country into areas where they had not previously operated, often spearheaded by small numbers of specially-trained fighters originally from each local area in the south, who as Derg soldiers in the 1980s had been taken prisoner by the EPRDF, and had subsequently joined the movement.

They quickly established local "peace and stability committees" from amongst local people. From the beginning, the EPRDF's strategy of political mobilization began a process of elision of party and state, simultaneously selecting proto-administrators in the process of promulgating the party's ideology and seeking to recruit members. The same people were targeted for both, and the training they received for both purposes was a political and ideological one given by the party. The seamless consolidation and expansion of both party and administration continued unconstrained and at breakneck speed throughout the south under the TGE banner of "peace and stability". Thousands of young recruits went through EPRDF's Tatek political training centre in 1991 and 1992, mostly drawn from Oromiya and the SNNPRS, though also from the pastoralist peripheries. Meanwhile, those who had been members of the Workers' Party of the former regime were excluded from government office, and a campaign to track down and arrest senior cadres suspected of involvement in Red Terror and War Crimes galvanized communities and detained several thousand people.

As these EPRDF activities began to run up against rival campaigns, tension mounted. The first instances of this were in Oromiya, where the OLF, and other Oromo opposition groups, were seasoned and determined competitors. The OLF nursed bitter memories of military and political collaboration with the TPLF in the early 1980s, and had been infuriated by the EPRDF's establishment of its own Oromo organization, the Oromo People's Democratic Organization, OPDO, in 1989/90. Violent clashes between the armed forces of the two movements escalated as a first round of elections approached. On the eve of the polls the OLF withdrew from the government, announcing its inability to work with the EPRDF and a decision to return to armed opposition. Civil war, which for several days threatened to engulf the country, failed to materialize. After three weeks the immediate military threat posed by the OLF had been effectively defeated, and 30,000 of its fighters taken prisoner in re-education camps.

As other non-EPRDF members of the government began to consider their positions, elections were held, and the EPRDF took control of local government across the four core regional states of Amhara, Oromiya, SNNPRS and Tigray. Realizing that, with federal elections, their influence and positions in government would vanish, other non-EPRDF members of the TGE began to protest against the non-level playing field, and several withdrew. Some joined forces with a diaspora-based opposition bloc, which had been excluded from the beginning. They began calling for a process of "national reconciliation" which would start the process of state constitution anew, incorporating those increasing numbers of actors who now operated outside the legal framework. Such attempts to undermine the legitimacy of their energetic reform process were anathema to the EPRDF, and the rump TGE moved harshly to expel from parliament and detain members who had been involved in "illegal" negotiations with armed opponents. Positions polarized. The remaining opposition parties were torn between risking all by withdrawing from the elections of 1994 and 1995 and lending a veneer of multi-party legitimacy to a process they now saw as vitiated, by continuing to participate in it. It is a quandary they have confronted ever since.

As TGE pluralism dissolved, observers questioned the capacity of the EPRDF to work in coalition with other political parties. By the end of the transitional period, the TGE no longer looked like the magnanimous mechanism for power-sharing some had envisaged. It had, however, served a number of ruling party purposes well, and the strategy is worth reflecting on in retrospect. First, it secured the support of representatives from communities all over the country, including all the major armed liberation movements, for the controversial new state structure of ethnic federalism. Secondly, the TGE won for the EPRDF a period of grace during which the new arrangement could be viewed by almost all sides (and especially the international community) as marking a distinct ideological break with the past, introducing pluralism, multi-partyism, inclusivity, and apparently "liberal" democracy. Finally, it won for the EPRDF an essential breathing space within which it was able to establish and activate an infrastructure for political mobilization in those core areas of the south of the country where it had not previously operated. Thus the transitional period, with the involvement and even, initially, approval of many outside the party, and with relatively limited visible recourse to violence, achieved the formula which has become entrenched over the subsequent decade: a highland core administered by EPRDF parties, with a lowland periphery administered by EPRDF affiliates or associates.

The trajectory of the transitional period from 1991 to 1995 illustrates the difficulties of contemporary assessment of who gains what from changes to Ethiopia's political arrangements. At the outset of the TGE era it seemed to most observers and participants that the many small ethnic parties and liberation movements that became partners in government had gained very considerably. By the end of the period, however, it emerged starkly that it was the ruling party, the EPRDF, that had gained greatly from the legitimating collaboration of these other groups in its reconstitution of the state.

Consolidation of power: the first federal government, 1995–2000. The first federal government came to power in a flurry of ruling party optimism. A poor harvest in 1994 was followed by three years of good crops, and over-heated talk of sustainable food self-sufficiency. The economy was further buoyed by high international coffee prices. Regional governments were now relatively well established in most areas. Whilst they enjoyed extensive powers on paper, regional states' inability to raise significant revenue left them heavily dependent on subsidies from the centre. Significant numbers of civil service jobs had been decentralized from the federal capital, or newly created in the regions. This won the enthusiastic support of young professionals from the various ethnic groups where local administration had been established. Many benefited from a dramatic expansion of local employment and education opportunities as the federal structure became entrenched, creating something of a social revolution.

Less enthusiastic, meanwhile, were more established civil servants, with family commitments in the capital, who saw public sector opportunities in Addis Ababa contract. Many moved into the expanding private, voluntary and international sectors, establishing private businesses and local NGOs. The capacity of the civil service, particularly in the federal capital, has continued to be affected by heavy losses of skilled professionals, attracted by the significantly higher salaries available outside the public sector. The outbreak of war with Eritrea brought complaints about the squandering of the "peace dividend", and renewed criticism of the Eritrean secession process; national mobilization, meanwhile, saw an unprecedented degree of patriotic unity.

The new federal and regional governments were regarded with resentment by the political opposition that had been comprehensively outmanoeuvred during the transitional period. Officers of a number of parties were harassed or imprisoned, including notably the chairman of the All Amhara People's Organization, who died soon after his release from a lengthy period of detention. The OLF continued sporadic guerrilla attacks, alongside a series of bombings in 1996 co-ordinated from southern Somalia. Ongoing Western diplomatic efforts to reconcile the OLF and the EPRDF ran into the sand in 1998 when a new generation of OLF leaders rejected federalism in favour of the struggle for an independent Oromo state, and allied with Asmara. International human rights monitoring organizations, meanwhile, protested at the large numbers of political opponents, particularly Oromos, kept in official and—allegedly—also unofficial detention.

Opposition came also from a series of professional associations of teachers, trades unions, and journalists. The Teachers' Association

(ETA) opposed the government's policy of encouraging primary education in local languages. In response, the government dismissed or detained the ETA's key members, including its chairman, who was arrested in 1996 and eventually released in May 2002. Another leading ETA member was shot and killed by police in May 1997, provoking a storm of protest. The Confederation of Ethiopian Trades Unions (CETU), meanwhile, also came under government pressure when it criticized privatization and restructuring initiatives.

Criticism of the government was often channelled through the private press. From 1974 until 1991, all media of communication in Ethiopia had been state owned. When a legislative framework to provide for the "freedom of the press" was introduced in 1992, weekly and monthly newspapers and magazines mushroomed overnight, many staffed by experienced former journalists of the Derg's media outlets who had been dismissed. The new publications were almost unanimously hostile to the new regime, and a climate of mutual antipathy resulted. Inexperience, political passion, and a culture of political exclusion led to exaggeration and misinformation, and gave the government excuses to crack down with fines, imprisonment of editors, and closure of newspapers, on the all too familiar charges of "dissemination of false information", "inciting racial hatred" or "damaging the national interest". During the 1990s, most private papers became the subject of legal proceedings for a range of alleged transgressions, large and small. At best, such cases drained the financial and human resources of the private press; at worst, they resulted in the imprisonment and bankruptcy of independent journalists and proprietors. From a peak of 128 publications registered in 1994, by 2000 only a few dozen remained.

Renewal and challenge: the second federal government, 2000–2005. International concern about federal elections in 2000 and regional and local elections in 2001 was relatively muted, with much greater focus on the impact of the ongoing war with Eritrea. Nevertheless, a number of key studies documented "shattered promises and hopes" and declared "democracy unfulfilled".[16] Analysis suggested that the operation of the political system in much of the country made it almost impossible for opposition parties to use the democratic institutions effectively to challenge the dominance of the ruling party. A range of tactics commonly disadvantaging the opposition prior to and during elections was documented: closure of their offices, harassment and arrest of candidates, refusal of some of their signatures of endorsement, last minute shifts in the regulations regarding the number of candidates to be fielded, suspension of candidates spuriously claimed to be "under police investigation", and so on.

These problems affected federal, regional and local elections. In local polls, electoral regulations made it difficult for smaller opposition parties to succeed. At *woreda* and *kebele* levels, for instance, it was in 2001 already necessary to field between 60 and 100 candidates in order for an organization's participation to be considered legal. Further reforms in 2007/8 raised the bar still further, increasing the required numbers of members of local parliamentary bodies, particularly at *kebele* level. This worked against independent candidates and small emergent groups. It also meant that local elections were about party support more than the merit of individuals as constituency representatives. As a result, the political system in Ethiopia began to be described as single-party dominant. In 2000, for instance, out of the 547 seats in the House of Peoples Representatives, the EPRDF held 481, or 88 per cent.

The opposition parties remained extremely weak in terms of size, organizational capacity, and material and human resources. Whilst most have agreed on their commitment to the private ownership of land, there has been much less common ground on federalism between ethnically-based and pan-Ethiopian organizations. Lack of agreement on this fundamental issue made it extremely difficult for the opposition to work collaboratively, and numerous attempts since 1991 to establish a coalition of forces foundered. Disturbances in and around the Addis Ababa University (AAU) campus in April 2001 may have marked the beginning of a chain of events that saw the weakness and lack of cohesion of the opposition start to shift. They resulted in the imprisonment of two senior AAU academics, who emerged in 2003 as driving forces behind the pan-Ethiopianist Coalition for Unity and Democracy (CUD), which fought the 2005 election with such unexpected success.

Apart from electoral issues, and continuing political polarization, the early years of the second federal government were overshadowed by the Ethio-Eritrean war and settlements signed at Algiers in June and December 2000, which seemed largely favourable to Ethiopia. An internationally sanctioned Boundary Commission held its first meeting in May 2001, and published its decisions on delimitation in April 2002. These placed the iconic town of Badme inside Eritrea, a decision at variance with the balance of power on the ground, which presented the Ethiopian government with a problem. It had already been criticized domestically for making too many concessions to Eritrea. To accept the loss of Badme, where the war started, and for which tens of thousands of Ethiopian soldiers had died, was politically impossible. The Ethiopian government, while continuing to claim it accepted the Boundary Commission's decisions, made clear its dissatisfaction with the details.

Even before the controversial ruling, Ethiopia's decision to co-operate with a negotiated process, instead of simply pressing the military advantage it held in May 2000, had catalyzed a division amongst the leaders of the EPRDF. In March 2001 a faction within the TPLF central committee attempted to win wider EPRDF and military support for a move against the Prime Minister. Disagreement over the handling of relations with Eritrea provided a trigger for the breakdown of relations, as well as a temptingly emotive vehicle for what became known as the "dissident" faction to try to garner support. A more likely cause of the split was a power struggle, between the leaders of two groups whose day-to-day interaction was no longer close enough to overcome diverging expectations and goals. The dissidents were rapidly outmanoeuvred, leaving significant bitterness, particularly amongst veterans and constituents in Tigray. A number of its protagonists remained in prison on corruption-related charges for several years, and on their release some joined the opposition political groups that now form part of the Medrek umbrella.

In the wake of the 2001 division, the government moved quickly to modernize, professionalize and bureaucratize the state, announcing new emphasis on capacity building, education, and urban development. Throughout the 1990s, the poor separation of party and state had dogged the democratization process, with the party operating as a mechanism of control and mobilization shadowing both government and state at every level. This double power structure facilitated and provided the vehicle for the schism within the TPLF in 2001. Under the rubric of a process of "renewal" its leaders now moved to curb the separate structures and activities of the ruling front, bringing many areas of erstwhile party activity under the purview of several powerful new ministries for rural development, federal affairs, and capacity building. Intensive processes of state-building began to consolidate the bureaucratic and physical infrastructure for *wereda*-level decentralization, with

IT systems for integrated budget management, *woreda*-net and school-net communication, and comprehensive business process re-engineering across the civil service. Whilst those at the apex of the state also retained their positions in the political leadership, with the two structures now effectively fused, further down the hierarchy the political party as a distinctive structure seemed to have disappeared, replaced with a highly politicized capacity building bureaucracy. In retrospect, the implications of this arrangement for electioneering were profound.

The 2005 elections and after. In the run up to a third round of federal and regional elections under the FDRE Constitution in May 2005, the ruling party, apparently confident in the extent of public support it commanded in the wake of internal reorganization and ideological renewal, opened up the electoral campaign to a series of televised multi-party debates. Several opposition groupings, and particularly the CUD with its swiftly and covertly communicable two-finger "victory" symbol, began to capture the mood, particularly in urban areas. Much to the surprise of the EPRDF, the CUD (and to a lesser extent the ethno-national opposition, especially the ONC, the SEPDC and the newer Oromo Federalist Movement, OFDM) not only swept the polls in Addis Ababa and a number of other ethnically mixed towns, but also made strong inroads amongst significant rural peasant constituencies, who normally were notoriously reluctant to vote against an incumbent government.

Various reasons have been advanced for this success. The period of the Ethiopian-Eritrean war (1998–2000) had been marked by an upsurge in pan-Ethiopian nationalist rhetoric,[17] which had brought a return of official legitimacy to views not considered "politically correct" since the demise of the Derg. The EPRDF was seen as weakened by the airing of internal grievances and high-level expulsions that resulted from the 2001 TPLF split.[18] As discussed above, the crisis saw the independent capacity of the EPRDF party organs substantially curtailed, with power consolidated in state structures in the period leading up to the 2005 elections.[19] In some rural areas of the north, the very fact of "sitting down with its enemies" to conduct televised debates was seen as a sign of terminal weakness which boosted the opposition vote.[20]

Rural Amhara and Gurage communities in particular responded positively to pan-Ethiopian nationalist suggestions that ethnic federalism threatened their interests in mobility and urban linkages. These anxieties were shared by educated elites, and an explicit ERPDF change of policy in 2002 to reverse its previous disregard of urban professionals came too late to address their grievances and merely gave them oxygen: the demolition of a series of prominent Addis Ababa neighbourhoods at the time of the poll in preparation for road construction was a physical manifestation of "too little too late". The CUD seems to have benefited from a strong protest vote against the incumbent government's record. In many urban areas, this has been conceptualized in terms of a preference for "civic" over "ethnic" nationalism.[21] The challenge was an existential one: not only to EPRDF rule, but also to the very ethnic federal nature of the state. It left the notion of a national consensus in tatters.

Violent dispute erupted over opposition claims to have won a national victory, as well as control of the capital, and core CUD opposition MPs refused to take up their seats. Several tens of thousands, mostly young urban men, were arrested, and protests in Addis Ababa in June and November 2005 dissolved into violence and several hundred deaths amidst mutual recriminations.[22] The leadership of the CUD was arrested alongside two NGO officials and a number of journalists, all charged and eventually found guilty of a series of "crimes against the constitution". Most were released and left the country only after petitioning for pardon several years later, whilst the leader of the successor UDJ was for some time subsequently rearrested, accused of breaching pardon conditions.

It is easy to overestimate the impact of the 2005 poll on EPRDF thinking: in fact the schism of 2001 seems to have had a much more profound effect on the long-term evolution of the organization's ideological commitments and strategies. Nevertheless there was one abrupt consequence of the EPRDF's poor showing at the polls: its immediate decision to reconstruct and reinvigorate the infrastructure of the party on a massive scale. Within weeks of the polling senior members of the organization were reassigned from state to party political roles, and over the next three years, intensive campaigns in rural and urban areas boosted membership to an alleged 6 million.[23] Recognizing the weakness of its support amongst wealthier and more highly educated groups, the party began to campaign in urban areas and on university campuses, establishing formally affiliated youth leagues alongside the reinvigorated mass associations, now set up as "community based organizations": formally divested but still strongly supportive of party activity.

Attempts to build a new national consensus began with the Ethiopian millennium celebrated in September 2007, which ushered in a new government narrative of renaissance and the achievement of middle-income status. For the first time, the Prime Minister surprised (and pleased) many in his audience by speaking of the longer history of the Ethiopian polity, over several thousand years back to Axum. A wave of popular economic nationalism culminated with the sale of national bonds to finance the Millennium Dam on the Nile towards the western border, construction of which began in 2011. Urban enthusiasm has been tempered by high levels of inflation since 2008, driven by global price hikes and rapid growth in domestic money supply to finance expansion of the state's investment programme, and more recently by insecurity about legislation to tighten state control of urban land leasing.

Dramatic new levels of investment in regional hydropower projects and road infrastructure have often been concentrated in the lowland peripheries, or on the edge of the escarpment. In combination with the federal granting of large-scale land leases to those investing in commercial agriculture in lowland areas with relatively sparse population, and attempts at the widespread resettlement of pastoral or transhumant farming populations, these massive infrastructure projects drew criticism for their likely impact on marginal populations and environments. The government reacted angrily, accusing international critics of double standards, and redoubling its efforts to expand the combined envelop of domestic investment by the state, FDI, and the subsidy for local service delivery under an ambitious five-year programme for Growth and Transformation (GTP), 2010–2015. Despite recent dispute over growth figures, all agree that rates have been impressive for the last ten years.

On the back of an intensive programme of local political mobilization in rural areas, the ruling party swept the board in local elections in 2008. The continuation of an assertive programme of local state capacity building saw the appointment of a new cadre of *kebele* managers, and the expansion of *kebele* representative council membership. Both have been key to boosting the presence of the local state—to the enhancement either of service delivery and accountability, or of political control, depending on one's political viewpoint: almost certainly both. Critics point to three pieces of legislation—curbing the activities of the media and civil society, and outlawing "terrorist" activities—that most observers see as having constrained the activities of political opponents, and "closed political space" (Abbink 2006). At least as important, but much less analyzed, have been the intensive activities of the reconstructed party in uniformly reoccupying the political landscape. In the run up to the 2010 election, it piloted a comprehensive approach to the mobilization of the population for political as well as developmental ends, and the melding of the twin objectives marks a new phase in the ruling party's dominance.

Ideology and control: liberalization and the developmental state

Whilst the architecture of federalism shapes the form of the state, the political economy of contemporary Ethiopia is increasingly shaped by the ruling party's twin commitments to revolutionary democracy and the developmental state. The latter first emerged in 2001, when the party finally abandoned its commitment to socialism (long in abeyance, but never until then formally renounced) in favour of a managed transition to "developmental capitalism" (*lematawi habt*). The developmental state project is premised on the belief that a government can both be developmentally activist and also avoid the "socially wasteful rent-seeking activities" associated with a dominant public sector (Meles Zenawi, 2012): it explicitly rejects the notion that markets represent the ideal tool for boosting production and allocating surplus in a transformatory developmental context. The EPRDF sees the developmental state system as achieving its legitimacy and hegemony from the single-minded pursuit of broad-based, long-horizon development, based on a "strong national consensus" broadly shared across the mass of the population.[24]

Believing this to be in the interests of accelerated socio-economic transformation for the majority of smallholder farmers, rather than the wealthy elite, the government is keen to preserve what Rodrik has called the "autonomy"[25] of the developmental state from private sector influence. It emphasizes the importance of government having the will and the capacity to discipline market and private sector forces, both domestic and international, which it sees as likely to threaten the integrity and pro-poor orientation of policy making and the bureaucracy. Critics have questioned the extent to which this "capacity and will" exist in practice at federal level, let alone in *kilil, woreda* and *kebele* regulation. What Kelsall has called the "technocratic integrity" of the civil service (2011) is open to question in terms both of the extent of corruption and of its willingness to "speak truth unto power", this last being consistently underdeveloped in Ethiopian political culture.[26] The problem is arguably compounded by limitations to the scope of the national consensus, which place the talents and energies of key educated groups outside the national development project.

Despite a modicum of liberalization of the economy, and privatization of state assets, implementation of the GTP thus remains overwhelmingly state-led.[27] Privatization has not been extended to infrastructure or services where national security implications are in play, and national security is broadly conceived. There is little evidence that the role of state-owned companies has shrunk, with new military-industrial enterprises expanding their activities. Party-affiliated endowment conglomerates form a significant proportion of the private sector, alongside the large, diversified, and strongly integrated MIDROC economic bloc. Expanding FDI has focused on commercial agricultural ventures, including some controversial land-intensive initiatives in the periphery, a number of which have reinforced concerns about the autonomy, integrity, and capacity of state regulation. State developmental and economic initiatives have been complemented by the activities of a range of politically allied institutions, including regional NGOs and development associations, mass membership bodies, micro-credit institutions, and co-operatives. The existence of this spectrum of state and non-state socio-economic actors, all strongly aligned with the government's vision, gives the leadership very extensive leverage over the development agenda. The developmental potential of an approach that takes a long-horizon pro-poor perspective, and succeeds in centralizing rents and rendering the policy environment predictable, seems clear. But its implementation by a civil service and political hierarchy largely unconstrained by external checks and scrutiny, and subject only to internal—often political—systems of evaluation and control, raises concerns about probity, integrity and sustainability.[28]

Under the vanguard leadership of the EPRDF, the developmental state is seen as being built on a direct "coalition with the people" (as opposed to the indirect "coalitions" between politicians characteristic of multi-party pluralism).[29] This is an all-encompassing project, under which the leadership seeks to unite state, party and population to form a so-called "developmental army", designed to mobilize communities and contributions in support of the GTP and MDGs. Piloted in Tigray in the run up to the 2010 elections, the strategy has since been adopted in other rural agricultural areas, and works on the basis of a hierarchy of "model" farmers, each followed by five "followers" who themselves provide model leadership to five others. This comprehensive form of mobilization also offers unique mechanisms for passing developmental and political messages right to the grassroots—and for evaluating and controlling performance and commitment, again both developmental and political. Similar initiatives have been mooted by *kebeles* in urban centres in the recent period.

Unlike many other parts of Africa, Ethiopia has a ubiquitous state presence which extends in much of the country to the local, even household, level: as has been discussed above, these structures have been strengthened in repeated phases of reform and capacity building under federalism. Citizens are heavily reliant on the lowest level of government, the *kebele*, for a wide range of services including identification cards and access to land (which remains under state ownership) and to water, education, health, and other services, as well as to food security and welfare safety nets. The state enjoys a near-monopoly on the distribution of resources and on decision-making in relation to service delivery. In this context EPRDF ideology embraces a form of "popular" or "revolutionary" rather than "liberal" democracy, in which unified mass participation is valued over individually-oriented pluralism. This has much in common with "proletarian democracy", apparently rooted in Leninist principles of organization that sought to bring the mass of the population into unmediated involvement with the activities of the state.[30]

Key to the EPRDF's conception of popular consensus has been the unified and mobilized participation of ethno-national communities. Similarly its commitment to self-determination of nationalities incorporates the notion that a vanguard party may legitimately grant self-determination to a community from above, in that process identifying and prescribing the "objective" ethnic criteria to define the group and demarcate administrative borders around it. Its approaches to "democracy" and to the "national question" are thus intimately linked. Inherent in the EPRDF's attachment to the idea of nationality-based mobilization, along with the idea that it is morally better than other forms (that is, that ethnic self-determination brings in democracy, emancipation and non-discrimination for the first time in Ethiopia's history), is the idea that it works better—that people are more responsive to political education and encouragement given to them in their own languages by their own children.

Given these ideological perspectives on ethno-nationalism and decentralization, democratic unity, and managed liberalization, then, it is not surprising that the EPRDF has never appeared as an organization committed to pluralism for its own sake, and has been resistant to the emergence of parallel (competitor) systems of political patronage or local resource delivery. A dominant view within the EPRDF is that disagreements over policy and perspective should generate competition rather than dialogue. This has contributed to a polarized political landscape, in which the ruling party has benefited little from the constructive criticism of outsiders. A further corollary is that elections have evolved as performative plebiscites designed to reinforce the national consensus behind the ruling party. Government spokesmen claim that revolutionary democracy will transform state-society relations, empowering citizens to participate in developmental decision-making; whether or not this is so, it has in the meantime entrenched the dominance of a party-state unity apparently stronger than it was 20 years ago, leaving little space for alternative voices.

For the future, the EPRDF promises to deliver an eventual transition from revolutionary to liberal democracy, in a context where growth and transformation have turned a majority of subsistence farmers into a broadly based middle class, likely to provide sustainable constituencies for plural political parties committed to representing their socio-economic interests. It argues that an incremental and managed transition will do more for the long-term interests of the poor than the competitive clientelism that has often resulted from "neo-liberal fundamentalism" elsewhere on the continent. Critics are unsurprisingly sceptical about a path to "renaissance" and profound political change that remains distant and ill defined. In the meantime, the interpretation of patterns of continuity and change—decentralization, democratization, and liberalization—is polarized and contested. Where most observers agree is on the ongoing concentration of state power in the hands of the ruling party—for good or ill.

BIBLIOGRAPHY AND FURTHER READING

Aalen, L., 2011, *The Politics of Ethnicity in Ethiopia: Actors, Power and Mobilisation under Ethnic Federalism*, Leiden: Brill.

Aalen, Lovise, and Tronvoll, Kjetil, 2009, "The End of Democracy? Curtailing Political and Civil Rights in Ethiopia", *Review of African Political Economy*, 120, pp. 193–207.

Abbink, Jon, 2006, "Discomfiture of Democracy? The 2005 Election Crisis in Ethiopia and its Aftermath", *African Affairs*, 105, pp. 173–99.

—— 2009, "The Ethiopian Second Republic and the Fragile 'Social Contract'", *Africa Spectrum*, 44(2), pp. 3–29.

Asnake Kefale, 2013, *Federalism and Ethnic Conflict in Ethiopia. A Comparative Regional Study*, London, New York: Routledge (Routledge Series in Federal Studies 20).

Beken, Christopher van der, 2012, *Unity in Diversity—Federalism as a Mechanism to Accommodate Ethnic Diversity: the Case of Ethiopia*, Zurich and Berlin: LIT Verlag.

Eshetu Chole, 1994, "Opening Pandora's Box: Preliminary Notes on Fiscal Decentralisation in Ethiopia", *Northeast African Studies*, 1(1) (new series), pp. 7–30.

Gebru Tareke, 2009, *The Ethiopian Revolution: War in the Horn of Africa*, New Haven, CT: Yale University Press.

Kelsall, Tim, 2011, *Developmental Patrimonialism? Rethinking Business and Politics in Africa*, Africa Power and Politics Policy Brief 02, June 2011, available at http://www.institutions-africa.org/filestream/20110610-appp-policy-brief-02-development-patrimonialism-by-tim-kelsall-june-2011 (last access on April 2014).

Lefort, René, 2007 "Powers—*Mengist*—and Peasants in Rural Ethiopia: The May 2005 Elections", *Journal of Modern African Studies*, 45(2), pp. 253–73.

Markakis, John, 1974, *Ethiopia: Anatomy of a Traditional Polity*, Oxford, Addis Ababa: Oxford University Press, Clarendon Press.

—— 1987, *National and Class Conflict in the Horn of Africa*, Cambridge: Cambridge University Press.

—— 1998, *Resource Conflict in the Horn of Africa*, London: Sage.

Medhane Tadesse and Young, J., 2003, "TPLF: Reform or Decline?", *Review of African Political Economy*, 30(97), pp. 389–403.

Paulos Milkias, 2003, "Ethiopia, the TPLF, and the Roots of the 2001 political Tremor", *Northeast African Studies*, 10(2) new series, pp. 13–66.

Pausewang, Siegfried and Tronvoll, Kjetil (eds), 2000, *The Ethiopian 2000 Elections: Democracy Advanced on Restricted?* Human Rights Report No. 3/2000, Oslo: Norwegian Institute of Human Rights.

Pausewang, S., Tronvoll, K., and Aalen, L. (eds), 2002, *Ethiopia Since the Derg: A Decade of Democratic Pretension and Performance*, London: Zed Books.

Peterson, Stephen, 2010, "Reforming Public Financial Management in Africa", *Faculty Research Working Paper Series*, 10–48, Harvard University, Kennedy School.

Rodrik, D., 1991, "Political Economy and Development Policy," *European Economic Review*, 36(2–3), pp. 329–36.

Smith, Lahra, 2013, *Making Citizens in Africa. Ethnicity, Gender and National Identity in Ethiopia*, New York: Cambridge University Press.

Teferi Abate Adem, 2004, "Decentralised There, Centralised Here: Local Governance and Paradoxes of Household Autonomy and Control in North-East Ethiopia, 1991–2001", *Africa 74* (4), pp. 611–32.

Turton, David (ed.), 2006, *Ethnic Federalism: the Ethiopian Experience in Comparative Perspective*, Oxford: James Currey.

Vaughan, Sarah, 1994, "The Addis Ababa Transitional Conference of July 1991: Its Origins, History and Significance," Centre of African Studies *Occasional Papers*, no. 51, University of Edinburgh.

—— 2006, "Responses to Ethnic Federalism in Ethiopia's Southern Region", in D. Turton (ed.), *Ethnic Federalism: the Ethiopian Experience in Comparative Perspective*, Oxford: James Currey, pp. 180–207.

—— 2011, *"Ethnic and Civic Nationalist Narratives in Ethiopia"*, in T. Harrison and S. Drakulic (eds), *Beyond Orthodoxy: New Directions in the Study of Nationalism*, Vancouver: University of British Columbia Press, pp. 154–82.

—— 2012, "Revolutionary Democratic State Building: Party, State, and People in EPRDF's Ethiopia", *Journal of Eastern African Studies*, 5(4), pp. 619–40.

Vaughan, Sarah and Mesfin Gebremichael, 2011, *Rethinking Business and Politics in Ethiopia: the Role of EFFORT*, Africa Power and Politics Research Report no. 2, August 2011, available at http://www.institutions-africa.org/filestream/20110822-appp-rr02-rethinking-business-politics-in-ethiopia-by-sarah-vaughan-mesfin-gebremichael-august-2011 (last access on April 2014).

Vaughan, Sarah and Tronvoll, Kjetil, 2003, *The Culture of Power in Contemporary Ethiopian Political Life*, Stockholm: SIDA.

Young, John, 1997, *Peasant Revolution in Ethiopia: The Tigray People's Liberation Front, 1975–1991*, Cambridge: Cambridge University Press.

12

ELECTIONS AND POLITICS IN ETHIOPIA, 2005–2010

Patrick Gilkes

The May 2005 elections marked a significant change in Ethiopia's political history, being the country's first genuinely contested elections.
Several opposition parties, despite expressing mistrust of the National
Electoral Board of Ethiopia (NEBE) and doubts about government
intentions, decided, under considerable international pressure, to participate rather than boycott as in 1995 and 2000. In all, a total of 35 parties contested the election, for both federal and regional assemblies.

The results, widely seen as the first real test of the EPRDF's
expressed commitment to democracy, provided a considerable surprise
to both government and opposition alike. Neither had expected the
extraordinary enthusiasm with which people went to the polls, or the
results achieved. Overall, the EPRDF which had taken over 90 per cent
of seats in the 547-seat House of Representatives in 2000 won less
than 60 per cent (327 seats), while the opposition increased its representation from 12 to an impressive 174 seats. Although the opposition
disputed the figures, they represented a major shift in Ethiopia's polit-

ical landscape, and one not confined to the federal parliament. There were similar changes in the regional councils. The largest opposition party, the four-party Coalition for Unity and Democracy (CUD), took all but one seat in the Addis Ababa council (as well as all of Addis Ababa's 23 seats in the Federal House of Representatives).[1] It also made substantial gains in the most important regional states, taking 106 seats (36 per cent) in the Amhara region, while the opposition as a whole took 150 seats (27 per cent) in Oromiya and 77 seats (22 per cent) in the Southern region.

The build-up to the election provided considerable political space for the opposition, and for civil society, despite a number of clearly expressed doubts about the impartiality of the proceedings, notably about the make-up of the NEBE itself. The government took the initiative to negotiate with the opposition and agreed to a number of electoral reforms to create conditions for a more acceptable process: these included changes in the electoral law to improve the registration process; the establishment, by the NEBE, of joint political forums to resolve problems; the creation of an NEBE website; guaranteed access to the state-controlled media; a civic education programme by civil society organizations; and a comprehensive code of conduct for the EPRDF and other parties.

An unprecedented level of open debate characterized the electoral campaign. The Public Forum, transmitted live for hours on both television and radio, allowed a much wider audience to gain some idea of party policies. The debates, sometimes aggressive, were avidly listened to and played a major role in giving voters, particularly in rural areas, an idea of the alternatives available and in encouraging voters' participation. The format, with EPRDF spokesmen presenting policy and opposition party leaders free to criticize rather than forced to define their own alternative programmes, favoured the opposition.

Despite the openness of these debates—welcomed by, among others, the EU which described it as launching a "sea-change" in Ethiopia's democratic process—the opposition parties made allegations of substantial intimidation during the campaign including numerous arrests and random killings. A Human Rights Watch report on the Oromo region alleged that the extent of repression made the election a "hollow exercise".[2] The government called these charges baseless, but the Prime Minister, Meles Zenawi, announced an investigation into alleged human rights abuses in Oromiya in January 2006.

One major factor encouraging a more open election was the significantly greater level of finance available to the opposition. The Donors' Ambassador Group provided funding, through the UK Electoral Reform International Services (ERIS), for opposition parties, independent candidates and the NEBE. The diaspora was also a major source of financial support. The All Ethiopia Unity Party, one of the main components of the CUD, set up a committee to raise funds from the diaspora in the US in 2003. It proved remarkably successful, obtaining hundreds of thousands of dollars using American techniques including plate dinners as well as direct donations. Others followed suit. Most of the parties in the United Ethiopian Democratic Forces (UEDF), the other main opposition coalition, were US-based, and much of its funding also came from the US.[3] The result was that the opposition had a much greater level of organization and impact, allowing it to campaign in almost all constituencies.

The donors from the diaspora, not surprisingly, expected and demanded some input into opposition policy. In the case of the CUD, the diaspora subsequently played a major role in pressuring the CUD to refuse to attend parliament when it opened in October. The decision to refuse was taken against the wishes of a majority of the central committee in Addis Ababa, and led directly to splits in the CUD, the confrontations of early November and the arrest of the CUD leadership. The decision of the UEDF leadership in Ethiopia to enter parliament, in order to represent the constituents who had elected them, ran into strong criticism from the diaspora. The leaders of the two main elements in the UEDF, Dr Merara Gudina of the ONC and Dr Beyene Petros of the SEPDC, lost much of their funding as a result.

In the 1995 and 2000 elections the government had not invited international observers, arguing that it did not need any "outside interference". This time, after strong encouragement by the international community, invitations were sent to the African Union, the Carter Center and the European Union, as well as other organizations and countries. A total of just over 300 observers were supplied. Three American organizations were ordered out shortly before the election, apparently for failing to register though the organizations concerned had a record of participation in a number of controversial episodes, including recent elections in Kyrgyzstan, Georgia and Ukraine. There were fewer local observers than expected. They were effectively limited by a ruling of the NEBE in April, though this was overturned by the courts in early May—too late, however, to allow many to participate.

The official allocation of 54 per cent of state media time for opposition groups, with 46 per cent for the EPRDF, helped provide for a more open campaign. Opposition coverage in terms of space however exceeded this overall, with the UEDF getting 26 per cent of TV coverage, the CUD 23 per cent and others 10 per cent, compared with the EPRDF's 41 per cent. The Oromo and Amhara language broadcasts were rather more balanced than those in Tigrinya. The state audiovisual media largely presented the EPRDF in a favourable light and its reporting of the opposition tended to be negative and to focus on its complaints about the electoral process.[4] In turn, the private Amharic press largely supported the opposition, producing stories, in a number of cases invented, to discredit the EPRDF. Several of the papers, including three private English language papers, *Capital*, *Fortune* and *Reporter*, had impressive election coverage.

The campaign was vigorous and outspoken. Observers criticized both EPRDF and opposition for abusive language. The EPRDF claimed the CUD was trying to spark off ethnic violence and organize a revolution on the lines of those in Ukraine, Georgia or Kyrgyzstan. The CUD alleged the government was intending to provoke violence in order to stop an opposition victory.

A critical factor in the final vote was the mass rallies in Masqal Square in Addis Ababa on 7 and 8 May, a week before the vote. The first was organized by the EPRDF. Estimates of those attending ranged from a quarter to three quarters of a million people. The next day, opposition parties brought significantly larger numbers into the square. The authority of the EPRDF government was severely dented. For the first time people began to believe that the opposition could make a real impact, and that they might be able to take control of Addis Ababa, and even win elsewhere.

Polling day itself went off largely without incident with some 90 per cent of registered voters turning out. The preliminary results indicated significant gains for the opposition as a whole and for the CUD in particular. And indeed the CUD swept Addis Ababa, taking all the 23 national assembly seats as well as all but one of the Addis Ababa city council's 138 seats. Despite this, the EPRDF quickly claimed an overall majority, as almost immediately did the CUD. A leaked internal European Union Election Monitoring Mission document suggesting that the CUD had won an overall majority on the basis of partial returns from Addis Ababa and the Amhara region, its main areas of support, encouraged CUD claims.[5]

Prior to the vote and on polling day, the CUD had originally suggested that the results would be entirely unacceptable because of what it claimed were massive irregularities. When it became clear that it had won overwhelmingly in Addis Ababa, it rapidly changed the focus of its criticisms to areas where it did not win and had expected to do better, notably the Amhara region. In fact, the CUD's victory in Addis Ababa was not totally unexpected as the city is a centre of internal migration and had very high unemployment. The EPRDF had assumed it would lose control of the city council, though it did not anticipate complete loss of all seats.

After the vote, the EU Observation Mission claimed that the elections were being undermined by the delays, and criticized the NEBE for slowness in counting votes and in the release of provisional results. Official results were only announced on 9 August, when the NEBE said that the EPRDF had won 296 seats. This figure rose to 327 after polling in 31 constituencies was re-run in August. The final figures for the opposition were: CUD 109; UEDF 52; Oromo Federal Democratic Movement (OFDM) 11; others 2.

International observers noted the allegations of intimidation in specific regions, and of post-election manipulation of votes. This gained some credence from the delays in the publication of the official results, but there was little support for opposition claims that it had won the election overall, or for the CUD's claim that the election had been stolen and its demands that the NEBE investigate irregularities in nearly 300 seats.[6]

Little work has been done on the analysis of voting patterns, but what there has been suggests that areas with Muslim majorities voted for the EPRDF; that areas producing *khat* tended to vote for the opposition following increased government taxes over the previous couple of years; that unemployment in urban areas favoured the opposition; that opposition support fell in areas where the proportion of people on food aid rose. While some results suggested voters believed that the EPRDF alone could ensure continuation of aid, constituencies with higher than average levels of fertilizer use tended to favour the opposition. This appears to contradict claims that voters were threatened with withdrawal of fertilizer or the recall of fertilizer loans if they voted for opposition parties. Claims that constituencies left out of ERPDF patronage network voted for the opposition or that voting was purely on an ethnic basis do not hold up.[7] There was certainly some protest voting but there were also significant levels of strategic voting. There is no doubt that a considerable number of voters saw the election in 2005 as a response to the EPRDF's economic record. This incidentally was even more obviously the case in 2010 when a central factor was again the failure of the opposition to offer serious alternative economic policies. In 2010 there was widespread appreciation of considerable economic growth over the previous five years, as well an almost complete failure by the opposition to get its act together.

Almost immediately after the voting, and in defiance of a ban on demonstrations, the CUD launched several public demonstrations. Student protests in Addis Ababa University were followed by stone-throwing demonstrations in the Mercato area. Security forces opened fire killing some 40 demonstrators; there was a three-day city-wide transport strike and several CUD leaders were briefly put under house arrest. The EU managed to broker a pact of non-violence accepted unequivocally by all parties. ERIS produced an agreement for investigation of disputed seats, providing for a Complaints Review Board that passed on 180 of the 300 complaints referred to it to Complaints Investigation Panels (CIP). These were each made up of three people, representing the NEBE, the complainant and the other party. There was the option of a further appeal to the courts. The process, however, appeared to favour the better-organized EPRDF rather than the opposition. Certainly, ERIS noted that the CUD proved unable to back up a very considerable number of its original complaints. The EPRDF gained 31 seats out of the process.

The CUD optimistically interpreted British government suspension of a proposed increase in the UK's budgetary support to Ethiopia as support for its criticisms of the NEBE and the CIPs. It also interpreted a highly critical preliminary EU election report as confirming its claims.[8] Certainly, some of the criticisms of the electoral process were valid, and accepted by the government, but it considered that the overall tone of the report, and some of the comments, were both unprofessional and partial, and that the mission had exceeded its mandate. Other observer missions were more balanced in their views.

It was against this background that the two opposition coalitions engaged in often highly public and acrimonious internal debates on whether to join parliament when it opened on 11 October. The UEDF argued for participation with the aim of building on its success in the 2008 local elections and providing a base for the next federal and regional elections in 2010. It also made the point strongly that a boycott would betray those who had elected members to participate in the parliament. The leadership of the CUD, in particular the chairman, Hailu Shawel, with strong support from the diaspora, backed a boycott on grounds that the results were fraudulent and that the EPRDF had no intention of allowing the opposition to play any realistic role in parliament. This, the CUD suggested, was underlined by the changes in parliamentary procedures requiring 51 per cent support to place items on the agenda rather than the previous requirement of 20 MPs.

The CUD decision to boycott parliament, taken in fact against the wishes of a majority of its own central committee, was one factor in the split that developed in the CUD during October. Another was the attempt to merge the four CUD parties into a single organization. The EUDP-Medhin in particular saw this as an attempt by Hailu Shawel and AEUP to take control of the CUD. The result of these manoeuvres was the withdrawal of the EUDP-Medhin from the coalition.[9]

Parliament met on 11 October. With nearly all CUD members refusing to take seats, though a majority changed their mind over the next few weeks, the new EPRDF government promptly lifted parliamentary immunity for those who boycotted the session. The CUD then announced plans for a general strike, fuelling a long-standing government fear that the CUD really intended to try for the sort of "orange revolution" called for by some in the diaspora: mass popular demonstrations to overwhelm the authorities, on the lines of events in Ukraine or Georgia.

The evidence of any such organized effort remained small. However, following the arrest of a number of CUD leaders in early November, the post-June calm was broken with two days of riots and violence in Addis Ababa in which seven policemen were killed and dozens injured, and 193 civilians died and thousands were arrested.[10] The US described the riots as a "cynical, deliberate" attempt to cause violence, and called on the opposition to refrain from inciting civil disobedience—though, like the EU, it also deplored the use of excessive and lethal force, and pressed the government for an inquiry into the deaths in the riots in both June and November. Over the following two weeks there were sporadic outbreaks of violence in a number of other towns, particularly in schools and universities; these carried on into January. There were a number of further deaths. Most of those detained in November were released within a couple of weeks but the government continued to hold the top CUD leaders, including ten CUD members of parliament. Others detained included a number of journalists and Ethiopian representatives of international NGOs. In mid-December, 131 people including a number of CUD leaders were formally charged with treason, genocide and other related offences. The CUD leaders were subsequently pardoned in 2007 at the time of the Ethiopian Millennium.

The CUD and the UEDF represented two very distinct strands of opposition to the EPRDF, and although temporarily linked in an electoral pact, they could never have collaborated for any length of time, nor worked together in government. In addition, both were themselves uneasy coalitions. The more successful element was the CUD which brought together the main lines of Amhara nationalism, split in the mid-1990s when the All Amhara Peoples Organization (AAPO) had fractured, together with elements of the business community in Addis Ababa, particularly among the Gurage, and the Amhara diaspora in the United States, exiles from the present regime and from the previous military dictatorship of Colonel Mengistu. The catalyst was a new party, Kestedamena (Rainbow), headed by two intellectuals, Dr Berhanu Nega and Professor Mesfin Wolde Mariam, which aimed to produce a more wide-ranging and organized opposition to the EPRDF, and an alternative to the UEDF. It was able to call on extensive dissatisfaction with the EPRDF, especially in Addis Ababa and other urban areas, and the widespread feeling that fourteen years of EPRDF rule had failed to produce sufficient alleviation of poverty, or jobs for the substantial numbers of unemployed in Addis Ababa. The CUD also gained from its criticisms of EPRDF policies towards Eritrea and its insistence that Ethiopia should, at the very least, have the use of the port of Assab. It made much of the "failure" of the government to take and hold Assab in 2000 following Ethiopia's success in the war that followed Eritrea's attack in 1998.

Formal ideological differences between CUD members, while important, remained less significant than the fact that the two main parties in the coalition, the AEUP and EUDP-Medhin, despite their claims to multi-nationalism, were in strong competition for Amhara support. The AEUP was the more successful in obtaining diaspora support and finance; the EUDP-Medhin, itself an amalgam of four parties, and largely representing a younger electorate, took 14 out of 23 National Assembly seats won by the CUD in Addis Ababa, while the AEUP won only four. The EUPD-Medhin also did significantly better in the Addis

Ababa city council, taking nearly two-thirds of the seats. Not surprisingly it resented the AEUP's subsequent efforts to take control of the CUD. With its younger support base, the EUDP-Medhin was also less influenced by the diaspora whose mixture of financial pressure and threats played a major role in discouraging AEUP and Rainbow leaders from entering parliament. Following the arrest of most leading figures in the AEUP and Rainbow in early November, EUDP-Medhin MPs began to trickle into parliament. Many of those from the AEUP and Rainbow gradually followed suit. By the beginning of 2006 at least 90 out of 109 CUD MPs had taken their seats. No opposition party, however, was able, or prepared, to muster a quorum to take up the administration of Addis Ababa.

The other main strand of opposition, the United Democratic Ethiopian Forces, included most of the other nationalities in Ethiopia in its ranks. The leading elements were the Southern Ethiopian Peoples Democratic Coalition, SEPDC, chaired by Dr Beyene Petros, itself a coalition of 14 small nationality parties, and the Oromo National Congress, ONC, chaired by Dr Merara Gudina. It was set up in Washington in 2003 as a broad-based coalition to fight the 2005 elections and originally included both the AEUP and the EUDP. Ideological and personal differences led to these two groups rejecting the leadership of Dr Beyene and Dr Merara and walking out after a few months. The UEDF and the CUD did make an electoral pact to fight the 2005 election, but their major policy differences would have precluded any long-term post-electoral links.

Central elements in CUD policy include suggested changes in the Constitution to limit regional autonomy, remove ethnicity from the federal status and replace the current regions by smaller structures, and remove Article 39, the article that allows the right of a regional state to secede. Another policy, favoured by many donors as a panacea to solve poverty, was privatization of land. This was widely interpreted as amounting to a return to the past, indeed to the structure of the imperial regime, offering a vision of a single Amhara-speaking Ethiopian polity. It was totally unacceptable to the UEDF's concept of a pluralist state. It was also significantly at odds with the EPRDF's own pluralist vision allowing for certain levels of self-determination for Ethiopia's different nationalities. While the EPRDF has extended democratic rights, if selectively, to those who agree with its methodology, the CUD continued to project itself as the sole exponent of the concept of "Ethiopia", and its policies were widely perceived as aiming to restore power to the Amhara. As such they were completely unacceptable to almost all other nationalities in the country, including those represented in the UEDF and the OFDM, as well as those parties allied to the EPRDF in the Afar, Somali, Benishangul-Gumuz and Gambella regions.[11] Together with the Tigreans, these amount to over 70 per cent of the population. This is why the CUD itself could never have won the election, despite the considerable support it received from the widespread "protest vote" against the EPRDF in urban areas.

The failure of the government to bring those detained in November to a speedy trial, and the violence of June and November, caused concern among donors; but attempts to pressure the government into releasing opposition leaders by dropping direct budget support had little effect. Although donors made it clear they did not intend to cut aid, it was clear that changes in delivery of aid would inevitably cause financial problems in 2006, and they were much resented. Cancellation of direct budget support had been an opposition demand and the timing of British announcements over aid in June 2005 and again in January 2006 appeared to offer support to the opposition. Similarly, the government felt donors made little effort to understand either the aims of the opposition or its own intentions. The attempt to put pressure on it stiffened the government's resolve not to tolerate violent opposition and to respond "appropriately".

Local elections in 2008; federal and state elections in 2010

Opposition parties and the EPRDF responded very differently to the electoral process and its aftermath in 2005. The CUD was effectively emasculated by the arrest of many of its leaders and by the continued ramifications of the disputes over whether or not to enter parliament. Following the pardons granted to its leaders in mid-2007, the leadership of the CUD indulged in a series of internal disputes which brought about the total collapse of the coalition. The results have continued to affect the subsequent activities of opposition parties, most of which have made no serious efforts to build up their organizational strength or party structures. Nor did they show any real attempt to campaign prior to the local elections in 2008 or the federal and regional elections in 2010.

In effect, in 2007 the CUD as an organization tore itself to pieces as different leaders tried to take control of the coalition and criticized each other over the events of 2005. Underlining the influence of the US diaspora on CUD policies, the infighting surfaced first in the United States, to which a number of leaders departed immediately after their release.[12] Once the dust had settled, Dr Berhanu Nega withdrew to teach in the United States where he subsequently set up his own organization, Ginbot 7. Rejected by other coalition leaders, Haile Shawel took his own AEUP out of the CUD. Birtukan Mideksa, with a number of other former CUD figures, continued as chairman of the party under the name of Unity for Democracy and Justice (UDJ or *Andinet*). They were unable to continue to use the name of the CUD as the National Election Board had given this to the CUD MPs who entered parliament in 2005/6. The parliamentary CUD was accused of betrayal by its erstwhile colleagues.

Leadership problems continued to plague all these bodies. Birtukan herself was rearrested in December 2008, accused of having publicly rejected the terms of her earlier pardon. After mediation by the Committee of Elders, she was again pardoned in October 2010, several months after the elections in May. While in jail, Birtukan proved unable to control the conflicts and rivalries that arose between UDJ leaders in her absence. Her re-arrest provided the party with a highly symbolic martyr, but at the same time it intensified the disarray within the party leadership. It damaged the party's effectiveness and produced two factions within the party, as well as a breakaway faction headed by Professor Mesfin Woldemariam. After her release, Birkutan decided to withdraw from politics and retired to the United States. She was replaced in early 2011 as chair of UDJ by the former president Negasso Gidada.[13] As an independent he had been one of the founders of Medrek, another opposition coalition set up in July 2008. The UDJ joined Medrek in 2009.

Medrek, the Forum for Democratic Dialogue in Ethiopia, was largely the brainchild of Gebru Asrat of ARENA (the Union of Tigreans for Democracy and Sovereignty). It included several of the "identity-based", or ethnically linked parties, among them the Oromo Federalist Democratic Movement, the Somali Democratic Alliance Forces, and the United Ethiopian Democratic Forces, in itself a coalition led by Professor Beyene Petros and Dr Merara Gudina, involving a number of ethnic parties. Also involved were two individuals, Dr Negasso, the former president, and Siye Abraham, former Defence Minister. Medrek subsequently listed the Oromo Peoples Congress (led by Dr Merara Gudina) and the Southern Ethiopian Peoples Democratic Coalition (led by Professor Beyene Petros) among its members. Of the multi-national opposition parties, the UDJ joined Medrek after protracted negotiations in 2009. Hailu Shawel's All Ethiopia Unity Party (AEUP) refused to join, arguing that the difference between the parties' concepts was too wide to be brought under one umbrella.[14]

In mid-2010 Haile Shawel, then 74, announced his intention to resign from the leadership of his AEUP, but he was subsequently elected chairman again at a congress at the end of the year. By the following September, the party had split into two factions, with one group accusing Haile Shawel of making appointments without reference to general assembly decisions while Haile himself was accusing his critics of conspiring behind closed doors.

Dr Berhanu Nega had set up Rainbow Ethiopia: Movement for Democracy and Social Justice with Professor Mesfin Woldemariam in 2004. Never a mass movement, it was never really more than an intellectual attempt to provide a unifying factor for the opposition, and despite its pretensions, it was never seriously able to compete for the leadership of the CUD. After his refusal to take up the position of Mayor of Addis Ababa, Berhanu was one of the CUD leaders arrested in November 2005. Along with others he was pardoned in 2007 after mediation by the Committee of Elders and requests for pardon. Losing out in the competition for the CUD leadership in 2007, Berhanu left Ethiopia for the United States. Taking up a teaching post, he also set up his own organization, Ginbot 7, the Movement for Justice, Freedom and Democracy, in May 2008. This has publicly committed itself to the overthrow of the government by any means possible, underlining this position by apparent co-operation with the Ogaden National Liberation Front and the Oromo Liberation Front, both involved in armed struggle, and by links with President Isaias Afeworqi of Eritrea. In April 2009, the government announced that it had foiled a coup attempt by Ginbot 7 and arrested 35 people. It subsequently revoked Berhanu's pardon and sentenced him to death *in absentia*. Ginbot 7, like the ONLF and the OLF, has now been declared a terrorist organization in Ethiopia. It is a curious alliance as the ONLF and the OLF want to secede from Ethiopia while Ginbot 7 wants to restore the unity of Ethiopia by doing away with the federal Constitution as well as taking Assab back from Eritrea.

After taking the UEDP-Medhin out of the CUD in late 2005, Lidetu Ayelew announced his "Third Way", claiming to create a functional democratic movement that could operate between the inflexibility and ineffectiveness of the old politicians and the various opposition parties and the authoritarian leftist elements of the EPRDF. He defended his stance over the post-2005 election crisis in a book, *Yearem Ersha* ("The Weed Farm"), but he was blamed by many for falling out with Haile Shawel and Berhanu Nega before he was ousted from the CUD in October 2005. The power struggle within the CUD between August and October 2005, and the disputes over whether to take up their seats in parliament, culminated in the suspension of Lidetu and his deputy Musa from the CUD council. The ostensibly reason was the issue of transition from a loose coalition to a full merger of the four parties, as well as disagreements over allocation of posts and the position of mayor of Addis Ababa, and personality clashes.

Lidetu's political reputation was badly damaged by the rumours that other CUD leaders circulated about him. The expulsion of Lidetu and Muse from the CUD, shortly after the CUD council had called on the public to demonstrate and carry out other forms of protest including actions interpreted as aimed at specific ethnic groups, saved them from the detentions and trials of CUD leaders. In 2007 the UEDF-Medhin changed its name to the Ethiopian Democratic Party (EDP). The EDP claims to be a multi-ethnic party with support in the Amhara region (Lidetu is from the Wollo area of the Amhara Regional State) as well as in the Southern Regional State (his successor as president of the party, Muse Seme, is a Gurage from the Southern Region and looks to acquire support from the Gurage business community, to make up for disappointment with Berhanu Nega who is also Gurage). Despite playing an active role in parliament after 2005, the party did badly in the local elections in 2008 and, like all other opposition parties, collapsed in 2010. Lidetu did not stand for any party post in 2010 after serving his allotted two terms as party chairman.

The contrast between the essentially dysfunctional opposition and the EPRDF could hardly have been more marked after 2005. The EPRDF took immediate steps to investigate the reasons for its less-than-expected results in some parts of the countryside and in urban areas in 2005. More important, it then responded to its findings on a substantial scale, making major organizational changes. It listened to the criticisms made by both party members and others and made sweeping changes in party organization and leadership, especially in areas where it done badly. It set up women's and youth organizations in most *kebeles* and *woredas* and launched a major recruitment campaign. In 2005, the EPRDF had some 700,000 members; by 2007, in advance of the local elections, there were over 4 million. By 2010 the number was well over 5 million. It has continued to grow, if more slowly. Underlining the point, the government tripled the size of the elective *kebele* councils in advance of the election, and the EPRDF put up candidates for virtually all seats. The numbers were staggering. In Oromiya there were 1.7 million *kebele* seats, there were 934,000 in the Amhara Regional State, 682,000 in the Southern Regional State and 166,000 in Tigrai, with 32,000 in Addis Ababa. In all, the EPRDF produced 3.7 million candidates for the *kebele* seats. The opposition was simply unable to cope, not least because the two largest parties pulled out of the election. In effect, no other party than the EPRDF was in a position to operate on any substantive scale in the elections in 2008, or indeed in 2010.

This has been coupled with major changes in the EPRDF's concept of "Revolutionary Democracy". This has steadily moved away from the party's original concentration on the poor peasantry and the proletariat during its struggle to overthrow the military dictatorship before 1991. It began to look towards recruitment of the wealthier peasantry and the urban petty bourgeoisie. Party spokespersons made it clear that "revolutionary democracy" did not contradict capitalism or multi-party democracy. This shift first appeared in the mid-1990s but did not begin to enter party policies until after about 2002. It only became really visible after 2005 when the pattern of recruitment began to focus on various specific groups able to provide competent leadership, including better-off peasants, secondary school graduates, college students and their lecturers as well as intellectuals and women and youth more generally. The 2006 Congress emphasized the development of Women and Youth Leagues in rural areas together with recruitment of moderate and well-off farmers. The party also produced the concept of deploying members in "armies" to assist in planting and irrigation activities in the *kebeles* along with a campaign of support providing fertilizer and other inputs.

Intensive training was given at all levels and over 300,000 were given leadership training in 2006–7 alone. In fact, a central aspect of EPRDF activities in the last seven years has been training programmes for new recruits and for all levels of the party's leadership. This was in response to some of the other weaknesses identified after 2005, which included the failure to maintain effective leadership or to deal with problems and mistakes promptly, particularly, though not exclusively, at the local level. A significant number of party leaders at all levels were retired. Indeed, this process has been extended up to the highest levels of the party with the policy of retiring senior figures, first launched at the congress in 2010. This has been coupled with enhanced promotion of younger cadres to leadership positions.

Other issues that surfaced during the election campaign in 2010 included the problem of landless youths, unemployment and the need for an efficient and fair judicial system to reduce litigation over land and allow land claims to be settled fairly. In urban areas, youth unemployment was highlighted, as was the need for the creation of more micro- and small-enterprises. Inflation was an issue, and has remained so. The post-election discussions at the 2010 Congress made it clear that all these issues had been noted and the party would try to respond. Since then the EPRDF has specifically emphasized the importance of local councils working to resolve issues of administrative injustice, particularly illegal land-grabbing by "rent seekers", and worked to control inflation (though with significantly less success than it would like). It has also shown awareness of problems arising over efforts to recruit a vanguard element in the high schools and universities, with too many students seeing membership as a possible short cut to advancement.

The result of these EPRDF activities and changes was a massive victory both in the local elections of 2008 and in the federal and state elections of 2010. The 2010 elections may have been criticized by the EU Observer Mission, concerned by the sheer volume of reports of intimidation and harassment and by the use of state funds by the EPRDF, but the mission did not believe these had affected the outcome. Other observers, both in 2005 and in 2010, all classified the elections as free and fair. In fact, the reports of international observers both in 2005 and in 2010 do make it clear that allegations of interference and harassment have some truth, but there were no indications on either occasion that these affected the final result.

In fact, it is clear that the EPRDF's victory in 2010, as in 2008, resulted from a number of factors in addition to the improved organization and extensive campaigning of the EPRDF after 2005. There was the steady economic growth for which the EPRDF could claim credit since 2004, with annual growth rates averaging 11 per cent.[15] This growth was accompanied by significant social developments within

Ethiopia, one of the few countries that appear likely to achieve all the Millennium Development Goals. Health and education services have been substantially extended throughout the country, coupled with some decentralization of authority and finance down to *woreda*, even *kebele* level. Given the virtual identity of the government and the EPRDF, the EPRDF gained significantly from such developments.

An independent survey of people's attitudes in advance of the 2010 elections supported these explanations of the EPRDF's success. It found that over 50 per cent of the population believed they were better off in 2010 than in 2005, and three quarters expected this improvement to continue to 2015. About half of those surveyed saw their own economic condition as positive and only a fifth classified the economy or their personal condition as "very bad", though 59 per cent did not see the general condition of the country as "satisfactory". Few saw crime or religious or ethnic conflict as serious problems; 70 per cent, however, were critical of unemployment and 40 per cent commented adversely on corruption. At the same time over 50 per cent felt they could have some say in what the government did.

As opposed to this, the opposition as a whole, and Medrek in particular, which had been expected to provide the strongest challenge, failed to offer anything approaching a sufficiently organized alternative, or indeed much in the way of coherent policy proposals. The creation of Medrek and the various leadership changes among the component opposition elements did not appear to make any real impact on the opposition's capacity, its preparedness or its willingness to operate between elections.[16] This attitude appears to have continued. As of mid-2012 Medrek, like the UDJ, appeared hardly aware that local elections were due in Addis Ababa later in the year; certainly its campaigning was invisible. With the next national elections not due until 2015, Dr Negasso, as chair of Medrek, seemed content to wait for an "Arab Spring" response, commenting in early 2012, "there are too many economic problems, inflation, unemployment…it may explode".

Addis Ababa is certainly the nerve centre of Ethiopia's political and economic activity, but even in that city there was no indication in the early part of 2012 that any of the opposition parties were prepared to make any real effort for the forthcoming elections or produce policies that might encourage their supporters. There was little indication that Medrek or any of its components had been making any effort to develop intra-election activity or long-term campaigning. Indeed, in mid-2012 there were press references to "an indolent opposition" and to the "veil of [opposition] inactivity" looming over the city: "No strategic political activities that normally foreshadow elections can be observed within the political space."

In 2010, given the government figures for growth and highly visible signs of development, it was hardly surprising that the voters were prepared to reject an opposition that largely confined itself to calls for regime change and offered little except possible rewriting of the Constitution and reorganizing of the regions, neither of which had widespread resonance outside Addis Ababa and parts of the Amhara regional state. Nor did the public appear to have much, if any, appetite for the inclination of some opposition politicians to go for confrontation rather than dialogue and participation. There was significant condemnation of the opposition's failure to take up the seats it had won in 2005. Rather than accepting the claim that it would be a betrayal to take up seats won in a flawed election, the more general attitude in Addis Ababa in 2010 was that the opposition's refusal in 2005 to take up seats in parliament was a betrayal of the public who had given them their votes. This view was reinforced by the internal bickering among the CUD leaders after 2007. In the last resort, people did as they always tend to do in Ethiopian elections: they voted for the winner.

Prime Minister Meles insisted that Ethiopia was being transformed into an effective democratic developmental state. The EPRDF, under his chairmanship, has established a highly pragmatic structure, bringing together party and government in a flexible administration that has committed itself to extensive pro-poor developments. The EPRDF has made it clear that it intends to restructure itself and move Ethiopia gradually away from its current "one party dominant" model, but it insists on doing this in its own way and at its own pace. Inevitably the overwhelming size of the EPRDF's victory has given rise to concerns that Ethiopia is becoming a one-party state. The diaspora opposition has certainly made such claims. In fact, the figures for the 2010 election are misleading. The EPRDF itself won 499 seats out of 547, and seven other parties allied to the EPRDF won another 46 seats. Nevertheless, overall opposition parties acquired 30 per cent of the vote nationwide and 41 per cent of the vote in Addis Ababa in 2010, even though it only managed to translate this into one seat in the House of Representatives; another single seat was taken by an Independent.

Ethiopia had the experience of a one party state in the past, the Derg's Workers Party of Ethiopia. The EPRDF is very aware that this has left Ethiopians with a very real distaste for any such idea. The EPRDF itself, after all, fought for years against such a concept. It would be politically difficult, even dangerous, to try to rebuild a single party state in Ethiopia. The EPRDF sees the development of a dominant party as the result of efforts to develop "a stable democratic system" through multi-party elections in 2005 and 2010. It identifies this as a major strategic advance in democratization. The next stage, however, must be a move to a more effective level of multi-party democracy in which two or more parties can continue to provide acceptable levels of constitutional stability irrespective of which wins an election. The EPRDF regards this as some years away, if only because of the weaknesses of the opposition.

Certainly, its own stability seems assured for the foreseeable future. Overall economic growth and pro-poor development have been impressive. The ruling party has successfully expanded and largely educated a vast increase in its numbers. Opposition parties remain weak and divided, and efforts to raise armed opposition have attracted little support. The continued successes of the EPRDF have given support to the view that it knows how to govern. It brought the country out of the economic shambles of the military regime and the negative growth of the late 1980s into a near-decade of double digit growth in the 2000s. It anticipates doubling growth and agricultural production in its ambitious Growth and Transformation Plan. For most of the population, as was apparent in May 2010, it offers an acceptable choice despite the questions that remain over inflation and food prices as well as some aspects of bureaucracy and governance, including human rights and the government's attitude to the press, both federally and regionally.

BIBLIOGRAPHY AND FURTHER READING

Aalen, Lovise and Tronvoll, Kjetil, 2009a, "The 2008 Ethiopian Local Elections: The Return of Electoral Authoritarianism", *African Affairs*, 108/430, pp. 111–20.
——— 2009b, "The End of Democracy? Curtailing Political and Civil Rights in Ethiopia", *Review of African Political Economy*, 36/120, pp. 193–207.
Abbink, Jon, 2006, "Discomfiture of Democracy? The 2005 Election Crisis in Ethiopia and its Aftermath", *African Affairs*, 105/419, pp. 173–99.
Africa Confidential, 2005, "Ethiopia: The Big Upset", *Africa Confidential*, 46 (1), pp. 1-2.

Alemayehu Geda, 2001, "Macroeconomic Performance in Post-Derg Ethiopia", *Northeast African Studies*, 8 (1), pp. 159–204.

Arriola, Leonardo, 2008, "Ethnicity, Economic Conditions, and Opposition Support: Evidence from Ethiopia's 2005 Elections", *Northeast African Studies*, 10 (1), pp. 115–44.

————— 2007, "The Ethiopian Voter: An Assessment of Economic and Ethnic Influences with Survey Data", *International Journal of Ethiopian Studies*, 3 (1), pp. 73–90.

Hagmann, Tobias, 2006, "Ethiopian Political Culture Strikes Back: A Rejoinder to J. Abbink", *African Affairs*, 105/421, pp. 605–612.

Lefort, René, 2010, "Powers—*Mengist*—and Peasants in Rural Ethiopia: the Post-2005 Interlude", *Journal of Modern African Studies*, 48 (3), pp. 435–460.

Lyons, Terrence, 2006, "Ethiopia in 2005: The Beginning of a Transition?", *CSIS Africa Notes*, January 2006.

Merera Gudina, 2003, *Ethiopia: Competing Ethnic Nationalisms and the Quest for Democracy (1960–2000)*, Addis Ababa: Shaker Publishing.

Pausewang, Siegfried, 2009, "Political Conflicts in Ethiopia—in View of the Two-Faced Amhara Identity", in S. Ege et al (eds), *Proceedings of the 16th International Conference of Ethiopian Studies*, vol. 2, Trondheim.

Samatar, A.I., 2005, "The Ethiopian Election of 2005: A Bombshell & Turning Point?", *Review of African Political Economy*, 32, 104/5, pp. 466–73.

Tronvoll, Kjetil, 2009, "Ambiguous Elections: The Influence of Non-Electoral Politics in Ethiopian Democratization", *Journal of Modern African Studies*, 47 (3), pp. 449–474.

————— 2011, "The Ethiopian 2010 Federal and Regional Elections: Re-establishing the One-Party State", *African Affairs*, 110/438, pp. 121–36.

Tronvoll, Kjetil and Hagmann, Tobias (eds), 2012, *Contested Power in Ethiopia: Traditional Authorities and Multi-Party Elections*, Leiden and Boston: Brill.

13

MAKING SENSE OF ETHIOPIA'S REGIONAL INFLUENCE

Medhane Tadesse

With the region's largest population and situated at its centre, Ethiopia was meant to be the Horn of Africa's most influential country. However, the make-up of the region itself, in both geographic and ethnographic terms, under-development, and a sense of insecurity have prevented Ethiopia from exercising the stabilizing and hegemonic role that its size and position might have allowed. Ethiopia remains the prisoner of history and geography. The ethnic question, access to the sea and the Nile issue have remained critical issues for hundreds, if not thousands of years, defining Ethiopia's future and its place in the Horn of Africa.

Successive Ethiopian regimes have followed a Metternichean realpolitik, carefully identifying their state security interests and resolutely pursuing them. This largely explains why Ethiopia remains a status quo power that focuses on maintaining internal peace and a balance of power in the region. The TPLF-led EPRDF government largely followed that tradition. The only difference is that in the early 1990s the

EPRDF took the notion of good neighbourliness at face value and downsized Ethiopia's military capacity to the detriment of its security. This created a regional power vacuum which allowed conflicts to fester unresolved all over the region, often directly threatening the country. These factors caused most of the failures of the EPRDF's foreign policy in the 1990s, and sowed the seeds of a future conflict.

Nonetheless, the EPRDF government quickly recovered and made a perilous journey to prove that it could react forcefully if its interests were threatened. As a result, Ethiopia began again to pursue its interests without waiting for nods of approval from major powers. The EPRDF-led government used military power and Africa's security organizations to breach some of the economic limits on its regional influence. The diplomatic move was more fruitful, if less dramatic, than the unilateral use of the military as a means of managing regional security. Apart from using these organizations as a vehicle to pressure and isolate hostile countries it also served to block the emergence of a coalition of countries antagonistic to it or its regional policy imperatives. This multiplicity of roles and initiatives seems to indicate a high degree of coordination at the national, regional, and global levels aimed at supporting economic development and security, and gaining influence and standing at the regional level.

EPRDF and the Horn in the 1990s: complexity and caution

Historically, Ethiopian foreign policy has been based on Westphalian principles with its emphasis on the security, territorial integrity and sovereignty of the Ethiopian state. This was complemented by a corresponding commitment on the part of Ethiopian leaders to the principle of non-interference in neighbouring countries unless they posed a clear danger to their security. The focus has been mainly on maintaining the status quo and the balance of power rather than supporting interventionism.[1] To the extent that the EPRDF had formulated a foreign policy before assuming state power, it involved non-alignment, a search for peace in the conflict-ridden Horn, and a genuine—if somewhat naive—commitment to good neighbourliness. Between 1991 and 1996 the TPLF-led EPRDF had been inward looking as far as the region was concerned, focusing on the restructuring of the Ethiopian state and searching for Western economic support to solidify it.

The conduct of EPRDF's foreign policy in the immediate post-1991 period (the transitional period) can only be understood in light of the ruling party's origins in the north of the country as a peasant based revolutionary movement, the relations it had established with the EPLF in the course of their revolutionary struggle and the traditional Ethiopian concerns with security in a volatile and often unpredictable region.[2] This is partly a reflection of a non-state actor assuming state power. Politically (as a negation of what it called the Derg's "aggressive" policies) the EPRDF applied a crude policy of good neighbourliness vis-à-vis its neighbours, a policy which later proved to be mistaken and which forced the EPRDF to make a U-turn of sorts within a few years. During this time the EPRDF was hot on rhetoric but cool in practice. Ethiopian diplomacy was marked more by its passivity and ideological rigour than by any true inventiveness or realism. The TPLF-led EPRDF was not naïve but political expediency coupled with its policies of ending the long antagonistic relations in the Horn and having good relations with its neighbours meant it had to fly low and focus on internal political transition, stability and nation building.[3]

Understandably, Ethiopia's regional policy during this period was one of adjustment to Eritrean independence and was largely based on the premise that any unnecessary conflicts with outside forces (mainly neighbours and especially the EPLF) would significantly damage or undermine the Ethiopian state.[4] This position was a direct response to new security and governance challenges. However, the EPRDF was very slow to appreciate the new features of the Horn's international relations.[5] The overthrow of the Derg not only produced a government of a very different political complexion in Ethiopia, it also produced a new country: Eritrea. In the decade after it was established, Eritrea had major difficulties in establishing its position and ranking in the Horn inter-state system, and its frequently contentious relations with its neighbours further complicated the foreign policy challenges facing Ethiopia's new rulers. It can be argued that Ethiopia's regional and foreign policy during this period was to a large extent influenced by history, ideology and immediate practical challenges facing the country. In the late 1980s and early 1990s Ethiopia was on the verge of fragmentation and decay. Poverty, underdevelopment and a sense of insecurity correlated with a cautious regional policy. TPLF leaders accepted the tremendous loss of power and influence and tried to "lead from behind". They became more preoccupied with domestic rather than foreign policy.

EPRDF policy on Eritrea was largely influenced by its almost mystical communion with what it defined as revolutionary democratic ideals such as self-determination, harking back to the days of its armed struggle.[6] One of the reasons behind EPRDF's policy towards Eritrea was the fact that even after assuming power, the EPRDF continued to operate largely as a revolutionary movement and not as a democratic party of government responsible for safeguarding the national interests of the country. The ultimate expression of this approach was the EPRDF's willingness to cede to the demands of the EPLF for a referendum on Eritrean independence and to accept the outcome, thus ensuring initially positive relations between Addis Ababa and Asmara.[7] This was a policy in stark contrast to the Westphalian tradition and nothing short of an abandonment of the offensive posture of its predecessors, which had been defensive in nature.

The major task of reconstructing the Ethiopian state based on a new model (ethnic federalism) and in the meantime maintaining its unity seems to have led its leaders to stay clear of conflict, war or indeed any sort of foreign involvement. Ethiopia's new leaders seemed inward looking and tired of war. Evidently, TPLF leaders saw Ethiopia less as a regional power than as a poor and conflict-ridden country on the verge of collapse. During this period Ethiopia's regional policy was largely immobilized, creating a vacuum in which the new state of Eritrea was able to punch above its weight. Ethiopia's regional policy suffered a brief moment of contraction. On the surface this was due to the fact that the TPLF-led EPRDF came to power committed to the development of the poverty-stricken rural economy, peasant empowerment, revolutionary democracy, and opposition to traditional domination of the Amhara, but gave little attention to foreign affairs. At another level, it was a matter of managing emerging power relations and the TPLF was mainly concerned with establishing its dominance in Ethiopia regardless of developments in Eritrea. The priority was internal power consolidation and external resource mobilization.

The TPLF-led EPRDF followed a policy of peaceful coexistence by respecting the sovereignty and territorial integrity of its neighbours, and appeared to concentrate on forming and protecting its own new political order and economic development, for which it also needed at least a respite from engagement in regional conflicts. The task of maintaining the unity of disparate ethnic groups in volatile and hostile surroundings seems to have made them apprehensive about the survival of the Ethiopian state; hence the emphasis on security. Decidedly, the priority lay in transforming Ethiopia from an impoverished disaster into a poor but more productive country. Ensuring the country's continuity and regional influence necessitated internal peace and economic growth. The EPRDF nonetheless went on to play a leading and positive role in the peace processes in Sudan and Somalia, Muslim neighbours with which Ethiopia has always had contentious relations. Regional actors moved in to take advantage of Ethiopia's apparent weakness, creating instability and uncertainty.[8]

Indeed, the sub-region saw the good gesture of the EPRDF as a sign of weakness and tried to provoke the regime and test its strength. The country found itself under assault from dissidents and Islamists operating from both Sudan and Somalia, and after many attempts to resolve these problems through reconciliation, the EPRDF responded militarily in what would prove to be highly effective operations.[9] Most significantly, after a few years Eritrea moved in to occupy Ethiopian territory: a breaking point in the post-1991 fledgling political order.[10] The National Islamic Front (NIF) saw the new situation in Ethiopia as an opportune moment to introduce its Islamist politics to the country's large Muslim population.

Sudanese leaders seem to have expected a "payback" from the EPRDF in the form of allowing a free hand for its cadres and Islamic NGOs in the country. This, undoubtedly, was another major cause of hostility between the two regimes when Islamist intrigue reached its height in mid-1995. In parallel to this, the Somali Islamist insurgent group conducted several attacks inside Ethiopian territory. Repeated terrorist attacks by al-Ittihad al-Islamiyya in eastern Ethiopia and Khartoum's efforts at exporting political Islam mainly in western Ethiopian regions convinced Ethiopian leaders to join the anti-Khartoum coalition at a later stage. The EPRDF came to that position circuitously, indicating its lack of sufficient knowledge about the different camps in Khartoum, its desire to end the long antagonistic relations in the Horn and its eagerness to have good relations with its neighbours. So, whatever level of commitment Ethiopia's new leaders might have had to peaceful coexistence and non-interference in the affairs of neighbouring countries, it was only a matter of time before they were drawn into the conflictual nature of the Horn's international system.

From non-interference to non-tolerance: 1996–2006

The attempted assassination of Egyptian President Hosni Mubarak in Addis Ababa in 1995 marked the end of the post-1991 period of caution for EPRDF-dominated Ethiopia. Ethiopian leaders saw the events surrounding the assassination attempt as a Sudanese bid to humiliate and weaken Ethiopia and thereby set the stage for conflict and instability. There was some truth to the Ethiopian perception. Ethiopia was shocked by the assassination attempt and felt humiliated. As a result the EPRDF shifted its policy towards the Sudan from cooperation to confrontation.[11] Only then did the EPRDF act, dramatically reducing the size of the Sudanese embassy, closing the consulate in Gambella, expelling Islamist NGOs, arresting many Sudanese in the country, and conducting a widespread purge, particularly in the infiltrated regional government of Banishangul-Gumuz. Not stopping with this the EPRDF reconciled with the SPLA and allowed it to establish military bases on its western border.[12] The policy on the Sudan based on a friendly and good neighbourly relationship ended and once again EPRDF's policy resembled that of the Derg.[13] The EPRDF suddenly became entangled in the conventional dictum "the enemy of my enemy is my friend" which characterizes the inter-state rivalries in the Horn as well as the common support for neighbouring states' uprisings. Ethiopian diplomacy and regional policy had made a perilous journey to reach this point with enormous consequences.

This turnaround in regional policy and military posture would ultimately result in Ethiopia having a measure of influence in Sudanese affairs. After what Ethiopia regarded as a regional attempt to further damage it, the EPRDF reverted to reasserting its influence in the neighbourhood. This came about from the effective use of its military power, but also the far-reaching influence of the regional organization IGAD. The EPRDF-led government's influence in the Horn of Africa, to the extent that it was exerted, largely involved the effective use of regional security organizations and stop-gap coalitions. Ethiopia joined the Kampala-Asmara–Kigali axis, an alliance aimed at changing the status quo in the Congo and Sudan. Ethiopia was much slower to move towards confrontation with Sudan than either Uganda or Eritrea, but when it did move after 1995, its role was potentially decisive. Very spectacularly, Ethiopia stepped up its military engagement with Sudan not only by providing full support to the Sudan Peoples' Liberation Movement (SPLM) but also by deploying its army units and directing SPLA military operations. Ethiopian engagement included upgrading the military skills of the SPLA so as to make it an effective fighting force capable of organizing and directing big military operations.[14] Ethiopia's first effort was undertaken to prevent the defeat of the SPLA in Equatoria; it was followed by a counter offensive in the Parajok operation. Ethiopian support had long-term consequences for the SPLA, the course of the war and the military balance of power in Sudan.

In February 1996 the SPLA and the Ethiopian military occupied Yabus at the southern tip of Blue Nile State in Sudan and defeated a Sudanese airborne counter-offensive. Then in 1997 the Ethiopians enabled the SPLA to conduct the Black Fox Operation that liberated the Kurmuk-Geizan area from government control—sending a shockwave to the leaders in Khartoum and creating a feeling that the days of the Sudanese regime were numbered. It is no exaggeration to say that were it not for the Eritrean-Ethiopian war the Sudanese regime would have come close to collapse.[15] Most importantly, Ethiopia altered the military situation in Sudan for a long time to come. The military balance of power between North and South Sudan, largely maintained by Ethiopia, was critical in cementing close relations between the two. It was also important for creating the conditions for peace negotiations, and provided the incentive for a political settlement. South Sudan was always grateful towards Ethiopia, particularly for the key military support during the recent war with the North, while the North came to recognize the disruptive nature of Ethiopian military power, seeing it as a major deterrent against Eritrean transgression. It is also said that the government in Khartoum came to be more comfortable with the predictability of the Ethiopian leadership compared to the unpredictable and reclusive nature of the Eritrean leader. Gradually the politics of water and oil would come into the picture, contributing to the development of trust and close relations between Khartoum and Addis Ababa.

Having close relations with both Khartoum and Juba put the TPLF-led government in a unique position of influence in both the North and the South.[16] This, coupled with the IGAD peace process, increased Ethiopian influence in Sudan; Ethiopian leaders played a critical role in authoring the Declaration of Principles (DoP) which served as a basis for the negotiations that led to the signing of the Comprehensive Peace Agreement (CPA). The IGAD peace process and its pitfalls could be considered as one arm of Ethiopian foreign policy and strategy on the Sudan. Dealing with immediate security threats by military means and turning them into a diplomatic asset with the help of regional mechanisms had been the defining feature of Ethiopia's regional policy. This would be replicated in the cases of Somalia and Eritrea, and will most probably be seen in the case of Egypt.

However, Ethiopia's most direct security threat came from Somalia.[17] Ethiopia responded with a cross border military operation in the Gedo region of Somalia, destroying al-Ittihad's main base in the locality of Luuq.[18] This was probably the earliest large-scale operation against a collection of international jihadists in the world. From this perspective the attacks of 11 September did not—as is widely claimed—impose a new course, but instead intensified existing trends. The security threat from Somali and al-Ittihad actions seemed to have dissipated until the outbreak of the Eritrean-Ethiopian war in 1998. However, Ethiopia remained on high alert, ready to move into Somalia any time it felt its security was threatened. Thus a consistent pattern in the EPRDF's regional policy was its commitment to change Ethiopia's age-old conflictual relations with its neighbours and its pursuit of a policy of good neighbourliness while it was steadily drawn ever deeper into the concerns of its neighbours as threats to its security grew.

Meanwhile, repeated attacks from Somalia led to successive interventions, which enabled Ethiopia to cultivate friends and interest group inside the war-torn country. During the Ethio-Eritrean war, Eritrea tried to open another military front against Ethiopia in Somalia. The shipment of armaments from Eritrea and the gathering of anti-EPRDF forces in Baidoa in 1999 invited a large-scale military offensive by Ethiopia inside Somali territory. This, apparently, led to the military decline of Mohamed Farah Aideed's United Somali Congress-Somali National Alliance (USC-SNA) in Somalia. It also marked a change in Ethiopia's policy towards Somalia.[19] Ethiopia's close relations with Somali clans and political forces in the autonomous region of Puntland, Bay, Bakol and Gedo are a direct result of this development. Beyond military intervention, Ethiopia decided to co-opt friendly Somali forces and enable them to take care of adjacent border areas as buffer zones for its own security. Subsequently, Ethiopia went on to play a leading role in the Somali peace processes, among which the 1996 Sodere Peace Process was the most prominent.

Through the National Salvation Council created at the Sodere talks, and by co-opting mainly Darod factions of the Somali National Front (SNF), Somali Patriotic Movement (SPM) and SSDF, Ethiopia succeeded in developing the capacity of friendly Somali forces and a pro-Ethiopian Somali camp inside Somalia. In the meantime Ethiopia would support the establishment of the friendly autonomous region of Puntland. In 1991 its roadmap for Somalia, supported by IGAD and the European Union as well as the US, aimed at establishing regional administrations: the so-called Building Block Approach (BBA). This gave it an opening to build close relations with Somali regions.[20] The BBA seeks to resolve the conflict in Somalia around the concept of "building blocks", using a decentralized approach to Somali unity, rather than the much-discredited efforts to produce a unified administration in one go. Like the DOP in Sudan, the BBA for Somalia helped Ethiopia to build relations with several Somali administrations without having to wait for a nod of approval or a protest note from Hawiya-dominated Mogadishu. As a result of this policy, Ethiopia gained support from the newly created Puntland administration, whose leaders were eager to seek Ethiopian support against the Hawiya-dominated south.[21] For much of the next decade several Somali groups, particularly Darod political and armed forces, looked upon Ethiopia for military support in a bid to strengthen their negotiating power vis-à-vis Hawiya-led factions.

Ethiopia had already cultivated sympathetic relations with the independent Republic of Somaliland. Like Puntland, Somaliland considered Ethiopia as the ultimate guarantor of its security and sovereignty. Hence, the relationship has remained very close for the largest part of Somaliland's years of independence. Ethiopia continues to have good relations with the Republic of Somaliland.[22] Ethiopian policy's primary intention was to create safe havens for its own security. Nurturing peace zones in Somalia was a major aspect of its regional policy. However, it became instrumental in establishing close relations and influence in Somalia's northern regions. There have also been initiatives by elements within breakaway Somaliland to unite their territory with Ethiopia and, while there is no indication that the EPRDF would welcome such a development, it is known to support the creation of a number of small Somali states, perhaps along the lines of Puntland. The support for the BBA by the international community is critical in this regard. Whatever they do in terms of a road map for peace in Somalia and Sudan, Ethiopian leaders have sought synergy and coherence with their neighbours, Africa's regional organizations and the West. This gave Addis Ababa international legitimacy to act militarily but also to play a leading role diplomatically.

In the late 1990s both the OAU and IGAD gave Ethiopia a mandate to monitor the Somali peace process, providing it with significant leverage in Somali affairs. This brought widespread sympathy and support for the Ethiopian regional policy even if such relations were mainly handled by the military, without proper oversight by the political leadership. In November 2006 Ethiopia launched an all-out war against the Union of Islamic Courts (UIC) and occupied many towns in Somalia including the capital Mogadishu. The main goal of the military intervention was to weaken Somali Islamists and deny them a permanent base or favourable environment from which they could launch attacks on Ethiopia, or serve as a launching pad for Eritrea. Until January 2009, for two years, the Ethiopian army stayed in Somalia. This led to the disintegration of the UIC and the continued presence of a Somali government, albeit weak, in Mogadishu. By inter vening militarily Ethiopia helped to relocate an internationally sanctioned Somali government inside Mogadishu, triggering internal splits within the UIC and ultimately blocking the emergence of a Somali government dominated by radical and violent Islamist groups.

Ethiopian intervention also prepared the ground for a UN-backed African peacekeeping force to be deployed in Somalia. Had it not been for the Ethiopian military the African Union Mission for Somalia (AMISOM) would not have been conceived, let alone parachuted into Mogadishu. While AMISOM continued to protect the infrastructure around Mogadishu the Ethiopian army remained responsible for the handling of difficult military operations against al-Shabaab. Its role has largely been to oversee and protect the African force stationed in Somalia. Ethiopia also played a critical role in co-ordinating the AU and IGAD roles in Somalia.[23] The war in Somalia once again proved Ethiopia's military primacy in Africa; its military remains self-sufficient, capable of conducting all kinds of cross-border military operations without waiting for external support.[24] Consequently IGAD, in which Ethiopia played a key role, continued to supervise developments in Somalia. In October 2008 the sub-regional organization established a Somalia Facilitator Liaison Office in Addis Ababa with the mandate to oversee critical aspects of support for the Transitional Federal Government (TFG) of Somalia.[25] The combined use of military muscle, diplomatic weight and deep knowledge and expertise on the situation helped Ethiopia play an unmatched role in Somali affairs. In both political and military terms Ethiopia slowly emerged as the main arbiter of the conflict in Somalia. This role, as well as Ethiopia's closeness to Camp Lemonier, Djibouti, the only permanent US military base in Africa, makes Ethiopia an important country for the West in its "war on terror".

The War with Eritrea and Ethiopia's Military Resurgence

Still trying to reorganize their regional security file, Ethiopia's leaders faced another embarrassment when clearly neither the party nor the Ethiopian armed forces were prepared for the Eritrean attack of May 1998 that resulted in heavy losses, both material and human. Compounding this was the early failure of the Ethiopian government to successfully challenge Eritrea's far superior defence of its case internationally. Ethiopia fought much of its war with Eritrea in direct opposition to the international community led by the US. Evidently, the policy of the EPRDF became increasingly influenced by the instability of the countries on its borders. The war with Eritrea brought this to a climax and, almost certainly, the EPRDF will eventually at some point conclude that its strict adherence to a policy of good neighbourliness has been a mistake and that Ethiopia's security necessitates sustained involvement.

The diplomatic effort of the EPRDF-led government became fully focused on creating friends globally in a bid to win the war against Eritrea, but the results were not impressive. Major actors in the international community failed to take official and clear positions on the war. Indeed some advised Ethiopia not to go to war. Ethiopian leaders rejected this partly because they considered it a legitimate war of self-defence. As a result there was a marked slowing down of international financing and aid flows to Ethiopia and a reduction in goodwill. The Americans were reported to have gone to the extent of warning Ethiopian leaders not to go to war or to cross the Eritrean border, saying that there would be bad consequences if they did.[26] From the EPRDF's perspective improved relations with the West would not be achieved by acceding to US or Western demands for a peaceful settlement of the war but instead by reversing Eritrean aggression, by military means if necessary. By aiming at this the EPRDF tried not only to demonstrate its independence and military prowess but also to show that outside powers should respect Ethiopian interests in the region and recognize it as a force of stability.[27] A military defeat of Eritrea was also expected to serve as a lesson to other forces in the region with intentions to destabilize the Ethiopian state. Ethiopia also sought to frustrate Eritrean hegemonic ambitions once and for all, and ensure Ethiopian military supremacy in the sub-region. This, basically, was the line of argument presented by the group that later opposed Meles during the 2001 crisis within the TPLF.

However, Ethiopian diplomacy succeeded in getting some sympathy, particularly in Africa. African mediation teams supported the call for the withdrawal of Eritrean forces from the occupied territory. The bloody and devastating conflict came to an end after both parties signed the Cessation of Hostilities Agreement in June 2000 and the Framework for the Comprehensive Peace Agreement (Algiers Peace Agreement) in December 2000. The Algiers agreement came about in large part because of Ethiopia's military victory, but also partly because of the pressures that the two regimes had been under. The Algiers "peace" could be considered largely an Ethiopian peace, as it was surely dictated by Ethiopia. The international community, headed by the US and the EU, had equally made it clear that the option of continued war was not acceptable. After an outright military victory Ethiopia cooperated fully with the United Nations, agreed to withdraw from Eritrean territory and allowed the establishment of a Temporary Security Zone (TSZ). The sense of humility after victory created confidence on the part of the international community that Ethiopia had no other intentions beyond defending its territory. Gradually Ethiopia would mend fences with the West. Also important in Ethiopia's increasing acceptance is its key role in the "war on terror" and the growing cooperation with Western and primarily US armed forces and intelligence services. This began before the 11 September attacks and the subsequent "war on terrorism", but has intensified since then. The "war on terrorism" was thus very fortuitous for Ethiopia because it came at a time when Ethiopia's relation with the West were at their lowest owing to complications created by the war with Eritrea.

Ethiopia evacuated Eritrean territory (the TSZ, allowing the UN force to come in), scaled down its hostile propaganda and military preparations and demobilized at least a third of its army. Meanwhile Eritrea moved in the opposite direction, speeding up its recruitment of additional military forces, accumulating a new military arsenal and continuing a policy of destabilization in a bid to weaken the regime in Addis Ababa. Later on Ethiopia would object to the ruling of the border commission and continued to define its interests irrespective of a series of protests from Eritrea, a position that created unpredictability in the peace process.[28] No wonder the high expectations that followed the April 2002 EEBC decision have not, so far, been fulfilled. The war redefined the regional power hierarchy. It became clear that Eritrea did not possess enough military power or reliable allies to uphold the ruling and overturn the post-Algiers order. Ethiopia's good will has been welcomed by Africa and the world, its readiness for peace duly recognized. Ethiopian leaders have always been careful not to go against the decisions and resolutions of the UN as well as Africa's regional organizations. This is a big source of strategic and diplomatic capital on which they have carefully continued to build and which has yielded superior results.

The war with Eritrea had a great deal of impact on Ethiopia's regional standing. It demonstrated Ethiopian military skill and sent a shockwave of threat to its neighbours. President Isayas of Eritrea was contemplating capitulation (indeed, he was on the verge of leaving the port of Assab as a ransom),[29] Egypt and Sudan were in total disbelief at the speed with which Ethiopia defeated the "mighty" Eritrean army and pushed deep into Eritrean territory. Even Kenya, not a party to the regional tension, was worried. Ethiopia's neighbours were actually so disturbed by the outcome of the war that the Ethiopian government had to send a military delegation to calm them down and explain the situation.[30] Initially caught totally unprepared but able to prevail, Ethiopia emerged from the war with Eritrea with renewed self-confidence. In the following years Ethiopia worked hard to isolate Eritrea using multiple avenues. Its diplomacy was aimed at familiarizing the international community with what it labelled "Asmara's destabilization strategy" in the Horn of Africa. It also created a regional alliance aimed at the regime in Asmara. To this effect Ethiopia helped create the Sana'a Forum with Sudan and Yemen, which served to isolate and weaken the regime in Asmara.[31] This diplomatic move was as fruitful, if less dramatic, as the unilateral use of the military.

Ethiopia's use of ad hoc coalitions and regional organizations in a bid to promote its position and isolate hostile countries has been exemplary. Such a strategy is also intended to achieve another goal: to block the emergence of a hostile camp in the neighbourhood. Looking at Ethiopia's attempt to ensure its security in Somalia and Sudan shows that what it cannot tolerate are tight borders without buffer zones and its neighbours united against it. This is why similar Ethiopian actions that took place later appeared aggressive but were actually defensive. Ethiopia's successful application of soft power through the use of regional organizations in support of its regional policy and national security interests is less recognized by many and appears, on the surface, surprising. But there seems to be an explanation behind this.

Beyond sticking to their resolutions Ethiopia's relationship with Africa's regional organizations has a deep and broad history behind it. As it is heir to an ancient state and played a critical role in African independence and unity, the cumulative diplomatic wealth of the Ethiopian state is quite enormous. The historicity of the Ethiopian state, its accumulated conduct of foreign policy and the tradition of statecraft have been useful in gaining an advantage over new countries like Eritrea. Its critical role in the revitalization of Africa's regional security organizations is another. Its place in the history of the Black Consciousness Movement and pan-Africanism is an additional asset. An age-old diplomatic arsenal and organizational culture also mattered. Ethiopia's new leaders have benefited a great deal from the collective memory, historical narrative and diplomatic potential of the Ethiopian state.

A degree of Ethiopia's influence in the region is an extension of its position and influence in African regional organizations and beyond. However, Ethiopian leaders were also helped by the behaviour of the Eritrean leadership. Eritrea worked hard to antagonize much of Africa and the rest of the world. Its gradual isolation is to some extent self-inflicted. It pursued angry and rejectionist diplomacy which perpetuated its own marginalization.[32] Unhappy with Ethiopia's influence in the African diplomatic landscape, Eritrea dissociated itself from both the AU and IGAD, leaving its regional diplomacy at the mercy of Addis Ababa. While Ethiopia increased its engagement Eritrea pursued disengagement. Aware of the benefits they provided, Ethiopia remained in constant conversations with regional organizations and gradually its leaders came to occupy centre stage in Africa's international relations. Although Eritrea has attempted to return to full IGAD membership, it has become extremely difficult partly due to Ethiopian influence. Eritrea has definitely been asked to pass through rigorous processes before securing admission to the regional organization.[33]

The war with Eritrea also helped Ethiopia to establish close economic and diplomatic ties with Djibouti. It had already forced Ethiopia to divert its import-export axis from Eritrean ports to the port of Djibouti. This coupled with the threat posed by Eritrea to both Djibouti and Ethiopia has led to a growing alliance between the two countries. The "war on terror" and instability from Somalia helped to cement their relationship. This is not the place to describe the multi-dimensional relationship between Ethiopia and Djibouti, but instead to show that closer security relations and the ever increasing volume of import-export trade make Djibouti the lifeline for Ethiopia and vice versa. The two countries have become much closer, to the extent that there have been talks about forming a union with Ethiopia and they have gone as far as bringing France into the discussions. This resulted in the progressive strengthening of Ethio-Djiboutian relations to the extent that Ethiopia played a key role in the conceptualization of Djiboutian economic policy and the Vision 2035 development plan.[34] This includes a vast cross-border industrialization programme as well a cross-border duty-free zone to integrate Djibouti's economy with Ethiopia's and provide a gateway to other economies in the region such as South Sudan.[35] The economic imperatives aside, the leaders of both countries have developed a great deal of intimacy.

The attempt by Ethiopia to regain primacy and reassert its influence has been multi-pronged. Primarily, it was concerned with internal stability and a growth-led strategy. This required thwarting any threat in the sub-region militarily and economically, bilaterally and multilaterally. The military component helped to keep the country from danger by dealing with hostile military attacks. However, it also served to create a first and second tier of buffers around its borders, creating the internal stability required for development. Playing a leading role in peace processes and peacekeeping operations has been very much part of the strategy. Ethiopian leaders consciously and aggressively pursued this strategy partly because it accords them support and recognition by the international community. It has also helped them to secure the goodwill of Western countries and financial institutions. Compounding this is the use of regional organizations for streamlining its foreign policy objectives. Hard power may be needed for blunting security threats and self-protection, but Ethiopia had to apply other mechanisms of soft power to look after its security interests. A critical element of this—something that has really been going on from the beginning—is that Ethiopia will always try to prevent anti-Ethiopian coalitions from forming. In this way the EPRDF's record in foreign policy is better than generally recognized.

However, partly in response to deep structural difficulties, most of the ingredients of Ethiopia's regional influence remain either outside the continent, or in the realm of economic development, or both. Indeed internal peace and economic development at home and regional peace and security initiatives have underlined the EPRDF's determination to come to grips with its regional status. As discussed previously the earlier focus was on survival, to be followed by economic development that could in turn lead to regional influence. Thus, the single most important focus of Ethiopian foreign policy has been economic development at home for which a secure region and Western economic support were critical.

Global Express: the quest for regional influence through economic diplomacy

Ethiopia has clearly identified poverty as its number one national security threat. Other countries implicitly acknowledge a similar concern but only Ethiopia has developed a coherent policy framework for addressing the issue. Success in this growth-based strategy demands access to external resources, at least in the short term, and a stable neighbourhood. The argument would be that there could only be a geopolitical shift in favour of Ethiopia if it is aligned with an economic shift. This requires transforming Ethiopia from an impoverished disaster into a more productive country. In this regard Ethiopian leaders have a long-term view of Ethiopia's influence in the sub-region. A country with a strong economy would be in a far better position to compete with and resist unfair pressures from countries like Egypt. This will only come if the country gets respite from regional conflicts and mobilises external resources.

The Ethiopian calculation could be that the strategic threat to the country is presented by Egypt, whose politics have been structured around its desire to control the headwaters of the Nile, and which has therefore sought to isolate Ethiopia and prevent an alliance of states in the Horn from emerging to challenge its sub-regional hegemony. While busy making long-term military preparations for an eventual confrontation with Egypt which could probably happen some time in the future, Ethiopian leaders were caught by surprise when in 1998 they were attacked by the least expected neighbour, Eritrea. The Ethiopian government had come to recognize that the country should first develop and development could come only, at least at the initial period, with the support of the West. And both should be handled with care and foresight. This was particularly important to deal with the threat that would inevitably come from Egypt. So, the assessment was that Ethiopia must first create economic strength. Militarily strong but economically poor is a bad position for nations to be in. If Ethiopia is to remain united and survive as a state, it must be in an economically strong position to protect its interests and shape its regional environment.

No doubt a major plank in Ethiopia's foreign policy, which was relatively successful in the immediate aftermath of 1991, was the development of positive relations with the West and particularly the US, which was seen as the ultimate guarantor of donor money. This was mainly at a time when bipolarity attracted limited global interest in the Horn of Africa, largely because of the region's insignificant economic contribution.[36] In economic terms Ethiopian diplomacy has been categorically global. Not surprisingly, the main global engagement of Ethiopia is dictated by its desire to extract resources from dominant power blocks so as to develop its economy within the realms of globalization. The Ethiopian leadership sees Ethiopia's future advance only through the input of enormous amounts of foreign aid and investment and that capital will only be forthcoming if Ethiopia wins the favour of the US and the IFIs over which it exerts most control. Indeed, the EPRDF has demonstrated considerable foreign policy skills at the global level, cleverly adapting to the US-dominated new world order and securing resources on conditions that allow it far more autonomy than most developing countries.[37] In effect, the EPRDF leadership had come to formally endorse globalization and its geostrategic implications. This has been mainly true after the split within the TPLF.

The Ethiopian government white paper on Foreign Policy and Security Strategy, reportedly written by the Prime Minister himself in early 2003, clearly stipulates that the main focus of Ethiopian foreign policy should be geared towards building a vibrant capitalist economy and a democratic order upon which the future survival of Ethiopia depends.[38] To realize this objective, the policy document argues that attracting investment, capital and aid to the country and upgrading Ethiopia's participation in the world market are crucial. Clearly the determinant of Ethiopian foreign policy has remained the domestic economic and political context. The new policy further underscores that Ethiopia's relations with any other country should be based on a clear assessment of its contributions or potential input to the eradication of poverty and the building of a democratic order. As a result, given their limited potential and capacity in the two areas of Ethiopian interest, neighbouring countries, except the Sudan with its oil-led economy, are not given priority. Hence, the focus on resources, particularly water.

Ethiopia's huge hydroelectric power projects are meant to facilitate not only economic development but also regional economic integration and stable relations with neighbours. They are aimed at consolidating Ethiopia's economic and diplomatic weight through water-led energy diplomacy.[39] Ethiopia is anxious to export electricity to all of its neighbours. Ethiopia's focus on economic development has regional objectives potentially contributing to energy-led integration in the Horn of Africa. Still, old economic ties dominate the region, except that Ethiopia's new model, exporting energy, will make these countries even more dependent than they were previously. These are the dynamics that Ethiopia is hoping it will take advantage of in order to reassert its sphere of influence. Ethiopia's economic influence in the region will become far more important over the next five to ten years.

Thus, limited by a dearth of resources and competing domestic concerns, the Ethiopian government seems to have chosen to actively participate in external realms. Its active role in the formative period of the AU, its energetic participation in NEPAD initiatives, its engagement and tiresome consultations with international financial institutions and quick flexibility in adopting to the principles of liberal democracy and the market economy, and its desire to appear as a force for stability in a volatile sub-region are all geared towards achieving its economic and political objectives. The primary goal is to guarantee unilateral advantages from privileged relations with external actors. It is a major part of a long process in which the EPRDF is trying hard to translate an international profile into political and economic resources that would serve domestic and regional purposes.

Occasionally lambasting Eritrean intransigence and Islamic terrorists, Ethiopia over the last ten years has focused on domestic economic concerns. The EPRDF's laser-like focus on economic diplomacy is certainly a sharp contrast to its predecessors. Effective use of aid money has only increased the acceptance of the Ethiopian government among the aid and donor community and ensured continued financial support. The whole exercise was considerably supported by the personal interventions of the Prime Minister. That Ethiopia was one of the largest recipients of international assistance in Africa and has gained the support of the US while the country is ruled by a vanguard party that has made only limited progress in democratization and privatization is on the surface a paradox, if not an enigma. To a large extent Ethiopian foreign policy was helped by the regional and continental profile of the

Prime Minister. The problems of the regime were masked by the extraordinary openness, charm and intellectual brilliance with which Prime Minister Meles Zenawi was able to engage the sympathies of leaders of international financial institutions and leading foreigners.[40]

His role in Africa's international relations, his place in the AU's New Economic Partnership for Africa's Development (NEPAD) and in Africa's climate talks at the international level, were meant to reinforce the same outcome.[41] This has been a major factor in attracting international attention to Ethiopia. This, coupled with its security role, has increased the regional influence of Ethiopia in that the country has become a critical player in regional diplomacy and security; a country that has to be listened to even by global powers. Thus it is not surprising that Ethiopia's relations with the West are strong, as indicated by the high level of aid that flows into the country and the unwillingness of Western countries to seriously criticize Ethiopia about its human rights abuses.[42] Ethiopia has been securing various funds from the international community, a major prerequisite for mobilizing international resources for the grand experiment that is transforming Ethiopia through a developmental state paradigm.[43] Evidently, the presence of a focused and dynamic government committed to economic development meant that greater utilization of the waters of the Blue Nile would become a government priority. Furthermore, the possibility that Ethiopia's economic development and the continued mobilization of external resources could enable the country to finance big economic projects has, as expected, presented a new set of challenges to Egypt.

The challenge from Egypt: Ethiopia and the regional power order

Even the military defeat of Eritrea and closer relations with the West did not make Ethiopia's economic development, security and dominance in the region inevitable. A major factor in the absence of a workable peace and security order in North East Africa is the absence of a regional power order. This is partly linked to the lack of an established regional power hierarchy, as reflected in the unfortunate geostrategic situation of the Horn of Africa—a region lacking an internal hegemon, but adjacent to Egypt. Ethiopia's power is constrained by underdevelopment. However, Egypt is a country whose body is in Africa but whose head is in the Arab world. The sub-region needs to reach an agreement on whether a robust security community requires an inter-state power order: some kind of constructive hegemon.[44] Behind the competition for regional hegemony is the long-standing conflict between Cairo and Addis Ababa over the use of the Nile waters. The contentious relations between the two are mainly historical and structural, but also deeply cultural and political. Conflicting myths and narratives compound this. Age-old strategic concerns such as control over the Nile waters, a cause of major wars going back hundreds of years, are still a major feature that continues to shape their respective positions and roles in the sub-region.

The EPRDF almost certainly sees the development of the Blue Nile basin as critical, probably central, to the long-term economic salvation of the country. This idea was quickly interpreted in Cairo as a threat and it has endeavoured to block Ethiopian plans for development of the Blue Nile basin waters. Egyptian policy towards Ethiopia and the Nile issue has always been guided by a two-track strategy: the politics of cooperation and the politics of destabilization.[45] Egypt's cooperative engagement on negotiations does not preclude its multi-faceted hostile actions against Ethiopia. Although Egyptian and Ethiopian leaders have repeatedly proclaimed a new era of co-operation in the sharing of Nile waters since 1991, Egypt has continued to fight hard to ensure that Ethiopia does not receive international loans for major (and even minor) water development projects. The Nile 2002 conferences and other initiatives have gone some way to ease tensions and make clear the gains to be made by all basin countries through co-operation, but it is unlikely that Egyptian objections can be overcome and the logjam broken without concerted regional pressure and the political will of the international community led by the US. Egyptian supremacy over the issue of the Nile is, however, dwindling and the tide is slowly turning against Cairo.

In 1999 the ten Nile riparian countries established the Nile Basin Initiative (NBI), the first cooperative institution in the basin to include all ten riparian states. This was meant to be a precursor for real and meaningful negotiations for a new legal and institutional regime for the shared and equitable use of the Nile waters that is referred to as the Cooperative Framework Agreement (CFA). However, the real negotiation was between Ethiopia, Sudan and Egypt.[46] To deal with the challenge Ethiopia deployed regional instruments, first cementing relations with Khartoum and then galvanizing upper riparian countries for the cause. Egypt's internal problems and the decline of its regional influence, added to uneasy relations with Washington, seem to have helped Ethiopia push the equitable share of the Nile waters as a major regional agenda. In this it was supported by new developments in the sub-region as well as its own resurgence in regional security affairs. The end of the Cold War has been marked by some dramatic swings in regional and international alignments in North-East Africa. The National Islamic Front (NIF) leadership in Khartoum which came to power in a military coup in 1989 increasingly distanced Sudan from Cairo and swiftly began pursuing an aggressive Islamist-based foreign policy.

Indeed, Cairo became increasingly aggrieved by the emerging hostile tendency of the new regimes in Khartoum, Asmara and Addis Ababa towards its hegemonic postures. Some of them were Islamist, others were nationalist; all of them were ideologically assertive (though there have been some changes in this regard in recent years). From this perspective it is not surprising to see that Cairo's hands have become increasingly tied and its influence narrowed. Moreover, the new regimes in the Horn were able to attract the attention of the US. After the defeat of the Derg the US turned to the governments of Ethiopia and Eritrea to provide regional stability as a bulwark against the expansionist Islamist aims of the National Islamic Front (NIF) in Sudan. After the second half of the 1990s Egyptian influence in the Horn of Africa was at its lowest. It has lost ground and control in Somali affairs and entered into antagonistic relations with Sudan.[47] This was followed by new economic and political developments in the countries of the region.

Increased political and economic stability in recent years has meant that upstream countries were now in a position to develop the hydro-power and irrigation potential of the Nile waters. In recent years, the "collective" power of upstream countries has been greatly enhanced. Many of them have continued to involve themselves in the process in the belief that negotiations will bring about a new legal agreement or the much-anticipated CFA as well as the much-needed financial investment by external donors for hydrological projects. The possibility of securing alternative external support from non-traditional sources (such as China) for Nile Basin projects compounded the new external element. These led to an important shift in terms of bargaining powers and not only in material terms. Moreover, upper riparian countries have decided to use their collective voice and streamlined position to get concessions from downstream countries, mainly Egypt. Ethiopia's quiet diplomacy has helped crystallize this common approach. The risk of going alone and refusing to cooperate on the Nile issue has become high for Egypt. Ethiopia has focused on creating a consensus in the region that development of the Blue Nile basin has positive economic and political spin-offs beyond Ethiopia, a position that would ultimately convince the rest of Africa and the West. The hope is that the US may come to discount Egypt's position and accept Ethiopian arguments that security in the Horn is ultimately dependent on development, and that this is conditional upon fully developing the waters of the Blue Nile basin.

With the turmoil in the Arab world and the alignment of forces in East Africa, Egyptian influence has declined and this can be expected to continue if the current political crisis in the country does not abate. Moreover, the emergence of a stable and strong Ethiopia and an assertive region means that the Americans may be less inclined to accept Egypt as the regional hegemon in the Horn. Given the emerging complications in the US-Egyptian relationship it is fair to assume that Washington would be easily attracted by Ethiopia's position as an alternative source of stability in North-East Africa. Its peace-keeping role around the region and effective use of its military for regional security frameworks mean that it is a regional power that should be taken seriously. Most important, Ethiopia has already begun to depend on its relative economic strength to develop the Nile Basin and influence the outcome of negotiations. The building of the Grand Ethiopian Renaissance Dam (GERD) started in April 2011, which would have been inconceivable a few years ago, is a telling illustration of the shifting balance of power in the sub-region in which Egypt is being increasingly pushed into a defensive position.[48]

Ethiopia's bold move to attempt such a grand scheme in the face of Egyptian opposition and galvanize regional support for the NBI points in one direction: its pivotal role in highly critical regional issues. By all accounts the GERD could symbolize Ethiopia's regional influence. It is highly probable that Ethiopia will continue to galvanize regional resources, ad hoc coalitions and Africa's regional organizations to further promote its position in a bid to thwart Egyptian obstructionism. The recent suspension of Egypt by the AU from July 2013 to June 2014 could indeed be a blessing in disguise. Nonetheless, the fact that the traditional proponents of the politics of destabilization within the Egyptian political establishment (that is, Egyptian military intelligence) have become the new masters of the Egyptian state since the 2011 revolution, and the regrettable views of the top leadership towards Africa, do not bode well for a peaceful resolution of the Nile issue.[49] Increased hostility and tension between Ethiopia and Egypt are very real.

Far more important will be Ethiopia's economic influence in the region over the next five to 10 years. In the next decade, Ethiopia will become increasingly wealthy (at least relatively to its past) but politically insecure. It will therefore use some of its wealth to create visibility and a military force appropriate to protect its interests. Ethiopia will not become the most powerful country in the next decade, but it has no choice but to become a major regional power in the sub-region. And that means it will clash with Egypt. The Ethio-Egyptian relationship and the regional power order in North-East Africa remain a fault line. Ethiopia is interested not in conquering or dominating the region, but in ensuring its security along its borders and reasserting its influence. From the Ethiopian point of view, this is both a reasonable attempt at establishing a minimal sphere of influence and—traditionally—a defensive measure.

BIBLIOGRAPHY AND FURTHER READING

Abbink, Jon, 2003, "Ethiopia-Eritrea: Proxy Wars and Prospects of Peace in the Horn of Africa", *Journal of Contemporary African Studies*, 21 (3), pp. 407–425.

Abdelwahab El-Affendi, 2009, "The Perils of Regionalism: Regional Integration as a source of instability in the Horn of Africa", *Journal of Intervention and Statebuilding*, 3 (1), pp. 1–19.

Carlson, Jon D., 2011, "Externality and Incorporation in the World System: Abyssinia—Anomaly or Palimpsest?" *American Sociological Association*, 17 (1), pp. 165–98.

Clapham, Christopher, 2009, "Post-war Ethiopia: the Trajectories of Crisis", *Review of African Political Economy*, 36, 120, pp. 181–92.

Connell, Dan, 2005, *Conversations with Eritrean prisoners of War*, Trenton, NJ: The Red Sea Press.

Guzzini, Stefano, 1998, *Realism in International Relations and International Political Economy. The Continuing Story of a Death Foretold*, London: Routledge.

Healy, Sally, 2011, "Seeking Peace and Security in the Horn of Africa: the Contribution of the Inter-Governmental Authority on Development", *International Affairs*, 87 (1), pp. 105–120.

ICG, 2003, *Ethiopia and Eritrea: War or Peace?* International Crisis Group, Africa Report 68.

—— 2008, *Beyond the Fragile Peace Between Ethiopia and Eritrea: Averting New War*, International Crisis Group, Africa Report 141.

—— 2008, *Somalia: To Move Beyond the Failed State*. International Crisis Group, Africa Report 147.

—— 2010a, *Sudan: Regional Perspectives on the Prospect of Southern Independence*. International Crisis Group, Africa Report 159.

—— 2010b, *Eritrea: The Siege State*. International Crisis Group, Africa Report 163.

Iyob, Ruth, 1993, "Regional Hegemony: Domination and Resistance in the Horn of Africa", *Journal of Modern African Studies*, 31 (2), pp. 257–76.

—— 2000, "The Ethiopia-Eritrean Conflict: Diasporic vs. Hegemonic States", *Journal of Modern African Studies*, 38 (4), pp. 659–82.

Medhane Tadesse, 1999, *The Eritrean-Ethiopian War: Retrospect and Prospects: The Making of Conflicts in the Horn of Africa, 1991–1998*, Addis Ababa: Mega.

—— 2002, *Al-Ittihad: Political Islam and Black Economy in Somalia: Money, Religion, Clan and the Struggle for Supremacy over Somalia*, Addis Ababa: Mega.

—— 2004, *Turning Conflicts to Cooperation: Towards Energy-led Integration in the Horn of Africa*, Addis Ababa: Friedrich Ebert Stiftung.

—— 2007, "The Conduct of Ethiopian Foreign Policy: From TPLF Political Bureau to Meles Zenawi", in K.G. Adar and P.J. Schraeder (eds), *Globalization and Emerging Trends in African Foreign Policy*, vol. 2, Washington, DC: University Press of America, pp. 53–70.

—— 2009, "UN Peace Keeping in the Horn: Problems & Prospects", in Adekeye Adebajo (ed.), *From Global Apartheid to Global Village—Africa and the United Nations*, Scottsville: University of Kwazulu Natal Press.

Kidane Mengisteab, 2011, *Critical Factors in the Horn of Africa's Raging Conflicts*, Uppsala: Nordiska Afrikainstitutet (Discussion Paper 67).

Reid, Richard (ed.), 2009, *Eritrea's External Relations: Understanding Its Regional Role and Foreign Policy*, London: Royal Institute of International Affairs.

Sharamo, Roba and Berouk Mesfin (eds), 2011, *Regional Security in the Post-Cold War Horn of Africa*, Pretoria: Institute for Security Studies (Monograph 178).

Thomas, Caroline and Wilkin, Peter (eds), 1999, *Globalization, Human Security and the African Experience*, Boulder, CO: Lynne Rienner.

Woodward, Peter, 2003, *The Horn of Africa: Politics and International Relations*, London: I.B. Tauris.

—— 2012, *Crisis in the Horn of Africa: Politics, Piracy and the Threat of Terror*, London: I.B. Tauris.

14

THE ETHIOPIAN ECONOMY

THE DEVELOPMENTAL STATE VS. THE FREE MARKET

René Lefort

Is there an Ethiopian Economic Miracle?

When a visitor comes to Addis Ababa these days his first reaction is one of shock. There are new roads, including modern four-lane freeways, running everywhere. New buildings, ranging from futuristic high rises to more modest popular dwellings, are growing, and even a combination tram/elevated railway is under construction, the first segment of a serious mass transit system in any African capital. The speed and ambition are prodigious. No other capital city on the continent has known such fast-paced and extensive modernization over the last few years. And similar processes are taking place in many provincial towns.

For any observer assessing Ethiopia from the angle of infrastructure and physical development, everything in sight confirms the government's repeated claim of double-digit growth, the highest rate for a non-oil-dependent African economy over the last eight years.[1] As even an opposition journalist had to admit, "the regime has been able to

357

crack the code of East Asia's rise and download it into an Ethiopian hardware."[2]

But the mistake is that almost all observers limit themselves to this obvious approach, which is blind to the realities of four-fifths of Ethiopians—those who still struggle to eke out a living from tiny undersize land holdings or "informal" activities. The Multidimensional Poverty Index of 2011 puts Ethiopia just above Niger.[3] The UNDP's Human Development Index (2011) ranks it 174th out of 187 countries, a slight improvement over 2003 (169th out of 175).[4] Ethiopia still needs some form of emergency or recurring food aid every year to prevent between ten and fifteen million Ethiopians (one in six or eight, mostly peasants) from starving.[5] And this proportion of assisted people has remained stable over the last thirty years. In monetary terms the cost of cereal imports has multiplied by three in ten years, going from 2 per cent to 4 per cent of imports, measured in volume.[6]

So what are we to make of the apparent contradiction between a sharply growing modern sector and the persistence of dire poverty mainly among the peasants? The present regime can certainly be praised for having finally managed to get the country moving—and moving fast and energetically—after the twilight years of the Haile Selassie regime followed by the catastrophe of the "communist" military regime. Ethiopia is not an "underdeveloped block" any more: islands of modernity have surfaced and its economy is now dual. But this duality makes difficulties for statisticians.

Statistics are supposed to be the ultimate test of reality. But in Ethiopia statistics are questionable and controversial. They are so optimistic that international financial organizations have at times hesitated and contradicted themselves—and contradicted their Ethiopian sources—over short periods of time. A joint assessment made by the IMF and the World Bank states that "staffs have not been able to confirm [the] very high growth rates reported in the official statistics (an average 11 per cent per annum during 2004/5 and 2009/10)[7] that appear to significantly overstate actual growth. Staff estimates suggest robust growth in the 7–8 per cent range". In addition, "official GDP growth rates imply productivity increases that appear implausible, casting doubt on some aspects of national accounts compilation".[8] The IMF reiterated its reservations in the years that followed.[9] Agriculture is particularly in the spotlight as official statistics purport to show that grain production has tripled in fifteen years, which seems unrealistic.[10]

Two recent (confidential) studies from international cooperation organizations conclude that grain production has been exaggerated by about 30 per cent.[11] Even some of the results of the last census (in 2007)—for example those dealing with the very sensitive areas of ethnic and religious repartition—have been questioned. Ethiopia's economic progress is undeniable, but it is often difficult to give an accurate quantitative measurement of it.

The early years of the new regime: the founding of a "party-state led economy"

The inheritance of the Derg years. In 1991, when the Tigray People's Liberation Front (TPLF) finally crushed the Derg's army, it inherited a country devastated by seventeen years of civil wars and a "socialist command economy", which was even poorer than it had been in the last years of the Empire. While agriculture accounted for two thirds of GDP[12] and nine tenths of the work force, its production per capita was lower than during the last years of Haile Selassie's reign.[13]

The Derg's land reform of 1975 was among the most radical that had ever been attempted in the world. Land confiscated from "feudal landlords" was equitably redistributed to peasant households, along with a non-transmissible right of usufruct. Land could not be rented and hired labour was forbidden. Peasant Associations were turned into a kind of local administration, in charge, *inter alia*, of implementing the land reform.[14] But they were left with very little autonomy by a strongly authoritarian government which tried to extract more and more from the countryside in order to wage its wars. As in other socialist countries, the regime imposed production quotas and fixed prices. At the same time the Derg neglected subsistence farmers, putting most of its resources into Soviet–style *Sovkhozes* (state-owned farms), which completely failed. By the mid-1980s famine and peasant sabotage had forced the government to backtrack: free market sales were allowed, land renting became possible and inheritance of the usufruct right was re-established. But it was too little too late.

In 1991, industrial and service sectors made up only 12 per cent and 23 per cent of GDP respectively.[15] The private sector was tiny. 48 per cent of construction, 72 per cent of transport and communications, 89 per cent of industry and mining, and 100 per cent of electricity, banking and insurance companies were in the hands of the state, which had proved to be a very bad manager.[16]

"Development is first of all a political process". Another problem came from the fact that the winning TPLF was itself a radical neo-Maoist pro-Albanian Marxist movement.[17] But with the fall of the Berlin Wall the world had changed, and the TPLF changed radically, almost overnight—at least in public. Meles Zenawi, then TPLF Chairman,[18] declared that he was "no longer a hard-line Marxist" and would from now on "work for free enterprise".[19] But this seems to have been a largely tactical move designed to gain the support of the Western powers. Inwardly, the leadership remained deeply influenced by Marxism and Leninist "democratic centralism", which fitted perfectly into the age-old Abyssinian culture of hierarchy and submission. This *Weltanschauung* tended to provide the basis for new economic policies, and probably still does. The lingering imprint of the command economy was first evident in two important documents from 1993, which were later softened in their formulation by Meles Zenawi himself.[20]

The supreme goal was still to push forward "revolutionary democracy", in short to promote "the rights of the masses". Hence the party line that "development is first of all a political process". The party retained the image of a "vanguard party", which made it the one and only organization with the legitimacy and capacity to take the fundamental decisions in any field, including that of the economy. Some Ethiopia specialists have even argued that the fusion between the state and the ruling party has led to the practical hegemony "of a monolithic party-state".[21] Though the regime stated at its inception that the economy should be "driven by market forces", in reality these "market forces" have been led and operated by one force, the party-state. After the "command economy" of the Derg, a kind of "party-state led economy" was put in place. And this is still the way things operate today, in the broad scheme of global economic systems.

The TPLF considered that Ethiopia was at a "pre-capitalist stage". And it still considers that the market suffers from "multiples failures" and that "the major free market economy forces are not fully matured".[22] Adopting the "neo-liberal paradigm" (the "Washington consensus") and even "a classical liberal economy" by "allowing the market to rule" would lead to a "dead end". That is, "shackling the state" to the point of rendering it "non-activist and non-interventionist"—reducing it to "a night watchman state"—while "unleashing the market" in the hope that it would "self-correct its own failures" would ultimately "reach a dead end". So the interventions of the so-called "developmental state" are vital "to fill the deficit of the market ... so as to create a conducive platform for developmentalism."[23] Only a developmental state, which should be "strong" and "independent of the private sector", will be able "to build the physical and institutional environment and to change the rules of the game" in order to ensure "the survival of Ethiopia as a nation".[24]

This "state leadership role" has four main elements:

(a) "The commanding heights of the economy will be owned by the government".[25] If these cannot be kept under state monopoly, "arrangements should be made in which the State will have a higher share". So the developmental state will be able to intervene as much as possible in the branches that need to be developed but from which the private sector, national and international, "shies away".

(b) In order to bring the market to maturity and because the "national bourgeoisie wants to promote its interests at the expense of the people", the private sector should be "directed", "guided", "disciplined", "motivated". So the state will "hold an upper hand in the processes of the private enterprises". It must "have the ability and will to reward and punish the private sector actors" in order to lead them from their preference for short-term selfish enrichment to participation in the country's long term development.

(c) The same applies to international actors. And if "we have no choice but to give access to foreign capital", it should never be allowed "to twist the state's arms".

(d) The mass of mostly "backward", "uneducated" and "unorganized" peasants need a "strong revolutionary democratic leadership" in order to develop.[26] No alternative to a "top down approach" has ever been considered,[27] and compulsory labour is still presented as "voluntary contributions"[28] to local infrastructure projects (roads, schools, health centres, reforestation). But how is it possible to reconcile the "strength" of this leadership with its supposedly "democratic" character? The key word is "participation". But "participation" is limited to that which will "convince and ... mobilize" social forces, and they are allowed at most "to bring some adjustments" to decisions coming from above.[29]

These dogmas are not only still in place, they have never been discussed.

1991's ambiguous liberalization. To keep the "commanding heights of the economy" in the hands of the state, privatization excluded whole areas. First of all, land was not privatized,[30] because otherwise "the peasants will be forced to sell their land when they face hardship and then they will enter a state of poverty from which they can never [escape]".[31] Key sectors were kept in the state's hands, especially the banking, insurance, communication and electricity sectors. In other cases, public companies were "privatized", but with some restrictions. The state kept control of parastatals through "endowments" managed by the Relief Society of Tigray (REST), the humanitarian arm of the TPLF during the war, which in 1995 gave birth to a conglomerate known as the Endowment Fund for the Rehabilitation of Tigray (EFFORT). All the key positions were in the hands of Tigrean officials and the general management remained assigned to a high-ranking TPLF member. This form of control "len[t] credibility to the popular perception that the ruling party and its members were drawing on endowment resources to fund their own interests or for personal gain".[32]

The first version of ADLI (Agricultural Development-Led Industrialization)

Agriculture as the cornerstone of development. The EPRDF (Ethiopian People's Revolutionary Democratic Front) internal document (1993) that presented the economic strategy of the new regime remained in line with the Albanian approach of armed struggle.[33] It stated that "in the struggle for our revolutionary democratic goals" "our main enemies are imperialism and the comprador class", while the "upper stratum ... of the national bourgeoisie" and even of the "urban petty bourgeoisie ... are antagonistic to our political goals". But, it added, recent "major changes around the world" force us to "make a few adjustments" so as to avoid "the mobilization of imperialist forces against us", but "without doing away with the pillars of our Revolutionary Democracy".

Considering that the export led and import substitution strategies of the two former regimes had failed, the TPLF reckoned that "an economy based on foreign markets ... becomes dependant on imperialism".[34] "The role of external forces can only be complementary to those of internal forces".[35] The key terms became "independent development", "self reliance" and "national market". Thus, development should rely first on "an extensive use of the natural resources and manpower of the country". This meant that the "rural development strategy ... is not dependent on capital and technology".[36] The centrality of the tens of millions of small holders/subsistence farmers became obvious. "Agriculture should be the starting point—the cornerstone—for initiating the structural transformation of the economy". The rallying cry of this strategy was a "broad-based growth process involving smallholder farmers".[37]

The first aim was to alleviate the extreme rural poverty that existed by achieving individual food self-sufficiency for all farmers. The regime wanted the mass of farmers to progress at an even pace in order to enable "a structural transformation in the productivity of peasant agriculture"; without this, "economic progress will remain a myth".[38] Paradoxically, agriculture, although impeded by its own low productivity, was seen as having the highest development potential. Its transformation was to be based on the "agricultural extension package", which was to provide farmers with new inputs (fertilizers, seeds, etc.) and train them to use these inputs efficiently; followed by a mobilization of the work force through its "organization".[39]

The regime's motivation was perhaps more political than economic. In a country where the industrial proletariat had always been a tiny minority, the TPLF could not base its rule on anybody but the most numerous and poorest class in the country, the class which had been most exploited and which had given its blood to overthrow the Derg— the peasant class.

Agriculture as a launching pad for industry. But agricultural growth was not seen as the ultimate aim. An "interdependent", "mutually supportive" objective was also "to streamline and reconstruct the manufacturing sector ... so that it makes extensive use of the country's natural resources in order to reduce dependence on external sources, and manpower" and "expands domestic markets for goods and services".[40] Agriculture was therefore seen as a launching pad for industrialization. This strategy had a name: Agricultural Development Led Industrialization (ADLI).

The rise in agricultural productivity, it was thought, would lead to an increase in the marketed surplus, first nationally and then for export. The most successful peasants would see their buying power increase and as a result would be able to buy basic consumer goods. This demand would lead to the emergence of simple industries, which would offer employment opportunities to the rural labour force, which would have to leave the land since productivity gains would mean fewer labourers would be required. Among the industries envisioned were several that would not only produce basic manufactured goods but also provide products for agriculture, such as fertilizers, pesticides, seeds and so on. Locally produced, these agricultural components would be cheaper than imported ones and would lead to a new rise in agricultural productivity which would in turn lead to more demand for industrial products. The virtuous circle of growth would be set in motion.

Private actors were considered to be incidental to this virtuous circle, and their operations were regarded with suspicion. They should only bring "a supplementary input in the economic sectors in which the State cannot be directly involved". The state must always "strive to control" them.

This "endogenous" development strategy, with its overall embrace of public power, its enormous amount of party-state activity, its tight control, its high degree of centralism focusing on the traditional peasantry, its systematic marginalization of private enterprise, was a unique approach to development.

The "renewal": a radically new approach, the same modalities

Two political shocks. By the beginning of the 2000s it had become obvious that ADLI was not working. Agricultural output per capita was still roughly the same as in the last few years of the Derg and less than in the last years of the imperial regime.[41] GDP was lower than at the end of the Derg (around $8bn against $12bn).[42] In 2002–3 bad rains had brought the food shortages to the same level as those of the 1984–5 famine. Massive deaths were avoided only because the emergency system was much better than seventeen years before. Industry was still not taking off,[43] exports had stagnated and the balance of payment remained in deficit.[44] The time had come for reassessment.

This realization was triggered by two major political shocks. The April 2001 regime crisis was the most serious internal rift the TPLF had faced since its birth twenty-five years before and it eventually resulted in Meles Zenawi's absolute political supremacy.[45] Then, four years later, the regime became convinced that it could win free and fair elections because it assumed that the mass of poor farmers was basically sympathetic to it. But many rural voters followed their local leaders who had decided to support the opposition because they rejected the authoritarianism of the regime, its harsh intrusions into their daily life, and what they considered to be its bias in favour of the Tigreans. The push of the opposition seriously shook up the regime.[46] Faced with poor economic results, significant disapproval in the countryside and crushing defeat in the towns during the election, the regime decided to completely review its perennially intertwined economic and political strategy. This is what became known as *Tehadeso* (Renewal).

ADLI's second version. The first reaction to the 2005 shock was a strong reassertion of the regime's political hegemony.[47] The previous discourse of political legitimacy based on "democratization" sank into further discredit. A new basis for legitimacy had to be found, and the party decided this would be the promise of massive economic growth.

Meles Zenawi—who boasted an MBA from the Open University of the United Kingdom (1995) and a MSc in Economics from the Erasmus University of the Netherlands (2004)—summarized his new vision as follows: in the age of globalization "it is impossible to limit and to hide from merciless competition". One must either "survive by inserting oneself in this competition" or "perish" like the African countries which had tried to duck the issue. "Ethiopia has no choice except employing free market economy."[48] This was a major *aggiornamento*.

To succeed in this "insertion", the peasant masses were now seen as less useful than the most advanced actors, the "new entrepreneurs" and "constructive investors" active in agriculture, industry and the service sector. The private sector had remained embryonic so far because it was discriminated against. Businessmen were seen as capitalists exploiting the working masses: "There was suspicion of putting trust in the private sectors".[49]

From now on these "new entrepreneurs" were going to be considered the engine of economic growth. A sort of trade-off set in: this social class had so far been chilly towards the EPRDF and the government thought this change of direction would warm up its attitude towards the party. The deal was implicit: stop politicking and we'll help you get rich. The party-state promised it was going to finally release its pressure on the private sector and entrepreneurial farmers.

This U-turn set up two opposing camps. On one side were the "new entrepreneurs"; on the other side were the "rent seekers" who were fighting against the rise of the free market in order to keep benefiting from the rent accruing to them "from their official position in the government" or from "their patron-client relationship with office holders" or even from "their corrupt relationship with officials".[50] To bring the free market to maturity "the struggle of the revolutionary democrats is to replace the rent seeking political economy by developmental and democratic political economy".[51] This same antagonism superimposed itself on the opposition between democratic and anti-democratic forces: the rent seekers could only operate in the absence of transparency and accountability, two pillars of democracy. In that way, the rise of a market economy and the march towards democracy would be one and the same thing, fusing into what Meles Zenawi called "developmentalist democracy".[52]

This was a genuine change of tack: the market, both national and international, became the alpha and omega of development. Since 1991 it had been mostly endogenous, based on getting the masses of small farmers *to feed themselves* through public support. From now on, development was going to be led by a minority—the economic upper class—who would essentially work for the market. And the approach also switched from endogenous to exogenous. But this U-turn did not mean that the basic rules of a market economy would be put in place. The way towards progress dramatically changed but the same mechanism was retained to propel the country forward: the authoritarian leadership of the ever-present party-state.

The "model farmers". The "leftist wing" of the ruling party was blamed for Ethiopia's agricultural failures, and its members were expelled.[53] This group had advocated "detaching the farmer from commercialisation".[54] It was now felt that there was "an urgent need to change from this hand to mouth mode of production approach to a market led one".[55] The main goal was "to capture the private initiative of farmers" so as "to intensify the marketable farm products".[56] This was important because sufficient means were not available to support the poor farming masses: "We can't afford to give new technology to all of the 12 million rural households in Ethiopia," a high-ranking official declared later.[57] Even though "agriculture first" remained the driving slogan, it was not the same agriculture, nor the same peasants who were now the core target.

The priority now was to focus on the rural elite while abandoning the broader peasant masses to market forces: "Those who take advantage of them will prosper, and the rest will lose mercilessly."[58] The upper tier, now promoted to the role of "model farmers", would get the main thrust of public help (access to new techniques, training and fertilizers) and would be relatively free from the former party-state constraints so as to fully allow its entrepreneurial spirit to flourish. But in return it would have to join the ruling party, give up any sign of political opposition and thus neutralize local expressions of rural dissent. As a consequence the ruling party started to grow enormously, and has at present (2013) nearly five million members, compared with around 700,000 before 2005. Its triumphs in the local elections of 2008 and the general election of 2010 are evidence of how efficient this "neutralization process" has been.[59]

The financial tools. Since the dip of 2000–3, which was caused by the Eritrean-Ethiopian War and climate difficulties, economic growth has jumped to heights never before known in the country, with an annual rate of growth of at least 7.3 per cent over the last eight or nine years.[60]

This growth was fuelled by three financial resources: the national budget, international aid and diaspora remittances. Together, these represent about a third of GDP. Qualitatively speaking, the various administrative authorities used that money with a mixture of resolve, efficiency, integrity and clear-sightedness that had no equivalent anywhere else in Africa.

The developmental state fully played its role. Out of a federal budget representing roughly a fifth of GDP ($7.7bn[61] out of around $35bn estimated for the year 2012–13), roughly two thirds has been devoted to what the government calls "poverty reduction programmes", which mainly target rural areas. They are divided roughly into three equal parts: food security and agriculture; health and education; and basic infrastructure (mostly roads, with a smaller outlay on water and electricity). When the authorities and international donors say that few African governments, if any, have ever done so much for the peasantry, this is the absolute truth.

How was this financed? The budget contributed, but a lot of money was also "created" by widely opening up banking credit and by printing money. It worked, but the downside was the start of the inflation nightmare (see below). In addition, there was a fairly large amount of foreign aid. Following the repression that accompanied the 2005 election, donors briefly reduced their disbursement. But the aid that was withdrawn from direct lending to the federal state soon resumed through the back door of monetary transfers directly disbursed to regional authorities. In 2010 the Net Development Assistance received was around $3.5bn, roughly 12 per cent of GDP, and development finance represented around a third of the national budget. It had doubled during the course of the last five years.[62] The United States was the largest contributor, followed by the United Kingdom and the European Union.[63] In absolute terms, Ethiopia was the second-largest beneficiary of international aid, right behind Afghanistan. But, relative to population size, Ethiopia was among the lowest recipients in sub-Saharan Africa.[64] The Protection of Basic Services programme finances mainly schools (53 per cent), agriculture (21 per cent), health (15 per cent) and roads at the district (*woreda*) level, for a total amount of about $1bn a year, largely financed by donors.[65] The Productive Safety Net Programme handed out cash or "food for work" to seven or eight million Ethiopians, at a yearly cost of around $300m.[66]

As for the diaspora, which is estimated at an upper range of 1.5 to 2 million people (who live mostly in the United States), it provides an estimated gross yearly income in the vicinity of $20bn.[67] At first it only sent money to family and friends in the old country. But over the years it slowly began to take note of the incentives to invest and answer the siren calls that the regime was aiming at it. But being mostly close to the political opposition, the diaspora kept away from the EPRDF, both for political reasons and because it resented the heavily bureaucratic economic approach of the regime. But slowly things began to ease and the diaspora progressively moved into investing in a variety of businesses and building or purchasing retirement homes. A large amount of the building boom of these last few years seems to have been financed by diaspora money, in amounts that are still hotly debated, ranging from about $1bn (in the estimation of the National Bank of Ethiopia) to the much higher figure of more than $3bn (estimated by of the World Bank).[68]

Major achievements. The high level of these resources, combined with their efficient use, has led to the successes the government loves to boast about. Officially, Ethiopia has developed at an exceptional rate, with a 10.6 per cent average annual rate of growth between 2004 and 2011.[69]

The service sector has been the most dynamic sector. It represents today almost half of GDP (46 per cent in 2010), more than agriculture (which was 41 per cent in 2010). It is that sector's growth (13.8 per cent on average over the last seven years) that has fed the general growth.[70] The contribution of agriculture to global GDP has steadily shrunk. In 2004, out of the 11.7 per cent GDP growth, 2.4 per cent came from services and 7.7 per cent came from agriculture. But by 2011 these proportions had been inverted: of that year's 11.4 per cent GDP growth, 4.7 per cent came from agriculture and 5.3 per cent came from services.[71] The service sector has been mostly supported by growth in the financial sector, and in the real estate, hotel and tourism industries.[72] Tourism, which started from practically zero after years of war and instability, is steadily growing (around 600,000 visitors in 2012 provided an income of about $500m).[73]

But industry still lags behind. Its annual rate of growth looked quite high at 10 per cent over the last seven years; but this is a deceptive figure since it started from a very low baseline. The leading sectors are construction, electricity and water, but the manufacturing sector still constitutes barely 5 per cent of GDP.[74]

Expenditure on infrastructure goes mostly on road building, a key element in trade. Since 1991, Ethiopia's road density has expanded from 17 km per 1,000 km^2 to 48.1 per 1,000 km^2,[75] at a cost of nearly $3.6bn over the last ten years.[76]

Electrical production has multiplied by three from 700 Mw in 2005 to 2,000 Mw in 2010,[77] mostly through a steadily increasing use of the country's massive hydroelectric potential. The number of consumers connected grew from 800,000 in 2005, to more than 2 million in 2011.[78] But supply is still insufficient for a population of roughly 95 million and power cuts keep seriously hampering industrial production. There are giant projects in the offing, ranging from the Gibe III and IV dams on the Omo River (planned outputs: 1,870 and 2,000 Mw respectively) to the Grand Renaissance Dam on the Blue Nile (see below).

Telecoms are something of a mixed bag. While the growth of the sector has been important over the last ten years (Ethiopian Telecom Company serves 15 million subscribers), fixed line access (at 1 per cent of population) and internet access (at 0.9 per cent of population) are still way too low. Relative to population size, these figures are still the lowest among Sub-Saharan African countries (as of 2011).[79] In a display of the control mentality that tends to underscore all public policy in Ethiopia, the government has stubbornly refused to open the field to the private sector, arguing that private investors would neglect the rural areas, an explanation which hardly makes any sense.

The spheres of health and education have seen much more creditable achievements, with a net primary school enrolment rate of 86 per cent compared to 52 per cent five years ago.[80] 264,000 primary school teachers have been hired in 2005–9,[81] and 34,000 health extension workers were deployed, so that there should now be a minimum of at least two trained workers in every health post in every *kebele*.[82] The infant mortality rate has halved over the last twenty years and in rural areas nearly two thirds of the population now have access to drinking water, compared to 24 per cent in 2000.[83]

This progress is usually summarized by quoting one central statistic: the percentage of the population living below the poverty line ($0.6 per day) has decreased from 44 per cent ten years ago to 30 per cent (that is, from 28 to 25 million people). As with all these statistics, this should be taken carefully, but the general trend is there. The problem is that today, since inflation is hitting this group particularly hard, it may have halted or even reversed, and the absolute number of poor people might be on the increase again.

Agriculture is still lagging behind. Agriculture, which was supposed to be the engine of development, has had only a 9.2 per cent average rate of annual growth, lower than the GDP rate. In addition, its GDP share diminishes every year, having shrunk from 11.2 per cent in 2004–6 to 7.7 per cent in 2009–11. Its average annual contribution to GDP growth over the last seven years has been only 4.2 per cent.[84]

While there is no doubt that "the [Ethiopian government] appears committed to developing the largest agricultural extension system in Sub Saharan Africa",[85] the official figures measuring that effort are ambiguous. Quite clearly there have been large amounts of training. Around 50,000 Agricultural Extension Agents have taken up posts throughout almost all of the rural *kebeles*.[86] But there is a Farmer Training Centre in only one *kebele* out of two (a total of 9,000),[87] and these often do not have the necessary equipment that would allow them to fully play their role.[88] In addition, the use of modern agricultural inputs does not seem to have played the role it was supposed to. There are not enough selected seeds, fertilizers are sold at prohibitive prices and limited credit constrains their use. The problem is exacerbated by the fact that their massive cost does not always lead to productivity increases that would justify the expense.[89] Fertilizer use has gone up from 271,000 tons in 2003 to a little more than 400,000 tons in 2011, and less than half the farmers actually use it. Selected seeds, used in only 3 per cent of the cultivated land, stagnate at around 20,000 tons per year.[90] Nevertheless, if the official figures were correct, Ethiopia would have experienced the fastest "Green Revolution" in the world.

If we start with the surge of the economy in 2003, every crop year since then has been, at least according to the statistics, a "bumper harvest", outpacing the record set the previous year, whatever the climate. Cereal and pulse production increased from a range of 8 to 9 million tons at the end of the 1990s to 25 millions tons in 2012, a threefold increase[91]—a figure which is hard to believe. Coffee production has risen from 170,000 to 360,000 tons (in 2011) over the last ten years,[92] which makes Ethiopia the fifth largest producer in the world and the largest in Africa.

Ethiopia remains an essentially rural country. At 17 per cent, the proportion of Ethiopians living in urban areas is one of the lowest in Africa.[93] Agriculture still represents roughly half of GDP (46 per cent, compared to a 12 per cent average for sub-Saharan Africa).[94] Two thirds of agriculture's value comes from cereals and leguminous plants, and a fourth comes from cattle (Ethiopia has the largest herd on the continent, with slightly more than 100 million cattle, sheep and goat).[95] Agriculture employs 82 per cent of the active population and provides more than 85 per cent of exports.[96] 13 million households share 13 million hectares but over half (56 per cent) cultivate less than 0.5 ha each.[97] Demographic growth (2.6 per cent per year) and very high densities in fertile areas (over 500 people per km^2 on the plateau) contribute to permanent land hunger. Commercial farms (3 per cent of national production) are only playing a marginal role in terms of grain output but occupy an important role for sugar and coffee.[98]

Some of the lowest agricultural incomes in the world. To be realistic, the main cause of low agricultural production in Ethiopia is its very harsh natural environment. Erosion and soil exhaustion make the land less and less productive, particularly in the central highlands but also now, progressively, in the western and south-western peripheries, which used to produce a regular yearly surplus. Three fourths of the highlands have gradients of at least 30 per cent. Communities tend to be very isolated and the average walking time to an all-weather road is four hours.[99] Irrigation is rare (only 1.3 per cent of all cultivated lands are irrigated)[100] and the use of fertilizers is limited (about thirty kilos per cultivated hectare).[101] High yield seeds are rarely used. Most farmers have almost no capacity to invest in improvements, which makes for the perpetuation of primitive agricultural techniques. This results in very low productivity and high dependence on weather conditions. Too much or too little rain, falling too early or too late, and ordinary plant blights can all spell disaster. Global average yields for cereals (maize, wheat or *teff*)[102] are at around 16 quintals per hectare,[103] compared with 60 to 100 in developed economies. The net income of a "rich" peasant household[104] is around $1,000 per year. But in "poor" peasant households income, including self-consumed production, can be as low as $200 per year. Three fourths of the Ethiopians who are victims of severe poverty live in the countryside.[105]

Into the future

The Growth and Transformation Plan (GTP) (2010/11 to 2014/ 15).[106] "Above all, Meles' policies were delivering results".[107] Based on this simple assessment, the regime opted to shift not its approach but its targets. The Growth and Transformation Plan, which covers the years 2010/11 to 2014/15, displays ambition that could be seen as verging on hubris: it projects a base case scenario of an 11.2 per cent yearly rate of growth, and hopes for a 14.9 per cent rate (its high case scenario), that is, a doubling of GDP in five years. No country in the world has ever reached that performance in normal circumstances.

For agriculture, the aim is to more than double main crop production (+219 per cent). "We have devised a plan which will enable us to produce surplus and be able to feed ourselves by 2015 without the need for food aid," declared Prime Minister Meles Zenawi.[108] It is planned that export values for coffee will quadruple, oilseeds and flowers will triple, and pulses be multiplied by seven.

But the lion's share of the growth will go to industry, which the government expects to expand twice as fast as any other sector, at 21.3 per cent per year, ending with an annual increase of 27.9 per cent in 2015 (high case scenario). Its share of GDP should rise from around 13 per cent at present to at least 19 per cent in five years. So in terms of a political economy paradigm, the GTP exacerbates the reorientation that took place in the move from ADLI 1 to ADLI 2. Indeed, although national planners keep ritualistically mentioning that the future economy has to include a "modern and productive agricultural sector with enhanced technology", they now insist that industrialization has to play "a leading role". This means that exports should significantly contribute to growth: as a percentage of GDP they should more than triple in five years (from 10 per cent to 31 per cent). Implicitly (and sometimes explicitly), official documents point in the direction of a development strategy that would no longer directly target the most vulnerable Ethiopians. The improvement of their situation is now expected to be indirect, coming as a consequence of economic growth driven by other actors and sectors.

Particular attention is paid to small and medium-sized enterprises (SME): "they are the foundation for the establishment and expansion of medium and large scale industries, and open opportunities for employment generation, expansion of urban development, and provide close support for further agricultural development." One of the main aims is to create jobs for the 2 to 2.5 million young Ethiopians who arrive each year on the labour market and whom traditional agriculture cannot always employ.[109] The unemployment rate is steadily increasing. It was officially 9 per cent in 2000 and seems (unofficially) to have reached 20 per cent in 2010,[110] and is as high as 50 per cent among the young urban population.[111] Meanwhile annual growth in manufacturing jobs has been a modest 4 per cent over the last three years.[112]

Concerning infrastructure, the government's targets are: to double the rate at which it builds new roads; to build 2,400 km of railway lines; to increase output of hydro power by five times; to increase the number of users of mobile phones by four times; and to increase the number of internet customers by twenty times. In the social sector, the targets are: a 100 per cent primary school net enrolment rate; a doubling of the secondary school gross enrolment rate; a 2.5 per cent increase in university student numbers; drinking water access for 100 per cent of the population; and primary health services coverage for 100 per cent of the population. Total Poverty Head Count (as a percentage of population) should drop from 29 per cent to 22 per cent. The aim is to achieve all of this within five years.

The Grand Ethiopian Renaissance Dam (GERD). The symbol of the government's ambitions is the construction of the "Grand Ethiopian Renaissance Dam" on the Blue Nile. Its cost is estimated at $6bn, and the aim is to produce 5,250 Mw.[113] It will be the largest dam in

Africa and the tenth largest in the world. It will roughly triple Ethiopia's electricity production and will enable it to export power to Sudan and Egypt.

But the project has suffered from serious problems ever since it began. First, it created diplomatic tension with Egypt, which is worried about the dam's impact on the flow of water to the Egyptian Nile, an issue that is loaded with geopolitical danger. Second, the contract allocation formula is opaque. Third, there is an absence of serious impact studies. Finally, financing is lagging behind. All of this has left Ethiopia in a delicate and isolated position. A gigantic fundraising campaign has been undertaken under the slogan: "Ethiopians at home and abroad should come together for the realization of the Great Millennium Dam".[114] The public has been persistently asked to subscribe to governments bonds, which have a yield much lower than the inflation rate. All civil servants had to "voluntarily" give up one month's salary in 2011. Private banks have been ordered to contribute by giving 27 per cent of their loans to the government at the pitifully low interest rate of 3 per cent.[115] With these "below market rates figures, this is tantamount to a tax on banks, and ultimately households that deposit money in the banks."[116]

Can all this be taken at face value? The GTP seems to be in the spirit the Maoist Great Leap Forward. In spite very high rates of growth, the targets of the preceding two plans were far from having been achieved and the strategy of agricultural growth leading to industrialization was unsuccessful. But it seems that the regime's thinking was that higher targets—even if they are unrealistic—lead to a deeper and more radical mobilization and are therefore worth pursuing even if the hope of achieving them is dim.

Large land transfers: a golden opportunity? Since 2008 a process of large land transfers has been underway. The aim is to expand mechanized agriculture using foreign financial investment in order to increase the production of marketable exports.[117] The initial impetus was the government's realization that the rise in world agricultural prices and the growth in biofuel use had created a vast global demand for arable land. The Ethiopian periphery, populated by nomads and marginal ethnic groups conquered by the Abyssinians at the end of the nineteenth century, began to look like an El Dorado, with millions of "virgin" or "empty" or at least "under-utilized" hectares.[118] 3.5 million hectares have already been allocated, most of it to foreign investors, with some of them acquiring up to 500,000 hectares at a time.[119] The target was "to transfer nearly 3.3 million ha of land to commercial farming investors in a transparent and accountable manner" by 2015.[120] Investors from India and the Arabian Peninsula got most of it, followed by those from developed countries such as the United Kingdom, Italy, the US and Israel.[121]

The land was leased on a long-term basis for up to ninety-nine years at $1 per hectare per year at the beginning. The minimum lease has recently been raised to $8, still a very low figure.[122] By contract the land tenant acquires an unlimited right to water and underground resources. The expulsion and eventual compensation of residents is to be carried out by the Ethiopian government.[123] Contracts include generous tax exemptions and large credit facilities that are often linked to the proportion of produce that is exported. This shows that despite the government's claims to the contrary, this programme is not really aimed at working towards food self-sufficiency. The obligations of investors towards environmental protection and local infrastructure are often very slight. Moreover "there are no laws, regulations or directives in place that are clearly articulated to ensure benefit sharing between the investor and the public".[124] The state lacks the necessary tools for controlling these large operations, and "benefit sharing mechanisms as well as environmental and social safeguards are virtually absent".[125] Some observers have gone as far as to call this process "land grabbing" and even "the great land give away".[126] In their opinion "the damage done ... outweighs the benefits gained".[127] Finally, these critics highlight a central paradox in the land transfer policy:

> The government of one of the most vulnerable countries in the world is handing over vast land and water resources to foreign investors to help the food security efforts of their home countries, or to gain profits for their companies, without making adequate safeguards and without taking into account the food security needs of its own people.[128]

The authorities respond by talking about "win win agreements", made "on the basis of clearly set out lease arrangements ... to make sure everybody will benefit from this exercise".[129] Five benefits are usually mentioned: job creation, infrastructure development, technology transfers, growth of internal agricultural production, and improvement of the balance of payments through increased exports.

Only the future will tell whether these benefits will be realized. The GTP does not mention any expected figure for financial returns.

Average agricultural returns with exports of around 50 per cent of what is produced would bring returns of nearly $10bn yearly. Given the structurally weak balance of payments and a GDP of around $30bn, this revenue may look attractive, but only a marginal share of the money (the part of the earnings that are not transferable abroad) would actually remain in Ethiopian banks.

Then why is there such an enthusiasm on the part of the government? The deep underlying reasons can probably be found in the ongoing transformation of the former revolutionary leadership into an elite group, concentrating in its own hands not only political power but also economic assets.[130] And, strategically speaking, this "land grab" has probably been seen as a golden opportunity to achieve quickly the supreme target: that of inserting Ethiopia into the world market. To such criticisms, Areba Deressa, then Minister of Agriculture, simply answered: "We cannot afford to close our doors to the global economy."[131]

The potential of mining. The other domain where Ethiopia still retains a high potential for rapid growth is the mining sector. International demand is huge and there are funds ready to be invested. Even though hopes centred on oil and gas have never materialized for security reasons, gold has provided high returns with exports worth $485m in 2011,[132] a 1,000 per cent increase over the last ten years. Annual gold exports have now reached $550m and should soon exceed coffee exports. Considerable deposits of tantalum and phosphates have been discovered. The government has issued fifty-four exploration permits in 2011 compared to only fifteen in 2006. "The prospect of reaching $1.36bn in annual mining exports by 2014/15 (and $1.8bn for all minerals) is thus very much within the realm of the possible."[133]

The GTP's weaknesses and associated risks

There are three major weaknesses that make the GTP vulnerable.

(1) *The balance of trade.* Goods and services exports represented 11 per cent of GDP in 2010, against 15 per cent five years before.[134] They just provide enough money to pay for the oil import bill. The gross percentage of exports in relation to GDP is only one third of the Sub-Saharan average, down to one eighth if this proportion is calculated on a per capita basis.[135] Meanwhile imports represent 33 per cent of GDP,[136] resulting in a negative balance of trade amounting to around

one sixth of GDP, close to the whole national budget. This is evidently not sustainable. So the GTP's target is to triple the percentage of exports vis-à-vis GDP, while increasing the imports at a lower rate in order to bring the deficit down from 17 per cent to 15 per cent of GDP.[137] Ethiopia is landlocked and the use of Djibouti harbour, through which 90 per cent of external trade has to transit, is extremely expensive (at least one billion dollars a year if internal land transport costs are included).

To diminish this trade imbalance, the projected increase in agricultural exports—even if the potential results of the large-scale land transfers are considered—will not be enough. Coffee is still the main export product and the top foreign currency earner ($832m out of $2.8bn in total).[138] Oil seeds ($470m in export earnings for 2011) rank third,[139] *khat* ($236m)[140] is fourth and cut flowers ($170m)[141] are fifth.

The inadequacy of agricultural exports means that manufacturing will have to achieve a proportional increase. Prime Minister Meles Zenawi thus advocated "an export-led industrialisation strategy"[142] and the implementation of a classical import substitution strategy for primary consumption goods. Meles said: "To further enhance the foreign trade which is crucial to economic development, it is necessary to gradually transform the economic base from agriculture to industry".[143] The planned engines of this growth are gold, manufacturing, sugar[144] and electricity, whose combined export values should represent a higher return than the totality of present exports by 2015.[145] Exports of manufactured goods are expected to increase seven times,[146] leather exports 6.5 times and textile and garment exports, very low at present, should grow thirty times, all within five years. The latter sector's growth rests on its trump card: the low cost of its manpower, which is about a third of the Sub-Saharan African average. But per capita worker productivity is also much lower (about a third of the average).[147]

(2) *Financing*. The GTP sums the problem up by saying: "success in GTP requires high investment". In 2015 this should represent nearly one third of GDP: 31 per cent compared to 24 per cent in 2010. The biggest share will have to come from the government and state-owned enterprises.

The GTP government investment programs total some 407 billion Ethiopian birr.[148] In addition, there is 'off-budget financing' of infrastructure and industrial development programs, totalling 569 billion birr ... Projected investments for the GTP period add up to 976 billion birr [almost $60bn].[149]

The African Development Bank mentions $77bn as the sum required, of which 55 per cent needs to come directly from the government's budget.[150] Three main channels are foreseen to provide such an enormous amount of money.

(i) The first is internal. "The investment needs of the GTP could be mobilized by increasing communities' participation in effective domestic revenue collection, saving and resources utilization". There are calls "to enhance citizens' awareness about tax" through "mobilization". That way gross domestic savings should triple in five years, going from 5 per cent of GDP to 15 per cent in 2015; the ratio of tax revenue to GDP should double. But is this realistic? Bank deposits have gone down from 31 per cent of GDP a few years ago to 21 per cent today.[151] Even if we agree that tax collection is not up to par, there are now more and more instances of harassment of tax payers, to a point where the IMF now warns of "rising financial repression",[152] increasing feelings of uncertainty among economic actors. Is it possible to promote "a culture of saving" while the inflation rate is 39 per cent and banks are serving interest rates lower than inflation? This is a situation in which all Ethiopians who have savings are rushing to the real estate market.[153]

(ii) The second "solution" is simply to print money. This is what was done after the 2005 elections, with dire consequences for the inflation rate. In 2008 inflation peaked at 61.6 per cent in August, driven by 79.2 per cent inflation in food prices; similarly, inflation in 2011 reached 40.7 per cent and 40.2 per cent in August and September respectively, at a time when food price inflation reached almost 50 per cent.[154] Meles Zenawi had to admit that "the Central Bank has injected excess money into the market causing the inflation".[155] In 2011 the Central Bank "released" almost $3bn to finance public expenses.[156] Meanwhile, the volume of banking credit had grown by 36 per cent in one year.[157] The often mentioned "imported inflation" only represented 15 per cent of the total rate.[158] Inflation went up again to 36 per cent in March 2012,[159] reaching 45 per cent for food prices.[160] It slowed down to 23 per cent (25 per cent for food prices) in December 2012.[161] The birr is now overvalued and could be devalued at any time. The last devaluation (16.7 per cent in September 2011) brought it down to 17.28 to one US dollar.[162] At the current valuation of birr, the federal budget has jumped from 64bn birr ($5.6bn)[163] for 2009/10 to 138bn ($7.7bn)[164] for 2012/13. 79 per cent of this budget comes from internal resources, owing to a large tax increase, and 21 per cent comes from external loans and grants.[165] International aid is expected to increase. "The good relationship between the government and development partners and the government's established commitment to eradicate poverty are expected to encourage increased external resource inflows".[166] There are indications in this direction: in September 2012 the World Bank gave Ethiopia $1.15bn in interest-free credit[167] and in December offered another $4bn to be given over the next four years.[168]

But even if tax increases bring in as much as the government hopes, if Official Development Assistance remains at its present level there will still be a nearly $1.5bn gap in the budget.[169] Meanwhile, the government has promised to achieve single digit inflation by reducing fiduciary creation and cutting down on its borrowing from the Central Bank. But "the government has two options: either to print money or to cut back on its expenditures".[170] So in order to achieve record growth, it seems probable that inflation will be allowed to run its course.

(iii) The third source of finance is radical. "Private sector investment growth" is a leitmotiv in GTP documents. Particularly targeted countries are India,[171] China and Turkey. To attract them, thereby "creating an enabling environment for private sector investment growth",[172] is seen as a must, although the exact contents of this requirement have never been spelt out.

(3) *An "anaemic" private sector.* Basically, it has not reached lift-off stage. "The key to the GTP's success is the shift in the driver of growth from the public sector to the private sector ... But this formula does not seem to be working".[173] "The ambition of the statements [made by the authorities] has been matched neither by the performance of the private sector nor by the level of ambition of reforms to support the sector."[174] The formal private sector represents a small part of the economy, generating only 2.7 per cent of GDP and employing just 5.8 per cent of the workforce.[175] Industry is stuck at 14 per cent of GDP (compared to 30 per cent on average in Sub-Saharan Africa).[176] Foreign Direct Investments (FDI) net inflow is extremely volatile ($550m in 2006, less than $100m in 2009, $184m in 2010, $626m in 2011) and, even in 2011, represented only one sixth of the Sub-Saharan African

per inhabitant average.[177] (And the United Nations Conference on Trade and Development gives a completely different figure: $206m for 2011, around 6 per cent of the same average.) The FDI stock amounted to $4.4bn (2011), 1.2 per cent of Sub-Saharan African stock.[178]

How can we explain this "anaemia"? First and foremost by reference to the hegemony of public power, exerted through public and para-public enterprises and, paradoxically, through its role in guiding and backing the private sector.[179] The World Bank's *Doing Business Ranking* (2013) ranks Ethiopia 127th out of 185 countries (111th out of 182 in 2012),[180] towards the middle of Sub-Saharan African countries. "Ethiopia's ranking has not improved significantly over the past few years and the pace of reforms is slowing down."[181] The result is a dubious investment climate. There are six factors brought forth to explain this:

(i) Far from diminishing, state dominance—and more precisely the concentration of this dominance at the top of the party-state—is unabashedly increasing. "The equivalent of two-fifths of total economic activity will be linked to public sector activity in the coming years".[182] Taking into account the weight of traditional agriculture, which is not public sector-controlled, two thirds of the rest of the economy—that is, the modern economy—is "linked" to the public sector. As a result, in the words of Eyesus Worq Zafu, president of the Ethiopian Chamber of Commerce and Sectorial Association, "when private sector businesses are engaged in similar activities as public enterprises ... preference is given to government companies. The playing field is not level."[183] The US Embassy wrote: "state-owned enterprises have considerable advantages over private firms, particularly in the realm of Ethiopia's regulatory and bureaucratic environment, including ease of access to credit and speedier customs clearance."[184] State-owned companies have, for example, privileged access to government credit allocation. During the last six years, the amount of credit extended to state enterprises and parastatals has multiplied by eight.[185] "Roughly two-thirds of all banking system credit is now directed to the public sector."[186] This means a quasi-permanent credit crunch for the purely private sector. The *Doing Business 2013* report ranks the difficulty of obtaining credit at the very top of the hurdles any private business has to clear. Hence the emergence "of a significant parallel market in loans to business firms", in which "loan sharks" loan hundreds of thousands of dollars at annual rates of 30 per cent or more. But even those have only a limited outreach, given the fact that the volume of business "has to be based on personal confidence and trust".[187]

(ii) Another problem is that at the centre of the public sphere there is a small group of oligarchs who have become important actors on the economic scene and who operate hand in hand with the state. At the forefront is MIDROC Ethiopia,[188] a conglomerate owned by the half-Ethiopian Saudi billionaire Sheikh Mohammed Hussein Ali Al-Amoudi. *Forbes* ranks him as the 63rd richest person in the world. He owns the biggest gold mine in Ethiopia and is the country's exclusive gold exporter.[189] He plans to invest $3.4bn in Ethiopian industry and agriculture over the next five years.[190] Apart from the companies now run by EFFORT, 60 per cent of those that were privatized "have been awarded to Al-Amoudi related companies ... Al Amoudi is known to have close ties to the ruling TPLF/EPRDF regime, and rumours persist of favourable treatment."[191]

(iii) Far from limiting itself to the public and para-public sectors, the state is also very directive and intrusive in the genuine private sector. It has handpicked certain firms for support:

"The government appeared to be following a strategy of attempting to 'pick the winners' of the private sector development race."[192]

"[D]ecisions are taken within the confines of the government (or the ruling party) and are neither systematically evidence-based nor participatory nor transparent."[193]

"The government deliberately employs a carrot-and-stick approach that differentiates between economic activities and firms, up to the point where targets for individual firms are sometimes negotiated on a case-by-case basis in exchange for public support."[194]

As a consequence, the private sector is focused on those "pockets of vitality" that are opened by "government-affiliated projects".[195] These tend to be limited both in terms of sector and geography to where public support promises particularly high returns. As a consequence, much of the population is excluded from this particular growth, depriving it of sustainability. The examples of underdeveloped countries which have achieved very high rates of growth over the recent period, such as the Asian "small dragons", show "that rapid growth in the developing world has been invariably associated with diversification of production into manufacturing and modern services."[196]

(iv) Moreover, the regime is used to imposing "a slew of abrupt, challenging, and sometimes erratic regulatory changes".[197] Two examples: worried about the risk that unrest caused by hunger could lead to an Arab Spring-type uprising, Meles Zenawi suddenly and without any prior consultation announced a price cap on seventeen basic food commodities (4 January 2011). Chaos resulted since the taxed prices were often lower than the production costs of the products. A black market briefly appeared and the cap was lifted in June. With the same suddenness, the government announced that coffee could only be exported in bulk containers even though coffee traders worldwide exclusively use 60 kg bags (14 November 2011). Importers immediately stopped buying and producers complained that "the directive is completely impossible to work with". It was lifted on 15 December after tens of millions of dollars were lost in missed exports.

"It is not clear when firms are eligible to get preferential treatment in term of access to licenses, land, credit and foreign exchange, on what condition ailing firms will be bailed out, and whether these conditions vary between state-owned enterprises, firms affiliated with the ruling political parties, and independent private firms."[198] In Ethiopia, laws governing business are a complex jungle.[199] Any private entrepreneur knows that the administration can at any time fault him for some obscure violation, whether real or engineered by a rival firm or an official trying to extract a bribe. Going to court is a risky process because the very existence of the firm could be at stake. Potential investors would appreciate knowing better where they stand and what the rules of the game are. Transparency and long term sustainability are becoming more and more necessary.

(v) The best way for a private investor to protect himself from this type risk in dealing with the state is to acquire the protection of a high-ranking person. But even this is not an absolute safeguard since the entrepreneur's security will depend on the continued status of his protector.

(vi) Finally, whole sectors of the economy remain closed to foreign investment, particularly banking and telecommunications. Prime Minister Zenawi used to frequently repeat that "since we care ...

for our finally nascent businesses ... a free and open market in Ethiopia would be a challenge to our traders to compete with the elephants."[200]

There are two other factors also at play, in a more limited way. First, the quality of the administration is eroding. Its turnover is exceptionally high and "it seems that the government ... still values political loyalty higher than merit. There is a general perception that party affiliation and loyalty have become even more important since the 2005 events."[201]

Secondly, corruption remains limited and the general financial behaviour of the civil service is quite far from the usual predatory behaviour of African administrations, but this is slowly changing. In spite of the creation of the Ethiopian Ethics and Anti Corruption Commission, Ethiopia, which in 2010 was ranked 59th (in ascending order of perceived corruption) out of 102 countries in the *Corruption Perception Index* of Transparency International, ranks today 113th out of 174 and 23rd out of 47 African countries.[202] According to Global Financial Integrity, Ethiopia's illicit financial flows were worth $5.6bn in 2010, and the average per year between 2001 and 2010 has been $1.7bn.[203] The most frequent scam is export over-invoicing, while about a third of corruption is attributable directly to state administration. The 2010 figure, however, represents 18 per cent of GDP, a percentage that casts doubt on its reliability. But clearly corruption becomes an "increasing challenge" when "rapid economic growth is coupled with significant government intervention in the management of the economy".[204] This new phenomenon is casting a shadow on Ethiopia's famed administrative honesty, which up to now had been a big plus in the eyes of international donors.

The risk of a "poor productivity trap". All these various distortions accentuate the separation between two economies, one that is either part of the power structure (public and parastatal companies) or operating within its orbit (the new oligarchs), and one that is independent and pays a price for this. The "privileged" sector could reach yearly returns on investment as high as 50 per cent or 60 per cent, thus creating a structural rent which contradicts the government's proclaimed aim to combat "rent seekers". The disadvantaged sector, divided into a multitude of small and medium-sized enterprises, experiences the greatest difficulties in developing, even with projects that are really profitable, which might give a rate of return on investment of 30 per cent per annum.[205]

This duality seems inscribed in stone. A recent study indicates that not even one of the fifty leading industrial firms in Ethiopia started as a small firm.[206] The bias in resource allocation and regulation means that not only is there an abyss separating the large-scale elite and the struggling mass of small businesses, but also that the small ones can hardly be reliable partners for the big ones. They cannot face what economists coyly call "transaction costs". Private independent Ethiopian entrepreneurs "do not have the deep pocket to deal with such costs".[207] In the successful Asian economies, which the Ethiopian authorities like to parade as examples, there is a pattern "characterized by a dense web of firms, with many small and medium-sized enterprises linking up with a relatively small number of large firms ... One key reason why Ethiopian manufacturers lag behind their competitors in China and Vietnam is the absence of extensive subcontracting networks and clustering."[208]

The second consequence of this structural rent cushioning the public sector is that not only does it prevent efficient resource allocation in an environment of relative scarcity, but it also "hinders open and fair competition".[209] In a market economy, such competition is the engine of innovation and productivity. Lacking these two factors, enterprises tend not to be very productive. Furthermore, since the protected sector is largely free from competition, increasing productivity does not rank very high in its order of priorities. The danger is that Ethiopia might lock itself in a "poor productivity trap".[210] Even if the cost of its manpower is only one third of that of China, its productivity is six or seven times less. "Without effective competition, it is almost certain that Ethiopia's productivity growth will remain slow. That is not a viable strategy."[211]

Given that there are few natural resources apart from land and hydropower potential, that the population is very large but has a very low purchasing power, and that the country is landlocked, the hopes for rapid industrialization, key to the GTP's success, are in fact "dim".[212] The IMF, in an internal note co-signed by the International Development Association, extended a formal warning:

> The main concerns stem from heavy financing needs that have not been secured, insufficient prioritisation, and the limited role envisaged for the private sector [as well as] ... [h]igh and rising inflation ... Financing needs for the public sector will likely crowd out private sector credit on the domestic side and strain debt sustainability on the external side.[213]

The note recommends, *inter alia*, "to prioritize public sector investment based on rigorous cost-benefit analysis ... promote competition ... contain inflation ... and improve data quality". Some of the GTP goals are described as "unrealistic",[214] and the plan in general is considered to be over-ambitious and even dangerous. These international organizations recommend more realistic targets and assorted means of implementation to aim at an annual growth rate of 6 to 8 per cent. Such results would in any case be quite remarkable.

An obsession with control. In a recent study the International Food Policy Research Institute (IFPRI) has evaluated the Agricultural Extension System.[215] It pointed out a series of missing elements—material, technical and human—but argued that "most of all, the farmers in Ethiopia need to be able to make decisions, voice demand, and play a part in developing extension's priorities and evaluating its outcomes—in short, they need empowerment".

Mutatis mutandis, the same requirement seems to be applicable to all other economic agents. The government, following what has always been the dominant trend in Abyssinian power relations, seems to find it extremely difficult to tolerate the autonomy of economic actors, even within the framework of a market economy. It tends to adhere to a systemic view of tutelage, including for private agents.

> Discipline and control are the main features of Ethiopia's national ideology. The question is a lack of bottom-up feedback, the tendency to only pass 'good news' to the rulers ... which may be the biggest blind spot for Ethiopia ... A system that is long on top-down discipline and control may be strong ... but it may be 'brittle,' as it is short on ability to adapt; it could break down when faced with a major crisis ... The country will need to expand the space in which different ideas are debated vigorously, to forge and sustain a national vision.[216]

Meles Zenawi reacted abruptly and closed this debate by saying: "Nobody can impose neo-liberal views on Ethiopia".[217]

Conclusion: is this an insuperable paradox?

The growth rate of Ethiopia is steadily declining, from around 11 per cent in 2004 to around 7 per cent in 2013. A recent IMF report projected Ethiopia's growth for the coming year at 5 per cent, less than the Sub-Saharan African average.[218] After tense discussions with the Ethiopian authorities, this figure has not been adopted in subsequent reports. There is still a paradox which seriously threatens the very aims of the nation's economic policy. On one hand, the ruling power is trying to achieve a high degree of economic growth in order to ensure its legitimacy—a way to enhance its durability. It proclaims that the only viable strategy to reach this goal is to integrate Ethiopia into the world market. This requires massive private investment. On the other hand, its behaviour is calculated to keep the party-state in a command position. It disdains the very tenets and essential rules that it would need to respect in order to achieve this integration.

What will private investors do? Will they consider that the high return they could get in Ethiopia outweighs all the obstacles they have to face which are absent elsewhere? Or will the regime try to overcome this paradox? If so, the kind of governance which has prevailed in Ethiopia for centuries would need a paradigmatic shift, amounting to no less than a cultural revolution. That is hard to envision, not least because making it effective would require weakening the public and parastatal sectors, key elements of political hegemony which bring huge material benefits for those at the top of the power structure. The future of the Ethiopian economy depends as much on the political and even cultural order of society as on a certain level of economic performance.

[January 2013]

Addendum: The Ethiopian economy at the end of the GTP 2010–14

The international media are in the process of transforming their coverage of Ethiopia. Media "buzz" now comes not from poverty or famine but from the proliferation of skyscrapers in Addis Ababa, the opening of clothing factories and the new cultivation of thousands of acres of arable land by Chinese, Arab, Indian and Turkish investors, without forgetting to mention the Grand Ethiopian Renaissance Dam, soon to be the largest hydroelectric dam in Africa. After the "Asian Tigers" it would seem we now have an "African Lion".[219]

It is true that the economy continues to register remarkable successes. But their pace is steadily decreasing because they were achieved through the developmental state, a concept whose centralized statist engine is finding it harder and harder to drive by itself the whole economic system. Nevertheless, the Ethiopian regime does not consider changing course because, in spite of its resounding declarations, it does not want to (or perhaps cannot) have recourse to an essential auxiliary engine, the private sector.

Economic statistics have to be taken with an increasingly large pinch of salt. The regime has reported an average annual GDP growth rate of at least 10 per cent over the last ten years. Even though it admits a slight reduction—to 9.7 per cent—for 2013, it forecasts 11.3 per cent growth in 2014 and at least that much, if not more, for the coming period. Financial institutions offer more sober estimates: a 3 per cent rate of growth over the last ten years and 6 to 7 per cent for the next three to five years.[220]

If the regime's statistics are accurate, Ethiopian farmers continue to achieve miraculous results in spite of climate problems. The yearly increase of their output has never been less than 5 per cent and the next "great crop" is supposed to produce 25.4 million tons of cereals, pulses and oil seeds—10 per cent more than the previous one.[221] Total agricultural production would have thus nearly doubled in ten years. That over eight million Ethiopians still need food aid to survive can be attributed to marginal poverty. But the causes and processes that have resulted in this remarkable apparent increase in productivity remain unexplained. Nor is there an explanation for the fact that food prices are increasing faster than the general rate of inflation,[222] or for Ethiopia remaining a net cereal importer and one of the main food aid recipients in the world.[223] Unless, that is, we turn to a fact that is discreetly mentioned at the end of an official report: "There are annual losses of up to 30 per cent post-harvest".[224] This colossal figure is left unexplained and bears no relationship to the general figures given for the rest of the productive process.

As for the general increase in agricultural production, it bears no causal relationship to the land leasing—or, as we have seen it dubbed, "land grabbing"—that the government hopes will see the new cultivation of nearly seven million acres by 2015. The results are highly contentious but even the Prime Minister has had to admit that only about 20,000 acres are at present under cultivation[225] and that the whole programme needs to be completely reframed. There are many reasons for this fiasco: the programme has been rushed, not enough preliminary studies were done, the distances between the fields and the administrative centres are prohibitively large, logistical costs are high, local populations are often hostile, foreign investors have proved unreliable and potential local investors have been passive, preferring to speculate on the price increase of their own landholdings. Some of the 400 Saudi investors who had pledged $3bn altogether—a highly dubious figure—

seem ready to withdraw because they can't get dependable support from the Saudi Kingdom Agricultural Development Fund.[226] There have been other mishaps. The Indian company Karuturi recently discovered that three fourths of the 220,000 acres it had rented were flooded for six months of the year.

As for the villageization process (regrouping local populations to make room for investors), it has caused a strong (at times armed) opposition as well as foreign hostility, which embarrasses some of the major donors such as the United States Agency for International Development (USAID), the World Bank and Britain's Department for International Development (DFID). These investors were slated to "bring in desperately needed foreign currency"[227] and it was hoped that they could boost the level of agricultural exports to $6bn by 2015, the planned date of GTP termination. But their overall results in 2013 only reached $3bn, a 2 per cent regression from 2012 figures.

This downward trend continues, mostly because "the nation's competitiveness has dropped sharply".[228] The fall in global coffee and gold prices (Ethiopia's first and fourth largest export items respectively) has played a role. But the commercial balance deficit is now about 20 per cent of GDP, instead of 5 per cent when the EPRDF came to power.[229] The current account deficit is increasing ($3bn, 7 per cent of GDP) and so is the external debt ($11bn).[230] At a little more than $3bn, external aid represents nearly half the current budget.[231] After a 6 per cent dip in the spring of 2013, inflation is again on the increase (8.8 per cent in March 2014).[232] As a result, it is now becoming evident that most of the GTP targets will not be achieved, something which was predictable given their exaggerated optimism.

But these failures should not divert from a major success: Ethiopia's rate of growth remains one of the highest in Africa and it is now drawing more and more attention from foreign investors. But achieving the official GTP target—turning Ethiopia into a middle income country by 2025—will need a sustained rate of economic growth, and the accompanying target, poverty reduction, presupposes success in achieving a modicum of labour intensive growth, which is not yet in sight.

The active population grows by 3.5 per cent per year, one of the highest rates in Africa, and unemployment among the working age population has increased sharply since 2005. Unemployment among the active population ranges between 19 and 36 per cent, depending on which source is consulted.[233]

Therefore it is probable that the present GTP will more modestly mark an economic transition: moving from an agriculture-led economy to an industry-led one. Yet even this transition is still somewhat in doubt. The media have focused on the new clothing factories that have appeared around Addis, but these are in fact sweatshops which are taking advantage of a workforce paid between $40 and $50 per month—less than workers in Bangladesh. *The Economist* even published an article entitled "Manufacturing in Africa: An Awakening Giant",[234] in reference to Ethiopia. The title might be somewhat exaggerated. During the first three years of the GTP the share of agriculture in GDP decreased from 45.6 per cent to 43 per cent, while services remained stable at 45 per cent and industry grew from 10.6 per cent to 12 per cent (in comparison, in the rest of Africa industry accounts for between 10 and 14 per cent of GDP).[235] But while industry was supposed to boost exports, it contributes only 9 per cent of Ethiopia's total exports, and it represents just 3 per cent of jobs compared to agriculture's 78 per cent.[236] Industrial employment has gone down by around a third over the last five or six years and its productivity is lower than that of agriculture.

The engine of growth remains services—mostly trade and real estate—which are far ahead of manufacturing. But we have to keep in mind that "apart from a few tax havens, there is no country that has attained a high standard of living on the basis of services alone".[237]

The authorities were counting on a foreign capital influx, and foreign investors were welcomed and treated with special favour. But net foreign direct investments grew by a billion dollars in 2013, which is less than 3 per cent of GDP, and only $627m in 2012 and $288m in 2011. If we look at these figures within the context of East Africa, this $1bn growth is five times less than that in Mozambique and about at the level of Madagascar. If we take the figure as relative to population size, Ethiopia's 2013 increase is just 25 per cent of the continental average.[238]

The obstacles remain the usual ones: the difficulty of accessing finance, logistical problems, taxation, bureaucratic red tape and corruption. The constant power failures and the inefficient telephone system are a constant grind. Of late the main question has been to try to understand why national investors do not want to invest. This is because during the last ten years investment has been carried out by the state (about 18 per cent of GDP),[239] which has mostly financed the big GTP public work programme (whose cost is estimated today at $57bn).[240] Four fifths of the money came from national sources: taxes (even though they are very low compared to the African average), so-called "voluntary contributions", borrowing and inflationary money creation. Meanwhile savings are down, with domestic savings at their lowest level in thirty years at 6 per cent of GDP.[241] This is quite under-standable since interest rates paid to depositors stand at around 5 per cent, much less than the inflation level.

Because of lack of liquidity, public enterprises siphon off the little credit left. Out of the $2.5bn given to the market, public enterprises received 83 per cent, compared to 17 per cent for private investors.[242] "The public investment rate of Ethiopia is the third highest in the world, while the private investment rate is the sixth lowest."[243] Consequently, the consolidated budget deficit is nearly 10 per cent of GDP, a hardly sustainable rate, creating a sharp credit crunch.[244]

Faced with such unfair competition, private entrepreneurs shun the manufacturing sector because it requires too high a level of investment. Instead they put their money into services, which require less invest-ment and give a faster and higher rate of return. "The failure to achieve the target set (by the GTP) for the manufacturing sector is primarily attributable to the negligible involvement of local investors in the sec-tor."[245] This is a major failure since only they can create the vast net-work of labour intensive small scale enterprises that is needed. The IMF representative in Addis Ababa recently declared: "I don't think Ethiopia will reach its goal of joining the middle income group of countries without first giving more space to the private sector".[246] This position is common among most market-oriented observers of the Ethiopian economy, and some see it as an ideological position.

Meles Zenawi, who died in August 2012, used to say that "neo-lib-eralism" would not dictate Ethiopian economic choices. Today his suc-cessors avoid the problem by asking for time. "Achievements in infra-structural investments can show us that structural transformation may not be far away ... Our focus is on transformation not just growth," declared Abraham Tekeste, the State Minister for Finance and Economic Development. But in what does this transformation consist? Is the move only from agriculture towards industry, or does it also involve a shift in emphasis from the public sector to the private sector? Once more, if there is an answer to be found, one has to look at poli-tics as well as economic conditions.

Since the death of Meles Zenawi, the top part of the power structure has exploded into a multiplicity of competing centres. All of them affect total loyalty towards the dead man's memory and political line because all are afraid that deviating from that line would open them up to attacks from a coalition of competing enemies.

Business as usual is taken care of but nobody dares to confront the major contradiction of the economic situation: the constant proclamation that the market economy is the only way towards development and the consistent refusal to play by its rules. Ethiopia at present is like a ship without a skipper, with a respectful but passive crew and a faltering engine. If we look at the first discussions about the next five-year plan, we can see no change in sight.

[May 2014]

BIBLIOGRAPHY AND FURTHER READING

Access Capital, 2011, *Ethiopia: Macroeconomic Handbook 2011/2012*, 30 December, 2011, Addis Ababa: Access Capital.

Aklog Birara, 2010, *Ethiopia's Endemic Poverty that Globalization Can't Tackle but Ethiopians Can*, Salt Lake City: Signature Books.

―――― 2011, *Ethiopia: The Great Land Giveaway (Yemeret neteka ena)*, Salt Lake City: Signature Book Printing.

Altenburg, T., 2010, *Industrial Policy in Ethiopia*, Discussion Paper, German Development Institute, Feb. 2010.

Aregawi Berhe, 2009, *A Political History of the Tigray People's Liberation Front (1975–1991)*, Los Angeles: Tsehai Publishers.

Ayele Kuris, 2006, *The Ethiopian Economy: Principles and Practices*, Addis Ababa: Commercial Printing Press.

Ayelech Tiruwha Melese and Helmsing, A.H.J., 2010, "Endogenisation or Enclave Formation? The Development of the Ethiopian Cut Flower Industry", *Journal of Modern African Studies*, 48 (1), pp. 35–66.

Clapham, Christopher, 2009, "Post-War Ethiopia: The Trajectories of Crisis", *Review of African Political Economy*, 36 (120), pp. 181–92.

CSA, 2012. Central Statistical Authority, *Agriculture in Figures—Key Findings of the 2008/9 2010/11 Agricultural Sample Surveys for all Sectors and Seasons*, Addis Ababa: CSA.

Davis, K. et al., 2010, *In-Depth Assessment of the Public Agricultural Extension System of Ethiopia and Recommendations for Improvement*, IFPRI Discussion Paper 01041.

De Waal, Alex, 2013, "The Theory and Practice of Meles Zenawi", *African Affairs*, 112 (446), pp. 148–55.

Dessalegn Rahmato, 2009, *The Peasant and the State. Studies in Agrarian Changes in Ethiopia 1950s-2000s*, Addis Ababa University Press.

—— 2011a, *Land To investors: Large-scale Land Transfers in Ethiopia*, Addis Ababa: Forum For Social Studies.

—— 2011b, *Understanding Land Investment Deals in Africa—Country Report Ethiopia*, Oakland, CA: The Oakland Institute.

EPRDF, 1993, *Our Revolutionary Democratic Goals and The Next Step*, internal document of the EPRDF, June 1993.

—— 2006: *Development, Democracy and Revolutionary Democracy*, August 2006. This internal EPRDF document is believed to have been drafted by Meles Zenawi himself.

—— 2007: *Strategy of Revolutionary Democracy, Tactics and the Question of Leadership*, January 2007. This internal EPRDF document is believed to have been drafted by Meles Zenawi himself.

Eshetu Chole, 1994, "Opening Pandora's Box: Preliminary Notes on Fiscal Decentralisation in Ethiopia", *Northeast African Studies*, 1 (1) (new series), pp. 7–30.

Ezega, 2012, "Ethiopia: Tourism Income Increasing Substantially", 26 February, http://www.ezega.com/news/NewsDetails.aspx?Page=news&NewsID=3224 (last access Jan. 2013).

Ezekiel Gebissa, 2004, *Leaf of Allah: Agricultural Transformation in Harerge (Ethiopia) 1875–1991*, Oxford: James Currey.

Food and Agriculture Organization of the United Nations, 2014, "The State of Food and Agriculture 2014", http://www.fao.org/publications/sofa/en/ (last access November 2014).

Geiger, Michael and Moller, Lars Christian, 2013, *Ethiopia—Second Economic Update: Laying the Foundation for Achieving Middle Income Status*, Washington, DC: World Bank.

Hall, R., 2010, "The Many Faces of the Investor Rush in Southern Africa: Towards a Typology of Commercial Land Deals", Working Paper No. 2, Institute for Critical Agrarian Studies (ICAS) and Land Deal Politics Initiative (LPDI), The Hague: Institute of Social Studies. http://www.tni.org/sites/www.tni.org/files/Hall%20ICAS%20WP%202.pdf (last access May 2014).

HRW, 2011. Human Rights Watch report: *Forced Relocations Bring Hunger, Hardship*, 17 January 2011.

—— 2012. Human Rights Watch report: *"Waiting Here for Death": Displacement and "Villagization" in Ethiopia's Gambella Region*, January 2012.

IDA-IMF, 2011, International Development Association and International Monetary Fund, *The Federal Democratic Republic of Ethiopia: Poverty Reduction Strategy Paper—Joint Staff Advisory Note on the Growth and Transformation Plan 2010/11–2014/15*, IMF Country Report, No. 11/303, October 2011, Washington, DC.

IMF, 2012, *Country Report No. 12/287*, International Monetary Fund, October 2012.

Kar, Dev and Freitas, Sarah 2012, *Illicit Financial Flows From Developing Countries: 2001–2010*, Global Financial Integrity, December 2012.

Lefort, René, 1981, *Ethiopia: The Heretical Revolution*, London: Zed Press.

———— 2007. "Powers—*Mengist*—and Peasants in Rural Ethiopia: the May 2005 Elections", *Journal of Modern African Studies*, 45 (2).

———— 2009, "Ethiopia's Famine: Deny and Delay", *Open Democracy Website*, 24 March 2009, http://www.opendemocracy.net/article/email/ethiopias-famine-deny-and-delay (last access May 2014).

———— 2010, "Power—*Mengist*—and Peasants in Ethiopia: the Post-2005 Interlude", *Journal of Modern African Studies*, 48 (3).

———— 2011, "The great Ethiopian land-grab: feudalism, leninism, neo-liberalism ... plus ça change...", *Open Democracy Website*, 31 December 2011. http://www.opendemocracy.net/ren%C3%A9-lefort/great-ethiopian-land-grab-feudalism-leninism-neo-liberalism-plus-%C3%A7-change (last access May 2014)

Martins, Pedro, 2014, *Structural Change in Ethiopia. An Employment Perspective*, World Bank, Policy Research Working Paper 6749.

Meles Zenawi, 2006, *African Development: Dead Ends and New Beginnings*. Internal EPRDF document August 9th 2006.

Ministry of Agriculture and Rural Development, 2010, *Ethiopia's Agricultural Sector Policy and Investment Framework (PIF) 2010–2020*, Addis Ababa.

MOFED, 2006. *Ethiopia: Building on Progress. A Plan for Accelerated and Sustained Development to End Poverty (PASDEP)*, Ministry of Finance and Economic Development, Addis Ababa, September 2006.

———— 2010a, *Performance Evaluation of the First Five Years Development Plan (2006–2010) and the Growth and Transformation Planning (GTP) for the Next Five Years (2011–15)*, Ministry of Finance and Economic Development, July 2010.

———— 2010b, *Growth and Transformation Plan 2010/11–2014/15*, Ministry of Finance and Economic Development, Addis Ababa, November 2010.

MoPED, 1993, *An Economic Development Strategy for Ethiopia. A Comprehensive Guidance & a Development Strategy for the Future*, Addis Ababa, September 1993.

National Bank of Ethiopia, *Annual Report 2010–2011*, Addis Ababa www.nbe.gov.et/publications/annualreport.html (last access May 2014).

Oakland Institute, 2011, *Understanding Land Investment Deals in Africa— Country Report: Ethiopia*, 2011.

Ohashi, Ken, 2009, "Is Ethiopia in a low productivity trap?," *Addis Fortune*, 4 December 2009.

———— 2011a, "The 'Middle Way' to GTP Implementation", *Addis Fortune*, 22 May 2011.

———— 2001b, "National Ideologies, National Blinders", *Addis Fortune*, 12 June 2011.

Pankhurst, Alula and Piguet, François, 2009, *Moving People in Ethiopia: Development, Displacement & the State*, Oxford: James Currey.

Paulos Milkias, 2003, "Ethiopia, the TPLF, and the Roots of the 2001 Political Tremor," *Northeast African Studies*, 10 (2), New Series, pp. 13–66.

Serneels, P., 2004, *The Nature of Unemployment in Urban Ethiopia*, Centre for the Study of African Economies, Oxford University, CSAE WPS/2004–01. Available at: http://economics.ouls.ox.ac.uk/13265/1/2004–01text.pdf (last access May 2014).

Spielman, D. J., 2011, *Seed, Fertilizer, and Agricultural Extension in Ethiopia*, ESSP II Working Paper 020.

Sutton, J. and Kellow, N., 2010, *An Entreprise Map of Ethiopia*, International Growth Centre.

Tewodaj Mogues et al., 2011, *The Wealth and Gender Distribution of Rural Services in Ethiopia. A Public Expenditure Benefit Incidence Analysis*, Washington DC, International Food Policy Research Institute, IFPRI Discussion Paper 01057.

UN, 2007, *Industrial Development for the 21st Century: Sustainable Development Perspectives*, UN, Department of Economic and Social Affairs, 2007.

────── 2012, *World Investment Report 2012: Towards a New Generation of Investment Policies*, New York and Geneva: July.

UNICEF, 2010, "In rural Ethiopia, health extension workers bring care to new mothers", 6 August, http://www.unicef.org/infobycountry/ethiopia_55449. html (last access Jan. 2013).

Ventures, 2012, "The Ethiopian Billionaire: Sheikh Mohammed Al Amoudi", 20 July, http://www.ventures-africa.com/2012/07/the-ethiopian-billionaire-sheikh-mohammed-al-amoudi/ (last access Jan. 2013).

World Bank, 2009, *Ethiopia: Towards the Competitive Frontier: Strategies for Improving Ethiopia's Investment Climate*, World Bank Report No. 48472-ET, June 2009.

────── 2010, *Rising Global Interest in Farmland. Can it Yield Sustainable and Equitable Benefits?* 7 September 2010.

────── 2012a, *Ethiopia at a glance*, 29 March 2012.

devdata.worldbank.org/AAG/eth_aag.pdf (last access January 2013).

────── 2012b, *Country Partnership Strategy for the Federal Democratic Republic of Ethiopia*, World Bank and International Monetary Fund, Report No. 71884-ET, August 2012.

────── 2012c, *Ethiopia Economic Update—Overcoming Inflation, Raising Competitiveness*, Washington, DC: World Bank.

World Bank and the International Finance Corporation, 2013, *Economy Profile: Ethiopia—Doing Business 2013—Smarter Regulations for Small and Medium Size Enterprises*, 2013, Washington, DC: World Bank.

Young, John, 1997, *Peasant Revolution in Ethiopia. The Tigray People's Liberation Front 1975–1991*, Cambridge University Press.

15

ADDIS ABABA AND THE URBAN RENEWAL IN ETHIOPIA

Perrine Duroyaume

Ethiopian towns are often resumed by the quick sketch of a paradoxical country of high population density with 82 million inhabitants but weak urbanization with only 16.5 per cent city dwellers.[1] But we should also pay attention to the high urban growth rates, some 3.49 per cent[2] in the 2005–10 period, with increased growth forecast in the next twenty years.

The current urban development of Ethiopian towns is inscribed in the context of spectacular economic growth with an annual GDP growth of 11 per cent[3] in the 2006–10 period, which has largely benefited the service sector. However, this economic miracle raises questions. The current government has for long decreed the development and modernization of agriculture a national priority, and in the face of a lack of a clear urban policy, cities did not see significant investment throughout the 1990s: they are neglected, reports speak of underdevelopment of spaces under pressure from resumed rural-urban migration. Urban centres are similar to shantytowns and present a run-

395

down aspect. In the last ten years, the Ethiopian authorities have broadcast a change of heart and new orientations have taken shape that favour urban development. The city is a space to invest (in) and reconstruct: preoccupations about the state of cities are shared by all and current policy aims at modernization of urban infrastructure so that theses spaces may fully enjoy their role in the emergence of a liberalized economy. Urban policies have been more determined since 2005 and are underscored by a strong return of the power of the state to the urban field.

The case of Addis Ababa, a capital city that has just turned one hundred, and is still very influenced by its urban heritage, illustrates the radical dimension of the transformations underway. What will be the price of the transformation of a poorly equipped city, with village-like qualities, into an international capital, a competitive metropolis? What are the mechanisms that enable the Ethiopian authorities to undertake urban works, to finance roads and dwellings? Being both the stage of politics and a city in the turmoil of urban dynamics, Addis Ababa, the "New Flower", offers a sketch for an Ethiopian urbanization model in which economic growth must provide answers to the underlying poverty.

Capitals in the history of Ethiopia

An urban history of Ethiopia would first feature Axum, Lalibela and Gondar, political and religious centres whose names symbolize important phases in the history of the Christian kingdom. After the decline of the Gondar period, the nineteenth century was marked by territorial conquests and the changing alliances of the Kings of Kings (Tewodros II, Yohannes IV and Menelik II), confronted with the obligation of defending and stabilizing an empire coveted by the Western powers at the peak of their colonial expansion. The control and subjugation of the provinces demanded that the sovereign and his troops often sojourned there. The seat of power was nomadic. These mobile capitals were similar to military camps, often situated in militarily defensive positions.[4] After occupying the sites of Ankober and Entoto, Menelik II decided to fix the seat of power: the creation of Addis Ababa in 1886 ushered Ethiopia into contemporary urban history and contributed to the state modernization project.[5] The creation of an urban network centred on the capital began partially at the end of the nineteenth century, with the territorial unification policy. The conquests undertaken in the southern provinces went hand in hand with the establishment of military garrisons, the *ketema*, where a petty bourgeoisie of the administration's civil servants and local traders was concentrated. At the centre of these new urban links, Addis Ababa, the "New Flower", was founded to endow the empire with a visible power base recognized both nationally and internationally.

Situated to the south of the Christian highlands, at a strategic crossroads opening onto the Rift Valley, Addis Ababa rapidly came to dominate the political and economic landscape. As early as 1890 it had the infrastructure demanded by the foreign delegations, such as international class hotels and banking establishments.[6] On the eve of the twentieth century, the project of a railway linking the capital to the port of Djibouti was launched with the support of France, the main investor; the line was inaugurated in 1917. It consolidated Ethiopia's trade and encouraged the industrialization of the country and its supplies. Having barely emerged from the fields, Addis Ababa was given a role on the international political scene by establishing the claim of an empire capable of opening up to modernity.

In domestic politics, the permanent seat of power attracted provincial lords, *ras* and *dejazmach*, who set themselves up on large plots next to the palace. The emperor, the official holder of all lands, sought the allegiance of high dignitaries by offering them advantageous plots situated close to his palace. A whole society organized itself around the life of the court: servants, traders, craftsmen, and soldiers made up the first population of Addis Ababa. They made houses on the slopes and at the bottom of the ravines, the high grounds being reserved to the residences of the dignitaries.[7]

The capital became a unique setting in a largely rural country and never ceased attracting more and more migrants, integrating themselves into neighbourhoods defined by provincial origin. Addis Ababa experienced a heady growth, which intensified in periods of political and food crisis.[8] While generating a climate of instability, the Italian occupation from 1936 to 1941 consolidated urban networks. Road building, one of the largest infrastructure projects undertaken by the Italians, facilitated transport and the city became a more and more accessible space, family and ethnic solidarity guaranteeing to newcomers a first port of call.

Addis Ababa on the eve of the revolution

From the 1960s onwards Ethiopia sought to invest in industry and to develop a modern economy. Cities became spaces to organize and the first master plans conceived at the end of the 1950s projected an urban ideal promised by the country's industrial and economic success.[9] Addis Ababa magnified the setting of imperial power and the city transformed itself to welcome new infrastructure and monumental administrative buildings such as the City Hall, dominating Churchill Avenue. Universities, and hotels catering to the diplomatic and business community, gave the city the aspect of an open and modern capital. Emperor Haile Selassie was able to promote the unique and historical position of Ethiopia, the only country of the African continent not to have been colonized, in order to convince the Organization of African Unity to establish its headquarters in Addis Ababa in 1963. This international standing obliged Ethiopia to satisfy the infrastructure conditions: hotels adapted to the needs of an international clientele, meeting venues equipped with current technology, an airport connected to the continent[10] have fulfilled for Addis Ababa its role as a diplomatic capital.

But behind cosmetic touches and the image of a modern city visible from its main thoroughfares, the popular city continued to grow. A real estate market emerged. Cities, and in particular the capital, offered opportunities to acquire land ownership to the small administrative and commercial bourgeoisie. Imperial dignitaries sold off parts of their large concessions. The gradual break-up of landholdings benefited an urban class composed of owners who were encouraged to build at the back of their lots, in the backyards, and offer the buildings for rent to new urban dwellers.[11]

Some neighbourhoods were densely built up, full of little rental houses and built without any real master plan. The rental market in expansion gave Addis Ababa's different neighbourhoods a garish make-up, without any coherence for a foreign observer,[12] with sumptuous dwellings alongside hovels of wattle and daub. The dense urban tissue consolidated local solidarity associations founded on good neighbourly relations: the *edirs*, funeral associations for the support of bereaved families in which the inhabitants of a same neighbourhood participate, and the *geber* tradition in which an affluent family invites neighbouring households to a banquet during religious festivals, are manifestations of a society hierarchized along class faultlines but also attentive to social links.

The nationalization of houses

Urban configuration would probably have evolved towards gradual improvement of popular housing, but a major event in urban and political history put a stop to the mechanisms of the real estate market at the source of an original urban pattern.

One of the founding acts of the 1974 revolution was the nationalization of farm land. The "Land to the Tiller" slogan was to find an echo in the city and the revolutionary leadership wanted to ensure the support of the urban classes: hence the "extra houses" nationalization law was proclaimed on the night of 4 July 1975.[13] All rental properties of the capital became public property: the tenants were to be freed from the yoke of the landlords and benefit from the advantages of a new paying system. Rents were slashed in half and the management of houses entrusted to two different institutions. The Rental Housing Agency was in charge of the management of high class houses, allotted to privileged civil servants, while the great majority of dwellings of poor standing, rented out for less than 100 ETB—the average being 15 ETB—were placed under the management of Urban Dwellers Associations, replaced as early as 1976 by the *kebele*,[14] a decentralized organ of the central administration, very efficient for the control of the population. Of the 200,000 dwellings that Addis Ababa counted in 1975, 140,000, or 70 per cent, were nationalized in this manner, regrouped over an approximate total surface area of 4,000 ha.[15] Real estate ownership was not abolished but severely restricted, each family only having the right to privately possess one dwelling, and rental practises being strongly curtailed during the whole Derg period.[16]

This rental housing stock enabled a majority of urban dwellers to find accommodation with a rental amount never readjusted since. One of the main measures of the Derg was also to control mobility and limit migratory fluxes. The collectivization of land, the control of the peasantry, and systematic file-keeping surveillance by the *kebele* rendered migration more difficult.

While urban growth figures decreased in the period after the Derg's rise to power, they were already on the increase again from the mid-1980s,[17] but the spread of the built-up surface did not really indicate a growing population.[18] The Derg period certainly marked a cut-off point in the urban development of Ethiopia, and the real estate and land ownership policies froze the urban structure inherited from the 1960s for several decades; in 1991, at the downfall of Mengistu, Addis Ababa retained its popular aspect, with neighbourhoods still functioning like villages.

Addis Ababa in the 1990s: government neglect and informal practices

The downfall of the Derg and the proclamation of a federal regime in 1994 did not entail an immediate urbanization of Ethiopia. The new governing party, the EPRDF, favoured agricultural development, and was suspicious towards cities in which uncontrolled growth could be a source of social unrest. Low interest in the urban question meant a constant degradation of the state of cities, which became like shanty towns. Reports and studies[19] describe a critical urban situation, with Ethiopian cities accumulating severe handicaps, including, most preoccupying, the dereliction of the housing stock, in particular dwellings managed by the *kebele*.

Built with immediate returns in mind, nationalized houses were not made to resist the wear and tear of time. 95 per cent of the houses were in wattle and daub, more than three quarters of them covered less than 40m^2 with high occupancy rates.[20] Although certain households had the desire and the capacity to invest in self-rehabilitation projects,[21] they were confronted by the *kebele* administration and complex and rigid legislation. Faced with an increase in family size and multiple forms of cohabitation linked to inadequate supply of accommodation, the *kebele* administration accepted (or turned a blind eye to) expansion encroaching on roads and extensions in height to the original structures.

The lack of accommodation was due to state control of the real estate promotion sector. Current legislation in Ethiopia gives the state sole ownership of land in the name of the common good of the nation. Public authorities parcel out land deeds, and renewable leases with lengths varying depending on the type of occupation, residential, commercial or industrial. There is no land market, apart from the one organized by the state. For households, legally acquiring a plot is an ordeal and the required conditions reach such levels of constraint that plots allotted by the municipality do not find takers.[22]

In the face of the low productivity of legal real estate venues, house-holds develop solutions themselves by taking over empty plots, build-ing on their land. Popular housing is informal, on the margins of legal-ity; households pay electricity charges and are registered with the *kebele*, but do not possess official land deeds, their presence is recog-nized but not their accommodation. The struggle against illegal hous-ing regularly appears in the discourse of the Addis Ababa Municipality, which tries to discourage people from seeking it. But squatting phe-nomena are really quite minor when compared with real estate prac-tices: they are authorized, and enable households to put a simple hut up for sale at a price way beyond its value, which in reality reflects the price of the land plot itself. In this manner, many neighbourhoods have been developed, bypassing the legislative framework, and some peas-ants have been able to profit from the high demand from urban classes by selling off marginal plots now urbanized and integrated into the city, for attractive prices.[23]

A "shantytown" capital

In the centre, while neighbourhoods progressively became more built up, access to basic services has not always kept pace: if the provision of water and electricity is relatively correct in the old neighbourhoods, shortcomings in waste management entail high sanitary risks. The hygiene situation is alarming, rates of access by households to basic services are overwhelmingly insufficient, and existing infrastructure was not conceived for the growing population densities of the neigh-bourhoods. For lack of follow up, a good deal of communal sanitary infrastructure has been abandoned, degrading the environment. Neighbourhoods have developed and become denser without any par-ticular planning, as needs and possibilities arose: the urban road net-work, tight and narrow, seems a labyrinth to the inexperienced passer-by. A few secondary non-asphalted roads open up onto endless lanes often finishing in culs-de-sac. This lack of thoroughfares is a major constraint for disposing of waste and putting out fires, as the alleyways are often inaccessible to motor vehicles.[24]

According to the studies regularly published by UN Habitat, more than 90 per cent of the housing is slum-like. These numbers conceal a variety of situations and urban forms, but feed a political discourse which, faced with such a massive problem, has to formulate radical solutions.

The shanty town is made up of people, and the urban question poses a very delicate economic and social question in Ethiopia. The issues of city development and access to housing are played out in a context of urban poverty. High unemployment rates (more than 30 per cent) barely conceal the importance of the informal economy, the great diversity of which enables the popular classes to increase their incomes and safeguard a purchasing power battered by the constant inflation that directly impacts on the prices of consumer prices.[25] In a context of wage fragility and work instability, the possession of capital, especially in the form of private housing, offers great opportunities to increase one's income.

Towards an urban renaissance?

All of the statistics produced over the last ten years reflect the steady urbanization of Ethiopia and raise questions about its effects on an urban system noted for its top-heavy capital. Historically, Addis Ababa has dominated urban demography: in the last census of 2007, of the 12 million urban dwellers of Ethiopia, 2.7 million (22.5 per cent) resided in the federal capital. Even so, Addis Ababa's supremacy in an urban system where the second city of the country numbers 230,000 inhabitants would seem to be in decline. The growth of regional capitals, begun with the constitution of 1996, is rapid and reveals that urbanization is being played out in areas boosted and developed by the federal regime.

Regional capital cities	Annual average growth rate	Number of inhabitants 2007
Mekele	9.4%	215,546
Bahar Dar	9.9%	220,344
Awassa	9.9%	159,013
Gambella City	8%	38,994
Dire Dawa	3%	232,854
Addis Ababa	2.3%	2,738,248

Source: Central Statistical Authority, 2007.

However, the current economic growth of Ethiopia, qualified as miraculous with 10 per cent annual growth, mostly takes place in the capital, the dominant economic centre since the Empire. Addis Ababa stands out as an international metropolis, at the centre of an economic growth pole. In a radius of 200 km, along road axes, many investments have emerged, mainly farms in the agro-industrial sector and flower farming with production geared to export, a sector that is being presented as profitable ($17 million for the 2009–10 period).[26] The Oromo region benefits from the capital's pull and participates in agricultural development policies in which important concessions are granted to foreign investors. These investments have a strong impact on the urban network, especially apparent in the spectacular growth of towns situated in this radius. By connecting the hinterland of the capital with the world economy, the development of peri-urban or urban areas redefines the relations between local and global scales. It is also shaking up a city that has to conform to worldwide urbanization standards and stake its claim to being a diplomatic capital.

Urban development: a political and economic project

Addis Ababa's status as an international metropolis is at stake and development policies now reflect orientations more favourable to the city. The urban sector holds an important position in the GTP (Growth and Transformation Plan) strategy that aims to reduce unemployment, eradicate shanty towns and develop industry.[27] The objectives are met by the implementation of a housing programme that boosts the labour intensive construction sector, energizes the private sector and offers urban dwellers a more decent and comfortable environment. Reflecting an opening up to economic liberalism, access to private home ownership for all social categories is becoming an important objective of development policies. The paradigm shift is clear and seems to repudiate the previous housing policy, inherited from the 1975 revolution, which shunted tenants into an urban class on their own, giving them a stake in the creation of a more just society where limited private ownership would limit social injustice. But behind this apparent radical change, one should nevertheless perceive continuity in the power and role of the state which, through control of land ownership, keeps a near total control over urbanization. Through a housing policy that favours the access to ownership, but remains programmed and defined by the public authorities, Ethiopia is inaugurating an untried form of state capitalism.

During the last parliamentary election campaign in 2010, the city came to the fore as a political theme. Posters prepared for this occasion showed workers busy laying out a road, with a backdrop of modern high rise buildings. The message is clear: a building site city is under way, built with the labour and support of the people, an industrious city that offers its inhabitants well-being and surges toward modernity. The imagery evokes the "renaissance" (*tensay*) of Ethiopia and finds an echo in another project initiated by the EPRDF, the Millennium Dam which is supposed to be financed solely by national funds, with the public's contribution.[28]

But how to mesh urban and economic growth inside the frame of urban poverty? What is the road to take to leave the shanty town behind and obliterate the sometimes rural and peasant like face of the capital? The government seeks to have Addis Ababa promoted to the rank of a modern metropolis and become economically competitive while maintaining social justice objectives. These ambitions may over-reach the means and hide the weaknesses of the Ethiopian urban development model.

Private real estate investors and promoters: new actors in the making of the city

Long described as a town of hovels, mostly underdeveloped, the capital seems to be closing a chapter of its history by beginning a radical transformation. The construction sector is experiencing a renewal without precedent and participates in the renovation of the centre of Addis Ababa.

The main instrument of urban policy is found in the landholding legislation. The leasing system was initiated in 1993 and amended in 2002 to answer investors' and the public's needs, responding to their wish to see a very closed real estate sector liberalized. But this liberalization is quite relative and applications for leases give the city government (AACG) the means to use its monopoly in the management of landholding grants. These grants are made by public auction, the lands being allotted to the highest bidder. This competition drives up prices and whets the promoters' appetites. By stimulating the real estate market, the authorities face the obligation of freeing up space to build on and offer to investors. Construction situated nearby important urban axes has to respect construction rules, and the owners of small lots

404

have to erect buildings of at least five stories. In the case of the Mercato, the large market and neighbourhood situated in the centre of Addis Ababa, traders sought to organize themselves to obtain the finance necessary for the construction of high rise buildings and face off promoters' appetites. But the residents' projects are stalled in the light of the sums available to investors who benefit from the easy credit offered to some of them by the banks.[29]

The construction sector regulations favour Ethiopian companies but permit foreign investors in the area of contracting, subject to authorization by the Ministry of Works and Urban Development; most of the foreign investors are Saudi Arabian. The promoters' investment logic and the origin of the funds are open to question. The building boom is linked to the development of the banks, a sector for which the press regularly reports considerable dividends.[30] Real estate investments are a way to acquire secure assets and avoid the effects of the devaluation of the birr and raging inflation. Real estate holdings are very seldom put up for sale and owners prefer to gamble on the strong demand for office and commercial space.

Behind the high rise towers and the top end villas, smaller buildings, with high returns, reflect the diversity of investor profiles. Without access to bank credit, these urban entrepreneurs activate their personal networks, often among diaspora Ethiopians, in order to collect the necessary funds. More generally, the injection of diaspora fund transfers now makes up an important part of popular incomes, as is evident from the multiplication of transfer agencies all over the city.

The centre's hunger for modernity leaks out to the periphery as well. For this the AACG has programmed development by leaning on private Real Estate Developers (RED). The Ayat Company was the first to offer suburban villa complexes in the residential neighbourhoods situated in the eastern periphery of Addis Ababa. The housing was sold at prices relatively accessible to the well-to-do middle classes.[31] From 2005 onwards the market was opened up to other promoters, and in just a year's time more than a hundred REDs, often created for the occasion, obtained licences as well as plots to build upon. The inhabitants of Addis Ababa were soon given advertising billboards to display the housing projects conceived by the architects: luxurious villas nested in secure neighbourhoods, high rises offering all of the trappings of a "Western" lifestyle, all participating in the erection of a new and modern city.

The REDs aim at an international clientele, in particular members of the diaspora who would like to establish themselves in Ethiopia but do not want to forego their daily luxuries. The advertised prices are disconnected from the local market: the price of a villa ranges from 5 million to more than 10 million birr, and a household interested in buying a studio in a building has to pay up at least 800,000 birr.[32] If the demand for very high end housing exists, it is very small, and it would seem that the opening given to RED was overestimated. Many projects never saw the light of day because of lack of demand and weak financial backing.

On top of this, some REDs seem to have benefited from the plots by reselling them directly to moneyed private individuals in a hurry. Confronted with this misconduct, the authorities increased control of the sector by taking back the licences from those who had remained dormant.[33] The new reform promulgated in October 2011[34] aims to provide a better framework for the development of a private real estate market and put a stop to speculative and corrupt practises in which real estate changes hands "under the counter". The main change is the generalization of the lease system to all landholding transactions. Fears have been expressed about the application of this reform. While it makes it possible to limit speculation and price increases in the informal markets, it gives urban dwellers a feeling of land insecurity: the prospect of having to renew their land title hinging on the consent of public authorities, and without any compensation in the case of refusal, could discourage households' real estate investments.

Urban renewal and the destruction of existing neighbourhoods

Addis Ababa's centre offers startling contrasts: facing 15-plus-storey high rises, a luxury reserved to a certain elite, there are popular bars famous for their night time bustle. In the Bole neighbourhood, yesterday's vacant lots today harbour malls full of Addis Ababa's happy few.

The AACG has undertaken since some ten years to "remake" the city by renovating whole neighbourhoods and offering investors attractive lots. This development is in agreement with the Growth and Transformation Plan: boosting the construction sector makes it possible to eradicate the shanty towns, to create jobs, and offers Ethiopia a modern capital, but at what price?

The first pilot projects were the construction of the Sheraton Hotel complex and the implementation of the Casa Incis Local Development

Plan.[35] Renovation was done with the total destruction of the pre-existing neighbourhoods. Such renovation programmes have been intensified over the last few years.[36] Neighbourhoods are completely renovated, like Lideta where close to 26 hectares have been totally demolished. The historic central districts like Arada and Arat Kilo are planned to disappear to liberate the plots required for private investors. In this fashion, the question of the shanty towns is resolved by radical town planning. The inhabitants' relocation obliges the public authorities to propose a minimum compensation, in the form of housing situated in the periphery. Impact assessments[37] show that maintaining a roof does not prevent the risk of pauperization. Owners obtained financial compensation calculated on the physical worth of the property, often ancient and therefore highly undervalued when compared with the informal market. The lots offered are situated in non-accessible neighbourhoods, on plots that are not equipped with basic services.

Kebele tenants, often the majority of inhabitants in the central historic neighbourhoods, are put in temporary housing, on the waiting list for possible access to a condominium dwelling. Their only recourse is often to find a new landlord. When housing is cleared for enlarging roads, an exceptional procedure has been put into place: instead of relocation, *kebele* tenants are given a sum corresponding to three months of rent in the private renting sector.[38]

The Integrated Housing Development Programme

One of the major projects of the Municipality is the collective accommodation construction programme, with access to ownership, involving condominiums. The programme was tried out in the Tigray region and was largely inspired the President of the time and future city mayor of Addis Ababa, Arqbe Oqbay. From 2004, a big information programme encouraged the inhabitants of Addis Ababa to put their names down on lists available in the *kebele*s and be eligible to participate in a lottery. Local authorities advise tenants to organize themselves to collect the necessary funds to make the first down payment.[39]

The large number of applicants shows the amplitude of the programme: at the start of the programme, there were 50,000 housing units foreseen annually, to reach a total of 350,000 units. Intensive production is supposed to solve the housing deficit aggravated by years of negligence. To a major and complex problem, that of the chronic lack of housing, the public authorities have found a massive and one-size-fits-all answer.

Condominiums are complexes of small high rise buildings. The outside corridors give onto a common courtyard. Collective facilities, such as kitchens and wash rooms, have been designed in order to meet the habits and customs of urban dwellers.[40] Each unit has individual access to water, and a private kitchen and bathroom. Septic tanks are set up to collect waste waters. Condominiums seem like islands, often enclosed neighbourhoods in the city. Condominium complexes sprout all over the city, creating a new landscape, between gigantic undertakings in the periphery[41] and small complexes of two or three high rises in the city centre, next to degraded neighbourhoods.

The allocation is done by a lottery, small units (studio and one bedroom apartments) being set aside for the poorer households with fewer funds, while the bigger units are reserved for better endowed households. Social plurality is in this way encouraged. The financing of the units with greater surface area is to cover a part of the costs for the smaller units. Despite their more affordable prices, the cramped conditions of the smaller units are little adapted to the often high number of persons per household.[42] Another ambition of the programme is to promote access to ownership, not only for financial reasons linked to recovering the costs, but also in order to promote a new economic and social paradigm: the state wants to create the conditions under which urban dwellers can leave behind the instability of renting by setting them up for the long term in the envied status of owner. But the ownership statutes of a condominium dwelling are regulated: on the one hand, a condition of ownership is that households must join the co-owners' association, and on the other, reselling the unit is only allowed five years after the date of purchase of the housing. Private ownership is in this manner kept in a collective framework. However, the financial conditions demanded in order to access condominium housing cause certain households, in particular the less well off, to refuse this unique opportunity to accede to ownership. Condominiums are addressed to the households of the middle classes, capable of paying a housing unit for which the minimal cost will rise to 400,000 birr. The public sector is progressively falling into step with the private one, distancing itself from the social ambitions it had first espoused.

Urban tensions and development weakness

The rebirth of the capital is made possible by an opening to a certain liberalism played out under state control, urban renewal being one of the main manifestations of a type of state capitalism specific to Ethiopia. On the one hand, public authorities wish to modernize the city by opening up to private capital, on the other, they play their role as a powerful controlling state. Popular urban preoccupations are an integral part of the modernizing urban policies and the condominium housing programme appears as a counterweight to the renovations in the capital. However, the development model shows cracks: real estate investments without a market, unaffordable social housing, and so on. Although there does exist a demand for office space, real estate investments seem to be destined to secure cash holdings. Many private promoters encounter difficulties in finding a market, and if the diaspora does wish to buy top-end housing the supply seems to exceed the demand. The financial balance of the public programmes is also under question as the Addis Ababa Municipality borrows from the banks to finance its housing policies which end up being largely subsidized.

The land ownership issue is situated right at the heart of this problem and of the tensions created by these infrastructure policies. It has become just about impossible for people to have access to plots in the system defined by the public authorities. Opportunities exist, for instance, for buying up plots in the direct periphery of Addis Ababa, in the Oromo region. But conflicts about the legality of these plots occupied by urban residents coming from Addis Ababa have surfaced. The recent creation of a special administration to manage this zone (the Oromiya special zone) is supposed to maintain peaceful relations while shedding light on the stakes involved in the metropolitization of Addis Ababa and its territorial development.

Increasing commercialization of housing and the emergence
of a "rental city"

In the opinion of the leaders, the question of access to ownership for the middle and lower classes has been resolved with the implementation of the condominium programme. Would land ownership tensions be resolved by public real estate promotion? Despite the intensive production of condominium housing, the doubling of the selling price over the last two years makes it difficult to access for the popular classes. A study by UN Habitat[43] confirms the difficulties for poor households to become owners. Repaying the loan represents a permanent worry for households unable to meet the monthly payments (a minimum of 100 birr for a studio) when their *kebele* housing cost them only 15 *birr* a month. Partial or total renting of housing is the easiest solution for nearly 70 per cent of owners of a condominium unit in order to face the challenges of ownership. The public housing policy has therefore had an unexpected impact: the emergence of a class of poor owners, their real estate only generating a small rent enabling them to establish themselves in a location. The demand for housing has found an answer in an increased commercialization of housing, not in sales but in rentals. The 2007 census[44] lays bare the importance of this phenomenon, letting one think that Addis Ababa has again become the "rental city" it was at the end of the 1960s.

The extraordinary growth of the private rental network reveals the frenetic efforts of owners to put their property up for rent or to transform a part of their housing (often the commons and the backyards) in order to produce often not negligible income. Some households can offer up to fifteen rooms, demanding from their tenants irreproachable conduct (even in their personal life) and prompt payment. These cohabitations often create conflicts between tenants and owners, the former not accepting the controls and intrusions of the owners, the latter experiencing difficulty with this cohabitation with strangers on their own land.

Rental agreements, when they exist, have no official worth and conflicts are resolved amicably. Most of the rental housing is not the subject of fiscal controls: below a certain threshold, owners are exempt from tax on the income they derive from their rents and many declare lower incomes. Fiscal policy seems to be rather lenient towards owner-landlords.[45] For renting households, residential trajectories become more complex and mobility more unstable, accompanied whether they like it or not by the ups and downs of employment. Households adapt their housing mode to their financial situation, whereas landlords see in their real estate financial security.

"Social safety nets" under pressure from new urban mobility

In a city mostly inhabited by tenants, deprived of secure residence, the roles and stability of "social safety nets" based on belonging to a neighbourhood are now in doubt. For example,[46] for certain households, the ownership of a condominium unit enables them to become part of a solidarity association (*iddir*), created upon the initiative of the community of residents. But faced by the paying constraints of the loan, many put their housing up for rent while still living near the condominiums in order to participate in their associative life and fulfil their ownership obligations. Others maintain links with the *iddir* of their old neighbourhood to which they will have contributed for many years, ensuring their social protection. For reasons of sociability and good neighbourhood relations, they also forge links with the *iddir* of their new residence. Residential mobility created by a growing renting housing stock and urban renovation programmes turns upside down the "social safety nets" born from the history of the Ethiopian town. Despite the recomposing strength of local associations, worries persist about the disappearance of an urban tissue that has underpinned a social equilibrium.

Conclusion

Addis Ababa has won its bet: bedecked with the attributes of modernity, it can claim its rank as an international metropolis. But if the capital is being built, the city is commercialized, becoming more difficult to access for the popular classes. The reinvestment in the capital by the public authorities is followed by popular practises, the rental or sale of housing and land plots by many urban owners profiting from an inexhaustible demand. While urban renewal takes place equally in the public, private and popular spheres, the weak articulation between real estate practices gives rise to strong tensions, the new territories of the commercialized city force mobility and turn upside down "social safety nets" inherited from a now interrupted urban history. Addis Ababa can be seen as the black box of the urban transformations under way in the country. Reconstruction mechanisms visible in the capital seem to be under way in secondary towns, which are also under pressure from radical town planning and the emergence of economic liberalism.

BIBLIOGRAPHY AND FURTHER READING

Addis Ababa Chamber of Commerce and Sectoral Associations (2011), *Assessment of Urban Development Practices on Business Expansion in Ethiopia*.

AACG, 2000, Addis Ababa City Government, Office for the Revision of the Addis Ababa Master Plan, *Addis Ababa Revised Master Plan Proposals*. Draft summary.

Addis Mulugeta, 2009, "Protecting the new flower's heritage," *Capital*, 8 June 2009. http://www.capitalethiopia.com/index.php?option=com_content&vi ew=article&id=11477:protecting-the-new-flowers-heritage&catid=12:local-news&Itemid=4 (last access in April 2012).

Bahru Zewde, 1986, "Early Safars of Addis Ababa: Patterns of Evolution", *Proceedings of the International Symposium of the Centenary of Addis Ababa*, Addis Ababa: Institute of Ethiopian Studies, pp. 43–55.

——— 1991, *A History of Modern Ethiopia: 1855–1991*, Addis Ababa University Press.

Berhanu Zeleke, 2006, "Impacts of Urban Redevelopment on the Livelihoods of Displaced People in Addis Ababa: the Case of Casainchis", Master's thesis, Addis Ababa University.

Berlan, E., 1963, *Addis Abeba, la plus haute ville d'Afrique. Etude géographique*, Grenoble: Imprimerie Allier.

CSA, 1994, Central Statistical Authority, *The 1994 Population and Housing Census of Ethiopia*.

Corrado, D. and Patassini, D., 1996, *Urban Ethiopia: Evidences of the 1980s*, Venice: Istituto Universitario di Architettura di Venezia.

De Poix, S., 2007, "Heurs et malheurs du grand marché d'Addis Abeba face à l'ouverture éthiopienne", *Les Cahiers d'Outre Mer*, 237, pp. 41–66.

Duroyaume, P., 2009, "Social Mix Facing Urban Changes in Addis Ababa", *Construction Ahead* (Addis Ababa), 15, pp. 42–9.

Elias Yitbarek, 2008, "Revisiting Slums, Revealing Responses, Urban Upgrading in Tenant-dominated Inner-city Settlements, in Addis Ababa, Ethiopia", PhD thesis, University of Trondheim, Norway.

——— 2009, "Between Renting and Owning: Saving and Credit Cooperative Based Tenure Transformation in the Inner-City 'Slums' of Addis Ababa", in S. Ege et al. (eds), *Proceedings of the 16th International Conference of Ethiopian Studies*, Trondheim, pp. 943–56.

ESA, 2009, Population Division of the Department of Economic and Social Affairs of the United Nations Secretariat, *World Population Prospects: The 2009 Revision Population Database*. http://esa.un.org/ wup2009/unup/ p2k0data.asp (last access in April 2012).

Esrael Tesfaye (2005), "Illegal Land Sub-division in Addis Ababa City", Master's thesis, University of Rotterdam.

Essayas Deribe, 2003, "La gestion foncière et le développement urbain dans les villes des pays en voie de développement: le cas de la ville d'Addis Abeba", Université Lumière-Lyon II, France, PhD thesis.

Ezana Haddis, 2007, "An Assessment of the Working Conditions of the Floriculture Industry: The Case of Four Flower Farms in West Showa Zone, Oromiya Regional State", Master's thesis, Addis Ababa University.

Garretson, P., 2000, *A History of Addis Ababa from its Foundation in 1886 to 1910*, Wiesbaden: Harrassowitz Verlag, Aethiopistische Forschungen 49.

Getahun Benti, 2007, *Addis Ababa: Migration and the Making of a Multiethnic Metropolis, 1941–1974*, Trenton, NJ: Red Sea Press.

Fasil Giorgis and Gerard, D., 2007, *The City and its Architectural Heritage: Addis Ababa 1886–1941*, Addis Ababa: Shama Books.

Mains, D., 2011, *Hope is Cut: Youth, Unemployment, and the Future in Urban Ethiopia*, Philadelphia: Temple University Press.

Meheret Ayenew, 2008, "A Review of FDRE's Urban Development Policy", in Taye Assefa (ed.), *Digest of Ethiopia's Nation Policies, Strategies and Programs*, Addis Ababa: Forum for Social Studies.

Meskerem Shawul Areda (2008), "La place accordée à l'existant dans la mise en pratique de modèles d'urbanisme: le cas d'Addis Abeba", Université Paris 1, France, doctorate thesis.

MOFED, 2010a, *Performance Evaluation of the First Five Years Development Plan (2006–2010) and the Growth and Transformation Planning (GTP) for the Next Five Years (2011–20015)*, Ministry of Finance and Economic Development, July 2010.

Tamru, Bezunesh, 2013, *Villes et territoires en Éthiopie*, Paris: L'Harmattan.

UN Habitat, 2003, *The Challenge of Slums. Global Report on Human Settlement*, London: Earthscan Publications Ltd.

UN Habitat, 2007, *Situation Analysis of Informal Settlements in Addis Ababa*, Cities Without Slums, Sub-Regional Programme for Eastern and Southern Africa, Addis Ababa Slum Upgrading Programme.

Wubshet Berhanu, 2002, "Urban Policies and the Formation of Social and Spatial Patterns in Ethiopia: the Case of Housing Areas in Addis Ababa", Trondheim University, PhD thesis.

THE MELES ZENAWI ERA

FROM REVOLUTIONARY MARXISM
TO STATE DEVELOPMENTALISM

Gérard Prunier

It is immediately possible to recognize the men of destiny who influence their time by the degree of passion and controversy they create. For his detractors, Meles Zenawi was a dictator and a disaster for Ethiopia. For his supporters and devoted followers he was a genius, a visionary and a world class leader. One thing is sure: he did not leave anybody indifferent. Given the short time since his death,[1] it is somewhat difficult for the historian to assess the record of a man who has had such an intense impact on the fate of his country. But one thing is sure: the extremes of spite and adulation that he has evoked are both misplaced. And another thing is sure: his imprint is likely to influence the destiny of Ethiopia for many years to come.

There are four men—Emperor Menelek, Emperor Haile Selassie, Dictator-Chairman Mengistu Haile Mariam and Prime Minister Meles Zenawi who, for better or for worse, shaped twentieth century

Ethiopia. And the very evolution of their titles, from Emperor to Prime Minister, is in itself a summary of the country's slow climb from a traditional quasi-medieval polity to an embryonic democracy. The road has been long, it has been full of chaos and ambushes and it is not yet over. But Ethiopia is an age-old political structure, the longest-lasting state in Africa and with Egypt and China, one of the oldest in the world still in existence today. It is the only African polity which managed to avoid colonization and the one which pioneered collective African political action. It is in that long-range perspective that the Meles Zenawi years have to be seen.

This chapter is not a research piece. It is rather a historical essay, one could almost say a kind of philosophical musing, where we will try to stake out the possible research field. It is an attempt at an outline of that period, centred around the man who dominated it. Neither God nor demon, he was a hard-boiled politician who tried to rise—rather successfully—to the level of a statesman. He was a lonely figure on the African continent where political "leaders" often tend to simply manipulate situations in the hope of retaining power, without any thought for the future. Meles wanted to remain in power of course, but he thought about his country's future. The question which sharply divides his admirers from his adversaries is: what kind of a future? Looking at his record should enable us to outline a certain profile, one that drastically changed over time in its manifestations but nevertheless kept a certain continuity in its style and inspiration and whose shadow still extended over Ethiopian politics well after his death.

Meles Zenawi as revolutionary (1975–91)

The status of the word "revolutionary" in this early part of the twenty-first century has been subjected to a massive reinterpretation. On the one hand the commercial vocabulary that dominates our times makes great use of the word: everything is "revolutionary", from genetically-modified crops to Dreamliner jets and from smartphones to bionic prosthesis. But this has trivialized the word, and, given the post-ideological world outlook which has become hegemonic, it has delegitimized the original political meaning of the term.

Revolutions occur in the destiny of societies when they have reached a point of blockage where the past is dying, the future is increasingly hard to imagine from simply extrapolating the past and the present is becoming unworkable. Then they explode. Social scientists (and politicians even more) are deeply divided on the historical status of revolutions. For some they are a catastrophe which sets societies back hundreds of years, for others (now a shrinking band, particularly since the death of Eric Hobsbawm) they are a progressive jump forward into the future. But these are ideological rather than analytical views. For true historians revolutions are only critical moments in the social transformation of societies. Their ultimate fate depends on their unfolding and not on some pre-ordained "verdict of history". And revolutions are, in themselves, a historically defined object. There were many fundamental revolutions in history (the development of Christianity in the second and third centuries A.D., the spread of Islam from the seventh-to-ninth centuries, *Magna Carta* in the thirteenth century, the conquest of the Americas in the sixteenth century) which were revolutions without that name being attributed to them. But if we narrow down that meaning to significant political upheavals, without judging of their ultimate consequences, "revolutions" as a clearly recognized syndrome began with the French Revolution of 1789 and are still today roaming the planet—that is, the ongoing Arab revolutions since 2010—even though they tend to enjoy a diminishing degree of political acceptance and cultural legitimacy in the contemporary world.

From Jean-Jacques Rousseau to Karl Marx, social thinkers have given revolutions their philosophical badge of honour. And contrary to superficial appearances, Joseph Stalin has probably been the greatest counter-revolutionary actor of modern times. But at each step in the history of man, if revolutionary actions were undertaken, it was always within the framework of what was *conceivable* at the time. Pre-ideological revolutions were *de facto* while modern ones, which tried to create *de jure* situations, were attempts at adapting (imposing?) an ideological gridlock on a concrete situation.

Ethiopia in the third quarter of the twentieth century had reached that point of concrete blockage where young Ethiopian men and women felt trapped and from which they tried—at times with Procrustean difficulties—to escape by using the framework of revolutionary Marxism.

It is impossible to understand the man Meles Zenawi without taking into account that particular time, to see him without understanding that *Zeitgeist*, even if that was an ill-applying framework. A mistake commonly made by contemporary analysts is to judge politicians *sui generis*, as if they were timeless a-historical characters. This is actually a disturbing trend which goes way beyond the Ethiopian question, concerning the loss of historical relativity and the whole benefit of the *Annales* school of social history. In the case of Meles this can result in a disastrous misunderstanding because he is a perfect illustration of the remark by the great historian Marc Bloch (1953): "Men are much more the sons of their time than the sons of their fathers". Meles Zenawi came from a family that was typical of the Ethiopian post-World War II petit-bourgeois elite of Haile Selassie's civil society. He was a perfect representative of the young men and women depicted in Randi Balsvik's (1985) study of the revolutionary student milieu of the 1950s-1970s.[2] This was a milieu that was deeply influenced by a few very basic feelings, often rationalized as ideas:

- Ethiopia, which had been the torch-bearer of the African continent since the days of Adwa and the creation of the OAU, was falling hopelessly behind. The failure of the 1960 coup by the Neway brothers was seen as a tragedy.[3]
- But this failure was seen by the students as explainable: the Neway brothers had been petty-bourgeois revolutionaries, they had not been guided by the invincible light of proletarian revolution.
- The Ethiopian student elite lived in an intellectual world where Karl Marx was God and his prophets were called Lenin, Mao-Zedong, Ho Chi Minh, Fidel Castro and Samora Machel.
- A particular problem of the revolution in Ethiopia was thought to be its ability to deal with the "national question" (in the sense given to this expression by a whole line of socialist thinkers going from Otto Bauer to Joseph Stalin by way of Vladimir Illyich Lenin, Karl Renner, the left-wing Zionists of Hachomer Hatzair and Andrés Nin). The one thing all had had in common had been to criticize the dominance of the state by a social/regional sub-group, whether the Austro-Hungarians, the "Great Russians", the Gentile reactionaries or the Castilians as the case might be. In the Ethiopian case it was the Amhara, usually called "the Shoans" to accentuate their sub-sub-regional nature. Given the haunting problem of the Eritrean insurrection, any revolutionary movement would have had to deal with that sore that infected the Ethiopian polity. The problem was that all the authors mentioned above had a disturbing tendency to disagree with each other and to differ on the nature of the remedies they advocated. This would bring the Ethiopian student revolutionaries

to painful—and at times tragic—disagreements on the subject. From the ELF to the EPRP and from Mei'son to the TPLF, the different interpretations of the accursed "national question" would lead to much bloodshed and to an array of rancour which is still far from extinguished today.

• In addition, all the would-be revolutionaries were fiercely nationalistic. They resented the nobility but idolized its national heroes— even if these got differential treatment depending on who was the admiring group: the contradictory views regarding such a major historical character as Ras Alula are a case in point.[4]

It is impossible to understand Meles Zenawi without seeing him in the global perspective of the five points mentioned above.

When the revolution finally broke out in 1974, it was in a turmoil of contradictions which did not resemble the sacralized "proletarian insurrection" of the Marxist model. It was a mixture of working class demonstrations embedded in an embryonic bourgeois revolution in the capital, the whole thing being framed inside a military revolt and a broader peasant *jacquerie*. All this silhouetted against the haunting background of a potentially secessionist sub-national armed insurrection and the prospect of half-a-dozen more in the making. It was not only the domination of the aristocracy that was cracking up but the makings of the Empire itself. Given this overwhelming nature of the national question, a lot of the revolutionary struggles happened not nationally—as was the case with Mei'son or the EPRP—but within sub-nationally defined constituencies, whether Oromo, Tigrayan, Eritrean or Somali. It was a mish-mash of social revolution, political upheaval, military coup and regionalist uprisings.

Meles Zenawi was Tigrayan, so he became a Tigrayan revolutionary. And being a Marxist like most of his young educated contemporaries, he became a Marxist Tigrayan revolutionary. Something neither clearcut nor easy to define. Part of the problem was that he was both very young and what the great Italian Marxist thinker Antonio Gramsci[5] called an "organic intellectual", that is, somebody who was half-educated (he had only started his first year at university) but whose social position and intellectual make-up enabled to express the deep unspoken aspirations and ideals of those less educated than him. The most immediate problem was how the global revolutionary struggle would be articulated with the problem of sub-national determination: to make it plain, should the organization he had just joined—the TPLF—

fight to revolutionize Ethiopia or to secede from it? In fact, inasmuch as we can know it given the fairly secretive nature of the TPLF, it seems that there was a progressive evolution of the top TPLF leadership circles on the question. In the early days—1975 to 1985—the outlook was more in favour of promoting a sort of "Tigrayan nationalist feeling" which did not exclude secession but did not clearly promote it.[6] The TPLF surfed on the memories of the abortive Tigrayan uprising of 1943 and its subsequent violent repression by Haile Selassie.[7] It called itself *"Kela'aye Weyane"* or "the second *woyane"* in order to base itself on what Tigrayan historian Gebru Tareke very aptly calls "a foundation myth".[8]

All myths are multi-faceted and open to variable interpretations and this was the case with *"Kela'aye Weyane"* which managed to slide slowly from Tigrayan ethno-nationalism to pan-Ethiopian nationalism. This would of course leave a long aftertaste and it remained ambiguous not only during the years of fighting[9] but even following the TPLF victory, even though by then the TPLF had enlarged itself into the multi-ethnic EPRDF.

What of Meles himself during this long period of nearly sixteen years? This is where the glorification/demonization of the man starts. For his enemies (including some Tigrayans like Aregawi Berhe) he was a wolf in sheep's clothing, hiding his secessionist aims under the mantle of a fake nationalism. But for his supporters, he had never been anything but an ardent Ethiopian nationalist. The truth obviously stands in the middle: Meles was a supreme tactician and he was remarkable at sensing how far he could go on a precise issue. Back in the pre-1985 days, the ambiguities of the ethno-nationalist myth suited him fine in that they were a key component of the Front's capacity to survive and grow in his peasant environment. But by 1985, the strengthening of the TPLF, the advent of *perestroika* in the Soviet Union, the weakening of the socialist camp in the Cold War and the visible failure of the Mengistu dictatorship at all levels—social, economic, military and diplomatic—all pointed to the same direction: a toning down both of the socialist rhetoric and of the ethno-nationalist agenda. Victory was at hand but victory for what? Some aims were obvious: an end to the war in Eritrea, an end to the internal violence of the dictatorship, a new diplomatic deal with the international community and a rebuilding of the economy. But within what regional/ national framework and through what kind of governance? That was not clear.

Meles Zenawi and the problems of early post-war Ethiopian governance (1991–98)

Ethiopia was then an age-old polity and Meles was a (somewhat subdued) young revolutionary. The problem was in marrying the two. This was particularly true if we understand that this revolution was unfinished. The case of a completely finished revolution applies to China, which in 1949 was free to open a completely new chapter of its long national saga. The fact that after 1976 it chose to re-interpret the meaning of what it had done between 1919 and 1949 is quite another story. Other choices could possibly have been made. But there were few *unavoidable constraints* on its choices. On the contrary, if we look at France as it emerged from its revolution in 1815, we can see that it was only half-digested. It took over half a century, till the showdown that led to the 1877 *de facto* marginalization of President MacMahon, to establish a stable regime that embodied the results of the revolution. And even then, pre-revolutionary hiccups would always be ready to re-emerge, such as when the collapse of the French Army facing German invasion in 1940 became an occasion to re-create a regime which, in many of its aspects, reincarnated many of the counter-revolutionary traits of pre-1789 France. Russia is an interesting case of a disintegrated revolution that finally brought the country to a point that would probably have been reached anyway, even if the revolution had never taken place, and later attempted to both disavow its revolutionary past while at the same time glorifying it. In the case of Ethiopia, the problem was different: the revolution had destroyed a certain social order but had failed to institutionalize a new one, it had violently upset the premises of the agrarian economy of yesterday but without giving it a new stability, and it had destroyed a governance system without creating an alternate one. Worse, it had addressed the fearsome "national question" but without solving it.[10] And even worse than all that, it had completely failed to create a living civil society.

This is the situation Meles Zenawi had to face in order to reorganize Ethiopia after 1991. The very fact that this last sentence can be written is a testimony to the depth of the problem. Why Meles Zenawi? Why only him? Why not the whole political movement he was associated in with his comrades? Because he was there and he had in his hands—and knew how to use it—that magical element of *Habesha* culture, *mengist*, that is, "power" or "control", the key to fifteen centuries of Abyssinian survival. And that was because *mengist* in Ethiopia

421

has never relied on a non-existent civil society or even on embryonic social classes, but rather on the army and on the state apparatus. Of course it is possible to fantasize on the feasibility of a different governance dispensation which would have been more democratic, more articulated around an extended network of governance agents reaching far into the social and political landscape. And here again we touch on the demonization/adulation directed at the man Meles: was it possible to imagine such a form of governance? Were there bases for the immediate creation of at least an embryonic democratic state? What were the social and human elements that were available to ensure the continuity of the Ethiopian state which is the be-all and end-all of all forms of governance since the days of Axum? Did Meles choose authoritarianism or could he have gone another way? What social forces could he have used to promote a different choice of governance?[11] There are no simple answers to these basic questions.

Back in 1991 the landscape was not very encouraging: there were various ethno-nationalist groupings, the TPLF army and guerrilla structure command, an embryo EPRDF which was little more than a gaggle of war prisoners and Johnny-come-lately politicians, a friendly but now distant Eritrea, frustrated remnants of the revolutionary groupings defeated by the Derg and a diaspora which had no sympathy for what it saw as Tigrayan control of the Ethiopian state, a kind of comeback which had somehow re-linked with the Tigrayan hegemony gone since the death of Yohannes IV in 1889. Worse, there was no social class ready to support the new regime—or to take over in case of its collapse. Once more, as many times in the Ethiopian past, it was a choice between an authoritarian order and the danger of state and national dissolution. In a cultured Ethiopian mind the ghost of *Zemene mesafint*, the princely anarchy of the late eighteenth and early nineteenth century,[12] remains as the ultimate existential fear. It is recalled somewhat like the anarchy of the Southern Song dynastic period or the warlord era of 1919–37 in China: death, death not only of men—these can be seen as replaceable in the long-term perspective—but the death of the state, the death of the nation itself, the demise of the common collective identity. This exact same phenomenon happening in neighbouring Somalia exactly at that same moment was a haunting shadow in the regional landscape.

These were the constraints of the times. Many of Meles' critics point out the authoritarian structure he put in place after 1991 and lament his not sufficiently promoting democracy. When kept within reason these criticisms do have a point. But a limited point only: 1991 Ethiopia was not a *tabula rasa* where the seeds of democracy were there, just waiting to be watered by a benign hand in order to sprout. 1991 Ethiopia was a mess and a nightmare to organize.[13] One had limited choices. Was Meles authoritarian by nature? This is a question that is hard to answer. But what he certainly was, in a most visible way, was a pragmatist. And he had remained both a "revolutionary" and a nationalist. A revolutionary definitely not in the Marxist sense of the word, even if this was not so much by choice as by force. The tools, the manner, the design of a Marxist "dictatorship of the proletariat" were still in his hands. But not the program. He had the instruments but no more clearly-known part to play as the world-wide "socialist camp" had collapsed in the meantime. And the public was far from being uniformly supportive. The strength of Meles in these difficult days was that his enemies were confused and divided, ranging from Western-oriented democrats to nostalgic far-leftists by way of disgruntled ethno-nationalists and opportunistic fellow-travellers who were looking for an opportunity to ditch him. Among his trump cards were his tight party organization, his military strength and his supreme skill at playing the international community to make it dance to his music. But was there a *real* choice at the time between "democracy" and "dictatorship" as many of his critics insisted? Probably not. "Democracy", in the Western sense of the word, was not a readily available option in Ethiopia in 1991 since none of its necessary underpinnings—a liberal bourgeoisie, a civil society, a semi-educated working class, an embryonic national political tradition (as was the case for example in neighbouring Sudan)—were even remotely operational. Obstacles were many and the tools to overcome them were all more or less authoritarian.

Just as Meles had successfully muddled through in his management of the TPLF fighting years, he was going to attempt to muddle through the power that had now finally fallen into his hands and those of his comrades. But he realized—and some of his friends also did—that some kind of coalition politics was now in order. But did "coalition" then mean power-sharing? This was the key difficulty. He had tried at first when the OLF[14] had been associated with the government as a separate and allied body. Within a few months, this alliance had proved impossible because the OLF wanted to bite more than it could chew. Given the demographic weight of the Oromo, there was a rough democratic logic to this. But given the internal confusion and contradictions the OLF represented that it was a practical impossibility since the OLF itself was incapable of locally carrying out the democracy that it demanded to see the Transitional Government practice.[15] If the OLF was too big and at the same time too confused and too unwieldy to be able to convincingly rise up to a partnership role in a coalition government, the political positioning of the Amhara (and even more of the "Amharized")[16] was quite distinct. Mengistu's policy of "nation building" had in fact been a "socialist" rehash of the old Amhara-centred centralist imperial policy practiced in Ethiopia since the death of Yohannes IV in 1889. This group, especially the "Amharized", was the strongest advocate of democracy and would indeed have been its main beneficiaries had it managed to be developed along Western lines. Their educational level and their degree of past political experience would automatically have put them at the top of the social pyramid. But Mengistu's reliance on them during the Derg years had been a two-edged sword: it ensured their social survival in a terrible time but also fed the resentment of the peripheral ethnic groups who were increasingly discriminated against in the name of the national(ist) interest. The bevy of ethno-nationalistic groups at the forefront of politics in 1991 was in itself a sub-product of the differential treatment the Amhara(ized) had enjoyed during the years 1977–1991. Handling that nexus of competing ethno-nationalisms garbed in democratic clothing was akin to handling a cactus without protecting gloves.[17]

Meles was in a paradoxical situation: he had to satisfy his primary Tigrayan clientele while trying at the same time to build a trans-ethnic alliance with Amhara who dreamed of eliminating the Tigrayans to regain their old dominant position, with Oromo who would have liked to eliminate both the Tigrayans and the Amhara and with a multiplicity of minor ethnic groups who saw "democracy" mostly in terms of regional/local autonomy and often failed to see any further. His (imperfect) answer was to keep power strongly centralized at the centre while subcontracting variable pieces of it to the regions/ethnic groups in the name of the "ethnic federalism" system.[18] This was far from the democratic image used for foreign consumption. But it was realistic in terms of dealing with the age-old problem of Ethiopian governance.[19] Particularly since we have so far spoken only about governance without mentioning the two other main problems that the Transitional Government was facing in those years.

First, at the domestic level, the economic situation was disastrous. At the time of the collapse of the Mengistu regime there were only a few million dollars of foreign exchange left, barely enough to pay for a week of imports. And on the debit side, there was a $7bn debt. The infrastructure was either damaged by the war or neglected in peaceful areas because all the financial resources of the communist regime had been absorbed at first in incoherent economic reforms, and later in the war. The men coming to power and put in charge of the economy, such as Kassu Ilala or Tamrat Layne, had no idea of how to deal with the situation. Their economic expertise was close to zero and many had spent years reading Marxist classics which had no relevance to the realities they were now supposed to be dealing with. Meles was roughly aware of this but did not yet comprehend all the complex elements that he was responsible for handling.[20]

In addition to these difficulties the new honeymoon with Eritrea which had started in 1988 was quickly turning bitter. Issayas Afeworqi had a crude vision of his "big brother/small brother" relationship with Ethiopia which was roughly that of Mussolini back in 1936: Eritrea had to be the industrial power base of the Ethiopian ensemble, with Abyssinia and the South constituting both a large market for Eritrean manufactured goods and a source of cheap agricultural products.[21] This view of institutionalized imperialist inequality might have been more or less feasible in 1936 but in 1991 it made strictly no sense. And this increasing tension ran, in part, around the importance of economic investment in Tigray. For reasons of domestic governance, Meles had reserved a large slice of the investment pie for Tigray[22] and this had led the relationship with Issayas[23] into a progressive slide from recrimination to threats, to military gesticulation and finally to a face-off that was going to result in open warfare. Paradoxically, although Meles Zenawi was routinely accused by his detractors of being an Eritrean puppet, his real position was completely contradictory: Issayas kept reproaching him for "ingratitude" and for "anti-Eritrean investments"[24] while many of his comrades saw him on the contrary as "soft on Eritrea". Why so? Mainly because (and that is only my own interpretation) he realized that a war would have no winners but only losers, which eventually proved to be the case. He tried to humour and pacify his northern cousin as much as he could. But when the Eritreans decided, out of counterproductive nationalistic feeling, to have their own currency, he insisted that the Ethiopian *birr* and the Eritrean *nakfa* should have a floating rate of exchange, knowing full well that a fixed one would play massively in Asmara's favour.

These were the broad constraints of the first seven years of the EPRDF regime in Ethiopia. During those years, Meles was not the overwhelming multi-dimensional leader that he was eventually to become later. A whole array of men such as Seye Abraha, Tewolde Wolde Mariam, Seyoum Mesfin, Sebhat Nega, Kinfe Gebre Medhin, Gebru Asrat, Abay Tsehay, Kuma Demeksa, Girma Biru, Bereket Simon, Samora Yunus or Tsadkan Gebre Kidan were vastly instrumental in defining the various policies of the state. But they soon were all plunged into a new war in May 1998, from which the role of the Prime Minister was eventually to emerge transformed and strengthened through the fiery blast of the conflict's furnace.

War and the emergence of Meles Zenawi as undisputed leader (1998–2005)

The 1998–2000 Ethio-Eritrean war was an undiluted disaster in that, after it killed a minimum of 50,000 people and wasted at least $4.5bn, no war aims of any kind had been attained by either side after two years of conflict. The war had given Meles an edge of authority in a situation where all opposition had suddenly disappeared (temporarily) for patriotic reasons. But another effect of the war was the impact it had on the domestic politics of both countries. We have already documented what happened in Eritrea in September 2001 in the relevant chapter. But in Ethiopia proper the effect was comparable, even if its consequences eventually proved much less severe.

The 2001 TPLF's internal crisis. In March 2001, a group of TPLF dissidents headed by former Defence Minister Siye Abraha tried to depose Prime Minister Meles Zenawi by way of an internal bureaucratic coup. There were roughly three issues: (1) the dissidents accused the PM of "being soft on Eritrea";[25] (2) they accused him of a rightward drift; (3) they said he had become too subservient to the United States.[26] They were eventually counterchecked by the PM's allies (even though it was a pretty close shave) and were all arrested. But the opposition used this political uncertainty to egg on the student community—which had quite a separate quarrel with the government and particularly its unpopular Minister for Education Gennet Zewde—and got the students to take to the street on 17 April. In the climate of tension resulting from the TPLF bureaucratic mutiny, the police lost all control, killed 41 demonstrators, wounded about 400 and arrested 3,000. In the following weeks several leading intellectuals were arrested (supposedly for having incited the students), many journalists were detained and the President of the Republic (Dr Negasso Gidada) was deposed and kicked out of the party. His was a largely honorary position but this action showed that the repression would not fear to strike high.

The next few months were spent in endless debates (the famous TPLF practice of *gimgima*, which is supposed to yield consensus through animated confrontation) but by September Meles had regained full control of the political scene and put his own trusted allies in key positions. Nevertheless, this had been a close call: many of the dissenters who had tried to eliminate the PM (Tewolde Wolde Mariam, Gebru Asrat, Betew Belay) were among his closest associates and it showed that the solidity of the state rested on a fairly brittle foundation. The TPLF was the core of the EPRDF and if it had broken into pieces, the whole structure of the party-state as it existed since 1991 could have fallen apart.

Nothing in the past experience of Meles Zenawi had pushed him towards democracy. As a guerrilla leader, as the leading member of a revolutionary state trying to rebuild something out of the ruins, and recently as a war leader, all his life and experiences had tended to place him squarely within the authoritarian tradition of Ethiopian governance that he had inherited from his forebears. The only democratic space he knew—a rather peculiar one—was the TPLF one. And within 48 hours he had been forced to realize that this democratic space which he thought he could trust could suddenly bend back and turn against him. What then could he expect from the opposition—which usually used a rather radical vocabulary, even if it was at the service of the most conservative causes—if his own and closest friends could plot his elimination *ahead* of a party congress? There is no doubt that intellectually Meles agreed with the necessity of democracy. But what did it actually *mean* for him in a polity where the dog-eat-dog approach seemed prevalent, in spite of all the nice politically correct discourses?

There is no doubt that the Ethiopian state, as it evolved from his hands after the March–April 2001 crisis, was authoritarian. Human rights were not his main concern—that is an understatement—and repressive legislation and practice (on the press, on personal rights, on political activity) were common. The question is *how did he see it?*

Was it for him a tool towards indefinitely staying in power or was it an instrument towards the transformation of Ethiopia? The opposition, particularly the diaspora opposition, would undoubtedly answer the first question affirmatively. And this could be understood: it was a daring and uncomfortable thing to stand in the way of Prime Minister Meles Zenawi. But if we look at what happened later—and particularly after 2005—this seems unlikely. The problem of Meles seems to have been this: he wanted both economic development and the growth of democracy. But which one should come first?

The 2005 elections. The 2005 elections were to bring things to a head. In an unprecedented move, the EPRDF regime—which since the March–April 2001 crisis had been largely a reflection of Meles' own decisions and philosophy—decided to finally opt for a free and fair election, no matter what the consequences might be.

Facing the EPRDF, the opposition managed to regroup itself into two broad coalitions, the Coalition for Unity and Democracy (CUD) and the United Ethiopian Democratic Forces (UEDF).[27] Neither of those were real "political parties". They were groupings which, in their diversity and contradictions, reflected the social, ethnic and historical inheritance of the Ethiopian past. Within the CUD the two main parties in the coalition, the AEUP and EUDP-Medhin—itself an amalgam of four parties—were both in competition for Amhara support. As for the UEDF, it was a regrouping of a large Oromo party, the Oromo National Congress (ONC) of Merera Gudina, and the SEPDC of the veteran anti-EPRDF opponent Beyene Petros. But the SEPDC itself was also a coalition of fourteen small ethnic parties. Thus, like a series of Russian dolls, the opposition forces were conglomerates of smaller units with different views and aims, which were only united in their desire to see the EPRDF lose power and which, even though temporarily linked by an electoral pact, could have no reasonable prospect of serious collaboration in an eventual government of national unity.

The CUD and the UEDF, the two largest units, represented two very distinct strands of opposition to the EPRDF. In their various incarnations which differed in age and social status, the parties making up the CUD wanted changes in the constitution limiting regional autonomy, removing ethnicity from the federal status and abolishing article 39 of the constitution which allowed the right of secession for a regional state.[28] This was largely seen as a return to the past, almost to the structure of the imperial regime, with the implicit vision of a single Amhara-speaking Ethiopian polity. And this was completely unacceptable to the UEDF which stood for the defence of the non-Amhara ethnic groups, a position paradoxically closer to the EPRDF's own pluralist vision than to that of its opposition allies. Thus the accursed "nationalities question" which had been a key element in the starting of the revolution had returned to haunt the first seriously contested democratic election of the post civil war years.

For the outside observers of the international community, this was quite difficult to perceive. They tended to see the electoral contest in terms of democracy (opposition) versus authoritarianism (EPRDF), which in itself was not an entirely false perception. But it was only a partial one since they did not realize the heavy historical baggage each side was lugging along. And Meles Zenawi, as a deeply Abyssinian structured political/historical personality, could not see it the same way. Yes, he represented an authoritarian form of rule. But he also represented the continuity of the Ethiopian state. Was the opposition capable of incarnating either a change or an alternative to that rigid survivalist choice? Back in May 2005, the question had been an open one. But the handling of its own success by the opposition threw this democratic alternative into disarray.

When official results were announced in August, the EPRDF was declared to have won 327 seats after 31 constituencies had to be re-run following contestations. The opposition was said to have won 174 seats (CUD 109, UEDF 52, OFDM 11 and others 2). It did not accept this tally and decided to contest it in the courts.

Whether this was right or not is hard to say since the results of the 2005 elections were never objectively and dispassionately examined. But the handling of these confused and contradictory results was in itself revealing.

Almost immediately after the voting, and in defiance of a ban on demonstrations, the CUD launched several public demonstrations. Security forces opened fire killing some 40 demonstrators. Then the two opposition coalitions engaged in a loud and acrimonious debate on whether to join parliament when it opened on 11 October or not. The UEDF argued for participation while the leadership of the CUD, and in particular its hapless chairman Hailu Shawel, backed a boycott on grounds that the results were fraudulent and that the EPRDF had no intention of allowing the opposition to play any realistic role in parliament. The CUD decision to boycott parliament led to a split in the CUD during October as many members and its executive council did not agree.

Then to make things even worse, there was an attempt to merge the four CUD parties into a single organization, which EUDP-Medhin saw as an attempt by Hailu Shawel and the AEUP to take control of the CUD. This was disastrous. The election had been free even though probably not fair. But instead of bringing the various strands of the opposition together to a high vantage point from which they could criticize the obviously defensive and not very democratic reactions of the EPRDF, it led to an explosion of factionalism which discredited the opposition at the very moment it should have risen to a responsible level that would have made it look like a believable alternative to the government. For example, in spite of the fact that the opposition had swept the floor of the Addis Ababa Municipal Council, no opposition party was able to muster the necessary quorum to take up the administration of the capital city.

The democratic progress which had been the most impressive fact in the strong opposition results was wasted because that same opposition could not decide whether it was revolutionary or democratic, capable of handling a partial victory or not, and prepared to participate rather than to boycott. The net result was that, in spite of the overreaction of the security forces,[29] the opposition spoiled its impressive showing by a display of contradictory factionalism betraying its immaturity. It was seen as not so much the bearer of new distinct policy elements but rather the expression of a visceral rejection of what had happened since 1991—and perhaps even since 1974.

Should this disaster for democracy be attributed to the Prime Minister or to the opposition? Probably to both. To the debit of Meles Zenawi one has to admit that he had done nothing in the preceding years to promote the kind of civil society which could have laid the ground favouring the growth of a pre-party social/political development. And as far as the opposition is concerned, it displayed neither long-term political maturity nor short-term tactical sense. In its defence one should remember that *absolutely nothing* in the country's modern history had prepared it to realistically deal with a genuine democratic contest. In a typically binary vision of good versus evil which borrowed its terms from Abyssinian religious culture, it did not see itself as a complement or even as a relative alternative to the regime it was challenging, but rather as *qeddus Giyorgis*, the Archangel in shining armour about to set right everything that had been done wrong. These were not democratic political terms but theological ones and the result was not so much a victory for the EPRDF as a defeat for democracy. The whole terms of the contest had been handled so poorly by both sides that the outcome was a setback for the very idea of democracy which, like "socialism" a few years before, began to look like a fake God from the point of view of the ordinary Ethiopian peasant masses. As for Meles himself, this probably comforted him in the view that democracy was a rich man's toy and that the true problem of Ethiopia was economic.

Towards a new economic strategy. The year 2002 had been the year in which the per capita income of Ethiopians had reached its lowest point since the revolution, whether we use the non-compensated direct dollar Atlas method ($120) or the compensated PPP method ($550).[30] The economy was a disaster as this had probably played an added role in the strong showing of the opposition during the election.

Now that the opposition had largely self-destroyed,[31] the Prime Minister could turn his attention to the economy. In a way, this was a reflection of his lifelong exposure to Marxism: all societies are a product of the arrangement of their forces of production. But this being said, it left the door open for various forms of interpretation of that basic dictum. And although he never acknowledged it in such clear terms it seems probable that his evaluation probably concurred with that of Deng Xiaoping when he had to deal with the heritage of Maoism. Like China, Ethiopia was the heir to centuries-old cultural traits, embedded in political traditions that remained the bedrock of any later political transformations, including "Marxist" revolutions. Like China it had to deal with a largely peasant economy and like China it feared that ditching the resilient elements of the existing one-party state could prove disastrous for the state itself in the long run. Like China it had to make sure it could feed its large peasant masses and like China it had to climb out of the underdevelopment ditch, at first by way of heavy infrastructure investments.[32]

The time had now come for the priority turning towards a main economic thrust. We will not examine here Meles' economic policies as this is done elsewhere.[33] But, in line with this attempt at assessing Meles Zenawi's global record, we have to understand what it meant within his own perspective. Meles Zenawi was both a pragmatist and a revolutionary. In his view this emphasis on the economy—which he doubtlessly considered as more important than his commitment to democracy—had to be both pragmatic and radical. Hence the groping for an overall strategy which, given its repeated partial failures, led him to move from ADLI to the present GTP by way of several other partial temporary attempts. For Meles it is clear that two things were out of the question:

1. A *laissez-faire* attitude that would wait till private partial initiatives would, of themselves and by themselves, concur in a "natural" development through the agency of Adam Smith's "unseen hand".
2. On the opposite side, joining the neo-liberal economic new world order promoted by the United States and its financial extensions, the World Bank and the IMF. From that point of view it is very typical to see how the disaffected former IMF Chief Economist Joseph Stiglitz warmly embraced Meles's policies, to the dismay of the opposition and the EPRDF's satisfaction.

Meles' switch to a mainly economic approach of Ethiopia's perennial problems was not a rupture in his line of thinking. His pragmatism had caused him to ditch the concept of a nationalized command economy back in the early 1990s. But it did not mean that this had led him to embrace the new economic world view of his American ally in exchange. Just as for the Chinese, state capitalism and a semi-command economy had become his chosen path towards economic development. In a variety of guises, this has been a fall-back path of choice for the BRICS, with an array of colours ranging from full-fledged state-capitalism in the case of China to a largely liberal approach in the case of India. Ethiopia is definitely closer to the Chinese model. And, just like its model, it is now bumping its head on a variety of dysfunctions accruing from the centralized control nature of the project. Lack of democracy, civil rights negligence, preference for numbers over quality in terms of training, a quantitative rather than a qualitative approach to progress, civil service corruption, all these "Chinese" problems exist on a smaller, rougher scale in Ethiopia.

The loneliness of the long-distance runner: Meles Zenawi's last years (2005–2012)

The late Prime Minister's adversaries will put all the dysfunctions of the system to his debit while his supporters will insist that the results are a nearly blameless tale of constant progress and undiluted successes. These are the views of polemics and of politics, not the judgement of history. And when we think of Meles, of his place and role in the long history of Ethiopia, it is difficult—and probably premature—to establish a firm and definitive diagnosis.

But one thing is sure: the man has put a strong imprint on his time, probably the strongest one in Ethiopia since Emperor Menelik saved his country from falling into the hands of the conquering European powers in the nineteenth century. Retrospectively, it is only too easy to establish the list of Menelik's shortcomings: his manipulative approach to his entourage, his almost complete lack of interest in the ordinary *gebbar* peasant population or his brutal subjugation of the Southern regions. But without him, or with a lesser man at the helm of the Empire in the 1890s, Ethiopia would most likely have disappeared, partitioned between Britain and Italy. The main problem of his age was what Sven Rubenson (1976) has felicitously called *The Survival of Ethiopian Independence*. But later, things changed. After World War Two and with decolonization, the parameters were transformed. The threat did not come from outside any more, it came from inside, from the difficulty of the African continent to rise to the level where it could handle its own problems in a reasonably autonomous way.

Meles was deeply conscious of the problem of economic backwardness, and in his post-Marxist revolutionary way did not want to attempt to solve it either through a nineteenth century "classical" national capitalist approach or through the globalized transnational financial version of the New World Order. He strove for an independent path of a somewhat "Chinese" state capitalist nature. This might work or it might not. We are still *in media res*, in the middle of things, at the time of writing. And the work of the contemporary historian is not to be a crystal ball gazing prophet but rather an attentive observer and record keeper of his times. But what we can already say is that Meles tried to shoulder a huge burden. His methods were definitely not choosy and his tactics were rough. But his strategy was daring and carried a vision. Hence his loneliness, because the top is always lonely. It is not certain that his successors clearly know what to do with his inheritance and their extreme praise of his memory might well be an effort at postponing things in the hope of finding a sequential strategy. Which is not an easy thing. Since the independence of the 1960s, how many African heads of state have had the courage, wisdom and lucidity to take things back to the drawing board? The rough attempts run from Kwame Nkrumah to Thomas Sankara by way of Julius Nyerere and they are littered with the corpses of disastrously false solutions on the Mugabe or Mengistu model. Meles imposed an authoritarian developmentalist vision on the Ethiopian landscape and definitely considered that this was the priority of priorities.

His human rights shortcomings have to be judged in this perspective. As the inheritor of a Marxist revolutionary tradition, he was obviously impatient with "bourgeois" rights. This was a grave shortcoming because the very nature of advanced development implies access and expansion to these rights as they condition the functioning of a free economy. This is a discovery the Chinese themselves are now painfully making. We can speculate that if Meles had lived longer he might have become aware of this necessity. Another area of complete neglect in his approach is the problem of demographic increase. Ethiopia had around 35 million inhabitants before the revolution and it has over 95 million today. Such a population explosion is not sustainable because it eats up the benefits of economic growth. Meles would answer remarks to this effect with the quip that another mouth to feed meant another pair of arms at work. This was a typically anti-Malthusian remark coming from his revolutionary background. Mao-Zedong used to reason along exactly the same line of thought but Deng-Xiaoping put an end to it with the single child policy; and one can consider that this has been one of the key factors that allowed the enormous expansion of the Chinese economy over the last thirty years. Meles Zenawi steered Ethiopia roughly in the right direction but a lot of such fine tuning— financing the GTP, reconciling a modicum of respect for human rights and democratic process with a firm sort of governance, a massive ecological effort without which the Ethiopian land resources will not survive population growth—remains to be done.

Meles' mastery of international and African affairs. In roughly sketching this major era of Ethiopian history, there is one element we have so far neglected: international relations. Why? Because international relations have probably been more peaceful and less threatening for Ethiopia in the Meles Zenawi years than they have been at any point since the *Zemene Mesafint* period. Since 1991 Ethiopia has known no threat comparable to the Egyptian attacks of Khedive Isma'il in the 1870s or the threat of the Mahdists in the 1880s. Post-Berlin Conference European imperialism, Italian fascism or the regional

THE MELES ZENAWI ERA

effects of the Cold War had been haunting problems. And Meles' rise to power coincided with the collapse of the international communist system while the later rise of Muslim fundamentalism—perhaps the greatest *internal* rather than external threat to the Ethiopian polity today—had so far spared Ethiopia. Ethiopia under Meles Zenawi has been roughly at peace and more or less assured of remaining so in the foreseeable future. This gave him an amount of leeway his predecessors would have envied.

Meles was a master player of the diplomatic game and he managed both to charm the international community and to use it for Ethiopia's benefit. Contrary to legend he was not the Horn of Africa tool of US policy that his adversaries tried to portray. He was *useful* to the Americans but he certainly got more from them in terms of economic aid and diplomatic support than he provided them with. His handling of global African issues put him in a kind of *primus inter pares* position vis-à-vis Africa and the rest of the world which was somehow reminiscent of Haile Selassie's. He stood for Africa (even if his *real* African concerns were solidly regional) and tried to interpret it to the rest of the world. This was not entirely convincing and he probably knew it. But it earned him a lot of goodwill accruing from the confused guilt feelings of the West and he used it to good advantage.

His twin (manageable) headaches were the Sudan and Somalia. He handled the Sudan masterfully, at first using the Islamist regime in his fight against Mengistu and then later diversifying his support for the Sudanese rebels to put sufficient pressure on Beshir's regime to smooth the post-CPA period after 2005 and sponsor the 2011 independence referendum. His handling of the relations with Juba prevented Eritrea, which had been a major sponsor of the SPLA in the late war years, to regain a serious foothold in independent South Sudan.

Somalia was a less successful endeavour. His support for Yusuf Abdullahi after 2004 was overoptimistic and resulted in failure. His handling of the Union of Islamic Courts regime was extremely complex and finally short-sighted. The foreign vision of his carrying out an invasion of the country in December 2006 at the behest of the Americans is completely false. On the contrary, the American administration tried to restrain him from action in Somalia, arguing that the US had enough problems with Muslim countries worldwide and did not look forward to more trouble with Somalia (there were burning memories of the US "Restore Hope" failure in 1993) at this time. Meles agreed but cleverly manipulated the situation so that he could intervene for reasons that had very little to do with fighting Islamic fundamentalism.[34] Just like the Americans themselves in Iraq, he had an easy success at first that turned into a final blockage in the longer run. He had to evacuate in 2009 after fulfilling only one part of his war aims while precariously balancing what had been left unresolved.[35]

* * *

This short, early and unavoidably incomplete assessment of a major period in Ethiopian history will be concluded on a human note. Meles, the man, had known that he was sick since 2003. He had said nothing and had kept working. Apart from a handful of close associates, nobody knew of his sickness. He tried to prepare his succession and at times mentioned, almost jokingly, that he was tired of politics and was seriously considering retiring after the 2015 elections. As a long-time visitor, resident and associate of Ethiopia where I was living at the time, I never took such remarks seriously. I was wrong. He knew that he would soon have to retire—for ever—and that he had to try to prepare the country for it. From later conversations with people who knew, he was hoping to have perhaps a little bit more time. Death overtook him somewhat earlier than he had hoped and his preparations were not all finished. But nothing of his tragic situation transpired. I have spoken with people who talked with him only days before he left Ethiopia for his last trip and he showed no sign, in his conversation or behaviour, of what he knew was going to happen to him. He had always been pitiless with others and he was similarly pitiless with himself. He died on 20 August 2012, at the ge of 57, with the dignity of a Roman Stoic.

His remarkable inheritance is today largely mythified by the regime. This is an understandable temptation but not a very useful one since it solves nothing. Meles cannot keep governing from the grave, as it often seems to be the case when one moves around Addis Ababa these days.[36] The elections of 2015—and their aftermath—will be a key moment in the country's history.

BIBLIOGRAPHY AND FURTHER READING

Abir, Mordechai, 1968, *Ethiopia: The Era of the Princes. The Challenge of Islam and the Re-unification of the Christian Empire, 1760–1855*, London, Praeger.

Cabestan, Jean-Pierre, 2012, "Ethiopia and China: Authoritarian Affinities and Economic Cooperation", *China Perspectives*, 4, pp. 53–62.

Bahru Zewde, 2014, *The Quest for Socialist Utopia: the Ethiopian Student Movement (1960–1974)*, London: James Currey.

Balsvik, Randi, 1985, *Haile Selassie's Students: the Intellectual and Social Background to Revolution (1952–1977)*, East Lansing: Michigan State University.

Bloch, Marc, 1953, *The Historian's Craft: Reflections on the Nature and Uses of History and the Techniques and Methods of Those Who Write It*, New York: A. Knopf (Original edition: 1949, *Apologie pour l'histoire ou le métier d'historien*, Paris: Armand Colin).

Erlich, Haggai, 1996, *Ras Alula and the Scramble for Africa: A Political Biography: Ethiopia and Eritrea (1875–1897)*, Lawrenceville, NJ: Red Sea Press.

Gebru Tareke, 2009, *The Ethiopian Revolution: War in the Horn of Africa*, New Haven: Yale University Press.

Gramsci, Antonio, *Selections from the Prison Notebooks*, London: Lawrence and Wishart. [There were eleven reprints of this excellent critical selection, between 1971 and 2005; the mentions/discussions of the concept of "organic intellectuals" can be found on pp 6, 12 15–18, 20, 60 and 330].

Paulos Milkias, 2003, "Ethiopia, the TPLF, and the Roots of the 2001 Political Tremor", *Northeast African Studies*, 10 (2), New Series, pp. 13–66.

Pausewang, S., Tronvoll, K. and Aalen, L. (eds), 2002, *Ethiopia since the Derg*, London: Zed Books.

Prunier, Gérard, 2010, "The 1943 Woyane revolt: a Modern Reassessment", *The Journal of the Middle East and Africa*, 1 (2), pp. 187–95.

Rubenson, Sven, 1976, *The Survival of Ethiopian Independence*, London: Heinemann.

NOTES

INTRODUCTION

1. The *Encyclopedia Aethiopica*, published by Harrassowitz in Wiesbaden under the direction of Professor Siegbert Uhlig since 2003. Vol. 1, 2003; vol. 2, 2005; vol. 3, 2007; vol. 4, 2010; vol. 5, 2014. There are some articles in the *Encyclopaedia Aethiopica* that deal with post-1974 Ethiopia (for example, the article "Revolution of 1974" and the other articles it refers to), but the events, political movements and figures of this period are not studied as systematically and carefully as those of previous periods of Ethiopian history.
2. Schwab, Peter, 1985, *Ethiopia: Politics, Economics and Society*, Boulder, CO: Lynne Rienner.
3. Prunier, Gérard, (ed.), 2007, *L'Ethiopie contemporaine*, Paris: Karthala.
4. The editors thank Miklos Gozstonyi and Yves Stranger for their contribution to translation work, and Michael Dwyer, Jon de Peyer, Jonathan Derrick and Alasdair Craig for their editorial care and patience. They are also grateful for the institutional support they received from the French Centre for Ethiopian Studies, the French Embassy in Addis Ababa, the French National Centre for Scientific Research (CNRS), and Addis Ababa University through the Institute of Ethiopian Studies, the Institute for Development Studies, and the Institute for Peace and Security Studies.

1. ETHIOPIANS IN THE TWENTY-FIRST CENTURY: THE STRUCTURE AND TRANSFORMATION OF THE POPULATION

1. This chapter is based on a chapter co-authored by Éloi Ficquet, Hugo Ferran, Arnaud Kruczynski and François Piguet in Prunier, 2007, the prototype in French for the present volume. We have shortened, revised, reorganized and updated it. The authors thank Wolbert Smidt, Yves Stranger and Thomas Osmond for their comments.
2. For general reflections on ethnic and linguistic diversity see J. Abbink,

"Languages and Peoples in Ethiopia and Eritrea", *Encyclopaedia Aethiopica* Vol. 5. Henceforth references to articles in the *Encyclopaedia Aethiopica* are given in the following form: *EAE* followed by the volume number (e.g. *EAE*1 refers to Volume 1).

3. The lifestyle of the Gurage is described in the section below. Some Gurage societies, in particular those who are Christians like the Kistane, share with the Habesha a strong sense of Ethiopian national identity and see themselves as sharing their origins with the Habesha.

4. Figures based on the 2007 Population and Housing Census of Ethiopia (CSA, 2010, pp. 91–2).

5. The territorial divisions include the boundaries of Gojjam, Wollo, Shoa, Gondar and so on for the Amhara subgroups, and Welqayt, Agame, Hamasen and so on for the Tigray subgroups.

6. For a general anthropological overview of Habesha societies, see Shack, 1974.

7. On social control and socialization see Molvaer, 1995.

8. On land tenure and social organization in Habesha society, see Hoben, 1973; Crummey, 2000.

9. On the ideological roots of Habesha domination, see Levine, 1974.

10. On Ethiopian reformist intellectuals in the twentieth century see Bahru Zewde, 2002. On literature see Molvaer, 1980. On the development of Ethiopian popular music see Falceto, 2001.

11. On Amhara social organization and culture see Levine, 1965; Messing, 1985; Leslau and Kane, 2001. Encyclopedia articles: D. Levine, "Amhara", *EAE*1; D. Appleyard, "History and Dialectology of Amharic", *EAE*1.

12. On self-designations of Tigrinya speaking groups see Smidt, 2010 and his encyclopedia article, "Təgrəñña-speakers", *EAE*4.

13. On Tigray social order see Bauer, 1977; Tronvoll, 1998.

14. For an ethnography of the Qemant see Gamst, 1969 and Gamst's encyclopedia articles on the Agäw groups: "Agäw Ethnography", *EAE*1; "Hamta", *EAE*2; "Kəmant", *EAE*3.

15. On the history of the Agäw see Tadesse Tamrat, 1988.

16. S. Kaplan, "Betä ᴣsraʾel", *EAE*1. On the debate on the origins of the Beta Israel see notably Abbink, 1990; Kaplan, 1992.

17. Abdukader Saleh, "Ġäbärti", *EAE*2.

18. On the Argobba see Abebe Kifleyesus, 2006, and the shorter article by the same author, "Argobba Ethnography", *EAE*1.

19. On the historical evolution of Harari society see Gibb, 1999; Carmichael, 2004; Osmond, 2014, and the articles in *EAE*2: T. Carmichael, "Harär from the Late 19th to the Late 20th Century"; A. Gascon, "Harärge"; C. Gibb, "Harari Ethnography"; J. Miran, "Harär under Egyptian Occupation"; E. Wagner, "Harär City Structure and Main Buildings" and "Harär History till 1875".

20. E. Wagner, "Abādīr ʿUmar ar-Riḍa", *EAE*1; F.C. Muth, "Aḥmad b. Ibrāhīm al-Ġāzī", *EAE*1.

21. The count of ethnic affiliations has been a thorny issue since the publication of

the results of the last Kenyan national census in 2009. There are an estimated 250,000 Boorana Oromo in Kenya.

22. Encyclopedia articles on Oromo society and culture in *EAE4*: G. Banti, "Oromiffaa"; J. Hultin, "Oromo Ethnography"; Ezekiel Gebissa, "Oromo History"; D. Bustorf, "Oromo Religion", G. Banti, "Oromo Oral Literature"; W. Smidt, "Early Writing in Oromiffaa"; P.T.W. Baxter and Gaddisa Birru, "Contemporary Writing in Oromiffaa".

23. In 1994 44.3 per cent of the population of the Oromiya Regional State were Muslims, 41.3 per cent Orthodox Christians and nearly 9 per cent Protestants (CSA, 1998, p. 132). These figures, taken from the published results of the national census, do not represent the religious affiliations of the Oromo ethnic group, but provide an approximation since 87.1 per cent of the population of Oromiya are Oromo.

24. For a sympathetic view of Oromo traditional religion see Bartels, 1983. For a critical perspective see Osmond, 2004.

25. This process of social and cultural change following the Oromo expansion has been thoroughly analyzed in Hassen, 1990.

26. For an analysis of the strategy by which a Muslim Oromo lineage of Wollo penetrated the Christian kingdom, see Ficquet, 2014, and his articles, "Wällo" (with Hussein Ahmed), *EAE4*, and "Yäǧǧu", *EAE5*.

27. On Afran Qallo and its role in the emergence of cultural Oromo nationalism see the notes by Falceto and Osmond in the booklet joined to the CD compilation of Ali Birra, 2013.

28. For a detailed description of the *Gadaa* system as it works in Borana-Oromo society see Bassi, 2005. For a comprehensive review of ethnographic literature on *Gadaa* see P.T.W. Baxter, "Gadaa", *EAE2*. See Legesse, 2000 for a conceptual definition of Oromo democracy based on *Gadaa* values, on the basis of ethnographic research done in the 1960s (Legesse, 1973).

29. For a regional comparison of age sets and generation sets see Kurimoto and Simonse, 1998.

30. On the customary political and judicial procedures of the Borana Oromo today see Bassi, 2005, and a shorter version in "Boorana", *EAE1*.

31. On the ancient polities and religious networks of south-east Ethiopia see the collection of essays in Braukämper, 2002.

32. On the history of the Arsi, see Gnamo, 2014; Abbas Haji Gnamo, "Arsi Ethnography", *EAE1*.

33. On the history of Islam in Bale and the spread of Salafi reform movements since the 1960s see Østebø, 2011.

34. On the relations between Harari urban dwellers and their Oromo rural neighbours and clients see Osmond, 2014.

35. On the history of *khat* production and commercialization in Ethiopia see Gebissa, 2004.

36. On the early conquest of Oromo lands by the Kingdom of Shoa see Ege, 1986. On the politico-religious authority of the *Qaallu* among the Metcha Oromo see Knutsson, 1967; J. Hultin, "Mäčča", *EAE3*; Tsega Endalew, "Tuulama", *EAE4*.

37. On the danger posed by the expansion of irrigated plantations for Karrayu pastoralism see Ayalew Gebre, 2001.
38. Tsaga Endalew, "Leeqa", *EAE*3, and "Wälläga", *EAE*4.
39. There are unfortunately few published studies on this region. An exception is a fascinating collection of Amharic documents, without translation, published by TesemmaTa'a and Alessandro Triulzi in 2004 (1997 Ethiopian calendar) at Addis Ababa University Press.
40. Hassen, 1990 is the major historical study on the Oromo kingdoms of Gibe. See also Lewis, 1965 on the Kingdom of Jimma Abba Jifar. Encyclopedia articles: Hassen, "Geeraa", "ǦimmaAbbaa Ǧifaar", "Gomma", "Guumma", *EAE*2; J. Abbink, "Limmu Ennarya", *EAE*3; H. Amborn, "Yäm Ethnography", *EAE*5.
41. For a general perspective on Ethiopian lowland peripheries see Markakis, 2011.
42. On the challenges faced by Afar pastoralists see Maknun, 1993; Haberson, 1978.
43. On the Afar-Issa conflict from an Afar point of view, see Yasin, 2007.
44. On the social organization of the Afar see Chedeville, 1966; Getachew Kassa, 2001. On the history of their toponyms and clan division see Morin, 2004. On their poetry and oral traditions see Morin, 1995. See also D. Morin, "Afar Ethnography", "Afar History"; D. Morin and Getachew Kassa, "'Adohyammára and 'Asahyammára", all in *EAE*1.
45. For an overview on the history of the Somali people see Casanelli, 1982. On Somali groups in or near Ethiopia see: T. Ofcansky, "Dir", *EAE*2; F. Declich, "Habar Awal", *EAE*2; T. Ofcansky, "Isaaq", *EAE*3; D. Morin, "'Issa", *EAE*3; S. Samatar, "Ogaden", *EAE*4.
46. On political developments in Ethiopia's Somali region see Hagmann, 2005.
47. Ibid., p. 512.
48. On craftsmen and their status in south-west Ethiopia see the case studies gathered by Freeman and Pankhurst, 2003. See also the discussion of the notion of caste applied to these groups in H. Amborn, "Handicrafts", *EAE*2.
49. For an overview of Gurage societies through the lens of the Chaha sub-group, see Shack, 1966. On the different groups composing the Gurage see Worku Nida, "Gurage Ethno-Historical Survey"; "Gurage Religions", *EAE*2; C.M. Ford and D. Bustorf, "Caha", *EAE*1; R. Meyer, "Dobbi", *EAE*2; D. Bustorf, "Ǝnär", "Ǝndägäñ Ethnography", "Ǝnnänmor Ethnography", "Ǝnnänqor", "Ǝža", "Geto Ethnography", "Gumär", *EAE*2; D. Bustorf, "Mäsmäs", "Mäsqan Ethnography", *EAE*3; A. Kruczinsky, "Muhər Ethnography", *EAE*3; Bahru Zewde, "Soddo Ethnography" *EAE*4; D. Bustorf, "Wäläne Ethnography", *EAE*4; R. Meyer, "Zay Ethnography", *EAE*5.
50. On the political organization of the Gurage see Bahru Zewde, 2002.
51. On Gurage urban migration see Baker, 1992; Worku Nida, 1996.
52. D. Bustorf, "Səlṭi Ethnography", *EAE*4.
53. On the ethno-history of the Hadiya, see the major ethno-historical study of Braukämper, 2012, plus the synopsis in Braukämper, "Hadiyya", *EAE*2. On Kambata see Braukämper, "Kambaata Ethnography", *EAE*3.

54. On the Sidama see Hamer, 1987; Brøgger, 1986; J. Hamer and Anbessa Teferra, "Sidaama Ethnography", *EAE*4.

55. Mekete Belachew, "Awasa", *EAE*1.

56. H. Amborn, "Burǧi Ethnography", *EAE*1; C. McClellan, "Gide'o", *EAE*2; Wolde Gossa Tadesse, "Konso Ethnography", *EAE*3; H. Amborn, "Koorete Ethnography", *EAE*3. On the social organization of the Konso see also Hallpike, 2008 (revised and self-published edition of the 1972 original book).

57. On the agrarian system of the Konso see Watson, 2009.

58. Azeb Amha, "Ometo", *EAE*4.

59. J. Abbink, "Wälaytta Ethnography", "Wälaytta Kingdom", "Wälaytta-Malla Dynasty", *EAE*4.

60. For an eye-witness account of the conquest of Welayta see Vanderheym, 2012.

61. On Welayta's agrarian decline see Planel, 2008; Dessalegn Rahmato, 2007.

62. On the political system of the Gamo see Bureau, 2012 and Abeles, 2012, which are most welcome English translations of works originally published in French (in 1981 and 1983 respectively). See also Freeman, 2002 for a more recent study of the impact of socio-economic changes on Gamo societies. See also Data Dea, "Dawro", *EAE*2; Wolde Gossa Tadesse, "Dorze Ethnography", "Gamo Ethnography", *EAE*2; Abbink, "Gofa Ethnography", *EAE*2, "Zayse and Zargulla Ethnography", *EAE*5.

63. On the ethno-history of Kefa see Lange, 1976 and 1982; J. Abbink, "Käfa History", "Käfa Ethnography", *EAE*3; Shiferaw Bekele "Käfa Dynasties (14th to end of 19th c.)", *EAE*3, "Šakačo Ethnography", *EAE*4.

64. The following section contains extracts, like this one, from the more detailed description written by Hugo Ferran in the collective chapter on Ethiopian peoples in the book edited by Prunier, 2007. We have translated these extracts. Unless otherwise indicated, take extracted quotations in this section to come from this source.

65. Selected ethnographic studies on these societies: Tornay, 2001 on the Nyangatom; Donham, 1994 on the Maale; Almagor, 1978 on the Dassanech; Strecker and Lydall, 1979 on the Hamer; Turton, 1988 on the Mursi. Encyclopedia articles: C.M. Ford, "Aari", *EAE*1; Wolde Gossa Tadesse and A. Pellar, "Arbore", *EAE*1; K. Masuda, "Banna", *EAE*1; S. Epple, "Bäsada", *EAE*1; I. Strecker, "Hamär Ethnography", *EAE*2; M. Hiroshi, "Kara", *EAE*3; Wolde Gossa Tadesse and H. Ferran, "Maale", *EAE*3; S. Tornay, "Murle Ethnography", *EAE*3; D. Turton, "Mursi", *EAE*3; S. Tornay, "Ñaŋatom Ethnography", *EAE*3; J. Abbink, "Ṣamay", *EAE*4.

66. On these peoples see Abbink, 1992, 1993, 1997, 2000 and 2002. See also, by Abbink, "Baale Ethnography", "Benč Ethnography", *EAE*1; "Dizi Ethnography", *EAE*2; "Me'en Ethnography", *EAE*3; C. Bader "Suri", "Tirmaga", *EAE*4.

67. This corresponds to what I. Kopytoff, 1987 called the "African frontier", that is, the reproduction of traditional African societies through processes of cultural fusion between migrant communities and their hosts.

68. On the impact of tourism see Abbink, 2000; Turton, 2004.

69. On the political, economic and social transformations in Ethiopia's western border territories see Young, 1999.
70. For a fuller exposition of people and politics in the Gambella region see Dereje, 2011.
71. For ethnographic descriptions of the Anuak see Evans-Pritchard, 1940b; Kurimoto, 1996; Perner, 1997; E. Kurimoto, "Añwaa ethnography", *EAE*1.
72. On heightened rivalries between Nuer, Anywaa and Amhara settlers, see the chapter by Vaughan in this volume.
73. P. Unseth, "Maǧaŋgir Ethnography", *EAE*3.
74. A. Triulzi, "Beni Šangul"; J. Abbink, "Berta Ethnography", *EAE*1.
75. J. Spaulding, "Fung", *EAE*2.
76. On the history of Beni Shangul see Triulzi, 1981.
77. Abbute, 2009, p. 155. See also J. Abbink, "Gumuz Ethnography", *EAE*2; S. Hummel and A. Meckelburg, "Komo Ethnography", *EAE*3.
78. U. Braukämper, "Migrations from the 15th to the 19th century"; J. Abbink, "Migrations in the South-west", "Migrations from the Late 19th Century until Today", *EAE*4.
79. On resettlement schemes in Ethiopia see Pankhurst and Piguet, 2009.
80. For an overview of the slave trade in Ethiopia in the nineteenth century see Fernyhough, 1989.
81. On foreign-educated Ethiopian intellectuals and their role in the modernization of the country see Bahru Zewde, 2002.
82. For a detailed account of the history of Ethiopian immigrants in America see Solomon Addis Getahun, 2007. For a comparison of Ethiopian immigrants in the USA and France, see Abye, 2004. On cultural creativity in the Ethio-American diaspora see Shelemay and Kaplan, 2006. See also E. Alpers and K. Koser, "Diaspora", *EAE*2.
83. On Ethiopian domestic workers in the Middle East see Fernandez, 2011.
84. According to the National Bank of Ethiopia's official estimate, the total value of remittances to Ethiopia was $661 million in 2010. According to projections by the World Bank the real value of remittances could reach as high as $3.2 billion in 2010. According to this study, 14 per cent of the adult population of Ethiopia received international remittance, regularly, at an average amount of $120 five times a year. This high figure may be an overestimation but it reflects the potential influence of remittance flows on the economy.
85. On political mobilization in the Ethiopian diaspora see Lyons, 2012.

2. THE ETHIOPIAN ORTHODOX TEWAHEDO CHURCH (EOTC) AND THE CHALLENGES OF MODERNITY

1. Ayele Teklehaymanot, 1988.
2. Crummey, 1974, p. 577.
3. Tedesci, 1999, p. 108.
4. Crummey, 1978, pp. 427–42.
5. Tedesci, 1999, p. 109.

6. Ayele Teklehaymanot, 1999, p. 192; Bairu Tafla, 1977, p. 153.
7. Haile Mariam Larebo, 1988, p. 3.
8. This was the first journey of an Ethiopian Metropolitan abroad, cf. Kaplan, 2007, p. 867.
9. Shiferaw Bekele, 2010, p. 139.
10. Erlich, 2000, pp. 23–46.
11. Marcus, 1987, p. 104.
12. Ibid., pp. 204–5.
13. Erlich, 2000, p. 28.
14. Boutros Ghali, 1991, p. 980.
15. Isaac, 1971, pp. 248–9. On the collaboration of Ethiopian clergymen with the Italian authorities, see Shenk, 1972, pp. 125–35.
16. Mersha Alehegne, p. 2010.
17. Murad, 1950–1957, pp. 1–22.
18. Perham, 1948, pp. 126–30.
19. Erlich, 2000; pp. 35–6.
20. Bairu Tafla, 2002, pp. 495–6.
21. Boutros Ghali, 1991, p. 982.
22. Erlich, 2000, pp. 38–42.
23. Haile Mariam Larebo, 1988.
24. This reform was particularly strongly implemented in Gojjam during the revolt of 1968. See Markakis, 1974, pp. 377–86.
25. Haile Mariam Larebo, 1988, p. 10. See also Goricke and Heyer, 1976, p. 186.
26. *Negarit Gazeta*, 25 October 1972.
27. Chaillot, 2005.
28. Haile Mariam Larebo, 1988, pp. 10–11.
29. Ibid., p. 22.
30. Boutros Ghali, 1991, p. 983.
31. Haile Mariam Larebo, 1988, p. 16.
32. Ancel, 2011a.
33. Though not canonical, as he and his supporters highlighted, the forced removal of *Abuna* Merkorios was in line with the historical process of the unification of the Church and its increasing supervision by the state. We have seen in this chapter that each governmental power transition needed the cooperation of the Church and involved some kind of accomodation with canonical law—or its more or less brutal violation.
34. Alexander, 2012.
35. Engedayehu, 2013, p. 9.
36. See Engedayehu 2013, pp. 14–15 for the list of the fifty-seven Ethiopian churches abroad affiliated to the Synod in exile.
37. Chaillot, 2002, p. 43.
38. Hermann, 2010.
39. See, for instance, Young, 1977.
40. Boyslton, 2012b.

3. THE ETHIOPIAN MUSLIMS: HISTORICAL PROCESSES AND ONGOING CONTROVERSIES

1. The author thanks Ahmed Hassen Omer and Dereje Feyissa for their comments on preliminary versions of this text.
2. Vangsi,1985 compares the different statistical data on religions available since the first national sample surveys (undertaken in 1964–7 and 1968–71) up to the first large-scale Ethiopian census of 1984.
3. Kemal Abdulwehab, 2011.
4. This ideal of fraternity within the community of Islam (the *Ummah*) is undermined, however, by the prevalence of racial and ethnic discrimination. For instance, many African pilgrims to Mecca are bitter about their experiences of being subjected to racial slurs such as *'abd* ("slave").
5. For comprehensive accounts of the history of Islam in Ethiopia see Trimingham, 1952; Abbink, 1998; Hussein, 2007. For a focus on the ethnohistory of southern and eastern Ethiopian societies see the collection of essays by Braukämper, 2002. For a historical overview of Islam in Eritrea see Miran, 2005.
6. The exact words are: "Leave Ethiopians alone as long as they leave you alone", according to the biography of the Prophet by Ibn Ishâq.
7. Complex processes of conversion are encapsulated in this short description. For a more detailed discussion of the role of traders and clerics in the dissemination of Islam, see Hussein, 1999.
8. For a comprehensive overview of Islam in Ethiopia in the Middle Ages, see Fauvelle and Hirsch, 2010.
9. *Ulama* is the plural form of *'alim* ("scholar"). *Awliya* is the plural form of *wali* ("saint, holy man").
10. Seri-Hersch, 2009.
11. Abbas Hajji, 2002: 106–9.
12. The first mosque in Addis Ababa was founded in the Abware area in the compound of an Indian Muslim architect working for the palace of Menelik II. The call to prayer was performed in a well dug for this purpose. See Kemal Abdulwehab, 2011: p. 312.
13. On the reign of *Lij* Iyasu see the essays gathered by Ficquet & Smidt, 2013.
14. Hussein Ahmed, 2006: pp. 6–7.
15. Hussein Ahmed, 1994: pp. 775–6.
16. See Erlich, 2007: p. 81, discussed in Østebø, 2012: pp. 131–2.
17. Carmichael, 1998; Østebø, 2012: pp. 190–191.
18. Hussein Ahmed, 1994: pp. 776–8.
19. Ibid., p. 779
20. Hussein Ahmed, 1998: pp. 11–2
21. Østebø, 2012: pp. 211–3.
22. Hussein, 1994: pp. 791–7.
23. The main centre of education for Ethiopian Muslims is the Aweliyya School and Mission Centre in Addis Ababa, established in the 1960s and supported

by the Saudi-based Muslim World League. This institution is not focused only on Quranic education: it includes an orphanage, a high school and a college that provides vocational training in accountancy, law and Arabic language. It plays an important role in the civil representation of the Ethiopian Muslim elite.

24. On Islamic literature in Ethiopia see Gori, 1995 and 2005; Hussein, 2009.
25. Haustein and Østebø, 2012: p. 755.
26. There are 200,000 Ethiopian domestic workers in Saudi Arabia and 60,000 in Lebanon. They are also found in high numbers in the United Arab Emirates and Kuwait. The total number of Ethiopians in the Middle East approaches 500,000. See Fernandez, 2011.
27. It is estimated that 120,000 Ethiopians emigrate per year. Between 70,000 and 80,000 Ethiopians fled to Yemen in 2011 and 2012 according to UNHCR (the United Nations Refugee Agency).
28. See Peebles, 2012.
29. See Dereje, 2011.
30. The term "Salafism" derives from the Arabic expression *as-salafi as-s'âlih* ("the pious ancestors", that is, the close companions of the Prophet Muhammad). A related common generic designation for certain sorts of Islamic reform movements is "Wahhabism", from the Arab theologian Muhammad ibn Abd al-Wahhab (1703–1792) who propounded the main doctrines of Salafism. However "Wahhabism" or "Wahhabiyya" is often used with a derogatory undertone; "Salafi" is the designation most followers prefer.
31. Østebø, 2007: p. 14. See also Ishihara, 1996, which provides an example of local arguments against Salafism in the form of poetic verses composed in the Oromo language by a sheikh of Jimma.
32. Another Islamic reformist movement that has gained followers in Ethiopia, on a smaller scale than Salafism is the Tabligh missionary movement that is centred on the Gurage Muslim community of Addis Ababa.
33. Østebø, 2007: p. 5.
34. Hussein Ahmed, 2006: pp. 12–14; Kemal Abdulwehab, 2011.
35. In October 2006 there were serious religious clashes in Jimma and Wellega. The conflict began in a mosque that was disturbed by the smoke from celebrations in a nearby Orthodox church. Local skirmishes were exacerbated by extremist groups and the tensions escalated into a larger scale conflict. See Dereje, 2013b: pp. 5–6; Østebø, 2012: pp. 279–80.
36. Hussein Ahmed, 2006.
37. See De Waal, 2004.
38. A brief account of this dispute between Harari religious figures is given by Kabha and Erlich, 2006. H. Erlich gave a presentation of his study on the al-Ahbash movement in 2008 at the Institute of Ethiopian Studies, provoking expressions of disagreement from Muslim students.
39. On the doctrinal roots of al-Ahbash see Hamzeh and Dekmejian, 1996; Kabha and Erlich, 2006.
40. Al-Ahbash followers are estimated to number around 100,000 in Lebanon, 10,000 in Australia between 50,000 and 70,000 in North America and Europe.

41. According to Haustein and Østebø, 2011: p. 762, "The hegemonic position of the EIASC [Majlis] has consequently impinged on the possibilities of forming alternative organizations, which has contributed to a situation in which Islam in Ethiopia is highly informal and de-institutionalized." See also the controversial analysis by Awol Allo and Abadir M. Ibrahim, 2012.

4. GO PENTE! THE CHARISMATIC RENEWAL OF THE EVANGELICAL MOVEMENT IN ETHIOPIA[1]

1. The article presents some of the findings of research undertaken in Ethiopia during the months of May–June 2010 and February–March 2011 with the support of the French Centre for Ethiopian Studies in Addis Ababa and the Fondazione CRT of Turin. I am particularly grateful to Jörg Haustein, Mauro Ghirotti, Vadim Putzu, and Federica Gentile for their insightful comments on a previous version of this article.

2. Federal Democratic Republic of Ethiopia (FDRE) Population Census Commission, *Summary and Statistical Report of the 2007 Population and Housing Census*, December 2008, Addis Ababa. Available on the Central Statistical Agency of Ethiopia website: www.csa.gov.et

3. Johnstone and Mandryk, 2010.

4. Tibebe Eshete, 2009, p. 2.

5. Anderson, 2004, p. 115.

6. Getachew Haile, Lande and Rubenson, 1998; Eide, 2000.

7. Tibebe Eshete, 2009.

8. Haustein, 2011.

9. Abbink, 2011.

10. Anderson, 2004.

11. In the absence of official statistics and rigorous studies, key informants credit the two biggest denominations, the Mekane Yesus and Kale Hywot churches, with more than 80 per cent of the total number of *Pente* believers. Similar data are presented in a research commissioned by the Evangelical Churches Fellowship of Ethiopia in partnership with Dawn Ministries: National Mission Research, 2005.

12. According to the 2007 Population Census Protestants account for 17.7 per cent of the total population in Oromiya Region, 55.5 per cent in SNNPR and 70.1 per cent in Gambella.

13. Haustein, 2008.

14. Tibebe Eshete, 2009.

15. For an annotated list of the most important Pentecostal churches in Ethiopia, see Haustein, 2009.

16. Anderson, 2004, p. 103.

17. Tibebe Eshete, 2009, pp. 146–7; Haustein, 2011a, pp. 229–32.

18. Donham, 1999.

19. According to Samson Estephanos, 2007. Data obtained from the author.

20. Anderson, 2004, p. 104.

21. In the last years, some experiences of Charismatic Renewal have spread to the Ethiopian Orthodox Church, although the groups promoting this approach, like the Emanuel United Church, have been condemned as heretical by the Patriarchate and rapidly expelled from its body.
22. See Ethiopian Economic Association, Ethiopian Economic Policy Research Institute, 2008.
23. For an analysis of the dogmatic character of international discourse on development and its political and economic consequences, see Hibou, 1998.
24. Although, according to official statistics of 2007 census, the numbers of Protestants in traditional Orthodox or Muslim areas are still particularly low: 0.1 per cent of the population in Tigray, 0.2 per cent in Amhara, 0.7 per cent in Afar and 0.1 per cent in the Somali region.
25. Tibebe Eshete, 2009.
26. According to official statistics the share of Protestants in rural areas is 19.6 per cent, while in urban areas it is only 13.5 per cent. I owe to Jörg Haustein this remark and calculation.
27. Anderson, 2004, p. 122.
28. Ibdi., p. 167.
29. Bahru Zewde, 2002.
30. Donham, 1999.
31. Tibebe Eshete, 2009.
32. Cox, 2006.
33. Marshall, 2009.
34. Corten and Mary 2000, p. 17.
35. Bayart, 1993.
36. Wolf, 1991.
37. Bax, 1987.
38. Tadesse Tamrat, 1972.
39. Ibid., 1998.
40. Tibebe Eshete, 2009, p. 104.
41. Corten, 2006, p. 135.
42. Tibebe Eshete, 2009.
43. Eide, 2000.
44. Haustein, 2009.
45. Tibebe Eshete, 2009, p. 185.
46. Haustein, 2011b, p. 49.
47. Constitution of the Federal Democratic Republic of Ethiopia, art. 39 (5).
48. Østebø, 2008.
49. Exodus, 19:6.
50. Abbink, 2011.
51. Accounting for instance for 55.5 per cent of the population in SNNPR or 70.1 per cent in Gambella, according to the 2007 census.
52. Haustein, 2011b, p. 50.
53. Like General Taye, Defence Minister, Shiferraw Wolde Michael, adviser to the Council of Ministers, and Negussie Teferra, member of the Economic Campaign and Central Planning Supreme Council.

54. Like Teshome Toga, former Speaker of the House of Federation, and Haile Mariam Dessalegn (Deputy Prime Minister at the time of writing).
55. Gascon, 2005.
56. See for instance Hussein Ahmed, 2006.
57. Ibid.
58. Abbink, 2011.
59. Tronvoll, 2009.
60. Abbink, 2011, p. 274.
61. Marshall, 2009.

5. FROM PAN-AFRICANISM TO RASTAFARI: AFRICAN AMERICAN AND CARIBBEAN 'RETURNS' TO ETHIOPIA

1. Throughout this paper the word Rastafari is used to refer to both the movement and individuals as is the standard use in the literature (for example, Chevannes, 1994; Price 2009; MacLeod, 2014). Words like "Rastafarian" or "Rastafarianism" are avoided.
2. For a detailed account of African American, Caribbean and Rastafari settlements in Ethiopia since the end of the nineteenth century, see Bonacci, 2010.
3. See the discussion on this verse by Ullendorf, 1997, pp. 5–15.
4. This has been studied by a number of scholars, see for example Drake, 1970 and Geiss, 1968.
5. While Garvey had a tendency to vastly exaggerate the numbers of his followers ("four hundred million blacks"), records show that in 1921 UNIA counted a total of 859 branches, and in 1926 six million persons were apparently registered members. (Martin, 1986: 15–17, quoted by Tete-Adjalogo, 1995: 248–256).
6. Garvey, 1986: 44.
7. Black Jews formed their own congregations in New York and Chicago in the first thirty years of the twentieth century. They associated with the Ethiopian Jews known then as Falasha or Beta Israel, but are not to be confused with them. See for example Brotz, 1964.
8. This mobilization has been very well studied by Scott, 1993 and Harris, 1994.
9. A map of the Shashemene land grant is published in Bonacci, 2010.
10. For an account of the early Rastafari movement, see Hill, 2001.
11. Bonacci, 2013b.
12. See Chevannes, 1998.
13. For an account of the wider Back to Africa movement in Jamaica, see Bonacci, 2010, pp. 165–215.
14. Speech of Emperor Haile Selassie in Jamaica, 21 April 1966, published in *Reggae & African Beat*, 1986, vol. V (5/6).
15. While the Gregorian calendar is used internationally, Ethiopia uses the Julian calendar, which sets the date seven to eight years "behind" the Gregorian calendar. There were therefore two millenniums.
16. A 2003 government census numbered slightly more than a hundred Rastafari

living in Shashemene. However, a number of them refused to fill in the census forms. In 2014, 800 Rastafari live in Shashemene, half this amount in Addis Ababa, and a couple hundred in other towns. Ethiopia's population is estimated at 82 million.

17. MacLeod 2014 studies in-depth, the narratives of the relationship between Ethiopians and Rastafari.

18. In February 2005, on the occasion of the 60th birthday of Bob Marley, a festival dubbed "Africa Unite" was organized by the Bob Marley Foundation and the Rita Marley Foundation in Addis Ababa. The cultural impact of the huge reggae concert on Mesqel Square is discussed by MacLeod 2014, pp. 126–66.

19. The flag of Imperial Ethiopia, red, gold and green with the Conquering Lion of Judah in its centre, is one of the symbols praised by Rastafari. However, the "Flag Proclamation N° 654/2009" outlaws its public display and indicates that any flag "related with a national historical phenomenon or event shall be kept at museums prepared for such purposes" (Art. 17/2).

20. Decision of the third extraordinary session of the Executive Council on the application of the diaspora initiative in the framework of the African Union, DOC. Ext/EX/CL/5, May 21–242003, Sun City, South Africa.

6. MONARCHICAL RESTORATION AND TERRITORIAL EXPANSION: THE ETHIOPIAN STATE IN THE SECOND HALF OF THE NINETEENTH CENTURY

1. See the chapter on the Eritrean question by Gérard Prunier in this volume.

2. On this period, see Abir, 1968 and the critical revision on the literature of this period by Shiferaw Bekele, 1990.

3. On power relations between regional authorities in the first half of the nineteenth century see Crummey, 1975.

4. On the residual imperial legitimacy and the meaning of the Solomonic line, see Crummey, 1988.

5. Henze, 2000, p. 121.

6. Among the plentiful studies on the reign of Tewodros II, see Rubenson, 1966. An interesting historical reconstruction on the ascension to power of Tewodros and his tragic end was published by Marsden, 2007.

7. On the Islamization of the Oromo polities of Wollo see Hussein Ahmed, 2001.

8. Among many accounts of the British expedition to Ethiopia and the battle of Meqdela, see Arnold 1992.

9. On the reign of Yohannes IV, see the monograph written by his great-grandson Zewde Gebre Selassie, 1975.

10. On the religious policies of the Ethiopian kings in the nineteenth century, see Caulk, 1972.

11. On the resistance of Wollo Muslims against their forcible conversion to Christianity, see Hussein Ahmed, 2001.

12. The most famous and influential foreign adviser of Menelik was the Swiss engineer Alfred Ilg who was the inevitable middleman between any foreign inves-

tor or diplomat and the king. For studies on the Menelik's time based on Ilg's archival collections, see Biasio 2004 and Bairu Tafla, 2000. On the first Ethiopian modern intellectuals, exposed to the West by their education and who became promoters of a reformist agenda, see Bahru Zewde 2002.

13. On the building of the Ethiopian empire under Menelik's leadership by resisting the hegemony of European powers and negotiating partnerships with them, see Caulk 2002.

14. On the conquest of the southern peripheries of Ethiopia see Donham and James 1986, in particular the introduction by Donham that elucidates the organization of the imperial state and setting-up of its domination. For a description of the violence of the conquest by an eye-witness, see Bulatovitch 2000.

15. On the conflict between the Islamic radical Mahdist state in Sudan and the Christian radical kingdom of Ethiopia under Yohannes' rule, see Caulk, 1971; Erlich, 1994; Seri-Hersch, 2010.

16. On this battle that was the first Ethiopian and African victory against colonial aggression see Taddesse Beyene et al., 1988; Erlich 1996.

17. On the treaty of Wichale and the consequences of its linguistic ambuigities, see Rubenson, 1964 and Caulk, 2002 (chapters 5 and 6).

18. For a detailed account of this battle see Jonas, 2011. For other studies on this event, its circumstances and its impact, see the collections of essays edited by Abdussamad and Pankhurst, 1998, and by Paulos Milkias and Getachew Metaferia, 2005.

19. See the chapter by Gérard Prunier on the Eritrean question in this volume.

20. On the sensitive issue of boundaries see the collection of treaties gathered by Brownlie, 1979.

21. On the history of the Ethio-Djiboutian railway see the book of historical photographs gathered and published by Fontaine, 2012.

22. On the aborted reign of *Lij* Iyasu in the international turmoil of World War I, see the volume edited by Ficquet and Smidt 2014.

23. On these see Gebru Tareke, 1991.

8. THE ETHIOPIAN REVOLUTION AND THE DERG REGIME

1. The only other revolution to have taken place on the African continent had been the Egyptian revolution of 1952. But its cultural context was radically different from that of the African countries and was linked to the transformations then affecting the Arab world. In a way, we have seen the same disconnect half a century later when the 2011 "Arab Spring" successively shook three African Arab countries—Tunisia, Egypt and Libya—without causing any political reverberation further south.

2. The modalities of this parallel could at times be perceived in a rather surprising manner, as when a Russian technician told this author in 1985: "The Ethiopians are the only ones who can be good Communists on this continent because they are Orthodox". A remark which would probably have surprised Karl Marx.

3. Two books are useful to understand the immediate pre-revolutionary situation:

First, Markakis' study (1974), which is probably the best analytical presentation of pre-revolutionary Ethiopian society. Then Kapuscinski's book (1978), which should not be seen as a "historical study" but rather as a kind of psycho-political subjective essay, recreating the unreal atmosphere of the Emperor's last years.

4. Before 1935 Ethiopia only had a very small standing army. The central state still relied on the old feudal system of public levies organized by the nobility in case of war.

5. In line with the post-World War II statist approach of the economy, Ethiopia had adopted a system of economic planning in 1957. This system had nothing to do with "socialism", it was quite the opposite. It was rather a system arbitrating between various private interests which competed for milking the imperial state. See Gill, 1974.

6. Lefort, 1983, pp. 36–40.

7. The monetary mass in circulation was extremely limited and stood at only about $60 per capita. Trade in the countryside remained essentially by barter.

8. See Balsvik,1985; Bahru Zewde, 2014.

9. Gebru Tareke, 1991 gives a detailed study of these insurrections which kept following each other at the four corners of the country between the 1940s and the 1970s, without ever reaching the level of an all-out revolutionary movement.

10. Pankhurst, 1986.

11. The BBC documentary by Jonathan Dimbleby in which the Emperor was shown feeding his pets from a silver platter while the population was starving had a massive counter-propaganda effect.

12. There was no tram service or underground urban railway and the bus service was notoriously insufficient.

13. Its cause was very symbolic of the state of the army: the water pump used by the soldiers had broken down and the officers had refused them the right to use theirs.

14. Aman Andom had a rare combination of qualities for the role *Ras* Imru wanted him to play: nicknamed "the lion of the Ogaden", he had been a hero of the war with Somalia in 1963–64. Being Eritrean he could talk directly to the Northern population; and finally he was politically both a moderate and a reformist. His one weakness seems to have been a certain lack of personal determination.

15. The PMAC mentioned the fantastic figure of over $15bn found in foreign deposits. None of that money seems to have existed.

16. The BBC Dimbleby documentary was shown on Ethiopian TV on 11 September.

17. See Del Boca, 1995: 321–3.

18. It was only years later, after the fall of the Derg, that the truth became public: Haile Selassie had been murdered by the military, suffocated between two mattresses.

19. It was to last seventeen years, till the fall of the Derg.
20. Keller, 1998, p. 192.
21. Moffa, 1980, p. 53.
22. The Derg remained a secret committee whose members' names were not made public.
23. In spite of some questionable conclusions Messay Kebede, 2011 is the first work that tries to go into an analysis of the various strands of that military power. His idea that it was the revolution that radicalized the army, rather than the other way around, is largely true.
24. In order to blur the distinction between military authoritarianism and civilian radicalism, the Derg favoured the creation of a whole bevy of pseudo-independent revolutionary groups (*Emalred, Waz* League, ECHEAAT) with Mengistu himself heading a supposedly "independent" group, *Abyotawi Seded* [the revolutionary flame]. All were eliminated after they had served their smokescreen purpose.
25. Amharic acronym of the Pan-Ethiopian Socialist Movement.
26. Its leader Haile Fida was French-educated, and married to a French wife, and had been a member of the French Communist Party.
27. Given the very complex situation of the land question in pre-revolutionary Ethiopia, the land nationalization decree had a very different impact in the north (where land was tightly controlled by a complex system of hereditary land holding) and the Menelik-conquered south where the conquered peasantry had seen their land taken by the Abyssinians to whom the Emperor had given vast properties. The 4 February decree was therefore much more of a revolutionary measure in the south than in the north and elicited a lot more support there.
28. The creation of the AETU had been typical of this ambiguity. The laws introduced by this "revolutionary" organization on work conditions and strikes were much more repressive than those of the Empire.
29. The use of the vocabulary was telling. The Derg wished to retain the monopoly of the revolutionary phraseology and to be able to label its enemies as "reactionaries". The army's own anti-guerrilla measures were officially labelled as "Red Terror".
30. The Ogaden had become Ethiopian only in 1887, less than a hundred years before.
31. This was probably what Teferi Bante had in mind and the reason why Mengistu had him shot.
32. The People's Democratic Republic of South Yemen, established on the territory of the former British Aden Colony and Protectorate, was at the time a communist state closely allied to the Soviet Union.
33. For an inside view of the famine, see Dawit Wolde Gyorgis, 1989.
34. For an assessment of this crisis see Clay and Holcomb, 1986; Pankhurst, 1992.
35. Some of the most hysterical writing at the time came from France where the Ethiopian tragedy was manipulated to advance a purely French political agenda (see Jean, 1986; Glucksman and Wolton, 1986). The Derg propaganda

can be found in RRC 1985. The most dispassionate approach is that of Dessalegn Rahmato, 1991.

36. This author was an eyewitness to some of the process, particularly in Wollega.

37. See Ergas, 1980. This author was living in Tanzania in the 1970s and was an eyewitness to this policy failure. The difference between Tanzania's villageization and its Ethiopian equivalent was the degree of force used. Ethiopia was much worse in terms of brutality.

38. When this author tried to demonstrate at the international conference of Ethiopian studies held in Paris in 1988 that it was materially impossible to carry out the population transfers with the budget available (see Prunier 1994) he was publicly attacked and denounced as an agent of imperialism, the CIA and Mossad.

39. Eshetu Chole, 2004, p. 135.

40. Gebru Tareke, 2009.

41. Saddam Hussein had fought Ayatollah Khomeini's Iranian revolutionary regime and earned himself the good graces of Washington. Since his equipment was Soviet-manufactured, it could be passed on to the Fronts without fear of traceability. In the Sudan, Nimeiry provided the missing link between foreign imports and transporting the equipment into Ethiopian territory.

42. Gebru Tareke, 2009, p. 247.

43. The East German Secret Police had a technical control over the Ethiopian Army Secret Service.

44. There were strong rumours at the time that the CIA had negotiated Mengistu's flight directly with President Mugabe. It has not been possible to either confirm or refute these rumours.

9. THE ERITREAN QUESTION

1. Eritrea constitutes such a delicate conundrum that even the words one uses to formulate one's approach can be problematic. I have chosen here to use the eloquent and simple phrasing employed by Zewde Retta as the title of his book: *Ye Eritrea Gudday*, Addis Ababa, 2000.

2. Article 4b enshrined respect for colonial borders for the newborn African independent nations. But by the time the United Nations was created in New York, the brief episode of the 1936–41 Italian occupation could be seen as part and parcel of World War II rather than a form of colonization (to which both France and Britain were still clinging) and was thus dismissed by the new world order then emerging from the defeat of the Axis powers.

3. High and medium altitude: hese are the key morphological structures of the Abyssinian highlands.

4. Corresponding to the Abyssinian *qolla* regions.

5. It is impossible to be more precise as there never was a census.

6. Most of them belong to the Orthodox Monophysite (*tewahedo*) Church.

7. Killion 1998: 8.

8. See *inter alia* Pateman, 1990 or Okbazghi Yohannes, 1991.

9. And this even though during certain periods of its history Aksum managed to extend a kind of protectorate over the lowlands and to reach the limits of the Meroitic kingdom in today's Sudan. The brief raid of the Aksumite Emperor Ezana who reached Meroe in 350 AD did not lead to a sustained occupation of the Nilotic kingdom. Nevertheless, as if to make everything more complicated, many ancient sources refer to Meroe as "the city of the Ethiopians". But the word "Ethiopian" in this context should be understood as loosely describing the ancient non-Egyptian populations of north-eastern Africa rather than those of present day "Ethiopia", which in any case was called "Abyssinia" up to its systemic transformation in the late nineteenth century (see on this question the chapter by Shiferaw Bekele in this volume).

10. The 2011 secession of Southern Sudan is a good reminder of the arbitrariness "Sudan's" borders.

11. And this even though the Emperor had created the position of "Governor of the *Ma'ikele Bahre*" ("Governor of the region between the waters"), that is, the area between the Mareb River and the sea.

12. This multiethnic Muslim state occupied the north-eastern part of today's Sudan. See O'Fahey and Spaulding, 1974.

13. This occurred because Britain, having occupied Egypt in 1882 for financial reasons (Cairo was bankrupt and owed huge credit balances to British banks), found itself the bemused heir to the Egyptian Empire in Africa. It tried to save it and failed. But the spectacular death of General Charles Gordon, its envoy to Khartoum, produced such a shock in an era of alleged White superiority that a new myth was born, driving the British—and other European powers—deeper into the African continent. Gordon was killed while the Berlin Conference was taking place and his death, both at a symbolic level and at the practical-diplomatic level, had a tremendous accelerating effect.

14. Today's Djibouti Republic.

15. The Italian trader Giuseppe Sapeto had bought Assab from an Afar Sultan back in 1869. The port had later been resold to the Italian state in 1882.

16. He was killed by the Mahdists in the battle of Metemma in 1889.

17. On the role of Britain in furthering Italian interests see Ramm, 1944.

18. They failed to understand that Bahta Hagos and his insurgents had nothing behind them that could be compared withthe Emperor of Abyssinia's capacity to raise levies.

19. The result was that very little land (around 2 per cent of total arable land) was taken in Eritrea, thereby radically limiting all the analysis "explaining" later Eritrean problems through colonial land alienation. On this Tekeste Negash, 1986.

20. The vast numbers of Italian colonists had never materialized, the Italians preferring emigration to the United States or Argentina.

21. This author remembers having experienced during his first visit to Eritrea some forty years ago food, behaviour and speech habits that were so "Italianized" that they had morphed into a kind of autonomous "Italo-Eritrean" culture. This had never been the case in Ethiopia proper, even among people strongly

influenced by Italian culture. For an Italian literary testimony on this, see Dell'Oro, 1988.

22. Although Eritrea represented only 4 per cent of the AOI territory, it hosted 55 per cent of its industrial investments. See Tekeste Negash 1987.

23. Although Arabic was the native language of only 1 per cent of Eritreans, it was an important religious and cultural language for the Muslim community. Owing to their Sudanese tropism, the British tended to be perhaps more open to the Muslim population than to the Christian one which they saw as troublesome agents of Ethiopian interference.

24. Britain's Foreign Secretary Ernest Bevin was a passionate advocate of Somali unity but less interested in the fate of Eritrea.

25. Created in June 1949, the Independence Bloc was the result of a coalition between the Muslim League, two small pro-Italian parties, the Liberal Progressive Party (a modern secularist movement) and the Party for the Independence of Eritrea led by Wolde Ab Wolde Mariam, the first coherent and outspoken nationalist leader.

26. Wolde Ab Wolde Mariam survived nine murder attempts. He ended up taking refuge in Egypt in 1953 after the last attempt on his life which had caused him to spend five months in hospital.

27. This was the new name of the Independence Bloc.

28. These communitarian elements are essential if one wants to understand the nature of Eritrean identity, and good care should be taken not to fall into an anachronistic reading of history, influenced by what happened later, particularly during the war. An interesting exception to this tendency is the work of the historian Tekeste Negash, particularly for what concerns us here. See Tekeste Negash, 1997.

29. Many of them were Eritreans. But most of them were sycophants who had built their careers on total submission to the Emperor. And the Emperor had a tendency to judge the Eritrean situation by the yardstick of his past dealings with an unruly nobility, which always tried to disobey him not because they represented any genuinely dissident voices but simply out of arrogance and personal ambition. The Emperor was by then sixty and set in his ways. He could not but see Eritrea as just another case of an unruly periphery trying to evade his centralized authority.

30. The Ethiopian President of the Executive Branch of the government.

31. Between 1945 and 1952 the Eritrean customs had provided 45 per cent of the government's tax base. Their appropriation by Addis Ababa since 1952 had deprived the Eritrean Executive of essential revenue.

32. F.O. 371/102635. Quoted in Tekeste Negash, 1997: 84.

33. Haile Selassie uses here the old expression referring to the "Eritrean space" in the fifteenth century, when it was more or less incorporated into the Abyssinian Empire.

34. There was a strong Abyssinian cultural base for that, the fear of a return to *zemene mesafint*, the times of feudal anarchy. And then there was an added layer to that, which had been provided by the Emperor's "adoptive father", the

French Bishop Mgr Jarosseau, who brought him up fully within the centralizing tradition of the French state, presented as the epitome of order and civilization.

35. The so-called "democratic institutions" (Parliament, Constitution) which he had developed since 1945 were only paper structures which he had developed to please foreign public opinion but which had little internal relevance. Contemporary political analysts said so with the necessary caution required when dealing with Ethiopian institutions. See Perham 1969, pp. 95–100 or Clapham, 1969, pp. 153–4.

36. The ELM had been multi-ethnic and strongly anchored on the left, its founder, Mahmood Said Naud, being a member of the Sudan Communist Party.

37. The ELF as a coherent organization disappeared in September 1981, but it left in its wake many surviving micro groups, some of which are still struggling today against the present Eritrean government, which is itself an offshoot of the Eritrean People's Liberation Front (EPLF), the organization that was to eventually lead the whole armed movement to victory in 1991.

38. Hamid Idris Awate was a Beni Amer and many of his men belonged to that tribe.

39. The new ELF leadership had by then supplanted the old ELM one. And the ELF presented itself as the Eritrean incarnation of "the struggle of the Arab people" in order to get the support of a number of Arab countries, mostly Egypt and Sudan. Haile Selassie fought back by supporting the Christian Southern Sudanese rebels.

40. See my chapter (4) on the Revolution in this volume.

41. The Derg forces wrought a brutal repression on the civilian populations in the areas they reoccupied.

42. During the 1978 debacle ELF troops which were in Saray province had withdrawn with their EPLF comrades towards the Sahel. They had stayed there and the ELF leadership was afraid that they would eventually melt down within the EPLF's stronger presence and end up being absorbed.

43. The Front dug underground clinics and workshops, on the model of the Viet Cong strategic installations. This enabled it to keep functioning even under the worst attacks of the Ethiopian Air Force.

44. The military equipment delivered to the Front by the Iraqi dictator was of Russian manufacture and thus impossible to tell apart from the weapons the EPLF was capturing from the Ethiopian Army. The Iraqi deliveries were shipped through Sudan whose dictator, Jaafar al-Nimeiry, was a close US ally.

45. On the TPLF see Young, 1997 and Aregawi Berhe, 2009, as well as Medhane Tadesse's chapter in the present volume.

46. The Americans probably negotiated Mengistu's flight to Zimbabwe where President Mugabe gave him political asylum.

47. Such a figure could look suspicious and it is actually still disbelieved today by an ultranationalist fringe in Ethiopia. The author of these lines, who was present on the ground at the time as an official observer, is nevertheless completely ready to vouch for the honesty of that impressive score.

48. Asmara accused Ethiopia of protectionism.

49. Asmara had been paying for Ethiopian coffee in birrs and then reselling it abroad to acquire foreign currency. The financing of that operation was achieved by Eritrea issuing "true-false" birrs, since there was no clear definition of who was officially authorized to print the currency.

50. In that capacity 70,000 Eritrean soldiers (12 per cent of the population of the colony) had been recruited and many were deployed as occupation troops in Ethiopia.

51. Killion 1998:399. *Makalay aylet* means "the sort who cut grass", that is, casual labourers who were not allowed to sit in the *shemagelle* village councils and who were considered second class citizens of the Eritrean highland communities. On the modern expression of such ethnic feelings, the work of Alemseged Abbay, 1998 is of serious interest.

52. *The Economist*, 11 July 1998.

53. The US, which was at the time a strong supporter of the two post-Derg regimes in Ethiopia/Eritrea, tried to mediate, with the help of Rwanda, but to no avail.

54. The war gave rise to a flood of impassioned propaganda literature. The most balanced coverage can be found in Tekeste Negash and Tronvoll, 2000 and in Jacquin-Berdal and Plaut, 2005.

55. Popular Front for Democracy and Justice. This was the new name for the old EPLF, chosen after its Third Congress in February 1994.

56. A poignant account of these terrible days can be found in Connell, 2005.

57. Only four "registered" religious faiths were allowed: the traditional *tewahedo* Monophysite Christianity, Catholicism, Islam and Lutheran Protestantism.

58. See Human Rights Watch, *Service for Life: State Repression and Indefinite Conscription in Eritrea* (April 2009).

59. Redeker Hepner, 2009. See also the testimony by the former EPLF high-ranking member Andebrhan Giorgis, 2014.

10. THE TIGRAY PEOPLE'S LIBERATION FRONT (TPLF)

1. Balsvik, 1979; Bahru Zewde, 2014.

2. TPLF, 1985.

3. Medhane Tadesse, 1992.

4. Although it started its armed struggle in Dedebit, located in the district of Shire, in the initial months the TPLF had active presence in eastern Tigray where most of the protracted armed clashes with the EPRP took place.

5. Ibid. Discussions with TPLF leaders over the years also attest to the overriding feeling at the time. Almost all analysts of the TPLF agree that because of the then-prevalent psycho-political hurdles, the sense of neglect and frustration and the divisions within Ethiopian society the TPLF leadership had lost hope of continuing to be part of Ethiopia and issued the "Manifesto".

6. Young, 1997.

7. In September 1984, the TPLF addressed to the 39th Session of the United Nations General Assembly, in September 1984, a document entitled "Tigray" that

reflected the importance of self-determination to the struggle launched by the movement.

8. On the history of the MLLT, see the article "Malelit Zelay", authored by Aregawi Berhe, published by the MLLT in June 1988.

9. Citing Marx's analogy of the struggle of the Irish people, *Weyin*, the newspaper of the TPLF, noted in 1977 that, if co-ordinated, an Irish-inspired nationalist struggle could also liberate the oppressed working classes of England.

10. Ibid. All informants asked about this period affirm that the TPLF emerged from the bloody war with EDU both heartened and hardened. TPLF leaders also believe that it was during this period that bravery and fearlessness became sealed as the dominant characteristic of TPLF fighters, which has been due in no small part to the character and leadership of the early military commanders, particularly Aregawi Berhe.

11. *Liberation*, vol. 5, 1978: 25. Discussions with Yemane Kidane who was the first EPLF militant to be dispatched to Tigray to try to help the TPLF.

12. Tesfatsion Medhanie, 1997, p. 115. A detailed discussion on the conflict between the TPLF and Eritrean fronts can be found in Medhane Tadesse, p. 1999, a book which came out only three months after the eruption of the war in May 1998. It provides a detailed background to the war.

13. Ibid.

14. Young, 1996, p. 113.

15. Medhane Tadesse, 1999.

16. In 1984–85 Meles put forward his thesis that the Front faced major dangers because of empiricism (the notion that the Front lacked scientific theories) and its acceptance of pragmatism (by which he meant opportunism).

17. TPLF's main source of supply of armaments were government forces themselves.

18. The battle of Af'abet was a turning point in the history of the protracted war in Eritrea.

19. The major and decisive war at the Shire front began on 28/12/1988 with offensive operation of the 604th Core Army of the government and was concluded on 19/02/1989 with the victory of the TPLF forces.

20. This has been widely cited by TPLF leaders and the documents of the Front as a major area that differentiates them from other armed movements in Ethiopia and elsewhere.

21. Dubbed the Convention of Nationalities for Peace and Democracy and chaired by the Chairman of the TPLF, Meles Zenawi, the Conference was attended by more than 22 movements which used to oppose the Derg, primarily along ethnic lines.

22. Abebe Zegeye and Pausewang, 1994, pp. 299–300; EHRCO Report 1995.

23. This author discussed this topic in "TPLF and International Financial Institutions: TPLF and Ethiopia National Sovereignty and Interest," A paper presented at the Symposium held on the 25th Anniversary of the TPLF, Mekelle, February 2000.

24. This has been reflected in the discussions the author had with Eritrean authorities weeks before the Eritrean army attacked Ethiopia.

25. The author was one of the few to hint at an impending Eritrean attack returning from a visit to Asmara only weeks before the outbreak of the war.
26. The Commission started work on 25 May 2001, and reported its ruling on 13 April 2002. Then a year later, when the commission clarified its ambiguities and said that Badme lay in Eritrea, the Meles government expressed regret but said it would not reject the ruling as a whole, but would seek adjustments by peaceful and legal means.
27. Conduct of the war was led by the Central Command in which Meles was a member and played an important, but not dominant, role. Indeed, the Politburo member Tewolde Woldemariam could be said to have led this militant group and it was he, not Meles, who was the most powerful person in the country during the war years, a situation that the latter has acknowledged.
28. Special Issue of *Renewal* (bi-monthly bulletin of the EPRDF), Addis Ababa, November 2001.
29. Young and Medhane Tadesse, 2003.

11. FEDERALISM, REVOLUTIONARY DEMOCRACY AND THE DEVELOPMENTAL STATE, 1991–2012

1. Markakis, 1987, 1998.
2. Gebru Tareke, 2009.
3. As a result of the defeat of the Derg, the Eritrean People's Liberation Front (EPLF) was able to press for secession, *de facto* in 1991, and *de jure* following a referendum in 1993. See Prunier (chapter 11) in this volume.
4. For a fuller discussion of economic policy and development see Lefort (chapter 10) in this volume.
5. The phrase originates with Stalinist and Soviet thinking on self-determination. In practice, little or no differentiation according to the three categories is made in contemporary Ethiopia.
6. Van der Beken, 2012.
7. This, for instance, is one reason given for the organization's rejection of the term "ethnic" in relation to what they prefer to call Ethiopia's "multinational" federalism. See Meles Zenawi's comments to the inaugural Tana African Security Forum, Bahr Dar, 14 April 2012.
8. Markakis, 1974
9. Young, 1997. The TPLF took on the evocative name "*weyane*" (meaning "rebellion" in Tigrigna), and it has become the common—and sometimes pejorative—means of referring to it throughout contemporary Ethiopia.
10. This contrasts with more recent government rhetoric which seems to prefer history over ethnicity.
11. See Prunier in this volume for a discussion of Eritrea, Ethio-Eritrean relations, and the war.
12. Teferi Abate, 2004.
13. Peterson, 2011.
14. Aalen, 2011.

15. Named after the 2005 election date.
16. Pausewang and Tronvoll, 2000; Pausewang, Tronvoll and Aalen, 2002.
17. Tronvoll, 2009.
18. Medhane and Young, 2003; Paulos, 2003.
19. Vaughan and Tronvoll, 2003.
20. Lefort, 2007.
21. Vaughan, 2011.
22. Aalen and Tronvoll, 2009; Abbink, 2006, 2009.
23. Aalen and Tronvoll, 2009.
24. Meles Zenawi, 2012.
25. Rodrik, 1991, cited in Meles Zenawi, 2012.
26. Vaughan and Tronvoll, 2003; Vaughan, 2012.
27. See Lefort in this volume for a fuller discussion of the economy.
28. Vaughan and Mesfin Gebremichael, 2011.
29. Vaughan, 2012.
30. Ibid.

12. ELECTIONS AND POLITICS IN ETHIOPIA, 2005–2010

1. The CUD, or Kinijit, set up in November 2004 was made up of the All Ethiopia Unity Party (AEUP); Rainbow Ethiopia—Movement for Democracy and Social Justice (Kestedamena); the Ethiopian Democratic League (EDL); and the Ethiopian United Democratic Party-Medhin (EUDP-Medhin). It might be noted that this coalition simply ignored a number of fundamental differences between its components: the AEUP's Amhara nationalism, the EUDP's "liberal democracy", Kestedamena's "social democracy", and the EDL's socialism. It was in fact a coalition of entirely different and incompatible groups and of highly unequal parties and even more highly ambitious leaders.
2. The fact that this report came out in advance of the election led the government to suspect that HRW was deliberately trying to influence the vote; HRW did exactly the same in advance of the election in 2010.
3. The UEDF, created in 2003, was made up of the following parties: Afar Revolutionary Democratic Unity Front (ARDUF); All Amhara Unity Party; All Ethiopian Socialist Movement (Meison); Council of Alternative Forces for Peace and Democracy; Ethiopian Democratic Union—Tehadiso; Ethiopian National Unity Front; Ethiopian People's Federal Democratic Unity Party; Ethiopian Peoples Revolutionary Party (EPRP); Gambella Peoples United Democratic Front (GPUDF); Oromo National Congress (ONC); Oromo Peoples Liberation Organization; Southern Ethiopian Peoples Democratic Coalition (SPDC); Tigrean Alliance for Democracy (TAND).
4. *Monitoring the Media Coverage of the 2005 Parliamentary and Regional Council Elections in Ethiopia*, Graduate School of Journalism and Communications, Addis Ababa University, Addis Ababa, May 2005.
5. This was one of the reasons why the government strongly criticized the EU mission and its head, Mrs Ana Gomes. It also argued with some justification that

she had failed to abide by her mandate to observe only and not comment on the election process. In private, at least, other observers were highly critical of the "unprofessional behaviour" of Mrs Gomes, as well as of the EU Ambassador, Tim Clarke, and their relations with opposition leaders.

6. There is no doubt that the EPRDF won. The CUD could never have won. It was widely perceived as intending to turn the clock back to a centralized, Amhara controlled state, doing away with the regional states, and removing Article 39 from the constitution. This was totally unacceptable to all the other main nationalities which constitute 75 per cent of the state. Some of these might have had their differences with an EPRDF-controlled government but they had no desire to overthrow the constitutional federal structure.

7. See e.g. Arriola, 2007 and 2008.

8. *Preliminary Statement on the Election Appeals' Process, the Re-run of Elections and the Somali Region Elections*, European Union Election Observation Mission Ethiopia 2005, Addis Ababa, 25 August 2005.

9. A significant element was also the dispute over who should be Mayor of Addis Ababa. Neither Dr Berhanu Nega, chairman of Rainbow, nor Dr Admassu Gebeyheu, chairman of EUDP-Medhin, had stood for parliament, only for the Addis Ababa city council. The pre-election presumption was that Dr Berhanu should be Mayor, and he agreed. However, the EUDP-Medhin won 14 parliamentary seats in Addis Ababa while Rainbow took 4; the EUDP-Medhin also took 64 of 135 council seats. It therefore suggested Dr Admassu had better credentials for Mayor. There were heated discussions before it was agreed that Berhanu should become Mayor with Admassu as deputy. In the event neither took up these positions.

10. Original estimates counted 42 deaths, but a Commission of Inquiry subsequently established that 193 civilians and seven police had died. Controversially, it exonerated the security force from using undue force.

11. None of the parties in the election offered any solution to the question of the constituency claimed by the Oromo Liberation Front (OLF), still ostensibly engaged in armed struggle. Prime Minister Meles announced after the election that he was prepared to talk to the OLF "without pre-conditions". This was widely seen as an attempt to co-opt Oromo support against the CUD's Amhara constituency. However, no subsequent progress appears to have been made with this initiative, despite the splits that have now occurred in the OLF.

12. There were allegations of misuse of funds raised by two different bodies, accusations of illegal decisions being taken by Chairman Hailu Shawel, and public disagreements between the Chairman and his deputy, Birtukan Mideksa. Within a couple of months of the pardons, Dr Berhanu Nega was suggesting that all should go their own separate ways. They did just that.

13. It might be noted that even at the press conference announcing Negasso's appointment, other members of the central committee lost no time in airing differences, with public comments to the effect that "actually, Mr. Chairman, we haven't agreed on that issue".

14. The AEUP, although it claims to be multi-national, is widely perceived as

essentially an Amhara organization. In 2010, the UDJ and AEUP discussed a merger but negotiations broke down over AEUP's demands that the UDJ withdrew from MEDREK and that AEUP leaders should take the lion's share of top positions in the merged organization.

15. The government's figures have often been criticized though not seriously challenged, and current output and figures suggest the government claims for growth 2004–2012 are essentially accurate. The IMF, using different criteria, has put average growth at nearer to 7–8 per cent, but even this is significantly higher than in most non-oil-producing African states.

16. It should, of course, be noted that opposition parties consistently claim with some validity that government agencies inhibit their activities and harass their members.

13. MAKING SENSE OF ETHIOPIA'S REGIONAL INFLUENCE

1. Ethiopia has always been at the forefront of these principles while giving birth to, and supporting the Organization of African Unity (OAU), later African Union (AU). Cf. Guzzini, 1998.

2. "The Foreign Policy of the Federal Democratic Republic of Ethiopia", Ministry of Foreign Affairs, November 1996.

3. Expediency included the expulsion of the Sudan Peoples Liberation Army (SPLA) from Ethiopian territory. Besides, the SPLA had tried to stop the advancing EPRDF army in western Ethiopia by siding with the Derg army in the final days of the war. Thus the military victory and coming to power of the EPRDF led to the expulsion of the SPLA from Ethiopia, which was warmly welcomed by the Sudanese government because it almost brought about the total military defeat of the SPLA and factionalism in the SPLM.

4. Ethiopia was the first to recognize Eritrean independence and the EPRDF entered various economic and security pacts with Eritrea that many felt better served Asmara's interests. To this could be added Eritrea's import, of coffee purchased in Ethiopian birr that it then exported for US dollars, and the many smuggling operations that were overlooked until Eritrea introduced its currency in 1997. The details of this episode can be found in Medhane Tadesse, 1999.

5. Ibid. Besides the name "State of Eritrea" had a security connotation attached to it, as in the State of Israel where unilateral security and brokering regional power become a defining character of foreign policy.

6. "Revolutionary Democracy on Eritrea and the Issue of Ethiopian Unity." Ethiopian People's Revolutionary Democratic Front (EPRDF), March, 1992.

7. Ibid.

8. Accepting the bone fides of the NIF and giving support to the EPLF, to the extent that this produced growing dissent within Ethiopia were also mistakes of considerable magnitude. Running down its military, while no doubt attractive to Western donors, was clearly mistaken when civil wars were in progress in neighbouring Sudan, Somalia, and Djibouti, and Eritrea continued to strengthen its military forces and maintain conscription.

9. Free movement of Islamic NGOs, Sudanese support to Islamist rebels in Benihangul Gumuz and successive attacks from Al-Ittihad al Islamia in the Somali region of Ethiopia.

10. Eritrea attacked Ethiopia presuming the EPRDF-led government to be weak and unstable.

11. Discussions with Dr Tekeda Alemu, State Minister for Foreign Affairs of Ethiopia, 18 June 2003. Sudanese intelligence services were believed to be behind the attack against President Hosni Mubarak of Egypt in June 1995 as he came to attend an OAU summit in Addis Ababa, an operation backed by the Sudanese security services.

12. The SPLA had been seen by the TPLF as a Mengistu ally and therefore black-listed and expelled from the Ethiopian territory after 1991.

13. Various discussions with Ali Seid Mohammed, Sudanese Ambassador to Ethiopia between 1998 and 18 June 2001.

14. Conversations with General Tsadqan Tinsae, former Chief of Staff of the Ethiopian Defence Forces since 25 March 2003.

15. Ibid., discussions with Arop Deng, SPLA representative to Ethiopia, September 2003.

16. This is reflected in the fact that Ethiopia alone constitutes a peacekeeping operation in the disputed Abyei region.

17. Starting from mid-1990s al-Ittihad launched a series of terrorist attacks in different Ethiopian cities. There was the bombing of the government-owned Ghion Hotel in Addis Ababa in January 1996, followed a month later by a bombing of the Ras Hotel in Diredawa. This was accompanied by a destabilizing act in Region Five (Somali region) of Ethiopia.

18. The significance of the battle of Luuq and Gedo in June 1997 is largely underestimated. Some mention is made about this in Medhane Tadesse, 2002.

19. Ibid.

20. The author was a witness to this development. The Ethiopian and Egyptian-sponsored conferences at Sodere (January 1997) and Cairo (October 1997) only succeeded in highlighting the divisions among Somali faction leaders, and among interested regional powers.

21. Discussions with Abdullahi Yusuf, President of puntland during March 1998 and January 2004, Addis Ababa.

22. This was mainly true until the Kulmiye party's leader Ahmed Silanyo became the president of Somaliland, after which the relationship faced minor problems as the new president became increasingly influenced by an Islamists clique: the Waddaad. The author had been at the centre of relations between Somaliland and Ethiopia for many years until early 2001 when the Ethiopian government formally took over.

23. These included, among others, cooperation with the AU in conflict resolution, the IGAD peacekeeping mission in Somalia (IGASOM), the establishment of Liaison Office to the AU in cooperation with IGAD and supporting regional efforts.

24. This was stated by top American Generals in a presentation at the US Military

Base in Stuttgart, Germany, January 2012. They hinted that the Ethiopian military acts like a US army in Africa.

25. The facilitator's office is mandated to: "facilitate reconciliation; assist institutional and capacity building efforts; assist the mobilization of financial and technical resources for the TFG II, as is the TFG II to fulfill its mandate as per the TFG and the Djibouti agreement."

26. Meles' resistance to the war, during the discussions within the TPLF Political Bureau, was partly attributed to the diplomatic wrangling with the West.

27. A series of discussions with Tewolde Woldemariam, the most powerful TPLF leader during the war with Eritrea, May 2002–July 2006.

28. EEBC's statement in response to the Ethiopian Prime Minister Meles' letter, 3 October 2003; Ethiopian Minister of Foreign Affairs, Press Release, 29 September 2003; Letter from the President of Eritrea to the UN Secretary General, dated 17 September 2003, shed light on the issue surrounding the border issue and the TSZ.

29. Connell, 2005. Almost all top officials of the Eritrean government who were later imprisoned by Isayas hinted that Ethiopian military incursion was a blow that forced discussions on such matters.

30. The Ethiopian government had to send a delegation, led by the Chief of Staff of the Armed Forces General Tsadkan Gebre Tensae, to reassure and calm neighbouring governments that Ethiopian military power will not be directed against them.

31. The Sana'a Pact, June 2001. Apart from marginalizing Eritrea diplomatically the Sana'a Pact stipulated economic sanctions as well as support to the Eritrean opposition. Though Sudan and Yemen joined for their own specific reasons the role played by Ethiopia was crucial.

32. "Africa Summary: IGAD's Role in Stability and Diplomacy in the Horn of Africa." Presentation by IGAD Executive Secretary Mahboub Maalim at Chatham House, London 9 May 2013. He described Eritrea as still a member state of IGAD, but on a self-imposed suspension.

33. Ibid.

34. The late Meles Zenawi played a crucial role in the discussions that led to the economic vision of Djibouti as affirmed by the Djiboutian President, Ismail Omar Guelleh, when he spoke to Sub-Saharan Informer, December 2013.

35. Djibouti's Minister of Economy and Finance, Moussa Dawaleh in New Africa, Wednesday, 20 June 2012 14:14.

36. See Thomas and Wilkin, 1999.

37. Discussion with Neway Gebreab, Chief Economic Adviser to the Ethiopian Prime Minister, January 2002.

38. A detailed analysis on this is found in Medhane Tadesse, 2005.

39. See Medhane Tadesse, 2004, a study that revolved around water and oil and was used as a road map by IGAD and several member countries.

40. According to Christopher Clapham, in an unpublished paper he wrote around 2000, this capacity for self-presentation has helped to create a belief in the donor community that the Prime Minister himself was a dedicated supporter

of the policy agendas promoting democracy, open markets and respect for human rights but that he was held back by "obstructionist" elements within his own party.

41. And with Nigerian and South African leaders leaving power before him, it was only a matter of time before Meles occupied a leading role in Africa's affairs and in the AU/NEPAD circuit. Meles was also instrumental in defining the newly evolving relations with emerging economies. The most important development in Africa's international system after the end of the Cold War is the increasing engagement of China in Africa. Here again Meles played a critical role in defining and articulating the terms of engagement on this new and complex phenomenon.

42. Discussions with Western diplomats in Addis Ababa over the years. It is not an exaggeration to suggest that the Ethiopian government was the only Third World government to mobilize a lot of resources from the west by maintaining its independence. It was labelled as the anointed leadership and was often referred to as project ownership by international financial institutions. This refers to the fact that the Ethiopian leadership's tough negotiating mechanisms with the IMF and its rejection of donors' aid conditions.

43. Meles had been a major foreign policy currency. Because of the role he had been playing in Africa's affairs and the way he positioned Ethiopia in securing peace and stability in Africa, and so on, his name had been instrumental in attracting international finance.

44. See Medhane Tadesse, 2009.

45. FES sponsored Cairo meetings on the Greater Horn of Africa. While the foreign ministry and foreign office tilted towards the politics of cooperation, the army and security services, particularly military intelligence, pursued the politics of destabilization. Egypt has been able to recruit all neighbouring countries, except Kenya, at different levels and different times in a way to execute hostile policies against Ethiopia.

46. "The Nile Issue: From the Unknown to the Uncertain", The Currentanalyst. com, June 2012.

47. The policy came to be largely restricted to Egyptian support for Eritrea and, more accurately, evidence of heightened Egyptian involvement in Somalia, to undermine Ethiopian influence.

48. The foundation stone for GERD was laid on 2 April 2011. Egypt has demanded that Ethiopia cease construction on the dam as a precondition to negotiations and sought regional support for its position. However, Ethiopia resisted the call; other nations in the Nile Basin Initiative have expressed support for the dam, including Sudan, the only other nation downstream on the Blue Nile, which has accused Egypt of inflaming the situation.

49. Field Marshal El-Sisi's world view is based on the Gulf where he spent most of his career, and if he has any view towards upper riparian countries, particularly Ethiopia, it is one of ignorance, contempt and perhaps hostility.

14. THE ETHIOPIAN ECONOMY: THE DEVELOPMENTAL STATE VS. THE FREE MARKET

1. From 2004 to 2011 economic growth has averaged around 10.6 per cent per year, more than twice the Sub-Saharan African average (World Bank 2012a).
2. "The journalist as terrorist: an Ethiopian story", Open Democracy, http://www.opendemocracy.net/abiye-teklemariam-megenta/journalist-as-terrorist-ethiopian-story (last access Jan. 2013).
3. "Policy—A Multidimensional Approach", Oxford Poverty & Human Development Initiative (OPHI), http://www.ophi.org.uk/policy/multidimensional-poverty-index/ (last access Jan. 2013).
4. United Nations Development Programme: Human Development Reports, http://hdr.undp.org/en/statistics/ (last access Jan. 2013).
5. "In 2009, over 22 per cent of the rural population was dependent on a combination of emergency food aid and safety net programs" (Dessalegn Rahmato, 2011). Emergency humanitarian aid amounted to about $600bn in 2010. The United States is the main donor. See Global Humanitarian Assistance, http://www.globalhumanitarianassistance.org/countryprofile/ethiopia (last access Jan. 2013).
6. Access Capital, 2011.
7. In Ethiopia, the fiscal year—and hence the budget—goes from July to July of the following year.
8. IDA-IMF 2011.
9. IMF 2012.
10. From between 8 and 9 million tons at the end of the 1990s to a forecast 25 million tons in 2013 (Central Statistics Agency of Ethiopia [CSA], www.csa.gov.et).
11. Interviews, Addis Ababa, October 2012.
12. MoPED, 1993.
13. Data, World Bank, http://data.worldbank.org/indicator/SL.AGR.EMPL.ZS?page=3 (last access Jan. 2013).
14. Lefort, 1981.
15. MoPED, 1993.
16. Ayele Kuris, 2006.
17. Young, 1997; Aregawi Berhe, 2009.
18. Meles Zenawi was both Chairman of the TPLF and head of the executive from 1991 until his death on 20 August 2012.
19. *New York Times*, 29 May–1 June 1991.
20. MoPED, 1993; EPRDF, 1993; Meles Zenawi, 2006. The following quotes are taken from these three documents.
21. Clapham, 2009.
22. EPRDF, 2007.
23. Ibid.
24. Ibid.
25. In addition to banking and insurance, the first list of these "heights" included

"rail, air and sea transport, electricity, telephone, water supplies, textile industry, engineering works, textile and chemical industries, metal foundries, mining, etc." (EPRDF, 1993).

26. EPRDF, 2007.
27. Dessalegn Rahmato, 2009 has fully developed this theme. For a rural case study see also Lefort, 2010.
28. Local authorities demand that the peasants spend at least 20 per cent of their time on collective labour called "development work" or "social work".
29. See the no. 3 Special Issue of *Renewal (Tehadso)*, the bi-monthly EPRDF magazine, dated April 2002, which summarizes a document called *The EPRDF's Rural Development Vision—An Overview*.
30. Article 40, paragraph 3 of the Constitution: "The right to ownership of rural and urban land, as well as of all natural resources, is exclusively vested in the State and in the peoples of Ethiopia. Land is a common property of the Nations, Nationalities and Peoples of Ethiopia and shall not be subject to sale or to other means of exchange."
31. EPRDF, 1993.
32. For more details on this form of control, see "Party-Statals: How the ruling party's 'endowments' operate", 19 March 2009, Addis Ababa US Embassy cable released by Wikileaks.
33. EPRDF, 1993.
34. Ibid.
35. MoPED, 1993.
36. Paulos Milkias, 2003, Meles's quote.
37. MoPED, 1993.
38. Ibid.
39. Ibid.
40. Ibid.
41. Shortly before Haile Selassie's fall, cereal production per capita was around 150 kg/person/year (see Lefort, 1981). In 2000, it was around 140 kg/person/year, and in 2003 it was 120 kg/person/year (CSA, 2012). It was only in 2005–6 that the 1974 level was reached again.
42. Data, World Bank, http://data.worldbank.org/indicator/NY.GDP.MKTP.CD/countries?page=2 (last access Jan. 2013).
43. Data, World Bank, http://data.worldbank.org/indicator/NV.IND.TOTL.ZS/countries?page=2 (last access Jan. 2013).
44. Data, World Bank, http://data.worldbank.org/indicator/BN.CAB.XOKA.GD.ZS?page=2 (last access Jan. 2013).
45. Paulos Milkias, 2003.
46. See Tronvoll and Hagmann, 2011; and for a local rural study Lefort, 2007.
47. Over 200 demonstrators were killed and thousands of political opponents, real or alleged, were arrested.
48. EPRDF, 2006.
49. Ibid.
50. Ibid. and EPRDF, 2007.

51. EPRDF, 2007.
52. Meles Zenawi, 2006.
53. This crisis led to a massive purge, with the removal of top historical Front leaders. Thousands of lesser party cadres were purged from their positions.
54. EPRDF, 2006.
55. EPRDF, 2007.
56. Address to the House of People's Representatives, 19 March 2009.
57. Esayas Kebede, head of the Agricultural Investment Agency, to Reuters (12 November 2009).
58. EPRDF, 2006.
59. Out of the over three million Municipal Councillors elected in 2008, less than a dozen belong to the opposition. Out of the 547 MPs elected to the Federal Parliament in 2010, there was only one independent and one member of the opposition.
60. Data, World Bank, http://data.worldbank.org/indicator/NY.GDP.MKTP.KD.ZG (last access on Jan. 2013)
61. Walta Information Centre, 7 June 2012.
62. Data, World Bank, http://data.worldbank.org/indicator/DT.ODA.ODAT.PC.ZS (last access Jan. 2013).
63. World Bank, 2012b.
64. Data, World Bank, http://data.worldbank.org/indicator/DT.ODA.ODAT.PC.ZS (last access Jan. 2013).
65. $3.4bn from 2009 to 2013. See details of Ethiopia Protection of Basic Services Program Phase II Project, World Bank, at http://www.worldbank.org/projects/P103022/ethiopia-protection-basic-services-program-phase-ii-project?lang=en (last access Jan. 2013).
66. Tewodaj Mogues et al., 2011.
67. Aklog Birara, 2010.
68. *Reporter*, 20 August 2011. A World Bank study states that "14% of Ethiopian adults regularly receive an annual average of $600 from abroad", *Afrika News*, 1 November 2010. Access Capital mentions $1.4bn, for 2012, $2.5bn for 2011.
69. World Bank, 2012c.
70. Statistics reported by the National Bank Of Ethiopia.
71. Ibid.
72. Ibid.
73. Ezega, 2012.
74. Access Capital, 2011.
75. National Bank of Ethiopia.
76. Reuters, 5 July 2011.
77. National Bank of Ethiopia.
78. Ibid.
79. World Bank, 2012b.
80. Ibid.
81. World Bank, *Ethiopia: Protection of Basic Services Project, Overview*, 17 September 2010.

82. UNICEF, 2010.

83. World Bank, 2012c.

84. National Bank of Ethiopia.

85. Davis et al., 2010.

86. MOFED, 2010b.

87. Ibid.

88. Davis et al., 2010.

89. Many peasants are not at ease with their use, weather uncertainty restricts their efficiency and their relatively uniform use often doesn't fit the extreme variety of Ethiopian climactic and ecological systems.

90. Spielman, 2011.

91. CSA, 2012.

92. Ibid.

93. Ibid.

94. Data, World Bank, http://data.worldbank.org/indicator/NV.AGR.TOTL.ZS/countries/1W-ET?display=graph (last access on Jan. 2013).

95. CSA, 2012.

96. World Bank, 2012b.

97. CSAn 2012.

98. Ibid.

99. World Bank, 2012b.

100. Access Capital, 2011.

101. Ibid.

102. *Teff* is a typical Ethiopian cereal used to prepare the basic food of the highlands, the large *injera* pancake.

103. Data, World Bank, http://data.worldbank.org/indicator/AG.YLD.CREL.KG/countries (last access Jan. 2013).

104. Usually defined as a household where all the members can eat three meals a day, throughout the year.

105. 'Policy—A Multidimensional Approach', OPHI, http://www.ophi.org.uk/policy/multidimensional-poverty-index/ (last access Jan. 2013).

106. All figures concerning the targets of the GTP and quotes without references are taken from MOFED 2010b.

107. De Waal, 2012.

108. Agence France-Presse (AFP), 15 September 2010.

109. World Bank, 2012b. The same source adds: "In the coming years, the number of young people entering the urban labor market will be almost ten times the number of people retiring".

110. Data, World Bank, http://data.worldbank.org/indicator/SL.UEM.TOTL.ZS (accessed November 2014). A survey made in 2012 by the author in a rural *kebele* showed that around three quarters of people aged eighteen to thirty are jobless or landless.

111. "Around 50% of the urban men between age 15 and 30 are unemployed, Ethiopia has one of the highest unemployment rates worldwide". Serneels, 2004.

112. World Bank, 2012b.
113. Reuters, 13 November 2012.
114. Walta Information Centre, 6 April 2010.
115. "Investing in Ethiopia—Monetary Policy Review", Access Capital, April 2011.
116. Ohashi, 2011a.
117. The best studies on this process are Dessalegn Rahmato, 2011; Oakland Institute, 2011; Imeru Tamrat, 2010.
118. See for example Prime Minister Meles Zenawi's interview on ITMN Television (26 June 2011).
119. Dessalegn Rahmato, 2011.
120. MOFED 2010b.
121. Dessalegn Rahmato, 2011.
122. Ibid.
123. These expulsions and the gathering of expellees in new villages ("villageization") have raised international concerns. See for example Human Rights Watch, 2012.
124. Ibid.
125. Ibid.
126. Aklog Birira, 2011.
127. Dessalegn Rahmato, 2011.
128. Ibid.
129. Meles Zenawi, ITMN Television, 26 June 2011.
130. For more details, see Lefort, 2011.
131. *L'Hebdo* (Switzerland), 3 September 2009.
132. Access Capital, 2011.
133. Ibid.
134. Data, World Bank, http://data.worldbank.org/indicator/NE.EXP.GNFS.ZS (last access Jan. 2013).
135. *Reporter*, 13 November 2010.
136. Data, World Bank, http://data.worldbank.org/indicator/NE.IMP.GNFS.ZS (last access Jan. 2013).
137. For example, Ethiopia is a member of the Common Market for East and Southern Africa (COMESA) and is set to join the WTO in 2014 (Walta Information Centre, 17 January 2013).
138. Walta Information Centre, 30 October 2012.
139. Walta Information Centre, 5 November 2012; Bloomberg, 7 September 2011; and Access Capital, 2012.
140. *Khat* is a mild drug grown and consumed in East Africa and parts of Arabia. See Ezekiel Gebissa, 2004.
141. Access Capital, 2011.
142. Reuters, 23 November 2010.
143. Ethiopian News Agency, 26 January 2006.
144. Sugar production is aimed to increase sevenfold and its export value to rise from nil to $661m in 2015.

145. Projections made by Access Capital, 2011.
146. Access Capital, 2011.
147. World Bank, 2009.
148. The Ethiopian national currency is the birr. When GTP was drawn up, the exchange rate was about $1 for 17 birr.
149. Ken Ohashi, World Bank Representative for Ethiopia and Sudan, Ohashi, 2011a.
150. Ethiopia, *Country Strategy Paper 2011–15*, African Development Bank Group, April 2011.
151. Access Ethiopia, 2011.
152. IDA-IMF, 2011.
153. See the chapter on urban renewal by Perrine Duroyaume in this book.
154. World Bank, 2012a. That means a price of more than 600 birr per quintal for maize (Food and Agriculture Organization of the United Nations, http://www.fao.org/giews/english/gfpm/index.htm, accessed November 2014), the cheapest cereal on the market. Given that the lowest wages in Addis Ababa hover around 500 birr per month, and that a family of five needs 75 kilos of cereals per month, then if the head of the family is the only one to work his or her whole income will have to be spent on simply feeding their family.
155. *Addis Fortune*, 18 July 2011.
156. Access Capital, 2011.
157. Ibid.
158. *Addis Fortune*, 7 July 2011.
159. CSA.
160. Food and Agriculture Organization, http://www.fao.org/giews/english/gfpm/index.htm (last access Jan. 2013).
161. CSA.
162. In 1991 the US dollar was worth 2.01 birr.
163. Reuters, 6 July 2009.
164. Walta Information Centre, 7 June 2012.
165. "House endorses 137.8 bln birr budget a week after schedule", *Capital* (Ethiopia), 23 July 2012, http://www.capitalethiopia.com/index.php?option=com_content&view=article&id=1424:house-endorses-1378-bln-birr-budget-a-week-after-schedule-&catid=54:news&Itemid=27 (last access Jan. 2013).
166. MOFED, 2010b.
167. "Ethiopia: World Bank Approves New Funding to Improve Delivery of Education, Health and Other Services for 84 Million People—Also Pledges Support for Ethiopia's Main Roads", World Bank press release, 25 September 2012, http://www.worldbank.org/en/news/2012/09/25/ethiopia-world-bank-approves-new-funding-improve-delivery-education-health-and-other-services (last access Jan. 2013).
168. Walta Information Centre, 22 December 2012.
169. *Capital*, 23 July 2012.
170. *Fortune*, 10 July 2011.
171. India's existing and expected investments are estimated to be $4bn.

172. MoFED, 2010a.
173. Ohashi, 2011a.
174. World Bank, 2009.
175. World Bank, 2012b.
176. Ibid.
177. Data, World Bank, http://data.worldbank.org/indicator/BX.KLT.DINV.
     CD.WD (last access Jan. 2013)
178. UN, 2012.
179. IDA-IMF, 2011. Public corporations still include: Ethiopian Air Lines,
     Ethiopian Shipping Lines, Ethiopian Telecoms, Ethiopian Electric and Power
     Corporation, Ethiopian Metal Engineering Corporation, Commercial Bank
     of Ethiopia, Development Bank of Ethiopia, and Construction and Business
     Bank (World Bank, 2012b).
180. World Bank and IFC, 2013.
181. World Bank, 2012b.
182. Access Capital, 2011.
183. Ohashi, 2011a.
184. US Embassy cable (15 January 2010), released by Wikileaks on 30 August,
     2011.
185. Access Capital, 2011.
186. Ibid.
187. Confidential Report on the Ethiopian economy, from a large international aid
     organization (2010).
188. MIDROC: Mohammed International Development Research and
     Organization Companies.
189. Ventures, 2012.
190. Bloomberg, 27 February 2012.
191. "Privatisation or monopolization in Ethiopia", Addis Ababa US Embassy
     cable (11 November 2008), released by Wikileaks.
192. Confidential Report on the Ethiopian economy, from a large international aid
     organization (2010).
193. Altenburg, 2010.
194. Ibid.
195. Access Capital, 2011.
196. UN, 2007.
197. Access Capital, 2011.
198. Altenburg, 2010.
199. The subtitle of the World Bank report *Doing Business 2013/Ethiopia* is
     "Smarter Regulations for Small and Medium Size Enterprises".
200. *Afrik*, 10 January 2011.
201. Altenburg, 2010.
202. Transparency International, http://cpi.transparency.org/cpi2012/results/#
     CountryResults (last access November 2014).
203. Kar and Freitas, 2012.
204. World Bank, 2012b.

205. Confidential Report on the Ethiopian economy produced by a large international aid organization (November 2010).
206. Sutton and Kellow, 2010.
207. Ohashi, 2011a.
208. Ibid.
209. Ohashi, 2009.
210. Ibid.
211. Ibid.
212. Altenburg, 2010.
213. IDA-IMF, 2011.
214. Ibid.
215. Davis et al., 2010.
216. Ohashi, 2011b.
217. *Addis Fortune*, 10 July 2011.
218. "Ethiopia: IMF On Retreat On Ethiopia's Growth Outlook", *Addis Fortune*, 17 June 2012.
219. "Ethiopia: An African Lion?", BBC, 31 October 2012.
220. Reuters, 8 October 2013.
221. Walta Information Centre, 4 February 2014.
222. Food and Agriculture Organization, http://www.fao.org/giews/pricetool/?seriesQuery=79 (last access November 2014).
223. Food and Agriculture Organization, 2014.
224. Ministry of Agriculture and Rural Development, 2010.
225. Bloomberg, 25 November 2013.
226. *Al Ayat*, 9 December 2013.
227. Interview with Essayas Kebede, the man in charge of these agricultural investments at the Ministry of Agriculture and Rural Development. *Deutsche Welle*, 20 March 2014.
228. Jan Mikkelsen, resident representative of the IMF, in *Addis Fortune*, 10 November 2013.
229. Data, World Bank, http://data.worldbank.org/indicator/NE.RSB.GNFS.ZS (last access November 2014).
230. Jan Mikkelsen in *Addis Fortune*, 10 November 2013.
231. Data, World Bank, http://data.worldbank.org/indicator/DT.ODA.ODAT.CD (last access November 2014).
232. CSA.
233. Martins, 2014. But even these figures are probably underestimated. A paper detailing some of my recent research in a rural area in northern Shoa in 2012–13 (still to be published) shows that three fourths of the 16- to 35-year-old males who are not in school do not have a sufficient income to lead a normal autonomous life. This proportion was confirmed by the local authorities.
234. *The Economist*, 11 February 2014.
235. *Addis Fortune*, 16 February 2014.
236. Martins, 2014.

237. Rick Rowden quoted in *The Economist*, 11 February 2014.
238. Calculated from statistics on the World Bank's website, http://www.world-bank.org/en/publication/global-economic-prospects/regional-outlooks/ssa (last access November 2014).
239. Geiger and Moller, 2013.
240. *Addis Fortune*, 10 November 2013.
241. Data, World Bank, http://data.worldbank.org/indicator/DT.ODA.ODAT.CD (last access November 2014).
242. Jan Mikkelsen in *Addis Fortune*, 10 November 2013.
243. Guang Zhe Chen, World Bank Country Director for Ethiopia, Press Release, 18 June 2013.
244. *Addis Fortune*, 10 November 2013.
245. *Addis Fortune*, 12 April 2014.
246. Jan Mikkelsen in *Addis Fortune*, 10 November 2013.

15. ADDIS ABABA AND THE URBAN RENEWAL IN ETHIOPIA

1. ESA, 2009.
2. Ibid.
3. MOFED, 2010.
4. Bahru Zewde, 1991, p. 60.
5. Ibid., pp. 68–71.
6. Fasil Giorgis and Gerard, 2007.
7. Wubshet Berhanu, 2002, pp. 103–5.
8. Wubshet Berhanu, 2002, p. 99. Between 1935 and 1941, the population of Addis Ababa grew from 100,000 to 143,000 inhabitants with an annual growth rate of 6.1 per cent.
9. Meskerem Shawul Areda, 2008, pp. 102–6.
10. In 1962 Bole airport was inaugurated, replacing the one at Lideta, unsuitable for the new planes. Ethiopian Airlines received an important boost with the opening of new African routes.
11. At the beginning of the 1960s, the city's population shared just 7 per cent of land, whereas about 60 per cent of the land was possessed by the royal family. The rest was owned by the church, the state and foreign delegations: Essayas Deribe, 2003.
12. Berlan, 1963, p. 63.
13. Proclamation n°47/1975.
14. Proclamation n°104/1976.
15. UN Habitat, 2007, p. 10.
16. Proclamation n°292/1986. In 1986, the government reintroduced the possibility of renting by the legalization of cohabitation practices.
17. Bezunesh Tamru, 2007, pp. 163–6. Average urban growth ratio in Addis Ababa was in the 1961–65 period 7.2 per cent; in 1965–84, 4.7 per cent; in 1984–94, 4.1 per cent.
18. According to Wubshet (2002:97), "the total developed area in this period was

about 6.500 hectares (or about 23 per cent of the total area of the City as of 1999".

19. UN Habitat, 2003.
20. CSA, 1994.
21. GTZ, 2003.
22. Esrael, 2005
23. Ibid.
24. UN Habitat, 2007.
25. In 2011, according to the CSA, the inflation rate was about 35 per cent.
26. Ezana Haddis, 2007.
27. MOFED, 2010, pp. 47–8.
28. http://grandmillenniumdam.net/ (last access on 23.02.12).
29. De Poix, 2007.
30. For the year 2010, the government collected about $88 million in profit taxes on public and private banks, that is to say 15 banking establishments of which three are nationally owned: "Banking business booming in Ethiopia" in www.newbusinessethiopia.com, 8 January 2010. Available at: http://newbusinessethiopia.com/index.php?option=com_content&view=article&id=56:banking-business-booming-in-ethiopia&catid=37:finance&Itemid=37 (last access on 12.12.11).
31. Data collected in field surveys undertaken in ten households residing in the Ayat development, in March 2008.
32. Data collected from interviews undertaken with four RED representatives in December 2009.
33. "City to release land", *Addis Fortune*, 7 August, 2011. http://www.addisfortune.com/Vol_12_No_588_Archive/City%20to%20Release%20610ht%20of%20Land.htm (last access 24.10.11).
34. Proclamation 271/2012. http://www.thereporterethiopia.com/Politics-and-Law/the-new-land-lease-proclamation-changes-implications.html (last access 31.01.12).
35. Elias Yitbarek 2008. LDPs are infrastructure tools that aim to restructure neighbourhoods delimited by guidelines that are supposed to address the preoccupations of their inhabitants and the need for modernization. In the case of Casa Incis, it seems to have justified a complete renovation of the complex. Inhabitants' testimonials evoke the brutality of the eviction and the absence of clear information.
36. Addis Ababa Chamber of Commerce and Sectoral Associations, 2011.
37. Berhanu Zeleke, 2006.
38. Source: Land Management Office of Addis Ababa City Government, October 2009.
39. At that time about 200 birr for a studio for which the price is 15,000 birr. Source: Office of the IHDP.
40. Such as injera cooking, washing, the preparations for religious festivals.
41. UN Habitat, 2010b.
42. Data collected from interviews with 35 households living in condominium apartments between November 2007 and December 2008.

477

43. UN Habitat (2010b).
44. CSA, 2007.
45. Proclamation n°286/2002. Under 1,800 ETB income received by a landlord for renting of housing is exempt from taxes. "Officially" declared rental income is often below this threshold.
46. Data issued from household-surveys undertaken with 35 households living in condominium housing between November 2007 and December 2008.

16. THE MELES ZENAWI ERA: FROM REVOLUTIONARY MARXISM TO STATE DEVELOPMENTALISM

1. This text was written in May 2013 and updated in August 2014.
2. Balsvik, 1985.
3. See in this volume the chapter by Christopher Clapham.
4. See Erlich, 1996.
5. Gramsci [see appended bibliography for the various dates]
6. See the TPLF 1976 *Manifesto*.
7. See Prunier, 2010.
8. Gebru Tareke 2009: 81
9. This author frequently visited Ethiopia during the war years and remembers very clearly that the true war aims of the TPLF were ambiguous to the public, both among the Derg supporters and among its enemies.
10. The Eritrean secession in itself was a non-solution. Not only could the various ethnonationalist strands making up Ethiopia not follow the same path, but Eritrea itself was eventually to degenerate into such a problem child of the Ethiopian situation that it could not be seen as part of the solution, but rather as a sad example of an errant orientation.
11. It would be interesting to study the birth and growth of social differentiation in Ethiopia ranging from the failure of Tewodros to the partial success of Haile Selassie. The problem of Haile Selassie is that he was defeated by his own success: he presided over the birth of a class society whose evolution he could neither understand nor control and which finally blew up in his face.
12. See Abir,1968. This key period of Ethiopian history falls outside the purview of this volume. But its centrality to the Ethiopian world view would deserve a serious treatment in another context.
13. This author was a JIOG observer in the 1992 elections and had the occasion to personally witness this situation.
14. The Oromo Liberation Front, the other main ethno-nationalist organization which had fought the Derg regime, seen as an "Amhara" regime, alongside the TPLF but independently from it.
15. See for example Pausewang, Tronvoll and Aalen, 2002: 32.
16. By this term we mean the mostly urbanized members of a group with multi-ethnic origins who had progressively identified more and more with global Ethiopian nationalism throughout the nineteenth century and for whom the Amhara culture, although not completely theirs, had become a symbol and a beacon of national identification.

17. This does not mean that the ethno-nationalistic movements were fake in their defence of democracy; it simply meant that their concept of "democracy" was often more ethnic and regional than truly nation-wide. The notion of trans-ethnic democratic citizenship was often more a politically correct verbal referent than an intimately lived feeling.

18. See the chapter by Sarah Vaughan in this book.

19. Since the days of Gondar, the problem of Abyssinia/Ethiopia, like that of most multicultural empires, had been the balance between centre and periphery, which permanently threatened to veer into tyranny or on the contrary to degenerate into anarchy.

20. This is exactly what led him later to study economics by correspondence, a move of almost touching modesty when one thinks of the (often unfounded) dominant feeling of economic omniscience among world leaders.

21. See footnote 21 in my chapter on the Eritrean question.

22. Given Tigray's state of extreme economic neglect since the end of World War Two, there was also an element of catching up.

23. Even though a collective leadership of sorts still existed in the EPLF/PFDJ in the mid-1990s, it was more nominal than real and the president's name could already be used as a summary of "his" country's political life.

24. This bizarre "economic" concept was indeed used in confidential memos issued by Asmara in 1997.

25. This was the price he had to pay for his moderation on the Eritrean issue.

26. The battles lines drawn in 2001 were not born overnight. They resulted from a slow accretion of pent-up political dissent within the TPLF, going back to at least 1995 (see Paulos Milkias 2003).

27. For a more detailed account of this election, see the chapter by Patrick Gilkes.

28. This was anathema to the hard core Amhara ethno-nationalists who saw in article 39 the hated symbol of Eritrean secession and an open door for other ethnic groups, such as the Oromo or the Tigrayans themselves, to secede if they strongly rejected the state's central authority. Article 39 was seen by the Amhara as a sword of Damocles hanging over the very existence of Ethiopia. But for the other nationalities, it was seen on the contrary as the ultimate guarantee against a return to pre-revolutionary Amhara domination.

29. Another bout of demonstrations in November 2005 led to the brutal killing of around 200 demonstrators (the exact numbers have never been clearly given) by the security forces.

30. The Atlas method is a rough-and-ready method, still widely used (World Bank), whereby the country's GNP is simply divided by its population. The PPP method (Purchasing Power Parity) is a much more sophisticated system as it takes the purchasing power of the local dollar and resets it within the framework of the purchasing power of that same dollar in the US, taking into account the price differences. PPP is higher than Atlas in most cases.

31. After hesitating about participating or not, the opposition MPs started to drift in small groups to the institutions they had initially refused to attend. This tactic of late and dispersed joining eventually resulted in complete political irrelevance.

32. For a comparison between authoritarianism and economic policy in China and Ethiopia, see Cabestan 2012.
33. See the relevant chapter on economics by René Lefort in this volume.
34. This is an absolutely fascinating piece of diplomatic double game which I intend to discuss—and hopefully clarify—in the work I am preparing on the recent history of Somalia since the fall of Siad Barre.
35. The present Somalia situation remains today stuck roughly at the point where it was in early 2009, in spite of the limited defeat of the radical al-Shabaab Islamist movement and the international community's subsequent hollow self-congratulation.
36. The personality cult that has developed around the dead Meles had no precedent when he was alive.

INDEX

INDEX

INDEX

www.ingramcontent.com/pod-product-compliance
Ingram Content Group UK Ltd.
Pitfield, Milton Keynes, MK11 3LW, UK
UKHW020657120225
455006UK00010B/119